SURVEYS OF
AFRICAN ECONOMIES

SURVEYS OF AFRICAN ECONOMIES

VOLUME 1: CAMEROON, CENTRAL AFRICAN REPUBLIC, CHAD, CONGO (BRAZZA-VILLE), AND GABON. 1968.

VOLUME 2: KENYA, TANZANIA, UGANDA, AND SOMALIA. 1969.

VOLUME 3: DAHOMEY, IVORY COAST, MAURITANIA, NIGER, SENEGAL, TOGO, AND UPPER VOLTA. 1970.

VOLUME 4: DEMOCRATIC REPUBLIC OF CONGO, MALAGASY REPUBLIC, MALAWI, MAURITIUS, AND ZAMBIA. 1971.

The price for each volume in the series is $5.00, but students, faculty members, and libraries of universities may purchase the volumes at a special price of $2.50 each.

SURVEYS OF
AFRICAN ECONOMIES

VOLUME 4: DEMOCRATIC REPUBLIC OF CONGO,
MALAGASY REPUBLIC, MALAWI, MAURITIUS, AND ZAMBIA

INTERNATIONAL MONETARY FUND

WASHINGTON, D. C.

1971

Preface

This fourth volume of the *Surveys of African Economies* covers five countries—Democratic Republic of Congo, Malagasy Republic, Malawi, Mauritius, and Zambia. The *Surveys* are based mainly on published sources, supplemented by data gathered by Fund missions from the central banks and national authorities, who have authorized their publication.

Unlike the earlier volumes in this series, the countries covered in this volume are not joined together by common institutions. Accordingly, the introductory chapter is limited to a brief description of the principal characteristics of the five countries, emphasizing the similarities and differences among them.

The names of privately owned enterprises and organizations in a language other than English have not been translated into English in the text; however, most government and other agencies that perform public functions, such as ministries, marketing agencies, and central banks, as well as international agencies, are referred to in English. A listing of all these bodies, in most cases in both languages, is given in the index. Abbreviations are used for certain organizations that are referred to frequently, e.g., EEC for the European Economic Community. These will also be found in the index, along with their full names. Equivalents of the weights and measures used, as well as the conventional symbols used in the tables, are given on page xxv.

This volume has been prepared under the direction of Mr. Charles L. Merwin, Deputy Director in the African Department, and Mr. U Tun Wai, Senior Advisor. The chapters were prepared principally by the following members of the African Department: Messrs. Lamberto Dini, S.E. Cronquist, Massimo Russo, Viktor R. Sertic, C. Victor Callender, Emmanuel K. Martey, Albert Misrahi, Alassane D. Ouattara, Madhav V. Rao, and Mandé Sidibé. Other members of the African Department who contributed to the work at various stages were Messrs. D. Boushehri, Kwame Kwateng, Francis d'A. Collings, Joachim W. Kratz, Naguib M. Abu-zobaa, W. Parmena, Brian Quinn, and Petrus J. van de Ven.

Members of other departments also participated in the work, including Messrs. J.H.C. de Looper, Bahram Nowzad, and Y. Onitsuka, of the Exchange and Trade Relations Department; Mr. Jean F. Garnier, of the Fiscal Affairs Department; and Mr. Grant B. Taplin, of the Research Department.

The volume has been edited by Mrs. Jane B. Evensen, with the assistance of Miss O. Mary Price, Mrs. Christine E. Waller, Mrs. Jennie Lee Carter, and Mrs. Janet V. Koch. The maps were prepared by Mr. Armando Vaccari.

June 1971   MAMOUDOU TOURÉ

Director, African Department
International Monetary Fund

CONTENTS

CONTENTS

3 Malagasy Republic (*continued*)   *Page*

3 Malagasy Republic (*continued*)

TABLES

3 Malagasy Republic (*continued*) *Page*

4 Malawi

4 Malawi (*continued*)

TABLES

4   Malawi (*continued*)   *Page*

5 Mauritius (*continued*) *Page*

TABLES

5 Mauritius (*continued*) *Page*

6 Zambia (*continued*) Page

DIAGRAMS

TABLES

6   Zambia (*continued*)   *Page*

Conversion Factors and Symbols Used in Volume 4

Exchange Rates

Congo zaïre 1.00 = US$2.00, *from June 23, 1967*
Congo francs 165.00 = US$1.00, *before June 23, 1967*

Malagasy francs 277.710 = US$1.00, *from August 11, 1969*
Malagasy francs 246.853 = US$1.00, *July 1, 1963–August 11, 1969*
CFA francs 246.853 = US$1.00, *before July 1, 1963*

Malawi kwacha 1.00 = US$1.20, *from February 15, 1971*
Malawi pound 1.00 = US$2.40, *November 20, 1967–February 15, 1971*
Malawi pound 1.00 = US$2.80, *before November 20, 1967*

Mauritian rupees 5.555 = US$1.00, *from November 18 1967*
Mauritian rupees 4.7619 = US$1.00, *before November 18, 1967*

Zambian kwacha 1.00 = US$1.40, *from January 16, 1968*
Zambian pound 1.00 = US$2.80, *before January 16, 1968*

Weights and Measures

1 foot = 0.3048 meter
1 mile = 1.609344 kilometers
1 square mile = 2.58999 square kilometers
1 acre = 0.404686 hectare
1 arpent = 1.043 acres
1 pound = 0.4535923 kilogram
1 metric ton = 2,204.6 pounds = 1.10231 short tons = 0.984207 long ton
Temperatures are given in Fahrenheit

In the Tables

A long dash (—) indicates zero or less than half the unit shown, or that the item does not exist
Dots (. . .) indicate that the data are not available

In the Tables and Text

A slash between years (1969/70) indicates a single fiscal or crop year
A short dash between years (1969–70) indicates a period of two or more years, though not necessarily calendar years
The word "billion" means 1,000 million

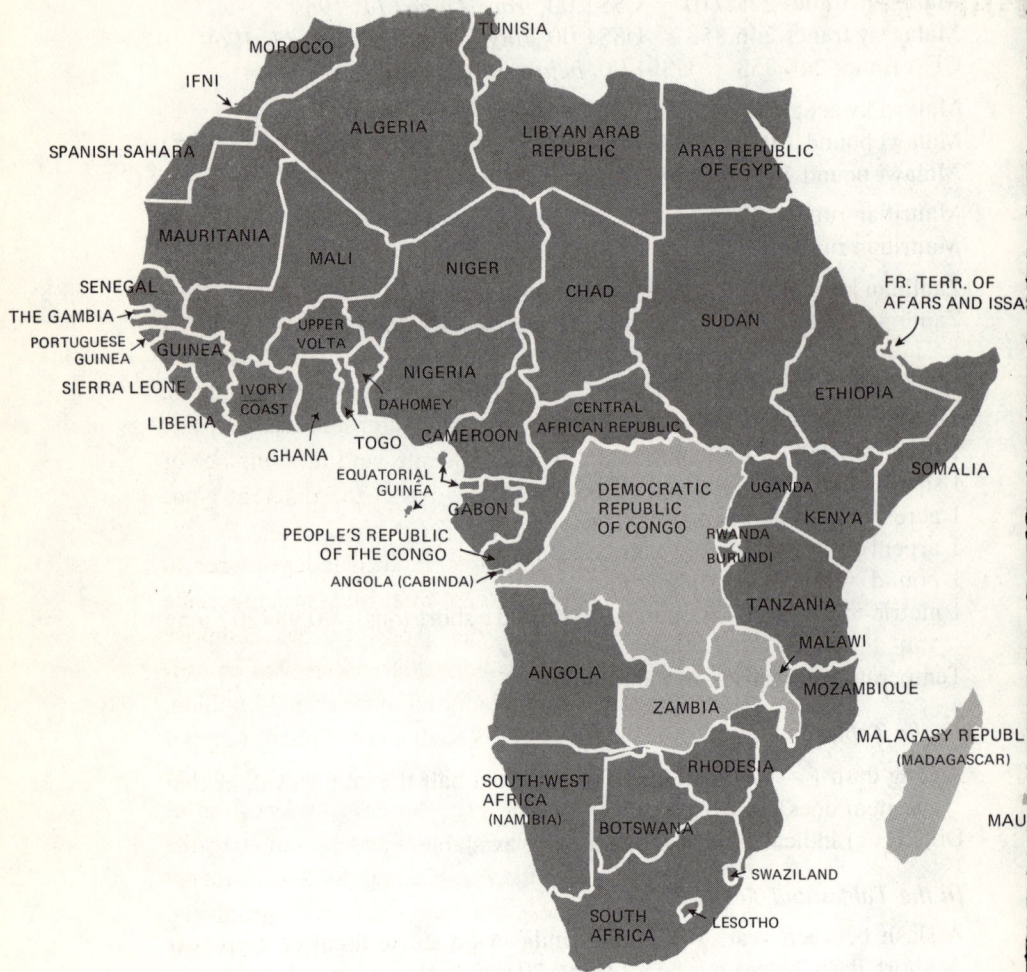

TUNISIA

MOROCCO

IFNI

SPANISH SAHARA

ALGERIA

LIBYAN ARAB
REPUBLIC

ARAB REPUBLIC
OF EGYPT

MAURITANIA

MALI

NIGER

CHAD

SUDAN

SENEGAL

THE GAMBIA

PORTUGUESE
GUINEA

GUINEA

UPPER
VOLTA

FR. TERR. OF
AFARS AND ISSAS

SIERRA LEONE

IVORY
COAST

NIGERIA

DAHOMEY

CENTRAL
AFRICAN REPUBLIC

ETHIOPIA

LIBERIA

GHANA

TOGO

CAMEROON

SOMALIA

EQUATORIAL
GUINEA

GABON

DEMOCRATIC
REPUBLIC
OF CONGO

UGANDA

KENYA

PEOPLE'S REPUBLIC
OF THE CONGO

RWANDA

BURUNDI

ANGOLA (CABINDA)

TANZANIA

MALAWI

ANGOLA

ZAMBIA

MOZAMBIQUE

MALAGASY REPUBL
(MADAGASCAR)

SOUTH-WEST
AFRICA
(NAMIBIA)

RHODESIA

MAU

BOTSWANA

SWAZILAND

SOUTH
AFRICA

LESOTHO

Introduction

This volume contains surveys of the economies of the Democratic Republic of Congo, the Malagasy Republic (Madagascar), Malawi, Mauritius, and Zambia. These countries, unlike those covered in earlier volumes in this series, are not joined together by any one common institution. They are all developing countries, though their economies differ markedly in size, structure, and growth rate, and in a number of ways they are illustrative of the different types of economies found in Africa.

All these countries attained independence in the early 1960s except Mauritius, which became independent in 1968. Together they comprise an area of 1.5 million square miles with an estimated total population of more than 30 million. The Democratic Republic of Congo (capital city, Kinshasa) is the largest country in the group; it straddles the south-central portion of the African continent and has an outlet to the Atlantic Ocean. Zambia and Malawi, situated farther to the south and southeast, respectively, are landlocked. The three countries form one contiguous area. The Malagasy Republic and Mauritius are groups of islands off the southeastern coast of the continent. The annual growth of the population in the area as a whole has averaged some 2.4 per cent over the past decade. There are, however, substantial differences in the average density of population, which ranges from 18 to the square mile in Congo to about 1,100 to the square mile in Mauritius.

These countries experienced varying rates of economic development during the 1960s. The expansion of real income exceeded the growth of population in Zambia, Malawi, and Madagascar but not in Congo or Mauritius. Over the period 1960–66, prolonged internal political disturbances resulted in virtual economic stagnation in Congo. Although there was a marked resumption of economic growth after 1967, with the restoration of economic stability, it is estimated that real per capita income in 1969 was still below the level of a decade earlier. In Mauritius, whose economy is almost totally dependent upon the production and export of sugar, exports have not expanded and there has been some fall in real per capita income in recent years. The acute scarcity of land and other resources has thus far hampered efforts at accelerating economic growth in Mauritius. Available data suggest that there are marked differences in per capita income in the countries under consideration, ranging from roughly $50 a year in Malawi to over $200 in Zambia.

The five countries being surveyed have certain broad structural similarities. Agriculture, chiefly of the subsistence type, constitutes the principal means of livelihood for the majority of the population. While the contribution of manufacturing to gross domestic product varies, it is nonetheless small and consists largely of the primary processing of agricultural or mineral products and the production of relatively simple consumer goods of the import-substitute variety. Each economy is an exporter largely of primary products, which may be mainly mineral in origin, as in Congo and Zambia, or agricultural in origin, as in Madagascar, Malawi, and Mauritius. The activities of the monetized sector in each economy are heavily oriented toward the export market, and the performance of exports, whether in terms of volume or of prices obtained on international markets, is therefore the most important single factor determining developments in the economy.

These similarities, however, cloak significant differences in the kinds of problems being encountered by each country as well as in its prospects for future growth. Thus, while each country's economy is heavily dependent upon the export of primary products, there are sharp differences in the extent of product diversification. Although Zambia and Congo are both primarily exporters of minerals, in 1969 copper accounted for 95 per cent of Zambia's exports, compared with about 60 per cent for Congo, which also exports a variety of other minerals, e.g., cobalt, industrial diamonds, tin, and zinc, as well as agricultural products, such as coffee, palm oil, and rubber. Therefore, while Zambia is basically a mining economy, its dependence on a single export commodity makes it closer in some respects to Mauritius, an agricultural economy, where exports of sugar account for almost 95 per cent of total exports. But Zambia, unlike Mauritius, has the potential for diversifying the agricultural and mining sectors and possesses an abundance of land. Madagascar and Malawi also depend largely upon agricultural exports. Unlike Mauritius, however, their exports are well diversified, consisting of coffee, vanilla, rice, cloves, sugar, and meat in Madagascar and tobacco, tea, groundnuts, and cotton in Malawi.

The problems of economic development faced by these five countries vary considerably, ranging from the need to strengthen the economic infrastructure in order to utilize the country's resources more effectively (as in Congo) to the need to broaden the production base (as in Mauritius). In addition, there are the problems common to all these economies of expanding the size of the monetized sector, promoting the growth of manufacturing and related activities to help absorb the increase in population, developing the agricultural sector, and reducing the vulnerability of export earnings through diversification. In sum, the problems to which these countries are addressing themselves are the ones that are being encountered by virtually every country on the African continent.

In reviewing the economic policies pursued by these five countries since they became independent, account should be taken of distortions that have resulted from particular political factors. The economic situation in Congo during 1960–66 was strongly influenced by internal political strife. As a consequence, there was an actual decline in aggregate output concurrent with a substantial expansion in government expenditure and in domestic credit. Subsequent policies were therefore concerned largely with the restoration of financial stability and of conditions under which the growth of the economy could resume. Economic policies in Zambia in recent years were strongly influenced by Rhodesia's unilateral declaration of independence. This resulted in a considerable diversion of investment resources toward the construction of alternate infrastructure, notably in the areas of transport and power, to the detriment of other sectors of the economy, particularly agriculture. The recent decline in agricultural output in Zambia has reflected not only this factor but also, since 1964, the departure of expatriate farmers who were largely responsible for the production of cash crops.

In general, the principal thrust of the economic policies of each country has been toward the strengthening of infrastructure, the diversification of the export sector, the broadening of the production base by encouragement of manufacturing industry, and the promotion of agricultural diversification. The success attending these efforts thus far has varied from country to country, the results reflecting not only differing resource endowments but also such factors as the inflow of foreign capital, fluctuations in export earnings resulting from natural causes or the behavior of prices on international markets, and the difficulties encountered in mobilizing domestic savings. In implementing their economic policies these countries have employed a variety of instruments, including direct state intervention and joint ventures with private foreign and domestic interests. Reliance on foreign official loans and grants has been substantial in the Malagasy Republic, Malawi, and Mauritius, not so great in Zambia, and relatively little in Congo.

Import and export taxes are the principal source of government revenue because foreign trade not only constitutes an important share of economic activity in these countries but also is comparatively easy to tax. However, the relative importance of the import and export sectors is not the same in all five countries. Export taxes are of primary importance in the revenue structures of Congo and Zambia; in addition, an important contribution is made in these two countries by income and corporate taxes levied on the mining sector. Income taxes paid by sugar producers are a major source of revenue in Mauritius. By implication, therefore, the fiscal situation in these three countries is significantly affected by fluctuations in output and in the earnings of the export sector. The revenue structures of the Malagasy Republic and Malawi, however, are characterized by a much greater dependence on import duties and hence on the level of imports. This difference in the revenue structures of Congo, Mauritius, and Zambia, on the one hand, and the Malagasy

Republic and Malawi, on the other, accounts for the greater potential instability in revenue collections in the former group, since exports of all these countries are generally subject to greater variations than are imports.

Malawi and Mauritius have made considerable progress in reducing the persistent deficits in their current budgets. In Mauritius the current budget is now in approximate balance. In Malawi the current budget deficit has been largely covered by foreign grants from the United Kingdom. All the five countries have generally been in deficit as regards overall budgetary operations (i.e., the current and capital budgets combined), though recourse to the banking system for the financing of such deficits has usually been relatively small. The ratio of central government tax receipts to gross domestic product at current prices varies quite markedly, from 10 per cent in Malawi to 34 per cent in Zambia.

With the exception of Congo, the monetary systems of these countries reflect their membership in larger currency areas—the French franc area in the case of the Malagasy Republic and the sterling area in the case of Malawi, Mauritius, and Zambia. However, unlike the countries covered in Volumes 1 and 3 of the *Surveys of African Economies*, which also belong to the French franc area, the Malagasy Republic has its own central bank. Its monetary system is governed by a cooperation agreement with France, according to which France guarantees the convertibility of the Malagasy franc into French francs.

With the exception of Congo in the period 1960–66, monetary policy in these countries has been successful on the whole in keeping the growth of domestic credit within acceptable limits, as evidenced by the generally moderate price movements that have taken place so far as well as by the continued maintenance of relatively liberal trade and payments systems. The situation in Congo was stabilized following the adoption in 1967 of a financial program that included the introduction of a realistic rate of exchange for the Congolese currency; this program was supported by a stand-by arrangement with the International Monetary Fund. The principal instruments of monetary policy employed in these countries thus far have been ceilings on commercial bank advances (e.g., in Congo), rediscount ceilings (e.g., in the Malagasy Republic), and changes in the rediscount rate (e.g., in Malawi).

Commercial banking in all these countries has been concentrated, as a rule, on the financing of trade and commerce and the short-term financing of crops; however, there is some short-term lending to other sectors, like manufacturing, largely for working capital. Commercial bank operations are subject to a certain degree of seasonality, particularly in those economies where agricultural exports are predominant. Most of the commercial banks are foreign owned, but in Malawi and Zambia the Government has recently taken a substantial participation in these banks.

Medium- and long-term credit is generally extended by the development banks that have been established in each country. The Government is the principal shareholder in all except the Congolese development bank, where the principal subscribers are a number of foreign and domestic financial institutions, including the International Finance Corporation. The lending activities of the development banks have for the most part tended to emphasize industrial ventures, though there has also been a modest amount of lending for construction. In Mauritius, however, the operations of the development bank have been directed primarily toward the agricultural sector, in particular the sugar growers, and in the other countries the development banks are beginning to pay more attention to the needs of the agricultural sector.

The geographic trading pattern of each country continues to reflect its ties with the country that administered it before independence (Belgium for Congo, France for Madagascar, and the United Kingdom for Malawi, Mauritius, and Zambia). About 25 per cent of Congo's imports are obtained from Belgium-Luxembourg, and 50 per cent of its exports are dispatched there. Over half of Madagascar's imports come from, and more than one third of its exports go to, France. Both of these countries are associated with the European Economic Community (EEC) under the Yaoundé Convention. The United Kingdom is the main trading partner of Malawi, Mauritius, and Zambia. However, all these countries except Mauritius have been progressively diversifying their trading relations.

The only countries of this group that have generally enjoyed a surplus in the balance of payments, both on goods and services account and overall, are Congo and Zambia. The other three have usually had a deficit on goods and services account, with the outcome for the overall balance of payments fluctuating between a surplus and a deficit depending on the size of the current account deficit and the magnitude and timing of transfer payments and capital inflows. The international reserves of both Congo and Zambia were on an upward trend until the second half of 1970. Madagascar's international reserves, after sustaining a sharp decline in 1969, recovered somewhat in the following year but still remain below the average of the several years preceding 1969. The international reserves of Malawi have held to a relatively steady level over the period of the 1960s. The international reserves of Mauritius fell off in 1967–68; a purchase from the International Monetary Fund in 1969 was followed by a repurchase in 1970 as the reserve position improved. All five countries are participants in the special drawing rights (SDR) facility established by the Fund, and their cumulative allocations (1970 and 1971) range from SDR 3.5 million for Malawi to SDR 27.2 million for Congo. Zambia and Congo have received SDRs in transactions with participants.

The trade system is generally liberal in all five countries, and they have few restrictions on current payments. Traders in Malawi, Mauritius, and Zambia may import most commodities freely from virtually all sources, whether under open general license or specific license. In the Malagasy Republic, imports from the French franc area and from EEC countries may be made freely; imports from other countries are subject to specific licensing but not normally to restriction. In Congo, most imports are free of licensing requirements irrespective of their origin.

In general, prospects for the continued economic development of these countries appear to be promising. This is particularly true of Congo, which has substantial and varied resources, both agricultural and mineral, and a low density of population. With a highly diversified agricultural base, an abundance of minerals, and a large domestic market, Congo has the prospect of developing into an important supplier of industrial and agricultural products. Although Mauritius is burdened by severe population pressure and heavy dependence on the production and export of sugar, there is potential for the development of other sectors, especially the tourist industry. The Malagasy Republic has varied agricultural and livestock resources and there is active prospecting for petroleum, bauxite, and nickel. Zambia is well endowed with mineral resources and possesses an agricultural sector which, though relatively undeveloped, has potential.

Malawi, though considerably smaller and with a greater density of population, also has the advantage of varied agricultural resources. In this respect and in its ability to export labor to southern Africa, it is favorably situated. In the case of the agriculturally based economies, future prospects are dependent on success in increasing productivity and altering the pattern of agricultural output to bring it more in line with demand. In all these countries except Congo, the small size of the domestic market places a limit on the expansion of manufacturing industry.

CHAPTER 2

Democratic Republic of Congo

GENERAL SETTING

The Democratic Republic of Congo, in central Africa, is bounded on the north by the Central African Republic and Sudan, on the east by Uganda, Rwanda, Burundi, and Tanzania, on the south by Zambia and Angola, and on the west by the Atlantic Ocean for twenty-five miles to the north of the Congo River estuary, by Cabinda, and by the People's Republic of the Congo (see map).

Congo, formerly the Belgian Congo, became an independent nation on June 30, 1960. The country is divided into eight provinces—Bandundu, Kongo Central, Equateur, Kasai Occidental, Kasai Oriental, Katanga, Kivu, and Orientale—each with its own governor. The largest urban centers are the capital city of Kinshasa (formerly Leopoldville), which forms a separate municipality in Kongo Central province, with a population estimated at 1.3 million in 1970; Lubumbashi (formerly Elisabethville), in Katanga province (318,000); and Kisangani (formerly Stanleyville), in Orientale province (230,000).

The country occupies an area of some 905,000 square miles astride the equator and embraces the larger part of the vast watershed of the Congo basin, which is formed by the Congo River and its tributaries. The Congo River alone is 2,900 miles long and drains an area of about 1,425,000 square miles. In the center of the country is an equatorial rain forest; to the east are forested mountains and lakes; forest parks and savannas are found in the north and cover most of the south. The climate is varied, ranging from intense heat and high humidity in the western and central areas, especially in the rain forest, to temperate and equable temperatures as the ground rises toward the eastern highlands and the Katanga escarpment. In the western and central areas, frequent torrential rains fall from April to November, and the mean annual rainfall is between 50 and 60 inches. In the areas to the south of the equator the principal rainy season occurs between October and June and the rainfall is much lower. On the whole, the land is not well suited to cultivation, the notable exceptions being along the cataracts of the Congo River, in southern Kasai Oriental and Kivu provinces, and in parts of the former provinces of Uélé, Ubangi, Mayombé, and Ituri.

The population was estimated at 16.1 million persons in 1968 and is believed to be increasing at an annual rate of 2.3 per cent.[1] The average density is 18 persons to the square mile, but because of the uneven distribution it is only about 3 persons to the square mile in over half of the country. Some 80 per cent of the people live in the rural areas adjacent to mineral deposits or along the main transport routes. The European population was estimated at between 40,000 and 50,000 in 1968, having declined from 110,000 in 1960.

There are three distinct ethnic groups among the indigenous population of Congo, namely the Negroid group (which include the Bantu, Sudanese, and Nilotes), the Hamites, and the Pygmies. The Bantu occupy most of the central basin as well as certain peripheral areas, while Sudanese and Nilotes inhabit the northern and northeastern parts of the country. Tribes having Arab characteristics are found in the

[1] A population count carried out by the Ministry of the Interior in the summer of 1970 shows that the population was 21.6 million, which implies an average rate of growth in population of 4.2 per cent a year.

region of Maniema and around Kisangani. Pygmoid tribes live in scattered areas in the Congo basin and in the area around Ituri in the northeast. Although there are numerous tribal dialects, there are four major vernacular languages. Kikongo is spoken in the province of Kongo Central from the sea to Kinshasa; Lingala is spoken throughout the Congo basin from Kinshasa to Kisangani; Kiswahili (a Bantu tongue with a strong Arabic influence) is spoken from the upper Congo River to the eastern regions; and Tshiluba is spoken in the south of the country. French is the official language and is spoken with varying degrees of fluency in the urban areas.

Before independence, education for Congolese was largely limited to an extensive primary school system. Enrollment in primary schools has increased since then and by the academic year 1969/70 was 3 million. Enrollment at the secondary level has increased nearly sevenfold since independence, and in 1969/70 was 264,000. Higher education is for the most part provided by universities located in Kinshasa, Lubumbashi, and Kisangani. Special professional training colleges have also been established in recent years in order to accelerate the training of lawyers, administrators, teachers, and other professional persons. Enrollment in these institutions expanded from 760 students in 1958/59 to 4,650 in 1966/67 and to 9,741 in 1969/70. Congolese students are also receiving advanced training in Belgium, France, and the United States.

Congo became a member of the United Nations on September 20, 1960. On September 28, 1963 it joined the International Monetary Fund (quota on May 31, 1971, $113 million), the International Bank for Reconstruction and Development (capital subscription on May 31, 1971, $96 million), and the International Development Association, and on April 15, 1970 it joined the International Finance Corporation. It is an associate member of the European Economic Community, a contracting party (effective September 1971) to the General Agreement on Tariffs and Trade, and a member of the African Development Bank, the Common Organization of African, Malagasy and Mauritian States, the United Nations Economic Commission for Africa, the Food and Agriculture Organization of the United Nations, and the United Nations Educational, Scientific and Cultural Organization.

The currency of Congo, the zaïre, is issued by the National Bank of Congo. The zaïre replaced the Congo franc on June 23, 1967 at an official rate of exchange of Z 1 = $2.00. The zaïre is divided into 100 makuta (singular form, likuta), and the par value agreed with the International Monetary Fund on September 2, 1970 is Z 1 = $2.00.

After attaining independence in June 1960, the Democratic Republic of Congo underwent an extended period of economic and financial disorder. Insecurity in many areas of the interior and disruptions of transport facilities and trade services resulted in considerable production losses and declining export earnings, especially in the agricultural sector. These developments, combined with large budgetary deficits, brought about inflationary conditions and pressure on the balance of payments, and external reserves were drawn down. Substantial increases in domestic prices, together with restrictions on foreign payments, led to a continuing depreciation of the Congolese currency on the black market and to clandestine exports.

Although several attempts were made to remedy the inflationary situation, these attempts were largely thwarted by political emergencies. With the restoration and consolidation of political stability in late 1965 and 1966, conditions became propitious for mounting a broad stabilization program, and this was adopted in June 1967. A general review of the economic situation from independence to the monetary reform is given in the following section, and the rest of the chapter is largely devoted to a survey of the Congolese economy after June 1967.

THE ECONOMY FROM INDEPENDENCE TO THE MONETARY REFORM OF 1967

At the time of independence, the economy of Congo was firmly based on a highly developed mining industry, a prosperous and diversified agriculture, and a smaller but expanding manufacturing industry. Production in mining and agriculture was largely export oriented, but the domestic market was expanding and investment was responding to the opportunities it offered. The infrastructure was fairly well developed, and the transport system and supporting commercial facilities were efficient.

Between 1960 and 1966, little change took place in gross domestic product (GDP). Real GDP is estimated to have declined by about 8 per cent between 1959 and 1964 but to have risen subsequently; in 1966 it amounted to the equivalent of some $1.3 billion, about 4 per cent larger than in 1959. Per capita GDP, which was estimated at the equivalent of $95 in 1959, had declined to about $80 in 1966, as the increase in population during that period was estimated at about 2.3 per cent per annum. Agricultural production, which supports some 70 per cent of the population, fell sharply during this period, particularly the production of cash crops for the domestic market and for export, and in 1966 receipts from agricultural exports were some 50 per cent below their pre-1960 level. Mineral output, which had declined up to the end of 1963, only slowly regained its 1960 level; in many parts of the country the mining industry suffered extensive damage during the civil strife. Production of copper did not regain the 1960 level until 1966. The only sector where limited expansion took place in this period was manufacturing, where rising prices, growing monetary incomes, and restrictions on imports created favorable conditions. The share of the government sector in GDP increased considerably, as outlays for government services and defense were expanded.

The principal cause of the inflationary conditions in the period 1960–66 was the government budgetary deficits, which were brought about largely by increases in expenditure and were financed principally by borrowing from the central bank. The increases in expenditure stemmed mainly from successive hikes in wages and salaries for government personnel, from an enlarged payroll, and from a virtual breakdown of controls on expenditure. Revised constitutional arrangements led to a surrender of power by the Central Government to the provinces, where the administrations did not always possess the qualified staff and organization needed, and this resulted in further excess spending and the accumulation of arrears. With treasury control over expenditure already weakened by the withdrawal of foreign personnel, budgetary policies—which in any case were often insufficiently formulated—could not be effectively implemented. In addition, the Katanga secession (July 1960–February 1963) and the ensuing political disruption deprived the Central Government of its most important source of revenue. Tax evasion and misappropriation of public funds were further factors which helped to widen the gap between revenue and expenditure.

In the period 1960–63, the deficit of the Central Government amounted to about one half of total budgetary expenditure. Following the exchange rate adjustment of November 1963, budgetary performance improved as new sources of revenue were created. With the renewed outbreak of rebellion in 1964, however, production continued to stagnate and government finances began to deteriorate again: in 1965 expenditure increased by more than 50 per cent and the budgetary deficit amounted to nearly 40 per cent of expenditure. In 1966, the increase in expenditure was small and, with rising budgetary revenue, the deficit was reduced substantially. However, progress was again cut short in the beginning of 1967 owing to an increase in the rate of spending and a fall in government receipts from taxes, following a dispute with Union Minière du Haut Katanga which led to the suspension of exports of copper and other minerals. By mid-1967, about one fourth of total government expenditure was being financed by central bank credit.

Consumer prices in the capital city of Kinshasa (then Leopoldville) rose by about two and one-half times between June 1960 and November 1963. Prices rose at a rate of about 12 per cent per annum in the two years 1964–65 and at a rate of 28 per cent per annum in 1966 and the first half of 1967. In June 1967 consumer prices were almost seven times higher than in 1960. The comparatively small increases in 1964 and 1965 reflected the relative price stability brought about, after an initial period of price realignment, by the exchange rate adjustment and stabilization measures introduced in November 1963. With improved supply conditions, prices remained virtually stable between September 1964 and June 1965; but in late 1965 they resumed their upward trend, and the rate of increase accelerated from the beginning of 1966 when the effects of higher wages and the large budget deficit of 1965 began to be felt. Quantitative restrictions on imports and inelasticity of supply of domestic products in the capital also affected prices in this period.

There were successive and substantial increases in wages and salaries in both the public and private sectors between 1960 and 1966. In the public sector, the largest increases were for the lower echelons, for which, in some cases, wages rose ninefold in this period. Minimum wages in the private sector were increased by about three and one-half times, and important wage rate differentials arose for comparable work between the private and public sectors. Comparison of money wages with prices in this period indicates that the successive wage increases were rapidly absorbed by the price increases and that wages in real terms declined markedly in the private sector.

Prior to independence and for a short time thereafter, central banking activities were the responsibility of the Central Bank of the Belgian Congo and Ruanda-Urundi. In August 1960, agreement was reached on the division of the assets and liabilities of the Central Bank between Congo and Ruanda-Urundi and on the establishment of two separate currencies and institutes of issue. The Congolese Government subsequently decided that in the period beginning from the liquidation of the Central Bank until the commencement of operations of a Congolese national bank, central banking responsibilities should be assumed by an interim institution, a monetary council, which was established on October 3, 1960. Statutes for a new central bank were later prepared, and the creation of the National Bank of Congo was announced on February 23, 1961. However, in view of the unsettled conditions in the country, the authorities decided to postpone commencement of operations by the National Bank. In fact, the Monetary Council acted as the institute of issue until June 22, 1964, when it ceased operations and its assets and liabilities were taken over by the National Bank, which then commenced operations. Parallel to these developments, a separate central bank, known as the National Bank of Katanga, was established in Katanga following the secession of that province from the Central Government in July 1960. The period of secession lasted until February 1963, at which time the province was reunified with the rest of the country and the operations of the National Bank of Katanga were terminated.

The money supply increased more than fivefold in the seven years ended June 1967. The principal expansionary factor throughout this period was a large increase in credit to the Government, which rose more than sevenfold. Most of this credit expansion was in the form of central bank advances, although commercial banks from time to time purchased treasury bills. Whereas before 1960 credit to the Government represented a small proportion of total central bank assets, such credit accounted for some 80 per cent of total assets in June 1967. Credit to the private sector also rose between June 1960 and June 1967, but only about threefold; at the latter date it accounted for under 15 per cent of total credit outstanding, its growth having been controlled through effec-

tive application of credit ceilings. Before June 1967, the overall change
in the net foreign assets of the banking system played a minor role as a
factor affecting the money supply; in relative terms, net foreign assets
did show some sharp fluctuations from one year to another, but in
absolute terms these fluctuations were rather small. Increases in quasi-
money and, in certain years, an accumulation of counterpart funds of
foreign aid were factors tending to contract the money supply.

The balance of payments in the years prior to independence had
shown relatively large surpluses on trade account, but there had been
deficits on account of goods and services and private transfers, generally financed by foreign aid. After independence, the balance of payments underwent structural changes owing to lower export earnings and
to the introduction of restrictions on imports and on payments for
invisibles. Exports fell by more than 30 per cent, to a low of some $320
million in 1962 and 1963, which was primarily the result of a fall in
agricultural exports. Clandestine exports, mainly of agricultural commodities and diamonds, were responsible for a loss in export earnings
of some $40–50 million annually. Receipts from agricultural exports
picked up in 1964, following the exchange rate adjustment of November
1963, but fell again in 1965–66. Largely because of a rise in world
copper prices and of increased mining production, total export receipts
rose from $373 million in 1965 to $483 million in 1966. Imports were
reduced from roughly $300 million annually before independence to a
low of some $210 million in 1963, despite the utilization of substantial
amounts of foreign assistance for import financing. With an improved
export performance, imports were raised to about $250 million in 1964
and 1965 and to about $300 million in 1966. During this period, im-
ports remained subject to restrictive licensing, and import quotas by
commodity categories were determined in accordance with established
priorities within a global allocation of foreign exchange for imports and
invisibles. Transfers of investment income were suspended in 1960. The
servicing of the foreign debt was also suspended in 1960, and virtually
no repayments of public debt were made until 1965. Private transfer
payments, though restricted, remained substantial owing to the relatively large number of foreign personnel employed in the mining and
industrial sectors.

As a result of the restrictions on all payments for current invisibles, the deficit on goods and services and private transfers in the years 1960–66 was generally smaller than in earlier years. On the other hand, net receipts from official transfers and from nonmonetary capital fell substantially, despite the relatively large amounts of foreign aid received. Gross official holdings of gold and foreign exchange, which had been drawn down considerably in 1959–60, remained relatively low during the period 1960–66 and totaled about $20 million at the end of June 1967, or the equivalent of about five weeks' imports financed by Congo's own external earnings and reserves. Total net foreign assets of the banking system amounted to $46 million at the same date.

In June 1967, a stabilization program was adopted which received the support of the International Monetary Fund in the form of a one-year stand-by arrangement for $27 million. The primary objectives of the program were the re-establishment of monetary stability and of con-ditions under which growth of the economy could be resumed. A new monetary unit, the zaïre, was introduced at an exchange rate that reflected a substantial depreciation of the currency. At the same time, stringent wage, fiscal, and credit policies were adopted to allow restora-tion of basic equilibrium in government finances and the liberalization of current international transactions. The stabilization effort was assisted by the very favorable market for copper, which resulted in sub-stantial increases in export proceeds and in government revenue. No drawings were made under the stand-by arrangement.

STRUCTURE OF THE ECONOMY

GROSS DOMESTIC PRODUCT

After years of virtual stagnation (see above), GDP at constant 1966 prices rose by about 8 per cent in 1968 and, according to preliminary figures, by a further 7 per cent in 1969 (Table 1). In the latter year, GDP at constant prices was only some 20 per cent above the level of 1959, an average rate of increase of less than 2 per cent a year. Since the population is estimated to have been increasing by about 2.3 per cent a year, it would appear that per capita GDP in real terms has declined since 1959.

In recent years GDP at current prices has increased much more rap-

TABLE 1. DEMOCRATIC REPUBLIC OF CONGO: GROSS DOMESTIC PRODUCT, 1966-69

(In millions of zaïres)

	At 1966 Prices				At Current Prices		Percentage Change at Constant (1966) Prices			Per Cent of Monetized GDP at Current Prices		
	1966	1967	1968	1969¹	1968	1969¹	1967/66	1968/67	1969/68¹	1966	1968	1969¹
Primary sector	48.52	51.11	56.29	55.45	159.51	175.06	5.3	10.1	−1.5	17.65	24.30	21.49
Agriculture (marketed)	27.12	29.63	34.79	32.96	86.21	85.33	9.3	17.4	−6.6	9.87	13.13	10.48
Mining	21.40	21.48	21.50	22.96	73.30	89.73	0.4	0.1	6.8	7.78	11.17	11.01
Secondary sector	59.91	59.39	61.63	68.69	169.17	216.40	−0.9	3.8	11.1	21.79	25.77	26.57
Processing of minerals	32.71	32.97	34.00	37.37	112.99	148.27	0.8	3.1	9.9	11.90	17.21	18.20
Manufacturing	18.41	17.96	16.75	18.43	32.11	37.09	−2.4	−6.7	10.0	6.70	4.89	4.55
Energy	2.29	2.01	2.98	3.41	7.07	8.09	−12.2	48.3	14.4	0.83	1.08	1.00
Construction	6.50	6.45	7.90	9.48	17.00	22.95	−0.8	22.5	20.0	2.36	2.59	2.82
Tertiary sector	87.84	84.30	92.94	101.85	193.20	238.85	−4.0	10.2	9.6	31.95	29.43	29.33
Transport and telecommunications	16.34	17.30	19.67	21.24	40.10	48.71	5.9	13.7	8.0	5.94	6.11	5.98
Banking and insurance	4.30	4.00	4.77	5.96	12.80	18.10	−7.0	19.3	25.0	1.56	1.95	2.22
Commerce	41.00	38.50	41.50	45.03	82.30	100.46	−6.1	7.8	8.5	14.92	12.54	12.34
Other services	26.20	24.50	27.00	29.62	58.00	71.58	−6.5	10.2	9.7	9.53	8.83	8.79
Domestic production at factor cost	196.27	194.80	210.86	225.99	521.88	630.31	−0.8	8.2	7.2	71.39	79.50	77.39
Indirect taxes	28.48	24.79	24.68	30.60	53.16	71.85	−13.0	−0.4	24.0	10.36	8.10	8.82
Domestic production at market prices	224.75	219.59	235.54	256.59	575.04	702.16	−2.3	7.3	8.9	81.75	87.60	86.21
Government services and defense	50.16	51.94	59.08	60.62	81.35	112.30	3.5	13.7	2.6	18.25	12.40	13.79
Monetized gross domestic product	274.91	271.53	294.62	317.21	656.39	814.46	−1.2	8.5	7.7	100.00	100.00	100.00
Subsistence agriculture	29.20	29.60	30.00	30.40	64.00	68.04	1.4	1.4	1.3	10.62	9.75	8.35
Gross domestic product	304.11	301.13	324.62	347.61	720.39	882.50	−1.0	7.8	7.1	110.62	109.75	108.35

Sources: Banque Nationale du Congo, *Rapport Annuel, 1968–1969*; and data provided by the Congolese authorities.

¹ Figures for 1969 are preliminary.

idly than at constant prices, especially in 1967 and 1968 when domestic prices rose sharply following the exchange rate adjustment in June 1967. In 1969 per capita GDP at current prices was equivalent to about $100, compared with $95 in 1959.

In real terms, GDP declined slightly in 1967 as the economy was adjusting to the new situation brought about by the new exchange rate and the introduction of stabilization measures. Although output originating in the primary and secondary sectors rose by about 2 per cent, this increase was more than offset by a reduction in the contribution of the tertiary sector. In particular, the contribution of commerce to GDP at constant prices declined by about 6 per cent, reflecting the sluggishness of economic activity and a reduction in the profit margins of traders.

In 1968, overall financial stability was restored and all sectors of the economy except manufacturing contributed to the 8 per cent growth in real GDP. Agricultural production rose by about 17 per cent, and there was an increase of about 10 per cent in the value added by the tertiary sector. The contribution of the government sector to GDP rose by about 14 per cent, owing mainly to the increase in the salaries of government employees, the larger role assumed by the Government in the field of education, and the growth of the armed forces.

The economy expanded by a further 7 per cent in 1969, despite a shortfall in agricultural production. The increase in GDP during that year resulted mainly from an increase in mineral extraction and processing, a recovery in manufacturing production, and a further expansion in the tertiary sector.

Between 1966 and 1969, the contribution of the primary and secondary sectors to monetized GDP at current prices rose from 39 per cent to 48 per cent. This was primarily due to the rise in copper prices on the world market, as the relative contribution of both sectors to GDP at constant prices remained approximately unchanged. The relative importance of the tertiary sector in monetized GDP at current prices declined during the same period from 32 per cent to 29 per cent; in particular, the contribution of commerce declined from about 15 per cent to 12 per cent.

It is estimated that GDP at constant prices increased by about 9 per cent in 1970 and that all sectors contributed to the expansion. Agricultural output is estimated to have expanded by about 7 per cent, mining by 5 per cent, manufacturing by 10 per cent, construction and public works by 20 per cent, and the service sector by 9 per cent.

Since 1966 gross domestic expenditure has been smaller than gross domestic product, and a surplus on exports of goods and services has been realized. Between 1966 and 1968, gross domestic expenditure at constant prices rose by about 4 per cent, compared with an increase of about 7 per cent in GDP, but in 1969 the rise in gross domestic expenditure was larger than that in GDP. Net exports of goods and services accounted for more than 5 per cent of total GDP at current prices in 1969, compared with 7 per cent in 1968 and 2 per cent in 1966 (Table 2).

Between 1966 and 1969, investment increased much more rapidly than consumption and contributed nearly three fourths of the increase in gross domestic expenditure. As a result, the share of investment in gross domestic expenditure at constant prices rose from 14 per cent in 1966 to 16 per cent in 1968 and 21 per cent in 1969. Gross fixed investment at constant prices rose by 16 per cent between 1966 and 1968 and by 44 per cent in 1969. Over these years, public investment rose at a much faster rate than private investment, accounting in 1969 for more than 30 per cent of total gross investment. In that year some 70 per cent of total gross investment was in the form of imports of transport equipment and other capital goods; construction and public works accounted for most of the remainder.

During this period, total consumption at constant prices rose by only 4 per cent. Private consumption declined by more than 6 per cent, while public consumption rose, and the share of the latter in total consumption at constant prices increased from 24 per cent in 1966 to 32 per cent in 1969. Disposable income also grew much less rapidly than GDP, mainly because of the increase in taxation.

Preliminary estimates for 1970 show a further substantial increase in gross fixed investment and public consumption, which at current prices rose by some 16 per cent and 26 per cent, respectively. Private consumption also rose in 1970, by some 13 per cent.

AGRICULTURE

Because of the wide variations in climate and topography, the agricultural sector is highly diversified. Palm oil, coffee, rubber, cotton,

TABLE 2. DEMOCRATIC REPUBLIC OF CONGO: NATIONAL INCOME AND EXPENDITURE, 1966, 1968, AND 1969

(In millions of zaïres)

	At 1966 Prices			At Current Prices		Percentage Change at Constant (1966) Prices		Per Cent of GDP at Current Prices		
	1966	1968	1969[1]	1968	1969[1]	1968/66	1969/68[1]	1966	1968	1969[1]
Consumption	257.6	261.7	268.5	531.3	617.0	2.6	2.6	84.7	73.7	69.9
Private	194.6	174.4	182.2	376.3	440.0	-10.4	4.5	64.0	52.2	49.9
Public	63.0	87.3	86.3	155.0	177.0	38.6	-1.2	20.7	21.5	20.0
Gross fixed investment	41.5	48.1	69.4	139.8	218.4	15.9	44.3	13.6	19.4	24.8
Private	34.8	36.0	47.8	104.5	150.4	3.4	32.8	11.4	14.5	17.1
Public	6.6	12.1	21.6	35.2	68.0	83.3	78.5	2.2	4.9	7.7
Gross domestic expenditure	299.1	309.8	337.9	671.1	835.4	3.6	9.1	98.4	93.2	94.7
Net exports of goods and services	5.0	14.8	9.7	49.3	47.1	19.6	-34.5	1.7	6.9	5.3
Gross domestic product	304.1	324.6	347.6	720.4	882.5	6.7	7.1	100.0	100.0	100.0
Net payment to factor income	-12.7	-16.6	-17.0	-55.5	-56.0	30.7	2.4	4.2	7.7	6.3
Gross national product	291.4	308.0	330.6	665.0	826.5	5.7	7.3	95.8	92.3	93.7
Indirect taxes	-44.3	-51.7	...	-143.8	-193.0	16.7	...	14.6	20.0	21.9
Depreciation	-27.4	-28.7	...	-83.5	-86.7	4.7	...	9.0	11.6	9.8
National income	219.7	227.6	...	437.7	546.8	3.6	...	72.2	60.8	62.0
Direct taxes	-10.4	-14.6	...	-28.0	-70.0	40.4	...	3.4	3.9	7.9
Disposable income	209.3	213.0	...	409.7	476.8	1.8	...	68.8	56.9	54.0

Sources: Banque Nationale du Congo, *Rapport Annuel, 1968–1969*; data provided by the Congolese authorities; and Fund staff estimates.
[1] Figures for 1969 are preliminary.

sugarcane, cocoa, groundnuts, tea, and other tropical commodities are produced; conditions are favorable for rice and wheat as well as for the staple cereals of maize and cassava; considerable areas are suitable for beef cattle; and the reserves of hardwood are the largest in Africa. At present about 1 per cent of the land is being used for agricultural purposes, such as cultivated crops and plantation products.

Traditional systems of ownership have remained unchanged. These vary between tribal areas; rights to hold or work land depend largely on whether the social system is patriarchal or matriarchal, but ownership is usually vested in the tribal unit. However, legislation adopted in 1966 (Bakajika Law) suspended tenure rights for all land acquired during the colonial period. Landowners seeking reconfirmation of their title deeds were required to submit applications to the Congolese Government showing how and at what price the land was originally obtained, and the extent to which it had been developed.

In 1966 the agricultural sector accounted for almost 20 per cent of GDP and supported some 70 per cent of the population. Production is divided between European-owned plantations and Congolese cash and subsistence farming. The produce grown on the plantations is mainly for export, supplemented to a limited extent by Congolese farmers working small holdings; in 1967, agricultural commodities accounted for about 20 per cent of total export earnings. Foodstuffs for domestic consumption are grown for the most part by small-scale farmers, a sector which merges into the subsistence sector. Land tends to be underutilized, since Congolese farmers make little use of fertilizer and instead let the land lie fallow for twice as long as it is cropped.

After years of regression and stagnation, agricultural production began to recover in 1967. Marketed production rose by 9 per cent in that year and by a further 17 per cent in 1968; it declined by about 7 per cent in 1969, mainly because of unfavorable weather conditions, but rose again by 9 per cent in 1970. Therefore, over the four years 1967–70 marketed production rose at an average annual rate of 7 per cent. Owing largely to the decline in output in 1960–66, marketed production accounted for about 10 per cent of monetized GDP in 1969, compared with 21 per cent in 1959. Production in the subsistence sector is estimated to account for just under half of total agricultural activity in that year (see Table 1).

Data on the value added for each of the main agricultural commodities are presented in Table 3. Food crops (mainly cassava, bananas, rice, maize, fruits, and vegetables), livestock, and fishing accounted for about 38 per cent of all marketed production, and production of other crops (for both export and domestic consumption) for the remaining 62 per cent, in 1968. Although output of food crops has increased in recent years, it still falls short of domestic requirements, and relatively large though declining quantities of maize, rice, and other staples continue to be imported.

Production for Export

Palm products, coffee, and rubber are the principal agricultural export products; in 1968 they accounted for about 75 per cent of all marketed production other than food crops. Production of these commodities rose between 1966 and 1968 but declined in 1969 and was still considerably smaller than in 1959 (Table 4). In 1969 exports of agricultural products totaled about Z 47 million (compared with Z 51 million in 1968 and with about Z 80 million in 1959), and accounted for less than 15 per cent of total export earnings. Clandestine exports of agricultural products have declined sharply since the adjustment of the exchange rate in June 1967.

Palm products, mainly palm oil, palm nut oil, and palm husks, are the most important agricultural export commodities. Although palm oil production has been recovering (206,200 metric tons in 1968 and 200,500 metric tons in 1969), it has still not reached the 1959 level (244,500 metric tons). The production of palm nut oil and of husks have followed a similar pattern. Exports have declined in recent years as an increasing proportion has been diverted to the domestic market for the manufacture of soap, margarine, and cooking oil. Whereas in 1959 just over 75 per cent of the palm oil produced was exported, by 1967 this proportion had fallen to 64 per cent. The amount of palm nuts exported is relatively small compared with 1959. Most palm products are grown on plantations where they are collected and marketed by CONGOPALM, a cooperative for the plantations.

Coffee is the second most important export crop; it is largely composed of robusta, although arabica is also grown, and is almost entirely

TABLE 3. DEMOCRATIC REPUBLIC OF CONGO: VALUE ADDED BY PRIMARY SECTOR, 1966-68

(In millions of zaïres)

	At 1966 Prices			At Current Prices	Percentage Change at Constant (1966) Prices		Per Cent of Total at Current Prices	
	1966	1967	1968	1968	1967/66	1968/67	1966	1968
Agriculture [1]	**27.13**	**29.63**	**34.79**	**86.21**	**9.2**	**17.4**	**55.9**	**54.0**
Foodstuffs	12.50	13.71	15.45	32.87	9.7	12.7	25.8	20.6
Food crops [2]	*8.53*	*9.28*	*10.65*	*22.32*	*8.8*	*14.8*	*17.6*	*14.0*
Livestock, fishing	*3.97*	*4.43*	*4.80*	*10.55*	*11.6*	*8.4*	*8.2*	*6.6*
Production for export	10.05	11.30	13.91	42.38	12.4	23.1	20.7	26.6
Palm products	*3.34*	*4.58*	*5.65*	*17.73*	*37.1*	*23.4*	*6.9*	*11.1*
Coffee	*3.52*	*3.73*	*4.71*	*13.38*	*6.0*	*26.3*	*7.2*	*8.4*
Rubber	*1.71*	*1.82*	*2.30*	*6.60*	*6.4*	*26.4*	*3.5*	*4.1*
Timber	*0.53*	*0.42*	*0.39*	*1.29*	*-20.8*	*-7.2*	*1.1*	*0.8*
Tea	*0.36*	*0.19*	*0.33*	*1.09*	*-47.2*	*73.7*	*0.8*	*0.7*
Cocoa	*0.16*	*0.22*	*0.20*	*1.24*	*-37.5*	*-9.1*	*0.3*	*0.8*
Other [3]	*0.44*	*0.33*	*0.32*	*1.05*	*-25.0*	*-3.0*	*0.9*	*0.7*
Production for domestic market	4.57	4.61	5.43	10.96	0.9	17.8	9.4	6.8
Palm products	*1.63*	*1.67*	*1.80*	*3.00*	*2.4*	*7.8*	*3.4*	*1.9*
Timber	*0.96*	*0.85*	*1.06*	*2.12*	*-11.5*	*24.7*	*2.0*	*1.3*
Cotton	*0.87*	*0.97*	*1.39*	*3.25*	*11.5*	*43.3*	*1.8*	*2.0*
Groundnuts	*0.55*	*0.52*	*0.55*	*1.35*	*-5.5*	*5.8*	*1.1*	*0.8*
Other [4]	*0.56*	*0.60*	*0.63*	*1.23*	*7.1*	*5.0*	*1.1*	*0.8*
Mining	**21.39**	**21.48**	**21.50**	**73.30**	**0.4**	**0.1**	**44.1**	**46.0**
Copper	10.04	10.10	10.28	34.70	0.6	1.8	20.7	21.8
Diamonds	3.48	3.61	3.46	14.13	3.7	-4.2	7.2	8.9
Other [5]	7.87	7.77	7.76	24.47	-1.3	-0.1	16.2	15.3
Total value added	**48.52**	**51.11**	**56.29**	**159.51**	**5.3**	**10.1**	**100.0**	**100.0**

Source: Banque Nationale du Congo, *Rapport Annuel, 1968-1969.*

[1] Excluding subsistence agriculture, i.e., marketed production only.
[2] Mainly cassava, bananas, rice, maize, fruits, and vegetables.
[3] Cinchona, copal, urena-punga fiber, rauwolfia, ivory, sisal, papaya extract, pyrethrum, cottonseed husks, and groundnut oil and husks.
[4] Coffee, rubber, tea, cocoa, tobacco, and sugarcane.
[5] Cobalt, zinc, cadmium, cassiterite (tin dioxide), gold, manganese, columbite-tantalite, niobium, wolframite, silver, coal, germanium, and iron ore.

TABLE 4. DEMOCRATIC REPUBLIC OF CONGO: AGRICULTURAL
PRODUCTION, 1959 AND 1966–69 [1]

(*In thousands of metric tons, except timber*)

	1959	1966	1967	1968	1969
Palm oil	244.5	146.9	178.9	206.2	200.5
Palm nut oil	61.1	37.1	41.8	48.5	45.8
Palm husks	67.0	41.9	45.7	54.4	52.9
Palm nuts	39.8	—	4.1	2.2	—
Robusta coffee [2]	52.0	29.8	37.2	46.1	43.9
Arabica coffee [3]	10.3	4.6	9.0	7.2	5.0
Rubber	40.2	30.4	32.3	40.9	36.6
Timber (logs) [4]	227.8	186.3	154.0	137.5	130.5
Timber (sawn) [4]	212.5	130.7	123.9	119.5	124.8
Cotton (fiber)	63.2	7.4	8.0	11.8	18.1
Cottonseed husks	27.6	2.2	3.6	3.7	6.1
Cottonseed oil	6.0	0.7	0.7	0.8	2.0
Groundnuts	28.8	28.0	...	...	...
Groundnut oil	8.2	1.3	1.0	0.9	0.5
Groundnut husks	11.9	1.9	1.4	1.3	0.7
Tea	4.2	6.0	4.5	4.7	5.1
Cocoa	4.5	4.1	5.6	5.1	4.4
Sugarcane [5]	38.6	31.9	34.7	38.4	36.0

Sources: Banque Nationale du Congo, *Rapport Annuel, 1968–1969* and *1969–1970;* and data provided by the Congolese authorities.

[1] Excluding food crops for domestic consumption—mainly cassava, bananas, rice, maize, fruits, and vegetables. Other products not shown in the table include bananas for export, ivory, sisal, urena-punga fiber, copal, rauwolfia, and cinchona.
[2] Excluding coffee exported through the eastern part of the country.
[3] Exports only.
[4] In thousands of cubic meters.
[5] Sugar equivalent.

for export. Robusta coffee is produced mainly in the areas around Isiro in the northeast. The greater part is grown on plantations, with about a fifth of the production being supplied by small-scale growers. Production declined from more than 50,000 metric tons in 1959 to a low of about 19,000 tons in 1965, mainly on account of the general insecurity that prevailed in these regions and of transport difficulties. Subsequently production increased, and in 1969 it was 44,000 tons. The recovery was due partly to Congolese farmers reworking abandoned farms, but also to reduced smuggling to neighboring countries and the relatively favorable price of coffee on the world market. Most of the crop is processed in Kinshasa. It is graded and certified by the Robusta Coffee Office, but marketing is carried out by private companies and by a producer cooperative (CAFECONGO). Arabica coffee is grown mainly in Kivu, where the altitude is higher. The coffee is processed and graded in the OPAK coffee factory in Goma, but because the capacity of the factory is limited, there are often long delays in delivery. It is believed that significant amounts of arabica are still being smuggled across the eastern frontier. Congo's basic export quota under the International Coffee Agreement for 1970/71 was initially set at 63,600 metric tons (or 1.06 million bags).

Rubber is largely produced on ten plantations in the northwest, and considerable losses were incurred during the 1964–65 rebellion. Production, which amounted to some 40,000 metric tons in 1959, had recovered to 41,000 tons by 1968 but declined in 1969 to 37,000 tons. Approximately 10 per cent of production is used domestically by two shoe manufacturers, and the rest is exported.

Tea is cultivated and processed in Kivu, and production is now estimated at 5,000 tons. The tea industry was started after World War II, and although Congo is still a small-scale producer in Africa, growing conditions are favorable. Cocoa is grown almost exclusively by Europeans. Production declined during 1965 and 1966, but it has been increasing recently.

Production for Domestic Market

Cotton used to be one of the principal cash crops, but after 1959 production fell rapidly and by 1965 had declined from 63,200 metric tons to 4,500 tons. By 1969 it had risen to just over 18,000 tons. Cotton is grown exclusively by Congolese farmers. Before independence, production was sufficient to meet the requirements of the local textile mills and also to supply 50,000 tons of fiber for export. In subsequent years cotton was imported to supply the demand of the local textile mills; but beginning in 1968 domestic production has been sufficient to meet the needs of the domestic textile industry and to provide a small surplus of fiber for export. An association of private marketing companies, the Compagnie Cotonnière Congolaise (COTONCO), collects and gins the cotton, which is purchased direct from the farmers.

Sugarcane is exclusively a plantation crop, the most important one for domestic consumption. It is grown and refined by the Société Générale

Sucrière du Congo (SOGESUCRE) at Moerbeke in the province of Kongo Central and in the area of Kwilu, and by Les Sucreries et Raffineries de l'Afrique Centrale (SUCRAF) in Kivu province. Sugar production was expanding rapidly in the years before independence, but the plantations suffered considerable material losses during the rebellions, especially in Kivu. However, production in Kongo Central has expanded in recent years, following new investment by SOGESUCRE. Current production meets about three fourths of domestic requirements.

Maize and cassava are the principal farinaceous foods of the population and are grown throughout the country. Rice, which is consumed to a lesser extent, is grown along the Congo River, mostly between Lisala and Bumba in the northwest. Before independence, production of foodstuffs, such as fruit and vegetables, was generally sufficient to supply the domestic market and at the same time to leave a surplus for export. However, production has declined considerably, particularly in Kasai Occidental and in parts of Katanga; on the other hand, it has increased sharply in Kongo Central, which was not affected by political disturbances. Although production has now recovered, substantial quantities of cereals and other foods continue to be imported.

Marketing and Pricing

There is no government institution responsible either for marketing agricultural produce or for protecting producers' incomes. However, there are offices for inspecting and grading the quality of agricultural commodities for export. Agricultural exports are for the most part marketed either by the individual producers, especially the large plantations, or collectively through cooperatives. Some commodities, such as palm nuts, coffee, and rubber, are sold by Congolese farmers to the plantations for subsequent processing and marketing. Foodstuffs are customarily marketed through wholesale merchants who in turn distribute them to retailers in the urban centers.

The Government establishes a minimum producer price for each of the principal agricultural commodities. This may vary between regions in order to take account of differences in transport costs. Merchants and those plantations that purchase from Congolese farmers are required to pay the minimum prices and are subject in principle to supervision by government inspectors. Producer prices for export commodities were raised in October 1967 following the adjustment in the exchange rate in June of that year, but they were generally raised less than in proportion to the change in the exchange rate. Since then, they have been kept unchanged in spite of changes in world market prices.

FISHING

The fishing industry is still relatively undeveloped although fish are an important source of protein for the greater part of the population. The catch, estimated at 85,000 tons annually, is insufficient to meet requirements, and between 30,000 and 40,000 tons a year are imported. Fishing in the fresh water lakes in the interior is carried out mainly by foreign companies using modern equipment and, to a lesser extent, by Congolese fishermen using rudimentary techniques. One company conducts trawling operations along the Angola coast; its annual catch is estimated at 13,000 tons.

FORESTRY

Following the development of the market in Europe for African hardwoods, Congo became an important supplier of timber, as its reserves are the largest in Africa. Production was centered mainly in the Mayombé region of Kongo Central province because of easy access to Atlantic ports. With the depletion of forest reserves in the area, however, production has declined in recent years and the proportion of timber exported has fallen. The export of logs has now been restricted in order to meet the demand from domestic factories.

MINING

The mining industry is Congo's principal foreign exchange earner and also the largest single source of government revenue. In 1969 the mining sector provided about 85 per cent of all export receipts and more than 50 per cent of government revenue. Between 1966 and 1969 mineral output (including processing) rose at an average annual rate of 3.5 per cent, most of the increase taking place in 1969 (9 per cent). Largely because of an increase in copper prices, the contribution of mineral output to monetized GDP at factor cost and at current prices rose from 19 per cent in 1966 to 29 per cent in 1969 (see Table 1). After copper, which accounted for about 70 per cent of the total value added in the mining sector in 1968, the minerals which make a significant contribution to the value of production are cobalt, diamonds, zinc, and tin (see Tables 3 and 5).

Copper

Congo accounts for about 6 per cent of the world's production of copper and is the sixth largest producer (after the United States, the U. S. S. R., Zambia, Chile, and Canada). Production tended to contract after 1960, and it was not until 1966 that it regained and exceeded the 1960 level. Production rose by 3 per cent between 1966 and 1968 and by 12 per cent in 1969, when it totaled 364,000 tons. The price of copper on the Brussels market rose from an average of $0.49 a pound in 1967 to $0.54 in 1968, $0.66 in 1969, and $0.73 in the first half of 1970. In the second half of 1970 it declined to an average of $0.53 a pound. Partly because of the higher price, copper exports accounted for about 65 per cent of total export receipts in 1969, compared with 57 per cent in 1966. At present about half of the copper produced is refined in the country; the balance, in the form of cathodes and raw copper, is shipped to Belgium for refining. The greater part of Congolese copper output is marketed in Europe.

The copper deposits in Congo are a continuation of the ore bodies that reach northward from the Zambian Copperbelt into southern Katanga. Unlike the concentrations that are found in Zambia, the Katanga ore bodies tend to be found in relatively small pockets near the surface and can therefore be worked by open pit operations. The ore has a high metal content, averaging between 4 and 5 per cent. There are three main groups of mines, about 60 miles apart: the western group, centered on Kolwezi; the central group centered on Jadotville; and the southern group, centered on Lubumbashi. The western group accounts for over two thirds of the ore recovered; mining is mainly by opencast excavation. The largest underground mine is in the southern group at Kipushi, almost on the Zambian border. Four concentrators serve the mines, of which the largest is at Kolwezi; the other three are at Kipushi, Kambove, and Kakanda. A washery at Ruwe which processes

TABLE 5.   DEMOCRATIC REPUBLIC OF CONGO: VALUE ADDED BY SECONDARY SECTOR, 1966–68

(In millions of zaïres)

	At 1966 Prices			At Current Prices	Percentage Change at Constant (1966) Prices		Per Cent of Total at Current Prices	
	1966	1967	1968	1968	1967/66	1968/67	1966	1968
Mineral processing	**32.71**	**32.96**	**34.00**	**112.99**	**0.8**	**3.2**	**54.6**	**66.8**
Copper	27.84	28.54	29.33	96.72	2.5	2.8	46.5	57.2
Cobalt	2.93	2.59	2.70	10.50	−11.6	4.2	4.9	6.2
Zinc	1.67	1.67	1.72	4.96	—	3.0	2.8	2.9
Tin and cadmium	0.27	0.16	0.25	0.81	−40.7	56.2	0.4	0.5
Manufacturing	**18.41**	**17.96**	**16.75**	**32.11**	**−2.4**	**−6.7**	**30.7**	**19.0**
Consumption goods	11.23	10.85	10.29	19.30	−3.5	−5.2	18.8	11.4
Foodstuffs	*1.75*	*1.86*	*1.94*	*3.50*	*6.3*	*4.3*	*2.9*	*2.1*
Beverages	*3.10*	*3.06*	*3.01*	*6.49*	*−1.3*	*−1.6*	*5.2*	*3.8*
Tobacco	*0.93*	*0.89*	*0.87*	*1.48*	*−4.3*	*−2.2*	*1.5*	*0.9*
Clothing	*1.14*	*1.07*	*0.88*	*1.70*	*−6.1*	*−17.8*	*1.9*	*1.0*
Shoes and leather	*1.35*	*1.24*	*1.08*	*1.73*	*−8.1*	*−12.9*	*2.3*	*1.0*
Chemicals	*0.92*	*0.86*	*0.90*	*1.62*	*−6.5*	*4.6*	*1.5*	*1.0*
Plastics	*0.28*	*0.38*	*0.42*	*0.58*	*35.7*	*10.5*	*0.5*	*0.3*
Metals	*0.46*	*0.42*	*0.31*	*0.49*	*−8.7*	*−26.2*	*0.8*	*0.3*
Other	*1.30*	*1.07*	*0.88*	*1.71*	*−17.7*	*−17.8*	*2.2*	*1.0*
Basic materials and equipment	7.18	7.11	6.46	12.81	−1.0	−9.1	11.9	7.6
Weaving and spinning	*2.82*	*2.76*	*2.39*	*4.55*	*−2.1*	*−13.4*	*4.7*	*2.7*
Basic chemicals	*0.93*	*0.97*	*0.95*	*1.70*	*4.3*	*−2.1*	*1.5*	*1.0*
Mechanical industries	*0.92*	*0.82*	*0.66*	*1.38*	*−10.9*	*−19.5*	*1.5*	*0.8*
Transport equipment	*0.43*	*0.34*	*0.38*	*0.80*	*−20.9*	*11.7*	*0.7*	*0.5*
Nonmetallic minerals	*1.50*	*1.74*	*1.55*	*3.38*	*16.0*	*−10.9*	*2.5*	*2.0*
Timber	*0.58*	*0.48*	*0.53*	*1.00*	*−17.2*	*10.4*	*1.0*	*0.6*
Energy	**2.29**	**2.02**	**2.98**	**7.07**	**−11.8**	**47.5**	**3.8**	**4.2**
Electricity	2.29	2.02	2.14	5.09	−11.8	5.9	3.8	3.0
Petroleum refining	—	—	0.84	1.98	—	—	—	1.2
Construction and public works	**6.50**	**6.45**	**7.90**	**17.00**	**−0.8**	**22.5**	**10.9**	**10.0**
Total	**59.91**	**59.39**	**61.63**	**169.17**	**−0.9**	**3.8**	**100.0**	**100.0**

Source: Banque Nationale du Congo, *Rapport Annuel, 1968–1969.*

breccia into concentrates is the latest installation to be put into operation. Electrolytic copper is produced in the refineries at Shituru and Luilu.

Copper and associated minerals, such as cobalt, zinc, cadmium, lead, and silver, are obtained from deposits in southern Katanga by the Générale Congolaise des Mines (GECOMINES). The company was established in December 1966 by the Congolese Government to assume control of the mining and metallurgical installations in Katanga of Union Minière du Haut Katanga, its subsidiary companies, and its other assets in the country.[2] Since February 1967, management of the GECOMINES installations in Katanga, as well as marketing of the minerals, has been entrusted to the Belgian company, Société Générale des Minerais (SGM), in accordance with a technical cooperation agreement concluded between that company and GECOMINES. The agreement was put on a more permanent basis in September 1969 by a new accord between the Congolese Government and the SGM which also provided for a financial settlement of the dispute over the nationalization of Union Minière's assets in Congo. The share capital of GECOMINES is held by the Congolese Government, and its head office is in Kinshasa.

Minerals Associated with Copper

Cobalt is found in association with copper ores, and Congo accounts for about 60 per cent of world production. After 1960 cobalt production fluctuated and in 1963 it fell to 7,400 tons. The subsequent expansion was due to an increase in world industrial demand, and production in 1969, at 10,600 tons, was 29 per cent more than in 1960. Commercial grade cathodes are produced which are either refined or exported; the cobalt granules are vacuum degassed and refined electrolytically, as a result of a new process which became operative in early 1963. The Cobalt Information Center, an organization of the principal cobalt producers in the world, has done much to foster wider use of the metal and has developed a number of cobalt alloys; UMCo 50, a cobalt-chromium-iron alloy, perhaps the best known alloy developed in Katanga, is used in the degassing furnaces.

---

[2] Union Minière, until 1966 the largest mining company in Congo, had had a concession dating back to 1906.

Zinc is obtained from the sulphide ores at the underground mine at Kipushi, where concentrates with a zinc content averaging about 56 per cent are produced. From these crude concentrates, sulphuric acid and sintered concentrates are produced; the latter are either refined into electrolytic zinc or exported.

Cadmium is obtained from the flue dusts in the Lubumbashi plant. These are processed at Kolwezi into cadmiferous cements which are then refined into electrolytic cadmium rods. Germanium too is found in the copper deposits at Kipushi and after concentration is refined in the electric smelter at Jadotville. The germanium is further refined into high purity metal at the Hoboken works in Belgium or is processed into germanium oxides. Although there is a growing use of germanium as a result of its application in the electronics industry, demand has been declining because of economies in its use, greater re-employment, and competition from other semiconductor metals.

Other metals found in raw copper ores in Katanga include lead, silver, palladium, and platinum; the metals are recovered during the course of refining operations at Hoboken.

Diamonds

Congo is the largest single producer of industrial diamonds in the world, accounting for almost half of world production. In 1969 Congo's official production amounted to 14.1 million carats, but there are clandestine exports and it has been estimated that actual production was more probably in the region of 18 million carats. About 3 per cent of Congolese production consists of gemstones; the rest are uncut industrial diamonds, mostly bort.

Diamonds are found in the Kasai provinces, where there are alluvial deposits between the Tshikapa and the Luebo Rivers (Kasai Occidental) and in the Lubilash River basin (Kasai Oriental). In the latter area there are also kimberlitic pipes at Bakwanga which are estimated to contain about 85 per cent of the world's known reserves of industrial diamonds. Production is almost entirely concentrated in the Lubilash-Bakwanga region, where it is highly mechanized and controlled by a concessionary company, the Société Minière de Bakwanga (MIBA). Other production consists mainly of gemstones obtained by small miners in the alluvial area of Tshikapa. MIBA's current annual capacity is about 18 million carats, but actual production is restricted by agreement so as not to depress the London market. In November 1967, the responsibility for marketing diamond production was placed with the British Congo Diamond Distributors (BRITMOND), which purchases all of MIBA's production. BRITMOND also established an office in Tshikapa to purchase diamonds produced by the small miners, but this was subsequently closed (see below).

Prior to the adjustment of the official rate of exchange in June 1967, considerable incentive was given to diamond smuggling by the existence of a large differential between the official rate of exchange and the parallel market. Since then the incentive for small miners to sell their production to BRITMOND rather than to export it clandestinely has been further enhanced by the reduction in the export duty on these diamonds to 2.5 per cent, compared with an effective rate of 24 per cent on diamonds produced by MIBA. Although diamond smuggling has been reduced—from an estimated 7.2 million carats in 1967 to 6.6 million carats in 1968 and 3.7 million carats in 1969—there continues to be an incentive for clandestine marketing, as BRITMOND is not able to offer prices to the diggers that can compete with the rate of exchange in the parallel market. Moreover, the purchasing office in Tshikapa was closed in February 1970 by order of the Governor of Kasai Occidental province, who also canceled the prospecting permits of small miners and asked them to leave the region.

Other Minerals

Other minerals produced in Congo include cassiterite (tin dioxide), which is found in the provinces of Kivu and Katanga, and wolframite and columbite-tantalite, which are found in association with cassiterite. Mining operations were severely curtailed as a result of the 1964/65 rebellion, but have since been regaining their former levels. Four companies operate a series of mines extending across the center of Kivu in roughly two parallel lines, where the cassiterite is found in both alluvial and veinous form. The stanniferous deposits in Katanga consist mostly of decomposed pegmatite; this is quarried, washed, and smelted, and the tin is exported in ingot form. Congo supplied just over 4 per cent of the world's supply of tin in 1969.

Manganese is found in southwest Katanga, where quarrying operations are carried out by the Société Minière de Kisenge. Despite the disruption and damage resulting from political troubles, production has increased steadily in recent years.

Production of coal during 1961 and 1962 suffered considerably as a result of the civil disturbances, but some opencast mining still continues at the Kaluka deposit. As the coal is unsuitable for coking, there has been difficulty in finding an adequate market since the privately owned company Chemins de Fer Bas Congo-Katanga (BCK) electrified the Tenke-Luena section of the railway line. There is also a small underground mine at Lakunga, on Lake Tanganyika.

Gold production has been declining, largely owing to the exhaustion of the alluvial deposits but also because of the insecurity and strife which have prevailed in the producing regions of Kilo-Moto in Orientale province since 1960. The 1964–65 rebellion, in particular, led to widespread damage of mining installations and to financial losses. Production fell to 2.1 metric tons in 1965 but increased to 5 tons in 1968 and to 5.5 tons in 1969, compared with 9.8 tons in 1960. Two thirds of the gold output is now supplied from the underground deposits of high-grade ore at Kilo. The Kilo-Moto company was dissolved in 1966, and a new public corporation, the Gold Mining Office of Kilo-Moto, was formed. Small quantities of gold are also mined in Kivu by Minière des Grands Lacs.

MANUFACTURING

The greater part of manufacturing industry is concentrated in the areas of Kinshasa and Lubumbashi. These areas are well supplied with electric power and are on the main transport routes. Except for limited exports of cement, tobacco, and beer to neighboring countries, manufacturing is almost entirely geared to the domestic market. About 60 per cent of production consists of consumer goods, and the remainder of basic materials and equipment. The most important manufacturing activity is the production of beverages, the producing units consisting of breweries and plants for bottling mineral water. The next most important activity is production of textiles, which is integrated through all stages from spinning to the production of printed cotton piece goods.

Manufacturing declined by about 2.5 per cent in 1967 and by 6.7 per cent in 1968, but increased by 10 per cent in 1969, regaining the 1966 level. The contribution of manufacturing to monetized GDP at constant prices declined from 6.7 per cent in 1966 to 5.8 per cent in 1969; at current prices the decline was somewhat larger, since prices for manufactured goods rose less than the average (see Tables 1 and 5).

The decline of manufacturing in 1967–68 followed the introduction of the stabilization measures of June 1967, when production was adversely affected by reduced domestic demand and by increased competition from foreign products subsequent to the liberalization of imports. The decline in production was widespread, affecting nearly all industries in varying degrees, but was more pronounced for such consumer goods as clothing, shoes, and leather articles, and for metal furniture, bed springs, gas stoves, refrigerators, bicycles, motor scooters, and portable transistor radios. Production of many of these articles had expanded rapidly during the period of inflation and severe import restrictions. The only industries that managed to increase output in 1967 and 1968 were those producing foodstuffs, for which demand proved relatively inelastic, and plastics, because a new factory started producing during the first part of 1968.

With rising domestic demand, manufacturing recovered in 1969. In that year, among the industries that showed an increase in production were those producing foodstuffs, beverages, and tobacco, as well as those producing chemicals and transport equipment. On the other hand, production of textiles and clothing and the output of the metal and wood processing industries not only failed to increase but remained well below the 1966 level.

In order to provide the textile and clothing industries with the opportunity to adjust to the new market conditions following the removal of quantitative restrictions on imports, protective tariffs were introduced during 1968 and reinforced in April and December of 1969, when a minimum specific duty was levied on imports of certain basic raw materials and finished products. Ad valorem duties are levied only when their application, in comparison with the minimum specific duties, results in a higher yield. The specific duties have applied particularly to low-priced textiles originating in the Far East and in Eastern Europe. These protective duties have been established for a period of up to four years during which they are to be progressively reduced in accordance with the expected increase in the productivity of domestic industries. The sugar industry continues to be protected from imports of sugar on the free market, and the domestic price of sugar is kept at a level considerably higher than the c.i.f. import price.

Manufacturing output is estimated to have increased in 1970 by about 10 per cent, with the industries that recovered during 1969 likely to remain in the lead. Among the industries working at near capacity and planning to expand are those producing foodstuffs, beverages, and cement. On the other hand, little progress is expected in the near future in those industries affected by deep-seated productivity problems. The Investment Code of June 1969 offers liberal fiscal benefits (see Economic Development and Prospects—Investment Code, below) and should provide these industries with additional incentives to modernize their operations.

ELECTRIC POWER

Practically all of the electric power generated in Congo is by hydrostations. The 31 hydroelectric plants operating in the country have a total installed capacity of 700,000 kilowatts. Eleven generating stations account for 94 per cent of this; the largest, Le Marinel on the Lualaba River, has a total installed capacity of 248,400 kilowatts. In addition, there are numerous thermal-generating plants, both diesel and steam, but their total capacity amounts to only about 26,000 kilowatts. Many of these thermal plants are either used for ancillary production or held in reserve; GECOMINES, for example, has 14 such units in reserve.

About three quarters of the generating capacity is installed in Katanga, where it was developed primarily to provide energy for the mines. By developing the considerable natural resources which were available for producing low-cost power hydroelectrically, a high degree of mechanization has been introduced into the mines, and it has also been possible to develop a sophisticated metallurgical industry. The greater part of the existing capacity has been installed since World War II, either in conjunction with the expansion of mining operations in Katanga, or as part of the Ten-Year Plan, 1950–59.

There is no centralized electricity authority to control production and distribution. The industry is administered by private or semipublic corporations on a regional basis. In Katanga, an associate company of GECOMINES, Société Générale des Forces Hydro-Electriques du Katanga (SOGEFOR), operates four hydroelectric stations which supply the mining industry, the public grid, and those sections of the Bas Congo-Katanga railway that have been electrified. Another subsidiary of GECOMINES, Société Générale Africaine d'Electricité (SOGELEC), is responsible for distribution. In the Kinshasa area, Société des Forces Hydro-Electriques du Bas Congo, in which the Government holds 80 per cent of the shares, operates the hydroelectric stations at both Zongo and Sanga. The latter is owned by a private company, COLEC-TRIC, which is the distributing agency for the area. The Société des Forces Hydro-Electriques de l'Est operates the stations at Kisangani, Bukavu, and Kalemi, and the Régie de Distribution d'Eau et d'Electricité du Congo (REGIDESCO) operates a number of thermal-generating plants and supplies some of the lesser centers in the interior. Most mines outside the Katanga complex have their own hydroelectric plants, and industrial and agricultural companies in the interior usually have their own generating plants.

Until 1966 domestic consumption of electricity was increasing at a rate of approximately 7 per cent per annum. In 1967 there was a slight decline, owing to reduced consumption by GECOMINES, but in 1969 and 1970 it rose at an average annual rate of almost 8 per cent. The mines and metallurgical works are by far the largest consumers and account for 70 per cent of the power generated; about half of the remainder is absorbed by industry. The growth of electricity consumption in Kinshasa has been particularly rapid and reflects the expansion which has taken place in the city since 1960.

Up to 1960, exports of electricity were running at some 700 million kilowatt-hours a year, but after the completion of the Kariba dam the Zambian copper mines ceased to draw part of their supplies from Le Marinel and exports fell by over 50 per cent. In 1967 only 26 million kilowatt-hours were exported, but 115 million kilowatt-hours were exported in 1969, following a new agreement with the Copperbelt Power Company.

The installed capacity is theoretically ample to meet the country's immediate requirements, even allowing for the fact that certain large stations are run in parallel to ensure continuity of supply. However, the geographical distribution of capacity is very different from the pattern of consumption that has emerged. While there is sufficient capacity in Katanga and in the interior to meet foreseeable needs for the next six years, the two hydroelectric stations now operating in the Kinshasa area are barely sufficient to meet present demand, especially during periods of little rainfall. A new diesel-powered generating plant is being installed, and this should be adequate to cover anticipated demand until 1972, by which time supplies should be available from the Inga project, which will have an initial installed capacity of 150,000 kilowatts (see Economic Development and Prospects—Inga Scheme and Related Industries, below).

TRANSPORT

The vast watershed of the Congo basin is served by the two riverine arteries of the Congo and Kasai rivers, which enable shipping to penetrate deeply into the interior. There are approximately 8,700 miles of navigable waterways, including the series of lakes which form a natural frontier on the east. The railway system is essentially complementary and provides the connection for those stretches of river that are not navigable. In the southwest, a railway line connects Kinshasa to the estuary ports of Matadi, Boma, and Banana; in the northeast, a line links Kisangani with Ponthierville; and further south, another line runs from Kindu to Kabalo. The circle of communications is completed at Kamina where the railway from Port Francqui, the transshipment point at the head of the Kasai River, joins the line from Kabalo before continuing south. The road system, on the other hand, is largely localized and provides the connections between the producing districts and the rail and river loading points. There are approximately 87,000 miles of roads, many of which are impassable during the rainy seasons; only about 1,240 miles have been hard-surfaced. Whereas the distances and the climatic and geomorphic conditions are unfavorable for interconnecting trunk roads, these same factors are particularly propitious for air transport. There are 34 airports, but only 2, those at Kinshasa and Lubumbashi, are capable of serving international long-range jet aircraft.

There are three main rail connections linking the country with ocean ports. In the south, the Katanga railway links Lubumbashi and Kolwezi with the Benguela railway which crosses Angola to Lobito Bay. Lubumbashi is also on the rail line to the south which connects the Zambian Copperbelt with Bulawayo in Rhodesia and Beira on the coast of Mozambique. In addition, Katanga is linked to the Atlantic Ocean by the national route (*la voie nationale*), an all-Congolese rail-river route to the port of Matadi, Congo's principal port and the terminal point for the river route serving the northern regions. The eastern provinces have access to the East African transport system by road and by ship across the lakes, to Burundi, Rwanda, Uganda, and Tanzania.

The transport system is administered by both public and private companies. The largest of these is the Office d'Exploitation des Transports au Congo (OTRACO), a public corporation which is responsible for the transport services on the Congo and Kasai rivers as far as Kisangani and Port Francqui. OTRACO operates the port of Matadi and the river terminal at Kinshasa, and manages the railways linking Matadi with Kinshasa (CFMK) and Tshela with Boma (CFM). There are three other main railway companies. The Office Congolais des Chemins de Fer des Grands Lacs (CFL), a semipublic corporation, operates the eastern system and maintains lake and river shipping services. The other two are privately owned companies: the Chemins de Fer Bas Congo-Katanga (BCK) operates the rail system in Katanga and is responsible for the line from Sakania to Port Francqui; the services provided by the Société des Chemins de Fer Vicinaux au Congo (VICICONGO) include a narrow-gauge railway linking northeastern areas with the river port of Aketi. Air services are managed by Air Congo, a public corporation.

In recent years, the rail and river transport companies have incurred losses and faced financial difficulties. Adequate financial provision for the replacement of equipment and installations has not been made. With the deterioration in operating equipment and infrastructure, bottlenecks have developed at key points, such as Matadi and the transshipment center of Port Francqui. Shortages of storage space and rolling stock and difficulties in getting repairs done are further factors which have caused operational delays. The transport companies have recently been buying equipment overseas, such as barges, locomotives, and aircraft, for the most part financed by suppliers' credits. Plans are under consideration to extend the railway line from Port Francqui to Kinshasa and to relieve the congestion at Matadi by developing the port at Banana (see also Economic Development and Prospects—Transport Projects, below).

The roads have deteriorated because of inadequate maintenance, and considerable investment now appears necessary to recondition them. Repairs have been financed mainly with counterpart funds derived from the U. S. aid programs, but this has only permitted keeping up some of the main roads. Maintenance contracts for certain of the more important roads are given to those with a direct interest in orderly communications, such as the principal road users. A limited amount of road development is being undertaken with financing from the EDF. Further details are given below: see Economic Development and Prospects—Transport Projects.

ECONOMIC DEVELOPMENT AND PROSPECTS

INVESTMENT ACTIVITY

Although no figures are available, there appears to have been little new investment in either the public or the private sector between 1960 and 1966. The government budget was essentially of a subsistence nature and, in the circumstances, it was not possible to undertake systematic expenditure under a capital budget. Some infrastructure investment was made, e.g., road maintenance and construction of buildings, for the most part with the use of counterpart funds of U. S. aid. Other investments included the completion of an oil refinery (SOCIR) as a joint venture of the Congolese Government and an Italian group. Disbursements of development assistance under the EDF and other programs were small. During this period a certain amount of disinvestment took place in transportation and in public enterprises. In the private sector there may well have been some net disinvestment, as considerable capital losses were suffered in both agriculture and mining, the result of years of civil strife, and capital assets were not always replaced. However, new investment was made in manufacturing, which expanded considerably during this period, and in construction.

Since 1966, with the restoration of law and order in the country and the general improvement in economic and financial conditions, there has been a revival of investment activity. As outlined earlier (see Structure of the Economy—Gross Domestic Product, above), gross fixed investment rose markedly between 1966 and 1969, especially in the public sector. In 1969 total gross investment was estimated at Z 218 million, of which about 40 per cent represented replacement of depreciated capital assets and 60 per cent new investment, and public investment accounted for about 31 per cent of total gross investment, compared with 16 per cent in 1966.

In 1968 and 1969 about three fourths of all public investment was financed from domestic sources, and the remainder from counterpart funds, grants by the EDF, and suppliers' credits. Complete data on the distribution of public investment by economic sectors are not available, but it appears that about half of total capital expenditure was allocated to public works, mainly the construction of public buildings, and to the purchase of machinery to re-equip the transport, urban water supply, and energy sectors. Capital expenditure included the purchase of military equipment and disbursements in connection with the hydroelectric project at Inga (see below), the construction of an airport at Bukavu, and the reconstruction of the city of Kisangani. Expenditure to improve the transport infrastructure (e.g., roads, bridges, and ports) was relatively small.

Aside from the replacement of depreciated assets, new investment in the private sector in 1968 and 1969 was directed mainly to housing and to equipment for agricultural and mining enterprises. The completion of a new copper concentrator by GECOMINES in late 1968 was the single most important investment in the mining sector. There was little new investment in manufacturing, as this sector was going through a period of readjustment following the removal of import restrictions in the second half of 1967.

INVESTMENT PROSPECTS

A coordinated investment program for the country has not yet been prepared. In the immediate future an important share of all public investment is likely to be allocated to public works and buildings, especially in Kinshasa. Other public investment will most probably continue to be centered on the hydroelectric scheme at Inga and the development of those basic industries that make heavy use of electric power. Re-equipment of the transport sector and of public productive enterprises is also likely to continue, and major development projects in transportation are contemplated for the years ahead. A program to expand the production of copper and associated minerals is being undertaken by GECOMINES, and the Government is encouraging private investment in productive enterprises. To this end, liberal fiscal and other benefits may be provided in accordance with the Investment Code of June 1969 (described below). However, low priority appears to be given at this stage to agricultural development. A description of the principal investment projects in progress or under consideration follows.

Inga Scheme and Related Industries

Completion of the scheme to develop the hydroelectric power potential of the Congo River at Inga, some 25 miles upstream from the port of Matadi, a project that was begun in recent years, will make available large amounts of cheap electric power. The first phase of the project calls for diverting part of the Congo stream into a parallel valley to be sealed off by a dam and for the installation of six generating units of 50,000 kilowatts each. The first subphase aims at completing by 1972 the installation of a station with a capacity of 150,000 kilowatts and the construction of high-tension transmission lines linking Inga with Kinshasa and some consumer areas in the Bas Congo region of Kongo Central. Completion of the subphase will make possible an increase in total electricity production of about 20 per cent.

A consortium of Italian firms (SICAI) made the final studies and engineering plans for this project, and a contract for the construction of the power stations was concluded by the Congolese Government with an Italian syndicate (ITALINGA) in April 1968. Financing the cost of the first subphase, which is estimated at $65 million, has been arranged. Italy is providing $20 million of eight-year credits at 6 per cent interest. The EEC is providing about $18 million to construct the transmission lines and connected transformer system, one half of which is a grant from the EDF and the other half a long-term, low-interest loan from the European Investment Bank. The balance of about $27 million is the responsibility of the Congolese Government. The first phase of the project is considered viable under the existing electricity tariff. But once this phase has been completed, average costs are expected to decline rapidly as production expands, although these economies of scale depend on the growth of consumption.

Among the industrial projects being considered that would justify expansion of electric power production at Inga are a steel complex, a caustic soda and PVC (polyvinyl chloride) factory, a nitrogenous fertilizer plant, and an aluminum smelter. The establishment of new mining industries in southern Katanga would also require additional power which could conceivably be transmitted from Inga.

For the most important of these projects, a steel complex, technical studies are at an advanced stage and a final decision by the Government is expected in the near future. The steel mill will be established at Maluku, about 65 miles upstream from Kinshasa, and will include facilities for the production of 280,000 tons of steel products a year— the estimated level of domestic demand by 1977. Production would be divided between bars and sections, hot and cold rolled products, such as rods and small profiles, and galvanized sheeting. In the first stage the raw material would be imported in the form of scrap and semifinished products. The idea of obtaining iron ore from deposits at Luebo, in Kasai Occidental, has been temporarily abandoned; this would have involved transporting the ore after concentration by cableway to the Kasai River and then mainly by barge to Kimpoko and Maluku.

Investment in the steel complex is estimated at about $90 million, not including the additional investment that may be required for roads and electricity. A German-Italian consortium will be responsible for constructing the steel mill, which is expected to be financed entirely by suppliers' credits and to be wholly owned by the Congolese Government. It is envisaged that a production and management company will be formed. This company will probably be owned by the Government (50 per cent) and by the German-Italian consortium together with the Italian steel company FINSIDER. The terms of the agreement between the consortium and the Government have not yet been made final, but it appears that the consortium will be receiving management fees as well as a participation in net profits. On the other hand, repayment of the suppliers' credits and any losses that may be incurred by the producing company will be the responsibility of the Government. Production is expected to begin in 1973 and to reach the planned 280,000 tons a year by 1976.

Among the other industrial projects connected with the Inga scheme, the most promising is the caustic soda and PVC plant. It will be designed to produce some 30,000 tons a year of caustic soda and PVC and will involve investments of some $20 million. The technical studies for this project have been made by SICAI but no agreement with the company interested in the realization of the project—the German group, Klockner—has yet been signed. The nitrogenous fertilizer plant would produce 26,500 tons of nitrogen; however, the realization of this project may be delayed until 1975 owing to the present limited domestic market for fertilizer. Plans for the establishment of an aluminum smelter to transform imported aluminum are also at a very early stage of discussion with an international consortium that would include French, German, Italian, and U. S. producers.

Copper Projects

During the period 1960–65, political disturbances and uncertainties allowed little incentive to raise copper capacity and the producing company, Union Minière du Haut Katanga, kept output at about 300,000 tons a year. Although production was increased by about 15 per cent between 1966 and 1969, in the latter year Congo accounted for about 6 per cent of the world's copper production, compared with 7 per cent in 1960. Projects which are expected to bring a rapid expansion of production in the next few years are being undertaken by GECOMINES and by the Société de Développement Industriel et Minier du Congo (SODIMICO). Another important copper investment at Tenke in southern Katanga is being studied by a consortium of international companies.

Under the GECOMINES investment program recently approved by the Government, the company's copper production is to be raised from 360,000 tons in 1969 to 450,000 tons by 1974 and to 560,000 tons by 1978, and production of cobalt will be raised from the present 11,000 tons a year to 14,600 tons in 1974. Under the recently approved program, not only will the rate of extraction be increased, but the concentrating, smelting, and refining plants will be expanded. The required investment in mining installations is estimated at some $80 million, and additional finance will probably be required to expand production of electricity. Of the total mining investment, about one half will be financed directly by GECOMINES from its own resources, and the balance will be obtained mainly from foreign long-term loans and suppliers' credits. The economic and profitability studies of the investment program have been based on an average copper price of $0.45 a pound in the next five years. If the price does not fall below this point, and with exemption until 1974 from taxation on copper and cobalt production over and above present production levels, GECOMINES will be able to repay by 1974 the loans and credits that will have been contracted and to provide for an adequate rate of return on capital investment after covering depreciation and replacement costs.

SODIMICO, a joint venture of the Nippon Mining Company and the Congolese Government, has been prospecting for copper and other minerals in the area of Sakania, in the southeast corner of Katanga, since 1968. The Government has received a 15 per cent capital participation in SODIMICO in return for the concession and holds the right to acquire up to 50 per cent interest in the producing company. SODIMICO has been assured the incentive of important tax advantages. On the basis of deposits so far ascertained, the company expects to develop an ore output equivalent to some 50,000 tons of copper a year by 1972–73, with a total investment estimated at about $75 million. Initially the ore will be smelted in Congo and exported in blister form for electrolytic refining in Japan. However, when copper output exceeds 60,000 tons a year (by 1975 according to current estimates), facilities for converting half or more of the blister into electrolytic copper are to be established in Congo. The Nippon Mining Company will have the right to buy all of the output at world market prices.

Transport Projects

When Congo became independent in 1960, it possessed an efficient and diversified transport system centered on river and rail connections linking the principal producing areas with the outside world. Since 1960 the country's transport infrastructure has generally deteriorated, owing to inadequate maintenance and replacement of physical assets and to deficiencies in management and operations. The deterioration has been particularly marked in the road system that connects the producing districts with the rail and river loading points, but bottlenecks have also developed at key clearing and transshipment centers. While immediate difficulties are being alleviated by a certain amount of road repair and replacement of depreciated equipment, transport difficulties are considered a serious obstacle to the growth of production and exports, especially in agriculture. Furthermore, with the delays, inefficiencies, and pilferage that occur in transit, transport costs have become a substantial element both in producer costs and domestic consumer prices. Considerable investment appears necessary to recondition the transportation network, particularly the river and road systems.

Aside from some road and other transport maintenance financed mainly through the current government budget and by use of counterpart funds of foreign aid, certain new projects to rehabilitate and develop the road system have been undertaken since 1968 with financing from the EDF, the World Bank, the IDA, and the UNDP. Under the EDF programs, about $10 million has been committed for road and other transport projects since 1967. The IDA and the UNDP are financing road rehabilitation and maintenance projects involving a total cost of $7.5 million, and a more extensive program of road building is likely to emerge once these joint projects are completed. The World Bank has acted as executing agency for a recently completed UNDP project study on the reorganization of the agencies which operate the main river transport services—OTRACO and the Inland Water Transport Services (Services des Voies Navigables)—as a result of which an investment program for the improvement of river transport is being drawn up which is expected to be financed by the World Bank with the possible participation of the U. S. Agency for International Development. The construction of a deepwater port at Banana on the Atlantic Ocean is being considered by the Congolese Government.

Two railroad projects have been put forward. The first involves extending the narrow-gauge railway in the north from the present western terminal of Aketi to the Congo River port of Bumba, 115 miles southwest of Aketi. Construction was started in 1970 and is expected to be completed in 1972. The cost, estimated at $14 million, will be financed entirely by the Government.

The second, and more ambitious, project is a railway between Port Francqui and Kinshasa, thus establishing an all-rail route between southern Katanga and the Atlantic Ocean and making it possible to transport a larger part of the country's mineral products to the Atlantic on national territory. At present more than half of Congo's copper and other minerals is carried from southern Katanga to ocean ports in Angola, Mozambique, and Tanzania. Preliminary studies for this rail link have been completed, and a preliminary engineering study is under way. The required investment is estimated roughly at $300 million. No decision on construction has yet been made by the Government, and less costly alternatives for handling more traffic on the Katanga-Matadi rail-river route are being studied with the assistance of the World Bank.

Other Projects

Other investment projects are being carried forward on the initiative of the private sector. By April 1970, about 40 projects, mainly related to processing, manufacturing, and the purchase of railroad equipment and involving a total investment of more than $160 million, had been submitted to the Investment Commission, of which 14 involving an investment of $16 million had already been approved and declared eligible under the Investment Code. The approved projects comprise mainly new investment in the production of cement, matches, plastics, electrical equipment, wheat flour, beer, papaya extract, and furniture and other articles made of wood, and the construction of new hotels. By April 1970 some 30 other investment projects involving an investment of some $50 million had been laid before the Commission but their consideration was deferred pending the submission of more complete documentation.

Of the investments being contemplated, only a few, totaling some $16 million, are in agriculture and they are still at an early stage of preparation. Some of these projects are likely to be submitted to the EDF for possible financing, while others are being studied jointly by the World Bank and the Food and Agriculture Organization.

INVESTMENT CODE

In order to promote investment and encourage the inflow of foreign capital, the Government enacted a new Investment Code on June 26,

1969. The code specifies the fiscal and other benefits that may be extended to eligible enterprises—whether privately owned or jointly owned by the Government and the private sector—undertaking new investment in Congo. The benefits are grouped in two categories that are eligible for preferential treatment: the general category (*régime général*), which is applied to investment by enterprises whose establishment, expansion, or modernization is recognized as contributing to the development of the economy; and the special agreement category (*régime conventionnel*), which is reserved for those enterprises whose investment projects, besides qualifying for the general category, are exceptionally large and are considered of major importance for the country's economic and social development. A minimum investment of Z 50,000 is required to qualify for the benefits of the Investment Code.

The contribution of a particular investment to the economic and social development of the country is assessed by taking into consideration the following criteria specified in the code: the importance of the estimated value added; the number of jobs to be created; the size of the investment and the means of financing it; the impact of the project on the development of other sectors of the economy; its effect on the balance of payments; the location of the investment; the importance of the training program and the promotion of Congolese nationals to positions demanding specialization and managerial responsibility; and the conformity of the project to the general orientation of the Government's economic policy.

The code specifies the fiscal benefits that are extended to enterprises declared eligible under the general category. These aim at reducing the cost of realization of the investment and the charges imposed on the enterprises during the first years of operation of the new investment. They include exemptions from the following fees and taxes: the fees on deeds incorporating new companies and on the increase in the capital of existing companies; the customs duties and the turnover tax on imports of machinery, tools, and other materials required for the new investment when these cannot be provided by domestic industry at equivalent prices and of comparable quality; the tax on company profits —exemption for a period of five years for new companies and for a period not exceeding five years for existing companies undertaking new investment (in the latter case the exemption from the tax is applied only to that part of the company profits that exceed the average profits realized in the three years preceding the acceptance of the new investment under the general category); the special tax on remuneration paid by new enterprises to their foreign personnel before the enterprise starts production; the tax on dividends relating to shares issued by existing companies to finance the new investment—exemption for a period of five years beginning with the year of issue of these shares; and the tax on land acquired by enterprises for the purpose of undertaking the new investment—exemption for a period of five years.

The code does not spell out the benefits that may be extended to the enterprises that are declared eligible for a special agreement. But it indicates that, on the basis of the expected contribution of the investment to the development of the economy and of the commitments undertaken by the promoters of the enterprise, the Government may extend benefits having the effect of reducing the costs of installation and operation of the enterprise, such as adjustments in direct and indirect taxation and, for an appropriate period, the guarantee of fiscal stability on the basis of the tax system in effect when the special agreement entered into effect.

For investments made by foreign enterprises under the terms of the Investment Code, the Government guarantees transfer of the annual profits resulting from such investment, transfer of the actual value of the investment in case of liquidation or cessation of operations, and transfer of the principal, interest, and other charges relating to foreign loans contracted by the enterprise. Furthermore, in order to encourage enterprises to reinvest their profits in the country, the code provides for a reduction of 50 per cent in the profits tax on that part of undistributed profits earmarked for agreed productive reinvestment.

Applications for benefits under the code are examined by the Investment Commission, which formulates recommendations concerning the projects. The Commission is chaired by a representative of the Minister of National Economy and includes representatives of the Minister of Foreign Affairs and Foreign Trade, the Minister of Planning, the Minister of Finance, the Minister of Social Security, the Office of the President, and the Governor of the National Bank. In respect of a request for admission to the general category of preferential treatment, the recommendation of the Commission, if taken unanimously, is sent to the Minister of National Economy and the Minister of Finance who issue jointly a decision of admission (*arrêté d'agrément*) or rejection. If the recommendation of the Commission is not unanimous, the decision of admission or rejection is taken by the Council of Ministers. For a project to be declared eligible for a special agreement, the recommendation of the Commission is submitted to the Council of Ministers for decision. The special agreements (*conventions*) are signed by the Minister of National Economy, the Minister of Finance, and, when appropriate, by other interested ministers, and must be approved by government decree. Decisions concerning the reduction of the profits tax on reinvested profits are taken by the Minister of Finance, in accordance with the recommendations of the Investment Commission.

PRICES, WAGES, AND EMPLOYMENT

PRICES

The available information on movements in prices in recent years is summarized in Table 6, which shows the evolution of consumer price indices for low-income and high-income families living in Kinshasa and Lubumbashi, the country's two main urban centers. Although local circumstances give rise to divergences between some regions, price movements in these two centers are regarded as representative of those in most of the country. Three indices are computed for Kinshasa, two aimed at measuring the changes in the cost of living for people having typically African consumer preferences—the greater part of the population of Kinshasa—and one for the high-income group. The Institute of Economic and Social Research (Institut de Recherches Economiques et Sociales—IRES) of the University of Lovanium and the National Institute of Statistics (Institut National de la Statistique—INS) compute indices based on prices in the African markets, and the IRES computes an index based on the European consumption pattern. For Lubumbashi, two indices are computed by the Statistical Office of Katanga province —one for the low-income groups and one for the high-income groups. The bases and composition of all these indices are described in the footnotes to Table 6.

Prices rose sharply in the 12 months after the introduction of the economic stabilization measures in June 1967, as the economy adjusted to the new exchange rate and the higher taxes. Between June 1967 and June 1968, the indices of consumer prices on the African markets in Kinshasa and Lubumbashi rose on the average by about 80 per cent. During the same period, the indices of consumer prices for high-income families in both Kinshasa and Lubumbashi rose somewhat less. Concurrently, the index of retail prices of imported products on the African markets of Kinshasa rose by 107 per cent—more than the average increase in prices but considerably less than the increase in import costs, which rose by 178 per cent on account of the exchange rate adjustment alone. This development suggests that the profit margins of importers and retailers were reduced following the liberalization of imports, which reintroduced competitive conditions at a time when consumer demand had slowed down.

In the second half of 1968 prices were generally stable: the IRES index of consumer prices on the African markets in Kinshasa declined by about 1 per cent. Retail prices of imported goods, according to this index, fell by more than 3 per cent, indicating a continued reduction in profit margins of importers and retailers. At the same time, prices of domestic agricultural products fell by about 4.5 per cent, reflecting improved supplies.

In the early part of 1969 prices in Kinshasa began to rise again, and by December of that year consumer prices on African markets were about 13 per cent above those of December 1968. All categories of goods contributed to the rise, with the largest increase taking place in the prices of domestic foodstuffs. The index of these foodstuffs, which comprises such basic staples as cassava, maize flour, vegetables, and fruits, rose by about 27 per cent, and the prices of some items almost doubled. The index of foodstuffs of mixed origin (foodstuffs that are both produced domestically and imported), such as rice, potatoes, and meat, rose by about 17 per cent.

The relatively large increase in food prices in Kinshasa is attributed mainly to a considerable rise in demand at a time when domestic production had declined because of adverse weather. Aggregate demand was stimulated in 1969 by a rapid expansion in government expenditure, and, in particular, by increases in wages and salaries. Food production in the Bas Congo region, which is the main source of supply for Kinshasa, was severely affected by drought, and moving food from other

TABLE 6. DEMOCRATIC REPUBLIC OF CONGO: INDICES OF CONSUMER PRICES, 1966–70

(Monthly averages; July–December 1968 = 100)

	1966 Dec.	1967 June	1967 Dec.	1968 June	1968 Dec.	1969 June	1969 Dec.	1970 June	1970 Dec.
KINSHASA: AFRICAN MARKETS									
IRES index [1]	**48.1**	**54.0**	**84.0**	**101.1**	**99.7**	**106.7**	**112.3**	**113.6**	**114.2**
Foodstuffs	48.3	54.6	85.3	102.1	99.4	107.9	115.2	117.0	116.8
Clothing	51.7	54.7	77.2	98.2	101.3	104.9	107.0	105.3	108.7
Household and sundry	44.6	51.5	85.4	100.1	99.4	104.1	106.9	109.5	110.2
Domestic products	48.4	52.6	81.8	100.2	98.8	107.3	112.4	113.7	115.9
Agricultural	*49.0*	*52.3*	*89.2*	*99.9*	*95.4*	*109.1*	*121.2*	*120.9*	*125.1*
Manufactured	*46.6*	*52.8*	*77.7*	*99.6*	*100.1*	*103.2*	*104.9*	*107.6*	*108.7*
Other	*51.1*	*52.7*	*80.5*	*101.6*	*100.6*	*113.0*	*116.1*	*117.0*	*118.5*
Imported products	43.5	49.7	87.4	102.8	99.3	102.3	106.9	106.8	102.4
Products of mixed origin	59.7	82.9	91.2	100.7	106.7	110.7	124.7	130.7	134.4
INS index [2]	**48.5**	**58.3**	**85.6**	**97.9**	**101.5**	**110.0**	**114.7**	**114.3**	**113.8**
Foodstuffs	52.9	66.7	95.9	100.3	96.6	108.9	112.9	110.9	109.3
Other goods and services	45.5	52.7	78.8	97.0	104.9	110.8	115.9	116.6	116.9
KINSHASA: EUROPEAN STORES									
IRES index [3]	**45.6**	**55.9**	**85.4**	**98.8**	**101.6**	**106.1**	**108.4**	**114.4**	**112.2**
Foodstuffs	43.8	57.2	91.3	99.3	101.1	105.4	105.4	108.8	107.0
Household and sundry	47.7	51.6	74.8	97.6	102.2	107.3	113.5	124.2	121.6

LUBUMBASHI

Low-income households [4]	51.6	53.4	76.5	98.3	99.2	102.6	103.7	104.1	...
High-income households [5]	55.2	57.9	79.2	94.5	100.2	102.7	105.4	107.9	...

Sources: Banque Nationale du Congo, *Rapport Annuel, 1968–1969, 1969–1970*, and *Bulletin*; and data provided by the Congolese authorities.

[1] This index is computed weekly by the Institute of Economic and Social Research (Institut de Recherches Economiques et Sociales—IRES) on the basis of the unweighted geometric average of individual retail prices of 61 items: 40 foodstuffs, 10 clothing, and 11 household and sundry. Of the 61 items, 42 are produced locally, 14 are imported, and 5 are of mixed origin. Of the locally produced goods, 13 are agricultural and 13 are manufactured. The movements in the index are regarded as representative of the changes in the cost of living for the greater part of the people who live in Kinshasa and have typically African patterns of consumption.

[2] This index is computed monthly by the National Institute of Statistics (Institut National de la Statistique—INS) on the basis of a weighted average of the retail prices of 57 items: 36 foodstuffs (weight of 36.8 per cent), 7 clothing, 6 medical care and household, 4 utilities, and 4 transportation and sundry. This index, like the one calculated by the IRES, aims at measuring the changes in the cost of living for lower-income families living in Kinshasa and having African consumption patterns. Besides the fact that the INS index is weighted, differences in the movements of the two indices arise mainly from the composition of the indices themselves and the frequency with which prices are observed.

[3] This index is computed monthly by the IRES on the basis of a weighted average of retail prices for 35 items: 21 foodstuffs (weight of 55.1 per cent) and 14 household and sundry.

[4] This index is calculated by the Statistical Office of Katanga province and aims at measuring the changes in the cost of living for the lower-income groups in Lubumbashi. It is computed monthly on the basis of unweighted averages of individual retail prices of 50 items: 26 foodstuffs, 9 household, 7 clothing, 3 transportation, and 5 others.

[5] This index is calculated by the Statistical Office of Katanga province and aims at measuring the changes in the cost of living for higher-income families in Lubumbashi. It is computed quarterly on the basis of the weighted average of retail prices in the most representative stores in the city. It comprises 109 items: 43 foodstuffs (weight of 45.7 per cent), 31 household (weight of 26.9 per cent), 15 clothing (weight of 12.4 per cent), and 20 transportation and sundry (weight of 14.9 per cent).

parts of the country was hardly feasible because of high transport costs and other difficulties. Imported foods are no real substitute for certain domestic products, as consumption patterns cannot be quickly changed. Prices of imported foods are also higher, as a rule, than their domestic substitutes. Greater demand and uneven supply during 1969 encouraged speculation among traders, and this factor was largely responsible for the increase in the retail prices of imported goods in Kinshasa, which rose by 7.7 per cent. Profit margins, which had declined after June 1967, rose again: for some domestic food products, the margins of wholesalers and retailers represented, on the average, 70 per cent of the retail price in December 1969.

Consumer prices in other parts of the country did not rise as much in 1969 as they did in Kinshasa. In Lubumbashi both of the consumer price indices rose by less than 5 per cent. The supply of foodstuffs remained about normal in this area, as a shortfall in the domestic production of maize was offset by larger imports from neighboring countries.

Consumer prices in Kinshasa remained virtually stable in 1970. In December the IRES index of consumer prices in the African markets in Kinshasa was less than 2 per cent above its level in December 1969, with prices of domestic products averaging some 3 per cent more than a year earlier.

In principle, the prices of all goods traded in Congo, whether domestically produced or imported, are subject to government control. In practice, only the prices of certain commodities are fixed directly by the Government and cannot be changed without prior authorization by the Ministry of National Economy; these include domestically produced beer, cigarettes, sugar, cement, and textiles, and imported petroleum products, maize flour, and specified kinds of preserved fish. For all other commodities, control of prices is confined to general rules intended to limit the profit margins that wholesalers and retailers may apply to the basic cost price; generally, these rules are not effectively enforced.

WAGES AND SALARIES

Minimum wages and family allowances are guaranteed to all workers in the private sector. Minimum wage rates per day are set by law according to skill and to salary zones (rates in urban areas are generally higher than in rural areas). The salaries of the permanent staff in government service (i.e., of full-fledged civil servants) are governed by a special scale; in addition, civil servants receive special fringe benefits, such as housing allowances and pensions. This special scale applies also to teachers and, with some adjustments, to the army, the police, and employees of public enterprises. The salaries of contractual workers in government service are based on the minimum wage rates applicable in the private sector.

In the 18 months after the introduction of the stabilization measures in June 1967, minimum wage rates and family allowances were raised twice, by 25 per cent in October 1967 and by 15 per cent in April 1968 for a total of 43.8 per cent. Because of larger increases in certain regions resulting from the reduction in the number of wage zones in October 1967, the increase in the minimum wage rates over the period averaged about 50 per cent. The legislation in October 1967 also provided for an increment in the minimum wage rate of 1 per cent for each year of uninterrupted service with the same employer. Moreover, certain categories of skilled workers received increases in total remuneration over and above the increases provided by the minimum wage legislation.

During the same 18-month period, the increase in total remuneration for the permanent staff in government service averaged less than 30 per cent. This increase resulted from the reintroduction in July 1967 of a housing allowance, ranging from 20 per cent to 36 per cent of the basic salary (i.e., excluding family allowances, special indemnities, and other fringe benefits), and from a general salary increase of 10 per cent in October 1967. The legislation also provided for a 3 per cent annual increment in the salaries of all permanent government staff, which has now become a standard annual increase.

A comparison of money wages with price movements indicates that real wages were considerably reduced between June 1967 and December 1968. According to calculations made by the National Bank, the December 1968 index of legal minimum wages for unskilled workers in real terms was some 22 per cent below the June 1967 index. For highly skilled workers, however, the decline was less than 7 per cent, as actual earnings for these workers have generally been higher than minimum

wage rates. During the same period, the total remuneration of permanent civil servants declined in real terms by 25–35 per cent, depending
on the grade (Table 7).

In July 1969 the minimum wage rates and family allowances in the
private sector were raised by 10 per cent, partly because of the rise in
domestic prices in Kinshasa, and in January 1970 they were raised by
20 per cent; the latter increase was not, however, applied to upper echelon staff in managerial positions. Salaries of permanent civil servants
were raised in January 1969, when a new salary scale was introduced
designed to correct distortions and to restore adequate differentials
between qualified and less qualified staff. Under the new scale, basic
salaries (excluding the housing allowance and other fringe benefits)
were increased by a minimum of 25 per cent for the lower echelons
and by more than 200 per cent for the higher echelons and the differential between the lowest and the highest grades was thereby increased
from 1 to 10 to about 1 to 17. In addition, special allowances were
granted to university graduates with expertise in certain fields.

Real earnings increased as a result of the 1969 adjustments, and for
most categories of employees they exceeded the level of June 1967.
By June 1970, real minimum wages for unskilled workers in the private
sector were 10 per cent below those of June 1967, but for highly skilled
workers they were about 8 per cent above. In the government sector as
well, real salaries for permanent employees in most grades were
restored to a level above that of June 1967; only for middle echelon

TABLE 7. DEMOCRATIC REPUBLIC OF CONGO: INDEX OF MINIMUM WAGES
AND SALARIES IN REAL TERMS, DECEMBER 1967–JUNE 1970

(June 1967 = 100)

	1967	1968		1969		1970
	Dec.	June	Dec.	June	Dec.	June
Private sector						
Unskilled workers	80.4	76.6	77.6	72.6	75.9	90.1
Highly skilled workers	96.3	92.0	93.2	87.1	91.1	108.1
Permanent government staff						
Assistant clerk	78.3	65.1	65.9	109.3	103.8	105.7
Clerk	89.3	74.2	75.2	87.5	83.1	84.7
Division chief	87.6	72.8	73.7	123.8	117.6	119.8
Secretary-general	86.2	71.6	72.6	194.4	184.7	188.2

Source: Banque Nationale du Congo, *Rapport Annuel, 1969–1970*.

employees, such as clerks, whose salaries had increased more than the average between 1960 and 1967, had real earnings failed to regain their June 1967 level. In the last few years, there has been a tendency to move from the system of minimum wage rates to wage contracts negotiated for each industry through collective bargaining.

EMPLOYMENT

Comprehensive and reliable statistics on employment are not available. According to information gathered by the National Bank on the basis of annual surveys, the relatively rapid expansion of economic activity in 1968–69 was not accompanied by a proportional increase in employment (Table 8). These data show that the number of wage earners employed by enterprises, after rising by about 6 per cent to

TABLE 8. DEMOCRATIC REPUBLIC OF CONGO: EMPLOYMENT BY SECTOR, JANUARY 1966–JUNE 1969

(In thousands of persons)

	Jan. 1966	Jan. 1967	Jan. 1968
Enterprises [1]			
Agriculture	346.3	368.8	363.7
Mining and mineral processing	59.0	59.3	56.7
Manufacturing	48.0	50.3	50.7
Construction	15.0	15.9	15.0
Transport and communications	51.5	56.7	60.1
Commerce, banks, other services	22.3	24.4	29.5
Total	542.1	575.4	575.7
African salaried workers	*303.6*	*326.4*	*332.4*
Foreign personnel	*10.8*	*10.9*	*9.8*
Other African workers [2]	*227.7*	*238.1*	*233.5*

	June 1968	June 1969
Government		
Permanent staff	160.4	170.4
Civil servants	*26.5*	*27.9*
Teachers	*60.0*	*66.5*
Army	*53.0*	*55.1*
Police	*20.9*	*20.9*
Contractual workers	150.0	150.0
Total	310.4	320.4

Source: Banque Nationale du Congo, *Rapport Annuel, 1968–1969.*

[1] Consists of "large" private and publicly owned enterprises only.

[2] Comprises "free workers," mainly in agriculture, who are linked to enterprises and are generally paid on the basis of their production.

575,000 at the beginning of 1967, was approximately unchanged in January 1968. The number of workers on the payroll of enterprises as registered with the social security system was some 500,000 at the end of 1968, an increase of about 2.5 per cent over 1967; however, these figures, which are reported by the enterprises themselves, tend to underestimate actual employment.

Between June 1968 and June 1969 the number of permanent employees in government service is estimated to have increased by about 6 per cent to some 170,000 persons, and the number of contractual workers in government service was roughly estimated at 150,000, of which about 15,000 were employed by the Central Government and the remainder by the provinces.

GOVERNMENT FINANCE

BUDGETARY SYSTEM

The Democratic Republic of Congo has a centralized form of government. The country is divided into eight provinces, each with its local administration. Although the provinces still possess certain fiscal powers, these have been steadily reduced and are now very limited, and responsibility for the main governmental functions and for raising and administering most public funds is vested in the Central Government. The provinces are dependent on central government transfers (representing in 1969 about 9 per cent of the total current expenditure of the Central Government) to meet those expenditures which remain under their jurisdiction, notably the wages of provincial government employees (some 65 per cent of the total expenditure of the provinces in 1968). For other types of expenditure, e.g., subsidies to private schools, payments are made directly by the Central Government. The transfer of funds from the Central Government to the provinces is made, as far as possible, directly to the regional accounting units.

The financial operations of the Central Government are conducted largely through the current budget and a capital budget. The current budget includes the normal departmental activities of the 21 ministries, and also of the offices attached directly to the Presidency. Furthermore, the current budget provides for servicing of the public debt, transfers to local governments (provinces, municipalities, and the City of Kinshasa), and transfers of fiscal receipts to the capital budget. It does not include those technical assistance costs (Z 14.9 million in 1968, Z 15.9 million in 1969) that are financed from foreign resources, largely through programs supported by the United Nations and Belgium. Certain other current expenditures, including some costs relating to road maintenance, are met from the counterpart funds of foreign aid and are likewise excluded from the budget.

The capital budget, in the absence of a national development plan, consists mainly of a consolidated list of departmental investment projects, of loans and subsidies to public enterprises, and of equity participations, which are to be financed from the Government's own resources or from foreign and domestic borrowing. In recent years, an unspecified amount of current expenditure has also been included in the capital budget.

The current budget of the Central Government runs for the calendar year. Beginning in 1970, the three-month supplementary period for collecting revenue and making payments relating to the budgetary year was abolished. Disbursements against outstanding commitments at the end of the year are paid out against the budget appropriations of the next year. The capital budget also runs for a calendar year, but outstanding commitments are carried forward without being included in the new capital budget appropriations. In recent years, a varying proportion of all budget revenue (including receipts from the profits tax paid by GECOMINES) has been deposited in separate treasury accounts to finance capital budget expenditure. For 1970 this proportion was fixed at 24 per cent, which represents the share of capital expenditure in total budget expenditure, according to the original budget estimates.

The Ministry of Finance is responsible for preparing and administering the budget, which must also be discussed by the Council of Ministers and then approved by the President. The detailed administration of the budget is conducted by the Ministry of Finance in accordance with general procedures governing expenditure commitments and disbursements. Payments are made by central government accountants (comptables d'état) who are responsible to the Minister of Finance, or by local government accountants (comptables provinciaux) for local expenditures. To strengthen central government control over disbursements by the provinces, local accountants have been brought under the direct authority of the Ministry of Finance. In recent years actual expenditure under such categories as defense, education, foreign affairs, and expenditure authorized directly by the President have generally exceeded budgetary appropriations by a wide margin.

Cash transactions of the Central Government are handled by the Treasury Service in the Ministry of Finance, operating through the agency of the National Bank. All fiscal receipts, whether from taxes, portfolio investment, or other sources, are paid into the Treasury's accounts at the National Bank. Ways and means available to the Treasury over and above normal fiscal receipts are limited to the net increase in deposits with the Post Office; the social security funds are excluded from treasury accounts and control. The Treasury may, however, obtain advances from the National Bank not exceeding 15 per cent of the annual average fiscal receipts in the previous three years; these advances may not be extended for more than 300 days in any one year.

STRUCTURE OF CURRENT REVENUE

The main feature of the composition of budget revenue in Congo (see Table 9) is the predominance of indirect taxes, which in 1966–69 yielded 75–80 per cent of total tax revenue. Of these, taxes on international trade, including the turnover tax on imports and exports, are by far the most important; in 1969 they yielded about 68 per cent of total tax revenue, with taxes on exports alone accounting for almost 47 per cent of the total. The dependence of Congo's tax revenue on international trade makes it vulnerable to changes in world market prices.

Direct Taxes

Direct taxes consist mainly of schedular income taxes (*impôts cédulaires sur le revenu*) and property taxes. There is also a head tax, but it is of minor importance as a source of revenue.

For income tax purposes, incomes and profits are divided into six categories to which different tax rates are applied: rent, interest and dividends, corporation profits, individual business profits, wages and salaries, and professional income. In 1969 revenue from the corporation profits tax and the individual income tax on wages and salaries

TABLE 9. DEMOCRATIC REPUBLIC OF CONGO: SOURCES
OF BUDGET REVENUE, 1966–70

(In millions of zaïres)

	1966	1967	1968	1969	1970 [1]
Income and profits taxes	10.60	12.19	30.55	69.55	71.85
Corporations	*7.36*	*4.80*	*18.19*	*43.09*	*44.62*
Wages and salaries	*2.17*	*6.17*	*10.16*	*20.60*	*18.90*
Other	*1.07*	*1.22*	*2.20*	*5.86*	*8.33*
Property taxes	0.10	0.13	0.84	3.60	2.82
Internal turnover tax [2]	2.75	5.50	12.28	17.59	18.04
Excise taxes	6.58	6.69	8.05	10.43	11.72
Alcoholic beverages	*3.11*	*3.62*	*3.64*	*4.62*	*5.31*
Tobacco	*1.47*	*1.51*	*1.40*	*1.67*	*2.03*
Gasoline	*1.46*	*0.86*	*2.16*	*3.49*	*3.57*
Sugar	*0.19*	*0.24*	*0.16*	*0.21*	*0.29*
Other	*0.35*	*0.46*	*0.69*	*0.44*	*0.52*
Taxes on foreign transactions	35.54	77.56	127.18	166.17	189.90
Import duties	*7.82*	*13.27*	*30.89*	*41.28*	*42.47*
Export duties	*11.39*	*38.23*	*68.45*	*91.82*	*113.20*
Export turnover tax	*—*	*15.16*	*20.64*	*24.07*	*23.93*
Statistical tax and miscellaneous	*2.10*	*3.68*	*7.20*	*9.00*	*10.30*
Exchange tax [3]	*14.23*	*7.22*	*—*	*—*	*—*
Other taxes	0.05	0.11	0.25	0.59	1.72
Total tax revenue	55.62	102.18	179.15	267.93	296.05
Other revenue	3.63	4.18	5.56	4.74	12.35
Portfolio revenue	*0.11*	*0.12*	*1.10*	*1.57*	*8.29*
Other receipts [4]	*3.52*	*4.06*	*4.46*	*3.17*	*4.06*
Adjustments [5]	2.60	−7.93	1.45	−3.19	6.88
Total revenue	61.85	98.43	186.16	269.48	315.28

Sources: Banque Nationale du Congo, *Rapport Annuel, 1969–1970;* and data provided by the Congolese authorities.

[1] Preliminary outturn.
[2] Consists largely of revenue from turnover tax on imports.
[3] Abolished in June 1967.
[4] Fees, service charges, receipts from government property, etc.
[5] These adjustments result (1) when positive, from receipts not yet classified by revenue category, and (2) when negative, from receipts received but not yet transferred to the central accounts of the Treasury.

represented about 85 per cent of total revenue from all taxes on incomes and profits.

Corporation Income Tax.—Under the reformed system of direct taxation that entered into effect from January 1968, a single rate of 45 per cent on corporate profits was introduced; this was reduced to 40 per cent in 1969. Since the depreciation allowances of companies were based on the 1961 value of their assets, they proved insufficient to enable companies to maintain the current value of their assets. Accordingly, in 1968 companies were given until June 1970 to revalue their assets on the basis of specified coefficients. To offset the loss in tax revenue that such upward adjustment implied, a capital gains tax of 5 per cent was imposed on the increased book value resulting from revaluation. In addition, to accelerate collections on the corporation income tax, companies were required to make by April 1 an initial payment equal to 50 per cent of the tax paid on the previous year's profits as an installment toward the current year's tax liability.

Individual Income Tax.—All personal incomes of more than Z 240 a year (Z 180 before 1970) are subject to a progressive tax ranging from 4 per cent to 60 per cent as income rises from Z 240 to Z 9,500 and above. On a salary of Z 1,000 a year, the effective tax rate is about 7.5 per cent; on a salary of Z 9,500 a year, the effective rate rises to 29.5 per cent. Family allowances apply up to a taxable income of Z 3,000.

All income earned in Congo is subject to tax irrespective of the nationality of the recipient. A special tax of 5 per cent on total salaries paid to foreign workers is levied on all employers; this is payable quarterly and is intended to represent the tax liability on that part of such salaries paid outside the country.

Other Direct Taxes.—The tax on interest and dividends (*taxe mobilière*), the rate of which was reduced from 25 per cent to 20 per cent in 1968, is levied on all interest and dividends and on a part of the income received by partners who are not active in the company. The tax on income from rent (*impôt sur les revenus locatifs*) ranges from 20 per cent to 60 per cent as income rises to Z 7,000 and above, and is levied on all property owners or rent beneficiaries. The property tax (*contribution réelle*) is a tax based on so-called status symbols, mainly property classified into three categories: land, buildings, and vehicles. A head tax or minimum personal tax (*contribution personnelle minimum*) remains in force and applies to all incomes of less than Z 240 a year. The revenue from this tax is collected and retained by the local authorities.

Indirect Taxes

Indirect taxation consists largely of export and import duties (both customs duties and fiscal duties), turnover taxes, and excise taxes.

Export Duties.—Export duties are levied on all exports, of which minerals, mainly copper, cobalt, diamonds, and zinc, are the most important. The nominal rate of duty is applied to the f.o.b. value of the product less the amount of the tax (*valeur de base*), so that the effective rate of duty is much lower than the nominal rate. For instance, with the present nominal rate of duty of 40 per cent on the f.o.b. value of copper exports, the effective rate is 28.5 per cent. From June 1969, a progressive surtax on copper has been levied on that portion of the price in excess of Z 550 a ton. The rate of the surtax is 10 per cent ad valorem and is increased by 5 per cent for each increase of Z 7 a ton in the *valeur de base* up to a maximum of 40 per cent. This means that with an average f.o.b. price for copper wire bars of Z 600 a ton, the total effective rate of duty is about 34 per cent, which rises to 39 per cent when the price reaches Z 800 a ton. Beginning May 1, 1969 the tax is assessed on the basis of the c.i.f. price prevailing in the second month preceding the month of export.

The nominal rate of duty on palm oil was reduced from 15 per cent to 2 per cent in October 1968, in order to alleviate the effect of declining export prices. In October 1969 the export duty on coffee was reduced from 10 per cent to 3 per cent, that on rubber from 10 per cent to 5 per cent, and the rates of duty on palm kernel products and timber were also reduced. With effect from January 1970 the nominal rate of export duty on manganese was reduced from 25 per cent to 5 per cent and that on diamonds from 40 per cent to 25 per cent, and a duty of 6 per cent was introduced on gold exports.

Import Duties.—Following the stabilization measures taken in June 1967, import duties on nonessential items and luxury goods were raised. At the beginning of 1968, a two-column tariff (customs duty and fiscal duty) was established, and the customs duty was raised to the maximum compatible with the convention of association with the EEC. In April and December 1969, import taxes on certain textiles were raised to protect local industry; the margin of protection is estimated to be equivalent to 50 per cent of the price of a given domestic product.

Turnover Taxes.—A turnover tax was introduced in 1966 at the rate of 7.5 per cent on the wholesale value of goods either imported (c.i.f. value plus customs duties) or manufactured locally and at the rate of

10 per cent on certain services. In June 1967 the tax was extended to apply to the proceeds from exports. Effective January 1970, the rates were reduced to 6.75 per cent on imports and on all exports except for copper, cobalt, diamonds, uranium, and zinc, for which the rate was reduced to 7 per cent. The tax on imports is collected by the customs, on exports by the commercial banks, and on services by the internal revenue service.

Other Indirect Taxes.—A statistical tax is levied on all exports at the rate of 1 per cent and on imports at the rate of 3 per cent. Excise taxes are also levied on a number of consumer items, the most important of which are alcoholic beverages, tobacco, sugar, cement, gasoline, and mineral oil. These taxes are collected by the customs.

Other Revenue

Other revenue consists of receipts from portfolio investments, fees, service charges, and receipts from government property (see Table 9).

BUDGETARY OPERATIONS, 1966–69

A consolidated statement of the Central Government's financial operations including those financed with foreign resources, such as technical assistance, use of counterpart funds of foreign aid, and foreign borrowing, has been prepared by the National Bank for the years 1966–70 (Table 10). The analysis of fiscal developments which follows is based on this consolidated statement.

One of the primary objectives of the stabilization program introduced in June 1967 was to restore basic equilibrium in public finances while increasing the share of budget revenue earmarked for capital expenditure and eliminating large and continuous recourse to the banking system for treasury financing. Over the period 1967–69 this objective was broadly achieved—in the context, however, of rapidly growing receipts and expenditures.

The total budget deficit (line 6 in Table 10), which in the period January 1963–June 1967 had been equivalent on the average to about 28 per cent of total budget expenditure, virtually disappeared in 1967 and was reduced to less than 2 per cent in 1968. The budgetary position improved further in 1969, when a surplus of Z 10.8 million was real-

TABLE 10. DEMOCRATIC REPUBLIC OF CONGO: CONSOLIDATED STATEMENT OF FINANCIAL OPERATIONS OF CENTRAL GOVERNMENT, 1966–70

(In millions of zaïres)

	1966	1967	1968	1969	1970 [1]
A. Budgetary operations					
1. Budget revenue	61.85	98.43	186.16	269.48	315.30
2. Current budget expenditure	−62.12	−92.75	−165.65	−206.49	−250.20
3. Surplus or deficit	−0.27	5.68	20.51	62.99	65.10
4. Capital budget expenditure	−4.60	−6.84	−25.71	−52.67	−70.30
5. Other transactions (net)	—	1.15	1.41	0.46	−1.30
6. Total surplus or deficit	−4.87	−0.01	−3.79	10.78	−6.50
B. Operations with foreign resources					
7. Receipts [2]	6.29	13.63	18.99	24.24	20.00
8. Current expenditure [3]	−8.80	−11.76	−16.19	−17.45	−19.80
9. Capital expenditure	−2.71	−7.59	−17.28	−16.60	−15.10
10. Surplus or deficit	−5.22	−5.72	−14.48	−9.82	−14.90
C. Overall surplus or deficit (6 + 10)	−10.09	−5.73	−18.27	0.96	−21.40
D. Financing					
Domestic	4.48	−2.28	8.17	−5.74	15.80
National Bank (net)	*5.67*	*7.61*	*3.75*	*−5.68*	*11.80*
Commercial banks	*—*	*−0.11*	*3.87*	*−0.14*	*0.20*
Post Office	*−0.20*	*0.26*	*−0.04*	*0.83*	*−0.20*
Other [4]	*−0.99*	*−10.03*	*0.59*	*−0.75*	*4.00*
Foreign	5.61	8.01	10.10	4.78	5.60
New loans	*6.21*	*10.06*	*13.96*	*10.75*	*12.00*
Long-term loans [5]	*(5.82)*	*(8.47)*	*(8.02)*	*(6.77)*	*(...)*
Suppliers' credits	*(0.39)*	*(1.59)*	*(5.94)*	*(3.98)*	*(...)*
Repayments	*−0.60*	*−2.05*	*−3.86*	*−5.97*	*−6.40*
Total	10.09	5.73	18.27	−0.96	21.40

Sources: Banque Nationale du Congo, *Rapport Annuel, 1969–1970;* and data provided by the Congolese authorities.

[1] Preliminary outturn.

[2] Mainly technical assistance grants and financial grants from the EEC and other sources.

[3] Mainly counterpart of technical assistance grants and military purchases.

[4] Changes in Congolese counterpart funds of foreign aid and in the outstanding balances on account of devaluation profits.

[5] Including loans in zaïres extended by the U.S. out of the counterpart funds of U.S. aid.

ized. As part of this improvement, the balance of budget revenue over current budget expenditure moved from a large deficit position prior to June 1967 to a surplus of Z 5.7 million in 1967 as a whole. This surplus increased to Z 20.5 million in 1968 and reached Z 63 million in 1969, when it was equivalent to 23 per cent of total budget revenue. With the achievement of this surplus, capital budget expenditure was sharply increased, and at the same time the Treasury's net borrowing from the banking system was reduced.

Between 1966 and 1969, government operations financed from foreign grants and loans also increased in terms of zaïres, but this increase was largely the result of the exchange rate adjustment. In relative terms, the importance of these operations declined from the equivalent of 17 per cent of total budget expenditure in 1966 to 13 per cent in 1969. Although foreign grants, other than technical assistance grants, increased between 1966 and 1969, borrowing abroad to finance capital expenditure also increased during this period.

Altogether, the Government's financial operations, which had shown overall deficits of Z 5.7 million in 1967 and Z 18.3 million in 1968, registered a small surplus of Z 1 million in 1969. The related financing operations are shown in Table 10. The changes in net borrowing from the banking system reflect essentially the budget outcome and public debt amortization, while the increase in borrowing abroad is largely the counterpart of capital expenditure financed from foreign resources other than grants. The Government's net borrowing from the banking system amounted to Z 7.7 million in 1967 (mostly net advances from the National Bank) and to Z 7.6 million in 1968. In 1969, however, the Government's indebtedness to the banking system was reduced by about Z 6 million. Net borrowing from abroad rose to Z 8 million in 1967 and to Z 10.1 million in 1968 but fell to Z 4.8 million in 1969. Suppliers' credits accounted for about 43 per cent of total new foreign borrowing in 1968 and for 37 per cent in 1969, compared with 16 per cent in 1967. Other domestic financing and changes in counterpart funds accounted for only a minor part of total financing operations during these years, except in 1967.

Revenue

Budget revenue, which amounted to about Z 60 million a year in the 18 months that ended in June 1967, rose to an annual rate of about Z 132 million in the second half of 1967 and amounted to Z 98.4 million in 1967 as a whole, to Z 186.2 million in 1968, and to Z 269.5 million in 1969 (Table 10).

During 1967 the increase in revenue was largely the result of the exchange rate adjustment of June 1967 and of the tax measures that were then introduced as part of the stabilization program. These measures included a substantial increase in the rate of export duty on the principal mineral products (e.g., copper, cobalt, and diamonds) and doubling the rate of duty on all other exports. In addition, the turnover tax was extended to apply to the proceeds from exports at the rate of 7.5 per cent, and a new schedule of import duties was introduced with higher rates for nonessential and luxury goods.

Budget revenue in 1968, at Z 186.2 million, was about 40 per cent above the annual rate realized during the second half of 1967 and about three times larger than the revenue collected in 1966. The increase in revenue during 1968 was widespread, reflecting the full effect of the measures introduced in June 1967, the subsequent expansion in foreign trade and domestic activity, and the income tax reform of January 1968. Revenue from taxes on foreign trade totaled Z 127.2 million in 1968, compared with Z 35.5 million in 1966, with most of the increase stemming from export taxes. Revenue from taxes on incomes and profits also increased substantially, from an average of Z 11.4 million in 1966 and 1967 to Z 30.6 million in 1968.

Under the income tax reform of January 1968, the tax on company profits was increased by introducing a single tax rate of 45 per cent; the former rates had ranged from 14 per cent to 40 per cent according to six tranches into which a company's share capital would be divided. At the same time companies were authorized to revalue their assets, and in order to offset the loss in revenue resulting from the increase in depreciation allowances, a capital gains tax of 5 per cent was imposed on the increase in book value resulting from revaluation. The individual income tax was also revised, and all personal incomes of more than Z 180 a year were made subject to a rescheduled progressive income tax, with rates ranging from 4 per cent to 60 per cent.

In 1969 a further rapid increase in receipts from export and income taxes accounted for about 75 per cent of the rise in total tax revenue, and receipts from taxes on imports and domestic transactions for most of the remainder. Receipts from export taxes rose by 30 per cent, to some Z 125 million, with most of the increase resulting from copper exports. During 1969 both the volume of exports and the world market price of copper increased—exports by about 12 per cent and average prices on the Brussels market by 22 per cent. Furthermore, a progressive surtax on copper exports was introduced, with effect from June 1969. Toward the end of 1968 and in 1969 the rates of export duty on the main agricultural exports were reduced in order to alleviate the effect of declining export prices, but this measure had only a relatively small impact on budget revenue. The export duty on palm oil was reduced from 15 per cent to 2 per cent in October 1968. Furthermore, in October 1969 the export duty on coffee was lowered from 10 per cent to 3 per cent and that on rubber from 10 per cent to 5 per cent; large reductions in the rate of duty on timber exports were also introduced. In 1969 the average rate of export taxes, i.e., export duties, export turnover tax, progressive surtax on copper, and statistical tax, totaled some 35 per cent (compared with 30 per cent in 1968), while the average rate of import taxes, i.e., import duties, import turnover tax, and statistical tax, totaled about 27 per cent.

Receipts from income and profits taxes rose by nearly 130 per cent in 1969, to about Z 70 million. Large payments of profits tax by GECOMINES, the effect of the 1968 income tax reform, higher wages and salaries, and improved tax collection, all contributed to this increase. Receipts from the profits tax on corporations rose from Z 18.2 million to Z 43.1 million, and receipts from the tax on wages and salaries increased from Z 10.2 million in 1968 to Z 20.6 million in 1969.

Taxes paid by GECOMINES have risen rapidly in recent years. In 1969 they amounted to Z 132.4 million, of which about Z 100 million was in export taxes. However, taxes paid by GECOMINES as a proportion of total budget revenue declined from 74.5 per cent in 1966 to 51.7 per cent in 1968 and to 49.4 per cent in 1969. The decline is even larger when related to total tax revenue. The principal factor behind this development appears to be a general improvement in the assessment and collection of taxes, especially direct taxes on individuals and enterprises other than GECOMINES.

Expenditure

Total budget expenditure, excluding public debt amortization, rose from Z 66.7 million in 1966 to Z 191.3 million in 1968 and Z 259.1 million in 1969 (Tables 10 and 11). The share of capital expenditure in total budget expenditure was increased substantially during this period. However, a detailed distribution of budget expenditure is not

TABLE 11. DEMOCRATIC REPUBLIC OF CONGO: ESTIMATED DISTRIBUTION
OF BUDGET EXPENDITURE, 1967–70

(In millions of zaïres)

	1967	1968	1969	1970 [1]
1. Current expenditure	**92.75**	**165.64**	**206.48**	**250.20**
General services	40.24	75.76	85.01	...
Defense	*13.45*	*21.92*	*23.16*	...
Foreign affairs	*3.26*	*7.48*	*7.34*	...
Community and social services	15.64	29.41	57.26	...
Education	*13.12*	*25.76*	*44.81*	...
Health	*1.20*	*1.46*	*7.91*	...
Economic services	5.93	7.87	9.63	...
Agriculture	*0.84*	*0.55*	*1.79*	...
Interest on public debt	2.96	7.66	6.32	...
Unclassified expenditure [2]	27.98	44.94	48.26	...
2. Capital expenditure	**6.84**	**25.71**	**52.67**	**70.30**
Loans, grants, and equity participations	...	5.29	6.26	...
Direct investments	...	17.74	46.47	...
Other [3]	...	2.67	−0.06	...
3. Total (1 + 2)	**99.59**	**191.35**	**259.15**	**320.50**
4. Public debt amortization [4]	**4.67**	**3.87**	**5.98**	**6.40**
5. Grand total (3 + 4)	**104.26**	**195.22**	**265.13**	**326.90**

Sources: Data provided by the Congolese authorities; and Fund staff estimates.

[1] Preliminary outturn.
[2] Including expenditure authorized by the Presidency.
[3] Purchases of durable goods minus interest and amortization payments on suppliers' credits.
[4] Repayment of principal on long-term loans and of interest and amortization on suppliers' credits. In 1967 it included also the repayment of Z 2.6 million to the National Bank of Congo financed by the use of part of the devaluation profits.

available, and it is to be assumed that an unspecified amount of expenditure of a current nature is included in capital expenditure.

Current budget expenditure, which had averaged some Z 75 million a year in the 18 months prior to June 1967, rose to an annual rate of Z 108 million in the second half of 1967 and totaled Z 92.7 million in 1967 as a whole. It then rose to Z 165.6 million in 1968 and to Z 206.5 million in 1969. The increase in current expenditure in 1967 was largely the result of the exchange rate adjustment of June 1967 and of the wage increases that became effective in the second half of that year. The estimate for 1968 expenditure, Z 165.6 million, was about 50 per cent above the annual rate that obtained during the second half of 1967 and about 2.7 times that of 1966. Available data can provide only a very rough approximation of the increase in current expenditure by categories. It appears, however, that a large proportion of the rising expenditure during 1968 resulted from expenditure on goods and services. According to national accounts data, expenditure in 1968 on wages and salaries totaled about Z 80 million, approximately 60 per cent more than in 1966. The increase in expenditure for purchases of goods and services abroad was much larger, and so was the increase in expenditure on transfers and subsidies.

In 1969 current expenditure increased by a further 25 per cent, to Z 206.5 million. According to national accounts data, expenditure on wages and salaries rose by an additional 27 per cent, to Z 103 million, in 1969, when it accounted for less than 50 per cent of total current expenditure, compared with nearly 70 per cent in 1966. The available distribution of expenditure by function shows the preponderant share of education (about 22 per cent in 1969), defense (11 per cent), and other general services in total current budget expenditure, 23 per cent of which is unclassified (Table 11).

In recent years current expenditure has substantially exceeded the original budget estimates. The principal factor behind this development has been new expenditure commitments authorized in the course of the year, as control over the execution of the budget has been improving. Among the steps taken by the Ministry of Finance to strengthen budgetary controls since 1969 are the introduction of mechanized accounting, the redefinition of the responsibilities of the public accountants, and the establishment of a corps of financial inspectors to supervise disbursements. Furthermore, a census of both permanent and contractual employees in government service has been undertaken.

Capital budget expenditure increased from Z 4.6 million in 1966 to Z 25.7 million in 1968 and to Z 52.7 million in 1969. As in the case of current expenditure, a detailed distribution by sector is not available. However, as explained above in the section on Economic Development and Prospects, it appears that about half of capital budget expenditure in 1968 and 1969 was allocated to public works and to re-equipping the transport and energy sectors. Capital expenditure included the purchase of military equipment (about Z 9 million in the two years 1968–69), disbursements in connection with the Inga scheme and the water supply (Z 5.6 million in 1969), the construction and equipment of airports at Bukavu and elsewhere (Z 2.8 million in 1969), the International Fair at Kinshasa (Z 2.8 million in 1969), the reconstruction of the city of Kisangani (Z 3.3 million in 1969), and building an agricultural station at Ndjili in the Kinshasa area (Z 3.7 million in 1969). Other expenditure was in the form of financial investments (Z 6.3 million in 1969), mainly participations in the capital of public and semi-public companies. About 30 per cent of total capital expenditure in 1968 and 1969 is estimated to have been allocated to general services and administration.

Operations Financed with Foreign Resources

Government expenditure financed by foreign grants and loans outside the government budget increased from Z 11.5 million in 1966 to about Z 34 million in 1968 and 1969 (Table 10). Although an important share of this expenditure represents the counterpart of technical assistance grants (Z 15.9 million in 1969), investment expenditure has increased. In 1969 capital expenditure financed by foreign resources totaled Z 16.6 million (Z 2.7 million in 1966), of which some Z 10 million was made through new long-term loans and suppliers' credits and the remainder represented mainly disbursements from the EDF.

BUDGET FOR 1970

Preparation of budget estimates is at present subject to a large margin of uncertainty inasmuch as the evolution of budget revenue is heavily dependent upon the movement of world market prices for copper, and budget expenditure is strongly influenced by the expenditure, current and capital, authorized in the course of the year over and above original budget appropriations. In recent years the original budgets have tended to underestimate substantially both revenue and expenditure, and therefore original budget figures have had limited significance. For example, the original 1969 budget provided for total revenue of Z 185 million, with current expenditure appropriations at Z 145 million and capital budget expenditure at Z 40 million, whereas according to the budget outturn, revenue in 1969 totaled Z 269.5 million, with current expenditure reaching Z 206.5 million and capital expenditure about Z 53 million.

For 1970 the original estimates of both revenue and expenditure were initially Z 215 million, or roughly 20–25 per cent below the actual level of revenue and expenditure in 1969. The revenue estimate was based on an average copper price of $0.50 a pound. Current expenditure was estimated at Z 163.5 million and capital expenditure at Z 51.5 million. However, preliminary estimates of the budget outturn put revenue for the year at about Z 315 million (an increase of 17 per cent over 1969), current budget expenditure at Z 250 million, and capital budget expenditure at Z 70 million. Including other transactions (net), budgetary operations showed a deficit of Z 6.5 million in 1970, as expenditure rose more rapidly than revenue (Table 10).

As shown in Table 9, most of the increase in budget revenue in 1970 stemmed from export taxes—which are estimated to have yielded some Z 147 million, compared with Z 125 million realized in 1969—and from portfolio revenue.

Several changes in taxation were introduced with the 1970 budget. To mitigate the adverse effect of declining world market prices on producing enterprises, the rate of export duty for manganese was reduced from 25 per cent to 5 per cent and that on diamonds from 40 per cent to 25 per cent. On the other hand, an export duty of 6 per cent was introduced on gold exports. The rate of the turnover tax on exports and imports was reduced from 7.5 per cent to 6.75 per cent except on exports of copper, cobalt, diamonds, uranium, and zinc, the rate for which was reduced to 7 per cent; the rate of the turnover tax on services was kept at 10 per cent. These measures were taken to alleviate the general tax burden on enterprises and the effect on domestic prices of the increase in wages that took place in January 1970. Furthermore, the minimum annual income exempted from the personal income tax was raised from Z 180 to Z 240. Certain changes were also introduced in the property tax in order to encourage construction and land development.

Although it is not possible to give a detailed breakdown of the anticipated increase in current budget expenditure over and above the original budget estimates for 1970, it appears that a large share of the increase was in expenditure for defense, police, and education, and in priority expenditure authorized by the President.

PUBLIC DEBT

As of December 31, 1969, total public debt outstanding was estimated at Z 271.8 million (about 31 per cent of GDP), of which

Z 140.35 million was foreign debt and Z 131.55 million was domestic debt. The foreign debt is analyzed below in the section on Balance of Payments—External Debt. Of the total domestic debt, Z 112.51 million represented gross advances from the National Bank to the Central Government, Z 17.03 million was in short-term treasury bills held by commercial banks, and Z 2.01 million represented deposits with the Postal Checking System.

MONEY AND BANKING

MONETARY SYSTEM AND BANKING OPERATIONS

The currency of Congo, the zaïre, is issued by the National Bank of Congo. The zaïre replaced the Congo franc on June 23, 1967 at an official rate of exchange of Z 1 = US$2.00, which represented a substantial depreciation of the currency. New statutes for the National Bank were also promulgated and became effective from that date, giving the Bank increased authority in matters relating to credit control and foreign exchange policy. On September 2, 1970, a par value of Z 1 = US$2.00 was agreed with the International Monetary Fund.

There are seven commercial banks operating in Congo. Although most of them are incorporated in Congo, they are essentially branches or affiliates of foreign banks. The capital composition and the relative importance of each are described below in the section on Structure and Operations of Commercial Banks.

Other financial institutions include a savings bank, the Caisse d'Epargne du Congo (CADECO), and a medium-term lending institution, the Société de Crédit aux Classes Moyennes et à l'Industrie. These two institutions have been relatively inactive in recent years, and plans for their reorganization are under way.

A new development bank, the Société Congolaise de Financement du Développement (SOCOFIDE), was established on January 10, 1970. Its functions and capital structure are described below in the section on National Development Bank.

Operations and Policies of National Bank

The operations of the National Bank from the end of 1966 to the end of 1970 are summarized in Table 12. The foreign assets of the Bank

TABLE 12. DEMOCRATIC REPUBLIC OF CONGO: ASSETS AND LIABILITIES OF NATIONAL BANK, 1966–70

(In millions of zaïres; end of period)

	1966 Dec.	1967 June	1967 Dec.	1968 June	1968 Dec.	1969 June	1969 Dec.	1970 June	1970 Dec.
Assets									
Foreign assets	3.08	9.89	33.79	62.27	68.90	88.09	99.09	110.68	92.63
Claims on government	68.66	79.59	80.97	84.98	89.79	108.97	112.51	139.77	164.84
Assets = liabilities	**71.74**	**89.48**	**114.76**	**147.25**	**158.69**	**197.06**	**211.60**	**250.45**	**257.47**
Liabilities									
Reserve money	50.91	58.23	63.10	77.23	94.47	111.27	107.60	128.13	142.07
Currency outside banks	*31.41*	*36.76*	*41.01*	*45.60*	*51.07*	*56.32*	*56.91*	*65.98*	*74.76*
Currency in banks	*0.30*	*1.45*	*0.96*	*1.50*	*1.31*	*2.20*	*1.75*	*2.68*	*2.01*
Bankers' free deposits	*13.93*	*13.65*	*11.16*	*21.08*	*34.33*	*44.47*	*36.98*	*45.97*	*53.68*
Private sector deposits	*5.27*	*6.37*	*9.97*	*9.05*	*7.76*	*8.28*	*11.96*	*13.50*	*11.62*
Bankers' restricted deposits	5.19	8.72	15.78	22.38	18.17	15.40	16.17	3.35	0.18
Time deposits and foreign currency deposits [1]	0.20	0.24	0.33	17.30	11.30	22.29	13.19	9.02	4.19
Government deposits	5.47	1.57	10.18	9.81	15.24	27.10	43.65	71.78	84.19
Profits from revaluation of foreign assets	—	5.97	5.70	5.57	5.63	5.61	5.44	4.55	4.36
Counterpart funds	5.99	7.60	8.23	6.46	7.40	6.99	7.96	6.29	5.75
Import prepayments	1.29	1.12	2.22	1.83	1.36	0.92	1.30	2.73	1.84
Foreign liabilities	0.54	0.52	0.56	0.55	0.55	0.55	0.76	0.74	0.75
Capital account	4.34	5.39	3.33	3.08	5.90	5.11	8.31	8.36	9.94
Other items (net)	−2.19	0.12	5.33	3.04	−1.33	1.82	7.22	15.49	4.20

Sources: Banque Nationale du Congo, *Rapport Annuel, 1969–1970*; and data provided by the Congolese authorities.

[1] Since June 1968 includes GECOMINES deposits with the National Bank, which were previously included in deposit money.

rose from Z 9.9 million at the end of June 1967 to Z 33.8 million during the second half of 1967 and continued to increase rapidly; at the end of 1969 they amounted to Z 99.1 million, equivalent to more than six months' imports on a c.i.f. basis, and at the end of 1970 they stood at Z 92.6 million, including the initial allocation of SDRs equivalent to Z 7.56 million. The Bank's foreign liabilities are very small and have remained virtually unchanged in recent years.

The National Bank acts as banker and cashier for the Central Government, the provincial governments, and public and semipublic organizations. The Bank may extend credit to the Government in the form of direct advances or by holding treasury bills. Direct advances may be granted to meet a temporary excess of expenditures over receipts, up to a maximum of 15 per cent of the Government's average annual fiscal receipts in the preceding three years. These advances may not be outstanding for more than 300 days during a calendar year, whether consecutive or not. The advances extended by the Bank to the Government before June 23, 1967, when the new statutes for the Bank became effective, were turned into a perpetual government debt of Z 75 million carrying an interest rate of 3 per cent per annum. The Bank is authorized to hold treasury bills that are freely negotiable and that have a maturity of one year or less. It may accept treasury bills as collateral for loans to banks and other financial institutions, but its holdings of such bills may not at any time exceed 20 per cent of the average annual fiscal receipts of the Government during the preceding three years.

The National Bank's total net claims on the Government, which had increased rapidly prior to June 1967, rose in 1968 by 5 per cent and declined in 1969 by 8 per cent, to Z 68.9 million. The decline in 1969 took place entirely during the last quarter of the year, as a result of a sharp increase in government deposits which more than offset the continuing increase in direct advances to the Government. Gross claims on the Government rose from Z 89.8 million at the end of 1968 to Z 112.5 million at the end of 1969. At the same time, however, government deposits at the National Bank rose from Z 15.2 million at the end of 1968 to Z 27.1 million at the end of June 1969 and to Z 43.6 million at the end of the year, reflecting a substantial increase in government receipts during the second half of the year. In the first six months of

1970, the Bank's net claims on the Government declined further, but rose sharply during the second half. For 1970 as a whole these claims rose by 17 per cent, to Z 80.6 million.

The National Bank is empowered to conduct credit operations with the commercial banks and possesses the necessary powers to control bank credit. The Bank may undertake discount and rediscount operations and determine the rate of interest to be applied to these operations. It may also fix the maximum and minimum rates of interest which banks and other financial institutions may apply to their lending operations or pay on deposits. In addition, it may require banks to maintain with it a certain proportion of their deposits. Furthermore, whenever it deems necessary, the Bank may impose selective controls on loans and investments by commercial banks and other financial institutions. In this connection, the Bank may define the purpose of the operations for which credit may or may not be extended, determine the nature of the collateral necessary to secure these loans as well as their maximum maturity, and establish ceilings for all categories of bank lending. The Bank is authorized to impose on banks a penalty of up to 1 per cent a day calculated on the amount of credit in excess of the ceilings.

The National Bank has so far relied on quantitative ceilings and selective controls to regulate credit to the private sector. A special Credit Information Department (Centrale des Risques) was established in the National Bank in 1967, to which all bank credits exceeding Z 3,000 have to be reported, indicating their nature and purpose. Moreover, the approval of the Bank is required for credits beyond Z 20,000. At present, interest rates do not play a role in the supply and distribution of credit. The commercial banks are not subject to reserve requirements or liquidity ratios, and because of their highly liquid position, rediscount facilities with the National Bank have not been established. In June 1967 the National Bank established a global ceiling of Z 20 million on commercial bank credit to the private sector, a level considered consistent with the immediate objectives set for the balance of payments. In view of the continued improvement in the external payments position, the reduced recourse of the Treasury to the banking system, and the increased demand for credit on the part of the private sector, the National Bank allowed credit to the private sector to expand during 1968 and 1969 while furthering its policy of selective controls with a view to redistributing credit to the more productive sectors of the economy.

To this end the National Bank in November 1967 established separate ceilings on commercial bank credit—one on priority credits of a self-liquidating nature (*plafond réglementé*) and one on all other credits (*plafond libre*). In April 1968 an additional ceiling was established to cover special operations (*plafond spécial*), mainly priority credits for reconstruction, agriculture, and industry; all credits under this ceiling require the prior approval of the National Bank. During 1968 and 1969 the *plafond réglementé* and the *plafond spécial* were progressively raised while the *plafond libre* was lowered. At the end of December 1969 the credit ceilings totaled Z 27.8 million, of which the *plafond libre* represented less than 16 per cent, compared with 48 per cent at the end of 1967. Because of the expected expansion in export receipts in 1970, and in anticipation of a further decline in the net indebtedness of the Government to the banking system, the National Bank in January 1970 excluded all crop financing from credit subject to ceilings, and in March it decided to raise the *plafond réglementé* by Z 7 million. Furthermore, the Bank approved Z 13.4 million of credits under the *plafond spécial*. With these various measures, credit to the private sector rose to some Z 41 million at the end of June 1970.

With a view to encouraging the collection of private savings and the use of medium-term credit to finance investment, the National Bank decided in July 1970 to exclude from the ceilings medium-term credit financed through savings deposits. In addition, it instructed the banks to maintain with the National Bank a cash deposit calculated in relation to their deposit liabilities, without, however, fixing a ratio. This measure was aimed at introducing a new and more flexible instrument of credit control.

The principal liabilities of the National Bank are reserve money, bankers' restricted deposits, and time and foreign currency deposits (Table 12). In the three years 1968–70 reserve money rose more than twofold, to Z 142.1 million, and in December 1970 it accounted for more than half of the National Bank's total liabilities. This increase reflected largely an expansion in currency circulation by more than 80 per cent, to Z 74.8 million, and an increase in bankers' free deposits at the National Bank from Z 11.2 million at the end of 1967 to Z 53.7 million at the end of 1970. Bankers' restricted deposits consist of the counterpart of import prepayment liabilities of the commercial banks for which the National Bank has provided foreign exchange cover. Following an increase of about Z 2.4 million in 1968, these deposits declined to Z 16.2 million in 1969 because of a decrease in imports subject to this requirement (i.e., imports for which payment is required upon shipment); in January 1970 the National Bank abolished the requirement altogether. Time deposits and deposits of foreign currencies held with the National Bank, which consist almost entirely of deposits by GECOMINES, have increased substantially since the end of 1967. The GECOMINES account with the National Bank is credited with the proceeds of the company's exports and is debited with the amounts required for the company's current operations by monthly transfers to the demand deposit accounts of the company with commercial banks. The total of time and foreign currency deposits with the National Bank rose from a negligible amount to Z 17.3 million at the end of June 1968 and to Z 22.3 million at the end of June 1969, but then declined, as GECOMINES used a part of its deposits to reduce its short-term indebtedness abroad and to pay profits taxes early in 1970.

The net accounting profits resulting from the revaluation of foreign assets and liabilities in June 1967, which amounted to Z 10.6 million, were partly used in that year, mainly to reduce the Government's indebtedness to the National Bank and to offset losses incurred by the National Bank. As of December 31, 1970, Z 4.4 million of these profits were still outstanding on the books of the National Bank.

Structure and Operations of Commercial Banks

Commercial banking activities are well developed and diversified. With 46 branch offices, the commercial banks cover virtually the entire country and are the most important financial intermediaries. Owing to a lack of specialized credit and financial institutions, the commercial banks also provide medium-term and long-term investment financing.

There are seven commercial banks operating in Congo: Banque du Congo, Société Congolaise de Banque, Banque Belge d'Afrique, Crédit Congolais, Banque de Paris et des Pays-Bas, Banque Internationale pour l'Afrique au Congo, and Banque de Kinshasa. All are incorporated in Congo.

The Banque du Congo is by far the largest commercial bank, with deposits accounting for more than 60 per cent of all commercial bank deposits. It was established in 1909 as the Banque du Congo Belge by a group of Belgian banks, and acted as the bank of issue until the former Central Bank of the Belgian Congo and Ruanda-Urundi was established in 1952. The capital of the Banque du Congo is Z 1.4 million. The principal single shareholder is the Société Générale de Banque (Belgium), with a capital participation of 15 per cent; the Congolese Government and the Morgan Guaranty Trust Company hold the next largest single minority participations. The bank maintains 22 branch offices—almost as many as those of all the other banks combined; 13 of these branches also carry out operations on behalf of the National Bank.

The Société Congolaise de Banque (SOCOBANQUE), the second largest bank, was established in 1947 and in 1966 took over the Congolese operations of the Belgian Banque de Crédit Commercial Africain (Kredietbank). Its share capital was increased from Z 0.6 million to Z 1.2 million in May 1969. More than half of SOCOBANQUE's capital is owned by a group of foreign banks—including Banque Lambert, Bank of America, Commerzbank, Banque Nationale de Paris, and Banca d'America e d'Italia—through the Société Financière pour les Pays d'Outre-Mer, a holding company with headquarters in Geneva. The remaining part of SOCOBANQUE's capital is owned by the Congolese Government and by private Congolese nationals. SOCOBANQUE is managed by Banque Lambert and has 9 branch offices located in the main commercial and industrial centers. It holds some 20 per cent of all commercial bank deposits.

The Banque Belge d'Afrique was established in 1929 by the Belgian Banque de Bruxelles. Its capital was increased from Z 0.4 million to Z 0.8 million in November 1968 when the British Standard Bank bought a 23.5 per cent capital participation. Other principal holders are the Banque de Bruxelles and the Congolese Government, which have participations of 23.5 per cent and 18 per cent, respectively. The bank maintains 6 branch offices, and its activities extend to nearly every region of the country.

The Crédit Congolais (CREDICO), established in 1951 by a group of Belgian banks and industries, has a capital of Z 40,000 and is now owned completely by Barclays Bank D.C.O. It has 6 branch offices, but its activities are largely concentrated in Kinshasa and Lubumbashi.

The Banque de Paris et des Pays-Bas, which has been operating in Congo since 1951, maintains 1 branch office in Kinshasa; its capital, which was increased from Z 30,000 to Z 170,000 in March 1970, is owned solely by the Compagnie Financière Internationale de Paris et des Pays-Bas.

The Banque Internationale pour l'Afrique au Congo and the Banque de Kinshasa were both established in 1970, with share capital of Z 150,000 and Z 300,000, respectively. The latter is the first commercial bank entirely owned by Congolese nationals.

The operations of the commercial banks are summarized in Table 13. During the years 1968–70, commercial bank reserves increased steadily, and at the end of 1970 they totaled Z 55.9 million, equivalent to more than half of the banks' demand deposit liabilities. Most of these reserves are held in the form of free deposits with the National Bank. The marked improvement in the liquidity position of the banks has resulted from a large increase in demand deposits, the limitations imposed by the National Bank on the expansion of credit, and the fact that banks are not allowed to invest their excess funds abroad. From 1967 to 1970, the foreign assets of the commercial banks did not in general change very much, since they are required to turn over to the National Bank all their foreign receipts beyond a level considered necessary as working balances.

Commercial bank credit to the Government, which is in the form of holdings of treasury bills, has not changed substantially in recent years except for an increase of nearly Z 4 million in October 1968. Since then, claims on the Government have remained at approximately Z 17 million. As explained earlier, the banks' claims on the private sector have been allowed to expand considerably since 1968.

The most significant development in the liabilities of the commercial banks has been the increase in demand deposits, from Z 40.5 million at the end of June 1967 to Z 81.1 million at the end of 1969, and to Z 97.8 million at the end of 1970. This increase resulted essentially from the impact on the liquidity position of enterprises, especially those

TABLE 13. DEMOCRATIC REPUBLIC OF CONGO: ASSETS AND LIABILITIES OF COMMERCIAL BANKS, 1966-70

(In millions of zaïres; end of period)

	1966	1967 June	1967 Dec.	1968 June	1968 Dec.	1969 June	1969 Dec.	1970 June	1970 Dec.
Assets									
Reserves	14.19	16.14	12.67	22.66	35.77	46.78	40.69	48.73	55.93
Restricted deposits with National Bank	5.19	8.23	16.02	22.43	18.17	15.40	16.18	3.35	0.18
Foreign assets	7.97	14.12	28.30	17.24	17.92	14.86	15.59	16.60	18.54
Claims on government	13.41	13.30	13.30	13.38	17.17	16.88	17.03	16.96	17.25
Claims on private sector [1]	12.32	17.24	16.40	20.07	20.21	27.03	27.79	41.15	42.68
Assets = liabilities	**53.08**	**69.03**	**86.69**	**95.78**	**109.24**	**120.95**	**117.28**	**126.79**	**134.58**
Liabilities									
Demand deposits	35.80	40.49	58.66	61.34	75.33	88.93	81.06	91.53	97.79
Time and foreign currency deposits	3.96	4.30	3.94	4.34	4.30	5.62	6.26	11.20	18.38
Counterpart funds	1.95	2.66	0.09	2.23	0.71	0.17	2.80	2.93	2.82
Import prepayments	6.12	11.80	15.14	22.40	18.62	15.73	16.61	10.34	8.11
Foreign liabilities	0.24	0.67	0.61	0.93	1.09	2.14	1.03	1.26	1.07
Capital account	3.75	4.14	3.85	4.41	4.54	8.18	8.15	10.22	10.51
Other items (net)	1.26	4.97	4.40	0.13	4.65	0.19	1.37	-0.69	-4.10
Related data: Private demand deposits with Post Office	0.97	0.96	1.23	1.30	1.20	2.17	2.01	1.97	1.85

Sources: Banque Nationale du Congo, *Rapport Annuel, 1969-1970*; and data provided by the Congolese authorities.

[1] Including public and semipublic enterprises.

engaged in export activities, of the large balance of payments surpluses
registered during the period June 1967–June 1970. Time deposits also
increased sharply in 1970.

National Development Bank

A national development bank, the Société Congolaise de Financement
du Développement (SOCOFIDE), was established on January 10, 1970
with an initial capital of Z 100,000, which was increased to
Z 2,000,000 in June 1970. The largest single shareholder is the International Finance Corporation, with a participation of 18.75 per cent. The
Congolese Government and the National Bank each have a minority
participation of 12.50 per cent. Some 14 foreign banking institutions
from six countries have subscribed shares equivalent to 26.25 per cent
of the capital, and the remaining 30 per cent is held by commercial
banks and private enterprises operating in Congo and by Congolese
nationals.

Besides its capital, SOCOFIDE is authorized to borrow at long and
medium term from the Government, international organizations, and
the private sector. It is not, however, authorized to accept deposits with
a maturity of less than 2 years. On March 31, 1970, the Government
made an interest-free advance of Z 1 million to SOCOFIDE and agreed to
make available to it Z 2 million for 40 years at interest of 1 per cent.
In June 1970 the IDA announced that it was extending a 50-year
interest-free loan of $5 million (Z 2.5 million) to the Government to be
re-lent to SOCOFIDE to cover the foreign exchange costs of projects
financed by it.

SOCOFIDE was established to provide financing to productive private
enterprises, primarily to the manufacturing and processing industries
but enterprises engaged in commercially oriented agriculture, forestry,
fishing, transport, and tourism are also eligible. In addition to lending
at medium and long term, SOCOFIDE may take up equity participations,
underwrite securities, provide guarantees, or combine any of these operations. It may also provide technical assistance in the preparation and
execution of industrial investment projects. Its lending and investment
policies must be in accordance with the general development strategy of
the Government. SOCOFIDE's interventions, however, are to be limited to

the financing of investments likely to provide an adequate rate of return and undertaken by private or mixed enterprises in which the Government's participation does not exceed one third of the capital.

STRUCTURE OF INTEREST RATES

In recent years, interest rates generally have remained stable and have not been used to influence the amount and allocation of credit. In June 1967 the National Bank established a minimum discount rate, but so far it has had no practical significance. As a general rule, the Bank has not intervened to determine the maximum and minimum rates of interest that banks may charge for loans or pay on deposits.

Interest rates applied by commercial banks have thus far been regulated by an interbank commission that is outside the direct control of the National Bank. On loans to the private sector, the interest rate ranges from 6 per cent to 8½ per cent per annum plus a commission of 2–3 per cent per annum, and is usually based on the customer's creditworthiness rather than on the type of operation or duration of the credit. The interest rate on treasury bills varies between 4¼ and 4¾ per cent. Commercial banks do not normally pay interest on demand deposits; on savings and fixed-term deposits the rate ranges from 1 per cent to 3¾ per cent.

MONETARY SURVEY

Since the monetary reform of June 1967, monetary and credit developments have been characterized by a fairly rapid expansion of the money supply. This was a reflection mainly of a large and continuing increase in the net foreign assets of the banking system, which in December 1970 stood at Z 109.4 million, compared with Z 112.9 million in December 1969 and Z 22.8 million in June 1967 (Table 14).

Between June 1967 and December 1969, the money supply rose by nearly 80 per cent (to Z 151.9 million), the increases in 1968 and 1969 being 22 per cent and 12 per cent, respectively. A comparison between the money supply and domestic prices shows that, despite the substantial increase in money, real cash balances at the end of 1969 were still below their June 1967 level (Table 15). Real cash balances declined by more than 22 per cent during the 12 months that followed the devaluation of the currency in June 1967, an indication of the

TABLE 14. DEMOCRATIC REPUBLIC OF CONGO: MONETARY SURVEY, 1966–70

(In millions of zaïres; end of period)

	1966	1967		1968		1969		1970	
		June	Dec.	June	Dec.	June	Dec.	June	Dec.
Assets									
Foreign assets (net)	10.27	22.82	60.92	78.03	85.18	100.26	112.89	125.28	109.35
Domestic credit	90.32	109.97	102.18	110.39	113.62	128.45	115.77	128.29	142.64
Claims on government (net)	77.57	92.28	85.32	89.85	92.92	100.92	87.90	86.92	99.74
Claims on private sector[1]	12.75	17.69	16.86	20.54	20.70	27.53	27.87	41.37	42.90
Assets = liabilities	**100.59**	**132.79**	**163.10**	**188.42**	**198.80**	**228.71**	**228.66**	**253.57**	**251.99**
Liabilities									
Money	73.45	84.58	110.87	117.29	135.36	155.70	151.94	172.98	186.02
Quasi-money	4.16	4.54	4.27	21.64	15.60	27.91	19.45	20.21	22.57
Profits from revaluation of foreign assets	—	5.97	5.70	5.57	5.63	5.61	5.44	4.55	4.36
Import prepayments	7.41	12.92	17.36	24.23	19.98	16.64	17.91	13.08	9.95
Counterpart funds	7.94	10.26	8.32	8.69	8.11	7.16	10.77	9.22	8.57
Other items (net)	7.63	14.52	16.58	11.00	14.12	15.69	23.15	33.53	20.52

Sources: Banque Nationale du Congo, *Rapport Annuel, 1969–1970*; and data provided by the Congolese authorities.

[1] Including public and semipublic enterprises.

TABLE 15. DEMOCRATIC REPUBLIC OF CONGO: INDEX
OF REAL CASH BALANCES, 1966–70

(*June 1967 = 100*)

	Currency [1] (1)	Demand Deposits [2] (2)	Money Supply [3] (3)
1966 Dec.	95.9	107.8	102.7
1967 June	100.0	100.0	100.0
Dec.	71.8	95.7	86.9
1968 June	66.3	84.9	77.7
Dec.	75.2	97.0	88.8
1969 June	77.6	109.5	97.9
Dec.	74.4	102.5	92.0
1970 June	85.3	109.3	101.5
Dec.	96.2	115.9	108.0

Sources: Banque Nationale du Congo, *Rapport Annuel, 1968–1969* and *1969–1970;* and data provided by the Congolese authorities.

[1] Ratio of index of currency in circulation to index of prices on African markets in Kinshasa (see Table 6, above).

[2] Ratio of index of demand deposits to index of prices in shops of European type in Kinshasa (see Table 6, above).

[3] Weighted average of cols. 1 and 2, the weights representing the proportions of currency in circulation and demand deposits in the total money supply.

absorption of the excess liquidity which had been created during the inflationary period that preceded the monetary reform of June 1967. Since June 1968 real cash balances have increased because the growth in the money supply, mainly in demand deposits, has been considerably larger than the rise in domestic prices. By December 1970 real cash balances exceeded by almost 8 per cent their June 1967 level. The absorption of excess liquidity is also reflected in the ratio of money supply to monetized GDP at current prices, which declined from 26.7 per cent in 1966 to 20.6 per cent in 1968 and is estimated to have declined further to 18.6 per cent in 1969.

Credit developments between June 1967 and December 1969 were only moderately expansionary. Total domestic credit declined during the second half of 1967 but rose by 11 per cent in 1968 and by less than 2 per cent in 1969. Prior to June 1967, the banking system's net claims on the Government had been the most expansionary component of domestic credit. Since then, net claims on the Government have fluctuated rather widely; at the end of 1969 they totaled Z 87.9 million, 5 per cent below the level in June 1967. Credit to the private sector, including public and semipublic enterprises, is extended exclusively by the commercial banks; after declining slightly in the second half of

1967, it rose by 23 per cent, to Z 20.7 million, during 1968 and was allowed to expand to Z 27.9 million during 1969. During 1970 total domestic credit rose by about 23 per cent: net credit to the Government rose by 13 per cent and credit to the private sector by 54 per cent, following the decision of the central bank to relax its credit policy.

Although during 1968 and 1969 the expansion of credit to the private sector was rather rapid, the high degree of utilization of credit in relation to the overall ceilings set by the National Bank indicates that tight credit conditions prevailed throughout this period. The application of selective ceilings produced a marked redistribution of credit among sectors: credit to agriculture increased substantially while the relative shares of commerce and industry declined (Table 16). The relative importance of credit for the financing of imports has also declined, as importers have been induced to seek external financing, viz., the sharp increase in guarantees (*crédits de signature*) given by commercial banks to importers on the financing they receive from foreign banks, which rose by more than Z 20 million, to Z 46.6 million, during 1969. There was also a considerable change during 1967–69 in the type of credit extended. The share of overdrafts in credit outstanding to the private sector declined from more than 90 per cent in June 1967 to about 48 per cent in December 1969, while in the same period the share of credit against documents (commercial paper, warrants, etc.) increased from 2 per cent to more than 50 per cent of the total.[3]

BALANCE OF PAYMENTS

Balance of payments statistics for 1966–69 and the first half of 1970 are shown in Table 17.[4] After having weakened considerably during the first half of 1967, when there was an overall deficit of $23 million, the

---

[3] The reader is referred to the International Monetary Fund's monthly statistical bulletin, *International Financial Statistics*, for later information on monetary and credit developments.

[4] The data are derived from the exchange records and incorporate foreign aid and other capital transactions, such as suppliers' credits. Estimates of transactions through the unofficial exchange market, which in 1969 were equivalent to about 6 per cent of export receipts, are also included; these consist on the credit side of receipts from clandestine exports, sales of foreign exchange by nonresidents, and private direct investments, and on the debit side of payments on account of imports, investment income, private transfers, and capital outflows.

TABLE 16. DEMOCRATIC REPUBLIC OF CONGO: DISTRIBUTION OF CREDIT TO PRIVATE SECTOR BY ECONOMIC SECTOR AND PURPOSE, 1966-70

	1966	1967 June	1967 Dec.	1968 June	1968 Dec.	1969 June	1969 Dec.	1970 June	1970 Dec.
Sector					*(Million zaïres)*				
Agriculture	3.28	3.89	3.20	8.52	8.15	11.71	12.37	13.63	13.87
Manufacturing	3.58	4.86	4.70	3.87	3.22	5.46	5.47	7.59	7.85
Trade	3.67	5.85	5.08	5.13	5.76	6.24	6.54	8.38	7.92
Transport	0.30	0.30	0.20	0.29	1.22	1.33	1.12	7.97	8.52
Other	1.31	2.07	2.13	1.53	1.62	2.10	2.09	3.16	3.78
Total	12.14	16.97	15.31	19.34	19.97	26.84	27.59	40.73	41.94
Purpose					*(Per cent of total)*				
		(Sept.)							
Production and stocks[1]		33.1		48.9	35.0	40.3	31.0	31.1	...
Working capital		19.5		20.6	21.3	20.3	28.0	21.8	...
Distribution of goods[2]		6.7		8.9	23.5	14.7	20.7	14.3	...
Imports		28.0		9.4	10.9	11.1	5.0	1.5	...
Exports		5.3		9.6	5.6	9.0	9.8	5.7	...
Investment		}7.4		0.9	1.6	3.8	4.2	21.9	...
Other				1.7	2.1	0.8	1.3	3.7	...
Total		100.0		100.0	100.0	100.0	100.0	100.0	...

Sources: Banque Nationale du Congo, *Rapport Annuel, 1968-1969* and *1969-1970*; and data provided by the Congolese authorities.

[1] Largely financing of crops and marketing of agricultural exports.
[2] Including domestic distribution of imported goods.

TABLE 17.   DEMOCRATIC REPUBLIC OF CONGO: BALANCE OF PAYMENTS,
1966–FIRST HALF 1970

(In millions of U. S. dollars)

	1966	1967	1968	1969	1970 [1]
A. Goods and services	**−5.0**	**21.4**	**70.8**	**62.4**	**32.8**
Exports f.o.b.	488.4	476.2	588.6	684.0	419.4
Imports f.o.b.	−320.8	−274.0	−309.0	−405.8	−260.2
Trade balance	167.6	202.2	279.6	278.2	159.2
Freight and insurance	−58.0	−45.8	−51.2	−66.6	−37.0
Other transportation	−11.8	−6.4	−3.8	1.0	2.0
Travel	−9.8	−13.8	−16.4	−8.0	−4.4
Investment income	−10.2	−5.0	−14.6	−21.4	−15.4
Other government	−53.2	−67.4	−78.6	−78.0	−45.0
Other	−29.6	−42.4	−44.2	−42.8	−26.6
Services (net)	−172.6	−180.8	−208.8	−215.8	−126.4
B. Unrequited transfers (net)	**10.8**	**−6.4**	**−20.0**	**−16.0**	**−12.8**
Private	−32.0	−44.2	−55.0	−63.4	−36.4
Central Government	42.8	37.8	35.0	47.4	23.6
Total (A + B)	**5.8**	**15.0**	**50.8**	**46.4**	**20.0**
(Goods, services, and private transfers)	(−37.0)	(−22.8)	(15.8)	(−1.0)	(−3.6)
C. Capital movements (net)	**27.4**	**26.0**	**0.8**	**7.6**	**−11.0**
Private	−4.6	3.8	−12.2	0.2	−15.6
Central Government	32.0	22.2	13.0	7.4	4.6
D. Allocation of SDRs	—	—	—	—	**15.1**
E. Net errors and omissions	**−6.8**	**9.8**	**−3.0**	**1.4**	**0.7**
Total (A through E)	**26.4**	**50.8**	**48.6**	**55.4**	**24.8**
F. Monetary movements (net)	**−26.4**	**−50.8**	**−48.6**	**−55.4**	**−24.8**
National Bank	0.2	−47.0	−70.2	−59.8	−23.2
Commercial banks	−26.6	−3.8	21.6	4.4	−1.6

Source: Banque Nationale du Congo, *Rapport Annuel, 1969–1970.*

[1] First six months only.

balance of payments moved into a large surplus ($74 million) during the second half of that year and remained in a strong position in 1968 and 1969, when it registered surpluses of $49 million and $55 million, respectively. During the first half of 1970, the balance of payments continued to show a relatively large surplus ($25 million), part of which, however, was accounted for by the first allocation of SDRs, which provided Congo with $15 million of additional international reserves.

The balance of payments surplus in 1967 was almost twice that in 1966 largely because of a decline in imports, following the introduction in June of the new exchange rate and the implementation of stabilization measures. In 1968–70, increased export earnings, mainly from copper, more than offset a substantial expansion in payments for imports, services, and private transfers, which resulted from the generally more buoyant economic situation and the liberalization of current external transactions. During the period 1967–70, Congo's balance of payments was characterized by relatively large and increasing surpluses on transactions in goods and services, as export receipts substantially exceeded import payments (f.o.b.) and the resulting trade surplus was more than sufficient to cover the deficit on payments for services. The balance on goods, services, and private transfers moved from a relatively large deficit in 1966 and 1967 ($37 million and $23 million, respectively) to a surplus of $16 million in 1968 and small deficits in 1969 and the first half of 1970, despite higher net private transfer payments following the liberalization of these transactions.

Official transfers and private and official capital transactions showed large, though generally declining, surpluses throughout the period 1966–69. In particular, the traditional net inflow of capital declined from $27 million in 1966 to $8 million in 1969, owing mainly to a reduced net inflow of official capital which was only in part offset by an increased utilization of suppliers' credits both by the Government and by public enterprises. If suppliers' credits are excluded, there was a relatively large net outflow of private capital in each year.

Table 18 shows the geographical distribution of foreign exchange transactions effected through the banking system. These data, which include only settlements effected through the banking system, show that more than 80 per cent of Congo's foreign exchange transactions are with the EEC countries, mostly with Belgium-Luxembourg. In 1969 Congo had an overall payments surplus of $195 million with Belgium-Luxembourg, resulting from an apparent trade surplus of $385 million and a deficit of $191 million on services, transfers, and capital transactions. The major part of Congo's exports to Belgium consists of copper (some $350 million in 1969), which is processed and almost entirely re-exported by Belgium.

During the first half of 1970, the balance of payments continued to be relatively favorable, despite a substantial further increase in imports. Export receipts totaled $419 million, compared with $317 million

TABLE 18. DEMOCRATIC REPUBLIC OF CONGO: EXCHANGE TRANSACTIONS BY COUNTRIES, 1969 [1]

(*In millions of U. S. dollars*)

	Merchandise, f.o.b.			Services			Private Transfers			Official Transfers and Capital			Total		
	Credit	Debit	Balance	Credit	Debit	Balance	Credit	Debit	Balance	Credit	Debit	Balance	Credit	Debit	Balance
Belgium-Luxembourg	588.2[2]	203.0	385.2	26.2	131.0	−104.8	0.5	70.2	−69.7	2.2	18.3	−16.1	617.1	422.5	194.6
Italy	4.9	16.0	−11.1	0.1	4.5	−4.4	—	1.2	−1.2	0.5	1.0	−0.5	5.5	22.7	−17.2
Germany	3.2	14.6	−11.4	0.2	2.4	−2.2	0.1	0.1	—	0.1	1.0	−0.9	3.6	18.1	−14.5
France	0.6	17.1	−16.5	1.0	6.1	−5.1	0.1	0.8	−0.7	0.5	—	−0.5	2.2	24.0	−21.8
Netherlands	1.6	8.1	−6.5	0.1	1.8	−1.7	—	0.2	−0.2	0.3	—	0.3	2.0	10.1	−8.1
Total EEC	598.5	258.8	339.7	27.6	145.8	−118.2	0.7	72.5	−71.8	3.6	20.3	−16.7	630.4	497.4	133.0
United States	17.6	27.6	−10.0	6.9	34.2	−27.3	0.6	0.1	0.5	2.3	21.4	−19.1	27.4	83.3	−55.9
United Kingdom	31.8	13.2	18.6	1.5	4.6	−3.1	0.1	0.2	−0.1	0.4	1.1	−0.7	33.8	19.1	14.7
Others	32.6	40.1	−7.5	2.9	31.8	−28.9	0.5	3.2	−2.7	2.8	—	2.8	38.8	75.1	−36.3
Grand total	680.5	339.7	340.8	38.9	216.4	−177.5	1.9	76.0	−74.1	9.1	42.8	−33.7	730.4	674.9	55.5

Source: Data provided by the Congolese authorities.

[1] Includes only exchange transactions effected through the banking system.
[2] Mainly copper, a large proportion of which is re-exported by Belgium.

during the first half of 1969. Imports (f.o.b.) amounted to $260 million, an annual rate 28 per cent above that of 1969. The balance on goods, services, and private transfers showed a deficit of almost $4 million, while the surplus on official transfers and private and official capital transactions amounted to nearly $13 million.

TRADE

In the years that followed independence in 1960, foreign trade suffered a severe setback, mainly as a result of economic dislocation, insecurity, and disruption of transport facilities. Moreover, the maintenance of a generally overvalued exchange rate and of exchange restrictions gave rise to a black market for currency and to smuggling. These factors affected primarily the agricultural export sector. Mineral production also tended to contract but did not decline markedly, and exports of minerals began to provide an increasingly important share of export earnings. With conditions of security generally re-established, the exchange reform of June 1967 restored profit margins in the export sector, especially in agriculture, and permitted the abolition of import restrictions, thereby eliminating shortages of consumer goods. At the same time, very favorable conditions on the world market for copper led to a substantial increase in export receipts.

Exports

Since 1966, export receipts have regained and exceeded the 1960 level. After having increased by almost 30 per cent in 1966, they declined slightly, to Z 235 million, in 1967 (Table 19): with lower copper prices, receipts from mineral exports declined by about 3 per cent, to Z 173 million, while receipts from agricultural exports rose by 10 per cent, to Z 47 million. In 1968 with the increase in copper prices, export receipts rose by 25 per cent, to the unprecedented high figure of Z 294 million. The rise of 33 per cent in receipts from mineral exports accounted for almost the entire increase. Receipts from agricultural exports, which rose by 8 per cent in 1968, accounted for only 17 per cent of total receipts and were still some 40 per cent below the level attained in the late 1950s. The continued rise in copper prices and a 12 per cent increase in the volume of copper exports led to a further expansion of export receipts in 1969. Receipts from agricultural exports

TABLE 19.   DEMOCRATIC REPUBLIC OF CONGO: FOREIGN TRADE,
1966–FIRST HALF 1970

(In millions of zaïres)

	1966	1967	1968	1969	1970 [1]
Exports f.o.b.	**241**	**235**	**294**	**342**	**210**
Mining products [2]	179	173	230	290	173
Agricultural commodities and other recorded exports	42	47	51	47	34
Unrecorded exports [3]	20	15	13	5	3
Imports c.i.f.	**192**	**163**	**183**	**237**	**150**
Financed by					
Congo's resources	144	117	140	191	126
Foreign aid	28	20	15	12	6
Private capital	20	26	29	34	18
Suppliers' credits	*2*	*9*	*10*	*19*	*4*
Parallel market	*13*	*12*	*15*	*12*	*10*
Other [4]	*5*	*5*	*4*	*3*	*4*
Trade surplus	**49**	**72**	**111**	**105**	**60**

Source: Banque Nationale du Congo, *Rapport Annuel, 1969–1970.*

[1] January–June.
[2] Includes some industrial products.
[3] Believed to be largely diamonds.
[4] Grants in the form of goods and private direct investments.

actually declined in that year, partly owing to unfavorable weather. During the first half of 1970 export receipts totaled Z 210 million, with both mining and agricultural exports continuing to rise.

The predominant factor in the Congolese economy in recent years has been the extremely favorable evolution of copper prices. Congo's copper receipts generally reflect changes in the Brussels price, after adjustment is made for transport and insurance. The average price for electrolytic copper on the Brussels market rose from the equivalent of about $0.35 a pound in 1965 to $0.54 in 1966, fell to $0.49 a pound in 1967, but rose again to $0.54 in 1968, to $0.66 in 1969, and during the first half of 1970, to $0.73.

The other major mineral exports of Congo are cobalt, diamonds, zinc, and tin. Taken together, these products accounted in 1969 for some 17 per cent of total export receipts as registered in the exchange records of the National Bank. Receipts from cobalt rose by more than 50 per cent in 1968 and by 20 per cent (to Z 20.5 million) in 1969 in response to an increase in the average unit price on the London market from Z 0.725 a pound in 1967 to Z 0.8375 in 1968 and Z 0.8958 in the second half of 1969. Receipts from exports of diamonds, after declining in 1967, rose to Z 13.5 million in 1968, largely as a result of an increase in price, and to Z 15 million in 1969, when smuggling was not so great. The increase in price was the result of an agreement in June 1967 with BRITMOND on the marketing of Congo's diamonds. Exports of tin have remained virtually unchanged in the last three years. Exports of zinc rose from about Z 7.5 million in 1967 and 1968 to Z 10.5 million in 1969.

Receipts from agricultural exports rose in 1967 and 1968 but declined in 1969. Although both the volume of production and the volume of exports have generally increased in recent years, export prices have been relatively weak, especially for palm oil and coffee. As a result, the Government progressively reduced the export taxes on agricultural products during 1968 and 1969.

The exchange rate adjustment of June 1967 re-established profitable operating conditions for the exporting sector. However, clandestine exports of diamonds and of some agricultural products in the eastern regions have continued, though at a reduced rate. Clandestine exports still appear to be profitable, mainly because of the differential between the official rate of exchange and the parallel market rate and because of the export taxes (which, however, have now been reduced). Transportation difficulties within Congo have been a contributing factor to clandestine exports of agricultural products across the eastern border. The value of smuggled exports, estimated at Z 17.5 million a year during 1964–66, fell to an estimated Z 15 million in 1967 and Z 13 million in 1968, following the liberalization of imports and other current transactions, and are estimated to have amounted to only Z 5 million in 1969, largely owing to reduced smuggling of diamonds. The value of diamonds exported clandestinely is estimated to have declined from more than Z 11 million in 1968 to Z 4 million in 1969, following the opening of a purchasing office in Tshikapa in November 1968 and the reduction of the export duty on diamonds sold by small miners to 2.5 per cent.

Imports

The value of imports (c.i.f.), including those financed by foreign aid and by private capital, fell substantially in 1967 but increased consid-

erably in 1968 and again in 1969, when they totaled Z 237 million
(Table 19). The intensification of exchange restrictions in the first half
of 1967, the exchange rate adjustment in June, and the policies of
wage, monetary, and fiscal restraint adopted within the framework of
the stabilization program, were the principal factors responsible for the
15 per cent decline in 1967. Internal demand, especially consumer
demand, was sharply curtailed, and stocks that had been accumulated
before the exchange rate adjustment were reduced. In 1968, owing to
the expansion of economic activity and the increase in investment,
imports rose by 12 per cent; in 1969 the continued expansion of
domestic demand led to an increase of 29 per cent. With the decline in
foreign aid, the proportion of imports financed through direct sales of
foreign exchange by the National Bank rose from 72 per cent in 1967 to
80 per cent in 1969. At the same time imports financed through suppliers' credits rose from Z 9 million in 1967 to Z 19 million in 1969.
During the first half of 1970, imports were running at an annual rate of
Z 300 million and an increasing proportion was being financed by
direct sales of foreign exchange.

No information is available on the commodity composition of
imports in recent years, owing to a substantial lag in the publication of
customs statistics. The partial data available show that imports of certain foodstuffs, manufactured consumer goods, and equipment
increased markedly in 1968 and 1969.

Direction of Trade

Available figures on the direction of Congo's foreign trade are shown
in Table 20. Belgium is Congo's most important trading partner, taking
more than one half of total exports and providing about one fourth of
total imports in 1968–69. Exports to Belgium consist chiefly of mineral
products, which, as mentioned above, are largely re-exported after
processing. The share of other EEC countries in Congo's total trade has
been increasing in recent years and these countries accounted for a declining share (26 per cent) of Congo's exports and a rising share (one
third) of its imports in 1969. The United States purchased 5 per cent
of Congo's exports in 1969 (mainly agricultural commodities); its
share in total imports fell from 24 per cent in 1966 to 12 per cent in

TABLE 20. DEMOCRATIC REPUBLIC OF CONGO: DIRECTION OF TRADE, 1966–69

(*In per cent of total*)

	1966	1967	1968	1969
Exports				
Belgium-Luxembourg	54	48	51	54
Other EEC countries	27	32	30	26
Italy	*9*	*12*	*11*	*10*
France	*10*	*11*	*9*	*8*
Germany	*6*	*7*	*7*	*5*
Netherlands	*2*	*2*	*3*	*3*
United States	9	8	7	5
United Kingdom	5	6	7	7
Others	5	6	5	8
Total	100	100	100	100
Imports				
Belgium-Luxembourg	26	23	24	24
Other EEC countries	26	31	33	34
Germany	*9*	*9*	*10*	*11*
France	*7*	*10*	*10*	*10*
Italy	*6*	*9*	*7*	*5*
Netherlands	*4*	*3*	*6*	*8*
United States	24	22	17	12
United Kingdom	6	9	7	7
Japan	3	2	7	}23
Others	15	13	12	
Total	100	100	100	100

Sources: Banque Nationale du Congo, *Rapport Annuel, 1969–1970;* and IMF and IBRD, *Direction of Trade.*

1969, reflecting the reduction of U. S. import assistance. The United Kingdom's share in Congo's exports (mainly diamonds) fluctuated between 5 and 7 per cent in 1966–69, while imports from the United Kingdom fluctuated between 6 and 9 per cent of total imports. Imports from Japan amounted to 7 per cent of total imports in 1968, compared with about 2 per cent in previous years, and presumably rose further in 1969.

CURRENT INVISIBLES

In the years 1966–69, net outlays for services and private transfers, including transactions through the parallel market, increased substantially, owing in part to the relaxation of restrictions since June 1967. For the year 1967 the deficit on account of services and private transfers rose by $20 million, to $225 million, owing chiefly to larger transfer payments (Table 17). In 1968 it rose to $264 million because of an increase of $28 million in net service payments, resulting mainly from larger freight and insurance expenditures connected with imports and from a rise in government expenditure abroad. Payments for travel also rose substantially in 1967 and 1968, reflecting not only the liberalization of travel allowances but also the practice of repurchasing at the official rate zaïres sold by travelers in Brazzaville and elsewhere. This practice, however, was abolished in 1969 because of the abuses to which it had given rise.

In 1969 the deficit on account of services and private transfers rose further, to $279 million, the increase compared with 1968 being partly the result of larger payments on investment income, following the removal of restrictions on these payments, and on account of private transfers. Payments for travel declined substantially.

Private transfer payments consist almost entirely of transfers of savings by foreign residents in Congo, both through official and unofficial channels. These transfers, which had averaged some $60 million a year prior to the liberalization measures of June 1967, amounted to $98 million in 1968 and $103 million in 1969.

PRIVATE CAPITAL

In 1966 private capital transactions continued to show a net outflow of some $5 million, owing mainly to a continued outflow of private capital through the parallel market. In 1967 and in 1969, however, there was a small net inflow of private capital (Table 17), resulting from greater utilization of suppliers' credits on the part of public and semipublic enterprises, which are included in the private sector. Drawings on suppliers' credits by these enterprises amounted to $11 million in 1967, $8 million in 1968, and $30 million in 1969, compared with only $2 million in 1966. The capital outflow through the parallel market remained relatively important (see Table 19).

OFFICIAL LOANS AND GRANTS

In 1966–69, net official transfers showed large but for the most part declining surpluses, reflecting the gradual reduction of import grants from the United States. Net receipts declined from $43 million in 1966, to $38 million in 1967 and $35 million in 1968, but rose to $47 million in 1969. Grants from the United States, which in 1964 had reached a peak of $32 million, declined to $8 million in 1965 and to less than $3 million in 1969.

Aside from U. S. grants, a substantial proportion of official transfer receipts represents the cost of technical assistance programs financed mainly by Belgium and the United Nations. The Belgian program alone involves annual grants of more than $20 million a year (Table 21). The cost of UN programs, which have involved both technical assistance and project financing, declined from an average of almost $9 million a year in 1966–67 to some $7 million in 1968 and 1969. Another important source of foreign assistance has been the EEC, which provides project grants mainly under EDF programs. Disbursements by the EDF, which averaged just under $3 million a year in 1966–67, rose

TABLE 21. DEMOCRATIC REPUBLIC OF CONGO: DISBURSEMENTS
OF OFFICIAL FOREIGN LOANS AND GRANTS, 1966–69 [1]

(In millions of U. S. dollars)

	1966	1967	1968	1969
Bilateral assistance	**77.6**	**62.3**	**49.1**	**45.8**
United States	43.9	27.1	19.4	13.8
Commercial imports	*22.1*	*11.3*	*6.3*	*6.1*
P. L. 480 commodities	*20.7*	*15.4*	*12.8*	*4.8*
Other	*1.1*	*0.4*	*0.3*	*2.9*
Belgium [2]	25.2	25.5	20.6	22.6
France	3.9	4.5	5.3	5.2
Other [3]	4.6	5.2	3.8	4.2
Multilateral assistance	**10.7**	**12.5**	**10.6**	**16.4**
United Nations	8.7	8.7	7.1	7.4
EEC	2.0	3.8	3.5	9.0
Total	**88.3**	**74.8**	**59.7**	**62.2**
Balance of payments support [4]	*46.6*	*28.1*	*20.7*	*10.8*
Project financing	*8.5*	*10.7*	*7.7*	*12.6*
Technical assistance grants	*29.8*	*32.7*	*28.4*	*35.8*
Other[5]	*3.3*	*3.3*	*2.9*	*3.0*

Sources: Banque Nationale du Congo, *Rapport Annuel, 1968–1969* and *1969–1970*; and data provided by the Congolese authorities.

[1] Excluding suppliers' credits.
[2] Mainly technical assistance grants and scholarships.
[3] Includes assistance from Canada, mainland China, Denmark, Germany, Italy, Netherlands, Switzerland, and United Kingdom.
[4] Largely in the form of commercial imports, in particular under U. S. aid programs.
[5] Mostly scholarships to Congolese students.

to $3.5 million in 1968 and to $9 million in 1969. France is providing aid ($5 million in 1969) in the form both of technical assistance and of project grants.

Receipts from official capital consist essentially of U. S. import loans (part of total commodity assistance) and in recent years of suppliers' credits. U. S. import loans became important ($20.5 million) in 1966 following a shift of U. S. import assistance from grants to long-term loans. Since then, however, this assistance has been decreasing, from some $25 million in 1967 and 1968 to about $11 million in 1969. The utilization of medium-term and long-term suppliers' credits increased from a negligible amount in 1966 to $12 million in 1968 and declined to $8 million in 1969.

Payments for official capital consist mainly of the amortization of the foreign public debt, largely to Belgium, and of reimbursements of suppliers' credits—$4 million in 1968 and $7 million in 1969. In 1967 there was also a payment of some $2 million representing Congo's contribution to the capital of the African Development Bank.

EXTERNAL DEBT

Estimates of the medium-term and long-term foreign debt of the Central Government and of public and semipublic enterprises are shown in Table 22. These estimates are based on the effective utiliza-

TABLE 22. DEMOCRATIC REPUBLIC OF CONGO: ESTIMATES OF MEDIUM-TERM AND LONG-TERM FOREIGN PUBLIC DEBT OUTSTANDING, 1966–JUNE 30, 1970

(In millions of U. S. dollars)

	1966	1967	1968	1969	1970 [1]
Central Government	**184.2**	**212.4**	**231.0**	**240.4**	**243.7**
Belgian-Congolese Amortization Fund [2]	135.8	133.7	130.7	128.7	126.7
Loans from World Bank	11.4	10.4	8.6	6.8	5.9
U. S. Government loans	23.3	48.3	62.9	74.0	77.7
Other official loans [3]	10.8	12.8	13.3	14.8	14.0
Suppliers' credits	2.8	7.2	15.5	16.2	19.4
Public and semipublic enterprises [4]	**2.8**	**13.3**	**19.1**	**41.8**	**39.4**
Total	**187.0**	**225.7**	**250.1**	**282.2**	**283.1**

Source: Banque Nationale du Congo, *Rapport Annuel, 1969–1970.*

[1] June 30, 1970.
[2] Exclusive of interest.
[3] From Belgium, Federal Republic of Germany, and Italy.
[4] Suppliers' credits only.

TABLE 23. DEMOCRATIC REPUBLIC OF CONGO: FOREIGN PUBLIC DEBT OUTSTANDING, 1969, AND DEBT SERVICE PAYMENTS, 1970–74 [1]

(In millions of U. S. dollars)

	Debt Outstanding, Dec. 31, 1969	1970		1971		1972		1973		1974	
		Principal	Interest	Principal	Interest	Principal	Interest	Principal	Interest	Principal	Interest
Central Government	**239.7**	**17.5**	**3.0**	**18.5**	**4.0**	**15.8**	**4.1**	**15.0**	**3.5**	**15.5**	**3.8**
Belgian-Congolese Amortization Fund	128.4	6.0[2]	—	6.0[2]	—	6.0[2]	—	6.0[2]	—	6.0[2]	—
Loans from World Bank	6.3	1.3	0.4	1.5	0.3	1.0	0.2	1.0	0.1	1.0	0.1
U. S. Government loans	74.0	1.4	0.7	2.9	1.6	3.2	2.2	3.7	1.7	3.9	2.4
Other official loans[3]	14.8	1.7	0.6	1.7	0.5	1.7	0.4	1.7	0.4	1.7	0.3
Suppliers' credits	16.2	7.1	1.4	6.3	1.6	3.9	1.3	2.6	1.3	2.9	1.0
Public and semipublic enterprises[4]	**41.0**	**8.6**	**2.6**	**7.4**	**2.2**	**7.9**	**2.0**	**6.9**	**1.4**	**5.7**	**0.7**
Total	**280.7**	**26.1**	**5.6**	**25.9**	**6.2**	**23.7**	**6.1**	**21.9**	**4.9**	**21.2**	**4.5**

Source: Data provided by the Congolese authorities.

[1] Totals may not equal sums of components because of rounding.
[2] Including interest.
[3] From Belgium, Federal Republic of Germany, and Italy.
[4] Suppliers' credits only.

tion of loans received and include only those loans to public enterprises for which a government guarantee has been extended. No firm estimates of other loans to public enterprises and to the private sector are available; however, they are not considered to be large, and the private sector's medium-term and long-term foreign indebtedness, consisting entirely of suppliers' credits, was estimated at $18 million at the end of June 1970.

As of June 30, 1970, total medium-term and long-term foreign public debt outstanding was estimated at $283 million. Of this amount, $244 million represented debt incurred by the Central Government and $39 million the debt of public and semipublic enterprises. From the end of 1966 to June 30, 1970, the Central Government's foreign debt increased from $184 million to $244 million, largely as a result of new disbursements of U. S. loans and of increased utilization of suppliers' credits in connection with the Inga project and purchases of equipment by various departments. The indebtedness (exclusive of interest) to the Belgian-Congolese Amortization Fund has gradually declined: at the end of June 1970 it amounted to $127 million—52 per cent of the total foreign debt of the Central Government, compared with 74 per cent in 1966.

During the years 1966–69, recourse to suppliers' credits by public and semipublic enterprises increased markedly, raising the outstanding debt from $3 million at the end of 1966 to $19 million at the end of 1968 and to $42 million at the end of 1969. For the most part, these suppliers' credits carry a rate of interest of at least 6 per cent and rarely extend for more than 5 years. Prior to June 1967, resort to this form of financing reflected mainly the scarcity of foreign exchange. Since then it has been due largely to difficulties in raising domestic resources to finance investment by OTRACO, Air Congo, Chemins de Fer Bas Congo-Katanga, and other public enterprises. All suppliers' credits exceeding $20,000 must be approved by an Economic and Financial Committee.

On the basis of commitments as of the end of 1969, Congo's main creditors were Belgium, the United States, Italy, France, and the World Bank. Suppliers' credits had been extended not only by Belgium, Italy, and France but also by Japan, the Netherlands, and the United Kingdom. Some 50 per cent of total debt commitments have a maturity of 40 years or more, and a further 25 per cent have a maturity of 10 years or less.

Service charges on the medium-term and long-term foreign public debt for the period 1970–74 are shown in Table 23. For this period, the total debt service on loans outstanding at the end of 1969 is estimated at some $30 million a year, equivalent to about 4 per cent of receipts from exports of goods and services in 1969. Interest and amortization on suppliers' credits total some $18 million a year, about 60 per cent of the total debt service.

INTERNATIONAL RESERVES

The banking system's gross holdings of gold and foreign exchange rose from $48 million in June 1967 to $229.6 million at the end of 1969 and $222.4 million at the end of 1970 (Table 24). Sight liabilities rose from $2.4 million at the end of June 1967 to $4.5 million at the end of 1970. The National Bank's gross holdings, including Congo's gold tranche position in the International Monetary Fund, rose from $19.8 million at the end of June 1967 to $198.4 million at the end of 1969, when they represented more than six months' imports on a c.i.f.

TABLE 24. DEMOCRATIC REPUBLIC OF CONGO: INTERNATIONAL RESERVES, 1966–70

(In millions of U. S. dollars; end of period)

	1966	1967 June	1967 Dec.	1968	1969	1970
A. Gross holdings	**73.6**	**48.0**	**124.3**	**173.6**	**229.6**	**222.4**
National Bank	20.5	19.8	67.6	137.8	198.4	185.3
Gold	*3.5*	*3.6*	*4.1*	*12.5*	*54.9*	*49.9*
SDRs	—	—	—	—	—	*15.6*
IMF gold tranche position	*3.7*	*6.1*	*6.1*	*14.3*	*22.5*	*28.3*
Foreign exchange	*13.3*	*10.1*	*57.4*	*111.0*	*121.0*	*91.5*
Commercial banks	53.1	28.2	56.7	35.8	31.2	37.1
B. Sight liabilities	**5.5**	**2.4**	**2.4**	**3.9**	**4.5**	**4.5**
National Bank	3.9	1.1	1.2	1.7	2.4	2.4
Commercial banks	1.6	1.3	1.2	2.2	2.1	2.1
C. Net total (A − B)	**68.1**	**45.6**	**121.9**	**169.7**	**225.1**	**217.9**
National Bank	16.6	18.7	66.4	136.1	196.0	182..9
Commercial banks	51.5	26.9	55.5	33.6	29.1	350

Source: IMF, *International Financial Statistics.*

basis. They totaled $185.3 million at the end of 1970, including the
equivalent of $15.6 million in SDRs. Since 1966, no significant change
has taken place in the composition of foreign exchange reserves. The
rise in the National Bank's gold holdings, including the gold tranche
position in the Fund, was more or less proportionate to the increase in
total holdings and accounted for about 42 per cent of the total at the
end of 1970.

EXCHANGE AND TRADE CONTROL SYSTEM [5]

RECENT DEVELOPMENTS

On June 23, 1967 Congo introduced a new currency, the zaïre,
abandoned the double rate structure, and adopted a unified rate of
exchange of Z 1 = US$2.00, which involved a substantial depreciation
of the currency. This exchange rate was agreed with the International
Monetary Fund as the par value of the zaïre on September 2, 1970.
Authority over foreign trade and payments, including authorization of
imports, exports, and transfers, was delegated to the National Bank of
Congo, which announced a policy of general liberalization of imports
and current payments.

In accordance with this policy, measures were introduced on June 23,
1967 to abolish the import quota system, the 10 per cent tax on
imports under quotas, and the requirement of a 40 per cent advance
import deposit. The system of retrocession of foreign exchange earnings
and of exchange allocation agreements was discontinued, as was that of
separate licenses for imports and import payments. Certain restrictions
on payments to nonresidents for services supplied to Congo were eliminated.

The limitations on the import and export of domestic and foreign
banknotes by travelers were abolished. Imports and exports of domestic
and foreign banknotes were also freed from restrictions. Payment in
Congo for tickets for travel abroad by Congolese nationals or by for-

---

[5] As of December 31, 1970. The reader is referred to the International Monetary Fund's *Annual Report on Exchange Restrictions* for later and more detailed
information on exchange and trade controls.

eign nationals returning to the country of their nationality could be made in local currency.

Since June 1968 controls on imports have been further relaxed, and most of the remaining restrictions on private current invisibles and transfers have been eliminated. In a general way, the controls still maintained are designed to distinguish current from capital transactions—which are still subject to restrictions—and at ensuring that income taxes have been paid on the income and profits to be transferred. The prior licensing requirement on the great majority of imports (some 90 per cent of the total) was abolished in June 1969, and these imports are now covered by a general import and payments license. The remaining imports are still subject to individual license or require the prior approval of the National Bank, either of which is, however, granted freely and without delay. Moreover, with effect from January 10, 1970, the National Bank abolished the import prepayment requirement that still applied to imports for which the exporter requested full or partial payment upon shipment.

With effect from January 1969, current profits of firms with foreign capital participation may be transferred, beginning with the profits realized during 1968. The amount of net profits that may be transferred is determined by the ratio of foreign capital to the total capital of the company. Payments for services performed by nonresidents may also be transferred, provided that they are shown in the profit and loss account of the firm involved, that they are recognized as such by the tax office, and that they pertain to operations of the firm requesting the transfer. Furthermore, in October 1968 the remaining quantitative limitations on transfers of salaries by foreign nationals were removed. These transfers are now authorized without restriction and may be made directly to accounts abroad of the persons concerned. On June 25, 1970 transfers of rents were also authorized. The National Bank maintains an *ex post* control over these transfers to ensure that the relevant income taxes have been paid.

Although the removal of restrictions on current international transactions is virtually complete, there continues to be a parallel market for the zaïre. This market is largely supplied by the proceeds from clandestine exports of diamonds and by transfers of funds by foreigners to cover expenses in Congo. The nature of the demand for exchange on this market is more difficult to ascertain. Generally, however, the demand seems to be generated by current invisibles and private transfers, mainly for reasons of tax evasion, and by capital outflow. Since the monetary and exchange reform of June 1967, the scope of the parallel market has been considerably reduced and in mid-1970 it was estimated not to exceed 6 per cent of export receipts.

A detailed description of the restrictive system as it applied at the end of 1970 follows.

EXCHANGE RATE SYSTEM

The par value for the zaïre, Z 1 = US$2.00, was established with the International Monetary Fund on September 2, 1970. From June 24, 1968 until November 16, 1970 the zaïre was quoted against the official cross rate for the Belgian franc (Z 1 = BF 100) and the rates of all other currencies listed by the National Bank were quoted on the basis of their average rates on the official exchange market in Brussels. Since November 16, 1970 the National Bank of Congo has maintained an official rate of exchange for the Belgian franc based on the rate of the zaïre quoted in the official exchange market in Brussels. The rate of the zaïre in this market does not differ by more than 1 per cent from the par value. The buying and selling rates for currencies other than the Belgian franc are based on the official market rates in Brussels for the zaïre and these currencies. Forward exchange transactions are prohibited.

REGULATIONS GOVERNING IMPORTS AND EXPORTS

Imports

Imports of a few items—mainly arms, ammunition, and narcotics— are prohibited on grounds of public policy. Imports of corrugated metal sheets are prohibited to protect local production, as are imports of cotton. The only goods subject to individual license are (1) jewelry, precious stones, and precious metals and (2) certain types of machinery and vehicles when valued at over Z 10,000. Licenses are granted freely for the second group but the prior visa of the National Bank is required for statistical purposes. For all other commodities (involving some 90 per cent of total imports), the National Bank has issued a general import and payments license, which guarantees the availability of foreign exchange when payments fall due provided that the importer files an import declaration with his bank once a purchase has been concluded.

For those imports for which a license is still required, applications are made initially to authorized banks in Kinshasa, are forwarded to the National Bank for approval, and are returned to the authorized banks for validation. Import licenses are validated by the authorized banks without undue delay and remain valid for customs clearance during a period of six months starting from the first day of the month following that in which validation by the commercial bank takes place. Foreign exchange is made available for all licensed imports. Since the validated license also constitutes an exchange license, the license remains valid as long as payment has not been completed. The counterpart of the value of goods imported under the U. S. import support program and the U. S. agricultural aid program must be deposited within 180 and 120 days, respectively, after shipment.

Exports

All exports require licenses, and export proceeds must be surrendered. Banks are normally authorized to grant licenses to exporters who submit a declaration undertaking to collect the exchange proceeds. The licenses are normally valid for three months; within this period, the proceeds must be received and surrendered. Most exports of minerals are subject to special regulations which take into account the time required for processing abroad.

For exports of mineral products, a provisional payment of about 70 per cent of the shipment's estimated value has to be surrendered within eight days after shipment from an ocean port. For exports of diamonds, two thirds of the value established at a preliminary examination in Congo has to be surrendered before the shipment is dispatched. Export proceeds from coffee have to be surrendered within 45 days after shipment. Receipts from other agricultural exports (which are usually made under consignment) must generally be repatriated within six months of shipment. The export proceeds of GECOMINES must be surrendered directly to the National Bank.

REGULATIONS GOVERNING INVISIBLES

Certain payments for invisibles are subject to authorization by the National Bank, which is given or refused on a nondiscriminatory basis; the authority to approve other current payments has been delegated to the authorized banks. The National Bank will not authorize exchange to pay commissions to shippers or purchasing agents or, except for imports payable on arrival, for insurance on imports. In principle, all other payments for services performed by nonresidents are authorized. Transfers abroad of salaries of foreign nationals are authorized freely provided that at least Z 100 a month is deducted for local living expenses and that all taxes have been paid. As a rule, transfers in respect of certain administrative expenses abroad by enterprises, interest on private loans, and certain portions of insurance premiums are authorized. Net profits of firms with foreign capital participation are transferable up to an amount proportionate to that participation. Incomes from rents are also transferable, provided all tax liabilities have been paid.

Fares for travel abroad may be paid in Congo in local currency; for resident foreign nationals, however, the fare must not exceed the price of a return trip by a direct route to their country of origin. Congolese nationals traveling abroad may buy foreign exchange in amounts up to the equivalent of Z 400 a trip, depending on the duration of the journey; applications exceeding this amount are subject to individual approval by the National Bank.

There are no limitations on the amount of domestic or foreign banknotes that travelers may take out or bring into the country.

To facilitate the exchange of zaïres abroad by Congolese nationals at the official rate of exchange, the National Bank of the Congo made arrangements in September 1967 with banks in Brazzaville for the repurchase of zaïres (*opération rachat de zaïres*). Congolese in possession of travel cards that were issued by the National Bank could sell up to Z 100 for each two-week period to banks in Brazzaville. These zaïres were repurchased by the National Bank at the official rate of exchange. The arrangement was extended to cover Belgium, Switzerland, the United Kingdom, and France, where up to Z 100 could be changed every ten days. In 1969 the National Bank repurchased some Z 9 million under the various arrangements. In view of the abuses to which this practice had given rise, the National Bank suspended the issuance of new cards in April 1969, and since May of that year no further repurchases have been effected.

CAPITAL TRANSFERS

The repatriation of new foreign capital brought in under the provisions of the Investment Code of June 26, 1969 is guaranteed, as is the transfer of profits and dividends on such capital. With minor exceptions, other transfers abroad of capital owned by residents or nonresidents are not permitted. In principle, the sale of real estate located in Congo can only be made to the Congolese Government against payment in zaïres; gratuitous transfers of real estate are subject to approval by executive ordinance. When the local currency portion is paid by the debtor, amortization of foreign loans can be transferred in accordance with the terms of contracts that the National Bank has endorsed to guarantee the availability of exchange for such transfers.

GOLD

Residents other than the monetary authorities, producers of gold, and industrial users are not allowed to purchase, hold, or sell gold in any form other than jewelry, at home or abroad. The import and export of gold in any form, except jewelry constituting the personal effects of a traveler, require the prior approval of the National Bank, and licenses for such imports are not normally issued. Producers are required to sell 10 per cent of their production at the official price of $35 an ounce to the National Bank.

REGIONAL ARRANGEMENTS

Congo is an associate member of the EEC in accordance with the Yaoundé Convention. Under this arrangement, Congo has applied preferential import taxation to the six member countries of the EEC since January 1968.

In April 1968 Congo, the Central African Republic, and Chad signed an agreement to establish the Union of Central African States (Union des Etats de l'Afrique Centrale). The agreement provided for the removal of trade barriers and exchange restrictions between the participant countries and for the establishment of a common system of transport and communications. The liberalization of trade was to begin with effect from January 1, 1969. Effective immediately, the three countries were to abolish customs duties on imports, while other taxes on trade were to be maintained. In December 1968 the Central African Republic withdrew from the Union, and so far only an agreement on air traffic has been concluded with Chad.

In December 1969 Congo, Rwanda, and Burundi began discussions to establish closer economic relations. Three commissions were established and charged with identifying areas of possible cooperation in the economic, social, and political fields, respectively.

TRADE AND PAYMENTS ARRANGEMENTS

Congo does not maintain any bilateral payments arrangements.

CHAPTER 3

Malagasy Republic

GENERAL SETTING

The Malagasy Republic comprises the island of Madagascar and small adjacent islands, situated off the southeast coast of Africa. Covering about 229,000 square miles, its territory is about equal in area to that of France, Belgium, Luxembourg, and the Netherlands combined. The island of Madagascar consists of an eastern coastal strip 30 to 50 miles wide, a high, mountainous, central plateau with peaks ranging from 3,000 feet to over 9,000 feet, a sedimentary area in the west created by changes in the water level of the Mozambique Channel through different geological periods, and a desert in the southwest.

The climate is tropical along the eastern coastal strip and in the west, but temperate in the central plateau. The average annual rainfall is more than 100 inches on the east coast and is fairly well distributed throughout the year. It declines progressively toward the central and western areas, which have more definite rainy seasons and variable temperatures.

The country is divided into six provinces (see map). The principal urban area is Tananarive, the capital, with a population of about

342,000. Important towns besides Tananarive are Tamatave (population about 50,000), Majunga (45,000), Fianarantsoa (40,000), Diégo-Suarez (40,000), and Tuléar (35,000), each situated in the province of the same name. The principal ports are Tamatave, Majunga, Diégo-Suarez, Tuléar, Nosi Be, Hellville, and Manakara.

The population of the Malagasy Republic [1] at the end of 1970 was estimated at 7 million. There were some 100,000 foreigners, of which 37,000 were Comorians, 33,000 French, 17,000 Indians, and 9,000 Chinese. The Malagasy people comprise 18 ethnic groups; the plateau-dwelling Merina (1.7 million) are the most numerous, followed by the Betsimisáraka (1 million) on the east coast and the Bétsiléo (0.8 million) in the southern portion of the plateau. The Merina people are presumably from Indonesia and Malaysia, while most of the other ethnic groups are largely of Melanesian or African origin. The principal languages are Malagasy and French.

Population density averages 30 inhabitants to the square mile but varies considerably among the regions; the most densely populated areas are the central plateau and the eastern part of Madagascar.

The population increases at an estimated rate of 2.5 per cent per annum, resulting from a birth rate of 37 per thousand, a death rate of 12 per thousand, and a negligible net migration. Infant mortality accounts for about 20 per cent of total deaths. More than half the population is less than 21 years of age. In 1969 the active population was estimated at 3.2 million; of these, however, only 9 per cent were employed in the modern money economy—232,000 in the private sector and 45,000 in the public sector.

About half of the total number of children aged 6–14 receive primary education. A university, the University of Madagascar, was established in 1961. In the school year 1967/68, total student enrollment at all levels from primary through university was 825,000, approximately 80 per cent more than in 1959. The number of students at the University of Madagascar was 3,800.

On June 26, 1960, Madagascar became an independent republic. It was admitted to the United Nations on September 20, 1960. On

---

[1] In this chapter, the terms Malagasy Republic and Madagascar are used synonymously.

September 25, 1963 the country joined the International Monetary Fund (quota on May 31, 1971, $26 million) and the International Bank for Reconstruction and Development (capital subscription on May 31, 1971, $20 million), as well as the International Development Association and the International Finance Corporation. It is an associate member of the European Economic Community, a contracting party to the General Agreement on Tariffs and Trade, and a member of the African Development Bank, the Common Organization of African, Malagasy and Mauritian States, the Food and Agriculture Organization of the United Nations, the United Nations Economic Commission for Africa, and the United Nations Educational, Scientific and Cultural Organization.

The Malagasy Republic is a member of the French franc area. Its currency is issued by the Malagasy Institute of Issue. The unit of currency is the Malagasy franc, which is divided into 100 centimes. The Malagasy franc is fully convertible into French francs at the official rate of exchange, FMG 1 = F 0.02, giving the relationship FMG 277.710 = US$1. Prior to August 11, 1969, the official rate in terms of the U. S. dollar was FMG 246.853 = $1.00.

The economy of the Malagasy Republic is primarily agricultural, and industry, which caters mainly to the domestic market, is limited to the processing of agricultural commodities. The economy grew at an average annual rate of 4 per cent during 1964–68. Output was adversely affected by a violent cyclone, Cyclone Dany, in the early part of 1969, and in 1970 there was another severe cyclone, Cyclone Jane.

STRUCTURE OF THE ECONOMY

GROSS DOMESTIC PRODUCT

Comprehensive official estimates of the national accounts are available for the years 1960 and 1962–66. Provisional and incomplete estimates have been prepared for 1967–68 on the basis of data provided by the Malagasy authorities (Table 1). According to these statistics, gross domestic product (GDP) at market prices increased at an average annual rate of about 5.4 per cent during 1965–68; in the latest two years, the growth rates were 7 per cent and 6 per cent, respectively. Data are

TABLE 1.   MALAGASY REPUBLIC: GROSS DOMESTIC PRODUCT
AT CURRENT PRICES, 1962–68

(*In billions of Malagasy francs*)

	1962	1963	1964	1965	1966	1967 [1]	1968 [1]
Agriculture, forestry, and fishing	52	52	54	54	55	59	61
Industry	14	14	16	17	19	22	24
Transportation	13	14	15	16	18	…	…
Commerce	29	29	31	31	32	…	…
Services	12	13	13	14	15	…	…
Administration	27	28	31	33	35	…	…
Gross domestic product	147	150	160	165	174	186	197
Private consumption	106	110	116	122	129	138	150
Public consumption	36	35	36	38	38	39	39
Fixed investment	12	15	17	16	17	18	19
Change in stocks	—	1	1	1	1	1	2
Foreign balances (net)	−7	−11	−10	−12	−11	−10	−13
Gross domestic product	147	150	160	165	174	186	197

Source: Data provided by the Malagasy authorities; and Fund staff estimates.

[1] Provisional estimates.

not available for 1969 and 1970, but despite the adverse effect of cyclones, growth continued.

Economic growth during the period 1965–68 was adversely affected by the performance of the agricultural sector, where the annual gain in output averaged about 3 per cent, i.e., slightly above the demographic growth rate (2.5 per cent). Only in 1967 was this rate considerably exceeded; in that year, growth in the agricultural sector amounted to 7 per cent. The share of agriculture in GDP declined from 33 per cent in 1965 to 31 per cent in 1968. Substantial growth, however, took place in industry as well as in the tertiary sector. In 1968, industry contributed 12 per cent of GDP, compared with 10 per cent in 1965.

The rise in aggregate expenditure in the period 1965–68 was mainly because of the continued expansion of private consumption, which accounted on the average for about three fourths of total expenditure. The growth in public consumption averaged only 2 per cent annually in this period as a result of prudent budgetary policies. Total investment, comprising fixed investments and changes in stocks, remained at about 10 per cent of GDP from 1965 to 1968.

Since the consumer price index rose by about 2.6 per cent annually in 1965–68 and the annual population growth is estimated at 2.5 per cent, real per capita income changed very little in the period. Per capita GDP in 1968 amounted to about FMG 29,000, the equivalent of about $115 at the official exchange rate prevailing then.

TABLE 2. MALAGASY REPUBLIC: SAVINGS AND INVESTMENT, 1962–68

(*In billions of Malagasy francs*)

	1962	1963	1964	1965	1966	1967 [1]	1968 [1]
1. Gross domestic product	147	150	160	165	174	186	197
2. Consumption	142	145	152	160	167	177	189
3. Domestic savings (1 − 2)	5	5	8	5	7	9	8
4. Import surplus	7	11	10	12	11	10	13
5. Gross investment (3 + 4)	12	16	18	17	18	19	21
Fixed investment	*12*	*15*	*17*	*16*	*17*	*18*	*19*
Changes in stocks	*—*	*1*	*1*	*1*	*1*	*1*	*2*

Source: Data provided by the Malagasy authorities.
[1] Provisional estimates.

Estimates of domestic savings and investment are shown in Table 2. Domestic savings tended to increase over the period 1965–68, averaging about FMG 7 billion a year. Gross investment averaged about FMG 19 billion annually in the same period, the gap having been financed mainly with foreign resources. Domestic savings consisted primarily of the current budgetary surpluses and some private monetary savings. The ratio of domestic savings to GDP remained in the range of 3–4 per cent during the period. Gross investment increased steadily, to FMG 21 billion in 1968, about 11 per cent of GDP. Most of this investment emanated from the public sector, a large part having been financed by the French Fonds d'Aide et de Coopération (FAC) and the European Development Fund (EDF). However, domestically financed investment expenditure increased sharply in 1968 and 1969 as a result of a conscious effort of the Malagasy Government to step up its own development expenditure.

AGRICULTURE

Agriculture accounts for slightly less than one third of GDP and for more than four fifths of the value of total exports, and employs more than four fifths of the active population. The value of agricultural production, based on the volume of production and the producer prices of 13 commodities, reached a record level of FMG 36.4 billion in 1967, owing to exceptionally good weather in that year. In 1968, the weather was less favorable and the comparable figure was FMG 33.4 billion. In 1969, although Cyclone Dany early in the year destroyed crops estimated at FMG 2.5 billion, the value of agricultural output for the year was FMG 34.8 billion. Early in 1970 Cyclone Jane inflicted damage in the agricultural sector estimated again at FMG 2.5 billion. Most of the cyclones that occur in Madagascar each year are accompanied by mild rains and have beneficial effects on agriculture.

Aid for agricultural production from the European Economic Community (EEC) has helped to increase the average yield of cash crops and to make several cash crops competitive. Under the Yaoundé Convention, the Malagasy Republic received during 1964/65–1968/69 FMG 7,800 million in production and diversification aid, including FMG 5,274 million in production aid for coffee, pepper, rice, and cotton. Several export crops receive preferential treatment in specific markets besides the tariff preference granted to Malagasy exports by the EEC in connection with the Yaoundé Convention: sugar still benefits from preferential treatment under the sugar agreement concluded among members of the Common Organization of African, Malagasy and Mauritian States (Organisation Commune Africaine, Malgache et Mauricienne—OCAM); bananas receive preferential treatment under private arrangements with French companies; the export quota and price of vanilla are determined by special agreements with U. S. and European importers; and rice is sold to France and its overseas territories at a price slightly higher than the world market price.

Marketing and Stabilization Offices

There are six price stabilization funds, dealing with cassava, aleurites, vanilla, coffee, cotton, and sugar and four marketing boards dealing with pepper, groundnuts, cloves, and rice paddy. The only marketing board which has actively intervened in the marketing process, however, is the Rice Marketing and Price Stabilization Board; all others, whether they are called stabilization funds or marketing boards, have aimed exclusively at the stabilization of producer prices. There is, however, a statutory difference between the two categories, as only the marketing boards are authorized to buy and sell commodities should the private sector be unable to carry out its role in this regard.

The management committees of these organizations determine the guaranteed price (*prix-plancher*) payable for crops delivered to local buying stations. In principle, this is determined on the basis of the level of existing crop inventories, crop forecasts, current and future world prices, and the level of available financial reserves to support prices if necessary. The actual price paid to producers varies from the buying station price according to the cost of collection and other related inter-mediary charges. After the guaranteed price is established, the manage-ment committees determine an equivalent f.o.b. price by adding the various charges connected with the transport and the handling of the crop. If the equivalent f.o.b. price is higher (or lower) than the actual f.o.b. world price, the stabilization funds or marketing boards subsidize (or tax) the purchasing agents or exporting firms, as the case may be, for the difference.

Both the stabilization funds and the marketing boards receive their resources from a share of export taxes levied on the commodities under their control, from operating surpluses generated during years when world prices are higher than equivalent producer prices, and from gov-ernment loans and grants.

Food Crops

Rice.—In terms of output and use of inputs, rice is by far the most important food crop in Madagascar. It is estimated that rice is grown by 80 per cent of the farmers on one third of the cultivated land; paddy production represents about 40 per cent of the total value of agricul-tural output. During the years 1965–68 paddy production increased by about 100,000 tons annually (Table 3). In 1968 it was more than suf-ficient for domestic requirements, estimated at about 1.3 million tons (about 750,000 tons of milled rice).

In 1969, despite the flooding of many fields in the southern part of the country by Cyclone Dany, causing a loss of 60,000 tons, and dry weather in other areas, production of rice was estimated to have

TABLE 3.   MALAGASY REPUBLIC: PRODUCTION OF MAIN AGRICULTURAL
CROPS, CALENDAR YEARS 1964–69

(*In thousands of metric tons*)

	1964	1965	1966	1967	1968	1969 [1]
Food crops [2]						
Rice (paddy)	1,320	1,240	1,360	1,470	1,550	1,600
Cassava (fresh)	750	760	780	780	800	825
Potatoes (white and						
sweet)	360	370	380	380	385	390
Bananas	15	15	17	17	18	18
Fruits	86	85	86	87	87	92
Vegetables	59	59	62	61	65	65
Beans (dry)	23	25	26	26	26	26
Peas	18	22	12	10	13	16
Maize	85	85	90	86	90	90
Sorghum	4	4	4	4	4	4
Groundnuts	31	35	26	39	41	46
Export crops						
Sugarcane (fresh)	1,250	1,200	1,210	1,220	1,250	1,250
Coffee	67	41	53	71	58	65
Sisal	29.4	29.8	24.4	22.5	22.1	25.0
Raffia	7.5	7.5	7.6	8.0	7.0	7.0
Tobacco (leaf)	4.5	5.0	3.7	4.8	4.6	5.0
Cotton (unginned)	4.9	5.8	5.4	9.1	11.5	14.0
Cloves	4.8	6.0	0.3	13.0	0.5	2.5
Pepper (processed)	1.8	1.4	2.2	2.5	2.9	2.6
Vanilla (processed)	0.8	0.8	1.0	1.2	1.0	0.9
Cocoa	0.5	0.6	0.7	0.7	0.8	0.8

Source: Data provided by the Ministry of Agriculture.

[1] Preliminary estimates.

[2] Small quantities are sometimes exported.

increased by 50,000 tons, to 1.6 million tons. Large public investments,
financed mainly by the FAC and the EDF, and the use of fertilizers
have resulted in greater productivity and have contributed significantly
to the increase in output. During 1964/65–1968/69, the EEC allocated
FMG 799 million for price support and FMG 780 million for improvements in rice cultivation methods, mainly in the Lake Alaotra area of
the central plateau of Madagascar. In July 1970, the International
Development Association extended a credit of $5 million to finance
part of the improvement and extension of irrigation works in the Lake
Alaotra area. Consequently, this project is expected to raise paddy production to 1.9 million tons by 1974; of this amount, 120,000 tons
would be exported. The project also includes the establishment of an
experimental farm for crop diversification.

Lower-quality rice is being imported in order to preserve the export market for good-quality rice in France and the French overseas territories of Réunion and the Comoro Islands. The producer price for ordinary paddy has remained unchanged since 1966 at FMG 14.50 a kilogram and that for high-quality paddy at FMG 15.50 a kilogram. The export prices are FMG 39.30 and FMG 59.60 a kilogram, respectively. Various taxes and charges and the profits of intermediaries absorb the difference between the realized export price and the producer price.

The Rice Marketing and Price Stabilization Board is, in principle, responsible for the marketing and stocking of rice and rice by-products. The Board started its marketing operations in 1965 at the time of a severe shortage in rice production. So far, its marketing activity has been limited to the Lake Alaotra area, which produces about one tenth of the country's total paddy production; however, of the 250,000 tons of paddy marketed within the country, some 80,000 tons come from the lake area. Outside the lake area, the Board performs the same functions as the stabilization offices for other crops. The Board's head office is in Tananarive. In the lake area, it deals through agencies acting as intermediaries between the growers and the millers. Each of the ten rice mills established in the lake area is assigned a specific quota up to which it can buy at a price established by the Board. The rice mills also generally handle rice exports according to the Board's instructions. The Board has accumulated small profits, derived mostly from marketing operations, which are deposited with the National Development Bank.

Plans call for the Board to open new marketing agencies in other rice producing areas. The Board is also expected to build up stocks of rice to satisfy domestic needs in times of crop failure. At the same time, it will pursue its policy of prospecting for new outlets abroad.

Cassava.—Cassava ranks second as a staple food, and it is usually consumed by the local population fresh or cooked with rice. Less than 10 per cent of what is produced is exported. Production statistics, although deficient, show a continuous increase in recent years, to 825,000 tons in 1969. No producer price is fixed for this commodity, which has been selling at about FMG 30–40 a kilogram. The Cassava Price Stabilization Fund has made small profits, part of which have been deposited with the Treasury.

Other Food Crops.—A variety of other foods is grown. These include potatoes (both white and sweet), bananas, maize, groundnuts, peas, beans, fruits, and vegetables. Production has been increasing in recent years, and further increases are being encouraged. Most of these crops were adversely affected in 1969 by Cyclone Dany, except for peas, which benefited from the flooding. This cyclone destroyed half of the projected 1969 banana crop. The stabilization agencies dealing with the marketing of some of these food crops (e.g., groundnuts) have not so far been very active, since production is mainly for domestic consumption.

Export Crops

Coffee.—Coffee, mostly of the robusta type, is the leading cash crop in the Malagasy Republic, and has accounted for about one third of total export receipts in recent years. Production reached a record high figure of 71,000 tons in 1967 owing to excellent weather, but declined to 58,000 tons in 1968 (Table 3). In 1969, production rose to 65,000 tons despite an estimated loss of 15,000 tons because of the destruction of trees by Cyclone Dany. Production has been stimulated by Opération Café, a program financed by the EEC and the Coffee Price Stabilization Fund to promote better care of coffee trees and to replace old trees with selected trees of higher yield; EEC aid, which covered the period 1964/65–1968/69, was for price support (FMG 1,519 million) and structural improvements (FMG 1,649 million). Production was expected to reach 80,000 tons by 1972, but, owing to the adverse impact of Cyclones Dany and Jane, this target has now been set for 1974.

The Coffee Price Stabilization Fund raised the producer price for coffee from FMG 102 a kilogram in 1966/67 to FMG 105 in 1967/68, and maintained it unchanged in 1968/69. Toward the end of 1969, when export prices rose sharply because of the frost that destroyed a substantial portion of Brazil's coffee crop, the producer price was raised from FMG 105 to FMG 135 a kilogram (Table 4); as a consequence, production is expected to increase considerably in the next few years. Since taxes and charges on coffee were increased only slightly, the rise in the cost price was less than the rise in the actual export price and the Coffee Price Stabilization Fund accumulated substantial profits. Its

TABLE 4. MALAGASY REPUBLIC: PRICE STRUCTURE OF THREE MAIN
EXPORT COMMODITIES, CROP YEARS 1966/67–1969/70

(*In Malagasy francs per kilogram*)

	1966/67	1967/68	1968/69	1969/70
Coffee				
1. Producer price	102	105	105	135
2. Taxes and charges	41	44	44	46
Export taxes	*19*	*19*	*19*	*. . .*
Transaction and other taxes	*5*	*3*	*3*	*. . .*
Handling and packaging	*7*	*7*	*7*	*. . .*
Other [1]	*10*	*15*	*15*	*. . .*
3. Cost price, f.o.b. (1 + 2)	143	149	149	181
4. Actual export price	162	163	166	200
Vanilla				
1. Producer price	185	130	150	170
2. Export taxes	68	70	73	73
3. Processing, packaging, and other				
charges [1]	206	165	171	176
4. Cost price, f.o.b. (1 + 2 + 3)	459	365	394	419
5. Actual export price	547	547	574	630
Pepper				
1. Producer price	170	140	120	100
2. Export taxes	9	8	8	11
3. Freight and other charges [1]	53	49	48	55
4. Cost price, f.o.b. (1 + 2 + 3)	232	197	176	166
5. Actual export price	209	172	162	255

Source: Data provided by the Malagasy authorities.

[1] Includes profits of intermediaries and exporters.

deposits with the Treasury amounted to about FMG 1.8 billion at the end of the 1969/70 crop year.

Vanilla.—The Malagasy Republic produces about two thirds of the world's supply of vanilla. Production, which had reached a peak of 1,200 tons in 1967, declined to 900 tons in 1969 as a result of the Government's efforts to concentrate vanilla cultivation in the northeastern region of Madagascar. With higher prices on the world market, the producer price was raised from FMG 150 a kilogram in 1968/69 to FMG 170 in 1969/70 and FMG 190 for the 1970/71 crop year. Following the destruction of 800 tons of excess stocks of green vanilla (from stocks of 2,300 tons) in 1967 and higher prices since then, the stocks amounted to only 1,100 tons in 1969, equal to about one year's exports. The volume and price of exports of vanilla are the subject of special agreements with U. S. and European importers (see Balance

of Payments—Trade, below). The cost price has been rising since
1967/68 (Table 4), mainly as a result of higher charges by and profits
to intermediaries. However, since the cost price has remained considerably below the export price, the Vanilla Price Stabilization Fund has
earned substantial profits. Most of the profits were used to repay part
of a loan of FMG 400 million that had been contracted with the
Treasury to finance the destruction of vanilla stocks in 1967.

Pepper.—Production of pepper rose continuously from 1,400 tons in
1965 to 2,900 tons in 1968, but declined to 2,600 tons in 1969, owing
to the adverse effects of Cyclone Dany. Most of the output is exported.
The Pepper Marketing and Price Stabilization Board lowered the producer price from FMG 140 a kilogram in 1967/68 to FMG 120 in
1968/69, thus reducing substantially the cost price in this period (Table
4). The producer price was lowered again in 1969/70 to FMG 100.
Later during the 1969/70 crop year, the export price rose to FMG 255
a kilogram, from FMG 162 in 1968/69. Although the export tax was
increased and freight and other charges rose, the financial position of
the Pepper Board improved dramatically. Substantial arrears were paid,
but the Board still owes FMG 98 million to the Treasury. Madagascar
received FMG 335 million from the EEC during the period 1964/65–
1968/69 for price support and structural improvements in the production of pepper.

Sugar.—Production of sugarcane, which had increased continuously
during 1966–68, remained at the 1968 level of 1,250,000 tons in 1969.
Although domestic consumption has been increasing, a substantial proportion of production is exported under various agreements, of which
the most important is the OCAM sugar agreement. The Sugar Price
Stabilization Fund, which is to deal primarily with the marketing of
sugar, started operations early in 1970. Since marketing difficulties are
expected consequent upon the withdrawal of Senegal from the OCAM
sugar agreement, there are no plans to increase production substantially.

Cloves.—Production of cloves normally follows a three-year cycle.
After a peak output of 13,000 tons in 1967, production fell drastically
in 1968 and 1969 (Table 3). As this decline in output was accompanied by a sixfold increase in the export price, the producer price was
raised from FMG 110 a pound in 1968 to FMG 250 in 1969.

Cotton.—Production of seed cotton (unginned cotton) more than doubled from 1966 to 1969, when it reached 14,000 tons. The Cotton Price Stabilization Fund has been active in supplying farmers with fertilizers and insecticides and has received FMG 172 million from the EEC for structural improvements in production. The Stabilization Fund obtains its profits essentially from the sale of unginned cotton abroad.

Other Cash Crops.—These include sisal, raffia, tobacco, and cocoa (see Table 3). Although a variety of cash crops is grown, further diversification is envisaged and larger public investments are being made in such crops as cocoa, oil palm, coconuts, and cashewnuts.

Livestock

Livestock breeding has not been emphasized in Madagascar despite the extensive grasslands and the absence of serious animal diseases that are common in mainland Africa. Livestock is raised in regions extending along the entire west coast and throughout most areas of the high plateau. In 1968 the livestock population was estimated at about 12 million, including 10 million head of cattle, and it was estimated that the annual slaughter of cattle represented about 10 per cent of the cattle population and that less than one third of the slaughter was controlled by the Minister of Agriculture. Most cattle slaughtering is still done by owners, outside official control. The slaughter rate is relatively low, partly because marketing arrangements and transportation facilities are poorly developed in most livestock areas. Moreover, the Malagasy herders have traditionally preferred to maintain the largest size herd possible, which means that during the dry season the cattle raising areas have not been able to support adequately the entire herd and, as a result, unit weight is reduced and the proportion of unhealthy livestock increases. The commercial market for meat products has been depressed in recent years because of reduced French army purchases of Malagasy meat, which have been only partially offset by increased exports of frozen meat to Europe as well as of live animals to the Comoro Islands, Réunion, and Mauritius.

Malagasy meat is of good quality, and efforts have been made to expand the industry to allow greater domestic consumption as well as to increase exports. In order to increase the yield and the rate of slaughter, six new slaughterhouses and refrigeration plants under government control have been built, and efforts have been made to improve marketing. Only livestock that equals the standards prescribed by the Government are to be accepted for slaughtering by these establishments, which should induce herders to employ better raising methods. Investments in ranching and the construction of slaughterhouses have been financed by the FAC, the EDF, and the World Bank.

FISHING AND FORESTRY

The importance of fishing has increased markedly since 1950, but still accounts for only 1 per cent of GDP. The largest increase has come from fresh water sources following the construction of numerous stock ponds and the establishment of fishing cooperatives on the inland lakes and the east coast lagoons. Exploitation of the ocean resources has been limited by the lack of vessels and inadequate storage and transport facilities needed to provision the urban areas in the interior. About 6,000 persons were engaged in fishing in 1968, of whom about 2,000 were commercial fishermen. The total fish catch was estimated at 45,800 tons in 1968, more than two thirds of which was derived from inland fishing. Domestic consumption amounted to about two thirds of the total fish catch. Other seafood, including shrimp, lobster, and crab, is largely exported. Industrial fishing and greater exports of seafood are presently being encouraged.

Forestry has hitherto not been emphasized in Madagascar, because of the general inaccessibility of most forest regions (which are along the east coast), the distance from world markets, and the lack of world demand for the types of timber grown in the country. However, important investments are now being made to supply the paper and match factories with raw materials, though the effects of these investments will not be felt for some years to come.

MANUFACTURING

Manufacturing in Madagascar is confined mainly to processing local agricultural products and producing import substitutes. The important industries are those producing sugar, meat, beer, cement, and textiles (Table 5).

The output of some industries deriving their inputs from the domestic agricultural sector (e.g., sugar, sacks, and starch) declined slightly in

TABLE 5. MALAGASY REPUBLIC: INDUSTRIAL PRODUCTION, 1965–69

(*In metric tons unless otherwise indicated*)

	1965	1966	1967	1968	1969
Food					
Sugar	105,002	109,175	96,617	98,625	98,050
Tapioca	4,909	3,851	6,477	5,348	5,620
Canned beef	11,500	11,598	9,276	9,730	9,473
Canned pork	450	369	327	325	406
Starch	901	971	1,271	1,685	1,646
Beer (*hectoliters*)	34,611	49,929	53,440	67,928	80,199
Other					
Cement	39,192	50,714	59,585	66,918	77,079
Textiles	2,613	3,030	3,649	4,516	4,800
Sacks	3,502	2,723	3,756	4,408	3,808
Soap	1,322	1,268	1,309	2,034	4,084
Cigarettes and smoking tobacco	821	869	901	971	925
Chewing tobacco	1,071	1,185	920	1,133	1,270

Sources: Ministère des Finances et du Commerce, *Situation Economique au 1er Juillet 1969;* and data provided by the National Institute of Statistics and Economic Research.

1969, due to the adverse impact of Cyclone Dany. On the other hand, production of beer, cement, soap, and textiles increased. Several industries (e.g., beer and petroleum) are operating near capacity; cement production exceeds normal capacity (Table 6). Sugar and match production satisfy fully domestic requirements, but less than half of the domestic consumption of soap and paper is supplied by local industry.

Investment in the industrial sector amounted to FMG 5.2 billion in 1968 and resulted in the creation of 1,900 new jobs. The important new industries included textiles (Société Textile de Majunga or SOTEMA, for an investment of FMG 2,550 million and employment of 975 persons, and Cotonnière d'Antsirabé or COTONA, for an investment of FMG 1,480 million and employment of 302 persons); edible oils (Société Nouvelle des Huileries de Tuléar—FMG 282 million and 150 new jobs); and soap (Savonnerie Tropicale—FMG 150 million and 18 new jobs).

In 1969, investment amounted to FMG 747 million, mainly for the expansion of existing industries, and about 700 new jobs were created. It was anticipated that FMG 2.8 billion would be invested in 1970, providing new industrial employment for 1,200 persons. Firms in many industries (e.g., sugar, cement, soap, beer, and textiles) contemplate

TABLE 6.   MALAGASY REPUBLIC: INDUSTRIAL CAPACITY AND PRODUCTION,
AND DOMESTIC CONSUMPTION, 1969

(In metric tons unless otherwise indicated)

	Capacity	Production	Domestic Consumption
Food industries			
Sugar	120,000	98,050	98,050
Tapioca	. . .	5,620	. . .
Starch	. . .	1,646	. . .
Beer (*hectoliters*)	90,000	80,199	112,960
Other industries			
Cement	75,000	77,079	140,140
Textiles	5,900	4,800	7,740
Sacks	. . .	3,808	5,360
Soap	9,000	4,084	12,760
Cigarettes and tobacco	1,000	925	1,300
Chewing tobacco	. . .	1,270	. . .
Paper	7,000	4,922	13,670
Petroleum (*cubic meters*)	143,000	128,936	143,260
Matches (*thousand boxes*)	70,000	60,105	60,105
Corrugated iron	20,000	9,053	10,400

Source: Data provided by the Malagasy authorities.

expanding production and capacity. The capacity of the petroleum refinery at Tamatave will be expanded by 25 per cent, since production at full capacity cannot satisfy both domestic and export demand.

The National Investment Company, a public institution, has been active in promoting industrial investment in the Malagasy Republic. This company was created in 1962 for 50 years to mobilize domestic savings by issuing shares. Its capital of FMG 1 billion is fully subscribed. Since 1965 it has served as the financial promoter of industrial investment in the country by supplementing the efforts of the private sector through the purchase of minority participations in local industrial ventures. Participation of the company in the capital of various enterprises rose from FMG 1,375 million on December 31, 1966 to FMG 1,859 million on December 31, 1967; in 1968, new participation was only FMG 28 million; in 1969, participation commitments were FMG 102 million, and total participations at the end of the year amounted to FMG 1,989 million. Since 1967, textile industries have accounted on the average for more than one fourth of the company's participations. The share of food industries, which received up to one third of these funds in 1966, declined to about 16 per cent in 1969.

The wood industries' share was about 17 per cent in 1969. Participation in the total capital of an enterprise is high in small manufacturing and construction firms, as these industries find it difficult to raise private domestic capital: the highest rates of participation in 1968 were in the hotel and wood industries.

Because it has participated in several industries that proved unprofitable and its shareholders must be paid a dividend of at least 4 per cent per annum on their subscription to the company's capital, the company is in financial difficulties and has been receiving advances and subsidies from the Treasury to cover its operating deficits.

MINING

Madagascar is the leading world supplier of high-grade graphite. Production has remained at 16,000–17,000 tons (Table 7) in recent years and exports have had to compete with synthetic substitutes. In 1969, both production and exports increased because of higher prices and greater demand on the world market. Mica production has increased continuously, reaching 1,182 tons in 1969. The chromite mine at Andriamena has been exploited by the Mining Company of Andriamena since July 1969, and production amounted to 45,000 tons of concentrated ore in 1969. Investments in this project amounted to FMG 4 billion. Production of several minerals has come to an end since 1967 as ore bodies were exhausted. Offshore petroleum exploration has been carried out by several companies since the Middle East crisis and the

TABLE 7. MALAGASY REPUBLIC: MINERAL PRODUCTION, 1964–69

(*In metric tons*)

	1964	1965	1966	1967	1968	1969
Graphite	13,200	17,000	16,400	16,405	16,071	17,114
Mica	681	630	716	741	838	1,182
Uranothorianite	560	420	359	—	— [1]	—
Monazite	964	1,085	850	24	— [1]	—
Beryl	212	20	12	30	77	...
Columbite-tantalite	4	4	1	—	—	—
Chromite	11,800	2,384	— [1]	—	—	45,000
Quartz	28	88	100	40	71	...

Source: Data provided by the Malagasy authorities.

[1] Production ceased in the year indicated because the bodies of ore ran out.

closing of the Suez Canal. Investments of FMG 6 billion are expected in this sector by 1972. Exploration is also under way for bauxite and nickel.

ELECTRIC POWER

About 75 per cent of commercial electric power is produced by the Electricité et Eaux de Madagascar, and the remainder by the Société d'Energie de Madagascar. The city of Tananarive consumes three fifths of the power generated. The rates charged are higher than in most English-speaking countries in Africa but are comparable to rates in most of French-speaking Africa south of the Sahara.

Generation of electric power increased at an average annual rate of 10 per cent during 1965–69, but owing to reduced demand because of Cyclone Dany, the rate of increase was only 8 per cent in 1969, when it amounted to 150 million kilowatt-hours.

Future development of electric power, to be carried out in the framework of the Second Five-Year Plan, will include expansion of the hydroelectric station at Mandraka, construction of a high-tension line between Tananarive and Antsirabe, and construction of a hydroelectric plant at Rogez.

TRANSPORT

The road network consisted of some 23,560 miles of roads in 1968, of which 5,208 miles were primary and 4,650 miles were secondary roads. About 1,860 miles, mainly of primary roads, were paved; only about 140 miles of secondary roads were paved. Feeder roads are being given emphasis, to provide links between primary roads and to facilitate the marketing of export products and the distribution of consumer goods in the interior. Freight transport by road is estimated to have increased by about 5 per cent annually between 1965 and 1969.

Madagascar has a network of 530 miles of government-owned railways. The main line connects Tananarive with the principal port of Tamatave. Passengers numbered about 2 million a year in 1967–69 (Table 8). Merchandise transported increased from 627,000 tons in 1966 to 869,000 tons in 1969, mainly because of heavier traffic on the Tananarive–Tamatave line; the exploitation of the chromite mine at

TABLE 8. MALAGASY REPUBLIC: PASSENGER AND FREIGHT TRANSPORT, 1967–69

	1967	1968	1969
Railroads			
Passengers (*thousands*)	2,270	2,294	2,099
Freight (*thousand tons*)	627	736	869
Air			
International			
Passengers	66,247	67,365	82,923
Freight (*tons*)	2,216	2,446	3,108
Domestic			
Passengers	113,115	120,623	119,000
Freight (*tons*)	6,213	5,733	3,720
Maritime freight (*thousand tons*)	1,715	1,919	...
Port of Tamatave	*958*	*1,133*	*1,360*
Port of Majunga	*252*	*282*	*302*

Source: Institut National de la Statistique et de la Recherche Economique, *Bulletin Mensuel de Statistique*.

Andriamena contributed significantly to the 1969 increase. The railroad company has made a profit in recent years, but not enough to finance capital charges and investments, and these have been financed in part by advances from the Government and by borrowing.

Domestic air transport, including flights to the Comoro Islands, is provided exclusively by the national airline, Air Madagascar, which operates an extensive network. The number of passengers transported on these flights declined slightly in 1969 (to about 119,000) and domestic freight fell by 2,000 tons (Table 8). International flights are operated to and from Europe, Mauritius, Réunion, and mainland Africa. Air Madagascar and Air France operate most of these flights under a pool arrangement, the two companies sharing revenues equally. The number of passengers transported on international flights increased sharply in 1969 (to 82,923), and the volume of international freight increased also. Air Madagascar has made large profits on its international operations, which have more than offset the losses on domestic flights.

Following the devaluations of the French franc and the Malagasy franc in August 1969, passenger fares for international flights to countries outside the French franc area were increased in proportion to the devaluation. Within the French franc area, freight and passenger tariffs also were raised, but only by the equivalent of the increase in cost for items such as spare parts and petroleum that were imported from countries outside the franc area. Domestic fares were not changed.

The volume of maritime freight rose substantially in 1967 and 1968, mainly because of greater activity at the port of Tamatave. This trend is believed to have continued in 1969 as shown by increases in freight handled at the ports of Tamatave and Majunga. The increased activity in the port of Tamatave reflects the operation of the petroleum refinery since the end of 1966. Imports continue to account for the greater part of total freight. On June 17, 1970, the International Development Association approved a credit of $9.6 million to the Malagasy Republic for improvement and enlargement of the port of Tamatave to handle the projected traffic in dry cargo (due to chromite exports) and in petroleum products. Freight charges have risen substantially since the currency devaluation.

ECONOMIC DEVELOPMENT AND PLANNING

Economic planning in the Malagasy Republic began with the elaboration of the First Five-Year Plan (1964–68) by the General Planning Commission. The Commission also coordinated the implementation of projects by different ministries. It operated mainly through interministerial committees chaired by a representative of the Planning Commission. In recent years, changes have been made from time to time in the administrative machinery responsible for planning. A State Secretariat for Development was created early in 1969 to supervise the work of the General Planning Commission and other commissions dealing with rural promotion and cooperatives, and a Ministry of Planning was established in September 1970.

FIRST FIVE-YEAR PLAN (1964–68)

The First Five-Year Plan (1964–68) was established from the perspective of a ten-year development program, which calls for an increase of 75 per cent in production between 1964 and 1973. In order to attain an average annual rate of growth of 5.5 per cent in GDP, total investment under the Plan was expected to amount to FMG 165 billion, of which FMG 151 billion would be monetary investment and the equivalent of FMG 14 billion would represent the imputed values of contributions of free labor within the framework of small development projects to be implemented by the agricultural community (*ras du sol* program). Of the FMG 151 billion in monetary investment, FMG 69 billion was to be provided by the Government, FMG 23 billion by public agencies, and FMG 59 billion by the private sector. Half of the total investment was allocated to infrastructure, nearly one fourth to agriculture, 17 per cent to industry, and 9 per cent to social and miscellaneous projects (Table 9).

Actual monetary investment during 1964–68 totaled FMG 90 billion, representing about 60 per cent of planned investment in that period. Statistics on the distribution of investments by main economic sectors are fragmentary. The tertiary sector, including infrastructure, health, and education, absorbed FMG 53 billion, or about 59 per cent of the total. The highest implementation ratio was achieved in the secondary sector, where the volume of investment was FMG 24 billion, against a target of FMG 27 billion. In the primary sector, monetary investment during 1964–68 was estimated at FMG 13 billion, about 41 per cent of the target of FMG 31.5 billion. However, commitments of public resources to agriculture during this period amounted to FMG 22 billion. The goals for production of most agricultural crops were met, e.g., rice, sugar, coffee, vanilla, and pepper.

TABLE 9.   MALAGASY REPUBLIC: PROPOSED EXPENDITURE
UNDER FIRST FIVE-YEAR PLAN (1964–68)

(*In billions of Malagasy francs*)

	Public			Contri-butions of Free Labor	Total	
	Govern-ment	Enter-prises	Private		Amount	Share of total
Agriculture	20.6	2.2	8.7	7.1	38.6	23.4%
Industry	2.2	3.1	22.6	—	27.9	16.9%
Infrastructure and transport	33.7	16.8	26.7	6.3	83.5	50.6%
Social	10.4	1.0	0.4	0.6	12.4	7.5%
Other	2.1	—	0.6	—	2.7	1.6%
Total	69.0	23.1	59.0	14.0	165.1	100.0%

Source: Commissariat Général au Plan, *Plan Quinquennal, 1964–1968*, October 1964.

Public investment (the Government and public enterprises) during the Plan period was FMG 62.8 billion, about 68 per cent of the target of FMG 92.1 billion (Table 10). Although the rate of execution was substantially above this average in most sectors, it was below for infrastructure, which absorbed 41 per cent of total public investment. Agriculture accounted for 35 per cent, industry for 7 per cent, and most of the remaining 17 per cent was devoted to education, health, and research.

Domestic resources of the Government and public enterprises financed FMG 23.3 billion of total public investment (Table 10). It had been expected that FMG 49.1 billion would be financed in this way, including FMG 23.1 billion from public enterprises. Government investment, generally disbursed through the National Development and Investment Fund, averaged FMG 4 billion annually during 1964–68 and was concentrated in transport and communications. In 1968 it increased sharply, to FMG 9.3 billion, owing to the Major Works Program, and the emphasis was shifted from infrastructure to agriculture. The second largest supplier of funds was the European Development Fund (EDF), which provided FMG 16.5 billion during 1964–68, compared with expected commitments of FMG 20 billion. Most EDF grants were directed to the agricultural sector, which received FMG 10.4 billion. The French Fonds d'Aide et de Coopération (FAC)

TABLE 10. MALAGASY REPUBLIC: FINANCING OF PUBLIC INVESTMENT, 1964–68 [1,2]

(*In billions of Malagasy francs*)

	Invest- ment	Domestic Financing	Foreign Financing			
			EDF	FAC	Other	Total
Agriculture	22.2	5.6	10.4	4.1	2.1	16.6
Industry and mining	4.6	1.3	—	0.5	2.8	3.3
Infrastructure [3]	25.9	11.7	4.3	2.1	7.8	14.2
Other [4]	10.1	4.7	1.8	1.5	2.1	5.4
Total investment	62.8	23.3	16.5	8.2	14.8	39.5
Plan target	92.1	49.1	20.0	10.0	13.0	43.0

Sources: Commissariat au Plan, *Cinquième Rapport sur l'Exécution du Premier Plan Quinquennal,* September 1969; and Fund staff adjustments.

[1] On the basis of commitments.
[2] Totals may not add due to rounding.
[3] Transport and communications.
[4] Mainly health and education.

provided FMG 8.2 billion, mainly for agricultural projects, during the same period, though its commitments had been expected to amount to FMG 10 billion. Other public resources were grants from the United Nations Development Program (UNDP), bilateral loans, and World Bank loans; these funds were used mostly for infrastructure and research.

Private investment, mainly foreign, was estimated at FMG 27 billion during 1964–68, compared with FMG 59 billion envisaged in the Plan, and was concentrated in industry. As recording private investment in less developed countries is difficult, actual private investment may have exceeded the estimates. Malagasy nationals have generally invested in housing.

During the Plan period, the growth in GDP at constant (1964) prices was less than the target. The value of industrial output, which had been projected to reach FMG 34 billion in 1968, was estimated at only FMG 25 billion in that year. Furthermore, because of a lag in the financing of the Plan, total investment in 1968 represented about 12 per cent of GDP, compared with a target of 21 per cent. On the other hand, consumption increased more than expected and the foreign trade deficit remained high.

MAJOR WORKS PROGRAM (1968–69)

The Major Works Program (Programme de Grandes Opérations) was initiated in 1968 to improve the overall results achieved under the First Five-Year Plan and to provide an investment program until the adoption of the Second Five-Year Plan (1970–74). Its main feature was a shift in emphasis from infrastructure to agriculture and industry. The financing required for implementation of the Program in the two years 1968–69 was originally estimated at FMG 17.4 billion and was subsequently revised to FMG 11.1 billion; these estimates did not include FMG 13.5 billion in normal budgetary allocations in the two years, for investment through the National Development and Investment Fund. Important projects were in livestock (ranching and building of slaughterhouses), forestry, and textiles. No data are available on the implementation of the Program. While some projects were abandoned, several were carried out, and the Government's contribution to development expenditure increased sharply in 1968 and 1969 (see also Government Finance—Operations of Central Government Budget, below).

The Second Five-Year Plan had been expected to be adopted by Parliament in 1970. Adoption was delayed, however, and projects prepared under the Major Works Program continued to be implemented.

INVESTMENT IN 1969 AND 1970

Although national accounts data for 1969 were not available when this chapter was prepared, it is believed that total investment continued to increase rapidly. Public investment rose by 15 per cent in 1969, to FMG 14.0 billion (Table 11). Agriculture accounted for 47 per cent of the total and infrastructure for 34 per cent. Domestic resources financed FMG 10.0 billion. The EDF and the FAC financed FMG 2.2 billion and FMG 600 million, respectively.

In 1970, the disbursement of public resources for investment was expected to increase to FMG 15.8 billion. According to the projection, agriculture was to be the main recipient of funds, but its share in the total was to decline. The Government was expected to be the main supplier of resources, followed by receipts from borrowing from abroad, which were expected to increase sharply.

TABLE 11.   MALAGASY REPUBLIC: PUBLIC INVESTMENT AND FINANCING, 1968–70 [1]

(*In billions of Malagasy francs*)

	1968	1969	1970 [2]
Expenditure by sector			
Agriculture	4.8	6.6	6.4
Industry	2.8	0.3	0.2
Infrastructure	2.0	4.7	5.4
Other	2.7	2.4	3.8
Total [3]	12.2	14.0	15.8
Financing			
Domestic	7.5	10.0	7.2
FAC	0.9	0.6	1.4
EDF	0.3	2.2	2.9
Other	3.5	1.1	4.3

Source: Data provided by the State Secretariat for Development.

[1] On the basis of commitments, except for 1970.
[2] Forecast of disbursements.
[3] Details may not add to totals because of rounding.

INVESTMENT CODE

Under an Investment Code promulgated in October 1961 and revised in 1962 and 1965, preferential treatment may be granted to agricultural, industrial, and mining enterprises of special importance for the development of the Malagasy economy, provided that these enterprises, at least in the long run, can produce on an internationally competitive basis. The enterprises must also offer adequate financial and technical guarantees and undertake to carry out an investment program laid down in advance.

Four categories of preferential treatment may be granted to eligible enterprises: (1) preferential treatment to approved enterprises (*entreprises agréées*), which can be extended up to 5 years; (2) preferential treatment to encourage foreign enterprises which do not qualify for "approved" status (*régime de classification et d'encouragement*); (3) the special long-term taxation regime, under which enterprises may be granted a stabilization of their fiscal charges for a period ranging up to 30 years; and (4) the founding agreement (*convention d'établissement*), which is the most exceptional treatment, extending benefits beyond those provided by the Investment Code and requiring the approval of Parliament. The extent to which privileges are granted to qualifying companies depends on such criteria as the company's value-added contribution to the national product, the degree of utilization of local natural resources, and the induced creation of other industries.

Preferential treatment of approved enterprises may include (*a*) fiscal privileges (partial or total exemption from taxes on certain imports and exports, from patent taxes, from the profits tax for a maximum period of 6 years, from certain real estate taxes, and from property transfer taxes, as well as the privilege of deducting 50–100 per cent of investment expenditure from the taxable profits); (*b*) financial privileges (subsidies given as an incentive to invest in specified regions, or as a protection against unfair competition from abroad, and rebates on debt service charges in the case of particularly large investment programs); (*c*) economic privileges (protective measures with regard to import tariffs and quotas, which are generally extended for periods of up to 3 years, and priority in the purchase of goods and services); and (*d*) social privileges (government assistance in recruiting and training labor and special authorization to employ foreign personnel). Encouragement is provided for existing enterprises which may need temporary protection to face abnormal competition or temporary aid for reconversion purposes. Enterprises in this status may be granted fiscal, financial, and economic privileges as mentioned above.

At the end of 1968 the larger companies, in general, had approved status, while the smaller ones received preferential treatment to encourage their operations. The petroleum refinery at Tamatave was the only company benefiting from a founding agreement.

From 1962 to the end of 1967, investments benefiting from the provisions of the code amounted to FMG 12 billion and were mainly in textiles, chemicals, construction, forestry and wood products, and the petroleum refinery at Tamatave. The direct employment effect of these investments was the creation of 5,745 jobs. Total output from the industries covered by the code amounted to FMG 11.4 billion, thus giving an average incremental capital-output ratio of about 1. Textile, chemical, and food industries seem to have increased production in the past few years as domestic demand for their products has risen. The petroleum refinery at Tamatave, in operation since 1966, is already producing at full capacity, and plans have been formulated to expand its facilities and increase capacity by 25 to 30 per cent.

In 1968, investments benefiting from the code were estimated at FMG 6.8 billion. This figure includes FMG 2.3 billion for the expansion of the textile factory at Antsirabe; FMG 2.55 billion for construction of a textile factory at Majunga; FMG 525 million for a shoe factory; and FMG 200 million for a soap factory, one of two major industrial projects owned by Malagasy nationals.

PRICES, WAGES, AND EMPLOYMENT

PRICES

Price movements are measured by two cost of living indices for Tananarive; one measures the cost of a group of items typical of the consumption pattern of a lower-income Malagasy family, the other that of a European family, which is also applicable for an increasing number of higher-income Malagasy families (Table 12). The index for lower-

TABLE 12. MALAGASY REPUBLIC: INDICES OF COST OF LIVING IN TANANARIVE, 1965–70

(Averages of monthly data)

	Weight	1965	1966	1967	1968	1969	Oct. 1969	Oct. 1970
		(January 1964 = 100) [1]						
Food	56.2	106.6	111.1	110.6	110.2	115.2	114.0	118.9
Fuel and electricity	9.2	101.9	103.5	104.5	104.7	106.7	107.8	111.3
Domestic services	2.1	109.2	110.0	110.0	119.2	120.0	120.0	120.0
Maintenance, clothing, medicine	23.0	104.9	106.5	110.8	115.0	119.9	121.8	125.8
Sundry items	9.5	100.5	101.2	102.2	102.9	103.9	103.7	103.7
General index	100.0	105.2	108.4	109.3	110.3	114.5	114.4	118.4
		(March 1962 = 100) [2]						
Food	46.1	108.8	111.0	113.2	116.7	128.6	130.6	137.0
Fuel and electricity	7.4	102.5	102.5	102.9	102.9	106.7	108.2	114.6
Domestic services	8.0	131.6	132.7	138.5	142.1	145.9	147.7	151.5
Maintenance, clothing, medicine	28.4	112.3	118.3	122.6	125.5	143.3	146.3	152.3
Sundry items [3]	10.1	107.5	110.6	113.1	117.7	126.7	130.0	134.7
General index	100.0	111.0	114.1	117.2	120.4	132.4	134.7	140.6

Source: Institut National de la Statistique et de la Recherche Economique, *Bulletin Mensuel de Statistique.*

[1] The index is based on the consumption pattern of a typical Malagasy family living in Tananarive. The prices of 73 items are taken into account: food, 35; fuel and electricity, 6; domestic services, 1; maintenance, clothing, medicine, 27; sundry items, 4.

[2] The index is based on the consumption pattern of European (and higher-income Malagasy) families living in Tananarive. The prices of 204 items are taken into account: food, 114; fuel and electricity, 6; domestic services, 5; maintenance, clothing, medicine, 63; sundry items, 16.

[3] Includes, inter alia, entertainment, services, and luxury goods.

income Malagasy families, which takes into account the prices of 73 items, was started in 1964 on the basis of January 1964 = 100. It comprises five different categories of goods and services: food (35 items), fuel and electricity (6 items), domestic services (1 item), maintenance, clothing, medicine (27 items), and sundry items (4 items). The index for European families, which is on the basis of March 1962 = 100, comprises the same categories of goods and services, but takes into consideration the prices of 204 items: food (114 items), fuel and electricity (6 items), domestic services (5 items), maintenance, clothing, medicine (63 items), and sundry items (16 items).

Both indices remained relatively stable during the years 1965 through 1968; the Malagasy index rose by 4.8 per cent over the four-year period, whereas that for European families rose by 8.5 per cent during the same time span, owing largely to rising costs of imported goods, which have a greater weight in this index. In 1969, however, there was a distinct departure from this record of a slow-rising price level. By the middle of the year, the cost of living index for lower-income families had risen by 5.7 per cent over the index for June 1968 —food items had risen by 8.1 per cent—and the index for higher-income families had risen by 10.9 per cent. The sharp price increases in the first few months of 1969 occurred mainly because many merchants used the replacement of a general turnover tax by a value-added tax in early 1969 as an excuse to mark up prices. In order to check this upward pressure on prices, the Government undertook a campaign to explain the new tax to the public, lowered the rate of the tax from 12 per cent to 6 per cent for certain commodities, and exempted some essential goods altogether. These measures were successful: the index for lower-income families fell in the third quarter of 1969, and that for higher-income families ceased to rise further.

In order to minimize the effects on prices of the devaluation of the Malagasy franc in August 1969, the Government tightened its system of price control. On August 12, 1969, a decree was issued freezing prices for all goods and services, regardless of origin, at their August 9 level. By the same decree, merchants were requested to report the volume, value, and origin of their stocks of specified commodities.

On March 3, 1970, after concluding that most of the stocks of goods imported before the devaluation had been depleted, the Government issued a decree lifting the price freeze and replacing it by specified profit margins. These were set forth in a separate order prescribing the margins for both wholesale and retail sales of basic consumer goods. The margins for wholesale transactions range between 6 per cent and 12 per cent and those for retail transactions between 10 per cent and 35 per cent. The margin for goods not specifically listed may not, in the absence of special authorization by the Minister of Finance and Commerce, exceed 40 per cent at any stage of the transaction.

Price increases in 1970 were moderate, and as of October 1970 the cost of living index for lower-income families was 3.5 per cent, and that for higher-income families 4.4 per cent, above the indices for October 1969.

WAGES AND SALARIES

A Labor Code promulgated on October 1, 1960 established the right of wage earners in the private sector and unskilled government workers to participate in the drawing up of rules governing working conditions and to be guaranteed a minimum hourly wage. In addition, workers benefit from accident insurance, maternity benefits and family allowances, medical care, and retirement pensions.

The minimum hourly wage rate (*salaire minimum interprofessionnel garanti*—SMIG) has remained unchanged since November 20, 1963, when it was raised by an amount ranging from FMG 1 to FMG 5.50, depending on the salary area, and the number of salary areas was reduced from eight to five. The five areas, and the SMIG that has been in effect since November 20, 1963 for each one, are as follows: Area I (municipalities of Diégo-Suarez, Joffreville, Tamatave, and Tananarive), FMG 29; Area II (municipality of Majunga), FMG 26; Area III (municipalities of Tuléar, Fianarantsoa, and others), FMG 23; Area IV (municipalities such as Fort-Dauphin, Morondava, and others, and districts such as those of Diégo-Suarez, Majunga, and others, excluding municipalities), FMG 20; Area V (districts such as Fort-Dauphin, Tuléar, Morondava, and others, excluding municipalities), FMG 19. The last previous change had been made in 1953, when the minimum wage paid in the Tananarive area was FMG 21 an hour, and that in Area V was FMG 15 an hour. Since 1953, the difference between the highest minimum wage in urban areas and the lowest minimum wage in rural areas has been reduced from 120 per cent to 53 per cent.

Guaranteed minimum wage rates for skilled workers are linked to indices which are based on SMIG = 100 and which rise according to the degree of skill. These indices were introduced in 1963 to re-establish wage differentials for skills—which had been eroded by legislation favoring less skilled workers—and were subsequently increased in three annual steps. Since January 1, 1966 wage rates for skilled workers have remained unchanged.

The salary scales for civil servants, who are not covered by the SMIG, have not been changed since 1964, with the exception of a 10 per cent increase in the salaries for the lowest categories that was implemented in March 1970. Also in March 1970, the monthly family allowance for

employees in the private sector was raised by 25 per cent, to FMG 500
for each child. The family allowance for government workers, which is
proportional to the employee's salary, has remained unchanged.

EMPLOYMENT

Comprehensive labor statistics are not available in the Malagasy
Republic. According to government estimates (Table 13), the labor
force (all persons over 15 years of age) represents about 44 per cent
of the total population. Over four fifths of the active population is still
engaged in agriculture, whereas the number of wage earners is only
now approaching 10 per cent. Between 1967 and 1969, the Government
added people to its payroll at a faster rate than that of any other
sector, hiring a number of school leavers and university graduates.
However, its share in the total number of office workers is smaller than
in other developing countries because alternative employment opportunities exist in the economy, especially in commerce and banking and in
other service occupations where employment expanded at a pace not
much slower than that in Government. Although the numbers of agricultural wage earners and servants have declined, the Government's
estimates indicate that unemployment decreased slightly in recent years.
Underemployment in the agricultural sector is mainly seasonal.

TABLE 13.   MALAGASY REPUBLIC: ACTIVE POPULATION, 1967–69

(*In thousands of persons*)

	1967	1968	1969
Salaried workers in private sector			
Industry	43	44	45
Agriculture	45	39	41
Commerce and banking	40	44	46
Domestic servants	45	38	40
Construction	17	15	16
Services [1]	35	42	44
Total	225	222	232
Government	34	41	45
Proprietors, farmers, and farmhands	2,535	2,747	2,820
Others, including unemployed	100	86	80
Total active population	2,894	3,096	3,177

Source: Data provided by the Malagasy authorities.

[1] Includes, inter alia, transport, communications, and utilities.

The Government is contemplating various resettlement schemes in fertile areas that are now sparsely populated. Such a program would relieve overcrowded rural areas without swelling the ranks of the unemployed in the cities. The Government has also continued its efforts to upgrade the skills of Malagasy workers through various training programs and has persuaded foreign employers to speed up and expand their training activities.

GOVERNMENT FINANCE

BUDGETARY SYSTEM

The budgetary system of the Malagasy Republic includes the general budget of the Central Government, the budgets of the 6 provinces, the annexed budgets of 7 autonomous public agencies, and the budgets of 41 urban municipalities and 735 rural municipalities. Except for the rural municipalities, the Treasury is responsible for the execution of these budgets.

The Central Government's budgetary operations are recorded in the general budget, which covers ordinary receipts—including an annual budgetary contribution from France—and current as well as capital expenditures. The accounting period for the budget is January 1 to December 31, and there is no carry-over of current expenditure appropriations from one budget year to another. All bills have to be settled before January 31 of the following year. A law of June 24, 1964 adopted in connection with the First Five-Year Development Plan requires that the annual growth of current expenditure be limited to 5 per cent.

Capital expenditures comprise those financed both from domestic resources and by borrowing from abroad. Projects that are financed entirely by grants from abroad are not included in the budget. A General Budget Law of July 15, 1963 provides for a National Economic Development Fund, the name of which was changed to National Development and Investment Fund in 1964. This is a budgetary account through which are channeled all capital expenditures, whether financed by budgetary resources, by borrowing, or by treasury resources. According to this law, budgetary resources earmarked annually for the Devel-

opment and Investment Fund must be at least a given proportion of
total domestic fiscal receipts, including the French budgetary contribution. This proportion, which is actually equivalent to the ratio
between budgeted capital expenditure and current budget revenue, was
to increase by 2 percentage points each year, from 10 per cent in 1964
to 22 per cent in 1970.

The 7 annexed budgets comprise revenues and expenditures of the
Malagasy National Railroad, the Malagasy National Radio and Televi-
sion Company, the Post and Telecommunications Office, the National
Printing Office, the Government Garage, the Public Works Department
Workshop, and the Harbors.

The budgets of the provinces and the municipalities record expenditures, which are financed mainly through locally collected taxes and
transfers from the Central Government. Most expenditures of the provinces are for education and health; most expenditures of the municipalities are for local administrative services, road maintenance, and participation in primary education.

The annexed budgets and the provincial budgets are approved by the
Minister of Finance. The operations of these budgets have been consolidated with the Central Government's budgetary operations in this
study, so as to present a more comprehensive picture of public finance
(see Operations of Consolidated Budget, below). The budgets of the
municipalities are only partly supervised by the Ministry of Interior
and, because of lack of information, cannot be consolidated with the
other budgets.

STRUCTURE OF CURRENT REVENUE

In both the central government budget (Table 14) and the consolidated budget (Table 15), current revenue is derived mainly from taxes,
both direct and indirect, although in the latter budget there are substantial receipts in respect of government property, services, and autonomous public agencies. Moreover, revenue from indirect taxes is more
than double that from direct taxes in most years.

Direct Taxes

Direct taxes include a general income tax, a tax on profits, and a tax
on capital (mainly on dividends); there are also business fees. All these

taxes accrue to the Central Government. Receipts from the head tax and the tax on livestock accrue essentially to the provinces, but some accrue to the Central Government and the municipalities. A tax on vehicles is earmarked for urban and rural municipalities; in 1966, however, the rate of the tax on vehicles was increased, and the additional revenue accrues to the Central Government. Real estate taxes on buildings and undeveloped land are levied for the provinces and the urban municipalities.

The taxes on incomes, profits, and dividends account for about half of the revenue from direct taxation in the consolidated budget.

The general income tax (*impôt sur le revenu*) applies to all incomes of individuals above FMG 90,000 a year, and is composed of a fixed amount and a progressive rate. There are 22 fixed amounts, ranging from FMG 1,000 for incomes of FMG 90,000–100,000 to FMG 37,000 for incomes of more than FMG 2.5 million a year. The progressive rate is 4 per cent for incomes of FMG 90,000–100,000, with a maximum of 40.5 per cent for incomes of more than FMG 3 million. There are allowances for families and additional charges for bachelors.

The tax on profits (*impôt sur les bénéfices divers*) applies to all income except from wages and salaries. The rate is 16 per cent for income of more than FMG 90,000 but the entire income is taxed when it exceeds FMG 300,000. Corporate income is taxed at a rate of 31 per cent. There are allowances for families.

Business fees (*patentes*) are imposed on all individuals and all companies engaging in any commercial, industrial, or professional activity. These fees are of two kinds: (1) a fixed fee, determined by the nature and conditions of the business and by the number of people living in the area where the activity takes place, and (2) a proportional fee, determined by the rental value of the buildings in which the business is carried on (stores, offices, factories, etc.).

The head tax (*impôt du minimum fiscal*) is levied on men of more than 20 years of age living in the Malagasy Republic. The rate of tax ranges from FMG 3,225 to FMG 3,450 for each adult male, according to the municipality where the tax is levied. Receipts from this tax contribute one third to total revenue from direct taxes in the consolidated budget.

TABLE 14. MALAGASY REPUBLIC: CENTRAL GOVERNMENT BUDGET, 1965–70 [1]

(In millions of Malagasy francs)

	1965	1966	1967	1968	1969 Budget estimates	1969 Preliminary results	1970 Budget estimates
Current revenue	**24,865**	**26,275**	**27,979**	**31,903**	**34,451**	**36,039**	**36,580**
Taxes	22,928	24,849	26,367	30,147	32,971	34,140	35,048
Income taxes [2]	*3,783*	*4,928*	*5,269*	*5,593*	*5,632*	…	*5,754*
Excise duties on consumption	*2,844*	*3,606*	*3,653*	*4,200*	*4,353*	…	*4,500*
Turnover tax [3]	*2,134*	*2,240*	*2,672*	*3,069*	*7,000*	…	*6,547*
Import duties and taxes	*8,947*	*9,084*	*9,435*	*11,969*	*10,531*	…	*12,730*
Export taxes	*2,155*	*1,660*	*1,748*	*1,970*	*1,830*	…	*1,700*
Other taxes	*3,065*	*3,331*	*3,590*	*3,346*	*3,625*	…	*3,817*
Nontax revenue	1,937	1,426	1,612	1,756	1,480	1,899	1,532
Current expenditure	**24,308**	**24,461**	**26,531**	**28,869**	**32,439**	**31,052**	**33,419**
Public debt service	816	549	639	1,092	1,504	…	1,668
Wages and salaries	10,995	12,091	12,778	13,679	14,928	…	15,736
Materials and supplies	3,760	3,254	3,957	4,255	4,746	…	4,466
Transfers and subsidies	2,500	1,939	2,704	3,031	3,076	…	3,401
Other	6,237	6,628	6,453	6,812	8,185	…	8,148
Current surplus	**557**	**1,814**	**1,448**	**3,034**	**2,012**	**4,987**	**3,161**
Capital expenditure	**3,619**	**4,924**	**5,164**	**9,106**	**13,077**	**10,919**	**10,046**
Overall deficit	**−3,062**	**−3,110**	**−3,716**	**−6,072**	**−11,065**	**−5,932**	**−6,885**

Source: Data provided by the Ministry of Finance and Commerce.

[1] For a description of the components of revenue and expenditure, see text.
[2] General income tax, tax on profits, and tax on capital.
[3] Replaced by a value-added tax in 1969.

Table 15. Malagasy Republic: Consolidated Budget, 1965–70 [1]

(In millions of Malagasy francs)

	1965	1966	1967	1968	1969 Budget estimates	1969 Preliminary results	1970 Budget estimates
Current revenue	**34,659**	**36,413**	**38,791**	**43,270**	**45,999**	**48,499**	**49,590**
Taxes	26,073	28,481	29,891	33,513	37,901	38,302	40,255
Direct	*8,561*	*10,175*	*10,244*	*10,604*	*10,963*	…	*11,376*
Indirect	*17,512*	*18,306*	*19,647*	*22,909*	*26,938*	…	*28,879*
Nontax revenue [2]	8,586	7,932	8,900	9,757	8,098	10,197	9,335
Current expenditure	**33,169**	**33,320**	**35,940**	**38,919**	**43,476**	**44,382**	**45,250**
Public debt	816	549	639	1,092	1,504	…	1,668
Administration	10,259	10,735	11,114	11,627	12,827	…	13,000
Social services	9,290	9,328	9,827	10,361	11,732	…	12,451
Education	*5,158*	*5,363*	*5,768*	*6,388*	*7,235*	…	*7,993*
Economic services	6,281	6,448	7,252	7,948	8,080	…	8,225
Industrial services	4,571	4,720	5,083	5,029	5,599	…	6,260
Other	1,952	1,540	2,025	2,862	3,734	…	3,646
Current surplus	**1,490**	**3,093**	**2,851**	**4,351**	**2,523**	**4,117**	**4,340**
Capital expenditure	4,108	5,786	5,952	10,403	14,372	12,091	11,504
Overall expenditure	37,277	39,106	41,892	49,322	57,848	56,473	56,754
Overall deficit	**−2,618**	**−2,693**	**−3,101**	**−6,052**	**−11,849**	**−7,974**	**−7,164**

Source: Data provided by the Ministry of Finance and Commerce.

[1] Comprises the general budget of the Central Government, the budgets of the six provinces, and the annexed budgets of seven autonomous public agencies.

[2] Receipts in respect of government property, services, and autonomous public agencies.

Indirect Taxes

Indirect taxes comprise taxes on international trade, excise duties on consumption, including imports, a license tax on the sale of alcoholic beverages, and a turnover tax.

Import duties and taxes, which comprise a customs duty (*droits de douane*) and an import tax (*taxe à l'importation*), constitute the largest single source of tax revenue, yielding on the average about one third of total tax receipts. The customs duty applies only to imports from countries outside the French franc area and the European Economic Community, at rates ranging from 5 to 10 per cent for essential goods and at a rate of 40 per cent for products that the Government intends to protect most (e.g., textiles). The import tax applies to imports from all countries at rates ranging from 3 to 50 per cent, except that for certain products, such as coffee, tea, pepper, vanilla, and spices, the rate is 100 per cent, and for brandy, liqueurs, and other spirituous liquors it is 135 per cent. Customs duties and import taxes apply to the c.i.f. value of the imported goods.

Export duties consist of a fiscal tax (*taxe fiscale*) on coffee (FMG 19 a kilogram), and on vanilla, cloves, black pepper, and meat (15, 11, 5, and 0.5 per cent ad valorem, respectively).

Excise duties are levied on certain products, mainly alcohol and manufactured tobacco, and on consumption. Exemptions are granted for products for agricultural and industrial use, intermediate goods, and manufactured exports. The tax is low for essential goods and very high for luxury goods, e.g., alcoholic beverages are taxed at FMG 850–1,200 per liter of alcohol. There are excise taxes on sugar produced locally and on profits earned by the Office of Tobacco and Matches, which has a monopoly on the sale of these products.

The general turnover tax (*taxe sur les transactions*), which was levied at a rate of 2 per cent on the total value of each sale including turnover tax paid by the seller, was transformed in January 1969 into a value-added tax (*taxe unique sur les transactions*), which is levied at a rate of 12 per cent, only on the value added by the seller. This rate is reduced to 6 per cent for some products, such as fertilizers, machinery, and some types of vehicles; for certain transactions, such as those performed by banks and insurance companies; and for the construction of buildings, the production of electricity, transportation, and building rentals. Exempted from the turnover tax are the import and sale of essential goods—rice, salt, milk, vegetables, fish, meat, liquid fuel, etc.; certain transactions of small enterprises, cooperatives, the Malagasy Institute of Issue, and agricultural credit associations; and all exports.

STRUCTURE OF CURRENT EXPENDITURE

Current expenditure, including debt service, represented on the average 86 per cent of overall expenditure in the consolidated budget in the period 1965–67 (Table 15). This ratio fell to about 79 per cent in 1968 and 1969, following intensified government efforts to increase public investment expenditure. Wages and salaries have been the largest single current expenditure category, generally accounting for nearly half of current expenditure in the Central Government (Table 14) and over two thirds in the provinces. Wage and salary payments include contributions by the Government to the costs of the French technical assistance programs in the country; these contributions, which amounted to some FMG 1.5 billion in 1967, have declined with the gradual replacement of French experts by Malagasy nationals, who are paid much lower salaries. Expenditures for materials and supplies made up the next largest category, accounting for about one sixth of the Central Government's current expenditure. Transfers and subsidies were mostly to the provinces and certain public agencies to finance their current budgetary deficits. Amortization and interest payments on the public debt, which are mainly on account of the foreign debt (see Balance of Payments— External Debt, below) are still modest, representing less than 5 per cent of current expenditure. Other current expenditures include outlays for the maintenance of buildings, for services, and for transportation.

OPERATIONS OF CENTRAL GOVERNMENT BUDGET

1966–69

Current revenue of the Central Government increased at an average annual rate of almost 10 per cent during 1966–69. In 1966, the system of direct taxation was extensively revised, leading to a rise of 30.3 per cent in revenue from income taxes in that year, to FMG 4.9 billion (Table 14). In 1967 and 1968, these revenues increased only moderately, and in the latter year represented about 18 per cent of current revenue. Revenue from import duties increased substantially in 1968—accounting for 38 per cent of total current revenue—following a steep rise in imports and an increase in the ratio of duties and taxes to imports (from 26 per cent in 1966 to 28 per cent in 1968). This development was the primary reason for an increase of 14 per cent in current revenue in 1968. After a sharp decline in 1966, revenue from export taxes rose to almost FMG 2 billion in 1968 because of larger exports of vanilla, cloves, and coffee—the products most heavily taxed.

After a period of moderate increases, receipts on account of the turn-over tax in 1969 were estimated to be more than double those in 1968. Early in that year the general turnover tax of 2 per cent had been replaced by a value-added tax of 12 per cent (6 per cent for some items —see Indirect Taxes, above). Owing to the problems encountered in the application of the new tax, and to the inflationary pressures it created in the Malagasy economy, the rate was reduced to 6 per cent for a broader category of goods in June 1969 and exemptions were also applied to all essential commodities. A preliminary classification of current revenue in 1969 showed that receipts from the value-added tax amounted to FMG 7 billion, compared with receipts of FMG 3 billion from the general turnover tax in 1968. Consequently, total current revenue increased by FMG 4 billion in 1969, or 13 per cent.

Current expenditure increased at an average annual rate of 6.4 per cent during 1966–69. The wage bill rose by 10 per cent in 1966 as a result of a substantial gain in the number of government employees and of regular promotions. As most other categories of current expenditure declined in that year, total current expenditure was less than 1 per cent higher than in 1965. However, wages and salaries continued to increase in 1967 and 1968, though at a less rapid pace, and total current expenditure rose by more than 8 per cent annually. This was partly explained by larger outlays for economic and industrial services in connection with the implementation of the First Five-Year Development Plan (1964–68) and the Major Works Program. Because of the need to intensify foreign borrowing to finance investments under the Plan and the Program, service on the public debt rose from FMG 549 million in 1966 to FMG 1,092 million in 1968, when it represented about 4 per cent of current expenditure.

In 1969, the increase in actual current expenditure of 7.6 per cent compared favorably with the increases in the two preceding years and that of 12.4 per cent estimated in the 1969 budget. The improved performance may be explained by the tighter control on expenditure, which minimized the recruiting of new personnel and made better use of budgetary credit for materials and supplies. In addition, payments for the servicing of the public debt were lower than anticipated.

As current revenue increased much faster than current expenditure, the Government accumulated substantial savings during 1966–69, which were used in part to finance capital expenditure. This expenditure, which had averaged FMG 4–5 billion annually during 1965–67, almost doubled in 1968 (to FMG 9 billion) as a result of launching the Major Works Program. There was a further increase (to FMG 11 billion) in 1969, but this was considerably short of the amount estimated in the budget (FMG 13 billion). This shortfall was caused by an overestimation of the capital spending capacity of the Government. Furthermore, several development projects were not sufficiently prepared to attract foreign lenders. As a result of the larger investments, the deficit in the central government budget was some FMG 6 billion in 1968 and 1969, compared with deficits of FMG 3–4 billion in previous years.

1970

Budget estimates for 1970 provided for current revenue of FMG 36.6 billion, current expenditure of FMG 33.4 billion, and a current surplus of FMG 3.2 billion. Since capital expenditure was budgeted at FMG 10 billion, the budgetary deficit was expected to amount to FMG 6.9 billion. The increase in current revenue was projected at 6.2 per cent over the 1969 estimated figure and at 1.5 per cent over actual current revenue for 1969. Receipts from the turnover tax were estimated to decline from about FMG 7 billion in 1969 to FMG 6.5 billion, owing to rate reductions. Revenue from export taxes was also expected to decline, but that from import taxes was forecast to be higher. Given the 1969 tax structure, previous trends, and some increases in the rate of import duties to protect domestic industries, actual receipts in 1970 were expected to be much higher than budgeted. Current expenditure, on the other hand, was budgeted to increase by

7.6 per cent (compared with the preliminary results for 1969), or at the same rate that actual expenditures increased in 1969. The estimated increase would have been much higher had the Government not applied selective austerity measures in the 1970 budget.

The austerity measures limited spending by all ministries to their appropriations in the 1969 budget, except for the Ministries of Health and Education, which were granted additional appropriations for demographic reasons. Consequently, current expenditure was budgeted in 1970 at only 3 per cent more than had been budgeted in 1969. In terms of the broad categories of spending, the growth of wage and salary payments was reduced and spending for materials and supplies was estimated to decline from FMG 4.7 billion in 1969 to FMG 4.5 billion in 1970.

Capital expenditure was also budgeted to decline substantially in comparison with the 1969 budget. However, this reflected a more realistic picture of the capital spending capacity of the Government in terms of the preparation of projects. The provision in the General Budget Law of July 1963 that capital expenditure of the Central Government should increase by 2 percentage points a year, from 10 per cent of fiscal receipts in 1964 to 22 per cent in 1970, has been fully met. The ratio of central government capital expenditure to total fiscal receipts, including the French budgetary contribution, in the 1970 budget was above 25 per cent.

OPERATIONS OF CONSOLIDATED BUDGET

More than two thirds of revenue and expenditure in the consolidated budget (central government, annexed, and provincial budgets) is accounted for by the Central Government. Consequently, the execution of the central government budget explains to a large extent developments in the consolidated budget. Total receipts and expenditures of the seven annexed budgets have normally been balanced at FMG 6–7 billion, and the budgets of the six provinces, with total expenditure (mainly for wages and salaries) also at FMG 6–7 billion, have shown only small deficits. The provinces derive their revenue from direct taxation (a head tax, a cattle tax, and a property tax) and from subsidies from the Central Government.

1966–69

Current revenue in the consolidated budget increased at an annual rate of 9 per cent during 1966–69 (Table 15). Most of the increase took place in 1968 and 1969, reflecting the rise in central government revenue during the same period. Receipts from direct taxes in 1966, at FMG 10 billion, were 19 per cent higher than in 1965, owing to a revision of the direct taxation system in that year and much larger collections by the provinces. In subsequent years receipts from this source increased more slowly, amounting to FMG 10.6 billion in 1968, or 25 per cent of current revenue. The growth in receipts from indirect taxes accelerated during the years 1966–68, as imports increased, and in 1968 contributed 53 per cent of current revenue. Nontax revenue, which declined in 1966 but increased in subsequent years, accounted for 22 per cent of current revenue in 1968.

Current expenditure in the consolidated budget increased at an average annual rate of 7.7 per cent during 1966–69, which was more than the rate of growth of GDP at current prices. According to preliminary results, current expenditure was 14 per cent greater in 1969 than in 1968, whereas the increase in central government current expenditure was 7.6 per cent. The provinces have substantially stepped up their outlays for wages and salaries, mostly because of increases in personnel for the Major Works Program and schools and hospitals.

The execution of the consolidated budget has generated public savings which have been used to finance investments. However, beginning in 1968 these savings have remained at about FMG 4 billion, with striking increases in capital expenditure. Consequently, the overall budgetary deficit rose from FMG 3.1 billion in 1967 to FMG 6.1 billion in 1968, and preliminary results for 1969 indicated a deficit of FMG 8 billion.

1970

As a result of the austerity measures adopted in the central government budget and extended to the provinces, consolidated current expenditure was budgeted at only 2 per cent more in 1970 than actual expenditure in 1969. Capital expenditure was expected to decline to FMG 11.5 billion, from FMG 12.1 billion in 1969. Therefore, overall expenditure in 1970 was expected to be about the same as in 1969.

Since current revenue was budgeted at 2.2 per cent higher, the overall budget deficit should be reduced to FMG 7.2 billion; however, it was probable that this deficit would be much smaller, as current revenue was likely to exceed the forecast owing to improved economic conditions and to a shortfall in capital expenditure.

TREASURY OPERATIONS

Treasury operations other than those related to budget transactions are recorded in three main groups: (1) Loans and advances are extended by the Treasury to public institutions, such as the chambers of commerce, price stabilization funds, and development or investment agencies; to local authorities (provinces and municipalities); to institutions such as state farms or cooperatives; and to other public and semipublic enterprises and organizations (advances are extended by the Treasury for a maximum two-year period and can thereafter be consolidated in the form of loans). (2) Participations consist of subscriptions by the Government to international financial organizations or to the capital of Malagasy public and semipublic enterprises and organizations. (3) Miscellaneous operations cover various accounts, such as the working capital account of the Malagasy Office of Tobacco and Matches, the operating accounts of the Senate and the National Assembly, the accounts of the Pension Funds, and accounts used in effecting payment for investment, equipment, or maintenance.

The Treasury also receives deposits from public institutions—such as the price stabilization funds, the Social Security and Pension Funds, and the Postal Checking System—and from some private individuals.

Treasury operations resulted in increasingly large net expenditures between 1965 and 1967, as substantial payments on account of loans, advances, and participations more than offset net receipts from miscellaneous operations (Table 16). The steep rise in loans and advances in 1967 was due to the fact that the Treasury had to support newly created institutions, such as state farms and cooperatives. It also advanced FMG 400 million to the Vanilla Price Stabilization Fund to finance the destruction of stocks. Participations almost doubled in 1966, largely because of an accounting adjustment for subscriptions to international organizations, especially payments connected with the increase in the quota in the International Monetary Fund. Net receipts from miscellane-

Table 16. Malagasy Republic: Treasury Operations and Financing, 1965–70

(In millions of Malagasy francs)

	1965	1966	1967	1968	1969 Estimates	1969 Preliminary results	1970 Estimates
Overall budgetary deficit	−2,618	−2,693	−3,101	−6,052	−11,849	−7,974	−7,164
Treasury operations	−468	−803	−2,069	−885	—	−421	−394
Loans and advances	−569	−103	−2,533	−1,174	−370	−1,745	−260
Participations	−490	−973	−295	−294	−400	−194	−400
Miscellaneous	591	273	759	583	770	1,518	266
Changes in deposits held with Treasury	−1,924	−51	386	251	531	1,792	275
Total treasury deficit	**−5,010**	**−3,547**	**−4,784**	**−6,686**	**−11,318**	**−6,603**	**−7,283**
Financing							
Foreign	2,237	4,405	2,217	2,809	5,105	3,222	4,741
French budgetary grant	1,720	1,700	1,650	1,600	1,650	954	1,500
Borrowing	517	2,705	567	1,209	3,455	2,268	3,241
Domestic	2,773	−858	2,567	3,877	6,213	3,381	2,542
Borrowing	—	173	326	98	3,747	589	475
Changes in treasury balances (increase −)[1]	2,773	−1,031	2,241	3,779	2,466	2,792	2,067
	5,010	3,547	4,784	6,686	11,318	6,603	7,283

Source: Data provided by the Ministry of Finance and Commerce.

[1] Treasury balances include cash holdings, deposits held with the Malagasy Institute of Issue, deposits held abroad, and customs duty bills discounted with the Institute of Issue.

ous treasury operations declined in 1966, but increased almost threefold in 1967, reflecting larger deposits by the Pension Funds and the deposit in special accounts of funds earmarked for the amortization of materials and equipment used in road construction.

In 1968, net expenditure on treasury operations declined sharply, to FMG 885 million, partly because of some repayments of loans and advances but mainly because of a reduction in the amounts of advances granted to public and semipublic institutions. Preliminary results for 1969 showed a further reduction, to FMG 421 million, in expenditure, an increase in loans and advances being more than offset by an increase in receipts from miscellaneous operations. Advances were mostly to state farms and to regional groupings of municipalities (*Syndicats de Communes*). The increase in receipts from miscellaneous operations reflected essentially larger profits of several public enterprises, e.g., state stores (*Magasins M*). Budget estimates for 1970 provided for a further decline in net expenditure on treasury operations, to be achieved through reduced disbursements of loans and advances. Public institutions are now encouraged to borrow direct from the banking system rather than seek advances from the Treasury.

Other funds deposited with the Treasury, representing essentially the accounts of public commercial agencies, e.g., price stabilization funds, increased slightly in both 1967 and 1968 but expanded by about FMG 1.5 billion in 1969 owing to large deposits by the Coffee Price Stabilization Fund, which made substantial profits toward the end of 1969 when coffee prices rose sharply. According to the 1970 budget, these deposits were expected to expand by FMG 275 million on a net basis in that year. Since the financial position of several price stabilization funds had improved, the outcome was likely to be significantly better.

The total treasury deficit widened from FMG 4.8 billion in 1967 to FMG 6.7 billion in 1968 as a result of the large overall budgetary deficit. Although the latter increased in 1969, it was more than offset by the improvement in extrabudgetary treasury operations, and, consequently, the treasury deficit in 1969 was slightly below that of 1968. In 1970, the forecast was for it to increase again, to FMG 7.3 billion, but the actual deficit was likely to be much smaller if the possibility of a smaller-than-forecast overall budgetary deficit and net receipts from all other treasury operations were taken into consideration.

Financing of Treasury Deficit

In the financing of treasury deficits, foreign loans have tended to play an increasingly important role since 1967. The disbursement of loans in 1969, although less than budgeted, nevertheless reached FMG 2.3 billion and was the main source of foreign financing (Table 16). The French budgetary grant, although still substantial, amounted to only FMG 954 million in 1969, owing to delays in disbursements. Domestic borrowing, after a sharp decline in 1968, rose in 1969 to a record high figure of FMG 589 million (which was, however, still far short of the budgeted amount of FMG 3.7 billion). Domestic borrowing was largely in the form of sales of treasury bonds, primarily to enterprises, insurance companies, and banks. Total subscriptions to treasury bonds from October 1968, when they were first issued, to May 31, 1970 amounted to FMG 800 million. There are three types of bonds: (1) those maturing in six months and bearing interest at 3¼ per cent per annum; (2) those maturing in one year with interest at 4 per cent per annum; and (3) those maturing in two years with interest at 4¾ per cent per annum. A lottery feature is applied to some of these bonds. As a result of disbursements of foreign loans lower than had been expected in 1968, the Treasury used FMG 3.8 billion from its own resources to finance the deficit in that year. In the following year, owing to intensified foreign and domestic borrowing, use of the Treasury's liquid funds was reduced to FMG 2.8 billion.

The 1970 budget estimates provided for foreign borrowing of FMG 3.2 billion and for domestic borrowing of FMG 475 million. Both these estimates appeared to be realistic. As the French budgetary contribution was expected to amount to FMG 1.5 billion, the projected use of treasury resources to finance the budgetary deficit was estimated at FMG 2.1 billion in 1970. A law (*loi rectificative*) passed by Parliament in June 1970, however, limits the recourse of the Government to treasury resources to FMG 1.6 billion in 1970; this law also permits switching among various categories of expenditure. The reduction from FMG 2.1 billion to FMG 1.6 billion would be made possible by reimbursement to the Treasury of the unused portion of an advance of FMG 900 million that was made to the National Development Bank in 1967.

PUBLIC DEBT

The public debt of the Malagasy Republic is largely external (see Balance of Payments—External Debt, below). Its outstanding amount as of December 31, 1968 was estimated at FMG 1.1 billion; of this, FMG 747 million represented short-term treasury bonds issued in 1968; FMG 234 million, two medium-term loans obtained from a group of insurance companies for the equipment and modernization of the railroad company; and FMG 81 million, two long-term loans obtained in 1960 from the former Société Malgache d'Investissement et de Crédit (now replaced by the National Development Bank) and from the Malagasy Savings Bank for the construction of buildings.

MONEY AND BANKING

MONETARY SYSTEM

The Malagasy Republic is a member of the French franc area. Its monetary system in many respects resembles those of the African countries that have as their currency the CFA franc, but in contrast to them includes a separate central bank, the Malagasy Institute of Issue.[2] The country's banking system also includes four commercial banks, a development bank, a savings bank, and the Postal Checking System. The Institute of Issue issues the Malagasy franc (FMG), which on July 1, 1963 replaced at par the CFA franc that had circulated in Madagascar since 1945. The Malagasy franc is equivalent to 0.02 French franc. No par value has yet been agreed with the International Monetary Fund, but for payment of the currency portion of the increase in the Malagasy quota, the Fund agreed on March 18, 1966 to a provisional rate of FMG 246.853 = US$1.00. This rate was changed with Fund approval to FMG 277.710 = US$1.00, effective August 11, 1969.

---

[2] The CFA franc countries are the members of the Central Bank of Equatorial African States and Cameroon (Cameroon, Central African Republic, Chad, People's Republic of the Congo, and Gabon) and the members of the Central Bank of West African States (Dahomey, Ivory Coast, Mauritania, Niger, Senegal, Togo, and Upper Volta); see Volumes 1 and 3 of the *Surveys of African Economies*.

The present institutional framework of the monetary system has evolved on the basis of a cooperation agreement with France, concluded on June 27, 1960, relating to monetary, economic, and financial matters. This agreement specified that the Malagasy Republic would establish a national central bank and a national currency, the Malagasy franc. The Malagasy franc would be linked to the French franc at a fixed parity, which could be changed only with the consent of both parties, France and the Malagasy Republic. Should France decide to change the value of the French franc in terms of third currencies, it would consult the Malagasy Republic for the purpose of negotiating appropriate measures to safeguard the legitimate interests of the Malagasy Republic. Under the terms of the same agreement, France guarantees full convertibility of the Malagasy franc into French francs, and freedom of transfers between the two countries is maintained. For this purpose, it was agreed that the French Treasury would carry on its books an operations account in the name of the Institute of Issue, on which the latter would have the right to overdraft facilities.

The rules concerning the use of the operations account were set forth in a separate convention between the French Treasury and the Institute of Issue on March 10, 1963, according to which the Institute would hold its exchange reserves exclusively in French francs in its operations account. The account reflects Malagasy payments and receipts in French francs, in other currencies of the French franc area, and in currencies of countries outside the franc area; conversion of the last-named are effected through the Paris exchange market. On credit balances in its operations account, the Institute earns interest equal to the discount rate of the Bank of France plus, since 1967, a bonus (*prime de stabilité*), but the combined rate can never be less than 2½ per cent.

STRUCTURE AND OPERATIONS OF BANKING SYSTEM

Institute of Issue

The Malagasy Institute of Issue was established on March 10, 1962, replacing the Banque de Madagascar et des Comores, which had previously served as the bank of issue. In March 1968, the Institute moved into new headquarters in Tananarive. The Banque de Madagascar and another commercial bank still act on behalf of the Institute in the provinces, where they are the paying and receiving agents for the Treasury. The Institute does not pay any interest on deposits lodged with it by the Treasury.

The Institute has a paid-up capital of FMG 500 million, subscribed equally by France and the Malagasy Republic. The Board of Directors consists of 8 members, 4 members appointed by each country for four-year terms. The president of the Board of Directors is elected by the Board in agreement with the French and Malagasy Governments. The Board of Directors has broad powers. It decides on overall monetary policy, including the establishment of rediscount ceilings and changes in the rediscount rate, and resolves all questions pertaining to the issuance of currency. Decisions of the Board are taken by a simple majority vote. A general manager is appointed by the Board in agreement with the French and Malagasy Governments to manage the daily operations of the Institute.

A National Credit Council was created on July 13, 1962, consisting of 20 members, mostly civil servants, and meeting only on rare occasions. On December 11, 1964 a Banking Control Commission was established consisting of 4 members (the president of the Board of the Institute, the president of the Accounting Section of the Supreme Court, the director of the Treasury, and the president of the Banking Association). The Banking Commission, a more active body than the National Credit Council, regulates commercial banking in the country.

The operations of the Institute during the years 1965–70 are summarised in Table 17. The most striking features during this period were the movements in foreign assets and in government deposits. From FMG 12.7 billion at the end of 1966, foreign assets fell steadily to FMG 3.2 billion in September 1969, after which they rose again, and had more than tripled by the end of 1970. A small part of the rise was due to the allocation of SDR 3.2 million (on January 1, 1970), the counterpart of which is frozen in a special account (included in "Other items (net)" in Table 17). Government deposits, which amounted to FMG 8 billion at the end of 1965 and FMG 8.4 billion at the end of 1966, were almost completely drawn down in 1967–70. In June 1969, when its deposits were already nearly depleted, the Government began to discount some of its customs duty bills. Such discounts reached a

TABLE 17. MALAGASY REPUBLIC: ASSETS AND LIABILITIES OF INSTITUTE OF ISSUE, 1965-70

(In millions of Malagasy francs; end of period)

	1965	1966	1967	1968	1969 Mar.	1969 June	1969 Sept.	1969 Dec.	1970 Mar.	1970 June	1970 Sept.	1970 Dec.
Assets												
Foreign assets [1]	12,316	12,708	10,602	7,629	6,660	4,441	3,236	5,383	7,901	9,476	9,577	10,314
Operations account	*11,699*	*11,836*	*9,739*	*6,160*	*5,307*	*3,093*	*1,418*	*3,716*	*5,886*	*7,444*	*7,488*	*7,766*
Claims on government	—	—	—	—	—	1,168	1,079	2,981	2,276	1,937	502	—
Claims on banks												
Advances	342	116	242	93	505	133	118	54	105	57	—	106
Rediscounts	12,148	13,044	14,853	14,308	13,201	15,403	17,617	13,896	12,134	11,156	14,951	17,209
Short-term	*11,717*	*12,023*	*13,554*	*13,504*	*12,025*	*13,071*	*15,122*	*11,079*	*9,391*	*8,250*	*11,617*	*13,345*
Medium-term	*431*	*1,021*	*1,299*	*804*	*1,176*	*2,332*	*2,495*	*2,817*	*2,743*	*1,906*	*3,334*	*3,884*
Other	—	414	377	—	—	—	—	—	—	—	—	—
Total claims on banks	12,490	13,574	15,472	14,401	13,706	15,536	17,735	13,950	12,239	11,213	14,951	17,315
Assets = liabilities	24,806	26,282	26,074	22,030	20,366	21,145	22,050	22,314	22,416	22,626	25,030	27,629
Liabilities												
Currency	15,766	16,771	19,145	19,334	18,171	19,597	20,359	20,552	19,621	19,811	22,396	23,841
In circulation outside banks	*15,592*	*16,506*	*18,938*	*19,097*	*17,956*	*19,314*	*20,092*	*20,343*	*19,331*	*19,533*	*22,162*	*23,561*
Held by banks	*174*	*265*	*207*	*237*	*215*	*283*	*267*	*209*	*290*	*278*	*234*	*280*
Bankers' deposits	56	39	29	47	80	377	95	34	47	82	148	14
Government deposits	8,027	8,399	5,702	1,427	635	31	5	1	1	1	2	1,485
Foreign liabilities	1	2	—	—	—	—	—	—	1	1	1	—
Capital accounts	831	963	1,108	1,287	1,287	1,287	1,318	1,318	2,282	2,414	2,414	2,417
Other items (net) [2]	125	108	90	-65	193	-147	273	409	464	318	69	-128

Sources: IMF, *International Financial Statistics*; and data provided by the Malagasy Institute of Issue.

[1] Foreign assets other than those held in the operations account with the French Treasury comprise the IMF gold tranche position, the allocation of SDRs on January 1, 1970, and a subscription to World Bank bonds.

[2] Beginning in 1970, includes counterpart of SDRs.

peak of FMG 2.9 billion in December 1969; they declined to FMG 1.9 billion in May 1970 and ceased in December 1970 when government deposits amounted to FMG 1.5 billion. The Government has so far not obtained any direct advances from the Institute.

Currency in circulation has shown a continuous rise from year to year. It expanded more in the good crop year of 1967, reflecting the more intensive use of currency as a means of transaction in rural areas; there was also a very large increase in 1970 (see Table 17). Owing to seasonal patterns, currency outside banks fluctuates fairly widely during the year, usually reaching its trough in March and its peak in September or the last quarter of the year.

Claims on banks outstanding at the end of the year were higher in 1966 and 1967 but fell in 1968 and 1969. From FMG 13.9 billion in December 1969, they continued to decline, reaching FMG 11.2 billion in June 1970. This downward trend was the result of a deliberate policy of greater restraint by which the monetary authorities wished to compensate for the drawing down of government deposits; stricter ceilings on rediscounts and raises in the rediscount rate in January and November 1969 were used. The downward trend in rediscounts would have been even more marked had the rediscounting of medium-term credit not risen from FMG 0.8 billion in December 1968 to FMG 2.8 billion in December 1969 and further to FMG 3.9 billion in December 1970, as part of the Government's program to induce the banks to participate more actively in the financing of certain development projects. In May 1970 nearly half of the medium-term credit extended by the banks had been rediscounted by the central bank. The rediscounting of medium-term credit continued to rise after May 1970, reaching FMG 3.9 billion in December. As this rise coincided with a renewed expansion of short-term rediscounts, claims on banks rose to FMG 17.3 billion in December 1970.

Capital accounts, including certain reserve funds, rose from FMG 0.8 billion in December 1965 to FMG 2.4 billion in December 1970.

Commercial Banks and National Development Bank

Four commercial banks operate in the Malagasy Republic, with branches in various parts of the country. They are the Banque de Madagascar et des Comores, the Banque Malgache d'Escompte et de Crédit, the Banque Nationale pour le Commerce et l'Industrie—Océan Indien, and the Banque Franco-Chinoise. These banks are owned mainly by foreign interests, largely French, but the Malagasy Government holds 35 per cent of the subscribed capital of the Banque Malgache d'Escompte et de Crédit and 12.5 per cent of the subscribed capital of the Banque de Madagascar et des Comores.

The Malagasy National Development Bank was created in 1963, replacing the Société Malgache d'Investissement et de Crédit, which had in turn succeeded the Crédit de Madagascar in 1960. The National Development Bank has a share capital of FMG 1 billion, of which FMG 650 million has been subscribed by the Malagasy Government and the remainder by the French Caisse Central de Coopération Economique (CCCE). It is administered by a council of 12 members, of whom 8 are representatives of the Malagasy Government and 4 are representatives of France.

The Development Bank may extend short-term, medium-term, and long-term credit to individuals, companies, and public institutions to promote economic development, particularly in agriculture. It may also finance handicraft industries, manufacturing, and housing and may provide consumer credit. Furthermore, it is authorized to contribute to the financing of capital equipment programs of rural development agencies, agricultural cooperatives, and other semipublic and public entities either through loans or through capital participation. The Bank's resources stem largely from medium-term and long-term borrowing—including loans from the Malagasy Treasury, the Postal Checking System, and the CCCE—from rediscounting with the Institute of Issue, and, to a lesser extent, from demand and time deposits. Average outstanding credit extended by the Bank rose from FMG 5.5 billion in 1966 to FMG 9.4 billion in 1969, with the largest expansion (FMG 1.8 billion) occurring in 1969. Between 1966 and 1969, the share of agriculture in average outstanding loans fell from close to 40 per cent to about 29 per cent, that of housing from 19 per cent to 14 per cent, and that of small-scale enterprises from 8 per cent to 4 per cent; on the other hand, the share of industry and commerce rose from 31 per cent to 52 per cent, and loans to the public sector remained virtually unchanged (2 per cent in 1965 and 3 per cent in 1969). Of the average outstanding credit in

1969, 42 per cent was long term, 35 per cent was medium term, and 23 per cent was short term. Industry and commerce accounted for the largest portion of long-term and medium-term credit, followed by housing and agriculture; 79 per cent of short-term credit went to the agricultural sector and 18 per cent to small-scale family enterprises.

The operations of the commercial banks and the short-term and medium-term operations of the Development Bank (hereafter referred to as operations of the banks) are consolidated and summarized in Table 18. The Development Bank's long-term operations are excluded from this table, but are consolidated with the operations of the Savings Bank (see Other Financial Institutions, below).

The banks traditionally keep low reserves, relying instead on relatively easy access to credit from the central bank or, in certain instances, from their head offices abroad. The ratio between reserves and demand deposits fluctuates, owing to seasonal requirements, between 1.5 per cent and 3 per cent. Because of favorable export performance since the autumn of 1969, foreign assets of the banks had risen to FMG 5.9 billion in December 1970, a 74 per cent increase over the previous year. Claims on the Government represent mainly credits in connection with government contracts and tended to decline between 1967 and 1969, when they amounted to FMG 1.7 billion. In 1970, however, they increased to FMG 2.9 billion.

Short-term bank credits to the private sector are mostly to finance crops and the discounting of commercial paper relating to exports and imports. The seasonal pattern—a trough in the first quarter and a peak in the last quarter—reflects the financing of agricultural crops, which for the most part are harvested during the second half of the year. Such credits rose by 17 per cent in 1967, mainly on account of the good agricultural crop. In 1968, because of credit restrictions by the central bank through reduction and closer scrutiny of rediscounting following the high level of credit on December 31, 1967, short-term credit expansion was limited to slightly more than 3 per cent. There was no seasonal decline in short-term credit from December 1968 to March 1969 because of speculative imports and stockpiling in anticipation of price increases in France. For the year 1969 as a whole the increase in short-term credit by the banks to the private sector amounted to FMG 1.1 billion (3 per cent), a rate comparable to that of the previous year and

TABLE 18. MALAGASY REPUBLIC: CONSOLIDATED ASSETS AND LIABILITIES OF COMMERCIAL BANKS, 1965–70 [1]

(In millions of Malagasy francs; end of period)

	1965	1966	1967	1968	1969				1970			
					Mar.	June	Sept.	Dec.	Mar.	June	Sept.	Dec.
Assets												
Reserves												
Currency	233	317	220	365	253	377	413	249	486	344	256	310
Balances at Institute of Issue	174	265	207	237	215	283	267	209	290	278	234	280
Foreign assets [2]	59	52	13	128	38	94	145	40	196	66	22	30
Claims on government	1,119	1,470	2,535	2,674	2,563	2,294	3,036	3,407	3,504	4,107	3,516	5,924
Claims on official entities	1,922	2,347	2,366	1,973	1,464	1,573	1,725	1,663	1,266	2,513	2,679	2,869
Claims on private sector	27,937	31,232	36,417	39,059	38,836	40,019	42,777	41,176	38,773	38,587	44,952	48,446
Short-term	26,036	28,330	33,235	34,382	34,709	35,154	37,442	35,517	32,742	32,376	38,419	41,555
Medium-term	1,901	2,902	3,182	4,677	4,127	4,865	5,224	5,659	6,031	6,211	6,533	6,891
Assets = liabilities	31,211	35,366	41,538	44,071	43,116	44,263	47,951	46,495	44,029	45,551	51,403	57,549
Liabilities												
Demand deposits	11,725	13,316	13,930	16,167	15,018	15,114	15,602	17,063	16,071	15,850	17,837	17,787
Time deposits	1,583	2,398	4,153	4,250	5,378	5,950	5,962	6,167	6,838	7,472	7,764	10,000
Government deposits [3]	1,638	1,836	4,429	5,561	4,960	5,382	5,605	5,725	6,154	5,590	4,978	5,774
Foreign liabilities [2]	779	1,015	1,489	1,513	2,129	1,407	1,708	1,826	1,259	1,658	1,861	2,529
Credit from Institute of Issue	12,444	13,625	15,629	14,613	13,865	15,608	17,821	14,059	12,148	11,253	15,160	17,227
Capital accounts	2,031	2,115	2,340	2,467	2,508	2,565	2,606	2,691	2,788	3,901	3,960	3,931
Other items (net)	1,011	1,061	−432	−500	−742	−1,763	−1,353	−1,036	−1,229	−173	−157	301
Related data: Postal checking deposits	1,916	1,830	2,027	2,046	2,166	2,185	2,141	1,992	2,202	2,089	2,104	1,998

Sources: IMF, *International Financial Statistics*; and data provided by the Malagasy Institute of Issue.

[1] Including short-term and medium-term credit operations of the National Development Bank.

[2] Foreign assets are overstated because of the inclusion of export credits, and foreign liabilities are understated because of the exclusion of certain import credits that are not available separately at present.

[3] Comprises deposits of public enterprises with commercial banks (FMG 2.0 billion on December 31, 1969), advances of more than six months by the Treasury and the Postal Checking System to the National Development Bank, and the Treasury's deposits for the *ras du sol* program.

a sign that the further curtailment in rediscount ceilings and the two upward changes in the rediscount rate had been effective.

During the first few months of 1970, and in contrast to developments during the same period of 1969, short-term credit showed the customary decline. By June 1970, it had fallen to FMG 32.4 billion, FMG 6.6 billion below the previous peak in August 1969 and FMG 2.8 billion below the level of June 1969. This development was largely the result of additional measures of restraint applied by the monetary authorities in 1970: rediscounts were subjected to closer scrutiny and, for the first time, an overall ceiling on short-term credits in excess of FMG 5 million was applied for each bank, with the exception of the National Development Bank. This new ceiling differentiates between two categories of credit: one, judged more essential, was related to the stocking of agricultural products, to exports, and to government contracts; the other was related to imports, consumer credit, and overdrafts. Average outstanding credit in the first category, which amounted to about one third of total credit, was allowed generally to exceed the 1969 average by 15 per cent; in the second category it was usually not to exceed the average level for 1969. During 1970 as a whole, short-term credit expanded by 17 per cent as a result of a more favorable export performance.

Since the end of December 1968 a more detailed classification of short-term credit is available as a result of the declarations submitted to the Credit Information Office (Centrale des Risques). From this source it becomes apparent that the restraining measures of the monetary authorities have had the desired impact on credit to the commercial sector, while credit to the agricultural and industrial sectors has been allowed to expand (Table 19).

Medium-term credit to the private sector is provided mainly to finance investments in industry and agriculture and the construction of housing. Such credit increased at an average annual rate of 25 per cent in the years 1967–70; the increase in 1968 was 47 per cent. Until the end of 1968, the major share of medium-term credit was extended by the National Development Bank, largely from resources raised through medium-term borrowing. In order to encourage greater participation by the commercial banks in medium-term operations, they were required to grant medium-term loans equal to at least 3 per cent of their deposit

TABLE 19.   MALAGASY REPUBLIC: SHORT-TERM BANK CREDIT
BY ECONOMIC ACTIVITY, 1968–MARCH 1970 [1]

(*In millions of Malagasy francs*)

	1968	1969				1970
	Dec.	Mar.	June	Sept.	Dec.	Mar.
Commerce	15,401	14,890	14,371	15,197	14,734	12,861
Agriculture, livestock, fishing, and forestry	5,465	4,812	4,970	5,718	6,523	6,746
Mechanical, metallurgical, and electric industries	3,526	3,596	3,995	4,062	3,899	4,287
Industries transforming local products	3,075	2,457	3,302	4,470	3,680	2,495
Textile industry	2,293	2,452	2,726	2,391	2,319	2,299
Petroleum, chemical, and pharmaceutical sector	1,244	1,400	1,316	1,309	1,102	992
Public works and housing	1,905	1,950	1,810	1,732	1,753	1,508
Mining	465	427	458	465	404	423
Transportation	269	532	502	399	270	218
Other	1,386	1,207	1,460	1,554	1,381	1,414
Total	35,029	33,723	34,910	37,297	36,065	33,243

Source: Data provided by the Malagasy Institute of Issue.

[1] Commercial bank credit to private sector. Data in this table are based on declarations to the Credit Information Office, and so differ slightly from data in Table 18, which are based on balance sheet entries.

liabilities by June 30, 1969 and equal to 5 per cent thereafter. This measure provided some relief to the Development Bank: certain of its medium-term loans were taken over by the commercial banks under the auspices of a newly created consortium, and in the second half of 1969 the commercial banks extended several new medium-term loans. As a further inducement, the Institute of Issue kept the rediscount rate for medium-term loans unchanged at 3¾ per cent when the basic discount rate was raised to 4½ per cent and later to 5½ per cent. Consequently, medium-term credit rose in 1969 by almost FMG 1 billion, to FMG 5.7 billion, and further to FMG 6.9 billion in 1970.

Changes in demand deposits lodged with the banks are largely a function of changes in credit and in foreign assets. The seasonal pattern broadly mirrors that of short-term credit to the private sector. After demand deposits rose by 16 per cent in 1968, the rate of expansion was more moderate in 1969 and 1970, viz., 6 per cent and 4 per cent, respectively.

Time deposits have shown a spectacular growth over recent years
and almost quadrupled between 1965 and 1969; the increase was 62
per cent in 1970. Successive upward shifts in interest rates to keep
them at levels higher than in France contributed to a steady growth of
time and savings deposits, especially in 1969 and 1970.

Government deposits as defined in Table 18 comprise, in addition to
certain deposits by the Treasury, deposits by public agencies, mainly
the price stabilization funds, and loans in excess of six months by the
Treasury and the Postal Checking System to the Development Bank
(government lending funds). The sharp rise in government deposits in
1967 was due almost exclusively to an increase in these loans to the
Development Bank, some of which were partially repaid in May 1970.
The increase in government deposits between March 1969 and March
1970 (FMG 1.2 billion or 24 per cent) is explained mainly by rising
deposits of the stabilization funds. In December 1970, government
deposits amounted to FMG 5.8 billion.

Foreign liabilities reflect, among other transactions, those between
the commercial banks and their head offices abroad. The fluctuations
are caused by the seasonal pattern of lending and by the degree of ease
or restrictiveness governing credit from the central bank. The absolute
level, although rising over the years, as well as the swings within each
year have remained relatively low compared with the banks' other liabilities and capital accounts.

Credit from the Institute of Issue to the banks is, from an analytical
point of view, one of the most important indicators, because it shows to
what extent the central bank has been willing to supplement the banks'
other resources, such as deposits by the private sector and the Government, access to head offices abroad, and the banks' own funds. From
Table 18 it becomes evident that recourse to the central bank—despite
allowances for seasonal needs—was restricted between 1967 and 1969
with the exception of rediscounted medium-term loans, which rose
rather markedly. In 1970, however, central bank credit was expanded
by 23 per cent, reflecting in part increased export financing and a larger
volume of medium-term rediscounts.

The item "Capital accounts" in Table 18 excludes the capital
account of the National Development Bank. As these accounts include

various reserve funds, they normally show a rise at the beginning of a calendar year, when part of the net income has been transferred to the capital account. The ratio of the banks' capital accounts to total deposits or to total credit to the private sector fell over the years 1965–69; in the latter year, solvency ratios [3] were introduced and the ratio of capital accounts to total deposits rose in 1970.

Other Financial Institutions

Other financial institutions include the Postal Checking System and the Savings Bank. In addition, however, the Treasury performs certain banking functions for public and semipublic institutions and provides credit to the private sector by accepting promissory notes in payment of indirect taxes and customs duties. The amount of such promissory notes fluctuates between FMG 2 billion and FMG 3 billion.

Table 20 provides a consolidation of the operations of the Savings Bank and the long-term operations of the National Development Bank (other operations of the Development Bank are included in Table 18, above). The claims on the Government are the counterpart of the savings deposits collected by the Savings Bank, the major part of which the Government has redeposited abroad. Savings deposits with the Savings Bank rose from FMG 1.3 billion in 1965 to FMG 1.8 billion in 1969, and to FMG 1.9 billion in September 1970. The interest rate paid on these deposits was raised in April 1970 from 3¼ per cent to 3¾ per cent.

Long-term credit to the private sector, which is granted exclusively by the Development Bank, rose from FMG 1.7 billion in 1965 to FMG 4.2 billion in 1969 and FMG 4.7 billion in September 1970. The major share goes to industry and commerce, followed by housing and agriculture. Foreign liabilities reflect long-term loans to the Development Bank from the CCCE (France) and the Kreditanstalt für Wiederaufbau (Germany). They rose from FMG 2.4 billion in 1965 to FMG 3 billion in 1969 and FMG 4.1 billion in September 1970. The item "Capital account" covers only that of the Development Bank.

---

[3] For a definition of the solvency ratio, see Instruments of Monetary Policy, below.

TABLE 20.   MALAGASY REPUBLIC: ASSETS AND LIABILITIES OF
OTHER FINANCIAL INSTITUTIONS, 1965–SEPTEMBER 1970 [1]

(In billions of Malagasy francs; end of period)

	1965	1966	1967	1968	1969	Sept. 1969	1970
Assets							
Claims on government [2]	1.26	1.34	1.45	1.68	1.81	1.81	1.94
Claims on private sector [3]	1.71	2.20	2.56	3.36	4.23	3.98	4.68
Claims on banks	0.14	0.17	0.18	0.18	0.18	0.18	0.18
Assets = liabilities	**3.11**	**3.71**	**4.19**	**5.22**	**6.22**	**5.97**	**6.80**
Liabilities							
Savings deposits	1.26	1.34	1.45	1.68	1.81	1.81	1.94
Foreign liabilities	2.38	2.71	1.96	2.53	3.03	2.66	4.14
Credit from commercial banks	...	...	0.06	0.02	—	—	—
Capital account [4]	1.16	1.28	1.07	1.07	1.07	1.07	1.06
Other items (net)	−1.69	−1.62	−0.35	−0.07	0.31	0.43	−0.34

Sources: IMF, *International Financial Statistics*; and data provided by the Malagasy authorities.

[1] A consolidation of the long-term operations of the National Development Bank and all operations of the Savings Bank.
[2] Largely redeposited abroad.
[3] Largely long-term loans.
[4] Development Bank only.

STRUCTURE OF INTEREST RATES

The Malagasy interest rate structure has, with a few exceptions, shifted upward as a result of two increases in the basic rediscount rate (i.e., the rediscount rate for short-term paper).

On January 2, 1969, the rate at which the Institute of Issue rediscounts short-term paper was raised from 3¾ per cent to 4½ per cent, except that the rate for export bills remained at 3 per cent, and that for bills secured by local products remained at 3¾ per cent. On the same date, the rate charged by the Institute of Issue on advances was raised from 4¾ per cent to 5½ per cent. The rate for medium-term rediscounting had been raised from 3½ per cent to 3¾ per cent in June 1968; but the commission was lowered simultaneously from ½ of 1 per cent to ¼ of 1 per cent (this commission has even been suspended for certain types of credit, particularly to public enterprises).

On November 17, 1969, the rediscount rate for short-term paper was raised from 4½ per cent to 5½ per cent, that for bills secured by local agricultural products from 3¾ per cent to 4¾ per cent, and that for export financing bills from 3 per cent to 4 per cent. The rate charged by the Institute of Issue on advances was also raised, from 5½ per cent to 6½ per cent. Only the rediscount rate for medium-term credit remained unchanged, at 3¾ per cent, consistent with the monetary authorities' desire to encourage medium-term lending.

Interest rates charged by commercial banks are determined by an interbank agreement. These rates were adjusted selectively following the increases in the rediscount rates, with more of the adjustment burden falling on credit for nonessential imports and nonrediscountable loans than on loans for the production, marketing, and exporting of local products. The prime rate, which was 5 per cent before January 2, 1969, rose to 5¾ per cent thereafter and to 6¾ per cent in November. Rates for operations that are not eligible for rediscount are generally 1¼ to 2 per cent higher, depending on the type of credit, than those for rediscountable credit. According to estimates of the Institute of Issue, the average cost of credit rose from 7½ per cent in 1968 to 9 per cent after November 1969. The National Development Bank charges either all-inclusive rates or interest plus commission. The inclusive rates range from 6 per cent to 12 per cent on short-term credits for small household equipment and subsistence agriculture, and from 3 per cent to 6 per cent for medium-term and long-term credit, while nominal interest rates range from 5 per cent to 8 per cent to which are added commissions of ½ of 1 per cent to 2 per cent per annum.

The interest paid by commercial banks on time deposits was also raised in November 1969, as follows: for deposits of six months to one year, from 3.70 per cent to 4.60 per cent; for deposits of more than one year, and up to two years, from 4.35 per cent to 5.15 per cent; and for deposits of more than two years, from 5.35 per cent to 6.15 per cent. These rates were deliberately set at a level higher than in France so as to discourage the outflow of funds from Madagascar. Rates on certificates of deposit (*bons de caisse*) were raised twice in 1969 and now range from 3.60 per cent on deposits of six months to less than one year to 5.50 per cent on deposits of five years or more. These rates, although nominally lower than those for certificates of deposit in France, compare favorably, in most cases, when allowance is made for the fact that they are tax exempt in Madagascar but taxable in France.

INSTRUMENTS OF MONETARY POLICY

Policy instruments available to the monetary authorities consist mainly of ceilings and other limits on credits to banks, changes in the rediscount rates, liquidity [4] and solvency ratios,[5] and ceilings on government borrowing.

Ceilings on Central Bank Credit to Banks

Ceilings on credit extended by the Institute of Issue to the banks are the most important means of credit control in Madagascar because the banks have to borrow heavily from the Institute to finance their short-term and medium-term credit operations.

Periodically—usually three times a year—the Board of Directors of the Institute meets to establish an overall rediscount ceiling for short-term credit (less than one year) to the banks, taking into account the existing resources of the banks as well as a projected, desirable level of short-term credit. This overall ceiling, which may vary from month to month to allow for seasonal needs, is divided into a separate rediscount ceiling for each bank, based on the volume of the bank's deposits, the level of any other resources, and the size of its loan portfolio. An exception is made for the Banque de Madagascar et des Comores, which, because of its previous central banking functions, did not hold sufficiently large private deposits in relation to its operations. Between meetings of the Board of Directors, the management of the Institute is authorized, in case of need, to adjust the rediscount ceilings for the commercial banks by 5 per cent and for the Development Bank by 10 per cent. Furthermore, outside their rediscount ceilings, the banks may obtain advances from the Institute at an interest rate which is 1 percentage point higher than the rediscount rate, and they may also borrow against collateral (*mises en pension*) provided that the paper matures in a period not exceeding 15 days.

---

[4] The ratio of liquid assets to short-term liabilities.
[5] The ratio of resources to lending.

The Board of Directors of the Institute also establishes, periodically, an overall ceiling for medium-term credit (from one to five years) based on investment forecasts and the general monetary situation. This ceiling is, however, only indicative in nature and is not divided into individual ceilings for each bank. Each request by a bank to rediscount a medium-term loan is considered by the Institute on its merits. In order to be eligible for rediscount, the medium-term paper must be related to the financing of investments in production, construction, and housing that have received the prior approval of the Institute, to assure that a proper balance is maintained between the bank's own and its borrowed resources: for investments in commerce, a minimum of 50 per cent has to be financed from the investor's own resources; for expansion of an existing enterprise, up to 70 per cent (and in certain instances even up to 80 per cent) may be financed by medium-term loans. As a general rule, the Institute is prepared to rediscount medium-term paper relating to imports of capital goods only if financing from abroad is not available.

The Institute's rediscount policy also includes the establishment of selective credit ceilings at the enterprise level, mainly to ensure sound financial management. These individual limits are thus based on the enterprise's creditworthiness and their total may exceed the overall ceiling on rediscounts. They are applied when certain minimum standards with regard to bookkeeping and general financial control are met. The individual limit for each enterprise is subdivided into seven categories: (1) domestic commercial bills; (2) foreign trade bills; (3) bills secured by government contracts; (4) bills secured by stocks of imported goods; (5) bills secured by stocks of local products; (6) paper related to prefinancing and overdrafts; and (7) paper related to consumer credit. In setting these individual limits for enterprises and in dividing them into categories, the Institute also pursues structural economic objectives favoring credits connected with the production, stocking, and marketing of agricultural products and restraining credits for imports, especially imports of nonessential goods or goods competing with domestic production. Lending by banks to enterprises beyond these established limits is at a penalty rate of interest, which is usually 1¼ to 2 per cent higher than the interest rate for rediscountable loans.

Changes in Rediscount Rate

For a number of years the Institute of Issue kept the basic rediscount rate (for short-term paper) unchanged. However, in 1969, when pressures on domestic prices persisted and net foreign assets declined, the Institute twice raised the basic rediscount rate: on January 2, 1969 from 3¾ per cent to 4½ per cent, and again on November 17, 1969 to 5½ per cent (see also Structure of Interest Rates, above).

Liquidity and Solvency Ratios

In December 1968, the Banking Control Commission introduced both liquidity and solvency ratios for commercial banks, which became effective in January 1969.

The banks are required to maintain a prescribed liquidity ratio, i.e., their liquid assets must equal a minimum proportion of their short-term liabilities. Liquid assets are defined as cash, foreign exchange, claims on government, and rediscountable short- and medium-term claims on the private sector. Short-term liabilities consist of demand deposits, liabilities to the Institute of Issue, and contingent liabilities of the banks on account of customs duty bills. This ratio was set at 70 per cent in 1969; it was raised to 73 per cent in 1970 and to 75 per cent in 1971.

The banks are obliged to maintain two solvency ratios (*coefficients de solvabilité*): (1) the sum of the bank's capital and reserves (*ressources propres*) must be equivalent to 7.5 per cent of the sum of all the bank's lending; (2) the sum of the bank's capital and reserves (*ressources propres*), less its fixed assets, doubtful claims, and claims under litigation, must be equivalent to 4 per cent of the sum of all the bank's lending. The accounts of the commercial banks are verified three times a year (on April 30, August 31, and December 31) to assure compliance with these requirements.

Ceilings on Government Borrowing

The Institute of Issue is authorized to extend direct and indirect short-term credit to the Government in the following forms: (1) direct advances to the Treasury at the prevailing rediscount rate for a period not exceeding 240 days, consecutive or not, in a calendar year—this period may be extended by a special waiver of the Board of Directors until the first working day of the following calendar year; (2) rediscounting and purchasing treasury bills, or making advances to banks against treasury bills having a maturity of less than 6 months, provided that the central bank credit extended indirectly to the Government in this way may not exceed for each bank 10 per cent of its average private deposits during the preceding 12 months; (3) discounting customs duty bills (promissory notes accepted by the Treasury from the private sector in lieu of payment of indirect taxes and customs duties) for the Treasury having a maturity of less than 4 months and having received a guarantee by a bank. The total amount of short-term credit granted to the Government through advances and treasury bill operations (but excluding discounting of customs duty bills) may not exceed either 10 per cent of average private deposits with the banks, the Postal Checking System, and the Treasury during 12 months, or 15 per cent (raised from 10 per cent in April 1970) of the fiscal receipts of the Malagasy Government during the preceding calendar year.

MONETARY AND CREDIT DEVELOPMENTS, 1965–70

Overall monetary and credit movements are summarized in Table 21, which is a consolidation of the balance sheets of the Institute of Issue, the four commercial banks, the short-term and medium-term lending of the National Development Bank, and the deposits of the Postal Checking System.

In the period 1965 through 1969, domestic credit expanded by 90 per cent, net foreign assets declined by 45 per cent, and the money supply increased by 35 per cent. Quasi-money showed a spectacular increase of 290 per cent. Domestic credit expansion reached its peak in 1967, when it rose by 22 per cent. Through stricter control of rediscount ceilings, successive selective rises in the rediscount rates, and the imposition of liquidity ratios, the rate of domestic credit expansion was reduced to 18 per cent in 1968 and 17 per cent in 1969. The monetary authorities had to curtail credit to the private sector in order to bring about this reduction since the Government, although in a net creditor position throughout almost the whole of this period, made increasing use of its previously accumulated deposits. As already explained, the authorities used selective credit controls so as to minimize the interfer-

TABLE 21. MALAGASY REPUBLIC: MONETARY SURVEY, 1965–70

(In millions of Malagasy francs; end of period)

	1965	1966	1967	1968	1969 Mar.	1969 June	1969 Sept.	1969 Dec.	1970 Mar.	1970 June	1970 Sept.	1970 Dec.
Assets												
Foreign assets (net)[1]	12,655	13,161	11,648	8,790	7,094	5,328	4,564	6,964	10,145	11,925	11,231	13,709
Domestic credit	22,110	25,174	30,679	36,090	36,871	39,532	42,112	42,086	38,362	39,535	45,257	46,054
Claims on government (net)	−5,827	−6,058	−5,738	−2,969	−1,965	−487	−665	910	−411	948	305	−2,392
Claims on private sector	27,937	31,232	36,417	39,059	38,836	40,019	42,777	41,176	38,773	38,587	44,952	48,446
Assets = liabilities	34,765	38,335	42,327	44,880	43,965	44,860	46,676	49,050	48,507	51,460	56,488	59,763
Liabilities												
Money	29,233	31,652	34,895	37,310	35,140	36,613	37,835	39,398	37,604	37,472	42,103	43,346
Currency in circulation	15,592	16,506	18,938	19,097	17,956	19,314	20,092	20,343	19,331	19,533	22,162	23,561
Demand deposits	11,725	13,316	13,930	16,167	15,018	15,114	15,602	17,063	16,071	15,850	17,837	17,787
Postal checking deposits	1,916	1,830	2,027	2,046	2,166	2,185	2,141	1,992	2,202	2,089	2,104	1,998
Quasi-money[2]	1,583	2,398	4,153	4,250	5,379	5,950	5,962	6,167	6,838	7,472	7,764	10,000
Other items (net)[3]	3,949	4,285	3,279	3,320	3,446	2,297	2,879	3,485	4,065	6,516	6,621	6,417

Sources: IMF, *International Financial Statistics*; and data provided by the Malagasy Institute of Issue.

[1] Foreign assets (net) are overstated because of the inclusion of export credits but the exclusion of foreign liabilities arising from certain import credits not separately available at present.
[2] Time deposits.
[3] Beginning in 1970, includes counterpart of SDRs.

ence with Madagascar's economic development. Table 22 indicates that in 1967–68 the larger part of the increase in domestic credit went to the private sector. By 1969, the restraining measures of the monetary authorities had had sufficient effect, and the increase in credit to the private sector was smaller than the expansionary effect from the continuous drawdown of government deposits and the discounting by the Government, commencing in June 1969, of customs duty bills. Both in 1968 and 1969 the central bank reduced its facilities to the banks. The selective character of the central bank's policy becomes apparent if one considers that its rediscounts of short-term paper decreased in 1969 by FMG 2.4 billion (18 per cent), while rediscounts of medium-term loans, which the bank wishes to encourage, increased by FMG 2.0 billion, or 250 per cent (Table 17).

The impact of credit expansion on the money supply was mitigated by continuous losses in net foreign assets of the banking system and by considerable increases in time deposits in at least two out of the three years under review. The money supply increased by 10 per cent in 1967, by 7 per cent in 1968, and by less than 6 per cent in 1969. The ratio of currency in the hands of the private sector to total demand deposits (including postal checking deposits) fell from 53 per cent at the end of 1965 to 51 per cent in May 1970. Postal checking deposits increased only modestly over the years compared with currency or demand deposits held with the banks.

After a small rise in 1966, net foreign assets of the banking system fell in each of the following years, in part reflecting the large domestic credit expansion. The decline was most marked in 1968 (24 per cent), when time deposits showed virtually no increase, a sign that depositors were unwilling to increase their monetary savings that year. In 1969, in contrast, the loss in net foreign assets was FMG 1 billion smaller, since almost FMG 2 billion of funds had been shifted into time deposits, at least partly in response to the rise in interest rates implemented by the banks early in 1969 and then again later in the year.

Beginning in the autumn of 1969, the monetary and credit situation showed a marked improvement, due in part to the policies pursued by the Malagasy authorities and in part to the favorable developments in world markets for Malagasy exports. For the 12 months ended May 1970 the rate of domestic credit expansion was down to less than 4 per

TABLE 22.   MALAGASY REPUBLIC: CHANGES IN MONEY SUPPLY BY MAJOR DETERMINANTS, 1967–70[1]

(In billions of Malagasy francs)

| | Expansion or Contraction (−) in | | | | | | |
| | 12 months ended December | | | | 12 months ended May | | |
	1967	1968	1969	1970	1968	1969	1970
Foreign assets, net	−1.51	−2.86	−1.83	6.75	−1.42	−3.90	4.60
Institute of Issue	−2.11	−2.97	−2.25	4.93	−2.08	−3.39	3.35
Commercial banks	0.59	0.12	0.42	1.81	0.66	−0.50	1.25
Domestic credit	5.51	5.41	5.99	3.96	7.24	6.05	1.41
Claims on government, net	0.32	2.77	3.88	−3.30	2.84	1.08	2.32
Claims on private sector	5.19	2.64	2.11	7.27	4.40	4.97	−0.92
(Financed by Institute of Issue)	(1.90)	(−1.07)	(−0.45)	(3.37)	(0.45)	(2.11)	(−3.51)
Time deposits (increase −)	−1.75	−0.10	−1.92	−3.83	−0.58	−1.50	−2.11
Other items, net (increase −)	1.00	−0.04	−0.17	−2.93	−0.16	0.10	−2.26
Net expansion	3.25	2.41	2.07	3.95	5.08	0.75	1.64
Money supply	3.24	2.42	2.09	3.95	5.09	0.75	1.64
Currency in circulation	2.43	0.16	1.24	3.22	2.08	0.65	0.60
Demand deposits	0.61	2.24	0.90	0.73	2.61	0.36	0.99
Postal checking deposits	0.20	0.02	−0.05	0.01	0.39	−0.27	0.05
Increase in money supply	10.3%	6.9%	5.6%	10.0%	16.8%	2.1%	4.6%

Sources: IMF, *International Financial Statistics*; and data provided by the Malagasy Institute of Issue.

[1] Items may not add to totals, and total of expansionary or contractionary factors may differ slightly from changes in money supply, due to rounding.

cent, and credit to the private sector had even decreased; net foreign assets rose by 61 per cent, money supply by less than 5 per cent, and quasi-money by 38 per cent.

For 1970 as a whole, domestic credit expanded by 9 per cent, reflecting only partly the large increase in credit to the private sector. Domestic credit expansion would have been greater had the Government not reverted to building up its deposits with the central bank. With a near doubling in net foreign assets and an increase of 62 per cent in quasi-money, the expansion in money supply was limited to only 10 per cent. Currency in circulation showed a greater rise, reflecting in part larger cash balances in the agricultural sector derived from higher producer prices and favorable crops, and the ratio of currency to the total money supply reached 54 per cent in 1970.[6]

BALANCE OF PAYMENTS

Except for a small surplus of $2 million in 1966, as measured by the changes in net foreign assets of the banking system, the balance of payments was in deficit each year in the 1965–69 period. In general, Madagascar has relied on inflows of official grants and loans to offset substantial trade deficits. As seen in Table 23, both the trade deficit and the net inflow of aid declined in 1967. The trade deficit expanded in 1968 and 1969, as the slow growth in exports failed to keep pace with expanding imports. The increase in grants and loans was modest and the balance of payments deficit widened to $11.6 million in 1968 and was approximately $7 million in 1969. In 1970, data for the first nine months indicated a sharp reduction in the trade deficit, resulting from a substantial expansion in exports accompanied by a slight reduction in imports. The change in net foreign assets of the banking system indicated a substantial balance of payments surplus for the year.

A striking improvement in the balance of payments began in the autumn of 1969. The foreign assets of the Institute of Issue increased from $10.6 million at the end of August 1969 to $37.3 million (includ-

---

[6] The reader is referred to the International Monetary Fund's monthly statistical bulletin, *International Financial Statistics,* for later information on monetary and credit developments.

TABLE 23.   MALAGASY REPUBLIC: BALANCE OF PAYMENTS, 1965–69

(In millions of U. S. dollars) [1]

	1965	1966	1967	1968	1969
A. Merchandise	**−21.52**	**−24.99**	**−22.89**	**−30.01**	**−40.28**
Exports (f.o.b.)	91.68	97.76	104.16	115.89	112.96
Imports (f.o.b.)	−113.20	−122.75	−127.05	−145.90	−153.24
B. Services	**−19.60**	**−21.73**	**−7.16**	**−7.26**	**−8.71**
Transportation	−14.36	−22.45	−19.67	−20.98	−25.51
Travel	−7.69	−4.05	−3.64	−3.73	−1.44
Investment income	−16.92	−17.92	−18.70	−14.85	−13.32
Other government	20.60	23.93	36.27	34.19	38.94
Other services	−1.23	−1.24	−1.42	−1.88	−7.37
C. Goods and services (A+B)	**−41.12**	**−46.72**	**−30.05**	**−37.26**	**−48.99**
D. Unrequited transfers	**25.76**	**42.73**	**37.71**	**44.05**	**47.70**
Private	−10.29	1.30	−1.57	−2.73	8.27
Government [2]	36.05	41.43	39.28	46.78	39.43
E. Nonmonetary capital	**9.36**	**11.41**	**3.58**	**4.23**	**7.90**
Government	0.40	6.91	1.15	2.95	7.16
Receipts from loans	*1.72*	*8.01*	*2.30*	*4.90*	*8.43*
Amortization	*−1.32*	*−1.10*	*−1.15*	*−1.94*	*−1.27*
Private	8.96	4.50	2.43	1.28	0.74
Long-term	...	...	...	*2.60*	*1.15*
Short-term	...	...	...	*−1.32*	*−0.41*
F. Total (C+D+E)	**−6.00**	**7.42**	**11.23**	**11.02**	**6.62**
G. Errors and omissions	**3.76**	**−5.37**	**−17.36**	**−22.60**	**−13.70**
H. Monetary movements (increase −)	**2.24**	**−2.05**	**6.13**	**11.58**	**7.07**
Institute of Issue	0.85	−1.58	8.52	12.04	8.70
Commercial banks	1.39	−0.47	−2.39	−0.46	−1.63

Source: Data provided by the National Institute of Statistics and Economic Research and the Ministry of Finance and Commerce.

[1] The original data in Malagasy francs were converted to U.S. dollars at the official rate of FMG 1 = US$0.004051 for the years 1965–68. For 1969 the conversion rate used was calculated as an average of that rate and of the new rate established on August 11, 1969 (FMG 1 = US$0.003601), weighted according to their respective periods of application during the year, and amounted to FMG 1 = US$0.003875.

[2] Consists of receipts of foreign grants as credit items, and Malagasy contributions to international organizations and for technical assistance as debit items.

ing the equivalent of $3.2 million of SDRs) at the end of May 1970, the highest level since January 1968; at the end of December 1970 they amounted to $37.1 million. The trade balance was the most important factor in this improvement. For the period October 1969–April 1970, exports were about $28 million higher than in the comparable period of 1968–69, while imports were below their earlier level. The trade deficit

was $24 million in the first nine months of 1970, compared with a
deficit of $67 million in the same period of 1969.

TRADE

Exports

Madagascar exports mainly primary products of various kinds.
In recent years, agricultural products have accounted for more than
two thirds of total exports, although both the share and the value
of these exports declined in 1969 (Table 24). Coffee, vanilla, rice,
sugar, cloves, and sisal are the most important export products, but
Madagascar also exports small amounts of minerals, animal and meat
products, and chemical products, all of which have been increasing in
recent years.

After gaining steadily for many years, exports of coffee, the most
important export commodity, declined by more than FMG 0.5 billion in
1969, to FMG 8.3 billion. Madagascar produces the robusta variety,
and for the 12-month period beginning October 1969 its export quota
was initially set at 44,000 tons by the International Coffee Organization
(ICO),[7] whereas the final quota for the previous 12 months had been
53,000 tons. The 1969/70 quota was increased by 4,000 tons during
the year, reflecting the impact of the frost in Brazil on world coffee
supplies. Prices for all types of coffee rose sharply: for robusta, the
ICO indicator price moved to $0.42 a pound during the second quarter
of 1970, from $0.30 a pound a year earlier. Although cyclones caused
damage to the 1969 and 1970 crops, Madagascar was able to meet its
quota from stocks.

Over one half of Madagascar's coffee exports are to EEC countries;
France, the principal purchaser, took 47 per cent in 1969. These ship-
ments, under the terms of the first Yaoundé Convention, are duty free.
The duty on coffee imported by EEC countries from nonassociated

---

[7] Quotas are allocated by the International Coffee Organization to the African
and Malagasy Coffee Organization, which in turn distributes the quotas among its
member countries (Cameroon, the Central African Republic, the People's Republic of the Congo, Dahomey, Gabon, Ivory Coast, the Malagasy Republic, and
Togo).

Table 24. Malagasy Republic: Composition of Exports, 1966–69

(Value in millions of Malagasy francs)

	Value				Per Cent of Total			
	1966	1967	1968	1969	1966	1967	1968	1969
Main agricultural products	**17,271**	**18,162**	**21,324**	**19,349**	**71.6**	**70.6**	**74.5**	**66.4**
Coffee	7,593	8,122	8,803	8,270	31.5	31.5	30.8	28.4
Sugar	1,485	2,138	1,575	1,656	6.2	8.3	5.5	6.7
Sisal	972	721	749	904	4.0	2.8	2.6	3.1
Rice	1,052	1,854	3,047	2,438	4.4	7.2	10.7	8.4
Vanilla	2,216	1,672	2,530	3,013	9.2	6.5	8.8	10.3
Tobacco [1]	1,267	711	594	763	5.2	2.8	2.1	2.6
Raffia	812	918	687	516	3.4	3.6	2.4	1.8
Groundnuts	295	364	301	247	1.2	1.4	1.1	0.8
Cloves	579	876	1,952	407	2.4	3.4	6.8	1.3
Pepper	260	259	492	565	1.1	1.0	1.7	1.9
Peas	545	340	516	521	2.2	1.3	1.7	1.8
Cassava	195	152	78	49	0.8	0.6	0.2	0.2
Minerals	**978**	**1,740**	**1,787**	**2,185**	**4.0**	**6.8**	**6.2**	**7.4**
Graphite	455	432	433	509	1.9	1.7	1.5	1.7
Mica	258	260	303	390	1.1	1.0	1.1	1.3
Petroleum products	166	982	985	1,043	0.7	3.8	3.4	3.6
Chromite				206				0.7
Other	99	65	66	39	0.4	0.2	0.2	0.1
Miscellaneous	**5,883**	**5,809**	**5,497**	**7,619**	**24.4**	**22.6**	**19.2**	**26.1**
Animal and meat products	2,001	1,839	1,874	2,436	8.3	7.1	6.6	8.4
Tapioca	246	240	245	199	1.0	0.9	0.9	0.7
Hides and skins	586	372	312	467	2.4	1.4	1.1	1.6
Wood products	153	123	168	222	0.6	0.5	0.6	0.8
Chemical products	594	555	884	1,100	2.5	2.2	3.1	3.8
Other exports	2,303	2,680	2,014	3,195	9.5	10.4	7.0	11.0
Total exports	**24,132**	**25,711**	**28,608**	**29,154**	**100.0**	**100.0**	**100.0**	**100.0**

Sources: Institut National de la Statistique et de la Recherche Economique, *Bulletin Mensuel de Statistique*, April 1970 and various other issues; and data provided by the Malagasy authorities.

[1] Including cigarettes.

countries was reduced from 9.6 per cent to 7 per cent in January 1971, when the second Yaoundé Convention entered into force. Madagascar plans to expand coffee production to about 80,000 tons by 1974.

Madagascar is the principal world supplier of vanilla, and that commodity ranked second among the country's exports in 1969. Exports totaled FMG 3 billion, an increase of nearly FMG 0.5 billion over 1968, with the bulk going to the United States and almost 20 per cent to France. Export prices and quotas are the subject of special arrangements with U. S. and European importers. For the United States, for example, a committee of U.S. and Malagasy representatives meets toward the end of each year to negotiate prices and quantities for shipments in the following year. In the face of strong competition from synthetics, future markets depend to a large extent upon the continued promotion of natural vanilla. The Vanilla Price Stabilization Board, with financial assistance from the Government, destroyed excess stocks in 1967; stocks are now maintained at about 1,100 tons, equal to one year's exports.

Production of rice in 1968 was 1.5 million tons and 69,000 tons were exported. In 1969, production was insufficient to meet domestic demand and the authorities imported 43,000 tons of lower-quality rice —the first rice imports since 1966. Nevertheless, Madagascar exported 52,000 tons of higher-quality rice. Although the principal customers for rice are France and the neighboring islands of Réunion and the Comoros, Madagascar may face increasing marketing difficulties in Réunion and France. Rice sold in France, as well as in other EEC countries, is taxed at a rate that may adversely affect imports from Madagascar. Prices in Réunion have fallen, in line with world market prices, and may continue to fall in the future. Nevertheless, Madagascar as a marginal supplier might have less difficulty in expanding its exports within the context of the fundamental adjustment of rice production trends and trading positions currently taking place.

Sugar exports rose in 1969 by 6,000 tons, while in value terms the increase was FMG 81 million (5 per cent). Three fourths of total sugar exports were sold under the terms of the sugar agreement of the Common Organization of African, Malagasy and Mauritian States, primarily to Senegal. In 1969, 7,755 tons of sugar were sold to the United States, and Madagascar had a slightly higher quota for 1970 in the

U. S. market. Other customers for Malagasy sugar include the Comoro Islands and France.

Cloves ranked fourth among agricultural commodities exported in 1968, but dropped to tenth in 1969. Clove production normally follows a three-year cycle, with crops usually being harvested in the autumn and exported some months later. Output reached a peak of 13,000 tons in 1967, and exports of 12,000 tons in 1968 earned almost FMG 2 billion. In 1968, production fell to 500 tons and exports in 1969 were 974 tons. With the severe contraction in supply, prices rose from $0.32 a pound in 1968 to $1.65 a pound in 1969. Production recovered in 1969 to 2,500 tons, however, and was expected to reach 3,500 tons in 1970. Malaysia and Indonesia are the chief purchasers, and future sales depend primarily on the success of market negotiations with these two countries.

Sisal exports advanced by 17 per cent in 1969, to FMG 900 million, France and other EEC countries being the principal customers. This performance reflected an average price increase of FMG 5 a kilogram, which more than offset a slight decline in tonnage shipped.

Madagascar's exports of animal and meat products totaled FMG 2.4 billion in 1969 and accounted for more than 8 per cent of total exports. A new chromite installation began operations during 1969, with a capacity of 120,000 tons; in the last half of 1969, 33,000 tons were exported valued at FMG 200 million. There were also increased exports of chemical products, hides and skins, wood products, various minerals in addition to chromite, and agricultural products other than those mentioned above. Petroleum exports are discussed below under Imports.

Imports

Consumer goods including foodstuffs account for a good share of imports (Table 25). However, with the development of industries producing import subsitutes, the proportion of raw materials and fuels in total imports rose from 25 per cent in 1966 to 28 per cent in 1969. Capital goods imports advanced strongly in 1968 and 1969, as the Government financed investments under the Major Works Program. Altogether, imports rose by 10 per cent, to FMG 46.2 billion, in 1969

TABLE 25. MALAGASY REPUBLIC: COMPOSITION OF IMPORTS, 1966–69

(*Value in millions of Malagasy francs*)

	Value				Per Cent of Total			
	1966	1967	1968	1969	1966	1967	1968	1969
Consumer goods	**8,532**	**18,299**	**21,106**	**21,204**	**53.0**	**50.8**	**50.2**	**45.9**
Foodstuffs	4,778	3,760	4,373	5,795	13.7	10.5	10.4	12.5
Automobiles and buses	1,052	1,160	1,441	1,394	3.0	3.2	3.4	3.0
Textiles and clothing	4,620	5,423	6,684	5,036	13.2	15.1	15.9	10.9
Pharmaceutical products	966	976	1,266	1,160	2.8	2.7	3.0	2.5
Paper products	952	1,182	1,366	1,384	2.7	3.3	3.3	3.0
Capital goods	**7,535**	**8,681**	**9,885**	**11,982**	**21.6**	**24.2**	**23.5**	**25.9**
Machinery and equipment	3,508	3,332	3,860	5,825	10.0	9.3	9.2	12.6
Trucks	775	1,235	1,535	1,617	2.2	3.4	3.7	3.5
Tractors	176	398	452	433	0.5	1.1	1.3	1.0
Other agricultural machinery	125	135	188	217	0.4	0.4	0.4	0.5
Electrical equipment	2,508	2,482	2,326	2,900	7.2	6.9	5.5	6.3
Raw materials and fuels	**8,864**	**8,904**	**11,034**	**13,012**	**25.4**	**24.8**	**26.3**	**28.2**
Crude oil	604	1,138	1,617	1,938	1.7	3.2	3.8	4.2
Other petroleum products	1,514	756	724	948	4.3	2.1	1.7	2.1
Cement	404	319	412	427	1.2	0.9	1.0	0.9
Fertilizers	111	269	458	476	0.3	0.7	1.1	1.0
Cotton fiber	141	180	270	214	0.4	0.5	0.6	0.5
Iron bars and plates	1,366	1,445	1,678	2,139	3.9	4.0	4.0	4.6
Total imports	**34,931**	**35,884**	**42,024**	**46,198**	**100.0**	**100.0**	**100.0**	**100.0**

Sources: Institut National de la Statistique et de la Recherche Economique, *Bulletin Mensuel de Statistique*, April 1970 and various other issues; and data provided by the Malagasy authorities.

after an increase of FMG 6.1 billion in 1968 and in comparison with annual increases of less than FMG 1 billion in 1964–67. The 1969 increase was evenly divided between imports of capital goods and raw materials, including fuels; imports of consumer goods edged upward by about FMG 100 million.

Some of the 1969 increase in imports reflected unusual, nonrecurring demand, such as the equipment and furnishings for the new Hilton hotel in Tananarive and delivery to Air Madagascar of a new jet aircraft. The increase in raw materials and fuels suggests, in part, stockbuilding by importers, perhaps in anticipation of higher prices in supplier countries. Stockbuilding might also have accounted for the FMG 461 million increase in imports of iron bars and plates. Imports of rice, the first since 1966, totaled 43,000 tons valued at FMG 1.5 billion, and were needed to satisfy domestic demand; this increase more than accounted for the rise in foodstuff imports. Textile and clothing imports declined by FMG 1.6 billion, to FMG 5.0 billion; their share in total imports dropped from 16 per cent in 1968 to 11 per cent in 1969.

In 1966 when the refinery at Tamatave was opened, Madagascar began to import crude oil and to process it for both domestic use and export. As seen in Table 26, imports of crude oil totaled FMG 1,938 million in 1969. Exports of petroleum products, purchased mainly by Réunion, reached FMG 1,043 million in 1969. The net deficit on trade in petroleum products, which had contracted sharply in 1967, grew in 1968 and again in 1969. Imports of other petroleum products, primarily

TABLE 26.   MALAGASY REPUBLIC: IMPORTS AND EXPORTS
OF PETROLEUM PRODUCTS, 1965–69

(*In millions of Malagasy francs*)

	1965	1966	1967	1968	1969
Imports					
Crude oil	—	6,604	1,138	1,617	1,938
Other petroleum products	1,642	1,514	756	724	948
Exports	—	166	982	985	1,043
Net imports	1,642	1,952	912	1,356	1,843

Source: Institut National de la Statistique et de la Recherche Economique, *Bulletin Mensuel de Statistique*.

refined, are still substantial, although considerably below the amounts in 1965 and 1966. The refinery capacity is inadequate to meet increased domestic and foreign demand, and will be expanded by 25 per cent.

Direction of Trade

As seen in Table 27, trade with France dominates the overall import-export picture of the Malagasy Republic. However, France's share has declined in recent years, while those of the other EEC countries and the United States have been enhanced.

The value of imports from France in 1969 was FMG 24 billion, a decline of about FMG 2.5 billion from 1968. France's share in the Malagasy import market declined steadily from 64 per cent in 1966 to 52 per cent in 1969, in spite of the devaluation of the French franc in August 1969, which improved the competitiveness of French goods. On the other hand, the large, one-time imports in 1969 of rice, an aircraft, and hotel equipment and furnishings were not from France. Furthermore, Madagascar is continuing to seek out suppliers offering the lowest prices. Of total Malagasy exports in 1969, about 36 per cent went to France, compared with 34 per cent in 1968, 37 per cent in 1967, and 46 per cent in 1966. The balance of trade between France and Madagascar shows large deficits for the latter, which, however, declined from FMG 16.8 billion in 1968 to FMG 13.4 billion in 1969.

Imports from the other EEC countries were freed from quantitative restrictions in 1968 and their share in Malagasy imports increased from 11.5 per cent in 1967 to 18.3 per cent in 1969. In value terms, imports from the EEC countries other than France totaled FMG 8.5 billion in 1969, an increase of FMG 2.9 billion over 1968. Germany has had the largest part of the gains. These EEC countries as a group have also been purchasing more of Madagascar's exports; their share was 7.6 per cent in 1969, compared with 7.2 per cent in 1966. Exports to these countries dropped off in 1967, but recovered in 1968 and reached FMG 2.2 billion in 1969. The Malagasy trade deficit with the EEC countries other than France grew from FMG 1.9 billion in 1966 to FMG 6.3 billion in 1969.

Imports from the United States, on the other hand, have fluctuated from year to year, but show a general upward trend and reached

TABLE 27. MALAGASY REPUBLIC: DIRECTION OF TRADE, 1966–69

(*Value in millions of Malagasy francs*)

	Value				Per Cent of Total			
	1966	1967	1968	1969	1966	1967	1968	1969
Exports	**24,132**	**25,711**	**28,608**	**29,154**	**100.0**	**100.0**	**100.0**	**100.0**
France	11,057	9,428	9,584	10,561	45.8	36.7	33.5	36.2
EEC other than France	1,744	1,280	1,925	2,207	7.2	5.0	6.7	7.6
Germany	793	731	1,038	1,112	3.3	2.8	3.6	3.8
Italy	555	331	449	603	2.3	1.3	1.6	2.1
Netherlands	269	155	331	277	1.1	0.6	1.2	1.0
Belgium-Luxembourg	127	63	107	215	0.5	—	0.4	0.7
United States	5,503	6,315	6,431	6,910	22.8	24.6	22.5	23.7
Japan	253	386	464	678	1.0	1.5	1.6	2.3
Réunion	1,858	2,715	3,369	3,560	7.7	10.6	11.8	12.2
Senegal	549	1,156	930	943	2.3	4.5	3.3	3.2
Ivory Coast	155	352	420	460	0.6	1.4	1.5	1.6
Imports	**34,931**	**35,884**	**42,024**	**46,198**	**100.0**	**100.0**	**100.0**	**100.0**
France	22,238	23,206	26,423	23,949	63.7	64.7	62.9	51.8
EEC other than France	3,623	4,122	5,612	8,469	10.4	11.5	13.4	18.3
Germany	1,775	1,933	2,587	4,323	5.1	5.4	6.2	9.4
Italy	667	894	1,474	1,859	1.9	2.5	3.5	4.0
Netherlands	752	809	902	1,307	2.2	2.3	2.1	2.8
Belgium-Luxembourg	429	486	649	980	1.2	1.4	1.5	2.1
United States	2,236	2,457	2,111	2,969	6.4	6.8	5.0	6.4
Japan	873	960	1,026	1,152	2.5	2.7	2.4	2.5
Senegal	720	528	1,087	1,093	2.1	1.5	2.6	2.4
Ivory Coast	39	22	123	157	0.1	—	0.3	0.3

Sources: Institut National de la Statistique et de la Recherche Economique, *Bulletin Mensuel de Statistique*, April 1970; and data provided by the Malagasy authorities.

FMG 3 billion in 1969; this included the new aircraft. Exports have moved steadily upward from FMG 5.5 billion in 1966 to FMG 6.9 billion in 1969. Coffee, sugar, and vanilla accounted for almost FMG 4 billion in the later year. The 1969 trade surplus with the United States of FMG 3.9 billion was about FMG 400 million less than in 1968, but marginally higher than that in 1967.

Exports to Réunion have advanced steadily in recent years, as have those to the Comoro Islands and Mauritius. Trade with Japan has also been stepped up. Imports from Japan totaled FMG 1.2 billion in 1969, up FMG 126 million from 1968; exports to Japan totaled FMG 678 million, and the trade deficit with Japan contracted from FMG 562 million in 1968 to FMG 474 million in 1969.

CURRENT INVISIBLES

Net payments for services, which averaged over $20 million annually in 1965–66, declined sharply, to some $7 million, in 1967–68 as receipts on account of government services expanded. Transportation charges showed a rising trend in this period with the increasing import volume. On the other hand, the outflow of investment income, which had increased from 1965 to 1967, dropped sharply in 1968. Payments on account of travel also declined, but payments on account of other services increased steadily during these years. In 1969, the continued receipts on account of government services and the decline in payments on account of travel and investment income were more than offset by the increases in transportation charges and in payments for other services. The deficit on goods and services also worsened in 1969, but it reflected mainly the sharp deterioration in the trade deficit, which rose to $40 million from $30 million in 1968.

PRIVATE CAPITAL

Private unrequited transfers, which consist of receipts from pensions, private scholarships and private education funds, and resident workers' remittances, behaved erratically over the period 1965–69. There was a substantial outflow of $10 million in 1965, but an inflow of $8 million in 1969.

Private nonmonetary capital declined steadily from $9 million in 1965 to $0.7 million in 1969. Detailed statistics are not available for the years 1965–67, but the data for 1968 and 1969 show that an outflow of short-term capital was offset by an inflow of long-term capital in both years.

OFFICIAL LOANS AND GRANTS

Foreign grants appear in the balance of payments as government unrequited transfers, whereas official loans appear as government nonmonetary capital (Table 23). Government unrequited transfers include, as a debit item, Malagasy contributions for technical assistance and to international organizations, which totaled about $5.6 million a year during 1966–69. Government nonmonetary capital in Table 23 consists of disbursements from foreign official sources on the credit side and of debt amortization on the debit side.

In general, receipts from foreign aid offset, to a considerable extent, the large deficit that Madagascar incurs on the goods and services account. Since 1967, the proportion received as grants has tended downward and greater reliance has been placed on official loans.

Total gross foreign grants amounted to $52 million in 1968 and to $44 million in 1969 (Table 28). France provided the greatest part of these funds, although that country's contribution declined from $36 million in 1966 to $27 million in 1969. Some of this decline has been offset by grants from the European Development Fund and the UN Development Program. Under the terms of the first Yaoundé Convention, the equivalent of $730 million in aid was made available to the Associated African States and Madagascar through the second European Development Fund. Most of this amount consisted of grants, on a project-by-project basis, and Madagascar received over $44 million in the period 1966–69. Under the second Yaoundé Convention and the third European Development Fund, $918 million will be available to the Associated States in the period 1971–75.

Disbursements of foreign loans were only $2.3 million in 1967 but rose to $4.9 million in 1968 and to $8.4 million in 1969, as Madagascar intensified its borrowing to finance investments (Table 28). The sources of borrowing have also been diversified. In 1965 and 1966, for example, Germany and France were the largest contributors of new credit, while in 1968 and 1969 the International Development Associa-

TABLE 28. MALAGASY REPUBLIC: DISBURSEMENTS OF OFFICIAL FOREIGN AID, 1965-70[1]

(*In millions of U. S. dollars*)

	1965	1966	1967	1968	1969	1970 [2]
Grants						
France	35.52	36.42	33.61	33.13	27.02	...
FAC	*3.10*	*5.22*	*4.28*	*4.86*	*2.44*	...
Budgetary contribution	*6.97*	*6.89*	*6.68*	*6.48*	*4.84*	...
Technical assistance	*18.64*	*17.77*	*16.76*	*16.14*	*14.10*	...
Other [3]	*6.81*	*6.55*	*5.89*	*5.65*	*5.63*	...
European Development Fund	11.00	8.95	10.02	12.05	13.54	...
United Nations	1.26	1.97	1.20	6.96	3.75	...
Other [4]	0.03	0.06	0.01	0.29	0.02	...
Total grants	47.80	47.40	44.84	52.43	44.33	...
Loans						
France	2.85	1.35	0.28	0.61	0.56	—
World Bank Group	—	—	0.37	1.80	2.98	8.79
United States	—	—	0.04	0.01	1.95	0.86
Germany	0.41	6.45	1.61	0.36	0.02	—
Italy	—	—	—	—	—	2.03
Israel	—	0.20	—	—	1.07	—
Public bonds	—	—	—	2.11	1.86	...
Total loans	3.26	8.01	2.30	4.90	8.44	11.67
Total foreign aid	51.06	55.41	47.13	57.33	52.76	...

Source: Data provided by the Malagasy authorities.

[1] The original data in Malagasy francs were converted to U.S. dollars at the official rate of FMG 1 = US$0.004051 for the years 1965-68. For 1969 the conversion rate used was calculated as an average of that rate and of the new rate established on August 11, 1969 (FMG 1 = US$0.003601), weighted according to their respective periods of application during the year, and amounted to FMG 1 = US$0.003875. The available 1970 data were converted at the new official rate.

[2] Estimated.

[3] Mainly assistance for the construction and operation of the University of Madagascar and other technical schools, and for scholarships.

[4] Italy and Germany.

tion (IDA) was the chief source of funds, although France, the United States, and Israel also disbursed considerable amounts. Disbursements by the IDA totaled about $3 million in 1969 and were for road construction. The United States provided close to $2 million for the improvement and extension of the telephone system and the railways. The $1 million from Israel was toward the construction of a hotel in Tananarive. Substantial amounts of undisbursed funds from several sources are still in the pipeline.

Malagasy officials have estimated that loan disbursements in 1970 would amount to $11.7 million, of which the World Bank Group was expected to provide $8.8 million, Italy $2 million from a loan of $5.8 million negotiated in 1969, and the United States $0.9 million. In the summer of 1970, the IDA announced loans equivalent to $9.6 million for the improvement of the port of Tamatave and $5 million for rice irrigation projects.

EXTERNAL DEBT

The outstanding foreign debt of the Malagasy Republic amounted to $88.6 million (FMG 24.6 billion) on December 31, 1969 (Table 29). Most of this debt was to foreign governments, the French Government accounting for $59.2 million. Debt owed to France includes FIDES loans granted by France before independence, which were consolidated in 1962 into a 1 per cent interest-bearing loan maturing over 40 years, and CCCE loans, most of which are for 11–20 years and bear interest of 2½ per cent. The second major creditor country was Germany, followed by the United States and Israel. At the end of 1969 disbursements by international organizations were limited to the World Bank Group; disbursement had not started on a loan of $1.9 million contracted with the European Development Fund in 1969. Privately held debt amounted to $9.4 million, of which $5.2 million was in the form of suppliers' credits. Total loans contracted, including undisbursed, amounted to $120 million (FMG 33.3 billion) on December 31, 1969.

In 1970, amortization and interest payments on foreign debt were expected to amount to $6.9 million, payable mostly to governments and the private sector. Thereafter, debt service payments are scheduled to be larger owing to increased repayments to governments and international organizations. However, they are not expected to be a heavy burden on the balance of payments in the next few years, since the ratio of debt service payments to exports is relatively modest.

INTERNATIONAL RESERVES

Madagascar's international reserves are largely in the form of balances held by the Malagasy Institute of Issue in its operations account with the French Treasury, but they also include the gold tranche position with the International Monetary Fund and, since January 1970, SDRs (the allocation on January 1, 1970 was SDR 3.2 million).

Madagascar began independence in 1960 with a comfortable level of

TABLE 29. MALAGASY REPUBLIC: OUTSTANDING EXTERNAL DEBT AS OF DECEMBER 31, 1969, AND SCHEDULE OF SERVICE PAYMENTS, 1970–75

(In thousands of U. S. dollars)

Creditor	Debt Outstanding December 31, 1969 [1]		Debt Service Payments [2]					
	Disbursed only	Including undisbursed	1970	1971	1972	1973	1974	1975
Private sector								
Publicly issued bonds	4,132	4,132	465	462	461	460	459	458
Suppliers' credits	5,204	5,204	823	1,401	699	571	554	538
Loans from financial institutions	36	636	11	10	43	75	71	67
Total private sector	9,371	9,971	1,298	1,873	1,203	1,106	1,084	1,062
International organizations								
European Development Fund	—	1,862	—	—	—	—	—	—
World Bank	220	11,100	31	155	279	479	656	689
International Development Association	4,851	14,500	59	89	100	109	109	109
Total international organizations	5,071	27,462	90	244	380	588	765	798
Loans from governments								
France	59,183	63,613	4,141	4,609	4,903	5,109	4,771	4,139
Germany	11,664	13,030	1,196	1,202	1,190	1,179	1,211	1,230
Israel	1,203	1,203	174	267	257	179	171	162
United States	2,081	4,757	14	105	185	200	200	200
Total loans from governments	74,132	82,603	5,524	6,183	6,536	6,668	6,353	5,732
Total external debt	88,574	120,036	6,912	8,300	8,118	8,362	8,202	7,592

Source: Data provided by the International Bank for Reconstruction and Development.

[1] Debt with an original or extended maturity of over one year.
[2] Calculated in August 1970.

reserves. Foreign assets of the Institute of Issue totaled $48 million at the end of 1962 and reached a peak of $54 million at the end of November 1966, an amount equivalent to about 40 per cent of 1966 imports. From that time until the end of August 1969 there was a steep downward trend, to $10.6 million (FMG 2.9 billion). The deterioration in the foreign assets position, particularly in 1968, reflected in part the deficit financing and related credit expansion associated with increased investments. A striking reversal took place after September 1969: by May 1970 the foreign assets of the Institute of Issue had increased by $26.7 million, to $37 million, and at the end of 1970 they again amounted to some $37 million, equivalent to about 22 per cent of 1970 imports.

Foreign assets of commercial banks were $16.2 million at the end of 1962 but were only $4.4 million at the close of 1965. Since that time, they have risen steadily from year to year, reaching $15 million in May 1970 and $22 million in December. Foreign liabilities followed a similar course, moving from a low of $3.2 million at the end of 1965 to $7.1 million in May 1970 and $9 million in December. Net foreign assets of the Malagasy banking system totaled some $50 million on December 31, 1970.

EXCHANGE AND TRADE CONTROL SYSTEM [8]

EXCHANGE RATE SYSTEM

The Malagasy Republic is a member of the French franc area, and its exchange regulations are based on those applied in France, adapted to fit its own particular requirements. Exchange control measures do not apply to transactions with (1) France and its Overseas Departments and Territories (except that of the Afars and Issas); (2) Monaco; and (3) any other country whose bank of issue is linked with the French Treasury by an operations account.[9] Hence, all payments

---

[8] As of December 31, 1970. The reader is referred to the International Monetary Fund's *Annual Report on Exchange Restrictions* for later and more detailed information on exchange and trade controls.

[9] These countries are Cameroon, the Central African Republic, Chad, the People's Republic of the Congo, Dahomey, Gabon, Ivory Coast, Mali, Mauritania, Niger, Senegal, Togo, and Upper Volta.

to these areas may be made freely. All other countries are considered foreign countries, and financial transactions with them are subject to exchange control.

No par value for the Malagasy franc has been established with the International Monetary Fund. The official rate which was established on August 11, 1969 is FMG 1 = F 0.02, giving the relationship FMG 277.710 = $1. The prior official rate was FMG 246.853 = $1. The Malagasy Institute of Issue, in transactions with commercial banks, is ready to buy and sell Malagasy francs against French francs at the fixed rate of FMG 1 = F 0.02, free of commission. Exchange rates for other currencies are based on the fixed rate for the French franc and the Paris market rates for the other currencies concerned and are subject to commissions.

Madagascar's foreign exchange reserves are held by the Institute of Issue in an operations account with the French Treasury. France guarantees the unlimited conversion of the Malagasy franc into French francs. To make a transfer to a country outside the franc area, a commercial bank first obtains French francs against Malagasy francs from the Institute, which debits the operations account for the transaction; the bank then exchanges the French francs for the required currency on the Paris exchange market. In practice, commercial banks maintain current accounts with their correspondents in France through which they offset purchases and sales of currencies other than franc area currencies.

After the reintroduction of exchange control (on November 25, 1968), the Institute of Issue temporarily suspended the redemption of its banknotes when presented by residents of foreign countries. Redemption was resumed late in 1970, when such banknotes could again be credited to convertible nonresident accounts in the names of authorized banks' foreign correspondents.

REGULATIONS GOVERNING IMPORTS AND EXPORTS

Imports

All imports from countries outside the EEC and outside the French franc area are subject to import licenses, which are issued in accordance with an annual import program (see below). As a rule, imports originating in and shipped from franc area and EEC countries are free from restriction. However, licenses are required for imports from the franc area if such goods originated from outside that area and were not processed in a franc area country in accordance with certain rules; and licenses are required for all imports from the French territory of the Afars and Issas. In order to protect infant industries, imports of edible oils, used jute bags, used empty barrels, secondhand clothing, shoes, blankets, confectionery and biscuits, tomato concentrates, cotton, and fibranne (a synthetic fiber) are subject to license irrespective of origin or port of shipment. Imports of certain types of beer, new jute bags, new barrels, old newspapers, small candles, and certain types of ploughs are either prohibited or have been suspended until further notice. Special restrictions apply to imports of certain wines and of electric batteries: import licenses are issued only when evidence has been submitted that a specified amount has been bought from local production. Imports of cement, household soap, large and small sardines, tuna fish, and pilchards are covered by regional arrangements (*jumelage* agreements) with Senegal and Ivory Coast: for cement an import license is issued only when evidence has been submitted that 55 per cent of the import value has been ordered from Senegal, and for soap, only upon evidence that 35 per cent of the import value has been ordered from Senegal and another 35 per cent from Ivory Coast. Imports from Rhodesia are prohibited.

All import transactions relating to foreign countries must be domiciled with an authorized bank. The import licenses (or import certificates for liberalized commodities) entitle importers to purchase the necessary exchange, provided that the shipping documents are submitted to the authorized bank.

Import Program.—The import program is determined by a joint French-Malagasy committee. It establishes annual import quotas that are applicable to all countries that are not members of the EEC and are outside the franc area. Special ceilings agreed in the committee are established for dairy products and automobiles imported from all countries outside the franc area; these ceilings are included in the import program.

Madagascar's import policy was substantially liberalized in 1968 by the removal of restrictions on imports from the EEC countries. Import

TABLE 30. MALAGASY REPUBLIC: IMPORT PROGRAMS, 1968–70

(*In millions of Malagasy francs*)

	Total Quotas	General Reserve	Grand Total
1968			
Quotas available	7,960	500	8,460
Licenses issued	6,796	335	7,131
Utilization rate	85.4%	67.0%	84.3%
1969			
Quotas available	8,814	500	9,314
Licenses issued	7,607	450	8,057
Utilization rate	86.3%	90.0%	86.5%
1970			
Quotas available	8,252	500	8,752

Source: Data provided by the Malagasy authorities.

quotas in respect of all other countries have generally been increased over the years. The quotas for 1970 were set at FMG 8,752 million, whereas they were FMG 9,314 million (at the predevaluation rate) in 1969 (Table 30). The 1969 quota included provisions for unusual, one-time imports of furnishings and equipment for a new hotel, a new aircraft, and rice. The utilization of import quotas increased from 84.3 per cent in 1968 to 86.5 per cent in 1969, reflecting in part a greater use of the reserve quotas. Those items for which the complete quotas were used in 1969 included foodstuffs, beverages other than beer, cement, metals, petroleum products, plastic goods, textiles, and household items. On the other hand, only small portions of the quotas for beer and fabrics were used.

Exports

Exports may be carried out freely with the exception of specified commodities. Coffee, vanilla, cloves, pepper, sugar, rice, petroleum, and petroleum products require exit permits (*autorisations de sortie*), which are issued by the appropriate price stabilization fund. Export licenses are issued by the Foreign Trade Office for re-exports of products previously imported from outside the franc area and having a value exceeding FMG 250,000 and of certain other items. Exports to Rhodesia are prohibited.

Export proceeds received in currencies other than of France or another operations account country must be surrendered; such proceeds normally must become due not later than 180 days after arrival of the goods at their destination. All export transactions relating to foreign countries (see Exchange Rate System, above) must be domiciled with an authorized bank and a commitment to repatriate the proceeds must be undertaken.

REGULATIONS GOVERNING CURRENT INVISIBLES

Payments for invisibles to France, Monaco, and other operations account countries in the French franc area are permitted freely; those to other countries are subject to the approval of the Office of External Finance or the Institute of Issue. Payments for invisibles related to trade are permitted freely when the basic trade transaction has been approved or does not require authorization. Transfers of up to FMG 15,000 may be made through authorized banks at any time, without indication of purpose, provided that they are not installments of larger payments. Transfers of income accruing to nonresidents in the form of profits, dividends, and royalties are also permitted freely when the basic transaction has been approved.

Following the reintroduction of exchange control on November 25, 1968, basic allocations were established for payments and transfers in respect of travel, family support, and education. The provision for tourist travel was modified, effective June 1, 1970, and again with effect from October 10, 1970. Tourists are allowed a foreign currency allocation equivalent to FMG 75,000 a person for each trip, which may be taken up twice a year. This allocation may be used either in several installments or all at one time and may be used to purchase foreign banknotes, travelers checks, or letters of credit before leaving the country. An additional FMG 75,000 may be obtained by heads of families for pilgrimages. A basic allocation of FMG 20,000 a person a day, subject to a limit of FMG 200,000 a trip, is granted for business travel; however, application may be made to the Institute of Issue for an additional allowance. Resident and nonresident travelers to foreign countries may take out up to a maximum of FMG 25,000 in Malagasy banknotes; travelers to France or other operations account countries may take out any amount in Malagasy banknotes. Nonresident travelers may take out foreign banknotes and coins up to the amount declared by them on entry, as well as foreign currency obtained by reconversion of Malagasy banknotes purchased after entry, but not more than FMG 25,000 may be so reconverted; they may also take out any foreign means of payment acquired in Malagasy from a nonresident account.

Proceeds from transactions in invisibles with France, Monaco, and other operations account countries in the French franc area may be retained. All amounts due from residents of other countries in respect of services, and in general all income or proceeds encashed abroad or paid by a nonresident, must be collected and surrendered within one month of the due date. Resident and nonresident travelers may bring in any amount of banknotes and coins issued by the Malagasy Institute of Issue, the Bank of France, or any bank of issue maintaining an operations account with the French Treasury, as well as any amount of foreign banknotes and coins (except gold coins) of countries outside the French franc area.

CAPITAL TRANSFERS

Capital movements between the Malagasy Republic and France, Monaco, and other operations account countries in the French franc area are free of exchange control; capital transfers to all other countries require approval, but capital receipts from such countries are permitted freely, subject to any formalities which may be required under the regulations applicable at any given time. Special controls are maintained over borrowing abroad, transactions in foreign securities, and direct investments, but these controls relate to the transactions themselves, not to payments or receipts.

Borrowing abroad requires prior authorization by the Minister of Finance. The following are, however, exempt from this requirement: (1) loans constituting direct investment; (2) loans directly connected with the rendering of services abroad; (3) loans contracted by banks or by credit institutions with special legal status; and (4) other loans when the total outstanding amount is FMG 50 million or less for any one borrower (but the contracting of and repayment of such loans of more than FMG 500,000 but less than FMG 50 million are subject to declaration to the Minister of Finance). Lending abroad is subject only to exchange control authorization and is restricted. The issue, advertising, or offering for sale of foreign securities in the Malagasy Republic requires prior authorization by the Minister of Finance. Exempt from authorization, however, are operations in connection with loans backed by a guarantee from the Malagasy Government and shares similar to securities whose issue, offering, or sale has previously been authorized. Foreign direct investments in the Malagasy Republic [10] and Malagasy direct investments abroad [11] must be declared to the Minister of Finance (i.e., to the Directorate of the Treasury in the Ministry of Finance and Commerce) when they are being made, unless they take the form of a capital increase resulting from investment of undistributed profits. The Minister has the right during a period of two months to request the postponement of the projects submitted to him. Total or partial liquidation of direct investment must also be declared.

Both the making and the liquidation of direct investments, whether these are Malagasy investments abroad or foreign investments in the Malagasy Republic, must be reported to the Minister of Finance within 20 days following each operation. Direct investments are defined as investments involving the purchase, creation, or expansion of a company or enterprise or involving control over it. Mere participation is not considered as direct investment, provided that it does not exceed 20 per cent of the capital of a company.

In accordance with the Investment Code, foreign or domestic enterprises of special interest for the economy may be granted preferential treatment in accordance with an "order of approval" (*arrêté d'agrément*). Such enterprises may benefit from specified advantages relating to import and export duties, income taxes, supplementary allocations above those allotted in the annual import program, the introduction of quotas for competing imports, etc. Exceptional treatment beyond the benefits provided for by the Investment Code and other

---

[10] Including those made by companies in the Malagasy Republic that are directly or indirectly under foreign control and those made by branches or subsidiaries in the Republic of foreign companies.

[11] Including those made through the intermediacy of foreign companies that are directly or indirectly controlled by persons in the Malagasy Republic and those made by branches or subsidiaries of companies in the Republic.

existing legislation may be granted in a founding agreement (*convention d'établissement*); such an agreement requires parliamentary approval. (See also Economic Development and Planning—Investment Code, above.)

GOLD

Residents are free to hold, acquire, and dispose of gold in any form in the Malagasy Republic. Imports and exports of gold require prior authorization from the Institute of Issue, although requests for such authorization are seldom received. Exempt from this requirement are imports and exports by or on behalf of the Treasury or the Institute of Issue and imports and exports of manufactured articles containing a minor quantity of gold (such as gold-filled or gold-plated articles). Imports of gold, whether licensed or exempt from license, are subject to customs declaration.

The local production of gold in 1969 amounted to about 20 kilograms. All newly mined gold must be surrendered to the Ministry of Industry and Mines, which, in principle, must deliver it, after processing, to the Malagasy Institute of Issue. However, since 1969 the Ministry has, for technical reasons, suspended the delivery of gold to the Institute.

TRADE AND PAYMENTS ARRANGEMENTS

The Malagasy Republic does not maintain any bilateral payments agreements. However, it has agreed to purchase a certain portion of its requirements of cement and soap from Senegal and Ivory Coast (see Regulations Governing Imports and Exports, above). These arrangements are related to the multilateral sugar agreement among member countries of the OCAM, under which the Malagasy Republic may sell part of its sugar production at a guaranteed price that is higher than the world market price.

CHAPTER 4

Malawi

GENERAL SETTING

The Republic of Malawi is a landlocked country in southeastern Africa, stretching along the western shore of Lake Malawi (formerly Lake Nyasa) and on either side of the Shire River almost to its confluence with the Zambezi River. It is bounded by Tanzania on the northeast, Mozambique on the southeast and southwest, and Zambia on the northwest. (See map.) The southern tip of the country is about 130 miles north of the Mozambique port of Beira on the Indian Ocean. Malawi is about 520 miles long and varies in width from 50 miles to 100 miles. The total area of the country is about 47,940 square miles, of which some 11,460 square miles are lakes.

The outstanding geographical feature of Malawi is that part of the Great Rift Valley which traverses the country from north to south; the northern section of the Rift is occupied by Lake Malawi and the southern section by the Shire River, which drains the lake. The Lake Malawi section of the Rift Valley, which averages 50 miles in width and is about 400 miles long, is formed like a great trough, with a maximum depth of 2,310 feet (760 feet below sea level). On the west side of the lake, various plateaus and elevations rise to altitudes ranging between 7,000 and 8,000 feet in the Northern Region and between 3,000 and 5,000 feet in the Central Region. The Shire River section of the Rift Valley, only 120 feet above sea level at the southern tip of Malawi, is flanked on the west by the Kirk Range and on the east by the Namwera Hills and the Shire Highlands, the latter ranging in elevation from 2,000 to 4,000 feet, with higher, isolated massifs—Zomba (6,846 feet) and Mlanje (9,843 feet).

Although Malawi is situated in the tropics, between the latitudes of 9° 22' and 17° 18' south, the sharp contrasts in relief and the resulting diversity of climate permit a wide variety of crops to be grown. The dry season generally extends from May to October. However, there are large localized differences in weather, and four main climatic zones may be identified. These are the Shire River Valley and the lakeshore areas around Karonga and Salima, where the climate is hot and dry and the mean annual temperature is over 75° F.; the lakeshore area in the extreme north and around Nkhata Bay, where the climate is hot and wet, the mean annual temperature is over 75° F., and the rainfall is between 50 and 120 inches a year; the Shire Highlands and the lower plateaus in the Central and Northern Regions, having a warm climate with a mean annual temperature of 70° F. and a moderate rainfall of 30 to 60 inches a year; and the higher plateau areas of Nyika, Vipya, Dedza, Zomba, and Mlanje, which have a warm, wet climate with a mean annual temperature below 65° F. and a rainfall of 50 to 130 inches a year.

Malawi, formerly Nyasaland, became independent on July 6, 1964 following the dissolution on December 31, 1963 of the Federation of Rhodesia and Nyasaland, of which it had been a part from September 1953 to the end of 1963, and became a republic on July 6, 1966. Zomba, the present capital, has a population of about 20,000 (1966 census); Blantyre-Limbe is the largest city (110,000 in 1966). The capital is to be moved in the near future to Lilongwe (19,000 in 1966), which is nearly 200 miles by road north of Zomba and is more centrally located.

The total population, estimated at 4.4 million in 1969, is increasing at an annual rate of about 3 per cent. The non-Africans in Malawi are mainly Asians and Europeans, estimated at 11,000 and 7,000, respectively, in 1966. The principal ethnic groups in the country include Chewa, Nyanga, Yao, Ngoni, and Tenbuka. Although the official language has been Chewa since September 1968, English is the language of commerce and industry.

The 1966 census recorded the median age of the population as 17½ years (males 16½, females 18½), with almost 44 per cent of the population under the age of 15 years and nearly 43 per cent of the females between the ages of 15 and 44. Given Malawi's 36,500 square miles of land area, the average density of population in 1966 was 111 persons to the square mile; the highest density is in the south—382 persons to the square mile compared with only 48 in the north. A considerable number of Malawians migrate to South Africa, Rhodesia, and Zambia in search of employment. In 1967, the total number of emigrants (including dependents) to these three countries was estimated at 280,000.

Malawi became a member of the United Nations on December 1, 1964. On July 19, 1965 it joined the International Monetary Fund (quota on May 31, 1971, $15 million), the International Bank for Reconstruction and Development (capital subscription on May 31, 1971, $15 million), the International Development Association, and the International Finance Corporation. It is a member of the Commonwealth, and the European Economic Community has agreed to offer Malawi associate membership if the United Kingdom joins the Community. Malawi is a contracting party to the General Agreement on Tariffs and Trade and a member of the African Development Bank, the Food and Agriculture Organization of the United Nations, the United Nations Economic Commission for Africa, and the United Nations Educational, Scientific and Cultural Organization.

The currency is issued by the Reserve Bank of Malawi. Until February 15, 1971, the unit of currency was the Malawi pound, which was divided into 20 shillings, and the par value agreed with the International Monetary Fund was £M 1 = US$2.40, that is, the Malawi pound was at par with the pound sterling. With effect from February 15, 1971 a new currency unit, the kwacha, equivalent in value to one half of the former Malawi pound, was introduced. The kwacha is divided into 100 tambala, and the par value agreed with the Fund for the new currency is MK 1 = US$1.20 or MK 2 = £ stg. 1.

The Malawian economy is predominantly agricultural. Although the importance of cash crops is increasing, subsistence farming still plays the major role. The country has no significant mineral resources except bauxite, but it is reasonably well endowed with forests and there is good potential in fisheries and tourism.

STRUCTURE OF THE ECONOMY

GROSS DOMESTIC PRODUCT

Gross domestic product (GDP) at current market prices rose by 9.5 per cent in 1969, compared with an increase of 7.7 per cent in 1968 and with an average annual increase of 6.7 per cent in 1966–69 (Table 1). In real terms, GDP is estimated to have risen in 1969 by 6.2 per cent, compared with less than 1 per cent in 1968 and an annual average of 4.7 per cent in 1965–69. Per capita income in real terms, which declined by 2 per cent in 1968, rose by almost 3 per cent in 1969; the fluctuation is explained mainly by the fact that the economy is basically agricultural and variations in weather have a big impact on the growth of the economy.

The main factors contributing to the high rate of growth in 1969 were improved agricultural production and a rise in fixed investment. The contributions to GDP of almost all sectors of the economy increased in value (Table 2). In particular, construction rose by 50 per cent, compared with an increase of 21 per cent in the previous year, and manufacturing rose by 15 per cent, compared with 12 per cent in 1968, reflecting increased production of both consumer goods and building materials. The general expansion in the economy was conducive to a significant rise (4.8 per cent) in the output of the services industry, although the rate of growth was slower than that attained in the previous year (15.7 per cent). There was a 7 per cent increase in agricultural production, compared with an increase of less than 1 per cent in 1968, reflecting both good weather and higher prices obtained for some crops.

TABLE 1. MALAWI: GROSS DOMESTIC PRODUCT AT MARKET PRICES, TOTAL AND MONETARY, 1965–69

	1965	1966	1967	1968	1969	Average Annual Increase
Estimated population ('000)	3,908	4,025	4,146	4,270	4,398	3.0%
Current market prices						
Total gross domestic product						
Total (*MK '000*)	180,938	187,266	198,986	214,326	234,600	6.7%
Per capita (*MK*)	46.2	46.6	48.0	50.2	53.4	3.7%
Monetary gross domestic product						
Total (*MK '000*)	90,058	105,726	114,122	119,490	136,600	11.0%
Per capita (*MK*)	23.0	26.2	27.6	28.0	31.0	7.8%
Constant (1964) market prices						
Total gross domestic product						
Total (*MK '000*)	163,504	175,346	184,120	184,994	196,552	4.7%
Per capita (*MK*)	41.8	43.6	44.4	43.4	44.6	1.6%
Monetary gross domestic product						
Total (*MK '000*)	85,608	94,200	101,322	99,798	108,600	6.2%
Per capita (*MK*)	22.0	23.4	24.4	23.4	24.6	2.9%

Sources: National Statistical Office, *National Accounts Report, 1964–68*; Office of the President, *Economic Report, 1969*; and data provided by the Malawian authorities.

TABLE 2. MALAWI: GROSS DOMESTIC PRODUCT AT FACTOR COST, 1965–69

	1965	1966	1967	1968	1969 [1]
	MILLIONS OF KWACHA AT CURRENT PRICES				
Agriculture, forestry, and fishing	63.2	68.2	71.2	71.8	76.8
Mining and quarrying	—	0.2	0.2	0.2	0.4
Manufacturing	10.0	13.4	15.4	17.2	19.8
Building and construction	6.0	8.6	7.6	9.2	13.8
Electricity and water	1.4	1.8	2.0	2.4	2.6
Transport, communications, and storage	6.6	8.4	9.8	9.8	10.6
Banking, finance, and insurance	0.4	0.2	0.4	0.6	0.6
Community services	16.4	19.0	20.2	21.2	22.8
Other services	70.0	57.6	61.2	70.8	74.2
Total	174.0	177.4	188.0	203.2	221.6
	AS PER CENT OF TOTAL				
Agriculture, forestry, and fishing	36.3	38.4	37.9	35.3	34.7
Mining and quarrying	—	0.1	0.1	0.1	0.2
Manufacturing	5.7	7.6	8.2	8.5	8.9
Building and construction	3.4	4.8	4.0	4.5	6.2
Electricity and water	0.8	1.0	1.1	1.2	1.2
Transport, communications, and storage	3.8	4.7	5.2	4.8	4.8
Banking, finance, and insurance	0.2	0.1	0.2	0.3	0.3
Community services	9.4	10.7	10.7	10.4	10.3
Other services	40.2	32.5	32.6	34.8	33.4
Total	100.0	100.0	100.0	100.0	100.0

Sources: National Statistical Office, *National Accounts Report, 1964–68*; and data provided by the Malawian authorities.

[1] Provisional estimates.

There have been certain changes in the structure of the economy since 1965. The share of the agricultural sector, which was 38 per cent in 1966, has since been decreasing steadily. On the other hand, the shares of manufacturing, building and construction, and transport and communications have been increasing, while the shares of finance and services have remained fairly stable. Subsistence (i.e., nonmonetary) activity accounted for 44 per cent of GDP in 1966 (compared with 50 per cent in 1965), but the share of that sector had declined to 42 per cent by 1969.

Consumption accounted for 76 per cent of aggregate demand in 1965 (Table 3). By 1969 this had fallen to 71 per cent, the share of private consumption falling and that of government consumption rising. With respect to gross domestic investment, the most striking change between 1965 and 1969 was the increase in private sector investment, which rose almost fourfold and accounted for about 5 per cent of aggregate demand in 1969, compared with 2 per cent in 1965. Exports

TABLE 3.   MALAWI: AGGREGATE DEMAND AND SUPPLY
AT MARKET PRICES, 1965–69

(*In millions of Malawi kwacha*)

	1965	1966	1967	1968	1969
	AT CURRENT PRICES				
Aggregate demand	**235.0**	**257.8**	**267.6**	**291.4**	**316.2**
Consumption	179.0	183.6	193.6	210.6	223.0
Government	*25.8*	*30.4*	*33.2*	*35.6*	*37.4*
Private monetary	*62.6*	*73.2*	*76.8*	*81.0*	*88.6*
Subsistence	*90.6*	*80.0*	*83.6*	*94.0*	*97.0*
Gross domestic investment	23.6	33.6	26.6	33.6	42.2
Fixed capital formation	*17.8*	*27.6*	*22.6*	*35.8*	*40.4*
Central government	*(9.0)*	*(12.4)*	*(9.4)*	*(11.6)*	*(11.8)*
Public enterprises	*(4.4)*	*(3.6)*	*(4.4)*	*(6.6)*	*(13.6)*
Private sector	*(4.4)*	*(11.6)*	*(8.8)*	*(17.6)*	*(15.0)*
Changes in stocks	*5.8*	*6.0*	*4.0*	*−2.2*	*1.8*
Exports of goods and nonfactor services	32.4	40.6	47.4	47.0	51.0
Aggregate supply	**235.0**	**257.8**	**267.6**	**291.4**	**316.2**
Gross domestic product	181.0	187.2	199.0	214.4	234.6
Imports of goods and nonfactor services	54.0	70.6	68.6	77.0	81.6
	AT CONSTANT (1964) PRICES				
Aggregate demand	**216.6**	**247.8**	**255.4**	**258.6**	. . .
Consumption	162.4	177.2	182.8	186.0	. . .
Government	*24.8*	*28.8*	*30.4*	*32.0*	. . .
Private monetary	*60.0*	*68.6*	*70.2*	*69.2*	. . .
Subsistence	*77.6*	*79.8*	*82.2*	*84.8*	. . .
Gross domestic investment	23.2	31.0	23.4	28.6	. . .
Fixed capital formation	*17.6*	*26.0*	*20.6*	*31.2*	. . .
Changes in stocks	*5.6*	*5.0*	*2.8*	*−2.6*	. . .
Exports of goods and nonfactor services	31.0	39.6	49.2	44.0	. . .
Aggregate supply	**216.6**	**247.8**	**255.4**	**258.6**	. . .
Gross domestic product	163.4	175.4	184.2	185.0	196.2
Imports of goods and nonfactor services	53.2	72.4	71.0	73.4	. . .

Sources: Office of the President, *Economic Report, 1969*; National Statistical Office, *National Accounts Report, 1964–68*, and *Balance of Payments, 1968*; data provided by the Malawian authorities; and Fund staff estimates.

of goods and services rose by 57 per cent during the same period, accounting for 16 per cent of aggregate demand in 1969.

Consumption in both the government and subsistence sectors rose less rapidly in 1969 than in 1968; private consumption excluding the subsistence sector increased more rapidly, as retail sales of consumer goods, particularly of nondurable goods like cigarettes, beer, and soft drinks, rose markedly toward the end of the year. Private fixed investment declined slightly (to MK 15 million) in 1969, after having doubled in the previous year when a number of large industrial projects were completed. The decline was, however, more than offset by increases in the investment expenditures of the Central Government and public enterprises, which more than doubled, to MK 13.6 million. Public fixed investment on roads and on the rail link with the Mozambique railway system at Nacala contributed to the increase in domestic investment expenditures. With the rise in exports of goods and services in 1969, to MK 51 million, the cash earnings of the agricultural sector increased markedly. Given the significant growth in aggregate supply and the declining rate of growth in aggregate consumption, private savings at the Post Office Savings Bank, the New Building Society, and the commercial banks combined rose by 21 per cent in 1969.[1]

In addition to the growth of GDP, a steady rise in imports of goods and services—from MK 54 million in 1965 to MK 77 million in 1968 and MK 81.6 million in 1969—contributed to the increase in aggregate supply.

AGRICULTURE

Malawi's agricultural production may be broadly divided into two categories, subsistence crops that are primarily intended for domestic consumption and cash crops that are largely exported. The principal subsistence crops are maize, rice, and pulses; significant amounts of these are also exported. The principal cash crops are tobacco, tea, groundnuts, cotton, and tung oil, of which tobacco and tea are the most important. Cash crops may in turn be divided into estate-grown crops and smallholder or small farm crops; tea and some varieties of tobacco are the most important estate crops. The smallholder crops are sold to the Farmers Marketing Board, which sells them both locally and abroad; the estate crops are marketed by private exporters (see Agricultural Marketing, below).

Export Crops

Tobacco.—Tobacco, which is by far the most important export crop, was introduced into Malawi in 1920 and by 1928 had become the

---

[1] The increase in institutional savings is partly attributable to a decreasing tendency to hoard by the rural population and partly to intensified campaigns by the commercial banks to mobilize these savings.

major export crop. It is grown mainly in the Central Region. Production
was at first confined to the flue-cured type grown on estates, but later
the dark-fired type was introduced and now constitutes about two thirds
of total production. The area under cultivation for all types of tobacco
is currently estimated at about 97,000 acres.

Production of the four main varieties of tobacco declined from a
record high figure of 49.2 million pounds in 1965 to 26.3 million
pounds in 1969 (Table 4). During this period the combined output of
flue-cured and burley tobacco increased from 8.5 million pounds to
13.7 million pounds, partly owing to higher market prices, and the production of dark-fired and sun-air varieties declined from 40.7 million
pounds to 12.6 million pounds, thus accounting for only 48 per cent of
the total in 1969, against 83 per cent in 1965. The Government's
attempt to shift production from dark-fired tobacco to flue-cured proved
difficult to implement because of the more complex technology and
greater capital investment involved. Although output of both types
increased in 1970, that of the former is estimated to have more than
doubled, accounting for a large part of the estimated increase in total
output of tobacco to 48.9 million pounds.

TABLE 4.   MALAWI: VOLUME OF MARKETED PRODUCTION
OF PRINCIPAL CROPS, 1965–70 [1]

	1965	1966	1967	1968	1969	1970 [2]
	(Million pounds)					
Tobacco	49.2	41.3	45.8	32.1	26.3	48.9
Flue-cured	*2.7*	*2.7*	*4.0*	*6.1*	*6.1*	*10.3*
Burley	*5.8*	*5.3*	*5.9*	*6.7*	*7.6*	*12.5*
Dark-fired	*31.3*	*27.2*	*33.4*	*16.9*	*10.6*	*22.0*
Sun-air	*9.4*	*6.1*	*2.5*	*2.4*	*2.0*	*4.1*
Tea	28.6	33.9	37.1	34.9	37.3	41.3
	(Thousand short tons)					
Groundnuts	25.2	46.5	47.3	25.1	40.9	29.6
Cotton (unginned)	22.6	14.6	13.2	12.8	20.2	23.5
Maize	24.4	62.5	100.0	92.2	58.1	9.1
Pulses	30.3	20.3	23.3	3.8	18.1	7.9
Sugar (raw)	—	3.7	18.1	21.9	29.6	36.1
Rice (paddy)	5.6	4.5	5.1	2.3	9.3	11.0

Sources: Office of the President, *Economic Report, 1969* and *1971*; and data provided
by the Malawian authorities.

[1] Except for flue-cured and burley tobacco (which is sold at auction), and tea and
sugar, the data represent purchases by the Farmers Marketing Board.
[2] Estimates.

The prices of all types of tobacco were higher in 1969 than in the previous year, bringing producers' total earnings from tobacco sales to MK 6.4 million (i.e., MK 5.2 million for burley and flue-cured, and MK 1.2 million for dark-fired and sun-air), compared with MK 5.2 million in 1968. The auction price for smallholder tobacco, at 26 tambala a pound, was 47 per cent higher than in 1968. Auction prices for flue-cured tobacco rose by 3.3 tambala, to 39.4 tambala a pound. The average price for burley reached a record high level of 36.9 tambala a pound, some 47 per cent higher than in the previous year.

As far as development of the tobacco industry is concerned, the immediate domestic need is to build more barns. With regard to marketing, the sales potential of burley tobacco is excellent. Potential markets are estimated at 14 million pounds, of which some 10 million pounds could be produced on estates and the remainder by smallholders under controlled settlement schemes. Marketing prospects for flue-cured tobacco depend on the Rhodesian situation, as prices for this type are likely to fall if international trade relations with Rhodesia become normal. In the case of smallholder tobacco, new areas are expected to be opened up for cultivation. The higher prices announced by the Farmers Marketing Board and the upward revision of quotas were expected to be effective incentives to achieving larger output. The possibility of expanding Malawi's markets beyond the traditional areas of the United Kingdom and Norway, e.g., entering the U. S. market, is also being explored.

Tea.—By 1902 tea growing in Malawi was developing in the high rainfall areas of the Mlanje and Cholo districts and has expanded steadily as an estate-grown crop. Output increased especially after 1950, when the limitations on production imposed under the International Tea Agreement were lifted. Tea is also grown on smallholdings, with government support. During the past decade yields have improved, owing to the introduction of high-yield varieties and greater use of fertilizers. Malawian tea is generally classified among the lower grades, and the industry is now concentrating on improving the quality by better plucking and improved growing techniques. Though the major portion of Malawian tea is sold in London, an increasing amount is being exported to the United States, Europe, the Middle East, and Australia.

After falling to 28.6 million pounds in 1965, production of tea rose to 33.9 million pounds in 1966 (Table 4), mainly on account of better weather. From 37.1 million pounds in 1967, production dropped to 34.9 million pounds in 1968 owing to cold and dry weather. However, export earnings declined only moderately in 1968, as temporary short-ages caused by dock strikes in the United Kingdom (where 40 per cent of Malawi's output is sold) led to an 11 per cent rise in the price for Malawian tea, in contrast to the general downward movement in the world market price.

The acreage under tea in 1969 is estimated to have increased by almost 4 per cent over 1968, to 37,100 acres. Together with the replanting of old gardens, this resulted in an increase in output of 7 per cent, to 37.3 million pounds. Prices of Malawian tea, in line with world market prices, fell early in the year, and although there was a recovery toward the end of the year, it was not sufficient to offset losses incurred earlier; the average price of Malawian tea was just over 23.3 tambala a pound. With the recovery of world prices in 1970, the price of Malawian tea auctioned in London rose to 36.2 tambala a pound. Output in 1970 is estimated to have increased to 41.3 million pounds.

Smallholder cultivation of tea started in 1967, under a program financed in part by the Commonwealth Development Corporation. A Smallholders Tea Authority was established to help Malawians holding a small acreage (which they would otherwise have employed in subsist-ence farming) to grow tea as their main occupation and thereby to raise their standard of living. The authority has nurseries at Mlanje (823 acres), Cholo (91 acres), and Nkhata Bay (28 acres) on which it nurtures seedlings until they are 30 months old and then sells the young plants to smallholders. The authority supervises the care of the trees in the smallholders' gardens, including setting, pegging, mulching, the establishment of master rows for windbreaks, and keeping a check on weeds and disease. There are at present 700 tea growers under the scheme. The acreage presently cultivated by smallholders is estimated at 645 acres and is expected to increase to 2,107 acres by the end of the first phase of the program in 1971. The second phase is expected to expand the area under cultivation to 4,732 acres by 1975. Another smallholder tea scheme covering an area of 611 acres is to be started this year in the Kawalazi area of Nkhata Bay with aid from the United Kingdom. To ensure that high-quality tea is produced, each farmer is being restricted initially to bringing one additional acre a year under cultivation.

Groundnuts.—Malawian groundnuts are particularly suitable for use in confections and enjoy a premium price over nuts produced for oil. The area under cultivation was estimated at 1.1 million acres in 1970. A factor limiting groundnut production appears to be the problem of shelling. At present, no organized market exists for groundnuts in the shell, and the average farmer apparently is reluctant to grow more than his family can shell by hand. The basic consideration, however, is still the price paid to the producer.

The production of groundnuts has increased steadily since the early 1960s, and rose from 25,200 short tons in 1965 to 47,300 tons in 1967, largely because of a guaranteed price scheme operated by the Farmers Marketing Board. The 1968 groundnut crop, however, was severely affected by disease and unfavorable weather, and marketed production dropped to 25,100 tons (Table 4).

In 1969, farmers planted more groundnuts, especially in the Central Region, than in the previous year. In spite of rosette disease and insufficient rain, marketed production was 40,900 tons, 63 per cent more than in 1968, and farmers' income from sales to the Marketing Board rose by MK 1.4 million, to MK 3.6 million. For 1970, output is expected to decline by almost 28 per cent, to 29,600 tons, because of the hot, dry weather early in the year.

Although prospects for oil nuts in the world market are not promising, the prospects for Malawian confectionery nuts are reported to be excellent. Malawi's main problem now is to achieve a sufficiently high and stable level of supply to meet this expanding world demand for confectionery nuts.

Cotton.—Cotton is grown mainly in the Southern Region along the shore of Lake Malawi. Malawi produces a medium-staple variety that is less vulnerable to price fluctuations than the long- and short-staple varieties. Furthermore, the medium-staple cotton produced in Malawi is in good demand on the world market. Output has varied considerably over the past five years as a result of bad weather and damage by pests. The Government has been encouraging new spraying methods against pests and diseases, however, and although the area under cultivation declined from 112,000 to 90,000 acres, output rose from 12,800 short tons (unginned) in 1968, the lowest level in five years, to 20,200 short tons in 1969 (Table 4) because of good weather and the adoption of spraying techniques by farmers. A further increase to 23,500 tons is estimated for 1970. Purchases of unginned cotton by the Farmers Marketing Board were MK 1.8 million in 1969 (50 per cent higher than in 1968) and MK 2.3 million in 1970 (Table 5). At present, the local textile industry is using part of the domestically produced medium-staple cotton; it has been found to mix very well with artificial fibers.

It is the intention of the authorities to increase cotton production to 100,000 tons (unginned) by 1985 through the application of modern methods. To attain this goal, and also to increase the output of other crops, an irrigation project—the Lower Shire Cotton Scheme—was inaugurated in 1968 with a loan of MK 3 million from the International Development Association. The scheme was started at Kasindula on the Lower Shire River and will eventually cover 130,000 acres. There are also cotton improvement projects under way at Salima and Chikwawa. To encourage the further adoption of pest control techniques, sprayers have been sold to growers at a subsidized price. It is also contemplated to provide credit to growers in the Chikwawa and Salima project areas. In view of the relatively low world market price for short-staple cotton, emphasis is being placed on production of long-staple cotton for export and the medium-staple variety for domestic processing.

TABLE 5.   MALAWI: VALUE OF PURCHASES BY FARMERS
MARKETING BOARD, 1965–70

(In millions of Malawi kwacha)

	1965	1966	1967	1968	1969	1970 [1]
Cotton (unginned)	2.2	1.2	1.0	1.2	1.8	2.3
Groundnuts	2.2	4.6	4.8	2.2	3.6	2.8
Tobacco	3.8	2.8	3.2	1.2	1.2	3.0
Maize	0.6	1.6	3.0	2.4	1.6	0.2
Other produce	1.8	1.4	1.6	0.4	1.6	1.4
Total [2]	10.6	11.6	13.6	7.4	9.8 [2]	9.7

Source: Office of the President, *Economic Report, 1969* and *1971.*

[1] Estimates.

[2] The slight differences for the years 1965–68 between these totals and the figures for payments to producers in Table 6 are due to rounding. However, the total for 1969 differs from the figure in Table 6 because the estimate of total purchases by the Board, but not the estimates of individual crop purchases, has been revised.

Tung Oil.—Tung trees (from the seeds of which oil used in paints and varnishes is extracted) are grown mostly on estates in the Shire Highlands and in the Northern Region. The area planted reached a peak of 19,000 acres in 1957 but since then has fallen steadily. In spite of the reduced acreage, however, production showed a small increase owing to the planting of high-yielding trees and greater use of fertilizers.

The production of tung oil remained static at about 1,700 short tons between 1965 and 1967, but was 2,100 tons in 1968. The world market had been depressed because of expanding production in Latin America and mainland China (the world's largest producer) and the increasing use of synthetics in paint. The price of tung oil on the world market rose in 1970, however, and the Farmers Marketing Board began to take a special interest in production. It acquired an estate owned by the Commonwealth Development Corporation at Katoto, the Corporation's tung oil factory at Mzuzu (following the closing down of the Corporation's Vipya Tung Estate Project), and other estates belonging to the Corporation. The Board cropped over 4,000 acres in 1970 and processed and exported about 259 tons of tung oil from the Katoto estate.

Food Crops

Maize.—Maize is by far the most important crop grown for domestic consumption, though increasing quantities are also being exported. As it is primarily a subsistence crop, there is no reliable information on total annual production; sample surveys, however, indicate that it probably amounts to some 700,000 tons in a good year. The crop varies widely, however, as does the portion that is bought by the Farmers Marketing Board for reserves or for export (see Tables 4 and 5). Malawian maize is in good demand by distilleries in the United Kingdom.

The quantity of maize marketed increased from 24,400 short tons in 1965 to 62,500 tons in 1966 and a record high figure of 100,000 short tons in 1967, and remained at the high figure of 92,200 short tons in 1968. The average price paid for maize by the Farmers Marketing Board was reduced from MK 3.00 a bag (200 pounds) in 1967 to

MK 2.70 in 1968, as a result of a decline in prices following bumper harvests in South Africa and Mexico.

Owing to adverse weather, there was a substantial shortfall in maize production in 1969. Marketed production was 58,000 short tons, almost 37 per cent less than in the previous year. Receipts by growers from sales to the Board, which had been as high as MK 3 million in 1967, fell to MK 1.6 million in 1969 (Table 5). The area planted increased to over 2.6 million acres in 1969, but unexpected dry weather at tasselling time caused output to fall. There was a further fall in output in 1970, and the Board's purchases were only 9,100 short tons in that year. To cover the shortage of maize for domestic consumption, some 100,000 short tons, valued at MK 5 million, were imported in 1970. The Marketing Board was to purchase surplus maize from domestic producers at MK 2.50 a bag of 200 pounds (half the price of imported maize) and sell it through the Board's main depots and selected permanent markets at MK 4.50 a bag. Where such markets were not available, sales were to be effected through District Commissioners. The same sales price was to apply throughout the country, with the Board bearing the cost (estimated at MK 1 million) of transporting the maize to remote areas.

Rice.—Rice is produced mainly in the low-lying areas along the west shore of Lake Malawi. The rice produced in Malawi is of good quality and is popular in markets in neighboring countries. Production varies considerably from year to year, according to the amount of rainfall. Marketed production, estimated at 5,600 short tons in 1965, has fluctuated markedly since then (Table 4). Mainly on account of adverse weather, production in 1968 was only 2,300 tons. The output of 9,300 tons in 1969 was attributed partly to an increase in acreage prompted by the announcement of higher buying prices by the Farmers Marketing Board and partly to good weather. Output for 1970 was estimated at 11,000 tons. Through a rebate on import duties, Malawi continues to receive prices above those prevailing on the world market for the rice that it sells in South Africa.

With respect to the future, rice production in Malawi is expected to be expanded substantially to meet the anticipated gradual substitution of rice for maize by Malawians as their living standards continue to improve. It is estimated that the long-run potential output is approximately 200,000 tons of paddy or 135,000 tons of milled rice. For 1975 a goal of 55,000 tons of paddy has been set. Some 35 per cent of this amount is expected to be produced under small irrigation schemes established by the Department of Agriculture; another 35 per cent will be produced by the Kasindula Irrigation Project; and the remaining 30 per cent will come from rain-fed production. Favorable guaranteed prices and the distribution of improved seed are the principal means by which this higher output is to be achieved. It is anticipated that South Africa, Rhodesia, and Zambia will provide markets for part of the projected increase in output.

Malawi is presently receiving foreign assistance from the Republic of China (Taiwan), Israel, and the Federal Republic of Germany to improve methods of cultivation and to reduce reliance on the weather.

Livestock and Livestock Products

Owing to the relatively high density of population and the intensive cultivation of crops in many areas, livestock is produced on only a limited scale and mainly by traditional methods in the Central and Northern Regions. Domestic meat supplies are not sufficient, and the country depends on imports. Hides and skins are of some importance as exports.

The principal livestock are cattle, goats, pigs, and sheep. The cattle population, estimated at 491,000 head in 1969, is increasing at the rate of more than 3 per cent a year. Cattle slaughtering is also rising, and was estimated at 56,000 head in 1969, about 2.3 per cent above the figure for 1968. The number of goats and pigs nearly doubled between 1956 and 1967. The numbers of other livestock, with the exception of sheep, have increased steadily in recent years. In 1969, imports of beef rose by 154,215 pounds (to 344,000 pounds), pork by 139,000 pounds (to 180,500 pounds), and mutton and lamb by 22,800 pounds (to 130,900 pounds).

In an effort to increase the number of livestock, the Government's policy is to reduce the rate of slaughter for the present. In addition, through its agricultural extension services, the Government is attempting to improve the quality of the meat produced. The programs of the Veterinary Department include preventing disease and improving the strains for breeding purposes. For example, the Veterinary Department has started a "staff feeding" system under which farmers are provided young cattle on credit for feeding on surplus agricultural produce and waste. When the farmers sell the cattle, they are permitted to keep the difference between the credit value and the price they obtain at the market. With the aim of self-sufficiency in dairy requirements in the near future, the Government is encouraging dairy farming and in June 1969 established its first series of depots for collecting, cooling, and pasteurizing milk. Pig raising, which had previously been a by-product of crop farming, is now mostly in the hands of state farms. An FAO team is in Malawi helping with livestock development plans, and the United Kingdom and Denmark are providing aid to develop the dairy industry.

In the past, because of marketing difficulties, there has been little incentive for farmers to increase their herds. With improvements in the marketing system, particularly through the establishment of more live-stock purchasing centers, it is expected that more farmers will take to raising livestock.

Agricultural Marketing

Crops which are grown on large estates, such as tea and flue-cured tobacco, are marketed by private exporters or groups—the Tea Association and the Tobacco Association, for example. The other important crops, principally those not grown on estates, are marketed by the Farmers Marketing Board, a statutory corporation charged with the responsibility for processing and marketing all the important agricultural produce of non-estate farmers in Malawi, i.e., farmers on "customary" or communally owned land. The Agricultural Production and Marketing Board (which had been formed by amalgamating the Tobacco Board, the Produce Marketing Board, and the Cotton Marketing Board) was given the name of Farmers Marketing Board after independence; it is planned to rename it the Agricultural Development and Marketing Corporation in the near future.

The chief aim of the Board is to stabilize the prices paid to producers by means of price stabilization funds. In order to ensure an expanding agricultural output, the Board also provides to farmers, at or below cost, such farming aids as fertilizer, spraying equipment, pesticides, and carts and tools. Furthermore, the Board seeks to improve the quality of crops and acts as implementing agency of the Government's agricultural policy, especially in regard to production, processing and storage, establishment of experimental farms, and distribution of seeds. Finally, the Board maintains small reserves of foodstuffs, principally maize, against domestic shortages.

The Farmers Marketing Board maintains a large number of storage and handling depots in various parts of the country, and operates a large number of markets for cotton and tobacco at which other types of produce are also purchased. All markets have the ancillary support of numerous buying points throughout the country. As regards the marketing of tobacco, the Board purchases only those varieties grown on "customary" land and grades them for sale at auction. It also operates a cotton gin, a center for grading groundnuts, and several other large grading centers.

In respect of both overall policy and the determination of producer prices, the Board operates under the general direction of the Ministry of Agriculture and Natural Resources. Prior to 1968 the Board's policy relating to producer prices was discussed with the Ministry every October before seeding time, and then made public. The following April these prices were revised or confirmed and were in effect for the entire season. The Board did not consciously seek to make a profit, and the general consideration guiding the fixing of producer prices was to pay as high a price as possible so as to provide an incentive for expanding production. Accordingly, the Board aimed at paying producers the so-called export parity price, i.e., anticipated export price minus handling charges, commissions to buying agents, and other market costs.

Since 1968 the Marketing Board has been following a system of announcing a floor price for tobacco at the beginning of each season and making a bonus payment to the producers that depends on the actual sales price realized by the Board. In effect this means that there is a guaranteed minimum price which is confirmed in March and revised upward when the crop is sold by the Board. Payment of a second installment at the time of the year when the farmers need fertilizer and other inputs to begin planting the following year's crop is intended to encourage an increase in production. So far this pricing

system, which is expected to be extended to coffee, appears to be
bringing about the desired effect. The Board also uses price differentials
to encourage production of better grades, a policy which has already led
to an improvement in the quality of dark-fired tobacco produced by
small farmers.

In 1967 the Board paid out MK 13.5 million (more than double that
in 1964), consisting of MK 4.8 million for groundnuts, MK 3 million
for dark-fired tobacco, MK 4.6 million for maize, beans, and pulses,
and MK 1 million for cotton (Tables 5 and 6). However, owing to the
lower world market prices for maize and dark-fired tobacco, the trading
position of the Board deteriorated seriously during the year and a loss
of MK 3.6 million was incurred. Large stocks, particularly of groundnuts and tobacco, had to be carried to the next year and the Board had
to depend heavily on the commercial banks to meet its obligations.
Credit extended by the banks increased from MK 0.5 million in December 1966 to MK 7.6 million in December 1967. In 1968, the poor harvest led to a reduction in the value of purchases by the Board to
MK 7.4 million, and it was able to dispose of almost MK 4 million of
its previously accumulated stocks and to make a small profit of
MK 120,000 on its operations. In 1969 the Board's net profit was
MK 1.1 million, the result of improved marketing and administrative
procedures coupled with a particularly favorable trading year. Payments
to farmers were MK 11.5 million, as payments for high-value crops

TABLE 6.   MALAWI: OPERATIONS OF FARMERS
MARKETING BOARD, 1964–69

(*In millions of Malawi kwacha*)

	1964	1965	1966	1967	1968	1969
Costs	9.54	15.68	16.46	19.76	12.72	18.92
Payments to producers [1]	6.24	10.82	11.68	13.52	7.40	11.54
Marketing	2.02	3.24	3.40	4.84	3.80	5.90
Overhead and administration	1.28	1.62	1.38	1.40	1.52	1.48
Sales proceeds	11.50	14.64	13.40	15.86	16.66	20.02
Gross trading surplus or deficit (−)	1.96	−1.04	−3.16	−3.34	3.94	1.12
Plus Net change in stocks	−1.22	1.64	3.08	−0.28	−3.82	—
Net surplus or deficit credited to reserves	0.74	0.70	0.02	−3.62	0.12	1.12

Source: Data provided by the Farmers Marketing Board.

[1] See footnote 2 to Table 5.

(groundnuts, tobacco, cotton, pulses) more than offset lower payments for maize.

Agricultural Credit

Apart from commercial bank credit (which is available almost exclusively to estate farmers), agricultural credit is provided by the Farmers Marketing Board, the Smallholders Tea Authority, and, until recently, the Central Farmers Loans Board.

The Farmers Marketing Board provides credit for the purchase of insecticides for cotton and of fertilizers for tobacco in the Southern Region. The cotton insecticide credit program was initiated during the 1963/64 cotton season and has been built up rapidly following the widespread adoption of spraying techniques. The average credit extended to each grower in any one season is about MK 60. Credit outstanding on this account at the end of the 1967/68 season stood at MK 103,600. A tobacco fertilizer credit scheme was started during the 1968/69 season, and total credit so far extended amounts to MK 5,000. In the 1970/71 season, however, the Board discontinued granting credit to farmers to purchase fertilizers and began to sell fertilizers to them for cash.

The Central Farmers Loans Board was established in 1966 by reorganizing the former Nyasaland African Loans Board with new capital of MK 230,000. The Loans Board was intended to help small farmers to make the transition from subsistence to market agriculture. Disbursements of about MK 64,000 were approved in 1968. In 1969 the Central Farmers Loans Board was amalgamated with the Industrial Loans Board, which has been financing newly established estates, particularly those producing flue-cured tobacco. An agricultural financing agency may be established in the near future.

The Smallholders Tea Authority, with financial assistance from the Commonwealth Development Corporation, provides credit toward the purchase of fertilizer to farmers wishing to establish tea gardens. Under the arrangement, the farmer is eligible for credit until his garden yields a sufficient cash return to enable him to buy fertilizer for cash; this period may be as long as four years.

FORESTRY

Although presently a net importer of wood and wood products, Malawi possesses a good potential in its forestry resources. Of the approximately 36,500 square miles of land in Malawi, nearly 9,000 square miles is forested. There are at present about 88,376 acres of plantations, and although the majority of the trees are less than 15 years old, seasoned and graded timber for construction, for crates and boxes, and for transmission and telephone poles is being produced in limited quantities.

The Government has embarked on an afforestation program to meet the anticipated increase in demand. The acreage planted in the principal forest estates has shown a fairly consistent average annual increase of some 3,000 acres over the past ten years. More than 5,800 acres were planted during 1965, owing to expansion on the Vipya Plateau, where conifer species are being planted under a plan to produce 100,000 tons of dry pulp each year to be used in a projected bleached kraft pulp mill on Lake Malawi. This mill is planned to come into production in 1975 and to export pulp for the manufacture of wrapping and packaging materials in Europe. The total area of pulpwood planted on the Vipya Plateau at the end of 1968 was 47,000 acres. In addition to an increase of 7,175 acres in pulpwood plantations on the Vipya Plateau, some 9,650 acres of new plantations were established in 1969, particularly in the Cholo area.

The production of sawn timber by government sawmills increased significantly in 1968. Sales of sawn timber from these mills rose by 30 per cent, from 164,400 cubic feet in 1967 (value, MK 157,200) to 214,000 cubic feet in 1968 (value, MK 280,400). In 1969, production of sawn timber by government sawmills rose by about 14 per cent, to 244,600 cubic feet (value, MK 318,000). As total domestic sales of sawn timber were valued at MK 510,000 in 1969, imports of sawn timber rose sharply; moreover, the price of imported timber was substantially higher. The value of timber exports fell to MK 16,000 in 1969, from MK 32,000 in 1968. The situation is not likely to change in the near future despite the replacement in 1969 of two old sawmills in Zomba and Dedza by new ones, since the amount of timber that can be produced from government plantations is not expected to show any significant increase until 1972.

FISHING

Fishing is concentrated mainly in Lake Malawi, although some fishing is carried on in Lake Malombe and Lake Chilwa. The annual catch of fish was estimated at 12,000 short tons, valued at MK 800,000, in 1965 and at 19,300 short tons, valued at MK 960,000, in 1966. In spite of the drying up of Lake Chilwa, the fish catch in 1968 was 19,800 short tons, 4,000 short tons (25 per cent) more than in 1967. With the filling up of Lake Chilwa early in 1969, fishing recovered rapidly, and the estimated catch was 26,000 short tons. Another factor contributing to the bigger catches was the modification of the gear used on trawlers in Lake Malawi to suit the capacity of the individual Malawian fisherman. The value of fish exports was MK 168,000 in 1969, and the value of imports of fish was MK 135,200. Thus, for the first time, Malawi became a net exporter of fish.

In order to make up the deficiency of animal protein in the diet of the people, a high priority has been given to the development of the fishing industry. New fishing techniques have been introduced to exploit new species. These efforts have benefited from the financial and technical assistance of the Malawi Development Corporation. Recent road construction has also contributed to the rapid growth of the industry. In 1969, a fishing company, Freshcold Fisheries, Ltd., was established as a holding company for the two local companies engaged in commercial fishing on Lake Malawi, in order to provide capital for more modern equipment. Freshcold is incorporated as a subsidiary of the Malawi Development Corporation, with a capital of MK 220,000.

MANUFACTURING

Manufacturing activity in Malawi originated in the processing of local agricultural export products, mainly tea and tobacco. Since 1965 new manufacturing enterprises have begun to produce consumer goods —such as sugar, soap, cigarettes, soft drinks, household utensils, and textiles. In 1968 tea and tobacco processing industries accounted for about 25 per cent of net manufacturing output at factor cost, whereas

the new industries accounted for 17 per cent. Total output of the manufacturing sector in 1968 was valued at MK 17.2 million, or 8.5 per
cent of total GDP at factor cost, compared with MK 9.8 million or
5.7 per cent of total GDP in 1965 (Table 7). Most of the industries
established since 1965 have relatively high capital-labor ratios.

Manufacturing took a strong turn upward in 1969, as demand
increased sharply because of the higher earnings of both the rural and
the urban population, following upon increased government expenditure
and higher payments to farmers by the Farmers Marketing Board. The
contribution of manufacturing to gross domestic product at factor cost
rose by 15 per cent. Among the principal companies that contributed to
this MK 2.6 million increase in output were the Carlsberg Brewery,
David Whitehead and Sons (Malawi) Ltd. (textile manufacturers), the
Bata Shoe Company, and the Leopard Match Company. The textile
company, which uses locally produced cotton and operates a vertically
integrated mill for printing, weaving, dyeing, and finishing, sold 10 million yards of textiles in 1969, compared with 7 million yards in 1968.
With the establishment of a new printing plant in 1970, its total output
is expected to increase by another 3 million yards. The shoe company
increased its output by 67 per cent, to 1 million pairs, in 1969; of this
total, some 60 per cent were made of leather, the rest of plastic. The
company also produced a wider range of shoes, and its exports to

TABLE 7. MALAWI: CONTRIBUTION OF INDUSTRY TO GDP
AT FACTOR COST, 1965–70

(In millions of Malawi kwacha)

	1965	1966	1967	1968	1969	1970
Manufacturing	9.8	13.4	15.4	17.2	19.8	24.0
Mining and quarrying	—	0.2	0.2	0.2	0.4	0.6
Building and construction [1]	3.6	6.0	5.4	6.6	11.0	11.0
Electricity and water	1.4	1.8	2.0	2.4	2.6	3.0
Total	14.8	21.4	23.0	26.4	33.8	38.6
Total as per cent of monetary GDP at factor cost	17.8%	22.3%	22.2%	24.4%	27.3%	28.6%
Total as per cent of total GDP at factor cost	8.5%	12.1%	12.2%	13.0%	15.3%	16.0%

Sources: Office of the President, *Economic Report, 1969* and *1971*; and data provided
by the Malawian authorities.

[1] These figures relate to the monetized sector only, and therefore differ from the
figures for building and construction shown in Table 2.

Zambia were valued at MK 500,000. The match company began operations in October 1969; by March 1970 the demand for its output had
increased at such a rate that production had climbed to 1,200 boxes
of matches a day. At present the wood splints used in the match factory
are imported from South Africa, but local wood is expected to be substi-
tuted when the poplar trees planted in the Cholo area are ready for use.
A maize flour mill, with a capacity of 25,000 tons of flour, was established in 1969.

MINING

Mining remains of minor importance, but in recent years both the
Government and private companies have undertaken geological surveys
in an effort to assess Malawi's potential mineral wealth, particularly in
respect to radioactive minerals. There has also been some prospecting
for diamonds, monazite, and strontianite, and small quantitites of apa-
tite, pyrite, kimberlite, and titanium have been discovered. Geochemical
drainage surveys indicate that commercial quantities of copper, tin-
molybdenum, nickel, niobium, and uranium may exist. Further detailed
studies are to be carried out to find the extent of these mineral deposits.

A feasibility study is being conducted by a private foreign company
on the quality and ore content of some bauxite deposits discovered on
the Mlanje Plateau. The deposits cover an area of 1 to 2 square miles
and are estimated to contain 50–60 million tons of bauxite. However,
the difficulty of access to the site—on the Mlanje Plateau at an altitude
of 6,500 feet above sea level—together with the costs of transport and
of electricity to process the bauxite, seem to preclude commercial
exploitation at present. There are no roads to the deposits, and the site
is some 340 miles from the port of Beira. Exploitation of bauxite might
also have to wait until the hydroelectric potential of the Shire River
in the Middle Shire Valley has been developed to a capacity of at least
200,000 kilowatts.

CONSTRUCTION

The value of building and construction in the monetized sector rose
from MK 3.6 million in 1965 to MK 6 million in 1966 (Table 7). In
1967, affected by a temporary decline in public investment, building and

construction declined somewhat, but in 1968 the value rose to MK 6.6 million, benefiting from an increase in both private and public investment. As an indication of the expansion, cement sales reached 56,000 tons in 1968, compared with 44,000 tons in 1967.

The building and construction industry experienced a boom in 1969: output rose by 67 per cent, to MK 11 million, as a direct result of the public sector's expenditures on the rail link with Nacala and the Zomba-Lilongwe road. The upsurge of activity in the economy as a whole was also indirectly reflected in the building industry, as the demand for residential housing rose. The expansionary impact of the building and construction activity was transmitted to the brick and cement industry, where output increased considerably; imports of building and other construction materials also increased. Cement sales rose by 50 per cent, to 84,000 tons in 1969, and the Portland Cement Company (Malawi), Ltd., embarked on an MK 2 million program to double its capacity.

Although the demand for high-income housing declined toward the end of the year, building and construction in the aggregate was not expected to level off in 1970. To meet the acute shortage of low-income housing, the Malawi Housing Corporation had a program to construct some 400 houses a year in the Blantyre and Lilongwe areas. In addition, the Government intended to continue to disburse funds for the construction of the new capital city at Lilongwe.

ELECTRIC POWER

The generation and distribution of electricity in Malawi are the monopoly of the Electricity Supply Commission of Malawi (Escom), a statutory body. Generating capacity was estimated in 1965 at 14,500 kilowatts, of which 90 per cent was produced by thermal-generating plants. By 1968 the installed capacity of electricity in Malawi was 34,000 kilowatts. Escom sold 93.9 million kilowatt-hours in 1968, almost double the sales in 1965 and 21.3 per cent above sales in 1967, when there had also been a substantial increase. This rapid expansion in sales was made possible by the expanded capacity of the hydroelectric station at Nkula Falls, from 16,000 kilowatts to 24,000 kilowatts in 1967, and by the completion of a transmission line to Mozambique in 1968 which made Malawi a small exporter of power. Power exports to Mozambique increased by 45 per cent, to 1.28 million kilowatt-hours, in 1970.

Consumption of electricity increased by 12.6 per cent in 1969, compared with an increase of 21.3 per cent in the previous year, apparently because the expansion in industrial activity in 1969 was in existing industries rather than in newly established industries. The rate of increase in consumption of electricity by households in 1969 (12.5 per cent) was also lower than in the previous year (16.4 per cent), probably owing mainly to the fall in the rate of increase in demand for electricity for domestic use in high-income houses, the construction of which declined toward the end of the year.

Early in 1970 the International Development Association (IDA) agreed to extend a 50-year, interest-free loan equivalent to MK 4.4 million to build a new hydroelectric station, with a capacity of 16,000 kilowatts, at Tedzani Falls on the Shire River. Additional loans are being provided by the African Development Bank (MK 2.5 million for 20 years) and the Commonwealth Development Corporation (MK 1 million for 16 years) to meet the foreign exchange costs of the construction of the related transmission lines. The funds will be re-lent by the Government to Escom at 7 per cent interest. Escom will provide MK 3.4 million from its own resources to meet the domestic costs of the project, which is expected to provide enough electricity to meet Malawi's requirements for the foreseeable future. As a temporary measure for three years, Escom has increased its tariffs by 3 per cent in order to raise part of the revenue needed to meet its share of the cost of the project.

TRANSPORT

Malawi has approximately 410 miles of railways and 7,000 miles of roads. In addition, Lake Malawi serves as a major water route between the north and the south.

The existing road system is considered inadequate both for the present and for the developing needs of the country. Hence, the Government has given high priority to improving the network of main roads and to expanding the system of feeder roads to allow for more efficient collection and distribution of agricultural products. Between 1965 and

1968, nearly MK 8 million was spent in adding 1,000 miles of new or reconstructed roads to the country's network. Construction of a 180-mile road between Zomba and Lilongwe, the proposed new capital, was begun in 1968. The project is estimated to cost MK 11.4 million, of which MK 9.6 million is to be financed by a long-term loan from the IDA, and is expected to be completed by August 1971. To improve the transportation of agricultural produce in the Central Region, some MK 1.24 million has been spent on the Central Region Lakeshore Development Project.

Fluctuations in agricultural production create serious problems for rail transportation in Malawi. The tonnage hauled by the Malawi Railways increased by 30 per cent in 1967; but in 1968, a poor crop year, the increase was only 7 per cent. Passenger traffic has also fluctuated since 1965, declining by 10 per cent in both 1967 and 1968. In addition to these problems, the company had heavy expenditures in 1968 for rolling stock and a dieselization program, and its net operating profits declined.

The railway system was used extensively during 1967 to assist Zambia in diversifying its trade routes, but the early completion of the Tan-Zam oil pipeline in July 1968 has virtually eliminated the transport of oil by rail. Zambian copper exports through Malawi have also dropped from 4,000 tons a month to less than 2,000 tons. In 1969 total tonnage hauled by the Malawi Railways declined by 33 per cent, primarily as a result of the loss of the Zambian transit traffic. This led to a 59 per cent decline (to MK 630,000) in the Railways' estimated operating profits.

A 63-mile railroad to Nova Freizo, to connect the Malawi rail system with that of Mozambique and thus to give Malawi access to the Indian Ocean port of Nacala, was begun in May 1968 and completed in August 1970. Some 90 per cent of the costs of construction and rolling stock was financed through a loan of MK 10.2 million from the Industrial Development Corporation of South Africa.

In addition to the expansion of the railway system, efforts are being made to improve shipping facilities on Lake Malawi, which is an important communications link between the Northern and Southern Regions of the country. Over the seven years 1960–66, the lake service carried an average of 17,000 tons of cargo a year, while the tonnage carried in 1969 was 23,000 tons. The number of passengers carried by the lake service rose from 41,000 persons in 1965 to 114,000 in 1969. Plans are under way to develop an efficient transport system on the lake.

Following the dissolution of the Central African Airways Corporation, Air Malawi, a government-owned commercial enterprise, assumed full responsibility for all of the former's domestic services from January 1, 1968. It also operates international flights between Blantyre and Salisbury, Johannesburg, Lusaka, Ndola, and Beira, in addition to its domestic services. In 1969 Air Malawi took delivery of two new aircraft and completed a new engineering base at Chileka airport.

TOURISM

Malawi, with its beautiful landscape, lakes, and wildlife, has a number of tourist attractions. Compared with the tourist traffic in East Africa, however, tourism is still in its infancy in Malawi. At present, an average of about 85,000 tourists visit the country annually, bringing in more than MK 2 million in foreign exchange. The majority of tourists come from South Africa, Rhodesia, Zambia, and Mozambique, traveling mostly by road.

On May 3, 1969 a privately owned tourist firm—the United Tourist Company Limited—was formed as a subsidiary of the United Transport Company (Malawi) Limited. The new firm has an authorized and issued capital of MK 10,000. The Malawi Development Corporation holds a 26 per cent interest in this company, which organizes package tours in Malawi. The Development Corporation has also invested in hotels and other tourist facilities; these investments, which increased by 22 per cent in 1970, to nearly MK 0.95 million, are expected to rise to MK 0.97 million in 1971 (Table 8).

The Portuguese Government has agreed to provide a loan to finance the construction of a road through Tete in Mozambique to southern Africa, in an effort to encourage the flow of tourists from that region. Malawi intends to start package tours for South African and Rhodesian residents to Lake Malawi. Though the conservation of wildlife in game preserves for the benefit of the tourist industry is not expected to be on a large scale, South African tourists are expected to patronize such preserves. The Government is about to undertake an economic evaluation of tourism in Malawi, with technical and financial assistance from the United Kingdom.

INDUSTRIAL PROMOTION

Since 1965 the Government, in pursuing an active policy of industrial promotion, has introduced the following measures: (1) provision of exclusive protection for a limited period to industries whose production is too large for the domestic market; (2) exemption from customs duty of imports of certain primary products and goods for industrial use; (3) initial depreciation allowances on capital expenditure varying from 10 per cent to 33.5 per cent, depending on the type of capital equipment; (4) an investment allowance for tax purposes of 10 per cent on new plant and equipment other than motor vehicles; and (5) physical incentives in the form of government-improved industrial sites, which are available for rent to prospective investors. Where local involvement is considered necessary, the Government's policy is to encourage participation by Malawians in foreign-owned enterprises rather than outright nationalization.

An important stimulus to the development of industry is provided by the Malawi Development Corporation, a wholly-owned government

TABLE 8.   MALAWI: INVESTMENTS BY MALAWI DEVELOPMENT
CORPORATION, 1968–71

(*In thousands of Malawi kwacha*)

Economic Activity	Investments Outstanding [1]				Assets of Beneficiary Companies [2]
	1968	1969	1970 [3]	1971 [4]	
Milling, food, beverages	1,380	1,684	1,696	1,696	3,000
Tourism, hotels, catering	726	778	948	966	1,720
Wholesaling, retailing	20	678	960	792	5,200
Finance, property	72	230	166	266	2,120
Agriculture, fisheries	450	454	548	822	460
Textiles, clothing	400	382	382	382	4,400
Construction materials	166	102	102	102	260
Metal products	88	88	88	88	920
Chemicals, paper, electronics	46	30	46	180	120
Total	3,348	4,426	4,936	5,294	18,200

Sources: Office of the President, *Economic Report, 1969* and *1971.*

[1] At end of year.
[2] I.e., the estimated total of the assets of the companies in which the corporation has invested.
[3] Provisional.
[4] Estimated.

institution. The corporation was established by the Government of Malawi in January 1964 with capital from its own resources amounting to MK 100,000, a grant of MK 1 million from the U. K. Government, and contributions of some MK 238,000 from other sources. Subsequent financial participation in the form of loans amounting to MK 4 million was obtained as follows: MK 794,000 (interest free) from the U. K. Government, MK 670,000 from the Malawian Government, MK 1.22 million (interest free) from the Danish Government, MK 76,000 from the Kreditanstalt für Wiederaufbau of Germany, and a long-term loan of MK 1.27 million from other financial institutions. The local commercial banks have also made loans to the corporation amounting to MK 1.2 million. On January 1, 1970 the corporation became a limited liability company, with a share capital of MK 2.2 million, wholly owned by the Government.

The aims of the Malawi Development Corporation are to encourage the agricultural, commercial, and industrial development of Malawi. As a general policy, apart from the complete take-over of certain trading firms formerly under government control, the corporation has limited itself to equity participation in private enterprises, usually as a minority shareholder. It has the authority to participate in industries through the provision of loans and grants or in an advisory capacity.

In 1966 the corporation completed investments totaling more than MK 1 million; by the end of 1970, its investments amounted to MK 4.9 million (Table 8). Excluding the hotel industry and the Nzeru Radio Company, Ltd., in which the corporation has 85 per cent and 60 per cent of the equity, respectively, its shareholdings range from 14 per cent in B and C Metal Products, Ltd., to 50 per cent in National Oil Industries, Ltd. (previously a wholly owned subsidiary of the Farmers Marketing Board). Other companies in which the corporation holds shares include Agrinal (Malawi) Ltd., which produces hoes; Carlsberg Malawi, Ltd., which brews beer; Malawi Distilleries, which makes gin; the National Trading Company, Ltd.; and David Whitehead and Sons (Malawi) Ltd., which produces textiles. The corporation's major activities in 1969 were concentrated on building hotels, wholesale and retail trading, and real estate.

The Malawi Development Corporation is financially supported in its industrial promotion functions by one major subsidiary—the Develop-

TABLE 9.   MALAWI: INVESTMENTS BY DEFINCO, 1968–71

(*In thousands of Malawi kwacha*)

Economic Activity	Investments Outstanding [1]				Assets of Beneficiary Companies [2]
	1968	1969	1970 [3]	1971 [4]	
Finance and property	820	872	872	872	1,340
Construction materials	—	512	512	512	4,000
Chemicals, paper, electronics	—	150	150	150	860
Total	820	1,534	1,534	1,534	6,200

Sources: Office of the President, *Economic Report, 1969* and *1971*; and data provided by the Malawian authorities.

[1] At end of year.
[2] I.e., the estimated total of the assets of the companies in which DEFINCO has invested.
[3] Provisional.
[4] Estimated. Excludes projects still to be approved, estimated at MK 86,000.

ment Finance Company of Malawi, Ltd. (DEFINCO), which in turn has as subsidiaries DEFINCO Investment Trust Ltd., Namiwawa Estates, Ltd., and City Development, Ltd. DEFINCO and its subsidiaries are collectively known as the DEFINCO Group.

DEFINCO was established in 1968 in partnership with certain lenders, with the Development Corporation holding 51 per cent of the equity. The remaining shares are held by Commonwealth Development Finance Company, Ltd., Barclays Overseas Development Corporation, Ltd., Standard Bank Finance and Development Corporation, Ltd., South African Mutual Life Assurance Society, New Zealand Insurance Company, Ltd., and other foreign companies. In 1969 DEFINCO raised some MK 1.12 million, mostly from foreign sources, for investment in industries in which the Development Corporation had a financial interest. DEFINCO's investments are shown in Table 9.

ECONOMIC DEVELOPMENT AND PLANNING

DEVELOPMENT PLAN, 1965–69

Soon after independence, the Government prepared a Five-Year Development Plan to guide public investment for 1965–69. A total outlay of MK 89.2 million was envisaged for the period, i.e., an average annual rate of expenditure of MK 17.8 million, which is equivalent to nearly 20 per cent of GDP. The Plan placed major emphasis on the development of agriculture, internal communications, and educational facilities and on the promotion of industrial enterprises, the largest allocation being for the development of internal communications, primarily the construction of roads.

Implementation of the Plan encountered a series of difficulties, ranging from delays in the delivery of equipment and in recruitment of staff to inexperience in handling international bidding and negotiation. Actual development expenditure rose from MK 9.4 million in 1965 (83 per cent of the budget estimate) to MK 12.8 million in 1966, but fell to MK 10.1 million in 1967 (69 per cent of the budget estimate). Agriculture, communications, and transport accounted for a substantial proportion of development expenditure, which was financed almost entirely by external loans and grants, for the most part from the United Kingdom.

In order to clarify and reformulate the development objectives, the Government decided to replace the remainder of the 1965–69 Development Plan with an interim, three-year "rolling" program [2] covering the period 1968–70. The objective of this interim program was, among other things, to lay the foundation for a more detailed and comprehensive plan covering the period 1970–75 which would also take private investment into account. The interim 1968–70 program envisaged total expenditure of MK 63 million: MK 22 million in both 1968 and 1969 and MK 19 million in 1970. Investments in social infrastructure and in the development of natural resources were to account for MK 14 million and MK 16 million, respectively.

The emphasis in the 1965–69 Development Plan on the need to develop natural resources, internal communications, and transport was continued under the new program. Expenditure on transport, which accounted for 22 per cent of total development expenditure in 1967, accounted for 32 per cent in 1968, when the total was MK 14 million, i.e., exceeding the total for 1966.

Development expenditure in 1969 was the largest on record: the total outlay for the 15-month period ended March 31, 1970 was estimated at MK 22 million, disbursed mainly in the areas of agriculture, transport, and education. Expenditure on agriculture for this period was

---

[2] A three-year rolling program is basically a three-year development plan to which an additional year is added at the expiration of the first year of the plan. In this way a perpetual three-year plan is maintained and revised every year in the light of varying domestic requirements and changing revenue prospects.

TABLE 10. MALAWI: THREE-YEAR DEVELOPMENT PROGRAM, 1970/71–1972/73, AND SOURCES OF FINANCING

(In thousands of Malawi kwacha)

	1970/71		1971/72		1972/73		1970/71–1972/73	
	External finance	Local finance	External finance	Local finance	External finance	Local finance	Total	Total as % of program
Directly productive activities	21,318	2,292	7,336	1,880	8,662	1,722	43,210	52.4
Agriculture	*4,182*	*1,132*	*3,716*	*928*	*6,548*	*1,160*	*17,666*	*21.4*
Fisheries, forestry, game	*756*	*100*	*778*	*88*	*788*	*86*	*2,596*	*3.2*
Finance, commerce, industry	*78*	*8*	*244*	*16*	*380*	*20*	*746*	*0.9*
Transport	*16,302*	*1,052*	*2,598*	*848*	*946*	*456*	*22,202*	*26.9*
Surveys and investigations	222	34	220	32	196	30	734	0.9
Power, water, sanitation	2,544	64	2,834	138	2,780	136	8,496	10.3
Power	*2,020*	*—*	*2,410*	*—*	*2,200*	*—*	*6,630*	*8.0*
Water and sanitation	*524*	*64*	*424*	*138*	*580*	*136*	*1,866*	*2.3*
Other economic infrastructure	844	470	870	470	756	444	3,854	4.7
Veterinary services	*424*	*58*	*442*	*44*	*450*	*26*	*1,444*	*1.8*
Administration and training	*420*	*412*	*428*	*426*	*306*	*418*	*2,410*	*2.9*
Social infrastructure	9,034	1,734	6,926	1,820	4,922	1,664	26,110	31.7
Education	*3,850*	*468*	*2,790*	*328*	*1,620*	*238*	*9,294*	*11.3*
Health	*276*	*60*	*108*	*150*	*400*	*462*	*1,456*	*1.8*
Housing	*224*	*264*	*300*	*320*	*300*	*440*	*1,848*	*2.2*
Community and social development	*8*		*16*			*120*	*144*	*0.2*
Government buildings	*40*	*720*	*28*	*918*	*66*	*324*	*2,106*	*2.6*
Miscellaneous services	*398*	*40*	*4*	*44*	*4*	*44*	*534*	*0.6*
New capital city	*3,000*	*92*	*3,000*	*22*	*1,834*	*—*	*7,948*	*9.6*
Post and telecommunications	*1,238*	*80*	*680*	*48*	*698*	*36*	*2,780*	*3.4*
Total	33,962	4,594	18,186	4,350	17,316	3,996	82,404	100.0

Sources: Office of the President, *Economic Report, 1969*, and *Development Programme, 1970/71–1972/73*.

approximately MK 4.6 million, against MK 2.4 million in 1968, and was allocated to extension services, pilot projects, control of disease in livestock, and a number of agricultural development schemes. Some MK 1.4 million was spent on education, mainly for technical and secondary schools, a teacher training college, and the University of Malawi. Expenditures on transport were MK 6 million in the 15-month period ended March 31, 1970, against MK 4.4 million in the calendar year 1968,[3] the principal projects being construction of roads and the rail link with Nacala.

Both the 1968 and 1969 programs were financed mainly from external loans and grants. Local resources were used to provide the local counterpart of external aid and for small projects that were not eligible for foreign aid.

DEVELOPMENT PROGRAM, 1970/71–1972/73

The development program for the three years 1970/71–1972/73 provides for total expenditure of MK 82.4 million, of which MK 43.2 million (52 per cent) is earmarked for directly productive activities, including MK 17.7 million for agriculture and MK 22.2 million for transport (Table 10). Some 10 per cent (MK 8.5 million) of the total will be spent on power, water, and sanitation, of which MK 6.6 million will be allocated to the generation of electric power; projected outlays on the Tedzani hydroelectric project account for this large expenditure on power. Major infrastructure projects are the Zomba-Lilongwe road, the main sections of the lakeshore road, the rail link with Nacala, the new capital city, and the University of Malawi. More than MK 9 million is to be spent on education, and MK 8 million is allocated to the new capital city. Expenditures on post and telecommunications and on government buildings are expected to be MK 2.8 million and MK 2 million, respectively, during this period. Expenditure on social infrastructure for the whole period is estimated at MK 26.1 million (32 per cent of the total program expenditure).

The program for 1970/71–1972/73, like previous ones, is expected to be financed mainly from foreign grants and loans (Table 10).

---

[3] The Government changed its fiscal year from a calendar year to an April–March year, beginning April 1, 1970.

Finance for the first year of the program is firmly secured, but projections for the second and third years are based on expected levels of foreign assistance. Some MK 34 million (88 per cent of total expenditure for 1970/71) is being financed from external sources. For each of the years 1971/72 and 1972/73, external finance is expected to account for 81 per cent of total expenditure.

The Government is preparing, for the 1970s, a set of targets based on the projected level of exports, current expenditure, capital expenditure, and consumption. The three-year rolling programs are to be operated concurrently with these targets and will set out in detail the general guidelines of the ten-year program.

PRICES, WAGES, AND EMPLOYMENT

PRICES

The only price indices available relate to exports, imports, and government wholesale purchases. This last index rose by some 2.6 per cent from 1968 to 1969. The import price index (1967 = 100) declined from 106.4 in 1968 to 105.2 in 1969, while the export price index (1967 = 100) rose from 111.1 to 118.3, suggesting an improvement in the terms of trade.

Although the Government has indicated its determination to intervene where necessary to stabilize prices, a number of fiscal and other measures adopted early in 1970 are likely to lead to price increases. In the budget for 1970/71, a sales tax of 5 per cent on both imported and locally manufactured goods was introduced and certain customs and excise duties were raised. The Electricity Supply Commission also raised its rates by 3 per cent. In addition, there are likely to be temporary dislocations in retail trade as a result of the relocation of Asian traders from rural to urban areas in keeping with the Government's policy of providing Malawians an opportunity to engage in retail trading. Moreover, the anticipated shortage of maize and the relatively higher cost of maize imports in 1970 was expected to exert upward pressure on the cost of living.

WAGES AND SALARIES

Statutory wage-fixing machinery guarantees a minimum wage to all workers. The Government decides the rate upon the advice of a National Wages Commission, to which separate recommendations are presented by the six Wages Advisory Councils and a Wages Advisory Board. The Councils represent workers engaged in road transport, repair and servicing of motor vehicles, retail trading, the tobacco industry, the tea industry, and construction; the Board meets the needs of the remaining workers.

The legal minimum wages set in 1966 are still in force, i.e., 37.5 tambala a day for the city of Blantyre, 32.5 tambala a day for the municipality of Lilongwe and the townships of Zomba and Mzuzu, and 23.3 tambala a day for the rest of the country. There are, however, qualifications to the above rulings. The law stipulating minimum wages (Regulation of Minimum Wages and Conditions of Employment Act) permits employers in the city of Blantyre to pay an allowance to employees whose daily wage is 50 tambala or less—4.2 tambala a day to employees 18 years of age and over and 3.3 tambala to employees below that age. Employers are also permitted to pay higher wages to workers with special skills.

Only the minimum wage is set by law. Actual wages are determined by collective bargaining between employers and workers. The latter are presently represented by 19 trade unions. In 1969 the Malawian worker shared in the general improvement in economic activity in the country: average annual earnings of the worker were estimated at MK 308, compared with MK 302 in 1968. The largest increase in the wage bill was thought to be in the construction industry, where average hourly earnings for both unskilled and skilled workers have been typically above the average for all industries.

The last general increase in both the wages of civil servants and the minimum wage took place in 1966. Since then wage increases appear to have been limited to workers with scarce skills and to specific industries, especially those undergoing rapid expansion. The general pattern of wage stability is explained by the policy of the Government, which emphasizes that, so long as rural incomes are below urban incomes, the need to improve rural living standards dictates that the level of wages set in 1966 should be maintained. In effect, the Government has been attempting to contain urban unemployment by reducing the wage differential between the urban and rural populations. Apart from inducing urban employers to adopt more labor-intensive techniques, this policy also has the advantage of discouraging migration from the rural to the urban areas and reducing the capital cost of development projects, hence maximizing the development returns from the Government's limited resources.

A paper on wage policy issued by the Government in November 1969 and circulated to employers' associations and trade unions did not revise the existing minimum wages but set up broad policies with respect to wage rates throughout the country. It stated inter alia that the Government's present policy is to maintain the volume of its own paid employment and the share of national income paid as wages to its employees; to adjust pay rates selectively so as to attract scarce skills and encourage private employers to pursue a similar policy of selective pay increases; and to maintain minimum wages for unskilled workers at present levels as the main incentive for employers to increase the volume of paid employment and to reward scarce skills and experience by the payment of significant differentials.

EMPLOYMENT

Of the resident African population of more than 4 million, an estimated 90 per cent are directly dependent on agriculture, while some 160,000 are in full and part-time wage and salary employment (as of March 1970; see Table 11). The latter are mostly employed by agricultural estates and factories, construction, and general commerce and trade. However, large numbers of Malawian workers (253,000, approximately) are employed in neighboring countries, mainly South Africa, Rhodesia, and Zambia.

Of the domestically employed labor force, available data indicate that about 40 per cent of the 130,000 wage earners in 1966 were employed in agriculture, 15 per cent in building and construction, and 10 per cent in trading activities. In 1968 only 33 per cent of the total employed labor force of 134,473 were employed in agriculture, forestry, and fishing (Table 11), the proportion employed in trading and allied occu-

TABLE 11. MALAWI: NUMBER OF PAID EMPLOYEES, 1968–70 [1]

	Dec. 1968	Dec. 1969	Mar. 1970
Private sector	**89,614**	**99,893**	**112,854**
Agriculture, forestry, and fishing	40,782	42,528	55,713
Mining and quarrying	271	705	542
Manufacturing	16,583	17,001	15,743
Construction	7,763	12,175	15,676
Wholesale, retail, and hotels and restaurants	9,393	10,975	8,385
Transport, storage, and communications	6,495	6,469	6,409
Finance, insurance, and business	866	1,116	1,194
Other services	7,461	8,924	9,192
Public sector	**44,859**	**46,607**	**45,228**
Agriculture, forestry, and fishing	3,367	5,753	3,404
Mining and quarrying	214	291	173
Manufacturing	654	690	306
Construction	7,544	5,018	5,014
Transport, storage, and communications	1,687	1,898	1,963
Other services	31,393	32,957	34,368
Total paid employment	**134,473**	**146,500**	**158,082**

Sources: National Statistical Office, *Reported Employment and Earnings, First Quarter 1970;* and Office of the President, *Economic Report, 1971.*

[1] Resident Africans only, i.e., Malawians working abroad and foreigners working in Malawi are excluded.

pations was 7 per cent, virtually all in the private sector, and manufacturing accounted for 12 per cent.

The rate of increase in employment in 1969, particularly in the monetary sector, appears to have been generally in line with the rise in output. Information derived from the number of vacancies filled through the Department of Labor indicate that 39.2 per cent of those looking for employment were provided with jobs, compared with 34.4 per cent in 1968, and the number of employed increased by 9 per cent. In the manufacturing sector, there was an estimated 3 per cent increase in employment; this apparently low rate of increase is explained by the fact that the new industries that have been established in the country in recent years have high capital-labor ratios. Although employment in the agricultural sector increased by 9 per cent, to 48,281, agriculture's share of total employment remained at 33 per cent. Employment in private construction is estimated to have increased by 57 per cent, to 12,175, as a result of the increase in construction activity. Total employment in the private sector showed a significant increase during the first quarter of 1970.

The level of employment of Malawians outside the country depends both on domestic economic conditions and on the intensity of demand for foreign labor in the neighboring countries. South Africa and Malawi have concluded a labor agreement effective from November 1967 under which Malawians work under contract in South Africa. The contracts provide for employment for a period of two years at a time, for remittances of income tax to Malawi, and for 60 per cent of earned pay to be deferred and transferred to Malawi where it can be claimed after the worker returns home. Workers may be given another two-year contract under the same conditions after having spent at least six months in Malawi. Implementation of this agreement is administered by the Employment Services Division of the Ministry of Labor of Malawi. The number of Malawians in South Africa in 1967 was estimated at 80,000 men, of which 46,000 were under contract. The number of Malawians in Rhodesia and Zambia in 1967 (both workers and dependents) was estimated at 155,000 and 45,000, respectively.

With the natural increase in population and the depressed condition of agriculture in 1968, the migration of Malawian workers, especially to South Africa, is believed to have increased toward the end of that year, although precise information is lacking. This increased migration is reflected in the increase in remittances by Malawians working in South Africa in particular, which rose from MK 3.5 million in 1968 to MK 5.7 million in 1969 (Table 12).

TABLE 12.   MALAWI: REMITTANCES BY MALAWIANS WORKING ABROAD, 1965–69

	1965	1966	1967	1968	1969
THOUSANDS OF KWACHA					
South Africa	3,090	3,046	2,802	3,484	5,748
Rhodesia	622	542	522	604	690
Zambia	346	668	646	218	478
Total	4,058	4,256	3,970	4,306	6,916
AS PER CENT OF TOTAL					
South Africa	76.2	71.6	70.6	80.9	83.1
Rhodesia	15.3	12.7	13.1	14.0	10.0
Zambia	8.5	15.7	16.3	5.1	6.9
Total	100.0	100.0	100.0	100.0	100.0

Sources: Government of Malawi, *Ministry of Labour Report*, 1963–67; and data provided by the Malawian authorities.

GOVERNMENT FINANCE

BUDGETARY SYSTEM

The fiscal year in Malawi runs from April 1 to March 31.[4] The Government's budget is divided into a current and a development budget, which indicate both sources of revenue and areas of expenditure. Current expenditure is further classified into "statutory" and "voted" expenditure. The former entails mainly public debt charges and pensions and gratuities, while the latter consists of the current expenditures of various government departments and ministries.

Both budgets are presented simultaneously to Parliament, which votes appropriations before the beginning of each fiscal year. Supplementary appropriations may be voted from time to time during the year as the need arises. Appropriations are approved by Parliament in a series of votes for different departments and agencies. Budgetary transfers between different votes are not permitted, although the Minister of Finance may authorize transfers between items within a single vote without obtaining prior approval from Parliament.

All normal revenues, as well as special revenues of a nonrecurrent type, accrue to a general Revenue Account, to which all current expenditures are debited. Development expenditures are financed from a separate Development Fund Account, to which are credited contributions from the current budget, loans and grants for development, and other revenue from miscellaneous sources earmarked for that account.

After the budget has been approved by Parliament, the Accountant General, who is responsible for all government disbursements, is authorized under a general warrant approved by the Minister of Finance to spend certain sums of money, which, however, need not equal the total budgetary appropriations. All expenditures are charged against this warrant, and there is no other separate, central preauditing of each expenditure request; the ministers are individually responsible for ensuring that their expenditures are in accordance with the budgetary appropriations. The Auditor General conducts a postaudit of all government expenditures, and his report, which is published after the end of each financial year, is scrutinized by Parliament.

---

[4] See footnote 5 below (p. 248).

To improve financial management and control, a procedure of "appropriations-in-aid" was adopted in 1969. Under this system, the gross expenditure against each vote is offset by reimbursements and direct departmental earnings and, although only the net sum is voted by Parliament as reflecting the net operating costs of the department, the gross sum is appropriated and controlled. An advantage of this procedure is the encouragement it gives to controlling officers and heads of departments to ensure that revenues and reimbursements are collected fully and expeditiously in order that they may be available to meet expenditures.

A major characteristic of Malawian public finance is the existence of persistent, though decreasing, large deficits on current account and the total dependence upon external grants and loans to finance not only these deficits but over 80 per cent of public development expenditures as well.

STRUCTURE OF TAX REVENUE

The taxes accruing to the Central Government may be divided into three groups: customs and excise duties, taxes on income, and other taxes. Customs and excise duties make a slightly higher contribution to revenue than do income taxes; other taxes make only a minor contribution. In 1965 import duties (not including a tax on gasoline and a fiscal payment from Rhodesia) accounted for 23 per cent of the Government's current revenue, excise taxes for 3 per cent, and income taxes for 28 per cent; at that time taxes on corporations and self-employed persons accounted for 10 per cent of current revenue. By 1969 the share of import duties in current revenue had increased to 29 per cent, that of excise taxes to 5 per cent, and that of income taxes to 33 per cent; taxes on corporations and self-employed persons increased more than threefold during the period, contributing some 17 per cent of current revenue in 1969 (Table 13).

Customs Duties and Excise Taxes

The administration of customs and excise taxes is entrusted to the Department of Customs and Excise, which has its headquarters in the Blantyre-Limbe area, the commercial center of the country. The

TABLE 13. MALAWI: CURRENT BUDGET REVENUE, 1965–1970/71

(In thousands of Malawi kwacha)

	1965	1966	1967	1968	1969 Original estimates	1969 Revised estimates	1970[1] Original estimates	1970/71[2] Original estimates
Taxes on income								
Minimum, graduated, and assessed taxes	1,974	2,000	2,232	2,478	3,100	2,832	644	3,160
Employed persons (P.A.Y.E.)	1,306	1,614	1,908	2,254	2,600	2,530	720	2,800
Corporations and self-employed persons	1,824	2,638	4,170	5,182	5,800	5,750	340	6,100
Total	5,104	6,252	8,310	9,914	11,500	11,112	1,704	12,060
Customs duties and excise taxes								
Import duties	4,164	7,102	8,876	8,940	10,500	9,622	2,450	10,346
Tax on motor spirits	810	938	—	—	—	—	—	—
Fiscal payment from Rhodesian Government	822	22	—	—	—	—	—	—
Excise duties	592	680	802	980	1,660	1,786	—	2,400
Sales tax	—	—	—	—	—	—	540	2,000
Other	8	14	176	28	18	24	10	26
Total	6,396	8,756	9,854	9,948	12,178	11,434	3,002	14,770
Licenses, fees, and stamp duties	994	1,154	988	1,206	1,590	1,574	366	1,706
Total tax revenue	12,494	16,162	19,152	21,068	25,268	24,118	5,072	28,538
Departmental services and reimbursements	1,452	1,550	1,892	2,692	4,164	4,704	⋮	5,394
Post and telegraphs	1,532	1,618	1,946	2,250	796	1,080	350	1,120
Interest and loan redemption	1,288	1,612	1,650	1,604	1,544	1,664	788	1,500
Rents	400	418	698	792	762	816	170	650
Miscellaneous receipts	1,178	826	1,346	1,436	1,182	1,346	800	1,258
Total nontax revenue	5,850	6,024	7,532	8,774	8,448	9,612	⋮	9,920
Total current revenue	18,344	22,186	26,684	29,842	33,716	33,730	⋮	38,458
Percentage increase in tax revenue	27.8%	29.4%	18.5%	10.0%		14.5%		18.3%
Tax revenue as per cent of monetary GDP	13.9%	15.3%	16.8%	17.6%		17.6%		18.7%
Total revenue as per cent of monetary GDP	20.4%	21.0%	23.4%	25.0%		24.6%		25.3%
Revenue from import duties as per cent of imports[3]	12.0%	16.7%	21.7%	21.1%	20.9%			20.5–21.0%

Sources: Government of Malawi, Financial Statements, 1967–1970/71, and Estimates of Expenditure on Revenue Account, 1970/71; Office of the President, Economic Report, 1967–1971; and data provided by the Malawian authorities.

[1] January–March only.
[2] Fiscal year April 1, 1970–March 31, 1971.
[3] Excluding investment goods.

department has recently adopted the Brussels tariff nomenclature and the Brussels definition of value.

Customs Tariff.—Import duties are the largest single contributor to current revenue. The customs tariff provides for three rates of duty—a most-favored-nation rate, an intermediate rate (predominantly for Commonwealth countries), and a special preferential rate for imports from the United Kingdom. Most raw materials intended for industrial use are admitted free of duty. The general tariff rate applied to most manufactured goods is 30 per cent, but a preferential rate of 20 per cent applies to goods from the United Kingdom and to many Commonwealth goods. In addition, most items are subject to a general surcharge of 8⅓ per cent, which was imposed in 1968 for revenue purposes. Higher rates are levied on goods particularly suited as revenue earners and to protect domestic industry. Protective duties, which affect primarily clothing, textiles, beer, and spirits, are considered moderate. Low rates (in the range of 1 to 5 per cent) are applied to semimanufactured goods and building materials. Some local industries enjoy a manufacturers' rebate on the duty paid on imported materials and components used in domestic manufacture. Such rebates (which in 1968 amounted to MK 240,000) represent the actual amount of the duty paid on these items, and are returned to the manufacturers after proof of use has been supplied.

Receipts from import duties rose from MK 4,164,000 in 1965 to MK 9,622,000 in 1969 (Table 13). The increase was partly due to a greater volume and value of imports; but it was also the result of upward revisions in the existing rates and changes in the customs and excise tax structure, in response to the economic effects of the abrogation of the trade agreement with Rhodesia in November 1965 and to the Government's policy of import substitution. Import duties represented 12 per cent of the value of imports (excluding investment goods) in 1965, 16.7 per cent in 1966, 21.7 per cent in 1967, and 21 per cent in both 1968 and 1969.

Excise Taxes.—Excise taxes have been a minor source of revenue, despite their threefold increase between 1965 and 1969. Goods subject to excise tax include soap, spirits, sugar, tobacco products, and beer. In 1968 tobacco products alone accounted for 76 per cent of the excise tax collected. The rates of excise tax are lower than the corresponding import duties, thus affording protective margins to local manufacturers.

Taxes on Income

Personal Income Tax.—The tax on incomes of individuals is payable on income from the previous year derived from sources within Malawi. The tax is calculated according to two different formulas, the larger of the two results being the amount payable. (1) Under the first formula no account is taken of a taxpayer's personal circumstances, such as marital status or size of family, but some allowable deductions, e.g., contributions to approved pension schemes, are permitted. The resulting income is subject to a scale of rates which rises in segments from a minimum of MK 3 on annual incomes of MK 122 or less to a maximum of MK 60 on incomes in excess of MK 2,400 a year. (2) Under the second formula, a taxpayer's personal circumstances are taken into account, and personal allowances are deducted from taxable income; these include an allowance of MK 600 per annum for a single person, MK 1,440 per annum for a married person, and MK 288 per annum for each child under 18 years of age. Tax is payable on chargeable income at rates which commence at 12½ per cent on the first MK 1,000 per annum and rise progressively to 40 per cent on income in excess of MK 13,000 per annum.

Incomes below MK 900 are classified as low incomes. They are taxed under one of three different procedures—"minimum," "graduated," or "assessed." A minimum (poll) tax of MK 3.50 per annum is payable by all male persons over the age of 18 who reside in Malawi and whose annual income is less than MK 122, unless they are liable to assessed or graduated tax, and by others in special circumstances, notably migrant workers in South African mines. Of the total levy, an amount of MK 0.70 is passed back to the local authority of the district in which the taxpayer resides. The graduated tax is a simple wage tax; it is imposed on the current wages of employees earning up to MK 900, at rates ranging from 4.1 per cent to 2.1 per cent. It is based on the first formula described above, and is administered through the use of graduated tax stamps and special tax cards. The assessed tax is a tax on income other than wages of individuals resident in rural areas and is primarily a tax on traders whose incomes do not exceed MK 900 per annum. The scale of rates is that of the first formula described above. Assessments are made by rural assessment boards appointed by the Minister of Finance.

Corporation Tax.—Companies are subject to tax at the rate of 40 per cent of chargeable income. Companies not incorporated in Malawi are subject to an additional 5 per cent tax, which also applies to profits distributed as dividends to nonresident shareholders of companies incorporated in Malawi. However, provision exists for the remission of the additional 5 per cent in special circumstances.

Undistributed profits are subject to a tax of 22½ per cent, but the authorities have announced their intention to abolish this tax, and the necessary legislation has been presented to Parliament.

Other Taxes

Items in this classification include motor vehicle, trading, and arms and ammunition licenses and stamp duties. Stamp duties have in the past made a relatively small contribution to revenue, but recently proposed legislation aims at doubling the yield from this source. In 1968, these licenses and stamp duties are estimated to have contributed only 5.7 per cent of total tax revenue, of which about three fourths was from motor vehicle and trading licenses.

Investment Incentives

Malawi does not grant tax holidays to attract new industries or to encourage the expansion of existing ones, but relies on investment incentives, in the form of allowances deductible from taxable income, which are granted under the provisions of the Income Tax Act (see Structure of the Economy—Industrial Promotion, above). Malawi is a party to double taxation agreements with Denmark, France, Norway, Sweden, Switzerland, the United Kingdom, and the United States.

Tax Administration

Tax administration is entrusted to the Commissioner of Income Tax, but the day-to-day work connected with the minimum, graduated, and assessed income taxes is carried out by district commissioners in the field under the advice and guidance of the Commissioner. The administration of the other taxes on income is carried out by a centralized taxation department with offices in Blantyre.

In spite of serious staff problems, the Income Tax Department is endeavoring to modernize and simplify the laws, systems, and procedures with a view to improving efficiency. A notable feature of the Income Tax Department has been the rapid growth in its activities since the dissolution of the Federation. The number of personal and corporate payers of income tax rose from 237 to 9,267 in 1964–68, and collections rose from MK 2.6 million to MK 7.4 million in the same period. Statistics for the latter year show that the wholesale and retail trade, with 1,518 individual taxpayers having net incomes of some MK 4.6 million and 107 companies with net incomes of MK 2.8 million, were the largest group of taxpayers, followed by agriculture with 73 individual taxpayers having incomes of MK 0.4 million and 41 companies with incomes of MK 1.8 million. Of salaried employees, the two largest groups were taxpayers in government employment (2,725) with incomes totaling MK 6.6 million, and those engaged in services (1,701) with incomes of MK 3.2 million.

The handling of these large numbers of taxpayers by a relatively small staff has been facilitated by the adoption of a simplified, noncumulative withholding scheme which had about 550 participating employers as of March 31, 1968. Precise figures on the cost of collecting income tax are not obtainable, but it is calculated to have declined from approximately 2.8 per cent of collections in the fiscal year ended December 31, 1964 to about 2 per cent in the fiscal year ended December 31, 1967.

While the revenue from the minimum, assessed, and graduated taxes rose from MK 1.9 million in 1964 to about MK 2.5 million in 1968, the administration of these taxes is known to leave room for improvement. Recent statistics indicate that some 8,000 pay the assessed tax, 150,000 the graduated tax, and 400,000 the minimum tax, but that levels of noncompliance and evasion are high. As regards the minimum tax, the total number of persons liable to pay may be as much as twice those now paying, and revenue may be undercollected to the extent of some MK 1 million a year. In the case of the graduated tax, which is now producing close to MK 1.2 million annually, considerable amounts are believed to be lost as a result of the employers' failure to deduct this tax from employees' earnings and to purchase tax stamps.

With a view to improving the system and increasing the yield from taxation, the President appointed a Tax Committee in March 1969 to review the tax structure. The committee comprised members of the private sector and officials of the Treasury. Most of the recommendations of the committee were accepted by the Government and legislation implementing them was enacted in 1969 and 1970 (see Tax Changes, 1969–70, below). In terms of revenue, the most important product of the committee's work was the recommendation of a sales tax on consumer goods.

Tax Changes, 1969–70

In 1969 and early 1970 a number of tax measures were introduced, partly reflecting programs that had been started in 1968, partly implementing the recommendations of the Tax Committee, and partly to make up for revenue shortfalls in the 1969 budget. A new Stamp Duty Act and a new Customs and Excise Act were enacted in April and June 1969, respectively, mainly for reasons of simplification and more efficient administration and to strengthen the tax authorities' powers to deal with tax evasion. Also in April 1969, amendments to the Income Tax Act provided for the repeal of taxes on undistributed profits, certain minor changes concerning exemptions, and some improvements in tax administration, including giving the assessing officers the power to impose penalties without having to go to the courts. In addition, steps were taken to eliminate the possibilities of tax evasion stemming from the different maximum rates for personal income taxes and profits taxes.

On the recommendation of the Tax Committee, legislation concerning both direct and indirect taxes was enacted, with effect from April 1, 1970. With respect to direct taxes, the main change was an amendment to the Income Tax Act, the chief features of which were a progressive reduction in personal income tax rates which cut the maximum marginal rate from 60 per cent to 40 per cent, separate assessment of incomes of working wives, and the raising of the corporation tax rate from 37.5 per cent to 40 per cent. In addition, the exemption limit for the payment of death duties was raised from MK 10,000 to MK 30,000. Revenue foregone on account of the personal tax reductions is estimated at MK 360,000, but during the first year of operation this will be limited to about MK 26,000—which is equal to the expected increment in revenue from the increased rate of corporation tax.

Also with effect from April 1, 1970, a general sales tax was introduced. The tax is levied at the rate of 5 per cent on all manufactures except those which would be free of customs duty if imported from Commonwealth countries. Hence all items considered as basic necessities, goods produced for export, and investment goods are exempt from sales tax. For domestic manufactures, the assessed value is the normal ex-factory selling price including excise duties. For imports, the assessed value is the value for customs duty purposes plus customs duties augmented by 20 per cent. The 20 per cent represents the hypothetical cost of transport from the border to the main consumption centers.

Besides these measures involving modifications of the tax system, several revenue measures were introduced in the course of 1969 when it became apparent that revenue from some sources was likely to fall considerably short of estimates. The new measures included excise duties on locally manufactured beer (5 tambala a gallon) and cloth (1.6 tambala a yard) and an increase in the rates on local gin (from MK 1.50 to MK 2.00 a gallon).

STRUCTURE OF CURRENT EXPENDITURE

The general outlines of current budget expenditure for the fiscal years 1967–69 (corresponding to the calendar years) and for the fiscal year 1970/71 (April 1–March 31) are shown in Table 14.

BUDGETARY OPERATIONS AND FINANCING, 1965–1970/71

Since the achievement of independence in 1964, the main feature of the fiscal situation in Malawi has been the steady curtailment of the current budget deficit (Table 15). While in 1965 current budget revenue covered only 57 per cent of current expenditure, this ratio is estimated to have risen to 85 per cent in the 1970/71 budget. Since 1964 current deficits have been financed by grants from the United Kingdom.

TABLE 14. MALAWI: CURRENT AND CAPITAL BUDGET EXPENDITURE, 1967–1970/71 [1]

(In thousands of Malawi kwacha)

	1967	1968	1969 Original estimates	1969 Revised estimates	1970/71 [2] Original estimates
Current expenditure					
General services					
General administration	5,564	5,166	6,630	5,996	6,222
Defense	1,118	1,122	1,192	1,204	1,264
Justice, police, prisons	3,906	4,050	4,126	4,006	4,176
	10,588	10,338	11,948	11,206	11,662
Natural resources					
Extension, conservation, disease control	1,340	1,242	1,520	1,370	1,580
Research, surveys, land and geological survey	762	844	978	946	1,222
Other	804	720	906	748	806
	2,906	2,806	3,404	3,064	3,608
Social services					
Education	6,460	6,930	7,718	7,730	8,112
Health	2,694	2,740	2,988	2,898	3,096
Young Pioneers and Community Development	612	1,024	1,070	1,248	1,208
	9,766	10,694	11,776	11,876	12,416
Communications					
Road maintenance	796	304	914	268	222
Post and telecommunications	1,548	1,634	954	848	942
Transport administration	458	408	532	520	526
	2,802	2,346	2,400	1,636	1,690

Economic services					
Works, water, sanitation	1,196	1,554	1,404	1,718	2,042
Plant and vehicles	1,292	1,100	1,236	1,232	1,468
Building maintenance	782	714	906	844	928
Other	802	734	854	876	1,176
	4,072	4,102	4,400	4,670	5,614
Public debt					
Interest	2,462	2,566	2,952	3,242	3,648
Redemption	1,532	1,460	1,688	1,672	1,844
	3,994	4,026	4,640	4,914	5,492
Pensions and gratuities	3,852	3,760	2,770	2,766	2,932
Other expenditure, unallocated	886	2,268	576	2,374	1,914
Total current expenditure	**38,866**	**40,340**	**41,914**	**42,506**	**45,328**
Capital expenditure					
Social services	958	1,844		1,744	4,656
Communications	2,720	4,910		6,642	18,646
Natural resources	2,450	3,702		5,342	7,204
Economic and other services	3,982	3,504		4,260	8,042
Total capital expenditure	**10,114**	**13,960**		**17,998** [3]	**38,548** [4]
(Total excluding Nacala railway)	(10,114)	(13,960)		(16,094)	(28,388)

Sources: Office of the President, *Economic Report, 1969*; Government of Malawi, *Estimates of Expenditure on Revenue Account, 1970/71*, and *Estimates of Expenditure on Development Account, 1970/71*; and data provided by the Malawian authorities.

[1] Because of a change in classification, comparable figures are not available for the years prior to 1967.

[2] April 1, 1970–March 31, 1971.

[3] Provisional results indicate actual development expenditure of MK 16.0 million.

[4] Actual expenditure on the Nacala railway in 1970/71 is estimated at MK 1.0 million. The remainder had been incurred previously and prefinanced by the contractors.

The steady improvement in the current budgetary position has been the result of a concerted effort on the part of the Government to restrain the growth of current expenditure while accelerating the growth of revenue. The estimated current expenditure for the fiscal year 1970/71 exceeds the 1965 level by 41 per cent, representing an average annual increase of 7 per cent, the same as the average rate of increase of total GDP. Moreover, most of the increment in expenditure has been allocated to economic and social services and to public debt, the latter reflecting the sharp rise in expenditure on capital account (Table 14). Over the same period, current revenue more than doubled, while tax revenue increased at an average annual rate of 18 per cent (Table 13).

Although the tax burden measured as the ratio of tax revenue to total GDP has remained low by international comparison, this must be attributed in part to the relatively large subsistence sector in Malawi. The ratio of tax revenue to monetary GDP, i.e., excluding the subsistence sector, was expected to reach 19 per cent in 1970/71, against 18 per cent in 1969 and 14 per cent in 1965 (Table 13).[5] Although import taxes remain the single most important source of revenue, the growth of this revenue source has since 1966 been smaller than that of taxes on income; the proceeds of the latter more than doubled between 1965 and 1969. For 1970/71 income tax was estimated at MK 12 million, of which MK 6 million was expected from corporations and self-employed persons. With the growth of the domestic manufacturing sector, revenue from import duties has increased only slightly in recent years. It was in order to obtain a source of revenue that would keep pace with the growth of consumption that the Government introduced the general sales tax, which was expected to yield over MK 2 million in the fiscal year 1970/71.

In contrast to current expenditure, capital expenditure has shown a sharply rising trend: between 1965 and 1969 such expenditure rose

---

[5] As a result of changing the fiscal period from a calendar year to a year beginning April 1 (effective April 1, 1970), the 1969 fiscal period covered 15 months, revenue and expenditure for January–March 1970 being covered by supplementary appropriations to the 1969 budget. In this discussion, however, and in the accompanying tables, budgetary operations in the calendar year 1969 are treated separately from those in January–March 1970, to facilitate annual comparisons.

from MK 9.4 million to MK 18 million (revised estimate), or at an average annual rate of 20 per cent. As a result, the overall deficit on current and capital budgets combined fluctuated in the MK 22–26 million range in the years 1965–69.

With an average of four fifths of the overall deficit in 1965–69 financed by foreign aid and a large part of the remainder by medium-term and long-term domestic borrowing outside the banking system (Table 15), the monetary impact of the budgetary deficits has been limited. Moreover, since part of the foreign financing received was used to cover local expenditure, the net adverse effect on the balance of payments has been minimized. However, an increasing proportion of the budgetary deficit has been covered by domestic and foreign borrowing, while foreign aid in the form of grants has shown a steady decline.

1969

The original 1969 budget estimates provided for a reduction of the current deficit to MK 8.2 million, from MK 10.5 million in 1968. The reduction was to be achieved partly through additional revenue measures affecting import and excise duties and certain fees, expected to yield MK 1.2 million. In addition, an expansion of economic activity brought about by higher investment and larger crops—following the below-average agricultural output in 1968—was expected to widen the tax base and thus contribute to the growth of revenue. Total revenue in 1969 was estimated at MK 33.8 million, representing an increase of 13 per cent over the amount collected in 1968.

On the other hand, the budgeted increase in current expenditure in 1969 was limited to 4 per cent, to reach a total of MK 42 million. Substantially higher provision, however, was made for several categories of expenditure, including general administration, education, and debt service, owing to a major saving achieved by reducing contractual lump-sum payments to retiring civil servants. Apparent savings of about MK 0.8 million were shown in the budget, reflecting merely a change in accounting procedures of the Department of Posts and Telecommunications.

Revised budget estimates for 1969, which on the basis of past experience should not differ more than fractionally from actual results, show

TABLE 15. MALAWI: FINANCING OF BUDGETARY DEFICITS, 1965–1970/71

(In thousands of Malawi kwacha)

	1965	1966	1967	1968	1969 Revised estimates	1970/71 Original estimates
Current budget						
Revenue (other than grants and loans)	18,344	22,186	26,682	29,842	33,730	38,458
Expenditure	32,272	35,468	38,874	40,340	42,506	45,328
Deficit [1]	−13,928	−13,282	−12,192	−10,498	−8,776	−6,870
Capital budget						
Revenue (other than grants and loans)	54	628	344	168	100	270
Expenditure	9,406	12,760	10,114	13,960	17,998	38,548
Deficit	−9,352	−12,132	−9,770	−13,792	−17,898	−38,278
Total budget deficit	−23,280	−25,414	−21,962	−24,290	−26,674	−45,148
External financing						
Grants on recurrent account	13,900	10,472	10,734	9,110	7,672	6,224
U. K. OSAS and BACS [2]	1,006	1,074	1,474	1,716	1,878	1,900
U. K. grants for retiring officers' compensation	812	824	846	886	94	22
U. K. budgetary grants-in-aid	11,896	8,486	8,330	6,390	5,600	4,200
Other U. K. grants	186	88	84	118	100	102
Grants on development account	7,190	898	342	174	214	966
United Kingdom	6,834	566	112	—	—	758
U. S. AID [3]	296	146	230	36	—	—
Other	60	186		138	214	208
Total external grants	21,090	11,370	11,076	9,284	7,886	7,190
Loans on recurrent account (U. K. compensation and commutation loan)	1,250	970	1,230	1,078	776	638
Loans on development account	142	5,170	5,680	7,456	14,426	32,110
United Kingdom	8	3,400	4,302	4,540	5,000	5,368
Denmark		154	262	710	920	986
Germany	14	1,442	918	236	520	1,116
IDA/AfDB [4]		54	176	1,802	4,860	9,156
South Africa					3,000	13,160
U. S. AID [3]				142	80	2,306
Other	120	120	22	26	46	18
	1,392	6,140	6,910	8,534	15,202	32,748

Sales of external assets and other capital transfers	500	520	300	20	—	—
Sales of shares in Trans-Zambezi Railway	—	520	300	20	—	—
Kariba Power Surcharge Fund	500	—	—	—	—	—
Total external financing	**22,982**	**18,030**	**18,286**	**17,838**	**23,088**	**39,938**
Domestic financing						
Borrowing outside banking system	1,328	2,308	1,918	1,454	3,128	…
Long-term government stock [5]	808	1,048	988	2,544	1,378	…
Treasury bills (net)	520	1,260	930	-1,090	1,750	…
Transfer from Zambezi Bridge Account	—	—	1,000	-2,000	1,400	…
Long-term government stock	—	—	1,000	2,000	—	…
Treasury bills and bonds	—	—	—	—	1,400	…
Loan from Farmers Marketing Board	420	800	566	2,000	1,044	…
Borrowing from banking system	-1,588	3,824	-36	2,656	1,760	…
Borrowing from Reserve Bank	-192	3,072	-112	1,576	122	…
Long-term government stock [5]	(180)	(652)	(-30)	(692)	(-1,030)	…
Treasury bills (net)	(-1,960)	(—)	(-118)	(-1,770)	-716	…
Changes in deposits	2,008	(-2,420)	(602)	(-886)	(—)	…
Borrowing from commercial banks	-1,000	752	602	1,080	-720	…
Long-term government stock [5]	(1,100)	(-300)	(400)	(764)	(—)	…
Treasury bills (net)	(-92)	(200)	(100)	(320)	(4)	…
Changes in deposits	—	(-252)	(102)	(-4)	—	…
Total borrowing and transfers	1,748	6,972	3,484	6,110	5,572	…
Net below-the-line receipts or expenditures (−)	+856	-974	-8	734	-1,584	…
Government domestic cash balances (increase −)	-600	+286	-16	-64	-402	…
Government external cash balances (increase −)	-1,706	+1,140	+216	-328	…	…
Total domestic financing	**298**	**7,384**	**3,676**	**6,452**	**3,586**	**5,210**

Sources: Office of the President, *Economic Report, 1969*; Government of Malawi, *Public Sector Financial Statistics* and *Budget Documents, 1970/71*; and data provided by the Malawian authorities.

[1] This presentation differs from that adopted by the Malawian Government since the latter does not include expenditure financed by U. K. Government grants and loans other than budgetary aid. Such expenditure relates mainly to the cost of U. K. technical assistance. In this table, the cost of such assistance is included in expenditure, while the corresponding grants and loans appear as a financing item.

[2] Overseas Service Aid Scheme and British-Aided Conditions of Service.

[3] U. S. Agency for International Development.

[4] International Development Association and African Development Bank.

[5] These figures differ from the figures in Table 16 because the amounts for borrowing through long-term government stocks shown here reflect gross sales of stock; repayments of government stock are included in recurrent account expenditure.

current revenue of MK 33.7 million, the same as the budget estimate, and current expenditure of MK 42.5 million, some MK 0.5 million above the budget estimate. Although total tax revenue was some MK 3 million (14.5 per cent) above the level attained in 1968, it was about MK 1.2 million below the original budget estimate. Revenue from import duties fell short of estimates because the growth of consumer imports was less than projected. In addition, there was some shortfall in income tax collections, particularly from the minimum tax which is levied on all males over the age of 18. Although collections improved from the 1968 level, when they represented about 50 per cent of the amount due, this ratio was less than two thirds in 1969. As noted, however, total current revenue attained the level estimated in the budget, with the shortfall in tax revenue offset by receipts in excess of estimates from other sources. Receipts from departmental services, reimbursements, and postal and telegraph services were markedly higher than the estimates—which was in part attributed to improvements in the system of accounting and control introduced with the 1969 budget.

The revised estimate of capital budget expenditure in 1969, at the record high figure of MK 18 million, was well below the budget estimate of MK 27.6 million but was MK 4 million higher than in 1968. The growth of capital expenditure was to a large extent for such items as extension services, crop development, and land improvement. It should be noted that the 1969 capital budget excludes most of the expenditure on the rail link with Nacala; only some MK 1 million was financed through the capital budget. Additional construction and the purchase of rolling stock, estimated to cost almost MK 8 million, has been temporarily funded by contractor financing. These expenditures have been included in the 1970/71 budget, during which time the project is scheduled to be completed and the South African loan, which will be used to repay the contractors, will be disbursed.

The combined deficit on the current and capital budgets amounted to MK 26.7 million in 1969, compared with MK 24.3 million in 1968 (Table 15). Despite the higher deficit in 1969, recourse to bank financing (MK 1 million) was considerably less than in 1968, as foreign loans for development projects rose sharply. The main source of foreign financing in 1969 was the United Kingdom, which disbursed MK 13.4 million. Domestic financing other than bank credit amounted to MK 3 million and consisted largely of the sale of government securities to statutory bodies and nonbank financial institutions.

January–March 1970

Revenue estimates prepared for the extended 1969 fiscal period, January–March 1970, were based on actual performance in the first half of 1969 taking into account the annual seasonal decline in revenue in the first quarter of the year and extraordinary receipts. Estimates of current expenditure were based on appropriations for 1969 and actual data for the first part of the year. No specific estimates were drawn up for the capital budget, but spending against 1969 appropriations was permitted to continue, as only MK 16 million [6] out of total appropriations of MK 27.6 million had been spent by the end of 1969.

It is estimated that current revenue and expenditure were MK 8.8 million and MK 10.2 million, respectively, during the first quarter of 1970, resulting in a deficit of MK 1.4 million. With actual capital expenditures estimated at MK 5.4 million, the overall deficit is estimated at MK 6.8 million. As foreign loans and grants received were equal to the budget deficit, the proceeds from the redemption of certain government-held foreign securities could be used to reduce the level of domestic borrowing.

1970/71

The budget for the financial year beginning April 1, 1970 continued to reflect the Government's policy of reducing the current budgetary deficit in the face of strong pressure to increase current expenditure, partly to meet the recurrent costs of past investments. At the same time, the rate of increase of public investment was scheduled to rise further. According to the budget estimates, current revenue would rise by 14 per cent over the 1969 revised estimates, to MK 38.5 million, and current expenditure would rise by 6.6 per cent, to MK 45.3 million (Table 15). Capital expenditure for fiscal 1970/71 was budgeted at MK 38.5 million. This amount, however, included almost the full cost of the rail link with Nacala, which, as mentioned above, was scheduled to be completed. The actual expenditure incurred in 1970

---

[6] See footnote 3 to Table 14.

on the construction of the railway was estimated at MK 1.0 million, compared with the estimate of MK 10.2 million in the 1970/71 budget. Excluding work on the railway carried out in earlier years, total expenditure to be incurred under the 1970/71 budget was estimated at about MK 28.4 million.

Most of the increase in revenue in 1970/71 was expected to come from indirect taxes (Table 13). The budgeted increase in income tax collections was based mainly on the increase in national income in 1969, but the improved tax administration procedures adopted in the course of 1969 were also a factor. The increase in receipts from import duties was based on some increase in imports of consumer goods and an increase (1.6 tambala a gallon) in the specific duty on diesel oil and petrol, while the 34 per cent increase in receipts from excise taxes reflected largely the full effect of the excise duty measures taken during 1969 and a higher excise duty on traditional beer introduced with the 1970/71 budget.

The main single source of additional revenue was the sales tax, introduced with the 1970/71 budget. With the gradual expansion of domestic manufacturing of import substitutes, imports of the relatively highly taxed consumer goods have tended to lag behind the growth of the economy, particularly personal consumption, and receipts from import duties have grown relatively slowly in recent years. Proceeds from the new sales tax may be expected to grow at least as fast as personal consumption and will not be adversely affected by Malawi's progress toward self-reliance in the field of consumer manufactures.

With respect to current expenditure, the highest rates of increase were in appropriations for public debt service, economic services, development of natural resources, and social services, while the increase in provisions for general services, communications, and other categories was considerably less than average (Table 14). A substantial part of the rise in expenditure was associated with past investment or with current development programs, including, in particular, agricultural services, education grants and teachers' salaries, building and vehicle maintenance, and tourist services.

Excluding the provisions for the rail link with Nacala, the programs included in the 1970/71 capital budget were in the fields of agriculture, tourism, road transport, telecommunications, and the construction of the new capital city at Lilongwe. The highest rate of increase in capital expenditure was for social services, reflecting the acceleration of development efforts in the provision of educational and health facilities.

The overall budget deficit for 1970/71 was estimated at MK 45 million (Table 15). The current budget deficit of MK 7 million was to be met almost entirely by grants from the United Kingdom, while foreign loans were expected to cover MK 32.7 million of the MK 38.3 million estimated deficit on capital account. Domestic financing requirements were estimated at MK 5.2 million, most of which was to be raised through the sale of long-term government securities outside the banking system.

After the budget was approved, it became clear that current revenue and expenditure estimates would have to be revised as a result of the expected shortfall in maize and groundnut production in 1970. It was expected that some 100,000 tons of maize would have to be imported by the Farmers Marketing Board to meet the deficiency in food production. Although the imported maize was to be sold on the market, the Government planned to offset part of the decline in real income of the population by subsidizing maize sales, and through employment-generating projects in certain areas that were most affected. In addition, a loss of revenue from excise and import duties was expected, reflecting reduced personal income and consumption. These factors were tentatively estimated to add MK 3–3.8 million to the budget deficit, for which no new revenue or external financing was expected to be forthcoming. Although financing might be obtained in part through borrowing from the Farmers Marketing Board, it was expected that the Government would have to resort to borrowing as much as MK 3 million from the Reserve Bank.

PUBLIC DEBT

With the continuous increase in capital expenditure, an absence of budgetary savings, and a decline in grants from abroad, the Central Government's outstanding indebtedness almost doubled between 1965 and 1969. Although most of the debt continues to be held externally, the proportion incurred domestically rose from about 10 per cent in 1965 to almost 20 per cent in 1969.

Total debt service has actually declined in the face of rising indebted-

TABLE 16. MALAWI: OUTSTANDING DOMESTIC DEBT OF CENTRAL GOVERNMENT
AND DEBT SERVICE PAYMENTS, 1965–69

(*In thousands of Malawi kwacha*)

	1965	1966	1967	1968	1969
Denominated in Malawi currency					
Medium- and long-term	3,446	5,334	6,742	10,012	11,728
Local registered stock sinking funds	*834*	*3,216*	*3,646*	*6,024*	*7,852*
Other local registered stock	*2,320*	*1,876*	*2,924*	*3,778*	*3,786*
Other	*292*	*242*	*172*	*210*	*90*
Short-term [1]	2,510	3,650	3,500	4,810	6,900
Total	5,956	8,984	10,242	14,822	18,628
Debt service [2]	1,110	934	236	1,778	1,470
Interest	*216*	*196*	*150*	*628*	*826*
Amortization	*894*	*738*	*86*	*1,150*	*644*

Sources: Government of Malawi, *Public Sector Financial Statistics;* Office of the President, *Economic Report, 1969;* and data provided by the Malawian authorities.

[1] Including securities held by the banking system.
[2] Including sinking fund payments.

ness, partly because most of the loans received have been on a medium-term or long-term basis, but also because of gradually improving lending terms. In 1969, public debt service represented 10.2 per cent of current budget expenditure.

The domestic debt incurred by the Central Government in 1965–69 is shown in Table 16. For details on the foreign debt, see Balance of Payments—External Debt, below.

MONEY AND BANKING

MONETARY SYSTEM

Between 1954 and 1956, Malawi (then Nyasaland) along with Northern and Southern Rhodesia was a participant in the currency area served by the Central African Currency Board. In 1956, the Central African Currency Board was replaced by the Bank of Rhodesia and Nyasaland, which served as Malawi's central bank until 1964, when the Reserve Bank of Malawi began operations. The Bank of Rhodesia and Nyasaland was formally dissolved on June 30, 1965, and its assets were divided, in proportion to the old currency redeemed from each territory up to the end of June 1965, among the three central banks that succeeded it, that is, the Reserve Bank of Malawi, the Bank of Zambia, and the Reserve Bank of Rhodesia. Malawi is a member of the sterling area. Under the Sterling Agreement with the United Kingdom, an agreed proportion of Malawi's external assets is held in sterling.

The currency issued by the Reserve Bank of Malawi was, until February 15, 1971, the Malawi pound, which was divided into 20 shillings. The par value agreed with the International Monetary Fund was £M 1 = US$2.40, that is, the Malawi pound was at par with the pound sterling. With effect from February 15, 1971 a new currency unit, the kwacha, was introduced, which is divided into 100 tambala. The par value agreed with the Fund for the new currency is MK 1 = US$1.20 or MK 2 = £ stg. 1.

STRUCTURE OF THE BANKING SYSTEM

Apart from the Reserve Bank of Malawi, the banking and financial system in Malawi consists of three commercial banks, the Post Office Savings Bank, a building society, a development finance company, and several life and other insurance companies.

The Banking Act of 1965 sets forth the conditions governing the operations of domestic and foreign commercial banks and financial institutions with regard to registration, the carrying on of banking business, minimum capital and equity participation, accounting procedures, and the issue of periodic statements. The paid-up equity capital and unimpaired reserve funds of a bank whose head office is in Malawi should not be less than MK 500,000. Banks with head offices outside Malawi may be required to maintain capital and reserve funds up to an amount not exceeding MK 500,000. Discount houses and financial institutions are required to maintain capital and reserve funds of not less than MK 100,000. The legislation also prohibits a bank from purchasing or making advances against its own shares or those of a company which controls its business and from engaging in wholesale or retail trade except for the collection of debts due to it.

Two of the commercial banks—the Standard Bank and Barclays Bank D. C. O.—are branches of U. K. banks; the third bank—the Commercial Bank of Malawi, established in early 1970 with an authorized capital of MK 500,000, is owned by the Banco Pintu & Sotto

Mayor, of Portugal (60 per cent), the Malawi Development Corporation (20 per cent), and Malawi Press Holdings Limited (20 per cent). There are at present 14 commercial bank branches and about 115 agencies, including mobile agencies, in Malawi. The commercial banks finance the major portion of the export crops. Demand for crop finance begins around May each year and rises to a peak in September–October when the crops are marketed. A large portion of this credit is channeled through the Farmers Marketing Board. During the slack season (November–March), the commercial banks keep their surplus balances in London, and draw upon them as well as borrow from their head offices during the busy season. Consequently, there are wide fluctuations in the net foreign asset holdings of the commercial banks. In addition to crop financing, commercial bank credit is used to finance wholesale and retail trade and manufacturing.

The Post Office Savings Bank, operated through the Post Office System, was established mainly to provide savings deposit facilities for small savers.

The New Building Society was formed in early 1964, when it took over the assets and liabilities of three existing building societies. The initial share capital of MK 60,000 was increased to MK 120,000 in March 1969 and to MK 240,000 in September 1969. The shareholders are the Malawian Government, Lonrho (Malawi) Limited, and the Alliance Assurance Company. The society provides mortgage finance for residential houses, flats, shops, and offices.

The Development Finance Company of Malawi, Ltd., and its subsidiaries, collectively known as the DEFINCO Group, was established in 1968 with an authorized capital of MK 1.0 million with a view to investing in commercial and industrial projects. The main shareholders are the Malawi Development Corporation and a group of foreign-owned development corporations, finance companies, and insurance companies.

Reserve Bank Functions and Operations

The ordinance establishing the Reserve Bank of Malawi was passed on July 23, 1964, and the new central bank began issuing its own currency, the Malawi pound, in November 1964. The main objectives of the Reserve Bank, as stated in the ordinance, are "to issue legal tender currency in Malawi, to maintain external reserves so as to safeguard the international value of that currency, to promote monetary stability and a sound financial structure in Malawi, and to act as banker and advisor to the Government."

The authorized capital of the Bank is MK 1.0 million, all of which is subscribed and paid up by the Government. As stipulated in the ordinance, a General Reserve Fund is being built up from the net profits of the Bank. That part of the net profits not paid to the General Reserve Fund or to other reserve funds is paid to the Government.

The Bank acts as the Government's banker and fiscal agent, accepts deposits and makes payments on behalf of the Government, and administers the public debt. It may also act as banker to the commercial banks and other credit institutions, accepting deposits from them and making payments on their behalf. It is authorized to make temporary advances to the Government to offset shortfalls in budgetary revenues. Such advances, repayable within four months from the end of the financial year for which they are made, may not exceed 10 per cent of the estimated revenue for that year and are subject to an interest charge determined by the Bank. The Reserve Bank may purchase, sell, discount, and rediscount treasury bills of the Malawian Government with a maturity not exceeding 93 days; and inland bills of exchange and promissory notes issued for bona fide commercial transactions or for the purpose of financing the transport, marketing, and processing of agricultural produce and minerals. The Bank is further empowered to purchase, sell, discount, and rediscount external bills of exchange, treasury bills maturing within 184 days, and securities of any country whose currency is freely convertible. It may grant advances for periods not exceeding three months against treasury bills, securities of the Government maturing within 25 years, gold, eligible bills of exchange, promissory notes, and warehouse warrants or other similar documents.

With respect to the provision of long-term credit, the Reserve Bank is authorized to purchase and sell government securities with a maturity not exceeding 25 years, provided that the total amount of securities with more than two years to maturity, excluding those in which the internal funds of the Bank have been invested and those held by the Bank as collateral, do not exceed 20 per cent of total demand liabilities. With the approval of the Minister of Finance, the Bank may also subscribe to the shares of any corporation set up with the approval, or under the authority, of the Government for the purpose of facilitating the financing of the economic development of the country. The total value of such shares held by the Bank must not exceed 10 per cent of the aggregate amount of its capital and General Reserve Fund.

As a means of controlling credit, the Reserve Bank may prescribe from time to time minimum cash reserve ratios which other banks in Malawi must maintain in the form of deposits at the Reserve Bank, and minimum ratios of specified liquid assets; the ratios are expressed as percentages of the demand and time liabilities of each bank and have to be uniform for all banks. The liquid assets include gold, cash, and balances with the Reserve Bank and with other banks in Malawi and abroad, treasury bills of the Malawian and U. K. Governments, Malawian bills of exchange payable within 90 days, and certain other specified assets.

The Reserve Bank is required to maintain a reserve of specified external assets equivalent to not less than 50 per cent of its total demand liabilities (currency and all other deposits). The specified external assets are to consist of gold, convertible currencies, treasury bills, and securities issued by or guaranteed by foreign governments whose currencies are convertible, up to a limit of 30 per cent of the Bank's external assets, one third of which should mature in a period not exceeding five years.

Operations, 1965–69.—The Reserve Bank began to issue a new currency, the Malawi pound, on November 16, 1964, in exchange for the old federal currency circulating in Malawi, and began to issue coins on January 25, 1965. When the currency redemption operation was completed in June 1965, Malawi had received, in exchange for the currency redeemed, about MK 15 million worth of foreign assets, constituting 18 per cent of the assets backing the currency liabilities of the Bank of Rhodesia and Nyasaland and the investment reserve funds. In addition, the Reserve Bank received MK 800,000 worth of treasury bills previously held for the account of the Government by the Bank of Rhodesia and Nyasaland. At the same time, Malawi assumed responsibility for 10 per cent of the federal debt, most of which consisted of external debt.

In accordance with its role as government banker, the Reserve Bank took over most of the Government's deposit accounts from the Standard Bank, which had previously acted as government banker. For the sake of convenience, however, a few accounts are maintained with commercial banks in the rural areas and with institutions abroad. The Reserve Bank acts as the Government's fiscal agent, handling 91-day treasury bills and medium-term and long-term government stocks and redeeming outstanding issues.

Foreign Assets of Monetary Authorities.—The level of Malawi's net foreign assets at different times of the year tends to reflect the seasonal fluctuations associated with the short-term flows of funds to and from abroad for crop financing and the timing of aid disbursements. The net foreign assets of the monetary authorities (i.e., the Reserve Bank and the Treasury) fell from MK 18 million in 1965 to MK 15.3 million in 1966, mainly as a result of a change in the pattern of aid disbursements. They then increased to MK 18.8 million in 1967, and after remaining stable in 1968, fell by 7 per cent in 1969, to MK 17.5 million (Table 17). Superimposed on the decline in foreign assets were seasonal fluctuations reflecting the inflow of crop financing during the second and third quarters associated with the Farmers Marketing Board's purchases of the fire-cured tobacco and groundnut crops.

Credit to Government.—The Government's net position with the Bank of Malawi is influenced by the seasonal pattern of government revenue and expenditure and the disbursement of foreign aid. Government receipts are usually higher in the second and third quarters when income taxes are collected and lower in the first quarter, while government expenditure tends to be heaviest in the final quarter toward the end of the fiscal year.[7] However, the seasonal fluctuation in government borrowing for the current budget is sometimes affected by the irregularity of foreign aid disbursements.

The pattern of Government borrowing changed considerably during the period 1965–69. In contrast to 1965, when the Government borrowed small amounts and maintained sizable deposits with the Reserve Bank, since 1966 it has not only drawn down its deposits considerably and obtained direct advances from the Bank, but also increased the

---

[7] The change in the fiscal period from a calendar year to a year beginning April 1 is likely to affect this seasonal pattern.

TABLE 17. MALAWI: ASSETS AND LIABILITIES OF THE MONETARY AUTHORITIES,[1] 1965–70

(In thousands of Malawi kwacha; end of period)

	1965	1966	1967	1968	1969				1970			
					Mar.	June	Sept.	Dec.	Mar.	June	Sept.	Dec.
Foreign assets (net)	18,020	15,294	18,754	18,758	16,568	19,390	17,816	17,500	19,900	21,150[2]	24,434[2]	24,336
Reserve Bank	15,018	13,596	15,054	14,410	12,452	16,404	14,926	14,148	16,858[2]	18,350[2]	21,146[2]	21,049
Government's holdings	2,842	1,698	1,666	2,002	3,170	1,880	1,934	2,406	2,096	1,854	2,742	2,341
(Balances held with Crown Agents)	(1,858)	(714)	(514)	(842)	(2,010)	(720)	(772)	(1,244)	(928)	(686)	(1,572)	(1,174)
(IMF gold tranche position)	(984)	(984)	(1,152)	(1,160)	(1,160)	(1,160)	(1,162)	(1,162)	(1,168)	(1,168)	(1,170)	(1,170)
Special account[3]	—	—	2,034	2,346	946	946	946	946	946	946	946	946
Reserve Bank's claims on government	454	1,838	1,776	3,720	4,196	3,008	4,306	5,120	1,750	5,618	1,866	2,620
Securities	274	958	1,076	1,800	1,516	988	716	1,882	1,330	3,568	1,866	2,620
Treasury bills	180	180	150	1,920	430	1,020	740	888	420 }	2,050 }	—	—
Loans and advances	—	700	550	—	2,250	1,000	2,850	2,350	}	}	—	—
Reserve Bank's claims on commercial banks	—	—	500	—	—	340	1,000	—	940	500	1,620	380
Assets = liabilities	18,474	17,132	21,030	22,478	20,764	22,738	23,122	22,620	22,590	27,268	27,920	27,336
Reserve money	11,274	12,484	13,566	13,480	13,016	16,416	16,284	15,154	13,418	19,290	17,562	16,530
Currency in banks	400	508	688	682	766	948	626	740	900	1,066	706	1,012
Currency outside banks	8,880	10,564	11,820	11,570	11,018	14,308	14,528	12,540	12,066	16,450	15,276	13,276
Commercial banks' deposits	1,994	1,412	1,058	1,228	1,232	1,160	1,130	1,874	452	1,774	1,580	2,244
Government deposits	4,802	1,938	1,874	2,546	3,406	2,120	2,174	2,632	4,112	2,084	3,830	4,369
At Reserve Bank	1,960	240	208	544	236	240	240	226	2,016	230	1,088	2,028
Counterpart of Government's holdings	2,842	1,698	1,666	2,002	3,170	1,880	1,934	2,406	2,096	1,854	2,742	2,341
Private sector deposits	160	250	2,358	3,056	1,460	1,216	1,298	1,266	1,542	1,144	1,376	1,244
Special account[3]	—	—	2,034	2,346	946	946	946	946	946	946	946	946
Other deposits	160	250	324	710	514	270	352	320	596	198	430	298
Other items (net)	2,238	2,460	3,232	3,396	2,882	2,986	3,366	3,568	3,518[4]	4,750[4]	5,152[4]	5,193

Sources: Reserve Bank of Malawi, *Economic and Financial Review*; IMF, *International Financial Statistics*; and data provided by the Malawian authorities.

[1] The Reserve Bank and the Government (Treasury).
[2] Includes Malawi's allocation of SDR 1.89 million.
[3] Special account covers the proceeds from the sale of the Zambezi bridge.
[4] Includes counterpart of Malawi's allocation of SDRs.

amount of its borrowing from the Bank through treasury bills and medium-term and long-term government stocks. During 1966, net claims on the Government by the Reserve Bank itself (i.e., excluding the counterpart of government holdings) increased by over MK 3 million (Table 17). This large increase in central bank lending to the Government arose mainly from the change in the pattern of aid disbursement (see p. 274, below). Net claims on the Government by the Reserve Bank increased from MK 1.6 million in December 1966 to nearly MK 3.2 million at the end of 1968. During 1969, partly as a result of delays in the disbursement of foreign aid, the Government intensified its recourse to the Reserve Bank, and the Bank's net claims on the Government reached a peak of MK 4.9 million at the end of 1969.

Securities Market.—In its attempt to develop a securities market, the Reserve Bank has handled, on behalf of the Government, treasury bills and medium-term and long-term government stocks. The 91-day treasury bills were introduced in March 1965 and are currently issued at an interest rate of 5.6 per cent per annum. The Reserve Bank absorbs any unsubscribed balances and frequently arranges for sales and purchases of sizable amounts of bills between the monthly issues. The main purchasers of these securities are the banking system, the Post Office Savings Bank, the New Building Society, statutory bodies and commissions, insurance companies, local authorities, corporations, sinking funds, and private individuals. As a result of the increase in the Government's demand for temporary finance to bridge the gap between receipts (including foreign aid) and expenditure, the total amount of treasury bills issued has been increasing. The amount of treasury bills outstanding rose from MK 1.8 million at the end of 1965 to MK 6.0 million at the end of 1969 (Table 18); it then rose to MK 7.0 million at the end of March 1970 before declining to MK 5.6 million at the end of August 1970. About 47 per cent of the outstanding bills were held by the private sector (mainly insurance companies, corporations, the Post Office Savings Bank, and the New Building Society), 25 per cent by the public sector (mainly the statutory bodies and commissions), 17 per cent by the Reserve Bank, and 11 per cent by the commercial banks. The holders of these bills adjusted their holdings to changes in their liquidity requirements throughout the period. The commercial banks normally reduce their holdings of treasury bills in the second and third

TABLE 18. MALAWI: TREASURY BILLS AND LOCAL REGISTERED STOCKS OUTSTANDING, 1965–June 1970

(In thousands of Malawi kwacha; end of period)

	1965 Bills	1965 Stock	1966 Bills	1966 Stock	1967 Bills	1967 Stock	1968 Bills	1968 Stock	1969 Bills	1969 Stock	June 1970 Bills	June 1970 Stock
Reserve Bank	180	306	180	958	150	1,072	1,920	1,764	890	1,882	1,430	2,138
Commercial banks [1]	1,100	1,392	1,300	1,314	1,400	1,714	1,720	2,478	1,000	2,478	500	3,178
Statutory bodies	30	110	1,070	190	2,070	1,090	1,190	2,010	1,450	2,150	...	} 13,962
Other financial institutions	490	} 2,070	850	} 3,430	1,380	} 4,334	410	3,888	630	4,428	...	
Other residents	—		—		—		760	} 1,796	2,030	2,972	...	7,754
Nonresidents	—	9,762	—	8,858	—	8,652	—	8,642	—	7,904	—	...
Sinking funds	—	318	—	298	—	612	—	750	—	952	—	—
Total outstanding	1,800	13,958	3,400	15,048	5,000	17,474	6,000	21,328	6,000	22,766	6,000	27,032
Canceled stock		622		886		962		1,108		1,170		1,300
Total stock issued		14,580		15,934		18,436		22,436		23,936		28,332

Sources: Reserve Bank of Malawi, *Economic and Financial Review*; and data provided by the Malawian authorities.

[1] Figures in this table are not comparable with figures for commercial banks' claims on government, as the latter include other government securities.

quarters to supplement their resources for the purpose of providing crop finance and increase them in the fourth and first quarters as loans are repaid.

As the rate of government spending on development projects increased, the Government found it necessary to mobilize a larger amount of domestic resources to meet the local costs of a number of projects that were not covered by foreign aid and the entire immediate costs of some projects for which it was later reimbursed by foreign donors. As a means of obtaining finance for such expenditure, the Government began issuing local registered stock ranging in maturity from 2 to 20 years. Between independence and the end of 1967, there were three issues of local registered stock totaling MK 6.50 million, with coupon rates ranging from 5 per cent for the 2-year stock to 6½ per cent for the 20-year stock. In the case of some of the longer-term issues, the Reserve Bank was left with about half the initial issue but later succeeded in disposing of a substantial proportion of its holdings. Three issues totaling MK 6 million with maturities ranging from 2 to 20 years and coupon rates from 6 per cent to 6½ per cent were made in 1968. The issue with a maturity of 2 years was designed to respond to the particular demand of the market at that time. The commercial banks switched from treasury bills into the 2-year stocks. One of the longer-term issues was primarily a conversion issue designed to finance the redemption of an earlier issue. In addition to the three issues of local registered stock, an issue of MK 2 million of treasury bonds was placed directly with a statutory corporation.

Three new issues of stock were made between January 1969 and March 1970. On April 1, 1969, the Government offered a redemption issue of MK 1.0 million bearing an interest rate of 6¼ per cent and with a maturity of 3 years. Most of this issue was taken up by the holders of the original issue. Another issue of MK 1.50 million bearing interest at 7 per cent and with a maturity of 7 years was made on October 15, 1969. This issue was intended to fill a gap in the range of yields and maturities available on the domestic capital market. The Reserve Bank purchased a part of this issue for its portfolio; most of the remainder went to the Post Office Savings Bank, the insurance companies, the statutory bodies and commissions, and private corporations and individuals. A third issue of MK 1.0 million bearing interest at

6½ per cent and having a maturity of 4 years was offered in March 1970. Most of this issue was taken up by the commercial banks.

Credit to Commercial Banks.—Lending by the Reserve Bank to the commercial banks fluctuates in accordance with the banks' needs to provide crop financing for the Farmers Marketing Board and the large estates. In 1967, when the commercial banks were unable to meet the heavy demand for credit out of their own resources or from those provided by their London head offices, they turned for the first time to the Reserve Bank (Table 17). As a result of the poor harvest in 1968 the demand for such credit was considerably less, and during the second half of the year the commercial banks repaid their outstanding loans to the Reserve Bank. In spite of the need to finance substantially larger crops of fire-cured tobacco and groundnuts, total commercial bank borrowing from the Reserve Bank was not as great as it was in 1968, the main reason being that the improved financial position of the Farmers Marketing Board enabled it to reduce its indebtedness to the commercial banks.

Operations, 1970.—The net foreign assets of the monetary authorities rose by MK 6.8 million in 1970. The main factors responsible for this rise were the receipt of Malawi's allocation of SDRs (SDR 1.89 million), the receipt by the Government of large amounts of foreign aid payments and of interest and other payments on debentures owned by the former Trans-Zambezi Railway, and the receipt of export proceeds temporarily held abroad by the Farmers Marketing Board. The aid and interest payments enabled the Government to repay its advances to the Reserve Bank and to attain a net credit position of MK 0.6 million (excluding the counterpart of Government holdings), compared with a net debit position of MK 4.9 million at the end of 1969. Commercial banks' borrowing from the Reserve Bank to provide the normal seasonal crop financing reached MK 1.6 million in September and then fell to MK 0.4 million at the end of December.

Commercial Bank Operations, 1965–69

The commercial banks expanded their activities considerably between 1965 and 1969. Bank credit to the private sector (excluding the Farmers Marketing Board) rose by 64 per cent during the period 1965 to 1968 and by 25 per cent in 1969. Table 19 provides a classification of

TABLE 19. MALAWI: COMMERCIAL BANK LOANS AND ADVANCES, 1965-70 [1]

(In thousands of Malawi kwacha; end of period)

	1965	1966	1967	1968	1969				1970			
					Mar.	June	Sept.	Dec.	Mar.	June	Sept.	Dec.
Agriculture	1,446	1,196	1,552	1,842	2,568	2,340	1,758	1,874	2,414	1,780	1,436	2,086
Manufacturing	2,868	3,018	2,662	3,028	3,494	3,882	4,670	4,316	3,948	3,722	4,840	4,524
Distribution	2,448	3,236	3,610	4,050	4,316	6,218	5,546	5,686	5,674	6,984	8,380	7,406
Building and construction	66	38	120	254	634	538	1,276	1,392	2,050	2,004	2,086	2,034
Farmers Marketing Board	134	500	7,586	2,436	1,750	3,506	5,100	966	930	1,514	1,694	448
Financial	14	170	836	1,590	1,104	690	278	1,102	1,036	748	1,152	1,922
Other	1,152	3,688	1,738	2,404	1,304	2,124	2,724	2,688	2,796	2,388	3,296	3,890
Total	8,128	11,846	18,204	15,604	15,170	19,298	21,352	18,024	18,848	19,140	22,884	22,310

Sources: Reserve Bank of Malawi, *Economic and Financial Review*; and data provided by the Malawian authorities.

[1] Excludes bills of exchange.

commercial banks' loans and advances (excluding bills of exchange) by economic sector. Credit to the distribution sector increased steadily, from MK 2.4 million in 1965 to MK 4.0 million in 1968, largely as a result of the rise in imports of intermediate goods, capital equipment, and building materials. Agricultural credit, mainly to the tea estates, the tung oil plantation, and the Sucoma sugar plantation, increased by MK 0.4 million between the end of 1965 and December 1968. Credit to the manufacturing sector, after a slight decline in 1967, rose by MK 0.4 million in 1968 as a number of new manufacturing industries came into operation. Credit to the Farmers Marketing Board increased sharply in 1967: in September it was at a record high level of nearly MK 10 million and constituted nearly 48 per cent of total loans and advances; it then declined in 1968 as the financial resources of the Board improved and enabled it to repay a substantial proportion of its loans to the commercial banks.

Total loans and advances rose by MK 2.4 million in 1969. The largest portion of this increase (MK 1.6 million) went to the distribution sector and represented mainly an increase in credit to the National Trading Company, which operates as a monopoly for the wholesale of certain commodities, including sugar, used clothing, and, in certain areas, cigarettes. In addition, there was an increase in the volume of wholesaling, reflecting a shift from Rhodesia as the center of wholesaling operations for Malawi to Malawi itself. Approximately MK 1.3 million of the expansion in credit went to the manufacturing sector, mainly to finance an increase in textile production of David Whitehead and Sons, an increase in shoe production by Bata for both domestic consumption and for export to Zambia, and an increase in the production of beer by the Chibuku and Carlsberg breweries. The increase in credit to the building and construction sector amounted to nearly MK 1.1 million. This expansion was due mainly to the acceleration of the road-building program under which projects financed by foreign aid were temporarily prefinanced by contractors who utilized local bank credit. An additional factor was the construction of a large amount of high-income housing in Blantyre. Credit to the Farmers Marketing Board fell substantially in 1969, reflecting its improved financial position. Credit for financial services, which includes automobile financing, also fell, partly as a result of a decline in the sales of new cars related to the increase in import duties in 1969. Agricultural credit, mainly to the tea estates and the Sucoma sugar plantation, rose slightly in 1969.

The commercial banks used the repayments by the Marketing Board to repay the advances received from their head offices (Table 20). Such advances had risen by MK 2.8 million in 1967 to provide the banks with liquidity needed for increasing their loans to the Marketing Board, which had incurred a large deficit in that year. In order to meet the demand for credit from the private sector, the banks reduced their holdings of treasury bills by nearly MK 0.8 million.

Demand deposits increased by 15 per cent in 1969, compared with an average annual rate of increase of 12 per cent during the period 1966–68. A high rate of increase in time and savings deposits was attained throughout the period, partly as a result of the success of the campaign to mobilize a larger amount of savings in the rural areas through the provision of more and better facilities and partly as a result of an increase in migrants' remittances from Rhodesia and South Africa.

Commercial Bank Operations, 1970

Bank credit to the private sector (excluding the Farmers Marketing Board) rose by 23 per cent in 1970 compared with 25 per cent in 1969. Most of the increase went to the distribution sector for financing imports of food and consumer durables, electrical supplies, farm implements, trucks, and building materials. Credit to the transport and communications sector (included in the category "Other" in Table 19) and to the building and construction sector rose moderately, reflecting the implementation of rail and road construction projects. Credit to the agricultural and manufacturing sectors also rose slightly.

Credit to the Farmers Marketing Board fell by about 54 per cent. The Board's improved financial position and the need to purchase smaller quantities of maize and groundnuts had reduced the amount of its financial requirements.

Demand deposits increased by nearly MK 3.9 million in 1970, compared with an increase of MK 2.2 million in 1969, and time and savings deposits rose by MK 2.2 million, or MK 0.4 million more than in 1969.

Other Financial Institutions

Deposits with the Post Office Savings Bank have risen steadily over the last few years (Table 21), reflecting the rise in the incomes of the

TABLE 20. MALAWI: ASSETS AND LIABILITIES OF THE COMMERCIAL BANKS, 1965–70

(In thousands of Malawi kwacha)

	1965	1966	1967	1968	1969				1970			
					Mar.	June	Sept.	Dec.	Mar.	June	Sept.	Dec.
Assets												
Reserves	2,394	1,920	1,746	1,910	1,998	2,108	1,756	2,614	1,352	2,842	2,256	3,256
Cash	400	508	688	682	766	948	626	740	900	1,066	706	1,012
Deposits with Reserve Bank	1,994	1,412	1,058	1,228	1,232	1,160	1,130	1,874	452	1,776	1,550	2,244
Foreign assets	1,282	1,776	1,040	836	188	670	444	468	288	508	272	648
Claims on government	2,544	2,668	3,170	4,198	3,848	3,198	2,798	3,478	4,978	3,678	3,878	4,018
Claims on private sector [1]	10,546	15,110	21,226	19,562	19,168	24,302	25,752	22,472	23,832	26,492	26,794	26,916
Farmers Marketing Board	134	500	7,586	2,436	1,750	3,553	5,100	966	930	1,514	1,694	448
Assets = liabilities	16,766	21,474	27,182	26,506	25,202	30,278	30,750	29,032	30,450	33,520	33,200	34,838
Liabilities												
Demand deposits	10,836	11,874	13,756	14,662	14,786	17,088	16,288	16,900	16,390	18,958	18,656	20,774
Time and savings deposits	6,250	7,798	8,570	10,376	10,706	10,888	12,340	12,216	12,804	12,136	13,460	14,442
Government deposits	356	104	2	6	10	10	10	2	—	—	—	—
Foreign liabilities	1,104	3,388	6,152	4,330	2,462	4,590	3,852	3,008	3,846	4,682	3,704	3,184
Credit from Reserve Bank	—	—	500	—	—	340	1,000	—	940	500	1,620	380
Other items (net)	-1,780	-1,690	-1,798	-2,868	-2,762	-2,638	-2,740	-3,094	-3,530	-2,756	-4,240	-3,942

Sources: Reserve Bank of Malawi, *Economic and Financial Review*; and data provided by the Malawian authorities.

[1] Includes bills of exchange.

TABLE 21. MALAWI: ASSETS AND LIABILITIES OF OTHER FINANCIAL INSTITUTIONS,[1] 1965–70

(In thousands of Malawi kwacha; end of period)

	1965	1966	1967	1968	1969				1970			
					Mar.	June	Sept.	Dec.	Mar.	June	Sept.	Dec.
Assets												
Cash	204	142	108	174	64	92	40	130	26	54	144	95
Foreign assets [2]	466	144	88	24	22	22	22	22	22	22	22	...
Claims on government	1,996	3,078	3,490	4,354	4,256	4,472	4,878	4,878	4,912	5,188	5,742	6,098
Post Office Savings Bank	*1,464*	*2,394*	*2,948*	*3,472*	*3,698*	*3,830*	*4,190*	*4,438*	*4,466*	*4,630*	*5,038*	*5,280*
New Building Society	*532*	*684*	*542*	*882*	*828*	*642*	*688*	*440*	*446*	*558*	*704*	*818*
Claims on private sector [3]	1,188	1,250	1,988	2,430	2,602	2,840	3,058	3,170	3,232	3,186	3,184	3,152
Assets = liabilities	**3,854**	**4,614**	**5,674**	**6,982**	**7,160**	**7,426**	**7,998**	**8,200**	**8,192**	**8,450**	**9,092**	...
Liabilities												
Time and savings deposits	3,884	4,594	5,644	6,732	7,128	7,328	7,768	7,990	8,032	8,302	8,638	8,812
Post Office Savings Bank	*2,084*	*2,548*	*3,054*	*3,456*	*3,702*	*3,856*	*4,104*	*4,414*	*4,404*	*4,638*	*4,932*	*5,024*
New Building Society [4]	*1,800*	*2,046*	*2,590*	*3,276*	*3,426*	*3,472*	*3,664*	*3,576*	*3,628*	*3,664*	*3,706*	*3,788*
Other items (net)	−30	20	30	250	32 [5]	98	230	210	160	148	454 [6]	...

Source: Data provided by the Malawian authorities.

[1] Post Office Savings Bank and New Building Society.
[2] Post Office Savings Bank only.
[3] New Building Society only.
[4] Also includes investment deposits and fixed deposits.
[5] Includes an increase in New Building Society shares from MK 60,000 to MK 120,000.
[6] Includes an increase in New Building Society shares from MK 120,000 to MK 240,000.

small farmers from an increasing output of cash crops and of the wage earners in the lower income group from employment generated by the development projects, the success of the program to mobilize a larger amount of savings in the rural areas, and the increase in the amount of savings from migrant laborers in Rhodesia and South Africa. In order to utilize domestic savings for development purposes, the bank continuously increased the proportion of its resources invested domestically: its holdings of local registered stock and treasury bills rose from less than MK 1.5 million at the end of 1965 to MK 5.0 million in September 1970, while its foreign assets fell from MK 500,000 to MK 22,000.

Total deposits of the New Building Society rose steadily from MK 1.8 million in December 1965 to MK 3.7 million in September 1969, declined by 2 per cent in the fourth quarter of 1969, and then rose steadily to MK 3.7 million in September 1970. The main reason for the decline in the last quarter of 1969 was the withdrawal of MK 260,000 of fixed deposits by the Government. The amount of loans outstanding increased from MK 1.2 million in December 1965 to a high of MK 3.2 million in the first quarter of 1970, reflecting the emphasis on residential construction for the high-income group; it then fell slightly in the two succeeding quarters. The average size of the mortgages taken up by the society increased from MK 6,000 in 1965 to MK 8,000 in 1969. Nearly two thirds of all mortgages have been for new residential houses, about one fourth for existing houses, and the remainder for the construction of flats, stores, and offices. About MK 0.6 million of the society's assets were invested in local registered stock at the end of 1969.

The Development Finance Company of Malawi, Ltd., and its subsidiaries (DEFINCO Group) had invested a total of MK 1,534,000 at the end of 1969, of which 57 per cent was in financial and housing enterprises, 33 per cent in the Portland Cement Company, and the remainder in a paper packaging company and a match company.

INTEREST RATES

The monetary authorities have aimed in the past at keeping interest rates relatively low so as to foster the development effort. However, because of the close financial ties between Malawi and the United Kingdom, the structure and movements of interest rates tend to be influenced by developments in the London money and capital markets. In late 1967 and in 1968 pressures mounted on the rate structure in Malawi until the Reserve Bank found it necessary on August 1, 1968 to raise the bank rate (which had remained unchanged since independence) from 4½ per cent to 5½ per cent. Following this change, the commercial banks raised their prime lending rates by ½ per cent, to 7½ per cent, and at the same time raised the various rates paid on time and savings deposits by ½ per cent in order to attract more savings. The Post Office Savings Bank later raised the rate it pays on savings deposits by ¼ per cent, to 3½ per cent. The increase in rates was introduced to bring them more in line with those prevailing in the London market and thus to discourage foreign-owned companies from financing their operations from domestic rather than foreign resources.

In April 1970, two further measures were taken to restrain the rate of credit expansion to the private sector, including nonresident-controlled companies with access to foreign financial markets. One was an exchange control measure involving the reduction in the ratio of domestic to foreign borrowing permitted to such companies and the other was the increase in the commercial banks' prime rate for loans and advances from 7½ per cent to 9 per cent. Other commercial bank lending rates were also raised by 1½ per cent, and the interest rate charged on housing mortgages was raised by ½ of 1 per cent. Concurrently with the increase in lending rates, interest rates paid by the commercial banks and the New Building Society on time deposits were raised by 1 per cent, to a range of 4 to 7 per cent.

On August 21, 1970, the bank rate was raised from 5½ per cent to 6 per cent and the commercial banks' prime lending rate was reduced by ½ per cent, to 8½ per cent, with a view to narrowing the margin between the bank rate and the prime rate.

MONETARY SURVEY, 1965–70

1965–69

The monetary survey represents the consolidation of the accounts of the monetary authorities and the commercial banks. From a close scrutiny of developments during the four-year period from the end of 1965 to the end of 1969, these salient features emerge: a substantial increase in domestic credit, particularly to the private sector, in 1966 and 1967 and again in 1969; the concomitant increase in the money supply in those years; and the seasonal fluctuations in the foreign liabilities of the commercial banks resulting from the need to provide crop finance (Table 22).

In the three years ended 1968, domestic credit by the banking system nearly tripled. Net claims on the Government rose by MK 7.5 million, of which 61 per cent occurred in 1966 and 31 per cent in 1968. The main reason for the sharp increase in net claims on the Government in 1966 was the change in the pattern of development aid disbursements by the U. K. Government from a system of payments in advance to payments after expenditures had been incurred. This led to a sharp reduction in the level of government deposits with the Reserve Bank and to an increased reliance on treasury bills by the Government for temporary accommodation; the total amount of treasury bills outstanding rose from MK 1.8 million at the end of 1965 to MK 3.4 million in December 1966. To finance larger development expenditures in 1968, the Government increased its borrowing from the banking system mainly through the issue of medium-term and long-term securities.

Claims on the private sector (including the Farmers Marketing Board) nearly doubled between 1965 and 1968. The entire increase took place during 1966 and 1967, as such claims actually fell by 8 per cent in 1968. While 97 per cent of credit to the private sector during 1966 had been to customers other than the Marketing Board, the situation was completely reversed in 1967 when borrowing by the Board increased by over MK 7 million and loans to other borrowers declined by nearly MK 1 million. Commercial bank lending to the Board reached a peak of almost MK 10 million in September 1967. The resources of the Board had been reduced considerably by the need to hold large unsold stocks of tobacco and the delay in obtaining receipts for certain crops exported.

Despite an increase of MK 3.5 million in loans to other customers during 1968, claims on the private sector fell as the Farmers Marketing Board, which was able to dispose of some of its accumulated stocks

TABLE 22. MALAWI: MONETARY SURVEY, 1965–70 [1]

(In thousands of Malawi kwacha; end of period)

	1965	1966	1967	1968	1969 Mar.	1969 June	1969 Sept.	1969 Dec.	1970 Mar.	1970 June	1970 Sept.	1970 Dec.
Assets												
Foreign assets (net)	18,198	13,682	13,642	15,264	14,294	15,470	14,408	14,960	16,342	16,976	21,002	21,800
Monetary authorities	18,020	15,294	13,754	18,758	16,568	19,390	17,816	17,500	19,900	21,150	24,434	24,336
Commercial banks	178	–1,612	–5,112	–3,494	–2,274	–3,920	–3,408	–2,540	–3,558	–4,174	–3,432	–2,536
Claims on government (net)	–2,160	2,464	3,070	5,366	4,628	4,086	4,930	5,964	2,616	7,212	1,914	2,269
By banking system (net)	682	4,162	4,736	7,368	7,798	5,966	6,864	8,370	4,712	9,066	4,656	4,610
Others (net) [2]	–2,842	–1,698	–1,666	–2,002	–3,170	–1,880	–1,934	–2,406	–2,096	–1,854	–2,742	–2,341
Claims on private sector	10,546	15,110	21,226	19,558	19,710	24,300	25,750	22,470	23,832	26,492	26,794	26,916
Farmers Marketing Board	134	500	7,586	2,436	1,750	3,506	5,100	966	930	1,514	1,694	448
Other	10,412	14,610	13,640	17,122	17,960	20,794	20,650	21,504	22,902	24,978	25,100	26,468
(Total domestic credit)	(8,386)	(17,574)	(24,296)	(24,924)	(24,338)	(28,386)	(30,680)	(28,434)	(26,448)	(33,704)	(28,708)	(29,185)
Assets = liabilities	26,584	31,256	37,938	40,188	38,632	43,856	45,088	43,394	42,790	50,680	49,710	50,985
Liabilities												
Money	19,716	22,438	25,574	26,232	25,804	31,406	30,826	29,440	28,454	35,408	33,932	34,048
Currency	8,880	10,564	11,820	11,570	11,018	14,308	14,528	12,540	12,066	16,450	15,276	13,274
Demand deposits	10,836	11,874	13,754	14,662	14,786	17,098	16,298	16,900	16,388	16,958	18,656	20,774
Quasi-money	6,410	8,046	10,928	13,430	12,164	12,104	13,620	13,482	14,346	13,280	14,844	15,686
Savings deposits	3,414	4,410	5,284	6,138	6,562	6,742	7,164	7,382	7,618	7,696	8,076	8,124
Time deposits	2,836	3,386	3,286	4,236	4,142	4,146	5,174	4,834	5,186	4,440	5,392	6,318
Reserve Bank's other deposits	160	250	2,358	3,056	1,460	1,216	1,282	1,266	1,542	1,144	1,376	1,244
Other items (net)	458	772	1,436	526	664	346	642	472	–10	1,992	934	1,251

Sources: Reserve Bank of Malawi, *Economic and Financial Review*; IMF, *International Financial Statistics*; and data provided by the Malawian authorities.

[1] A consolidation of the balance sheets of the monetary authorities and the commercial banks (Tables 17 and 20).
[2] Covers the counterpart of government holdings in Table 17.

of tobacco, improved its financial position and reduced its indebtedness to the commercial banks by nearly MK 5.2 million.

Net foreign assets fell from MK 18.2 million at the end of 1965 to MK 15.3 million at the end of 1968. They fell sharply, by MK 4.5 million, in 1966, partly because of the drawing down of the Government's foreign balances and the utilization of some of its deposits with the Reserve Bank to acquire foreign exchange. As mentioned above, this was caused by the change in the pattern of foreign aid disbursements. The increase in the reserves of the monetary authorities in 1967 (arising mainly from the receipt by the Government of the proceeds from the sale of the Zambezi bridge) was more than offset by the large increase in the foreign liabilities of the commercial banks, and total net foreign assets declined slightly. In order to provide the necessary crop financing, particularly to the Farmers Marketing Board, the commercial banks had to draw heavily on their head offices and on facilities provided by the central bank. The net foreign liabilities of the commercial banks reached a record level of over MK 6.8 million at the peak of the crop season in September 1967. Net foreign assets rose by MK 1.6 million in 1968 as the commercial banks reduced their indebtedness with their head offices.

As a result of the developments in foreign assets and domestic credit, money and quasi-money combined rose by MK 13.5 million (52 per cent) between 1965 and 1968 (Table 23). The money supply increased by MK 6.5 million (33 per cent) while quasi-money, including the deposits from the sale of the Zambezi bridge held in a special account, rose by MK 7 million. Most of the increase in the money supply occurred in 1966 and 1967 (14 per cent in each year), when domestic credit was the main expansionary force. Largely as a result of the substantial reduction in domestic credit in 1968, the rate of increase in the money supply fell to less than 3 per cent.

In the first quarter of 1969, domestic credit fell slightly (2 per cent), compared with an increase of 5 per cent in the comparable period of 1968. Net claims on the Government fell by nearly MK 0.8 million. Despite a decline in the Farmers Marketing Board's borrowing from the commercial banks, credit to the private sector as a whole rose as much as in the previous year and, owing to the drawing down of the special bridge account to finance the current budget deficit, foreign assets fell

TABLE 23. MALAWI: CHANGES IN MONEY SUPPLY AND ITS DETERMINANTS, 1966–70

(In thousands of Malawi kwacha)

	1966		1967		1968		1969		1970	
	MK	%	MK	%	MK	%	MK	%	MK	%
Foreign assets (net)	−4,516	−24.8	−40	−0.3	1,622	11.9	−304	−2.0	6,840	45.7
Claims on government (net)	4,624	...	606	24.6	2,296	74.8	598	11.1	−3,695	62.0
Claims on private sector	4,564	43.3	6,116	40.5	−1,668	−7.9	2,912	14.9	4,446	19.8
Farmers Marketing Board	366	273.1	7,086	1,517.2	−5,150	−67.9	−1,470	−60.3	−518	53.6
Others	4,198	40.3	−970	−6.6	3,482	25.5	4,382	25.6	4,964	23.1
(Total domestic credit)	(9,188)	(109.6)	(6,722)	(38.3)	(628)	(2.6)	(3,510)	(14.1)	(751)	(2.6)
Other items (net)	314	68.6	664	86.0	−910	−63.2	−54	−10.6	779	65.0
Money and quasi-money	4,358	16.7	6,018	19.7	3,160	5.1	3,260	8.2	6,812	15.9
Money	2,722	13.8	3,136	14.0	658	2.6	3,208	12.2	4,608	15.7
Quasi-money	1,636	25.5	2,882	35.8	2,502	22.9	52	0.4	2,204	16.3

Source: Table 22.

by 6 per cent. As a result of these developments, money and quasi-money combined fell slightly, the decline in currency more than offsetting the increase in demand, savings, and time deposits combined.

In the second and third quarters of 1969, domestic credit increased by 26 per cent, compared with 10 per cent for the same period of 1968. More than half of this expansion represented increased credit to the Farmers Marketing Board; most of the remainder went to the distribution and manufacturing sectors. The Marketing Board utilized its credit to purchase the larger output of groundnuts and cotton. The rise in the level of credit to the distribution sector financed larger imports of petroleum products, wheat flour, packaging materials, and other intermediate consumer goods, while the increase to the manufacturing sector went to the textile, shoe, and beer industries. There was a slight rise in net claims on the Government as the latter increased its borrowing from the Reserve Bank. At the same time it drew down a substantial proportion of its balances with the Crown Agents and utilized a portion of the counterpart funds to reduce its indebtedness to the commercial banks.

The increase of MK 1.2 million in the net foreign assets of the monetary authorities between April and September 1969 resulting from foreign aid receipts in the second quarter of the year was almost offset by an increase of an equivalent amount in the net foreign liabilities of the commercial banks, as the banks borrowed from their head offices to provide funds for crop financing.

The large increase in domestic credit had an expansionary effect on money and quasi-money, which rose by 17 per cent in 1969, compared with 14 per cent in 1968. More than half of the increase occurred in currency in circulation, with demand deposits and quasi-money each accounting for about 23 per cent.

In the fourth quarter of 1969 domestic credit fell by more than 7 per cent, entirely as a result of the decline in credit to the Farmers Marketing Board, which repaid its loans for crop financing to the commercial banks; net credit to the Government rose slightly as the commercial banks and the Reserve Bank increased their purchases of treasury bills. The impact of the decline in domestic credit more than offset the increase in foreign assets (4 per cent), and money and quasi-money combined fell by nearly 4 per cent. Currency in circulation fell by nearly MK 2 million, while demand deposits rose by MK 0.6 million and quasi-money fell slightly.

1970

Despite an increase in credit to the private sector (including the Farmers Marketing Board) of over 6 per cent in the first quarter of 1970, total credit continued to decline as net claims on the Government fell sharply. The Government utilized foreign aid receipts and interest and other payments on the debentures owned by the former Trans-Zambezi Railway to liquidate completely the outstanding loans and advances from the Reserve Bank and attain a net credit position. Net foreign assets rose by 9 per cent, reflecting the extraordinary aid and other receipts mentioned above, the receipt of Malawi's allocation of SDRs, and the transfer to Malawi of export proceeds by the Marketing Board. As a result of these developments in domestic credit and foreign assets, money and quasi-money combined fell slightly, the decline in money (MK 1.0 million) more than offsetting the increase in quasi-money (MK 0.9 million).

In the second quarter of 1970, domestic credit rose sharply as the seasonal increase in private sector borrowing by the agricultural and distribution sectors was reinforced by a large increase in government borrowing from the Reserve Bank to meet the costs of increasing development expenditure. More than 50 per cent of the increase in credit to the private sector went to the distribution sector. The increase of MK 1.2 million in the net foreign assets of the monetary authorities was partially offset by the increase in net borrowing by the commercial banks from their head offices for the purpose of financing domestic agricultural marketing operations and imports. The combined effect of the sharp increase in domestic credit and the slight rise in net foreign assets was reflected in the sharp increase of 20 per cent in the money supply.

The receipt of foreign aid in the third quarter of 1970 enabled the Government to reduce its indebtedness to the banking system by MK 4.4 million and its overall indebtedness by MK 5.3 million, which led to a considerable decline (15 per cent) in domestic credit. Net foreign assets increased by more than MK 4 million, reflecting the increase in foreign aid receipts and the reduction in the commercial banks' liabilities to their head offices. As a result of these offsetting movements in domestic credit and net foreign assets, the amount of money and quasi-money combined hardly changed.

In the fourth quarter of 1970 total domestic credit rose by MK 0.5 million (less than 2 per cent). Credit to the private sector (excluding the Farmers Marketing Board) rose by MK 1.4 million but credit to the Farmers Marketing Board fell by MK 1.2 million and total credit to the private sector hardly changed. Net credit to the Government rose by nearly MK 0.4 million. Net foreign assets increased by MK 0.8 million. As a result of these developments, money and quasi-money rose by 4 per cent, most of the increase occurring in quasi-money, however, as the money supply increased only slightly.[8]

BALANCE OF PAYMENTS

Malawi's balance of payments has been volatile because of fluctuations in agricultural production, in world market prices, and in receipts of foreign aid. After a substantial surplus of $9 million in 1965, the balance of payments deteriorated to a deficit of $7.7 million in 1966, largely as a result of a very sharp increase in imports and a fall in transfer receipts (Table 24). The balance of payments improved substantially in 1967 and further in 1968, when a surplus of $1.7 million was achieved. In 1969 there was an overall deficit of $1.6 million, owing to a widening of the deficit on goods and services and a decline in the inflow of private capital. Provisional estimates for 1970 indicate a balance of payments surplus of about $8 million.

TRADE

The importance of foreign trade to the Malawian economy has increased in recent years. The ratio of the value of total exports (including re-exports) to GDP rose from 16 per cent in 1965 to 19 per cent in 1969, while the ratio of the value of imports to GDP rose from 23 per cent to 26 per cent. During the five years 1965–69 the value of exports rose at an average annual rate of 13 per cent.

---

[8] The reader is referred to the International Monetary Fund's monthly statistical bulletin, *International Financial Statistics*, for later information on monetary and credit developments.

TABLE 24. MALAWI: BALANCE OF PAYMENTS, 1965–69

(*In millions of U. S. dollars*)

	1965	1966	1967	1968	1969
A. Goods and services (net)	**−35.0**	**−49.6**	**−39.4**	**−44.7**	**−48.5**
Exports f.o.b.	39.9	48.4	55.3	48.0	52.2
Imports f.o.b.	57.2	75.7	68.7	68.4	73.2
Trade balance	−17.3	−27.3	−13.4	−20.4	−21.0
Freight and insurance	−5.4	−6.0	−5.2	−7.0	−8.0
Other transportation	−1.9	−2.0	−2.2	−1.8	−2.0
Travel	−3.2	−3.1	−2.6	−2.0	−2.7
Investment income	−8.1	−9.8	−11.1	−9.4	−11.1
Other government	−2.2	−3.3	−3.7	−4.0	−4.3
Other	3.1	2.0	−1.2	−0.1	0.6
Services balance	−17.7	−22.3	−26.0	−24.3	−27.5
B. Unrequited transfers (net)	**35.5**	**21.2**	**22.1**	**17.8**	**17.9**
Private	1.4	1.0	1.8	1.9	1.8
Official	34.1	20.2	20.3	15.9	16.1
Total (A plus B)	**0.5**	**−28.4**	**−17.3**	**−26.9**	**−30.6**
C. Capital movements (net)	**6.6**	**19.3**	**18.4**	**28.4**	**29.2**
Private	7.1	12.2	10.9	19.5	13.5
Long-term	*7.5*	*9.2*	*11.6*	*17.1*	*12.9*
Short-term	*−0.4*	*3.0*	*−0.7*	*2.4*	*0.6*
Official	−0.5	7.1	7.5	8.9	15.7
Long-term	*−0.5*	*7.1*	*7.5*	*8.9*	*15.7*
Short-term	—	—	—	—	—
D. Net errors and omissions	**1.9**	**1.4**	**−2.5**	**0.2**	**−0.2**
Total (A through D)	**9.0**	**−7.7**	**−1.4**	**1.7**	**−1.6**
E. Net monetary movements [1]	**−9.0**	**7.7**	**1.4**	**−1.7**	**1.6**
Central monetary institutions	−12.2	4.8	−4.0	—	1.5
Other monetary institutions	3.2	2.9	5.4	−1.7	0.1

Sources: IMF, *Balance of Payments Yearbook;* National Statistical Office, *Balance of Payments, 1969;* and data provided by the Malawian authorities.

[1] Net monetary movements in this table are not comparable with movements of foreign assets (net) in Table 22 because the figures for central monetary institutions in this table include also externally registered stock held by the Post Office Savings Bank and the figures for other monetary institutions cover, in addition, Malawian commercial banks' loans to nonresidents and deposits held by nonresidents.

Exports

Exports are concentrated on a few agricultural commodities. Before 1966, tobacco, tea, groundnuts, and cotton accounted for about 80–85 per cent of total exports of domestic products. Since 1966 maize has replaced cotton as the fourth major export commodity. The world market for Malawi's major exports in the past few years has remained relatively favorable, and changes in the level of exports of these principal products have been determined mainly by the volume of domestic production.

After remaining at about the same level in 1968 as in 1967, the value of exports (excluding re-exports) rose in 1969 by 9 per cent, to MK 36.6 million, because of higher prices and greater output for most crops (Table 25). Despite a lower volume of tobacco exports, the value rose by 20 per cent as world prices for burley, fire-cured, and air-cured tobacco increased substantially. The value of tea exports fell slightly, reflecting lower prices on the world market, while a rise in both volume and price increased the value of groundnut exports. Despite a sharp decline in the price of cotton (11 per cent), the value of exports increased by 36 per cent because of greater volume. Higher prices for maize only partially offset the sharp decline in volume, and the value of exports fell by 30 per cent. Exports of pulses and tung oil showed small increases, while the value of cassava exports declined. Re-exports, consisting mainly of Zambian tobacco imported for processing and of petroleum products in transit to Zambia, rose by 16 per cent, to MK 7.4 million, mainly as a result of higher tobacco prices.

Exports for 1970 were valued at MK 40.3 million, and re-exports at nearly MK 9.0 million. The value of tobacco exports, reflecting both larger volume and higher prices, rose by 31 per cent, while the value of tea exports, benefiting from higher prices, rose by nearly 15 per cent. The value of cotton exports rose from MK 1.7 million in 1969 to nearly MK 2.8 million in 1970. As a consequence of drought in the early part of the year, the value of groundnut exports fell by 24 per cent and no maize was exported.

Imports

In addition to the sharp increase in the value of imports between 1965 and 1969, there was a change in the structure of imports. The proportion of consumer goods to total imports fell from half in 1965 to less than 31 per cent in 1969, while the proportion of goods for intermediate consumption rose from 27 per cent to 33 per cent and the proportions of capital equipment and construction materials rose from 15 per cent and 7 per cent, respectively, to 25 per cent and 10 per cent (Table 26). This increase in the proportion of capital equipment and

TABLE 25. MALAWI: VALUE, VOLUME, AND UNIT PRICE INDEX OF EXPORTS OF DOMESTIC PRODUCTS, 1965–70 [1]

	Tea	Tobacco	Groundnuts	Cotton	Maize	Pulses	Tung Oil	Cassava	Other	Total
				THOUSANDS OF MALAWI KWACHA						
1965	7,536	10,260	3,278	2,158	34	1,858	606	136	1,218	27,084
1966	8,898	9,042	2,574	2,168	1,570	1,248	344	692	1,134	27,670
1967	8,982	8,452	6,868	1,384	3,278	1,528	410	532	1,670	33,104
1968	9,700	10,570	4,616	1,274	3,008	862	246	1,384	1,898	33,558
1969	9,526	12,646	5,590	1,730	2,132	1,022	306	638	2,980	36,570
1970	10,916	16,450	4,242	2,776	—	1,038	412	724	3,782	40,340
				SHORT TONS						
1965	14,548	19,449	20,876	5,123	1,120	…	2,030	5,817	…	…
1966	16,780	17,680	16,369	5,332	48,896	…	1,374	27,485	…	…
1967	18,563	18,307	56,262	3,471	100,800	…	1,941	23,523	…	…
1968	17,407	17,753	33,064	2,742	95,872	…	1,036	52,572	…	…
1969	19,012	16,072	37,765	4,205	5,244	…	1,257	24,211	…	…
				UNIT PRICE INDEX (1967 = 100)						
1965	107.1	106.3	128.6	106.7	93.4	…	141.2	…	…	…
1966	109.6	99.7	128.8	102.9	98.7	…	118.6	…	…	…
1967	100.0	100.0	100.0	100.0	100.0	…	100.0	…	…	…
1968	115.6	108.0	114.3	117.6	106.0	…	112.2	…	…	…
1969	103.6	135.7	121.4	104.1	125.7	…	115.6	…	…	…

Sources: Office of the President, *Economic Report, 1969* and *1971*; and data provided by the Malawian authorities.

[1] The values of exports shown here are based on customs records.

TABLE 26. MALAWI: IMPORTS BY MAIN CLASS, 1965–70 [1]

(Value in thousands of Malawi kwacha)

	1965		1966		1967		1968		1969		1970	
	Value	% of total	Value	% of total	Value	% of total	Value	% of total	Value	% of total	Value	% of total
Consumer goods												
Motor cars and bicycles	1,968	4.8	2,128	3.9	2,236	4.4	2,048	3.5	2,054	3.3	2,428	3.4
Piece goods	6,498	15.9	5,318	9.8	4,430	8.7	3,996	6.9	3,776	6.1	3,416	4.8
Motor spirit	534	1.3	578	1.0	682	1.3	900	1.5	1,014	1.7	1,040	1.4
Other	11,452	28.1	12,514	23.1	12,754	25.1	12,626	21.7	12,002	19.5	12,786	17.9
Total	20,452	50.1	20,538	37.8	20,102	39.5	19,570	33.6	18,846	30.6	19,670	27.5
Intermediate goods												
Petroleum products	1,070	2.6	1,426	2.6	1,546	3.0	2,156	3.7	2,432	4.0	2,580	3.6
Parts, tools, etc.	794	2.0	1,106	2.1	1,258	2.5	1,624	2.8	1,840	3.0	2,594	3.6
Other	8,942	21.9	14,874	27.4	13,362	26.3	13,392	23.0	15,782	25.7	22,406	31.4
Total	10,806	26.5	17,406	32.1	16,166	31.8	17,172	29.5	20,054	32.7	27,580	38.6
Capital equipment												
Transport equipment	2,636	6.5	4,970	9.2	4,986	9.8	7,024	12.1	7,380	12.0	8,570	12.0
Other	3,526	8.6	6,914	12.7	4,968	9.8	8,762	15.0	7,954	12.9	8,622	12.1
Total	6,162	15.1	11,884	21.9	9,954	19.6	15,786	27.1	15,334	24.9	17,192	24.1
Construction materials	2,746	6.7	3,428	6.3	3,446	6.8	4,334	7.5	6,198	10.1	5,388	7.5
Miscellaneous	638	1.6	1,534	1.9	1,184	2.3	1,320	2.3	1,046	1.7	1,606	2.3
Total imports	40,804	100.0	54,290	100.0	50,852	100.0	58,182	100.0	61,478	100.0	71,476	100.0

Sources: Office of the President, *Economic Report, 1969* and *1971*; and data provided by the Malawian authorities.

[1] The values of imports shown here are based on customs records.

construction materials reflects the emphasis on the strengthening of infrastructure through the development projects undertaken during the period, while the increase in the proportion of intermediate goods reflects partly the import of semifinished goods for further processing.

The value of total imports increased by 6 per cent in 1969, to MK 61.5 million, compared with an increase of 14 per cent in 1968 and an average annual increase of 23 per cent over the three years 1965–67. Imports of consumer goods, mainly textiles, clothing, footwear, sugar, and beer, declined by 4 per cent, reflecting greater domestic production of such products. Imports of goods for intermediate consumption rose by 17 per cent in 1969 mainly as a result of increases in imports of petroleum products, packaging materials, unmanufactured tobacco from Zambia for further processing, oils and fats, and wheat flour in bulk. Imports of capital equipment, which had risen sharply in 1968 as a result of the more rapid pace of road and rail construction, fell slightly in 1969 but remained well above the level of 1965–67. Imports of construction materials associated with the Development Program rose by 43 per cent in 1969, compared with an increase of 26 per cent in 1968.

The value of imports for 1970 was MK 71.4 million, about 16 per cent higher than in 1969. Imports of intermediate consumer goods rose by 38 per cent, largely as a result of the need to import more maize because of the partial failure of the maize crop. Imports of capital goods increased by 12 per cent, reflecting mainly the purchase of an aircraft for Air Malawi, while imports of construction materials fell by 13 per cent as a result of the slowdown in building and construction associated with the completion of the rail link with Nacala and the near completion of the Zomba-Lilongwe road. Imports of consumer goods rose by 4 per cent.

Direction of Trade

The United Kingdom and Rhodesia are Malawi's main trading partners. Most of Malawi's tea and a substantial proportion of its groundnuts and tobacco are exported to the United Kingdom. The value of Malawi's exports to the United Kingdom reached a peak of MK 18.2 million in 1967 and then declined to MK 16.8 million in 1969, when it represented 46 per cent of exports (excluding re-exports), slightly less than in 1965 (Table 27). The value of exports to Rhodesia, consisting mainly of vegetables, groundnut cake, rice, cotton, and tobacco, fell between 1965 and 1968 and then rose sharply in 1969, to MK 2.4 million, i.e., nearly 7 per cent of exports (compared with 10 per cent in 1965). Exports to the EEC countries, consisting of groundnuts, tobacco, and cassava, reached a peak of MK 3.7 million in 1967 and then fell to MK 3.1 million in 1969, constituting 8 per cent of total exports. Exports to Zambia quadrupled in 1969, mainly as a result of larger exports of maize, rice, and tea and, to a lesser extent, increases in exports of manufactured articles, particularly cattle cake and footwear. Exports to the United States, consisting mainly of tea, have increased steadily over the period; in 1969 they accounted for 6 per cent of total exports.

In 1970, exports to the United Kingdom as a proportion of total exports rose to 49 per cent (MK 19 million), from 46 per cent in 1969, a reflection mainly of the increased value of exports of tea and tobacco. Exports to Rhodesia and South Africa also rose, to MK 3.2 million and MK 1.7 million, respectively, while exports to the United States fell by almost half, to MK 1.2 million.

The United Kingdom and Rhodesia are also the main sources of Malawi's imports. Imports from the United Kingdom, consisting mainly of capital equipment and manufactured goods, have risen steadily; in 1969 they were valued at MK 18.2 million, nearly 30 per cent of the total. Rhodesia's role as the chief supplier of manufactured products to the other members of the former Federation of Rhodesia and Nyasaland has diminished in recent years. The abrogation of the trade agreement with Rhodesia in November 1965 and the devaluation of the Malawi pound in November 1967 (making imports from Rhodesia more expensive) were important factors in the reduction in Rhodesia's share of total imports from 36 per cent in 1965 to 17 per cent in 1969. South Africa has become the third most important source of Malawi's imports, providing 14 per cent of the total in 1969 compared with less than 6 per cent in 1965. Most of the increase occurred in 1968 and 1969 and reflected substantial purchases of capital equipment, iron and steel sheets, railway equipment, and other building and construction materials associated with the rail link with Nacala and the capital city of Lilongwe. Other important sources of imports are Japan (mainly tex-

TABLE 27. MALAWI: DIRECTION OF TRADE, 1965–69

	Thousands of Malawi Kwacha					As Per Cent of Total	
	1965	1966	1967	1968	1969	1965	1969
Exports [1]							
United Kingdom	12,834	13,338	18,214	16,996	16,816	47.4	46.0
Rhodesia	2,760	1,560	1,270	1,564	2,364	10.2	6.5
Zambia	214	448	776	786	3,054	0.8	8.3
EEC countries	2,916	3,408	3,670	3,558	3,082	10.8	8.4
United States	726	810	1,072	1,610	2,292	2.7	6.3
South Africa	1,128	954	914	1,544	1,210	4.1	3.3
Others	6,506	7,152	7,188	7,500	7,758	24.0	21.2
Total	27,084	27,670	33,104	33,558	36,576	100.0	100.0
Imports							
United Kingdom	10,338	16,840	14,466	17,898	18,236	25.3	29.7
Rhodesia	14,860	12,334	10,646	10,490	10,446	36.4	17.0
Zambia	722	5,230	3,532	2,312	2,636	1.8	4.3
EEC countries	2,496	3,302	3,528	4,750	4,876	6.1	7.9
United States	1,092	1,714	1,408	3,272	2,356	2.7	3.8
South Africa	2,252	3,928	3,920	6,414	8,820	5.5	14.3
Japan	2,738	2,690	4,276	2,814	3,212	6.7	5.2
Others	6,306	8,254	9,076	10,230	10,896	15.5	17.8
Total	40,804	54,292	50,852	58,180	61,478	100.0	100.0

Source: Office of the President, *Economic Report, 1969*; and data provided by the Malawian authorities.

[1] Exports of domestic products, i.e., not including re-exports.

tiles, iron and steel products, motor cars and trucks, and miscellaneous manufactures), the EEC countries, and the United States.

Although imports from the United Kingdom and South Africa increased in absolute terms (to MK 19.1 million and MK 8.9 million, respectively) in 1970, their shares of total imports declined to 27 per cent and 13 per cent, from 30 per cent and 14 per cent in 1969. Imports from Rhodesia rose by 48 per cent (to MK 15.5 million) in 1970, reflecting entirely imports of maize.

CURRENT INVISIBLES

With the exception of 1968, when it improved slightly, the net services account has deteriorated steadily in recent years, largely as a result of increasing interest and dividend payments and net payments for freight, insurance, and transportation. Although there was a large increase ($3 million) in migrants' remittances from South Africa and Rhodesia in 1969, the deficit on services rose by $3.2 million, to $27.5 million (Table 24). The main factors responsible for the larger deficit were increased remittances by foreign contractors employed in the construction industry, a rise in interest and dividend payments stemming from larger profits of foreign-owned companies, and a fall in receipts from freight and insurance as a result of the decline in the transit trade between Zambia and Malawi upon the completion of the Tan-Zam oil pipeline. Net receipts from other services rose, mainly as a result of an increase in net earnings of migrant workers.

Net transfers remained almost unchanged in 1969. Budgetary grants from the United Kingdom, including grants under technical assistance schemes, fell by nearly $2 million, but this was more than offset by the reduction in Malawi's contribution for the compensation of expatriate civil servants.

PRIVATE CAPITAL AND OFFICIAL LOANS AND GRANTS

After a slight decline in 1967, net receipts of official and private capital combined rose by $10 million in 1968 and by $0.8 million in 1969, to $29.2 million (Table 24). The net inflow of private capital rose sharply in 1966, declined by $1.3 million in 1967, and then rose by $8.6 million in 1968. In 1969, despite an increase of $4.7 million in long-term loans received by the private sector, the net inflow of private capital fell by $6 million, to $13.5 million, as direct investment by private firms fell sharply. One of the reasons for the decline in foreign investment was the increase in payments on short-term intercompany accounts. Long-term loans were received for Air Malawi, the Mudi River Water Board, the Nkula Falls hydroelectric scheme, and also by private firms from foreign contractors.

The net inflow of official capital rose sharply in 1966, to $7.1 million. It continued to rise moderately in the following two years, but again rose sharply in 1969, by $6.8 million, mainly as a consequence of the receipt of $2.9 million constituting the first tranche of the South African loan for the construction of the capital at Lilongwe, and Danish and German loans for the development of telecommunications, transport, sewerage facilities, and agricultural projects.

EXTERNAL DEBT

The outstanding foreign indebtedness of the Central Government increased from $48.6 million in 1965 to $81.7 million in 1969; at the same time, other public sector debt guaranteed by the Central Government rose from $9.6 million to $13.6 million (Table 28). Until 1968 the United Kingdom was the main source of foreign loan funds, but in 1969 disbursements from the International Development Association (for projects in the fields of agriculture, transport, and education) exceeded disbursements from the United Kingdom. It is anticipated that South Africa, which has extended loans for both the rail link with Nacala and the new capital city of Lilongwe, will have become the main lender in the fiscal year 1970/71.

Despite the rising debt, the service on that debt declined between 1965 and 1969. The weighted average interest rate fell from 4.7 per cent in 1965 to 3 per cent in 1969, and the average maturity rose from 17.3 years to 20.2 years. It is to be expected, however, that there will be some deterioration in the average terms after the loans for the rail link with Nacala and the capital city have been disbursed. The service payments on the Central Government's external debt, including the debt of other public agencies guaranteed by it, amounted to $4.5 million in 1969, the equivalent of 9 per cent of exports.

TABLE 28. MALAWI: OUTSTANDING EXTERNAL DEBT OF CENTRAL GOVERNMENT
AND DEBT SERVICE PAYMENTS, 1965–69 [1]

(In thousands of U. S. dollars)

	1965	1966	1967	1968	1969
Denominated in foreign currency					
United Kingdom	31,324	35,902	39,931	45,677	50,134
Sinking funds	*13,677*	*13,152*	*12,353*	*11,755*	*10,870*
Other	*17,647*	*22,750*	*27,578*	*33,922*	*39,264*
IDA	—	65	322	2,484	7,226
South Africa	—	—	—	60	5,141
Germany, Federal Republic	—	1,730	3,305	3,588	4,656
Denmark	154	338	696	1,548	2,568
United States	168	132	312	432	379
	31,646	38,166	44,566	53,789	70,104
Denominated in Malawi currency					
Local registered stock sinking funds	12,007	11,179	10,951	10,250	9,485
Other local registered stock	247	5	7	120	—
Commercial finance	2,722	2,765	2,402	554	542
Other	1,982	1,886	1,786	1,685	1,574
	16,958	15,835	15,146	12,610	11,602
Total outstanding	**48,604**	**54,001**	**59,712**	**66,399**	**81,706**
Debt service [2]	**4,159**	**3,266**	**3,617**	**3,000**	**3,442**
Interest	2,234	2,121	2,270	2,053	2,314
Amortization	1,925	1,145	1,346	936	1,128
Weighted average terms of outstanding debt					
Interest (*per cent*)	4.7	4.3	3.8	3.2	3.0
Maturity (*years*)	17.3	18.1	18.5	18.6	20.2
Other public sector debt guaranteed by Central Government					
Amount outstanding	9,636	10,843	12,026	11,885	13,622
Debt service	557	739	1,109	998	1,008

Sources: Government of Malawi, *Public Sector Financial Statistics;* Office of the President, *Economic Report, 1969;* and data provided by the Malawian authorities.

[1] Medium-term and long-term debt only.
[2] Including sinking fund payments.

INTERNATIONAL RESERVES

The foreign exchange reserves of the monetary authorities (including the gold tranche position in the International Monetary Fund) fluctuated on a seasonal basis throughout the period (Table 29, column 5). On an annual basis, they fell by $3.6 million (to $18.5 million) in

TABLE 29. MALAWI: INTERNATIONAL RESERVES, 1965–70

(*In thousands of U.S. dollars; end of period*)

	Reserve Bank (1)	Net Foreign Assets of Commercial Banks (2)	Net Banking System (cols. 1 + 2) (3)	Government-Related Institutions [1] (4)	Official Foreign Exchange Reserves (cols. 1 + 4) (5)	Total Foreign Exchange Reserves (cols. 3 + 4) (6)
1965 June	19,229	−2,155	17,074	2,172	21,401	19,246
Sept.	20,030	−1,483	18,547	5,638	25,668	24,185
Dec.	18,214	214	18,428	3,984	22,198	22,412
1966 Mar.	14,431	4,354	18,785	2,364	16,795	21,149
June	21,302	−1,870	19,432	3,163	24,465	22,595
Sept.	18,154	−3,878	14,276	2,678	20,832	16,954
Dec.	16,315	−1,934	14,381	2,230	18,545	16,610
1967 Mar.	13,944	−2,090	11,854	1,668	15,612	13,522
June	18,727	−5,746	12,981	4,284	23,011	17,265
Sept.	17,318	−8,246	9,072	4,567	21,886	13,639
Dec.	18,065	−6,134	11,931	4,546	22,610	16,477
1968 Mar.	14,894	−5,230	9,665	4,642	19,536	22,946
June	15,720	−3,900	11,820	4,714	20,434	16,534
Sept.	16,310	−4,704	11,606	4,058	20,369	15,665
Dec.	17,292	−4,193	13,099	5,246	22,538	18,346
1969 Mar.	14,942	−2,729	12,213	4,942	19,884	17,155
June	19,877	−4,704	15,173	3,394	23,270	18,566
Sept.	17,923	−4,090	13,833	3,456	21,379	17,289
Dec.	16,978	−3,048	13,930	4,022	21,000	17,952
1970 Mar.	20,230 [2]	−4,270	15,960	3,643	23,873	19,603
June	22,020 [2]	−5,009	17,011	3,360	25,380	20,371
Sept.	24,895 [2]	−4,118	20,777	4,426	29,321	25,203
Dec.	25,260 [2]	−3,043	22,217	3,941	29,201	26,158

Sources: Reserve Bank of Malawi, *Economic and Financial Review*; and data provided by the Malawian authorities.

[1] Includes foreign securities held by the Treasury and administered by the Crown Agents in London, foreign securities held by the Post Office Savings Bank, foreign exchange holdings of the Treasury with the Crown Agents, foreign exchange holdings in a special account for the sale of the Zambezi bridge, and gold tranche position in the International Monetary Fund.

[2] Includes Malawi's allocation of SDR 1.89 million.

1966, mainly as a result of the change in the pattern of aid disbursement mentioned above, rose to $22.6 million in 1967, and then fell to $21 million in December 1969. The net foreign liabilities of the commercial banks also displayed seasonal fluctuations, reflecting the seasonal credit requirements of the agricultural sector of the economy. On an annual basis, they rose sharply in 1967 because of the banks' borrowing from their head offices to lend to the Farmers Marketing Board, and then fell steadily to $3 million at the end of 1969.

In the first three quarters of 1970, receipts by the Government of foreign aid disbursements and interest and other payments on debentures owned by the former Trans-Zambezi Railway, together with the receipt of Malawi's allocation of SDRs, helped to increase the official exchange reserves to $29.3 million, about $7.9 million higher than at the end of September 1969. Net foreign liabilities of the commercial banks hardly changed over the period from September 1969 to September 1970, and total foreign exchange reserves amounted to $25.2 million, the equivalent of nearly four months' imports. The foreign exchange reserves held by the Reserve Bank at the end of December 1970 amounted to $25.3 million, constituting 130 per cent of its total demand liabilities.

EXCHANGE AND TRADE CONTROL SYSTEM [9]

Exchange control in Malawi is applied in accordance with the Exchange Control Instructions which are issued by the Reserve Bank of Malawi and are based on the Exchange Control Act that came into effect on June 1, 1965. Although exchange control is administered by the Reserve Bank, much of the authority for approving normal current payments has been delegated to local commercial banks. Malawi is a member of the sterling area and maintains prescription of currency requirements similar to those of the United Kingdom.

Until February 1971, Malawi's currency unit was the Malawi pound, which was at par with the pound sterling, giving the relationship

---

[9] As of February 15, 1971. The reader is referred to the International Monetary Fund's *Annual Report on Exchange Restrictions* for later and more detailed information on exchange and trade controls.

£M 1 = US$2.40. Effective February 15, 1971, Malawi introduced a
new monetary unit, the kwacha, to replace the Malawi pound. The new
unit is equivalent to ten shillings of the old currency, i.e., one half of
the previous monetary unit. With effect from the same date, a par value
of MK 1 = US$1.20, or 1.06641 grams of fine gold, was agreed
between the Government of Malawi and the International Monetary
Fund. The local commercial banks base their rates for currencies other
than sterling on the current London market rates.

REGULATIONS GOVERNING IMPORTS AND EXPORTS

With effect from July 1969, all firms and individuals proposing to
import or export goods could be required to be registered under the
Control of Goods Act, which authorized the Minister of Trade and
Industry to issue import and export licenses. Certain imports and exports are subject to licensing irrespective of country of origin or destination. Most imports from sterling area countries and GATT countries may
be brought in freely; virtually all imports from other countries are
subject to special licensing requirements.

Imports

Import licenses are required for such goods as clothing, sugar,
cement, and arms and ammunition. In general, however, all other goods
originating from GATT countries outside the sterling area may be imported under an open general license, and goods from the sterling area
may be imported free of license. Import licenses are normally issued
for a period of six months, after which they automatically lapse; but
provision exists for extension of the licensing period.

Payments for imports from all countries must be made within six
months after the date of import. For such imports, foreign exchange is
automatically granted by the authorized exchange dealers, although advance payments require individual exchange control approval. Imports
from all sources are subject to a customs surcharge of 8⅓ per cent of
the import duty applicable to the commodity concerned when imported
from a Commonwealth country other than the United Kingdom.
Furthermore, a surtax of 5 per cent is levied on most goods imported into Malawi, irrespective of their origin; the surtax is calcu-

lated on 120 per cent of the sum of the value for customs duty purposes and any customs duty payable.

Exports

Exports of goods exceeding MK 100 in value are prohibited, unless the Controller of Customs and Excise is satisfied that payment has been made or will be made to a resident of Malawi not later than six months after the date of exportation. Certain goods, such as petroleum products and nickel, are subject to export licensing, mainly to ensure an adequate domestic supply. Export proceeds in foreign currency must be sold to an authorized exchange dealer.

REGULATIONS GOVERNING INVISIBLES

Exchange to pay for invisibles related to imports and also, up to certain limits, for other purposes is provided by the authorized exchange dealers without prior reference to the exchange control authorities. The basic exchange allowance for travel is MK 20 a day for an adult, with a maximum of MK 600 a calendar year, and MK 10 a day for each child under 18 years of age, with maxima of MK 300 a calendar year for children between 10 and 18 years of age and MK 200 a year for children under 10. The allowance is not cumulative but may be increased by up to 50 per cent if the traveler has not applied for a travel allowance during the preceding three years. These allocations are subject to a combined maximum of MK 2,000 a year for a family traveling together. Exchange for other purposes, such as education, medical treatment, family remittances, and business travel, is also provided subject to certain limits. Applications for amounts exceeding the standard allocations may be submitted to the exchange control authorities. Travelers may take out up to MK 20 in Malawi currency and the equivalent of MK 20 in foreign currency in addition to their basic travel allowance.

In general, all foreign currency earnings in respect of invisibles must be offered for sale to an authorized exchange dealer. Although there is no limit on the amount of foreign currency notes and coins that may be imported by travelers, no more than MK 20 in Malawi currency may be imported.

CAPITAL TRANSFERS

There are no restrictions on imports of capital into Malawi, with the exception that borrowing abroad requires prior exchange control approval. Outward transfers of capital, including those to other parts of the sterling area, are controlled. Nonresidents are, however, permitted to repatriate their investments, provided that they satisfy the authorities that the original investment was made with funds brought into the country from sources outside Malawi. The transfer abroad of dividends and profits of any foreign-owned company is permitted if no recourse is being made to local borrowing.

Generally, residents are not permitted to transfer capital abroad and, with certain exceptions, are required to offer for sale to an authorized exchange dealer any foreign exchange which accrues to them. Residents may, however, purchase foreign securities (except bearer securities) that are quoted on recognized stock exchanges in the sterling area, provided that certain specified conditions are met. Moreover, all income earned from these investments must be repatriated, and the corresponding foreign exchange must be sold to an authorized dealer.

Emigrants are granted foreign exchange according to age, marital status, and size of family. Exchange granted ranges from MK 3,000 to MK 15,000; all applications to transfer such funds require the approval of the exchange control authorities. Similarly, residents require prior approval to lend to nonresidents or to resident firms controlled directly or indirectly from outside Malawi. In April 1970 the ratio of domestic to foreign borrowing permitted to nonresident-controlled companies operating in Malawi was reduced from 1:1 to 1:2½. A ratio of 5:1 is allowed to companies engaged in tea and tobacco production, and a ratio of 2:3 for industries producing import substitutes.

All nontransferable capital in Malawi currency which accrues to nonresidents normally is deposited in blocked accounts, balances on which usually may be invested in Malawi securities. The interest on blocked account balances is freely transferable to the account holder's country of residence.

GOLD

In general, residents other than the monetary authorities and authorized industrial users are not allowed to hold or acquire gold in any form other than jewelry, at home or abroad. As an exception, residents may purchase, hold, and sell gold coins in Malawi for numismatic purposes. Imports of gold in any form other than jewelry require licenses issued by the Minister of Trade and Industry. Such licenses are not normally granted except for imports by or on behalf of the monetary authorities and industrial users.

TRADE AND PAYMENTS ARRANGEMENTS

Malawi is not a member of any regional trade group and maintains no bilateral payments agreements.

CHAPTER 5

Mauritius

GENERAL SETTING

The State of Mauritius comprises an island of about 720 square miles some 500 miles east of Madagascar, and several other small islands, situated in the Indian Ocean. The main island, which is roughly pear-shaped, is 38 miles long and measures 29 miles at its widest point. It is of volcanic origin with no known mineral deposits. From the north, an extensive undulating plain rises toward a central plateau, which then drops sharply to the southern and western coasts. Bordering the central plateau are three mountainous ridges with rocky peaks, the highest of which is 2,700 feet. The central highlands are mostly covered with forest and scrub, which preserve and regulate the water resources. Numerous small rivers are found throughout the island; most of these are short, fast-flowing torrents descending from the central plateau to the sea. Some of the large waterfalls have been harnessed to supply hydroelectric power.

Mauritius has a subtropical maritime climate with two main seasons, a summer from November to May and a winter from June to

October. Temperatures are relatively mild, with the mean ranging from 74° F. at sea level to 67° F. at an altitude of 2,000 feet. Rain falls mainly in summer, but there is no clearly defined dry season. The average annual rainfall varies from 35 inches to 200 inches, depending on the region. Mauritius is in the tropical cyclone region of the Indian Ocean. Cyclones usually occur between November and May, with the greatest frequency during January and February; however, the March cyclones are more dreaded as they can inflict considerable damage on the maturing sugarcane crop.

Of the several small islands in the Indian Ocean that also form part of the State of Mauritius, Rodrigues, 350 miles to the east, is the principal one; it is a mountainous island of volcanic formation with an area of 40 square miles and is populated by farmers and fishermen. Agalega, 580 miles to the north, consists of two small islands and is the main source of copra for the edible oil industry of Mauritius. The archipelago of Cargados Carajos, 250 miles to the northeast, is a fishing station. (See map.)

At the end of 1969, the population of Mauritius was estimated at about 807,000 of whom about 42 per cent were under 15 years of age. With an average density per square mile of some 1,120 persons, Mauritius is one of the most heavily populated agricultural areas in the world. The urban population totals some 357,000, of whom about 39 per cent reside in Port Louis, the capital. During 1956–66, the average annual increase in population was 2.9 per cent, but during 1967–69 the rate of increase averaged only 1.6 per cent a year. The relatively rapid increase in population during 1956–66 resulted from high birth rates and from a sharp decline in mortality since World War II following the eradication of malaria, for long a leading cause of death on the island. The decline in the rate of growth of the population since 1966 has been brought about mainly by an increase in emigration and a decrease in the birth rate. The number of emigrants increased from less than 1,000 in 1963 to 4,600 in 1967 and some 5,900 in 1968. On the other hand, the birth rate declined from about 4 per cent in 1963 to approximately 3 per cent in 1967–69. It is estimated that the population will approach 1 million by 1980, unless emigration increases further.

The Government has attempted to moderate the rate of population growth by encouraging organized efforts to promote birth control and family planning. Two voluntary organizations, the Mauritius Family Planning Association and Action Familiale, initiated a family planning program in 1964, to which the Government has given both technical and financial support. In order to intensify and expand the family planning campaign, the Government has adopted a five-year program, the objectives of which are to increase the number of women of childbearing age who follow one of the approved methods of family planning from the present 15 per cent to at least 50 per cent and to reduce the birth rate to not more than 2 per cent a year.

The people are of diverse racial origin and comprise the Indo-Mauritians (about 69 per cent of the population), the people of European descent and of mixed and African descent (28 per cent), and the Sino-Mauritians (3 per cent). The official language is English, but French is used extensively. Creole (a French patois) and Chinese, as well as a number of Indian languages, are also spoken.

Primary education is virtually universal in Mauritius and the literacy rate is very high. From 1962 to 1969, the number of pupils enrolled in secondary schools increased by 58 per cent. A large number of primary and secondary schools are run by private institutions, some of which are subsidized by the Government. Higher education is available at the College of Agriculture, the Teachers' Training College, and the newly established University of Mauritius.

Mauritius, a former British dependency, became an independent country on March 12, 1968. It was admitted to the United Nations on April 24, 1968. On September 23, 1968 it joined the International Monetary Fund (quota on May 31, 1971, $22 million) and the International Bank for Reconstruction and Development (capital subscription on May 31, 1971, $18.8 million), the International Development Association, and the International Finance Corporation. It is a member of the Commonwealth, a contracting party to the General Agreement on Tariffs and Trade, and a member of the Common Organization of African, Malagasy and Mauritian States, the Food and Agriculture Organization of the United Nations, the United Nations Economic Commission for Africa, and the United Nations Educational, Scientific and Cultural Organization.

The unit of currency is the Mauritian rupee, which is divided into 100 cents. The official rate of exchange is Mau Rs 1 = £ stg. 0.075, which corresponds to Mau Rs 5.55555 = US$1. Prior to August 14, 1967, when the Bank of Mauritius (the central bank) began operations, the currency was issued by a Currency Fund. In November 1967 the rupee was devalued by 14.3 per cent.

The economy is predominantly agricultural. Sugarcane is the most important crop, and the sugar industry accounts for about 30 per cent of gross national product and about 95 per cent of exports. The general level of economic activity therefore follows closely fluctuations in earnings from sugar. Manufacturing excluding the sugar industry consists of a number of small private industries which produce almost exclusively for the domestic market.

STRUCTURE OF THE ECONOMY

GROSS NATIONAL PRODUCT AND EXPENDITURE

The gross national product (GNP) of Mauritius is subject to considerable variations from year to year because of the economy's heavy dependence on sugar. During 1961–68, GNP at current prices rose at an average annual rate of about 3 per cent, and in 1968 per capita GNP at current prices was about $190. As the annual rate of population growth averaged 2.4 per cent a year and prices rose on average by about 2 per cent, real income per capita declined. In 1963, with a bumper sugar crop and high export prices, GNP rose by 30 per cent, to a record high figure of Rs 900 million, but it declined by 16 per cent in 1964 (Table 1). It was estimated at Rs 879 million in 1969, when the sugar crop was about 12 per cent larger than in 1968 and export prices were more favorable.

The proportion of GNP contributed by the primary sector, which is mainly agricultural, declined from 27 per cent in 1961 to 23 per cent in 1968. The contribution of the manufacturing sector, which includes sugarcane processing, fell by more than 1 percentage point, to 15 per cent, in 1968. Construction, which in 1961 accounted for nearly 8 per cent of GNP—reflecting the repair and reconstruction following the 1960 cyclone—accounted for about 6 per cent in 1968. On the other hand, the share of government and other services (including ownership of dwellings) increased from 23 per cent to 27 per cent. Commerce

TABLE 1. MAURITIUS: GROSS NATIONAL PRODUCT AT CURRENT PRICES, 1961–68

(In millions of Mauritian rupees)

	1961	1962	1963	1964	1965	1966	1967	1968	Per Cent of GNP 1961	Per Cent of GNP 1968
Agriculture, forestry, hunting, and fishing	182	174	296	180	198	190	203	193	27.0	23.4
Mining	1	1	1	1	1	1	1	1	0.1	0.1
Manufacturing	111	115	176	119	129	121	130	124	16.5	15.1
Construction	52	52	49	53	55	52	59	49	7.7	6.0
Energy, water, and sanitary services	14	17	21	22	25	26	30	30	2.1	3.6
Transport, storage, and communications	78	84	92	95	102	99	100	102	11.6	12.4
Commerce and banking	84	84	95	102	103	100	106	108	12.5	13.1
Ownership of dwellings	52	55	57	59	61	63	65	66	7.7	8.0
Government services	30	32	34	38	40	41	43	44	4.4	5.3
Other services	75	80	85	91	94	99	104	110	11.1	13.4
Gross domestic product at factor cost	679	694	906	760	808	792	841	827	100.7	100.4
Sugar industry	222	214	395	213	246	220	245	228	32.9	27.7
Net factor income from abroad	–5	–4	–6	–2	–6	–1	–5	–3	–0.7	–0.4
Gross national product	674	690	900	758	802	791	836	824	100.0	100.0

Source: Central Statistical Office, *Bi-Annual Digest of Statistics.*

and banking, which are well developed, account for about 13 per cent
of GNP, and transport and communications account for a further 12
per cent. The contribution of the sugar industry considered as a whole,
including the value added by sugar mills and transport services provided by the industry, declined from 33 per cent in 1961 to 28 per cent
in 1968.

During 1961–68, total consumption increased from 82 per cent to 90
per cent of gross domestic product (GDP), with a peak of 91 per cent
in 1964 following the bumper sugar crop of 1963 (Table 2). Public
consumption increased more rapidly than private consumption, and in
1968 accounted for 16 per cent of GDP, compared with 13 per cent in
1961. During the same period, gross investment as a percentage of GDP
fell from 20 per cent to 15 per cent, with private investment declining
from 14 per cent of GDP to 10 per cent.

TABLE 2.   MAURITIUS: SUPPLY AND USE OF RESOURCES, 1961–68

(*In millions of Mauritian rupees*)

	1961	1962	1963	1964	1965	1966	1967	1968
Consumption	629	682	701	803	772	806	851	865
Private	*528*	*574*	*586*	*677*	*634*	*654*	*688*	*711*
Public	*101*	*108*	*115*	*126*	*138*	*152*	*163*	*154*
Gross investment	155	146	160	177	155	133	145	141
Private	*107*	*89*	*87*	*126*	*107*	*86*	*87*	*94*
Public	*48*	*57*	*73*	*51*	*48*	*47*	*58*	*47*
Net exports of goods and services	−15	−35	157	−102	−5	−27	−27	−40
GDP at current market prices	769	793	1,018	878	922	912	969	966
Indirect taxes minus subsidies	−90	−99	−112	−118	−114	−120	−128	−139
Net factor income from abroad	−5	−4	−6	−2	−6	−1	−5	−3
GNP	674	690	900	758	802	791	836	824
Consumption as per cent of GDP	82	86	69	91	84	88	88	90
Private	*69*	*72*	*58*	*77*	*69*	*72*	*71*	*74*
Public	*13*	*14*	*11*	*14*	*15*	*16*	*17*	*16*
Gross investment as per cent of GDP	20	18	16	20	17	14	15	15
Private	*14*	*11*	*9*	*14*	*12*	*9*	*9*	*10*
Public	*6*	*7*	*7*	*6*	*5*	*5*	*6*	*5*

Source: Central Statistical Office, *Bi-Annual Digest of Statistics.*

AGRICULTURE

The total land area of Mauritius is 460,800 acres. About 56 per cent is farmland, most of which is under intensive cultivation; the rest is mostly forest, scrub, and grassland. Land rights are still governed by the Code Napoléon, which provides for the equal division of property among heirs and has been responsible for fragmentation of land owner-ship. However, further fragmentation has been checked through the grouping of land holdings into company estates. Apart from Crown land, about 70 per cent of all land is now owned by companies and private estates; the remainder is owned directly by farmers, mainly Indo-Mauritians. In addition to freehold tenure, land is also held on lease and under sharecropping agreements.

Sugarcane covers about 200,000 arpents (1 arpent = 1.043 acres), i.e., 95 per cent of all the land that is under intensive cultivation. In recent years the Government has sponsored various schemes for expanding the production of tea; but so far production has been small and sugar remains the mainstay of the economy. The Government is also encouraging the cultivation of food crops in an effort to reduce the country's heavy dependence on imports.

Sugar

The soil and climate of Mauritius are particularly suited to the culti-vation of sugarcane. The sugar industry, in addition to providing about 30 per cent of GNP, contributes about 95 per cent of total export receipts. The majority of the population derives its monetary income from the sugar industry, and the general level of economic activity therefore depends greatly upon earnings from sugar.

Production.—Most of the sugarcane is produced on plantations. In 1969, 22 large sugar estates with licensed factories (mills) produced 61 per cent of the total crop on 52 per cent of the area harvested. The remaining 39 per cent of the crop was produced by some 29,000 plant-ers (largely owner-planters), of whom about 26,000 had plots of less than 5 arpents and harvested less than 20 per cent of the total area under cultivation.

The volume of sugar produced, after averaging 553,000 metric tons in the two years 1958–59 and declining sharply in 1960 because of a

TABLE 3. MAURITIUS: SUGAR PRODUCTION AND YIELDS, 1961–69

Crop Year	Total Area Under Cultivation	Total Area Harvested	Cane Produced	Sugar Produced	Average Yield of Sugar per Arpent	Share of Cane Recovered as Sugar
	(thousand arpents)		(thousand metric tons)		(metric tons)	(per cent)
1961	201	187	4,943	553	2.95	11.2
1962	205	194	4,624	532	2.74	11.5
1963	204	194	5,747	686	3.53	11.9
1964	207	195	4,380	519	2.66	11.8
1965	205	195	5,984	664	3.41	11.1
1966	207	196	4,843	562	2.87	11.6
1967	205	192	5,814	638	3.32	11.0
1968	203	189	5,152	596	3.15	11.6
1969	205	188	5,824	669	3.55	11.5

Source: Mauritius Chamber of Agriculture, *The President's Report, 1968–69.*

severe cyclone, rose to a record 686,000 tons in 1963 (Table 3). Production averaged 608,000 tons during 1964–69, but reached 669,000 tons in 1969. In 1970 it declined, however, to 576,000 tons. Throughout the 1960s the area under cane remained at about 200,000 arpents and the average yield of cane per arpent increased only slightly. There is, however, a wide range between the higher yields on the estates and those on small plantings. Efforts are being continued to increase productivity, particularly on the smaller plantings. The sugar industry benefits from the Mauritius Sugar Industry Research Institute's continuing work on methods of eliminating cane diseases and development of suitable fertilizers and better adapted cane varieties.

Marketing.—Sugar is harvested from July to the end of November. The cane produced by planters is delivered to the area mill by the planters themselves, or through cooperative societies and intermediaries who collect the cane from the planters. The sugarcane is processed into raw sugar in the sugar mills. Agreements concluded with the millers specify the milling charge (presently 32 per cent of the sugar and sugar by-products recovered) and the name of the sugar broker who is to represent the producer in dealing with the Mauritius Sugar Syndicate, a nonprofit, private organization and the sole agency for the marketing of sugar. The sugar content of the cane is assessed upon delivery by representatives of an Arbitration and Control Board, which is also responsible for the control of the mills, the assignment of the mill areas, the inspection of weights, and the settlement of disputes. The intermediaries are also required to make contracts with the planters from whom they purchase the cane specifying the form and conditions of payment, which are generally based on the average net price obtained by the Sugar Syndicate. About 70–75 per cent of the sugar is sold in preferential markets, the most important of these being the United Kingdom under the Commonwealth Sugar Agreement.

The most important by-products obtained from sugar are molasses and bagasse, a fibrous material that remains after the cane is crushed. Part of the molasses is exported and the remainder is distilled to produce alcohol. Exports of molasses account for some 3 per cent of total exports. Bagasse is used as fuel in the sugar mills and, beginning in July 1971, it will also be used in the manufacture of particle board by a recently formed company.

The Commonwealth Sugar Agreement was signed in December 1951 between the United Kingdom and representatives of sugar producers in the Commonwealth. The agreement guarantees imports of specific quantities of sugar by the United Kingdom at negotiated prices. The basic quota of Mauritius under the agreement is 470,000 long tons, but the negotiated price quota in recent years has amounted to 380,000 long tons, more than 60 per cent of Mauritius's total exports of sugar. The 1951 agreement provided for annual extensions and for annual adjustments in the basic negotiated price quotas in accordance with domestic consumption in the United Kingdom. However, at the conference on the agreement which ended in December 1968, it was agreed that the agreement would henceforth be of indefinite duration but subject to review every three years. The first such review was scheduled for 1971. It was also agreed that changes in the provisions of the agreement, other than those that can be mutually agreed on at any time, would be subject to three-year notice (to be given in the year of review), except for changes relating to the negotiated price quota, where six years' notice is required. In the event that the United Kingdom successfully completes negotiations for entry into the European Economic Community, it will not be committed to continuing contractual obligations under the Commonwealth Sugar Agreement after 1974. However, assurances have been given that, in this event, the United Kingdom would seek means of fulfilling its obligations to the sugar exporting countries of the Commonwealth.

Price Structure.—Mauritius's negotiated price quota under the Commonwealth Sugar Agreement remains fixed at 380,000 long tons. The negotiated prices for the three years 1969–71 were fixed at the same level as for the three preceding years—a flat rate of £43.50 a long ton f.o.b. and stowed bulk 96° pol. for all exporting countries, with a special price supplement for developing countries. This supplement consists of (*a*) a fixed payment of £1.50 a long ton, representing the former Colonial Certificated Preference System, and (*b*) a variable price supplement, established as an inverse proportion of the world free market price, which amounts to £2.50 a long ton when the world price is below £31.00 and to zero when the world price is above £39.00 a long ton.

In addition to the negotiated price quota under the Commonwealth Sugar Agreement, Mauritius sells some of its sugar on the U. K. market at the world price plus the Commonwealth preferential tariff, which is equal to £3.75 a metric ton. Additional quantities of sugar are exported to Canada at the world price plus Canada's preference for Commonwealth sugar, which amounts to about £5.25 a metric ton. Furthermore, Mauritius has a quota of about 17,000 short tons for export to the United States. The price received on the U. S. market is some 20 per cent higher than the price received under the Commonwealth agreement.

Mauritius is also a party to the 1968 International Sugar Agreement, which became effective on January 1, 1969 and which will remain in force for five years and will be subject to review before the end of the third year. One of the main objectives of this agreement is to stabilize the price of sugar in the international free market within a range of 3.25 to 5.25 U. S. cents a pound (f.o.b. stowed Caribbean port) by regulating supply, mainly through variations in export quotas and stockpiling operations. The agreement also makes provision for the redistribution of shortfalls and for contingency allocations (Hardship Fund). These allocations are mainly for the benefit of small developing member countries whose total export earnings are heavily dependent upon the export of sugar. During the first three years of the International Sugar Agreement, Mauritius's basic annual export tonnage will amount to 175,000 metric tons. However, for 1969 and 1970 all basic export tonnages were reduced by 10 per cent in order to achieve the price objectives of

the agreement. In 1969 Mauritius benefited from a contingency allocation under the Hardship Fund of 35,000 metric tons, bringing its effective quota for that year to 192,500 metric tons.

The price paid by the Mauritius Sugar Syndicate to all producers is a
weighted average of the prices obtained in the different markets, net of
all marketing expenses, the 6 per cent export tax, and contributions to
special funds, such as the Cyclone and Drought Insurance Fund. The
price paid to producers reached a peak in 1963, when world market
prices were exceptionally high, and declined in subsequent years
(Table 4). In 1970, the price was about 21 per cent lower than in
1963.

The decline in the price received, combined with rising production
costs, has reduced the profitability of the sugar industry in recent years.
Labor costs, which account for 40–50 per cent of total costs of production for the sugar estates, have risen by more than 30 per cent since
1963. Increases in import prices and import duties have also contributed to the rise in costs for the industry. The low profitability has been
partly responsible for the decrease in capital expenditure by the sugar
estates. This expenditure, mainly on replacement of equipment, declined
from Rs 33.4 million in 1964 to Rs 14.3 million in 1968.

Tea

Tea is grown on the higher land of the island. The area under tea
has risen from 4,200 arpents in 1960 to 8,100 arpents in 1968 and

TABLE 4. MAURITIUS: SUGAR SALES AND PRODUCER PRICES, 1961–70

Crop Year	Exports	Domestic Consumption	Total Sales	Producer Price	Producer Price Index
	←————(thousand metric tons)————→			(rupees per ton)	(1958 = 100)
1961	525	28	553	438.2	95
1962	507	26	533	445.2	96
1963	659	27	686	590.9	128
1964	492	27	519	433.1	94
1965	633	31	664	409.3	88
1966	532	30	562	421.5	91
1967	607	31	638	424.4	92
1968	566	30	596	428.4	93
1969	637	31	668	445.3	96
1970	582	32	614	468.0 [1]	101 [1]

Source: Mauritius Chamber of Agriculture, The President's Report, 1968–69.
[1] Provisional.

1969, of which about 5,000 arpents represents land developed since 1956 under the tea development schemes sponsored by the Government. Under these schemes, Crown lands are developed by the Government and then leased to smallholders. The private sector has also been active in recent years in the development of tea, and some sugar estates have turned over certain marginal cane lands to tea cultivation. Since it takes about ten years for a tea bush to become full bearing, however, production has not increased in proportion to the expansion of the area planted.

Mauritian tea is considered of good quality, especially for blending. In 1969, production of manufactured tea amounted to 3,200 metric tons (Table 5). In the same year the value of tea exports was Rs 14.6 million, less than 4 per cent of total exports. Until 1966 almost all the tea was exported to the United Kingdom at world market prices. Since then, world prices have declined and markets have been found in South Africa at preferential prices. In 1969, more than 50 per cent of the tea exported went to South Africa.

The current development scheme aims at planting 5,370 arpents over the three years 1971–73, and on April 1, 1971, the International Development Association approved a loan of $5.2 million for this purpose. The Government plans to add another 14,380 arpents over the following six years.

The fall in the price of tea on the world market in recent years, which has been mostly the result of overproduction, has induced the major tea producers of the world to seek an international agreement to regulate production and marketing. Recently, conferences have been

TABLE 5.   MAURITIUS: TEA PRODUCTION, 1955, 1960, AND 1965–69

	Area Under Cultivation	Manufactured Tea
	(arpents)	(metric tons)
1955	2,800	600
1960	4,200	800
1965	6,300	1,700
1966	6,800	2,000
1967	7,500	2,200
1968	8,100	2,300
1969	8,100	3,200

Source: Central Statistical Office, *Bi-Annual Digest of Statistics.*

held under the aegis of the Food and Agriculture Organization (FAO) to develop a scheme aimed at stabilizing tea prices at equitable and remunerative levels. Pending the conclusion of a long-term arrangement, exporters agreed to a proposal for a 7 per cent reduction in supplies of tea on the world market in 1970 through the establishment of an arrangement for temporary quotas. Mauritius's quota was fixed at about 4,300 metric tons.

Food Crops

Mauritius depends entirely on imports for rice and wheat flour, its staple foods, and imports of these two commodities accounted for 20.7 per cent of total imports in 1969. Production of food crops (mainly potatoes, vegetables, bananas, and groundnuts) varies considerably from season to season (Table 6).

The possibilities of developing the water resources of the country are being explored, with a view to facilitating irrigation and agricultural diversification. With the financial assistance of the UN Development Program, an FAO team has conducted feasibility studies on two main irrigation schemes, the Northern Plain Irrigation Scheme and the Western Coastal Region Irrigation Scheme, each of which covers about 18,000 acres. The development of the latter, which has proved more economically attractive, would increase considerably the areas suitable for the production of food and other crops, including rice, and would

TABLE 6.   MAURITIUS: PRODUCTION OF FOOD CROPS, 1960–69

(*In thousands of metric tons*)

	1960	1961	1962	1963	1964	1965	1966	1967	1968	1969
Potatoes	4.3	2.9	4.4	5.7	6.4	4.4	8.8	9.4	9.8	6.0
Tomatoes	6.1	3.2	6.8	5.7	5.4	5.4	5.7	10.5	8.8	8.6
Other vegetables [1]	36.3	14.9	22.8	23.4	14.7	20.7	21.4	19.9	18.2	18.5
Bananas	...	...	...	5.4	3.0	10.3	9.0	9.9	10.8	11.5
Groundnuts	0.4	0.3	0.3	0.4	0.5	0.6	0.8	0.9	0.6	0.8
Maize	0.3	0.2	0.2	0.1	—	0.3	0.3	0.4	0.4	0.5
Cassava	0.4	0.3	0.5	0.6	0.2	0.3	0.3	0.4	0.2	0.2
Ginger	—	0.4	0.8	0.7	0.5	0.4	0.8	1.0	0.9	1.2
Total	47.8	22.2	35.8	42.0	30.7	42.4	47.1	52.4	49.7	47.3

Sources: Department of Agriculture, *Annual Report*, and Central Statistical Office, *Bi-Annual Digest of Statistics*.

[1] Includes eggplant, beans and peas, eddoes, cucumbers, pumpkins, squash, beets, cabbage, carrots, cauliflower, garlic, onions, leeks, and lettuce.

also release land now occupied by sugar for other purposes. In addition, the Mauritius Sugar Industry Research Institute is constructing a "land capability map," which will indicate competing suitable crops for every given land area.

Output of potatoes increased from 5,700 tons in 1963 to 9,800 tons in 1968, when it met all domestic requirements. The increase was brought about mainly through the introduction of better seed, improved control of pests and diseases, and greater use of fertilizer. In 1969, production declined by about 39 per cent, mainly because of plant disease and adverse weather. The sugar estates are participating in the scheme to expand potato production, since experiments have shown that intercropping of potatoes and sugarcane does not significantly reduce the yield of sugar.

The Agricultural Marketing Board, established in 1964 to organize the marketing of food crops, has been developing both the production and marketing of potatoes. The sugar estates have assisted the Board by establishing their own marketing organization, which regulates sales through various retailing points in urban markets and rural areas. The Board is expanding its cold-storage facilities in order to regulate supplies to the market and stabilize prices.

Other vegetables are also grown extensively in Mauritius, where the soil and climate are suitable for a wide variety. However, owing to a succession of bad seasons, production, including tomatoes, has not expanded in recent years and in 1969 totaled 27,000 tons (Table 6).

Bananas are produced for domestic consumption. The principal variety grown is the dwarf banana. Following a substantial increase in acreage planted, production rose from 5,400 tons in 1963 to 10,300 tons in 1965. Output declined in 1966 because of damage caused by the cyclone, but by 1968 it had completely recovered, and in the following year totaled 11,500 tons (Table 6).

Groundnut production is still small, although it more than doubled between 1963 and 1967, when it reached 900 tons; output declined to 600 tons in 1968 but partly recovered in 1969 to 800 tons. Production has so far been for local consumption. Crude vegetable oils are imported and refined for the domestic market by the Mauritius Oil Refineries Ltd., which plans to set up a crushing plant to process locally produced groundnuts. Furthermore, the Sugar Industry Research

Institute has undertaken experiments to determine the most suitable varieties of groundnuts for domestic consumption and export.

Rice, the single most important staple food in the country, is presently entirely imported. During 1963–69, imports of rice averaged 66,000 metric tons a year and accounted for more than 10 per cent of the total value of imports. Efforts to develop rice cultivation are still in the experimental stage.

Other Crops

Tobacco is grown by small farmers on plots of land totaling less than 1,000 arpents. Output, which has averaged about 500 tons of leaf in recent years, reached 700 tons in 1968 but was only about 400 tons in 1969. All of the output is processed and blended with imported tobacco for domestic consumption. Production by the two cigarette factories amounted to 580 tons of cigarettes in 1969.

Fiber extracted from aloe plants (similar to sisal) is used in a government-owned factory to manufacture sacks and rope. About 1.5 million sacks a year are produced. Most of the production is sold to millers for bagging sugar; the remainder is exported.

OTHER PRIMARY PRODUCTION

The livestock industry is not developed in Mauritius. The cattle population, estimated at some 20,000 head, produces a negligible amount of milk. Except on a few estates, cattle are raised in a traditional manner as backyard animals by individual families who collect fodder from the roadside and from wasteland. Mauritius imports most of its requirements of milk and meat, meat being imported largely as live cattle from the Malagasy Republic. The Government is encouraging the production of beef and dairy products and is receiving assistance from the FAO in preparing a five-year program designed to make the country self-sufficient in both beef and milk.

Fishing is still relatively undeveloped. Fishing in the lagoons affords a livelihood for some 2,800 fishermen; however, stocks in the lagoons are being gradually depleted and the annual catch has been declining, amounting to some 1,300 tons in 1969. About 200 persons are engaged in small-scale deep-sea fishing on banks 300 miles northeast of Mauritius; the deep-sea catch amounts to about 1,500 tons a year. As domestic consumption of fish is not very great and is growing slowly, the future expansion of the fish industry depends on the development of markets abroad. The possibilities of fishing beyond the reefs and of expanding deep-sea fishing are being examined by an FAO survey team. A Japanese firm has been active in long-line tuna fishing and has signed an agreement for the expansion of tuna fishing and for establishing a processing plant in Mauritius. A protocol agreement with the U. S. S. R. for the development of fisheries in Mauritius and the expansion of fishing in the Indian Ocean was signed in 1969.

The forest areas, including scrub and grassland, cover about 35 per cent of the island's total area and are for the most part privately owned. Only part of the forest is productive and Mauritius imports more than 60 per cent of its timber requirements.

MANUFACTURING

The manufacturing sector, excluding the sugar industry, consists of a number of small private industries which produce almost exclusively for the domestic market—principally food, beverages, tobacco, footwear, repair and assembly of machinery and transport equipment, a micro-jewel factory, and a sack factory. Protection is afforded to a number of established industries by restricting imports of competing commodities. In September 1969 it was estimated that 7,800 persons were employed in industries with 10 or more employees.

The Government, in its efforts to provide more employment opportunities, is encouraging the expansion of industries producing import substitutes and the establishment of export-oriented industries. To this end a number of investment incentives are offered (see Economic Development and Planning—Investment Incentives, below). Expansion of the port facilities at Port Louis and establishment of an industrial free zone there are also expected to contribute to industrial development in the future. Among the major new industries is a fertilizer plant involving a total investment of about $10 million. The factory is expected to begin production in mid-1972, with a capacity of 100,000 tons of nitrogenous and compound fertilizers a year. On the basis of past consumption in Mauritius, about half of the capacity production will be available for export.

ELECTRIC POWER

Electricity is the most important source of energy in Mauritius. There are six hydroelectric plants and two thermal-generating plants. Production and distribution of electricity are controlled by the Central Electricity Board, which comprises representatives of the various interested parties, including the Government, and operates under the supervision of the Ministry of Commerce and Industry. In addition, each sugar factory operates its own power station. The Board supplements its output by purchasing surplus power from some of the sugar estates, mainly during the cropping season when rainfall is low. During 1960–65, sales of electricity by the Board increased at an average annual rate of 17 per cent; since then, the rate has averaged 5.5 per cent, mainly because by 1965 most of the household consumers were connected to the general grid. Future expansion of demand is expected to come largely from industrial consumers. The present capacity of the entire country—75,000 kilowatts including the new hydroelectric plant at Ferney—is considered sufficient to meet all demands for the next few years.

TRANSPORT

Mauritius has a good and extensive road network, consisting of 380 miles of main roads and 420 miles of rural roads, of which more than 500 miles have been asphalted. Passenger bus service connects all parts of the island. With the closing down of the Mauritius Government Railways in 1959, road traffic has increased substantially; in 1969 there were 24,736 registered motor vehicles. Under the Reconstruction and Development Program, 1960–66, expenditure on road construction and maintenance amounted to Rs 34 million.

The Plaisance International Airport, about five miles from Mahébourg in the southeast of the island, is the only airport in the country. The airport is managed by the Department of Civil Aviation and can accommodate long-range jets. Air traffic has been growing steadily in recent years. Between 1963 and 1969 the number of passengers arriving and departing increased from 26,000 to 68,000. The Government is considering the alternatives of building a new airport in the northern part of the island or expanding the existing one. A feasibility study by

French experts envisages expansion of existing facilities in three stages over ten years.

The harbor at Port Louis, the only port in Mauritius, has a loading capacity of about 7,500 tons a day. Traffic has been increasing steadily over the years, especially since the closing of the Suez Canal in 1967. In 1969 more than 1,300 vessels entered the port, compared with 718 in 1966. Projects under consideration include enlarging the harbor, constructing an additional deep-water quay, introducing bulk-handling facilities, and accelerating the land reclamation that was begun in 1963. Part of the reclaimed land is being used for the industrial free zone (see Manufacturing, above). The provision of bulk-handling facilities is required not only to reduce costs for the sugar industry but also in connection with the establishment of the fertilizer plant.

TOURISM

Mauritius has a good potential for the development of tourism. The country offers many natural attractions and a temperate climate. However, its geographic location has so far been a limiting factor. The number of tourists has grown in recent years, and in 1969 totaled about 20,600, compared with about 7,000 in 1963. The majority of the tourists have so far come from the neighboring islands of Réunion and Madagascar, but the number from South Africa, Australia, France, and the United Kingdom has increased more rapidly than the average in recent years. The peak tourist seasons are July–August for tourists from Réunion and Madagascar and December–March for tourists from northern countries.

The development of tourism is actively encouraged by the Government. In 1966, Mauritius, together with the Malagasy Republic, Réunion, and the Comoro Islands, formed the Alliance Touristique de l'Océan Indien, which aims at promoting tourist trade in the area by providing improved amenities. A Tourist Advisory Board, comprising representatives of both public and private organizations, makes recommendations to the Government on all matters related to tourism. Various measures designed to encourage tourism, such as the relaxation of customs regulations for tourists, have been adopted in Mauritius. Assistance in the form of soft loans and exemption from customs duty on hotel equipment has also been provided to the tourist industry.

There were about 375 hotel rooms in Mauritius in 1969. To meet the growing demand for hotel accommodations, the Government envisages the addition of about 600 hotel rooms by 1973. The New Mauritius Hotels Company, in which the Government holds a minority interest, in association with Lonrho Limited, is considering the creation of a company to build two hotels, each with a capacity of 100 rooms, and to set up other facilities and amenities. In addition, the New Mauritius Hotels Company plans to expand the existing hotel facilities. The building of a modern hotel at Port Louis is also being considered with the participation of the Development Bank of Mauritius.

ECONOMIC DEVELOPMENT AND PLANNING

EARLY DEVELOPMENT PLANNING

In 1957 the Economic Planning Committee prepared a five-year Capital Expenditure Program to commence in July 1957, with priority given to infrastructure. During the first three years total expenditure, almost wholly financed from internal sources, amounted to some Rs 96 million, of which 42 per cent was for infrastructure. Because of the damage caused by the 1960 cyclone, and after consultation with Professor J. E. Meade's Economic Survey Mission, the Government decided in June 1962 to abandon the Capital Expenditure Program and embark on a new five-year program, the Reconstruction and Development Program, 1960–65. This program, which was later extended to 1966, was based largely on the recommendations made by Professor Meade in his report, which emphasized the need for Mauritius to start a process of economic development on a scale that would absorb the growing population without a serious decline in its standard of living, and recommended specific projects and measures.[1] Priority was to be given to secondary industries, the development of a diversified agriculture, and infrastructure. Measures such as tax holidays and tax exemptions,

---

[1] J. E. Meade and others, *The Economic and Social Structure of Mauritius* (London, 1961).

designed to create a favorable climate for private domestic and foreign investment, were also suggested.

By the end of 1966, total expenditure under the Reconstruction and Development Program amounted to Rs 324 million, an average yearly investment of Rs 54 million, or nearly 20 per cent less than originally envisaged. About 14 per cent of the total was absorbed by economic services, 49 per cent by infrastructure, and 37 per cent by social services, mainly housing (Table 7). Delay in the preparation and completion of projects rather than a shortage of funds appears to have been the principal factor that kept total expendtiure below that initially envisaged. Those schemes which were not completed were carried forward to the development program for 1966–70.

DEVELOPMENT PROGRAM, 1966–70

The primary objective of the Public Sector Development Program, 1966–70, was to provide additional employment opportunities for the rapidly growing labor force. Investment in the directly productive sectors was to be accelerated and expenditure on infrastructure and social services reduced, investment in infrastructure being limited to that required to support the productive sectors. Priority was given to industry and agriculture, particularly agriculture other than sugar. Emphasis was placed on projects which combined the creation of permanent jobs with an increase in the supply of locally produced goods, for which there is continuing demand.

The program called for total expenditure of Rs 337.5 million, an average of Rs 84 million annually, compared with an average annual investment of Rs 54 million realized in the period 1960–66 (Table 7). Nearly 44 per cent of the planned expenditure was allocated to productive activities, mainly agriculture and industry, with tea development schemes absorbing about 27 per cent of the expenditure for agriculture. The planned expenditure under the tea schemes was for clearing and planting about 1,000 arpents a year and purchasing seeds, machinery, and equipment. The implementation of these schemes was expected to increase employment by about 2,600 persons during the period of the program. The expansion in manufacturing industry, to be financed through government loans to the Mauritius Development Bank, was

TABLE 7. MAURITIUS: PUBLIC SECTOR EXPENDITURE UNDER DEVELOPMENT PROGRAMS, 1960–66 AND 1966–70

(Amounts in millions of Mauritian rupees)

| | 1960–66: Actual Expenditure | | 1966–70: Planned Expenditure | | | | | |
| | | | Total | | Amount each year | | | |
	Amount	Per cent	Amount	Per cent	1966/67	1967/68	1968/69	1969/70
Economic services	**45.8**	**14.1**	**147.3**	**43.6**	**32.4**	**42.4**	**35.7**	**36.8**
Agriculture and forestry	37.7	11.6	86.2	25.5	20.3	27.0	19.3	19.6
Tea		..	23.3	6.9	5.2	5.5	6.6	6.0
Industry	6.6	2.0	60.2	17.8	11.8	15.2	16.1	17.1
Tourism	1.5	0.5	0.9	0.3	0.3	0.2	0.3	0.1
Infrastructure	**158.1**	**48.8**	**82.8**	**24.5**	**25.7**	**19.8**	**18.9**	**18.4**
Power	43.0	13.3	7.0	2.1	2.0	2.1	1.4	1.5
Roads	33.6	10.4	16.7	5.0	2.4	2.8	4.1	7.4
Water supply	12.2	3.8	15.3	4.5	4.0	3.6	3.8	3.9
Sewerage	24.6	7.5	12.5	3.7	2.0	4.1	4.3	2.1
Other	44.7	13.8	31.3 [1]	9.2	15.3	7.2	5.3	3.5
Social and government services	**120.2**	**37.1**	**107.4**	**31.9**	**33.2**	**30.2**	**27.4**	**16.6**
Education	14.0	4.3	20.8	6.2	5.3	6.6	5.6	3.3
Health	3.1	1.0	38.3	11.3	10.7	11.2	12.8	3.6
Housing	59.2	18.3	17.3	5.1	11.9	4.6	0.4	0.4
Administration (central and local)	21.8	6.7	25.1	7.5	3.9	6.5	6.8	7.9
Other	22.1	6.8	5.9 [2]	1.8	1.4	1.3	1.8	1.4
Totals	**324.1**	**100.0**	**337.5**	**100.0**	**91.3**	**92.4**	**82.0**	**71.8**

Sources: U. K. Foreign and Commonwealth Office, *Mauritius: Report for the Year 1966*; and Mauritius Economic Development Planning Committee, *Public Sector Development Programme, 1966–70*.

[1] Rs 5 million represents the Government's contribution to the capital of the Bank of Mauritius; this sum was to be used for the purchase of a site and construction of buildings.

[2] Rs 5 million was allocated to labor-intensive works.

expected to absorb about 18 per cent of total expenditure, and the creation of additional employment opportunities thus depended primarily on private initiative in making use of the available funds.

Outlays on infrastructure were projected to amount to only 24 per cent of the total, representing a substantial reduction when compared to investment in infrastructure in the 1960–66 program. The proportion of resources devoted to social services was to remain at about 23 per cent. The new program also placed greater emphasis on technical education. A Trade Training Centre for vocational training was to be established, and the new University of Mauritius was to be geared to the development needs of the country. In order to encourage labor-intensive activities, the program made a special provision of Rs 5 million to finance capital projects with a 75 per cent labor content.

The Public Sector Development Program, 1966–70, was adopted with a gap in resources, and actual expenditure remained considerably below what was planned. The sources of financing listed in the program consisted of those domestic resources which were expected to result from surpluses on the current budget and from domestic borrowing, and the foreign resources which had been secured or had been committed at the time the program was adopted.

Most of the investment by the public sector is included in the capital budget of the Central Government. In the three financial years 1966/67–1968/69, capital budget expenditures averaged Rs 53 million a year, compared with an average annual expenditure of Rs 84 million anticipated under the program. The revised estimates for the 1969/70 capital budget provided for expenditure of Rs 60 million, but actual expenditure is likely to remain below the estimates.

The principal factors responsible for the slow rate of implementation of the program appear to have been a shortage of financing and administrative difficulties in employing available resources. With the deterioration in the current budget, no transfers of resources to the capital budget have been made since 1965/66 (see Government Finance—Budgetary Operations, below). In certain cases difficulties have arisen in utilizing official foreign assistance tied to imports from the donor country. Delays in project implementation have occurred because of the acute shortage of qualified personnel in the Economic Planning Unit. With respect to the execution of the program by sector, investment in economic services appears to have lagged behind targets proportionately more than other major categories of investment.

DEVELOPMENT PLAN, 1971–75

In December 1970, the Ministry of Economic Planning and Development published a document, *Development Strategy, 1971–80,* in which the attainment of full employment is set as the primary objective of development planning. It is estimated that if full employment is to be realized by 1980, some 130,000 new jobs will have to be created during the decade. GDP at factor cost, computed at 1970 prices, would increase from an average of Rs 850 million for the period 1967–69 to Rs 1,835 million in 1980, or an average rate of growth of 7.3 per cent a year. Gross investment is expected to rise from about 17 per cent of GDP to about 20 per cent. Total investment during the decade is estimated at Rs 2.6 billion and will be made mainly in directly productive sectors, particularly manufacturing, and in tourism. Manufacturing, including the processing of sugar and tea, is expected to expand at a rate of 11 per cent a year, and tourism at 20 per cent.

A detailed Four-Year Development Plan is to be implemented beginning in July 1971 as the first phase of the ten-year program. The Plan calls for investment of some Rs 800 million, or about 30 per cent of the ten-year goal. Priority will be given to the provision or expansion of infrastructure necessary for increased industrial and agricultural production and exports and for the expansion of tourism. In addition to the development of water resources and of port and airport facilities, the projects envisaged include expanded production of electricity and an increase in the land under cultivation by smallholders, particularly for tea. The Plan is expected to create 60,000 permanent jobs.

As part of the 1971–75 Development Plan, the Government in January 1971 embarked on a program called "Travail pour Tous," designed to cope with the present unemployment. The program, which will gradually replace the present system of part-time relief work, is expected to provide employment for about 20,000 persons a year. It envisages a wide variety of directly productive projects, such as tea cultivation, cleaning stone from canelands, and replanting, and of indirectly productive projects, such as building primary schools and health centers.

The cost of the "Travail pour Tous" program is estimated at about Rs 47 million a year.

INVESTMENT INCENTIVES

There is no investment code as such in Mauritius. However, a number of measures have been taken by the Government in order to create a favorable investment climate and to stimulate the establishment and growth of secondary industries.

The income tax law was amended in 1961, 1964, and 1966 to provide the necessary inducement to investment. Industry is now able to claim against assessable income an initial depreciation allowance of 40 per cent on plant and 20 per cent on industrial buildings. To encourage the development of the tea industry, the initial agricultural allowance for projects other than sugar has been increased to 40 per cent of qualifying expenditure in the first year, together with an annual allowance of 10 per cent in each of the succeeding five years.

A further incentive to industrial development is provided to such new enterprises as the Government may consider to be beneficial to the economic development of the country and to which a so-called development certificate is given. This incentive is in the form of two alternative types of exemption from income tax: a tax holiday of eight years with normal depreciation allowances but no initial allowance; or a tax holiday of five years with the initial allowance on capital expenditure applicable to the tax holiday period, becoming deductible from the first year after the tax holiday. Furthermore, from 1966 onward, dividends received from any of these new enterprises are exempt from the individual income tax during the first five years of the tax holiday.

With similar ends in view, the customs tariff has been revised since 1960. The objectives have been to reduce the rates of import duty on raw materials and semiprocessed products used by local manufacturing industries, to provide rebates of import duty for selected industries, and to protect recently established industries by raising import duties on a number of finished products. The Government maintains a generally liberal policy toward foreign private investment; there are no restrictions on the transfer of profits and dividends, but capital transfers are subject to a stamp tax of 35.70 per cent.

PRICES, WAGES, AND EMPLOYMENT

PRICES

Price movements are recorded in a cost of living index which is computed monthly on the basis of retail prices in both urban and rural areas. The index is based on the prices of 223 goods and services, of which 108 are foodstuffs with a weight of 49.3 per cent. The group of items was determined by a family budget inquiry conducted from June 1961 to June 1962. The survey covered 1,016 households, representing all sections of the population except those in which the principal wage earner received more than Rs 1,000 a month; about 94 per cent of all households in Mauritius have average monthly incomes below this amount.

During 1962–67, the index of consumer prices showed an average increase of 1.3 per cent per annum. In 1968 it rose by 7 per cent, in 1969 by 2.3 per cent, and at the end of 1970 it was 1.5 per cent higher than at the end of 1969 (Table 8). The principal factors behind the rapid increase in prices in 1968 were the 14.3 per cent devaluation of the rupee in November 1967, the imposition of a 5 per cent surcharge on import duties applied from November 1967, and the gradual increase in the retail price of imported rice from Re 0.30 per one-half kilogram in August 1967 to Re 0.46 in June 1968. Except for the prices of rice and wheat flour, which are fixed by the Government, there are virtually no price controls. Controls on the prices of some

TABLE 8.   MAURITIUS: COST OF LIVING INDEX, 1963–70 [1]

(Averages of monthly data; January–June 1962 = 100)

	Urban Areas	Rural Areas	General Index
1963	98.5	98.5	98.5
1964	100.5	100.2	100.3
1965	102.3	102.0	102.1
1966	105.0	104.5	104.7
1967	106.6	106.6	106.6
1968	113.0	114.9	114.1
1969	115.6	117.6	116.7
1970	117.6	119.2	118.5

Source: Central Statistical Office, *Bi-Annual Digest of Statistics.*

[1] Based on the prices of 223 items (of which 108 are foodstuffs with a weight of 49.3 per cent) consumed by a family in which the principal wage earner earns Rs 1,000 a month or less.

foodstuffs were introduced in November 1967 following devaluation, but most of these have since been lifted.

WAGES

As a rule, wages and other conditions of employment for each category of worker in the private sector are fixed by Wage Regulation Orders issued by the Minister of Labor. In certain industries, however, wages are determined by bilateral agreements between the trade unions and the employers. There is no legal minimum wage for the country as a whole.

Under the provisions of the Regulation of Wages and Conditions of Employment Ordinance, No. 71 of 1961, and subsequent amendments, the Minister of Labor may from time to time appoint Minimum Wage Boards to inquire into and make recommendations concerning the wages and terms of employment of workers; these Boards may also inquire into the need to fix a basic minimum wage in respect of workers generally, or of any category of worker, in any area of the country. Furthermore, the Minister, if he is satisfied that no adequate machinery exists for the effective regulation of the remuneration or other conditions of employment of the workers in any trade, industry, or occupation, may establish Wage Councils to deal with these matters. The Wage Councils may submit to the Minister proposals concerning wages and salaries and other conditions of employment. The recommendations of the Minimum Wage Boards and the proposals of the Wage Councils are made to the Minister in the form of wage regulation proposals. After consideration by the Minister, and with the approval of the Council of Ministers, these proposals may be implemented, with any amendments and modifications that the Council of Ministers may authorize, by Wage Regulation Orders issued by the Minister. The members of the Minimum Wage Boards and of the Wage Councils are appointed by the Minister of Labor and comprise independent persons and representatives of employers and of workers in equal numbers. Wage Councils have been established for most industries, trades, and occupations. For the sugar industry there are two, the Wage Council for Agricultural Workers and the Wage Council for Non-Agricultural Workers.

Other benefits, such as annual leave, sick leave, maternity allowances, housing allowances, and grants to families of deceased workers, are also determined by the Minister of Labor through Wage Regulation Orders. The Workmen's Compensation Ordinance provides for compensation to injured workers amounting to 80 per cent of wages for temporary incapacity and to eight years' wages for permanent incapacity. The maximum sum payable to the dependents of a deceased workman is equivalent to six years' wages.

Wage rates for both monthly and daily laborers were raised considerably in 1963. In that year Wage Regulation Orders for the sugar industry introduced statutory minimum remunerations which involved a general increase in wage rates of approximately 25 per cent, and similar increases were extended to wage earners in other industries. In October 1968 a Wage Regulation Order raised wage rates in the sugar industry by a further 5 per cent and provided for a sizable increase in fringe benefits. Although this wage increase was later extended to day workers in the public sector, it has not been generally applied in all other industries. The practice of payment on the basis of piece work is still widely followed in industry. Government salaries are determined by direct negotiation between employees' associations and the Government. Wage increases in the private sector do not entail automatic increases in salaries for civil servants.

EMPLOYMENT

The economically active population (i.e., persons between the ages of 15 and 65) who are working or seeking work is estimated at 240,000, or 30 per cent of the total population. Surveys of employment and earnings conducted each year in March and September by the Central Statistical Office cover employment on sugar plantations of 25 arpents or more, tea plantations of 5 arpents or more, industries employing 10 persons or more, and government. Between March 1967 and March 1968 the number of employed persons rose by 2 per cent, to some 124,000 (Table 9). Most of the increase was in the sugar industry, which in March 1968 provided employment for about 51,000 persons; employment also rose in manufacturing, but declined in construction. Between March 1968 and March 1969 employment declined by 4.5 per cent, reflecting mainly a further reduction in the number of relief workers employed by the Government and a 5 per cent decrease in employ-

TABLE 9.   MAURITIUS: EMPLOYMENT BY SECTOR, 1967–69 [1]

(*In thousands of persons*)

	1967		1968		1969	
	Mar.	Sept.	Mar.	Sept.	Mar.	Sept.
Agriculture and fishing	53.4	57.0	56.3	61.7	53.7	58.7
Sugar industry	*48.5*	*53.3*	*51.2*	*57.4*	*48.4*	*54.5*
Mining and quarrying	0.2	0.2	0.2	0.2	0.2	0.1
Manufacturing	7.2	7.5	7.7	7.7	7.8	7.8
Construction	2.8	2.7	2.3	1.6	1.7	2.0
Electricity	1.3	1.3	1.3	1.3	1.2	1.3
Commerce	3.1	3.3	3.1	3.7	3.7	3.8
Transport, storage, and communications	4.1	4.7	4.4	5.1	4.4	5.6
Government services	46.7	59.0	46.0	41.4	42.1	41.8
Relief works	*19.3*	*30.9*	*17.8*	*13.4*	*13.5*	*12.4*
Other services	3.2	3.1	3.1	3.9	4.0	4.1
Total	122.0	138.8	124.4	126.6	118.8	125.2

Source: Central Statistical Office, *Bi-Annual Digest of Statistics.*
[1] Based on biannual surveys; see text.

ment in the sugar industry, although employment in the construction sector also continued to decline.

Reliable statistics of unemployment are not available. The number of persons registered for employment, about 15,000 in December 1969, provides only a partial indication. Total unemployment is estimated to be in the range of 30,000 to 35,000. According to projections made by the Central Statistical Office, between 8,000 and 9,000 workers will enter the labor market each year in the period to 1977, considerably more than the number of new jobs that have become available annually in recent years.

To alleviate unemployment, the Government embarked on a relief works program. The number of relief workers rose from less than 1,000 in September 1964 to a peak of almost 31,000 in September 1967 and then was reduced to 13,400 in September 1968 and to 12,400 in September 1969. After May 1968 relief work was reduced to three or four days a week and the wage to Rs 4 a day.

In view of the pressing unemployment problem, labor legislation designed to mitigate unemployment has been passed in recent years. The 1966 Ordinance on Security of Employment, which applies only to the sugar industry, provided that every person who has worked on 80 per cent or more of the working days during the crop season is entitled to be offered employment during the intercrop season; if he has worked between 55 and 80 per cent of the working days, he is entitled to be offered employment on four days a week during the intercrop season. This ordinance, however, was amended in May 1968 to require the sugar industry to provide employment throughout the year to a "regular labor force," defined as the number of workers employed during the 1967 harvest who qualified for employment in the subsequent intercrop season. Employers who hire more workers during the harvest of a given year will have to offer employment during the intercrop season to a "supplementary labor force" equal to 15 per cent of the difference between the total number of workers employed during the harvest of a given year and either (1) the "regular labor force" or (2) the average number of workers who qualified for employment during the 1965–67 intercrop seasons, whichever is larger. This amendment has resulted in increased employment in the industry; sugar estates employed 8,000 more workers during the 1968 harvest.

The Termination of Contracts of Service Ordinance, enacted in 1963, and subsequent amendments, provides for the payment of a severance allowance by all employers in all industries and by statutory and corporate bodies. For dismissals resulting from the employer's reduction of the work force that are considered justified by a board appointed by the Minister of Labor, the severance allowance is payable at the rate of two weeks' wages for each year of service. Where dismissals are considered unjustified by the board, the severance allowance is payable at the rate of twelve weeks' wages for each year of service.

GOVERNMENT FINANCE

BUDGETARY SYSTEM

The public sector in Mauritius consists of the Central Government, the local governments, and a number of statutory bodies which are under the jurisdiction of the Central Government and certain of which, although financially autonomous, depend on the Central Government for direct subsidies and for guarantees of their borrowing.

The local governments include the municipality of Port Louis, 4 town councils (Beau Bassin-Rose Hill, Quartre Bornes, Curepipe, and

Vacoas-Phoenix), 3 district councils, and 98 village councils. The budgets of the local governments are financed from local taxes (e.g., taxes on housing, water distribution, irrigation, advertisements and placards, and entertainment) and from subsidies from the Central Government's budget.

The budgetary operations of the Central Government are recorded in a current budget and a capital budget. The financial year runs from July 1 to June 30, and unexpended appropriations for the current budget may not be carried forward to the following financial year. The current budget derives its resources primarily from customs duties and income taxes. The capital budget has been financed from domestic borrowing, from foreign grants and loans, and, until the financial year 1965/66, from surpluses on the current budget.

The Accountant General is responsible for recording in appropriate accounts all financial transactions, budgetary and nonbudgetary, of the Treasury. The current budgetary receipts and expenditures of the Government are recorded in the Consolidated Fund, and transactions related to the capital budget are recorded in the Capital Fund. The balances held in these two funds, which until recently have been invested in foreign securities, have derived from past accumulated budget surpluses and have varied in recent years with the surpluses and deficits in the two budgets. The Consolidated Sinking Fund is credited with contributions to, and debited for payments for, public debt amortization, and therefore also reflects certain budgetary operations. The balances in this fund are invested in foreign securities in respect of public debts repayable in foreign exchange and, generally, in securities of the Mauritian Government for domestic public debts. The Accountant General also maintains certain Special Funds to record nonbudgetary financial transactions of the Government, such as deposits received and advances extended by the Treasury to a number of private and public institutions, including principally the Post Office Savings Bank. Balances held in these funds have also until recently been invested in foreign securities, mainly in London.

STRUCTURE OF CURRENT REVENUE

Historical factors have played an important role in shaping the tax structure of Mauritius. Income taxation was developed under the British administration and now accounts for more than 20 per cent of all tax revenue. On the other hand, certain taxes, such as business licenses and registration fees, were introduced by the French administration in the early nineteenth century and are still in effect. Indirect taxes, mainly customs duties and excise taxes, account for nearly 60 per cent of total revenue, and reflect the importance of international trade in the Mauritian economy.

Direct Taxes

Direct taxes consist mainly of income taxes levied on individuals and companies. In addition, there is a tax on wealth in the form of a succession duty, but it has little significance for revenue. Until July 1970, when changes in the structure of personal and company income taxes became effective, there was a development contribution tax, levied at a rate of 25 per cent on retained profits of companies in addition to the company income tax, and there was a 5 per cent surtax on the company income tax.

The tax rates on individual incomes are 20 per cent on annual taxable income of up to Rs 15,000 and 35 per cent on income in excess of Rs 15,000. In addition, there is a surtax applied by income bracket at rates of 15 per cent on incomes between Rs 35,000 and Rs 45,000, 30 per cent on incomes between Rs 45,000 and Rs 55,000, and 45 per cent on incomes of Rs 55,000 and above. The provision for earned income relief, abolished in July 1970 when the tax structure was revised, was compensated by increases in the personal allowance (from Rs 2,500 to Rs 3,500), the allowance for a wife (from Rs 1,500 to Rs 2,500), and the deductions for children (from Rs 700 for the first child, Rs 600 for the second, and Rs 500 for the third, to Rs 1,000 for each of the first three children). Allowance for life insurance premiums is granted by deducting 20 per cent of such premiums from the income tax otherwise payable, subject to certain overall limitations. Contributions to superannuation funds are allowable as deductions from taxable income. All income accruing to nonresidents of Mauritius is exempt from taxation in Mauritius, whether brought into the country or not. Also exempt from income tax is the imputed income arising from the annual value of immovable property used as a residence.

The income tax on companies and corporate bodies is levied at a rate of 45 per cent on all companies regardless of the nature of their activities. An allowance is granted for capital expenditure on agricultural land, buildings, or works in the form of a simple direct deduction of the entire expenditure in the year in which it occurred; prior to July 1970, the deduction was made from taxable profits over a certain, variable number of years. In addition, deductions are allowed for expenditure on market research and feasibility studies relating to the establishment of new industries in Mauritius.

The succession duty is levied on the aggregate value of all property passing at death, at rates dependent upon both the value of the estate and the relationship to the deceased. Legislation is being prepared to revise the succession duty. The revision would not involve alteration of existing rates, but would attempt to improve the procedures for assessment and collection of this duty.

Indirect Taxes

Indirect taxes consist essentially of import and export duties and excise taxes. There are also taxes on commerce and industry (*licences*), on transportation (drivers' and conductors' licenses and motor vehicle licenses), and on gambling (taxes on sweepstakes, lotteries, and betting). Until January 1, 1970, when a new customs tariff conforming to the Brussels nomenclature was introduced, there was a package tax, applied either ad valorem or according to the number of packages imported.

Export duties consist of a specific duty of Re 1.00 a metric ton on goods re-exported in transit or in bond, an ad valorem duty of 6 per cent on sugar exports (assessed on the sales price), and a tax of 5 per cent on molasses exports. In 1968/69, the ratio of export duties to the value of exports f.o.b. was about 4 per cent. In addition to export duty, sugar exports are subject to a number of other levies, the proceeds of which accrue to certain institutions related to the sugar industry, such as the Sugar Industry Research Institute (Re 0.34 a kilogram) and the Sugar Industry Reserve Fund (Re 0.10 a kilogram).

Import duties are classified according to the Revised Standard International Trade Classification and include ad valorem and specific duties. Preferential rates apply to Commonwealth countries, South

Africa, Ireland, and Burma. The general rates apply to all other countries which are contracting parties to the General Agreement on Tariffs and Trade (GATT) as well as to non-GATT countries. In 1968/69, the ratio of import duties to the value of imports c.i.f. was about 16 per cent.

Excise taxes provide about 15 per cent of total tax revenue and are levied mainly on the consumption of rum (tax equivalent to 7.8 per cent of retail price), local wine (Re 0.60 a liter), and tobacco (Rs 26.00 or Rs18.00 a kilogram according to quality).

Licenses (*licences,* originating from the French *patentes et licences*) consist of fixed fees that are levied on all individuals or enterprises engaged in commercial activity. They generally amount to Rs 500 a year, but they can be as low as Rs 100 a year and, as in the case of sugar mills, as high as Rs 6,000 a year. Special licenses are issued for dealers in and producers of alcoholic products. There has recently been a revision of the commercial code which will have the initial effect of reducing revenue collections from licenses by altering the licensing categories for commercial concerns and by reducing stamp taxes. It is expected, however, that this revision will stimulate commerce and thus in time broaden the tax base.

Registration Fees and Stamp Taxes

Registration fees and stamp taxes provide about 3 per cent of total tax revenue. The registration fees apply to all legal acts which have to be recorded by the Registrar's General Office. They include a fixed fee and proportional fees in specified cases.

STRUCTURE OF CURRENT EXPENDITURE

Expenditures on social services averaged some 44 per cent of current expenditure in recent years, reflecting the Government's efforts to mitigate the decline in living standards through social programs. Expenditures on general administration (including defense and police) averaged 17 per cent of the total, and outlays on economic services and public debt payments represented 16 per cent and 11 per cent, respectively. The general structure of current expenditure is shown in Table 10. Changes in the pattern from year to year are described in the following section on Budgetary Operations.

TABLE 10. MAURITIUS: CURRENT BUDGET, 1963/64-1970/71 [1]

(In millions of Mauritian rupees)

	1963/64	1964/65	1965/66	1966/67	1967/68	1968/69 [2]	1969/70 Original estimates	1969/70 Preliminary results	1970/71 Original estimates
Revenue	**184.6**	**231.7**	**182.2**	**199.3**	**215.1**	**228.7** [2]	**242.0**	**228.0**	**253.0**
Direct taxes	41.2	90.5	37.5	45.7	49.1	49.3	53.9	52.0	54.0
Income tax	38.0	87.2	34.1	41.3	45.5	45.2	50.2	...	50.0
Succession duty	1.5	1.5	1.5	2.3	1.5	1.9	2.0	...	2.0
Contributions to Social Security	1.7	1.8	1.9	2.1	2.1	2.2	1.7	...	2.0
Indirect taxes	112.5	106.5	106.0	111.6	121.1	126.5	131.6	129.0	136.0
Import duties	53.4	57.4	52.3	56.6	62.2	64.1	66.8	64.0	67.0
Export duties	22.6	12.9	15.2	13.4	15.3	14.6	15.3	17.0	17.0
Excise taxes	25.7	25.1	25.6	27.8	29.4	30.5	31.8	31.0	33.0
Registration fees and stamp taxes	5.5	5.2	5.2	6.1	6.7	8.9	7.6	...	9.0
Receipts from public utilities	10.9	11.6	13.7	14.1	18.4	21.0	22.1	21.0	23.0
Receipts from public services	5.3	5.6	5.7	5.8	6.1	6.3	8.5	7.0	10.0
Rental of public property	1.6	1.8	1.6	1.8	1.6	1.9	2.3	...	2.0
Other	7.6	10.5	12.5	14.2	12.1	14.8	16.0	18.0	19.0
Expenditure	**168.9**	**185.7**	**202.0**	**221.0**	**232.3**	**241.6**	**241.7**	**227.0**	**249.0**
General administration	32.5	35.0	35.6	37.9	39.5	38.7	40.8	...	48.0
Defense and police	10.1	10.2	10.6	11.7	11.6	12.0	13.4	13.0	15.0
Economic services	31.3	35.6	33.5	35.7	35.6	33.9	38.2	...	40.0
Agriculture, forestry, and fisheries	7.8	8.1	7.4	7.1	8.3	6.5	8.1	7.0	9.0
Transport	4.5	4.2	3.8	3.9	3.8	3.8	4.3	3.0	5.0
Post and telecommunications	6.0	6.0	5.8	5.7	7.2	7.0	7.4	6.0	6.0
Other	13.0	17.3	16.5	19.0	16.3	16.6	18.4	...	20.0
Social expenditure	73.0	77.0	91.4	103.2	109.5	100.3	99.9	...	93.0
Education	24.9	26.0	26.9	28.5	29.3	29.6	31.3	31.0	35.0
Health	19.2	19.7	20.9	21.8	22.0	21.9	26.1	24.0	28.0
Social Security	28.9	30.9	33.1	34.0	33.5	28.8	30.0	30.0	28.0
Relief works	...	0.4	10.5	18.9	18.9	9.0	9.0	...	2.0
Subsidies for rice and wheat					5.8 [3]	11.0	3.5		
Public debt and pensions	23.3	27.5	30.6	32.9	36.3	58.2	51.3	47.0	56.0
Public debt service	11.9	13.7	16.1	18.3	20.6	41.4	33.7	29.0	37.0
Local governments	8.8	10.6	10.9	11.3	11.4	10.5	11.5	8.0	12.0
Surplus or deficit (—)	**15.7**	**46.0**	**—19.8**	**—21.7**	**—17.2**	**—12.9**	**0.3**	**1.0**	**4.0**

Sources: Ministry of Finance, *Financial Reports*, and *Estimates as Passed by the Legislative Assembly, 1969–70* and *1970–71*; and data provided by the Mauritian authorities.

[1] Financial years ending June 30. [2] Net of Rs 13.9 million of borrowing for redemption of a Development and Welfare Loan.

[3] ... Rs 2.2 million on account of the 1966/67 budget.

BUDGETARY OPERATIONS

Current Budget

The current budget, which was in surplus during 1963/64 and 1964/65, showed marked deficits during the next two years (Table 10). Revenue fluctuated from one year to another, and in 1966/67 was only 8 per cent larger than in 1963/64. On the other hand, expenditure increased steadily and at a fairly rapid rate. The current deficit in 1966/67, at almost Rs 22 million, was equal to about 10 per cent of current expenditure. Measures aimed at reducing the deficit were introduced during the 1967/68 financial year and, as a result, the deficit declined to Rs 17 million in that year and to Rs 13 million in 1968/69, equal to about 5 per cent of current expenditure. The deficits in these two years were financed by resources provided by the United Kingdom.

Current revenue responds with a significant lag to changes in GNP, mainly because company income taxes are assessed on the taxable income of the previous year. Following the sharp expansion of GNP in 1963, current revenue rose by about 25 per cent (to about Rs 232 million) in 1964/65, and then fell to Rs 199 million in 1966/67. New tax measures introduced in the latter part of 1967, expected to yield an additional Rs 8–9 million a year, included a 5 per cent surtax on company income taxes and a 5 per cent surcharge on all import duties as well as on most fees and charges for government services. Largely as a result of these measures, together with an increase in receipts from public utilities, budgetary revenue rose by 8 per cent, to Rs 215 million, in 1967/68. Additional revenue measures were introduced in the 1968/69 budget, including higher charges for certain public services (e.g., telephone service) and for commercial and liquor licenses. Receipts from the tax reserve certificates (i.e., advance payments on income taxes), which until then had been credited to extrabudgetary accounts, were included in the current budget. The 1968/69 budget also provided for charges to be made for public health services. Actual collection of current revenue in 1968/69 totaled Rs 229 million, an increase of 6 per cent over the previous year.

Current expenditure rose at an average annual rate of almost 10 per cent between 1963/64 and 1966/67 (Table 10). All categories of expenditure contributed to the expansion, but a large share of the increase was in expenditure of a social nature, which rose by 41 per cent over the period. Among the rapidly growing items of social expenditure were the wages paid in connection with relief works programs, which rose from a negligible amount in 1963/64 to Rs 19 million in 1966/67. Expenditure on public debt service and pensions also rose more rapidly than the average over the period, reaching 15 per cent of total current expenditure in 1966/67.

In 1967/68 the rate of increase in current expenditure was reduced to 5 per cent, despite subsidy payments for rice and wheat flour, a further increase in expenditures for public debt and pensions, and continuing high expenditures on the relief works program. The economies introduced were estimated to save some Rs 4.5 million, and included reducing overseas leave for civil servants and holding vacant positions in government service unfilled.

Further measures to contain the growth of expenditure were adopted in the 1968/69 budget. These included (1) reduced outlays for the relief works program (from Rs 19 million in 1967/68 to Rs 9.5 million), to be attained by reducing the number of workers, their wages, and the number of workdays; (2) reducing the cost to the budget of family allowances (from Rs 9.3 million to Rs 3.4 million) by lowering the allowance which is paid where family income does not exceed Rs 225 a month from Rs 15 to Rs 12 monthly; and (3) a reduction of about Rs 1 million in grants and subsidies to secondary education and to local authorities. With the implementation of these measures, current expenditure other than for public debt service was budgeted to be reduced by some Rs 6.5 million below the level attained in 1967/68, despite the expectation of a further sharp rise in subsidies for rice and wheat flour.

Actual current expenditure in 1968/69 totaled about Rs 242 million, an increase of 4 per cent over the previous year. The further reduction in the rate of increase was attained despite a sharp rise in public debt service from Rs 21 million in 1967/68 to Rs 41 million, mainly owing to repayment of a Development and Welfare Loan in August 1968. The accumulated sinking fund for this loan fell short of the amount required for redemption by Rs 13.9 million, and this amount was raised by borrowing in London from a syndicate of private banks and the Crown Agents. Subsidy payments for rice and wheat flour rose by some

Rs 5 million in 1968/69 because of higher import prices. There was, however, a sharp decline in expenditure on relief works: at Rs 9.0 million, this was less than half the amount recorded in the previous year. As a whole, current expenditure excluding public debt service was actually reduced in 1968/69.

The original budget estimates for 1969/70 provided for approximate balance, with revenue and expenditure at about Rs 242 million. Compared with the results of the 1968/69 budget, these estimates indicate an increase in revenue of 6 per cent and no change in expenditure (see Table 10).

The increase in revenue was expected to come mainly from taxes, both direct (Rs 4.6 million) and indirect (Rs 5.1 million), and from enforcement of the collection of health fees (Rs 2.2 million). The higher receipts from direct taxes were expected to derive from the general revision of the income tax code for individuals and companies, which, it was estimated, would produce Rs 2 million, and from higher company profits in 1968/69—on which taxes were to be paid in 1969/70—which were expected to produce another Rs 2 million. Receipts from customs and excise duties were estimated to be 4 per cent higher than in 1968/69, largely as a result of greater economic activity. The adoption of the Brussels tariff nomenclature was expected to have only a marginal upward influence on collections from these duties in 1969/70; this upward influence was due to the rounding-off process involved in grossing up the rates to include the fiscal surcharge and the package tax (both of which were discontinued in July 1970), as well as to the slight general upward effect resulting from the rationalization of the rate structure.

The 1969/70 budget provided for no overall increase in current expenditure. However, if public debt charges are omitted, outlays were estimated to increase by about 4 per cent. This increase derives partly from small increases in the salaries of civil servants in the lower grades. The budgeted increases in expenditure for defense and police (Rs 1.4 million), education (Rs 1.7 million), health (Rs 4.2 million), and Social Security (Rs 1.2 million) were to be largely offset by reductions in expenditure on the price subsidies for rice and wheat flour, estimated to fall from Rs 11.0 million in 1968/69 to Rs 3.5 million in 1969/70. This reduction anticipated the benefits to be derived from lower import prices for these commodities and from the devaluation of the French franc, in which certain wheat contracts are expressed. The estimated increase in expenditure on health services reflected the expectation that the Sir Seewoosagur Ramgoolam Hospital would be open and operating fully throughout 1969/70. Expenditure on the relief works program was to be kept at the 1968/69 level, while public debt service was expected to decline from Rs 41.4 million in 1968/69 to Rs 33.7 million in 1969/70. It should be noted, however, that about Rs 13 million for the redemption of a debenture stock falling due in 1970 was not included in the 1969/70 current budget, but rather in the capital budget.

Preliminary results show that the current budget for 1969/70 was in approximate balance, with both revenue and expenditure remaining 6 per cent below original budget estimates. Revenue totaled Rs 228 million, about the same as in 1968/69, and expenditure Rs 227 million, about 6 per cent less than in 1968/69. Revenue failed to increase mainly because of a decline in receipts from income taxes. The shortfall was in part attributable to the fact that the revised income tax code for individuals and companies did not, as had been expected, become effective during the fiscal year. The reduction in expenditure was mainly the result of savings on subsidy payments for rice and wheat and of a decline in public debt service payments.

The original estimates for 1970/71, with revenue at Rs 253 million and expenditure at Rs 249 million, provided for a current surplus of Rs 4 million (see Table 10). Revenue was expected to increase by 11 per cent over the preliminary results for 1969/70, mainly as a result of higher receipts from indirect taxes. Receipts from public services, as well as interest and royalties, were also expected to increase.

Current expenditure was set at about 10 per cent above preliminary results for 1969/70. Most of the increase was in appropriations for the establishment of new ministries and the staffing of existing services, greater expenditures on education and health, and larger debt service payments. The increases in these categories were to be partially offset by economies on food subsidies, which were no longer required following the decline in import prices for rice. Moreover, appropriations for relief works totaling Rs 7 million were transferred to the capital budget following the Government's decision to employ relief workers on labor-intensive development projects.

Capital Budget

Between 1963/64 and 1966/67 capital budget expenditures averaged Rs 54 million a year and showed little change from one year to another. In 1967/68, however, expenditure rose by 15 per cent, to more than Rs 62 million, with notable increases in expenditure on projects in agriculture and public health. With completion of these projects, together with a fall in capital receipts and the emergence of certain administrative difficulties, capital expenditure in 1968/69 declined by 30 per cent, to Rs 43.4 million, compared with the estimate of Rs 67.3 million (Table 11). Outlays for public health fell from Rs 13.8 million in 1967/68 to Rs 4.5 million, largely as a result of the completion of the work on the Sir Seewoosagur Ramgoolam Hospital, and only in the area of transport did development expenditure increase in 1968/69. The decline in the Government's development activities also reflects the acute shortage of personnel who are equipped to mount and sustain a public development program.

Capital budget revenue since 1963/64 has fluctuated sharply from one year to another, reflecting mainly variations in disbursements of foreign loans and grants. Receipts from abroad have been almost entirely from the United Kingdom—largely official grants and loans— averaging more than Rs 20 million a year (Table 11). The unusually large amount in 1965/66 reflected compensation for the sale of the Chagos Islands to the United Kingdom (Rs 40 million). Revenue from domestic sources has also fluctuated, although within narrower limits. Transfers from the current budget reached a peak of Rs 20 million in 1964/65, but were discontinued beginning in 1965/66 leaving tap loans and other loans issued locally by the Government as the major source of domestic funds. Receipts from these loans reached Rs 20 million in 1967/68, but fell to Rs 3.4 million in 1968/69. Subscriptions came principally from commercial banks and certain local companies, but in recent years increasing interest has been displayed by local pension funds and insurance companies operating in Mauritius.

The balance on the capital budget has changed substantially from year to year. From a surplus of Rs 21.5 million in 1965/66 it moved to a deficit of Rs 27.4 million in 1966/67. In 1968/69, there was a deficit of Rs 22.9 million despite lower expenditure than any recorded for sev-

TABLE 11. MAURITIUS: CAPITAL BUDGET, 1963/64–1970/71 [1]

(In millions of Mauritian rupees)

	1963/64	1964/65	1965/66	1966/67	1967/68	1968/69	1969/70	1970/71
							Original estimates	
Revenue	**72.6**	**44.4**	**73.5**	**27.0**	**57.0**	**20.5**	**90.2**	**89.8**
Domestic sources	19.9	27.9	12.1	14.1	21.7	5.8	40.1	50.2
Current budget	*12.0*	*20.0*	*—*	*—*	*—*	*—*	*—*	*4.0*
Borrowing	*6.7*	*5.8*	*10.9*	*11.4*	*20.2*	*3.4*	*38.0*	*40.0*
Other	*1.2*	*2.1*	*1.2*	*2.7*	*1.5*	*2.4*	*2.1*	*6.2*
External sources	52.7	16.5	61.4	12.9	35.3	14.7	50.1	39.6
U. K. grants	*6.2*	*4.9*	*3.5*	*4.2*	*15.5*	*10.2*	*11.6*	*10.2*
U. K. loans	*31.1*	*0.6*	*12.8*	*8.7*	*19.6*	*2.4*	*13.5*	*27.9*
World Bank loans	*15.4*	*10.9*	*4.9*	*—*	*—*	*—*	*—*	*—*
Other	*—*	*0.1*	*40.2* [2]	*—*	*0.2*	*2.1*	*25.0*	*1.5*
Expenditure	**53.7**	**56.4**	**52.0**	**54.4**	**62.4**	**43.4**	**78.9**	**87.8**
Economic services	35.6	37.7	34.5	31.5	33.0	28.8	63.4	64.7
Agriculture, forestry, and industry	*4.6*	*8.1*	*8.3*	*9.9*	*13.3*	*8.8*	*11.5*	*19.2*
Transport and infrastructure	*30.6*	*26.5*	*23.2*	*14.1*	*12.0*	*16.3*	*34.9*	*35.0*
Loans to Development Bank and other	*0.4*	*3.1*	*3.0*	*7.5*	*7.7*	*3.7*	*17.0* [3]	*10.5*
Social services	15.3	13.9	12.7	18.4	19.1	8.3	9.8	7.2
Education	*3.1*	*2.8*	*3.3*	*2.7*	*2.2*	*1.4*	*5.8*	*5.0*
Health and welfare	*0.2*	*0.9*	*1.1*	*9.7*	*13.8*	*4.5*	*1.3*	*1.5*
Housing	*12.0*	*10.2*	*8.3*	*6.0*	*3.1*	*2.4*	*2.7*	*0.7*
Central administration and local governments	2.2	4.2	4.2	4.5	10.3	6.3	5.0	15.9 [4]
Other	0.6	0.6	0.6	—	—	—	0.7	—
Surplus or deficit (−)	**18.9**	**−12.0**	**21.5**	**−27.4**	**−5.4**	**−22.9**	**11.3**	**2.0**

Sources: Ministry of Finance, *Financial Reports*; and data provided by the Mauritian authorities.

[1] Financial years ending June 30.
[2] Includes Rs 40 million for the sale of the Chagos Islands to the United Kingdom.
[3] Includes redemption of a debenture stock (1970) in the amount of Rs 13 million which was to be financed by issuing a new debenture stock in the same amount, the proceeds of which are included in domestic borrowing.
[4] Rs 7 million represents expenditure on relief labor force to be redeployed on productive and labor-intensive development projects. Prior to 1970/71, expenditure on relief works was included entirely in current budget expenditure.

eral years, owing to exceptionally low receipts, both foreign and domestic.

The estimates for 1969/70 set revenue at Rs 90.2 million and expenditure at Rs 78.9 million, leaving an estimated surplus of Rs 11.3 million (see Table 11). Both revenue and expenditure included an entry for redemption of treasury debentures falling due in the amount of Rs 13 million. Appropriations exceeded those for 1968/69 in most major categories; transport and infrastructure more than doubled, and total expenditure was estimated to be almost double, compared with actual expenditure in 1968/69. Domestic sources were expected to provide some Rs 40 million (44 per cent of total receipts), largely in the form of the above-mentioned treasury debenture issue, medium-term loans (Rs 15 million), and tap loans (Rs 10 million). Foreign sources were expected to provide Rs 50 million, compared with only Rs 15 million in 1968/69. Receipts from U. K. grants and loans were estimated at Rs 25.1 million, while additional loans totaling Rs 25 million were expected from other countries or international organizations. Data on the execution of the capital budget show that actual expenditure totaled Rs 57 million, substantially below the budgeted amount of Rs 78.9 million.

The capital budget estimates for 1970/71 provided for expenditure of Rs 87.8 million (see Table 11). Domestic sources, which for the first time since 1964/65 included a transfer (Rs 4 million) from the current budget, were expected to provide about 56 per cent of total receipts, largely in the form of borrowing. Receipts from external sources would be mainly in the form of loans and grants from the United Kingdom.

TREASURY FINANCING

The financing operations of the Treasury moved from a surplus position of some Rs 34 million in 1963/64 and 1964/65 to approximate balance in 1965/66. There were deficits of Rs 49.1 million in 1966/67, Rs 5.3 million in 1967/68, and Rs 21.9 million in 1968/69 (Table 12).

The capital account inclusive of budgetary grants and loans of Rs 32.3 million showed a surplus of Rs 21.5 million in 1965/66, which corresponded closely to the deficit of Rs 19.8 million incurred in the current budget, and there was only a small change in other assets and

TABLE 12. MAURITIUS: BUDGETARY AND TREASURY OPERATIONS, 1963/64–1968/69 [1]

(*In millions of Mauritian rupees*)

	1963/64	1964/65	1965/66	1966/67	1967/68	1968/69
Current budget revenue [1]	184.6	231.7	182.2	199.3	215.1	228.7
Current budget expenditure	−168.9	−185.7	−202.0	−221.0	−232.3	−241.6
Surplus or deficit	15.7	46.0	−19.8	−21.7	−17.2	−12.9
Capital budget revenue [1]	13.2	22.1	41.2 [2]	2.7	1.5	2.4
Capital budget expenditure	−53.7	−56.4	−52.0	−54.4	−62.4	−43.4
Deficit	−40.5	−34.3	−10.8	−51.7	−60.9	−41.0
Overall surplus or deficit	−24.9	11.7	−30.6	−73.4	−78.1	−53.9
Budgetary grants and loans						
Current budget	—	—	—	—	17.2	13.9
Capital budget	59.4	22.3	32.3	24.3	55.5	18.1
Treasury surplus or deficit (−)	**34.6**	**34.0**	**1.7**	**−49.1**	**−5.3**	**−21.9**
Treasury financing			**−1.7**	**49.1**	**5.3**	**21.9**
Short-term borrowing from abroad			—	16.4	25.8	−22.3
Advances from domestic banks			—	10.0 [3]	−10.0 [3]	14.7
Sale of treasury bills			—	—	—	8.9 [4]
Changes in deposits (decrease −)			5.0	−10.8	5.2	−0.8
Changes in investment portfolio (increase −)			−11.1	30.6	0.4	−4.7
Advances and remittances			−1.1	−7.4	−9.9	10.3
Changes in cash balances (increase −)			1.2	5.6	−9.8	13.9
Other items (net)			4.3	4.7	3.6	1.9

Sources: Ministry of Finance, *Financial Reports;* and data provided by the Mauritian authorities.

[1] Budgetary receipts derived from domestic borrowing and external grants and loans are shown separately from other budget revenue, and the Treasury's financing operations reflect all other changes in the financial position of the Treasury.

[2] Includes Rs 40 million for the sale of the Chagos Islands to the United Kingdom.

[3] Represents a short-term advance from the Currency Fund in 1966/67 and subsequent repayment in 1967/68.

[4] Includes Rs 4.9 million which was purchased by the commercial banks.

liabilities of the Treasury. The situation was reversed in 1966/67, when the capital account inclusive of budgetary grants and loans showed a deficit of Rs 27.4 million; this deficit, combined with a deficit on current account of Rs 21.7 million, necessitated overall treasury financing of Rs 49.1 million. Moreover, the Treasury's liquidity was further strained by a decline in funds held on deposit totaling Rs 10.8 million and by net advances and remittances of Rs 7.4 million. The required financing was provided by selling foreign portfolio investments (Rs 30.6 million), by short-term borrowing from abroad (Rs 16.4 million), by a short-term advance from the Currency Fund (Rs 10.0 million), and by drawing down the cash and other balances of the Treasury.

In 1967/68, treasury financing declined to Rs 5.3 million, as the current budget deficit was met by a grant from the United Kingdom and the deficit on the capital budget inclusive of budgetary grants and loans was reduced. The Treasury borrowed Rs 25.8 million from commercial banks in London and obtained other funds from an increase in deposits (Rs 5.2 million). Despite a further increase in net advances and remittances of Rs 9.9 million, the Treasury was able to repay the Rs 10 million borrowed from the Currency Fund in 1966/67, and to increase its cash balances by Rs 9.8 million.

In 1968/69 the situation was reversed and treasury financing rose to Rs 21.9 million, as the deficit on capital account inclusive of budgetary grants and loans rose substantially and more than offset the surplus realized in the current budget transactions including a foreign loan in the amount of Rs 13.9 million. In that year the Treasury also provided resources for the repayment of foreign short-term loans amounting to Rs 22.3 million. On the other hand, transactions in advances and remittances registered a surplus of Rs 10.3 million. The required financing was provided by borrowing from the banking system (Rs 14.7 million), by issuing treasury bills (Rs 8.9 million), and by reducing the cash and other balances of the Treasury.

PUBLIC DEBT

Outstanding Debt

The total outstanding medium-term and long-term debt of the Central Government rose from Rs 184 million on June 30, 1963 to Rs 321 million on June 30, 1969, an average annual rate of over 12 per cent; however, during 1968/69 there was a decline of about Rs 20 million. The debt on June 30, 1969 was divided fairly evenly between domestic and foreign liabilities, the domestic debt amounting to Rs 146.5 million and the debt contracted and repayable in foreign currency totaling Rs 174 million (Table 13). The decline in outstanding debt in 1968/69

TABLE 13.   MAURITIUS: PUBLIC DEBT OUTSTANDING ON JUNE 30, 1969

	Outstanding June 30, 1969 (*million rupees*)	Repayment Period	Interest Rate (*per cent*)
Domestic debt	**146.5**		
Publicly issued loans			
Tap loans [1]	94.6	. . .	5.00
Development and Welfare Loan, 1950	3.1	1971–81	3.00
Development Loan, 1953	14.4	1964–74	4.25
Development Loan, 1962	15.0	1973–83	5.75
Development Loan, 1966	5.0	1971–76	6.00
Treasury debenture, 1968 [2]	14.0	1969–70	6.00
Other loans			
Cyclone and Drought Insurance Board	0.4	1969–74	—
Foreign debt	**174.0**		
U. K. loans, publicly issued			
Development Loan, 1950–53	27.9	1972–77	4.75
Development Loan, 1963	27.9	1973–75	6.50
U. K. loans, official			
Colonial Service Vote Loans [3]	9.6	1962–84	5.50–7.50
Exchequer Loans [4]	49.3	1963–94	5.50–7.38
Compensation and Commutation Loans, 1968 [5]	1.0	1974–99	7.50
Loan for Development Scheme No. 1, 1968	8.3	. . .	. . .
Loan for Development Scheme No. 2, 1968	2.1	. . .	. . .
London bank syndicate loan	13.9	1970–75	9.00
Total U. K. loans	140.0		
World Bank loan, 1963	34.0	1966–86	5.50
Total	**320.5**		

Source: Data provided by the Mauritian authorities.

[1] Tap loans have been issued in every year since 1959 and may be redeemed at the option of the subscriber.

[2] Consists of short-term treasury bonds issued in the first half of 1968, the proceeds of which were included in the 1967/68 capital budget receipts.

[3] Interest and amortization combined in 15 equal yearly installments.

[4] Interest and amortization combined in 25 equal yearly installments.

[5] Loans to finance the compensation of and the commutation of pensions owed to expatriate civil servants following Mauritius's independence. Interest is due only on the commutation part of the loan.

occurred principally in the foreign debt; the total domestic debt of the Central Government remained almost unchanged. Almost 65 per cent of the domestic debt consists of tap loans; these have been issued every year since 1957, carry an interest rate of 5 per cent, and are redeemable at the option of the subscriber. A further 26 per cent of the domestic debt is accounted for by four long-term loans issued between 1950 and 1966 and bearing interest ranging from 3 per cent to 6 per cent.

Of the total outstanding external debt on June 30, 1969, over 80 per cent represented debt denominated in pounds sterling, largely from loans issued publicly in the United Kingdom (Rs 56 million) and official loans (Rs 70 million) from the United Kingdom. Other foreign debt is confined to an outstanding liability equivalent to Rs 34 million in respect of a World Bank loan of $7 million made in 1963 to finance electric power stations. The publicly issued loans consist of two medium-term loans raised on the London market in 1950–53 and 1963 at interest of 4¾ per cent and 6½ per cent. A similar loan was due for redemption in 1968; at that time, however, the accumulated sinking funds for its redemption fell short of the amount required by Rs 13.9 million, and the Government found it necessary to borrow that amount from a group of private London banks and the Crown Agents. This loan carries an interest rate of 9 per cent and is repayable over a 5-year period beginning in February 1970. Official loans consist mainly of Colonial Service Vote Loans and Exchequer Loans contracted more or less annually between 1957 and 1967. The former bear interest at between 5½ and 7½ per cent and are repayable in 15 equal annual installments. Interest rates on Exchequer Loans range from 5.5 to 7.38 per cent and repayment is in 25 equal annual installments. Certain loans in both categories are re-lent by the Central Government to public institutions, such as the Central Electricity Board, and to state-aided schools, in some cases free of interest.

In 1968, Mauritius signed two loan agreements with the United Kingdom equivalent to Rs 8 million and Rs 19 million, at an effective interest rate of about 9 per cent, to finance agreed development projects. Further loan agreements in pounds sterling were signed with the U. K. Government during 1969 for the equivalent of Rs 13 million and Rs 65 million. These loans, which are also for the financing of agreed development projects, are free of interest and are repayable in 25 years with a 2-year grace period and graduated repayments of principal for the first 5 years.

Debt Service

Charges for interest, amortization (contributions to sinking funds and repayments of principal), and management of the public debt are gen-

TABLE 14.   MAURITIUS: PUBLIC DEBT SERVICE, 1965/66–1969/70

(*In millions of Mauritian rupees*)

	1965/66	1966/67	1967/68	1968/69 Original estimates	1969/70 Original estimates
Domestic debt	**7.7**	**8.1**	**8.8**	**11.3**	**24.8**
Interest and management charges	5.4	5.7	6.2	7.4	7.5
Contributions to sinking funds	2.3	2.4	2.6	2.8	3.3
Repayments of principal [1]	—	—	—	1.1	14.0 [2]
Foreign debt	**10.2**	**13.7**	**14.8**	**32.1**	**21.9**
Interest and management charges	5.8	8.4	9.0	8.4	9.5 [3]
Contributions to sinking funds	2.3	2.3	2.3	3.8	7.2
Repayments of principal [1]	2.1	3.0	3.5	19.9 [4]	5.2
Total debt	**17.9**	**21.8**	**23.6**	**43.4**	**46.7**
Through current budget	16.1	18.3	20.6	43.4 [5]	33.7
Through other accounts	1.8	3.5	3.0	—	13.0

Sources: Ministry of Finance, *Financial Reports*, and *Estimates as Passed by the Legislative Assembly, 1969–70;* and data provided by the Mauritian authorities.

[1] Excludes capital repayments out of the sinking fund.
[2] Includes Rs 13 million redemption of treasury debenture.
[3] Includes Rs 0.5 million for interest payments on treasury bills issued.
[4] Includes Rs 15 million on the 3½ per cent Development and Welfare Loan, 1965–68.
[5] The figure for public debt service in Table 10 is from the final budget outturns, and therefore differs from the original estimate given here.

erally included in the current budget (Table 14; see also Table 10). However, prior to the financial year 1968/69, a small part of the debt service was not effected through the current budget, but through extra-budgetary accounts. This covered a number of interest-free loans from the United Kingdom for the benefit of various institutions, including aid to schools and local authorities.

In the financial year 1968/69, expenditure on debt service amounted to Rs 41.4 million (final outturn; see Table 10), about 18 per cent of current budget revenue. In 1966/67 and 1967/68, the debt service represented 9 per cent and 10 per cent, respectively, of current budget revenue. The high debt service payments in 1968/69 resulted from the redemption of a Development and Welfare Loan, which raised the total debt service in that year by Rs 15 million.

In 1969/70, debt service payments declined to Rs 29.0 million (preliminary results; see Table 10), 13 per cent of current revenue. This total excludes a transaction to redeem a treasury debenture of Rs 13 million due for repayment during the year. The bulk of this repayment will be refinanced through a reissue of the debenture, the new issue having a maturity of two years; this refinancing will be repeated at two-year intervals, with the total outstanding debenture declining by Rs 2 million each time. In the 1969/70 budget, the transaction appeared in the capital budget, with the refinancing appearing as a capital receipt.

Expenditure on debt service was expected to increase to Rs 37 million in 1970/71 and to Rs 44 million in 1971/72. In part, this increase anticipates new loans which the Government hopes to raise in connection with its proposed development program, but it also reflects the fairly rapid growth in the public debt over the past five years.

MONEY AND BANKING

MONETARY SYSTEM AND BANKING STRUCTURE

The banking system comprises a central bank (the Bank of Mauritius), five commercial banks, a development bank, a cooperative bank, a housing corporation, and the Post Office Savings Bank. In addition, there are numerous sugar brokers, middlemen, and shopkeepers who engage in lending operations. The currency, the Mauritian rupee, is issued by the Bank of Mauritius. A par value has not yet been established with the International Monetary Fund; however, the official rate of exchange is Re 1 = £0.075, corresponding to Rs 5.55555 = $1. Mauritius is a member of the sterling area. Before the Bank of Mauritius began operations on August 14, 1967, the currency was issued by a Currency Fund against minimum deposits of 70 per cent in sterling, and sterling was provided in exchange for rupees.

Bank of Mauritius

The Bank of Mauritius was established under the provisions of Ordinance No. 43 of 1966 to exercise the functions of a central bank, and began operations on August 14, 1967. In December 1968, by the Bank of Mauritius (Amendment) Act, No. 56 of 1968, the statutes of the Bank were amended, enlarging the scope of the Bank's operations and its powers to regulate credit and the banks, and relaxing the requirement that the Bank keep a 50 per cent cover for its currency issue exclusively in gold or convertible currencies.

The Bank has an authorized capital of Rs 10 million; the paid-up capital amounts to Rs 5 million and is entirely subscribed by the Government. The general policy and administration of the Bank are entrusted to a Board of Directors composed of the Governor, who is the chairman of the Board, the Managing Director, and other Directors the number of whom may vary between three and five. The Governor and the Managing Director, in consultation with the Board, are responsible for the formulation and execution of the monetary and credit policy of the Bank.

The Bank has the exclusive right of issuing Mauritian currency notes and coins; it is required to keep reserves equal to no less than 50 per cent of the currency in circulation and its other sight liabilities. These reserves may consist of convertible foreign currencies and such securities of the Government of Mauritius as the Board of the Bank may determine. Most of the official foreign assets are now held by the Bank: during 1968 and 1969 it took over the principal foreign assets of the Government and official entities, including those of the Post Office Savings Bank, and the remaining official foreign assets (mainly sterling investments held by sinking funds for loans denominated in rupees and certain other small government sterling investments) were to be gradually centralized in the Bank.

The Bank of Mauritius acts as banker and financial advisor to the Government. Although under the Bank's statutes the Government may continue to maintain accounts with other banks in Mauritius, government deposits are gradually being taken over by the Bank of Mauritius. Credit to the Government may be extended by the Bank through either direct advances or the purchase of government securities. Direct advances to the Government may be granted for the purpose of meeting temporary deficiencies in budget revenue, at such rate of interest as the Bank may determine. The total amount of such advances may not at any time exceed 10 per cent of the estimated current budget revenue for the financial year in which the advances are granted, and must be repaid not later than four months after the end of that financial year; any part of these advances which is not repaid within the prescribed time is deducted from the amount allowed under this facility in the ensuing financial year. The Bank may buy and sell securities of the Government with maturities of not more than 20 years that form part of an issue also offered to the public. The Bank's holdings of such securities may not at any time exceed 30 per cent of the estimated current budget revenue for the relevant financial year, excluding government securities inherited from the Currency Fund and those held by the Bank for the account of staff funds and other internal funds of the Bank.

The Bank may grant short-term credit to the economy (i.e., for periods not exceeding 3 months) by purchasing, discounting, and rediscounting commercial paper and promissory notes, the latter bearing two or more acceptable signatures. Transactions of the Bank in this respect are subject to the provisions of the Stamp Ordinance of 1927, under which a stamp tax is levied on promissory notes ($\frac{9}{100}$ of 1 per cent ad valorem) and bills of exchange (Re 0.15 irrespective of value). The Bank may also purchase, sell, discount, and rediscount commercial paper drawn or issued for the purpose of financing seasonal agricultural operations, including fishing, animal husbandry, and marketing and processing agricultural produce, maturing within 12 months from the date of acquisition by the Bank. Short-term advances (for periods not exceeding 3 months) may be extended by the Bank against gold, commercial paper eligible for rediscount, warehouse warrants, and eligible government securities maturing within 20 years.

With the approval of the Minister of Finance, the Bank may subscribe, hold, and sell shares of any corporation set up with the approval of, or under the authority of, the Government for the purpose of facilitating the financing of economic development. The total value of the Bank's holdings of such shares may not exceed 50 per cent of the capital and general reserve fund of the Bank.

The instruments of credit control at the disposal of the Bank include changes in discount and rediscount rates, the establishment of reserve requirements, and the fixing of selective and overall ceilings on the commercial banks' credit operations. The Bank may require all authorized banks to maintain such minimum cash balances as it may determine; these balances may not, however, exceed 25 per cent of each bank's total deposits and other liabilities. The Bank may also publish instructions regulating the type, maturity, and guarantees to be obtained by commercial banks in respect of their loans, advances, or invest-ments. In addition, the Bank may determine the maximum and mini-mum interest rates which the authorized banks may apply to their credit operations or pay on deposits. The Bank's regulatory powers over the control of credit to the economy may also, with the prior approval of the Minister of Finance, be applied to other credit institu-tions in addition to the authorized banks.

The Bank has not imposed reserve requirements or applied other restrictions to bank credit. It has extended credit only to the Govern-ment, and is gradually taking over from the commercial banks the deposits of the Government (Table 15). A clearinghouse arrangement for commercial bank transactions was established in 1968 under the auspices of the Bank of Mauritius. In addition, the Bank established a call-money market through which the commercial banks may satisfy their day-to-day needs for liquidity. Under this arrangement, the banks may make available to one another overnight money at interest of 4 per cent per annum. The Bank of Mauritius may also make overnight money available against government securities, but has not operated this facility. During 1969 the Bank took steps toward the creation of a market in government securities in Mauritius by conducting limited pur-chases and sales of government paper with commercial banks and other customers.

In 1968, at the request of the commercial banks, the Bank of Mauri-tius decided to provide the banks with forward cover in sterling to alle-viate uncertainties concerning the stability of the exchange rate. Under this facility the Bank of Mauritius undertakes to provide forward cover for commercial banks in an oversold position, and in this connection to sell forward sterling to the banks at an interest charge of 1 per cent per annum. To qualify for use of this facility, a commercial bank is required to maintain each month a spot oversold position at least as great as that of the average of the corresponding months of the last 3 years. In addition, during the life of any forward contract, the banks are required to maintain an oversold position at least as large as the amount for which forward cover has been taken. At the same time, rec-ognizing the difficulties experienced at times by the commercial banks in employing all funds borrowed abroad, the Bank of Mauritius offered to sell government securities to the commercial banks at the appropriate

TABLE 15. MAURITIUS: ASSETS AND LIABILITIES OF THE BANK OF MAURITIUS, 1965–70 [1]

(In millions of Mauritian rupees; end of period)

	1965	1966	1967	1968	1969				1970			
					Mar.	June	Sept.	Dec.	Mar.	June	Sept.	Dec.
Assets												
Foreign assets	87.3	84.0	73.8	89.0	85.9	112.4	151.9	180.0	210.3	190.5	195.3	246.6
Claims on government	22.1	23.5	40.9	39.9	51.7	39.2	33.3	34.6	10.2	19.6	7.7	3.1
Discounts and advances	—	—	6.9	15.9	22.9	15.2	12.8	19.7	2.8	10.8	6.3	2.6
Government securities	22.1	23.5	34.0	24.0	28.8	24.0	20.5	14.9	7.4	8.8	1.4	0.5
Assets = liabilities	109.4	107.5	114.7	128.9	137.6	151.6	185.2	214.6	220.5	210.1	203.0	249.7
Liabilities												
Reserve money	99.0	98.3	100.3	97.1	89.2	86.0	92.6	106.6	97.4	94.4	101.8	114.7
Currency outside banks	93.2	93.0	93.3	89.2	82.8	79.1	84.2	97.2	89.9	86.3	93.2	104.7
Currency in banks	5.8	5.3	7.0	7.9	6.4	6.9	8.4	9.4	7.5	8.1	8.6	10.0
Demand deposits	—	—	0.5	3.1	9.5	8.3	19.8	9.5	10.6	8.4	10.1	12.4
Central Government	—	—	—	1.4	0.7	0.6	1.6	2.9	2.9	1.9	2.6	3.3
Other official entities	—	—	0.5	1.7	8.8	7.7	18.2	6.6	7.7	6.5	7.5	9.1
Time deposits	—	—	—	21.0	30.2	26.4	44.9	67.1	82.1	64.5	75.9	108.8
Post Office Savings Bank [2]	—	—	—	—	—	—	19.7	...	...	...	...	...
Other official entities [3]	—	—	—	21.0	30.2	26.4	25.2	...	...	...	...	...
Foreign liabilities [4]	—	—	—	—	—	22.2	22.2	22.2	22.2	22.2	...	...
Other items (net)	10.4	9.2	13.9	7.7	8.7	8.7	5.7	9.2	8.2	20.6	15.2	13.8

Sources: Bank of Mauritius, *Quarterly Review*; and data provided by the Bank of Mauritius.

[1] Data for the period before August 1967, when the Bank of Mauritius was established, refer to operations of the Currency Fund.
[2] Consists of the local currency counterpart of the foreign assets of the Post Office Savings Bank, which were transferred to the Bank of Mauritius in September 1969.
[3] Consists of the local currency counterpart of the foreign assets of the Cyclone and Drought Insurance Fund, which were transferred to the Bank of Mauritius in December 1968.
[4] Arising from a purchase from the International Monetary Fund in April 1969, and a repurchase transaction in August 1970.

market rate. These facilities were introduced for an initial period of 3 years, subject to annual review by the Bank of Mauritius and the commercial banks. In practice, the bulk of the forward cover taken up by the commercial banks has been provided by the Mauritius Sugar Syndicate, with the Bank of Mauritius providing only marginal extra amounts.

Commercial Banks

With 5 commercial banks operating 32 branches and 35 mobile units to serve a population of just over 800,000, Mauritius has a relatively highly developed commercial banking system. Only one of these banks, the Mauritius Commercial Bank, is owned and incorporated locally; the four foreign-owned banks, Barclays Bank D. C. O., the Mercantile Bank, the Bank of Baroda, and the Habib Bank, operate as branches of overseas banks. The Mauritius Commercial Bank is also the largest commercial bank, accounting for roughly half of all banking business transacted in Mauritius. Barclays Bank is next, with about 25 per cent of total business, while the Bank of Baroda and the Habib Bank together are responsible for less than 10 per cent.

The Mauritius Commercial Bank, incorporated by Royal Charter in 1838, has a total capital of Rs 6 million; the head office is located in Port Louis and the bank maintains branches in ten other localities. Barclays Bank D. C. O. has expanded considerably since its establishment in 1919 and is represented throughout the island. The Mercantile Bank, a subsidiary of the Hong Kong and Shanghai Banking Corporation, took over the activities of the Bank of Mauritius Ltd. in 1916. The Bank of Baroda commenced operations in Mauritius in 1962, and the Habib Bank first opened a branch in Mauritius in 1964.

The activities of the commercial banks in Mauritius are regulated by the Banking Ordinance of 1958, the Banking (Amendment) Ordinance of 1965, and the Bank of Mauritius (Amendment) Act of 1968. Under the ordinance, companies licensed to undertake banking activities are obliged to have a minimum capital issued and paid up in cash and outstanding of Rs 1 million. The provisions relating to capital apply to the banking corporation as a whole, whether incorporated in Mauritius or overseas. Foreign banks operating in Mauritius are therefore under no legal obligation to assign capital funds to their branches in Mauritius, and may finance their fixed assets in Mauritius entirely from resources raised locally; in early 1970 these assets were estimated at some Rs 10 million. Each commercial bank is also required to maintain a reserve fund, the annual contribution to which is fixed at 50 per cent of net profits until the fund reaches the equivalent of half the paid-up capital, after which a minimum of 20 per cent of net profits must be transferred to the reserve fund until the fund is equal to the paid-up capital. The provisions of the Banking Ordinance apply only to commercial banks and do not regulate the activities of other financial institutions.

The credit operations of the commercial banks consist primarily of short-term financing of crops, mainly in the form of overdrafts. The banks also provide short-term credit to finance domestic and foreign trade and, to a lesser extent, industry. Whereas credit for nonagricultural purposes remains fairly stable throughout the year, credit to the agricultural sector is subject to considerable seasonal variations. Bank loans to the commercial sector appear to be principally for the financing of domestic trade, and the commercial banks do not seem to be heavily engaged in financing foreign trade. Virtually all proceeds from sugar exports under the Commonwealth Sugar Agreement, which represent approximately two thirds of all sugar exports, are paid to the Mauritius Sugar Syndicate within a few days of shipping. Imports of rice and wheat flour, which in recent years have been made directly by the Government, are financed through banks in London; most other imports are financed by the suppliers. In view of the limited financing of foreign trade by commercial banks and the local preference for credit in the form of overdrafts, discounting of commercial paper constitutes a very small part of bank credit in Mauritius.

Barclays Bank and the Mauritius Commercial Bank provide small amounts of medium-term credit, mainly through subsidiaries, to finance fixed or working capital needs of industry, but the absence of legal provisions permitting the assignment of equipment and machinery as collateral has limited the scope of the commercial banks for extending credit to industry.

Commercial bank credit to the agricultural sector is extended primarily in connection with the planting, cropping, and marketing of sugar. Payments to sugar producers by the Mauritius Sugar Syndicate are

TABLE 16. MAURITIUS: ASSETS AND LIABILITIES OF THE COMMERCIAL BANKS, 1965–70

(In millions of Mauritian rupees; end of period)

					1969				1970			
	1965	1966	1967	1968	Mar.	June	Sept.	Dec.	Mar.	June	Sept.	Dec.
Assets												
Foreign assets	62.1	58.7	54.3	40.7	34.6	10.5	31.2	47.2	33.6	29.4	44.4	34.2
Cash	5.8	5.3	7.0	7.9	6.5	6.8	8.4	9.5	7.5	8.1	8.6	10.0
Claims on government	2.3	3.6	2.9	7.9	6.0	16.4	16.8	20.0	17.0	17.9	27.0	50.1
Government securities	—	—	—	—	—	11.5	13.1	17.4	16.0	15.3	20.0	42.3
Treasury bills	2.3	3.6	2.9	7.9	6.0	4.9	3.7	2.6	1.0	2.6	7.0	7.8
Claims on private sector	160.9	163.9	185.2	194.5	187.5	222.3	194.2	201.5	208.7	222.9	204.4	214.4
Loans and advances [1]	145.1	146.4	166.2	180.5	173.0	205.2	178.9	185.7	181.4	171.0	157.3	177.4
Investments	3.5	3.4	3.8	3.9	3.8	3.8	4.3	4.3	8.3	8.3	8.3	8.8
Discounts	12.3	14.1	15.2	10.1	10.7	13.3	11.0	11.5	19.0	43.6	38.8	28.2
Assets = liabilities	231.1	231.5	249.4	251.0	234.6	256.0	250.6	278.2	266.8	278.3	284.4	308.7
Liabilities												
Demand deposits	128.4	148.8	139.7	104.4	112.7	96.2	102.7	120.5	104.0	110.5	114.9	126.3
Private sector [2]	104.4	125.6	128.0	100.7	104.3	87.7	95.6	116.7	100.5	104.1	110.4	123.8
Public sector	24.0	23.2	11.7	3.7	8.4	8.5	7.1	3.8	3.5	6.4	4.5	2.5
Time and savings deposits	70.4	56.2	72.2	98.6	96.0	92.8	99.5	119.3	127.6	125.9	140.3	171.1
Private sector	70.4	55.0	66.7	95.5	...	...	...	...	...	...	...	...
Public sector [3]	—	1.2	5.5	3.1	...	...	...	...	...	...	...	...
Foreign liabilities	13.9	3.5	16.3	19.2	7.4	45.8	34.5	6.0	8.1	10.8	13.6	10.6
Other items (net)	18.4	23.0	21.2	28.8	18.5	21.2	13.9	32.4	27.1	31.1	15.6	0.7

Sources: Bank of Mauritius, *Quarterly Review*; and data provided by the Bank of Mauritius.

[1] For 1965 and 1966, includes unspecified loans and advances to the Central Government.

[2] For 1965 and 1966, consists of deposits of the Central Government and other official entities; from 1967 on consists of deposits of official entities only.

[3] Deposits of official entities only.

made through sugar brokers in the form of an advance payment of Rs 300 a metric ton upon delivery of the sugar to the broker, about four or five installment payments from October to February, and a final payment in June. The advance and installment payments are partially financed through bank advances, which reach a peak in September of approximately Rs 30 million and are reimbursed by April of the following year. Producers normally use the advance payments and installment payments to repay the credit they have obtained during the intercrop season from the brokers or, in the case of small planters, from the cooperative societies. In most cases, producers require new advance payments from the brokers before the end of the crop season, so that there is a continuous rollover of credit from one year to the next. The assets and liabilities of the commercial banks are shown in Table 16.

Development Bank

The Development Bank of Mauritius was established on March 1, 1964 (Ordinance No. 34 of 1963) to facilitate the industrial, agricultural, and economic development of Mauritius. It incorporated the business of the Mauritius Agricultural Bank, which had been in operation since 1936. The Development Bank's operations are largely in the form of long-term and medium-term loans, but it is also authorized to make equity investments in suitable cases. Furthermore, the Bank is prepared to give technical and financial advice and to assist in the preparation and initial study of agricultural and industrial projects.

The ability of the Development Bank to encourage sugar production is limited by the provision which restricts new loans to sugar planters to amounts repaid on previous loans. An experimental scheme for extending small industrial loans of up to Rs 5,000 has been established by the Bank under the supervision of the Minister of Education. Loans made by the Bank are normally secured by mortgages or fixed assets. In addition, for industrial loans exceeding Rs 2 million, the Bank requests government guarantees. Under existing legislation, the Bank is prevented from accepting as collateral equipment bought with the proceeds of its loans.

The Development Bank derives most of its resources from loans from the Government and public bond issues, but it also has at its dis-

posal resources in the form of savings and short-term deposits. The
Bank pays interest of 3½ per cent per annum on savings deposits and
5½ to 6½ per cent per annum on one-year and three-year deposits.
Loans from the Government, which amounted to Rs 23 million at the
end of June 1969 (Table 17), are extended through the capital budget
at an interest rate of 2½ per cent. Other long-term borrowing by the
Bank amounted to Rs 18 million at the end of June 1969 and consisted
of loans taken over from the Agricultural Bank, which carry interest
rates averaging 4½ per cent.

The lending operations of the Development Bank have not shown a
pronounced expansion in recent years. At the end of June 1969, long-
term loans outstanding stood at Rs 38.1 million, compared with
Rs 26.8 million on June 30, 1965. The largest share of the Bank's
resources is invested in loans to agriculture (Rs 22.5 million at the end
of June 1969). These loans, most of which had been made by the Agricultural Bank and largely to the sugar sector, are for ten years and bear
interest at 7½ per cent. It has been the policy of the Development
Bank in recent years to limit new loans to the sugar industry to the

TABLE 17. MAURITIUS: ASSETS AND LIABILITIES OF THE DEVELOPMENT
BANK OF MAURITIUS, JUNE 1965–JUNE 1969

(In millions of Mauritian rupees; end of period)

	June 1965	June 1966	June 1967	June 1968	June 1969
Assets					
Cash	2.6	1.7	1.5	1.1	0.8
Long-term loans	26.8	29.7	36.9	36.9	38.1
Agriculture[1]	*23.8*	*23.7*	*24.0*	*23.6*	*22.5*
Industry	*2.5*	*5.6*	*12.6*	*12.6*	*15.5*
Housing	*0.5*	*0.4*	*0.3*	*0.7*	—
Share participations	—	—	1.4	1.4	1.6
Industrial buildings	—	—	0.6	1.5	1.6
Other assets	5.0	5.5	4.6	8.2	12.0
Assets = liabilities	**34.4**	**36.9**	**45.0**	**49.1**	**54.1**
Liabilities					
Deposits	4.1	3.7	3.3	3.2	3.0
Long-term borrowing	23.6	26.1	32.9	36.7	41.0
From Government	*4.2*	*7.2*	*14.5*	*18.7*	*23.0*
Reserves	6.2	6.6	7.2	7.9	8.5
Other liabilities	0.5	0.5	1.6	1.3	1.6

Source: Development Bank of Mauritius, *Report and Accounts*, 1965–69.
[1] Including the tea industry.

equivalent of 50 per cent of repayments of existing loans to the industry. In this way, the Bank supports the efforts of the Government to diversify the economy and also accumulates sinking funds for the repayment of its borrowings from the private sector.

The Development Bank is also financing agricultural diversification, mainly projects related to tea growing and processing. At June 30, 1969, loans to industry amounted to Rs 15.5 million; these are generally extended for ten years, at interest rates ranging from 4½ to 7½ per cent, and include loans to local enterprises manufacturing razor blades, cardboard boxes, and other consumer goods. Outstanding investments in share participations and industrial buildings totaled Rs 3.2 million (Table 17).

Other Financial Institutions

The Mauritius Cooperative Central Bank was established in 1948 to perform banking activities and certain other services (including the marketing of goods) for its members, which essentially comprise registered cooperative societies. At the end of February 1969 there were 229 member societies of the bank, including credit and other societies representing about 12,000 sugar planters producing not less than 1,000 tons of cane. At that date, the bank's resources totaled Rs 11.2 million. Since 1950 the bank has been authorized to accept savings and time deposits both from its members and from the general public. As a result, deposits have grown fairly rapidly, reaching almost Rs 6 million in February 1969. The opening of current accounts was, until 1969, restricted to member societies, and deposits on current account amounted to only Rs 1.5 million at the close of 1968/69. In June 1969, however, the Banking Ordinance was amended to authorize the bank to accept demand deposits from the general public.

Most of the Cooperative Bank's operations take the form of loans for seasonal financing of the sugar crop. The bank lends up to 60 per cent of the value of the anticipated crop, based on an agreed price. This proportion is estimated by the bank to represent the cost of upkeep of land employed, including the cost of fertilizer. It also extends longer-term loans for the capital expenditures of sugar planters, secured by a signed bond assigning the land to the bank. At the end of February

1969, loans and advances outstanding amounted to Rs 6.9 million, including crop loans (Rs 4.7 million), medium-term loans for purchase and improvement of land (Rs 0.9 million), and housing loans (Rs 1.2 million). The volume of crop loans fluctuates widely, varying from about Rs 4 million in February to Rs 8 million in July, when the bank is obliged to supplement its own resources with advances from Barclays Bank.

The Mauritius Housing Corporation, established in 1962 to take over the housing credit activities of the Agricultural Bank, specializes in mortgage lending for low-cost housing. It provides long-term credit for up to 90 per cent of the purchase price, under a ceiling of Rs 30,000, at an interest rate of 8 per cent. Repayments, which may not exceed 25 per cent of the borrower's income, are deducted from salary. The corporation's loans totaled Rs 28 million at the end of 1967. They were financed by long-term borrowing, mainly from the Mauritian Government (Rs 15 million), the U. K. Government (Rs 3.5 million), and the Commonwealth Development Corporation (Rs 6.7 million). The Housing Corporation has recently concluded borrowing arrangements with insurance companies and the Sugar Pension Fund amounting to Rs 11 million, for 20 years, at interest of 7 per cent.

The Post Office Savings Bank is operated by the Post and Telegraph Department through 32 post offices in the country. Savings deposits, which since April 1969 earn 4 per cent a year (previously 2½ per cent), have remained fairly stable in recent years, at Rs 29 million. Deposits are limited to Rs 7,000 a year, with an overall limit of Rs 20,000. The funds collected by the Post Office Savings Bank are deposited exclusively with the Treasury (under Special Funds), which is responsible for their utilization.

According to the provisions of the Post Office Savings Bank (Amendment) Ordinance of 1968, investments in government securities are limited to 40 per cent of the total assets of the bank. The other assets of the bank are invested in foreign securities or kept in deposits at call in London. At the end of June 1969, the foreign investments of the bank were valued at Rs 18.9 million (market value). However, in August 1969, the foreign assets of the Post Office Savings Bank were sold to the Bank of Mauritius in exchange for rupees, in accordance with government policy. The proceeds of the sale were placed on deposit with the Bank of Mauritius to the account of the Post Office Savings Bank, and will attract interest at a rate 1 per cent lower than the discount rate. The Post Office Savings Bank also maintains a Reserve Account, equal to almost 15 per cent of its deposits. Under the Post Office Savings Bank Ordinance of 1950, the Government may require the transfer of any profits that bring the bank's reserves above 15 per cent of its liabilities.

STRUCTURE OF INTEREST RATES

All of the commercial banks operating in Mauritius have adhered to an interbank agreement which sets out common and fixed rates of interest to be charged for loans and advances, as well as bank charges and commissions, and the maximum interest rates to be paid on deposits. As of December 1970, interest rates on loans ranged from 7½ per cent to 9½ per cent per annum, and interest on deposits varied from 4 per cent for savings accounts to 5¼ per cent for 12-month deposits. The agreement does not cover the interest rate to be paid on fixed deposits of more than 12 months, but the volume of such deposits has so far been small. While the interbank agreement prevents banks from competing in terms of interest charges, it leaves them free to compete in terms of services.

MONETARY AND CREDIT DEVELOPMENTS, 1965–70

Monetary and credit developments in Mauritius display a marked seasonality, arising principally from requirements for crop financing. Bank credit to the economy expands during the first six months of the year, reaches a peak in June–September when the sugarcane is harvested and processed, and declines to a seasonal low in December. At the peak of the sugar season, loans to the agricultural sector account for nearly 50 per cent of outstanding loans and advances, declining to about 30 per cent in December. Credit to commerce is less subject to seasonal variation and accounts for one third of the total. Loans to manufacturing comprise about 10 per cent of total bank credit.

Because of the seasonal variations in bank credit, the commercial banks borrow fairly large amounts of funds from overseas to support their lending activities at the peak of seasonal demand, and invest substantial amounts overseas when seasonal demand for credit is at its lowest point. During January–June, the commercial banks supplement their local deposits by Rs 30–45 million by borrowing from external sources, principally the head offices of the foreign banks operating in Mauritius. After September, the banks begin to repay these liabilities, and by December their net foreign assets are generally at their highest annual level.

Over the three years 1965–67 bank credit rose by 24 per cent (Table 18). Credit to the private sector, consisting mainly of loans and advances, increased by 15 per cent, to Rs 185.2 million. Net credit to the Government, mainly from the Currency Fund, appears to have increased from Rs 24.4 million to Rs 43.8 million, but the figures do not include changes in government deposits with commercial banks, for which separate data for this period are not available. The expansion in total bank credit was accompanied by a decline in the net foreign assets of the banking system, which fell from Rs 135.5 million in 1965 to Rs 111.8 million in 1967, and by a 5 per cent increase in the money supply, which rose to Rs 233.5 million.

In the two years 1968–69, total bank credit rose at a rate of 5 per cent a year. In 1968, credit to the private sector and net credit to the Government rose at about the same rate. In 1969, the rate of increase in net credit to the Government was more than three times that of credit to the private sector, resulting mainly from larger holdings of government securities by commercial banks whereas net credit by the Bank of Mauritius continued to decline. Total net foreign assets of the banking system, which fell slightly in 1968, rose by 80 per cent in 1969, to Rs 199 million. In 1968, the decline of 43 per cent in the commercial banks' net foreign assets was partially offset by a 21 per cent increase in the foreign assets of the Bank of Mauritius (see Tables 15 and 16). This increase resulted from the transfer to the Bank of the foreign exchange holdings (Rs 21.0 million) of the Cyclone and Drought Insurance Fund. During 1969, net foreign assets of both the commercial banks and the Bank of Mauritius rose sharply. For commercial banks, the improvement reflected an increase in assets as well as a reduction in liabilities. In addition to the large surplus in the balance of payments, the substantial increase in the net foreign assets of the Bank of Mauritius reflected the transfer to the Bank of the foreign exchange holdings of

TABLE 18. MAURITIUS: MONETARY SURVEY, 1965–70

(In millions of Mauritian rupees; end of period)

					1969				1970			
	1965	1966	1967	1968	Mar.	June	Sept.	Dec.	Mar.	June	Sept.	Dec.
Assets												
Foreign assets (net)	135.5	139.2	111.8	110.5	113.1	54.9	126.4	199.0	213.6	186.9	226.1	270.2
Claims on government (net)	24.4	27.1	43.8	46.4	57.0	55.0	48.5	51.7	24.3	35.6	32.1	49.9
Claims on private sector	160.9	163.9	185.2	194.5	187.5	222.3	194.2	201.5	208.7	222.9	204.4	214.4
Assets = liabilities	320.8	330.2	340.8	351.4	357.6	332.2	369.1	452.2	446.6	445.4	462.6	534.5
Liabilities												
Money	221.6	241.8	233.5	195.3	204.3	183.0	205.1	224.3	201.6	203.3	215.6	240.1
Currency outside banks	93.2	93.0	93.3	89.2	82.8	79.1	84.2	97.2	89.9	86.3	93.2	104.7
Demand deposits	128.4	148.8	140.2	106.1	121.5	103.9	120.9	127.1	111.7	117.0	122.4	135.4
Quasi-money [1]	70.4	56.2	72.2	119.6	126.2	119.2	144.4	186.4	209.7	190.4	216.2	279.9
Other items (net)	28.8	32.2	35.1	36.5	27.2	29.9	19.6	41.5	35.3	51.7	30.8	14.5

Sources: Bank of Mauritius, *Quarterly Review*; and data provided by the Bank of Mauritius.

[1] Time and savings deposits.

the Government and of certain official entities. In that year, the foreign
assets of the Bank of Mauritius were augmented by the transfer of the
foreign assets of the Post Office Savings Bank (Rs 19.7 million) and
of certain assets of the Government and the Sugar Industry Labour Welfare Fund, totaling Rs 16.4 million. The Bank's foreign assets also benefited from a drawing on the International Monetary Fund equivalent to
Rs 22.2 million in April 1969. The money supply, which fell by 16 per
cent in 1968, rose by 15 per cent in the following year. Quasi-money
increased substantially in each of the two years, reflecting in part the
counterpart liability of the repatriation and transfer to the Bank of
Mauritius of the foreign exchange holdings mentioned above.

In 1970, net credit to the Government fell by 3.5 per cent: net credit
by the Bank of Mauritius declined by Rs 32 million, whereas that by
commercial banks rose by almost the same amount, reflecting a substantial increase in their holdings of government securities. As a whole,
total bank credit rose by 4 per cent during the year and was accompanied by a sharp expansion in net foreign assets, reflecting a marked
improvement in the balance of payments. The money supply rose by
only 7 per cent, and quasi-money increased by 50 per cent.[2]

BALANCE OF PAYMENTS

In recent years the balance of payments of Mauritius has been subject to sizable fluctuations because of swings in the trade balance,
reflecting mainly variations in earnings from sugar exports and the
lagged effect of these earnings on imports (Table 19).

In 1965 there was an overall deficit of $11.9 million as a result of a
marked deterioration in the trade balance. In 1966 a surplus of $4.9
million was achieved, mainly because of the reappearance of a trade
surplus ($8.4 million) and of an extraordinary receipt in respect of
central government transfer payments. But in 1967 the balance of payments deteriorated by $19.9 million, largely because of the worsening
of the trade balance (by $13.9 million). In each of the following two

---

[2] The reader is referred to the International Monetary Fund's monthly statistical
bulletin, *International Financial Statistics,* for later information on monetary and
credit developments.

TABLE 19. MAURITIUS: BALANCE OF PAYMENTS, 1965–70

(*In millions of U. S. dollars*)

	1965	1966	1967	1968	1969	1970 [1]
A. Goods and services	**−10.1**	**−1.9**	**−15.2**	**−5.4**	**4.7**	**3.5**
Exports f.o.b.	66.8	71.0	63.1	64.6	66.1	68.0
Sugar and products	*62.1*	*66.8*	*60.9*	*59.9*	*60.5*	...
Imports f.o.b. [2]	−67.2	−62.6	−68.6	−64.9	−59.2	−64.9
Trade balance	−0.4	8.4	−5.5	−0.3	7.0	3.1
Freight and insurance	−9.9	−8.4	−10.0	−7.7	−7.4	−8.1
Other transportation	—	—	1.3	2.6	2.5	0.9
Travel	−3.2	−2.9	−1.9	−1.5	0.1	1.1
Investment income	−1.2	−0.4	−1.2	−0.7	−0.2	1.5
Other government	1.0	1.6	1.8	1.7	1.5	2.2
Other services	3.6	−0.2	0.3	0.5	1.2	2.8
B. Unrequited transfers	**−1.3**	**7.2**	**1.2**	**4.4**	**2.6**	**2.8**
Private	−2.4	−1.9	−1.4	−0.9	0.3	0.7
Central Government	1.1	9.1 [3]	2.6	5.3	2.3	2.1
Total A + B	**−11.4**	**5.3**	**−14.0**	**−1.0**	**7.3**	**6.3**
C. Capital movements	**−2.3**	**1.9**	**2.7**	**2.8**	**2.4**	**1.7**
Private	−1.0	—	−1.0	−0.5	2.8	1.1
Central Government	−1.3	1.9	3.7	3.3	−0.4	0.6
D. Other capital, and errors and omissions	**1.8**	**−2.3**	**−3.7**	**1.6**	**0.6**	**2.6**
E. SDR allocation	**—**	**—**	**—**	**—**	**—**	**2.7**
Total A through E	**−11.9**	**4.9**	**−15.0**	**3.4**	**10.3**	**13.3**
F. Monetary sectors [4]	**11.9**	**−4.9**	**15.0**	**−3.4**	**−10.3**	**−13.3**
Commercial banks	10.6	−1.5	4.7	3.1	−3.2	3.6
Central institutions	1.3	−3.4	10.3	−6.5	−7.1	−16.9

Sources: IMF, *Balance of Payments Yearbook;* and data provided by the Bank of Mauritius.

[1] Provisional.
[2] Including nonmonetary gold.
[3] Including compensation for the sale of the Chagos Islands to the United Kingdom.
[4] There are some overall discrepancies between these figures and those that may be derived from the monetary data (Table 18) and the exchange reserves data (Table 24) which cannot be reconciled.

years the trade balance improved, and there were overall balance of payments surpluses of $3.4 million and $10.3 million, respectively. Because of the special arrangements regarding sugar exports, the devaluation of the rupee at the end of 1967 appears to have had little direct effect on the 1968 balance of payments. Rather, imports declined by 5 per cent and the net deficit on services account was substantially reduced, partly on account of higher earnings from invisibles, particularly in respect of increased bunkering and other services for ships after the closing of the Suez Canal. Also, the surplus on transfers rose substantially as a result of a budgetary grant of $3.1 million from the

United Kingdom. In addition to the large trade surplus in 1969, the further decline in the deficit on the services account contributed to the overall surplus. In 1970, despite a 10 per cent increase in imports, the trade balance registered a surplus of $3.1 million. This, combined with the elimination of the deficit on the services account, contributed to the overall balance of payments surplus of about $13 million (including the allocation of SDR 2.7 million).

TRADE

The balance of trade of Mauritius has fluctuated in recent years. Variations in the size of the sugar crop and in sugar prices have caused fluctuations in exports, while the lagged effect of sugar export earnings on expenditure has been an important determinant of imports. Another important factor affecting the balance of trade in recent years has been a worsening in the terms of trade, which have deteriorated sharply since 1963 as export prices have declined and import prices have increased steadily (Table 20). In 1968 the deterioration in the terms of trade was largely the result of higher prices for imports of rice and wheat flour and the 14.3 per cent devaluation of the Mauritian rupee in November 1967.

Exports, as registered by the customs, reached a record high value of Rs 427.8 million in 1963, owing to a large volume of sugar exports at favorable prices. In subsequent years exports declined considerably, falling to Rs 354 million in 1968 (about 17 per cent below the 1963 level), but recovered to Rs 365 million in 1969 (Table 21). Sugar and

TABLE 20.   MAURITIUS: INDICES OF VOLUME AND PRICES OF EXPORTS
AND IMPORTS, AND TERMS OF TRADE, 1963–68

(1965 = 100)

	Exports		Imports		Terms of Trade
	Volume	Prices	Volume	Prices	
1963	100	136	97	93	146
1964	99	118	111	95	124
1965	100	100	100	100	100
1966	103	105	90	100	105
1967	91	108	99	102	106
1968	106	106	98	117	91

Sources: Central Statistical Office, *Bi-Annual Digest of Statistics;* and data provided by the Mauritian authorities.

TABLE 21. MAURITIUS: COMPOSITION OF TRADE, 1963–69 [1]

(*In millions of Mauritian rupees*)

	1963	1964	1965	1966	1967	1968	1969
Exports f.o.b.	**427.8**	**366.9**	**313.4**	**337.6**	**306.8**	**354.0**	**365.2**
Sugar	400.2	344.2	290.3	306.4	281.3	320.7	326.0
Molasses	13.5	8.8	5.0	11.5	8.5	11.9	10.1
Tea	5.5	4.4	5.9	6.5	8.4	9.6	14.6
Other	1.8	2.5	2.2	4.1	2.4	4.0	7.6
Re-exports	6.8	7.0	9.9	9.0	6.1	7.7	7.0
Imports c.i.f.	**333.1**	**388.9**	**367.3**	**333.2**	**371.1**	**421.1**	**376.0**
Foodstuffs	94.7	105.9	108.0	109.6	118.5	135.5	132.6
Rice	*38.3*	*39.2*	*39.3*	*37.5*	*44.2*	*55.7*	*54.9*
Wheat flour	*12.1*	*13.5*	*14.4*	*13.1*	*15.3*	*17.6*	*23.0*
Beverages and tobacco	7.9	7.4	6.8	4.9	4.8	5.7	5.3
Animal and vegetable oils and fats	12.1	11.3	14.9	17.7	18.3	18.5	12.5
Raw materials	5.6	6.5	6.7	5.4	7.1	7.8	5.6
Fuels, lubricants, etc.	14.2	17.0	17.7	15.4	25.4	35.9	31.7
Chemicals	39.7	46.4	47.1	45.6	42.6	49.0	43.0
Manufactured goods	70.8	88.5	78.6	70.2	78.5	77.6	72.4
Machinery and transport equipment	55.7	70.3	56.3	36.9	43.7	56.5	44.7
Miscellaneous manufactures	31.7	35.5	31.0	27.4	32.1	34.6	27.9
Other	0.8	0.1	0.3	0.2	0.1	0.1	0.2

Source: Central Statistical Office, *Bi-Annual Digest of Statistics.*
[1] Components may not add to totals because of rounding.

sugar by-products account for about 95 per cent of total exports. Exports of tea have increased in recent years, but they still represent only about 4 per cent of all exports. The bulk of export receipts is received toward the end of the year when sugar is shipped. About two thirds of the sugar is sold under the Commonwealth Sugar Agreement to the United Kingdom, and under other arrangements, at preferential prices. As noted above, Mauritius is also a party to the International Sugar Agreement.

Imports c.i.f., which in 1963 totaled Rs 333 million, rose to Rs 389 million in 1964, fell back in the subsequent two years, rose in 1967 and 1968, but declined to Rs 376 million in 1969. Foodstuffs, beverages and tobacco, and oils and fats account for about 40 per cent of all imports. In 1969, rice alone was equivalent to about 15 per cent of the total. Other important groups were manufactured goods (19 per cent), machinery and transport equipment (12 per cent), and chemicals (11 per cent).

On average, about 80 per cent of exports go to the United Kingdom. Canada is the second largest purchaser, followed by the United States

TABLE 22.   MAURITIUS: DIRECTION OF TRADE, 1963–69

(*In per cent of total value*)

	1963	1964	1965	1966	1967	1968	1969
Exports							
United Kingdom	69	76	78	82	87	77	71
Canada	15	15	10	9	3	12	17
United States	11	1	4	5	5	6	5
Other	5	8	8	4	5	5	7
Total	100	100	100	100	100	100	100
Imports							
United Kingdom	28	29	27	24	21	24	20
EEC	9	8	10	12	12	12	11
Burma	10	7	6	7	7	10	2
South Africa	9	8	9	8	8	7	8
Australia	6	8	6	7	7	6	7
India	4	4	3	3	2	3	3
Japan	3	4	4	4	4	3	4
Iran	3	3	3	3	5	3	5
Thailand	1	3	5	4	4	2	12
Hong Kong	4	3	3	3	3	2	2
Other	23	23	24	25	27	28	26
Total	100	100	100	100	100	100	100

Source: Central Statistical Office, *Bi-Annual Digest of Statistics.*

(Table 22). Imports from the United Kingdom account for about 25 per cent of the total on average. Imports from the European Economic Community (mainly France and Germany) increased from 9 per cent in 1963 to about 12 per cent in 1966–69. Other important sources are South Africa and Burma, the latter being the main supplier of rice. Rice is imported in bulk by the Government and generally on a cash basis.

CURRENT INVISIBLES

The deficit on the services account, which was about $10 million in the three years 1965–67, was gradually eliminated and in 1970 a small surplus of $0.4 million was achieved. The closing of the Suez Canal at the end of 1967 resulted in a greater number of ships calling at Port Louis and hence greater earnings in respect of bunkering and other services to ships. Improvements in the other items of the services account also contributed to the reduction of the deficit, and there was improvement in respect of travel, resulting from some increase in tourism in Mauritius and reduced overseas leave by Mauritian public servants. The reintroduction of exchange controls in 1966 also affected the travel account.

The large surplus in respect of transfer payments in 1966 was due to the receipt from the United Kingdom of compensation for the sale of the Chagos Islands. Also included under government transfer receipts are budgetary, development, and technical assistance grants, while government transfer payments include payments in respect of pensions. The deficits in private transfer payments in 1965–68 reflected mainly transfers by those leaving the country as emigrants and transfers in respect of lotteries and pools.

PRIVATE CAPITAL AND OFFICIAL LOANS AND GRANTS

The balance on net capital account has improved over the past few years, owing mainly to higher capital receipts by the Government. These have basically consisted of loans from the U. K. Government and from the Commonwealth Development Corporation (Table 23). In

TABLE 23.   MAURITIUS: AID FROM UNITED KINGDOM, 1965/66–1968/69 [1]

(In thousands of pounds sterling)

	Disbursements			
	1965/66	1966/67	1967/68	1968/69
Grants				
Technical assistance	120	132	243	215
Budgetary	—	—	750	550
Development	144	162	1,003	904
Disaster relief	156	—	88	—
Food aid	—	—	—	166
	420	294	2,084	1,835
Loans				
Development	—	480	775	626
Compensation	—	—	—	29
Commutation	—	—	—	45
Disaster relief	1,050	—	175	—
	1,050	480	950	700
Total grants and loans	1,470	774	3,034	2,535
Investment by Commonwealth Development Corporation	125	125	150	53

Source: Data provided by the U. K. Ministry of Overseas Development.
[1] U. K. financial years (April–March).

1965 there was a heavy net capital outflow in respect of direct investment, but since then capital movements for this purpose have been
much smaller.

EXTERNAL DEBT

At the end of June 1969, Mauritius's external debt amounted to the
equivalent of about $31 million. With the exception of the World Bank
loan, the debt was denominated in pounds sterling. The repayment
schedule calls for fairly stable debt service payments of $3–4 million a
year for the next five years. The debt service ratio (i.e., debt service as
a proportion of receipts from goods and services) was equal to about 4
per cent in 1969 and was expected to remain about the same in 1970.
For further details, see Public Debt, above (pp. 339–43).

INTERNATIONAL RESERVES

Mauritius's foreign exchange reserves are subject to pronounced seasonal fluctuations: they reach a peak in October–November, when most
of the receipts from sugar exports are received, and a trough during
March–September. The seasonal decline in the official exchange
reserves has so far been moderated by borrowing abroad by commercial
banks.

The balance of payments deficits in 1965 and 1967 were financed
by drawing down the foreign exchange holdings of the monetary authorities, and by variations in the foreign assets and liabilities of the commercial banks. By the end of 1968, the gross foreign assets of the Bank of
Mauritius had fallen to $16 million, from $18.3 million at the end of
1965 (Table 24). The declining foreign reserve position led the authorities to draw $4 million from the International Monetary Fund (IMF)
in April 1969 in order to strengthen confidence in the currency while
corrective financial measures were being implemented to redress the
balance of payments position. Reflecting this drawing and the impact
of the measures that were taken, as well as the transfer to the Bank of
Mauritius of the foreign assets of the Post Office Savings Bank ($3.5
million), the Accountant General's capital and revenue accounts ($2.0
million), and the Sugar Industry Labour Welfare Fund ($0.9 million),
the gross foreign exchange position had recovered to $32.4 million at

TABLE 24. MAURITIUS: FOREIGN EXCHANGE RESERVES, 1965–70

(In millions of U. S. dollars; end of period)

	1965	1966	1967	1968	1969	1970
Assets						
Bank of Mauritius [1]	18.3	17.6	13.3	16.0	32.4	44.4
Post Office Savings Bank	6.1	6.3	4.2	4.2	— [2]	—
Commercial banks	13.0	12.3	9.8	7.4	8.5	6.2
Total	37.4	36.2	27.3	27.6	40.9	50.6
Liabilities						
Bank of Mauritius [3]	—	—	—	—	4.0	—
Commercial banks	2.9	0.7	2.9	3.6	1.1	1.9
Total	2.9	0.7	2.9	3.6	5.1	1.9
Total net reserves	34.5	35.5	24.4	24.0	35.8	48.7

Source: Data provided by the Bank of Mauritius.
[1] Figures for 1965–66 relate to the former Currency Fund.
[2] The foreign assets of the Post Office Savings Bank were taken over by the Bank of Mauritius in August 1969.
[3] Liabilities in 1969 consist of a drawing on the International Monetary Fund.

the end of 1969. In spite of the discharge of a repurchase obligation to the IMF in the amount of $4 million in August 1970, the gross foreign assets of the Bank of Mauritius increased to $44.4 million at the end of December 1970 (including the allocation, on January 1, 1970, of SDR 2.7 million). The gross foreign assets of the commercial banks declined from $13 million at the end of 1965 to $6.2 million at the end of 1970.

A substantial part of official foreign exchange reserves is held in sterling securities, and the level of reserves is subject to autonomous changes resulting from fluctuations in the market prices of these securities. The Bank of Mauritius revalues all its foreign assets at the end of each month on the basis of the market values of the securities held. The foreign assets outside the control of the Bank of Mauritius are revalued once a year.

EXCHANGE AND TRADE CONTROL SYSTEM [3]

Mauritius maintains a relatively liberal system of trade and current payments. The basic exchange control legislation is the Exchange Con-

---

[3] As of December 31, 1970. The reader is referred to the International Monetary Fund's *Annual Report on Exchange Restrictions* for later and more detailed information on exchange and trade controls.

trol Ordinance of 1951 (which was based on the U. K. Exchange Control Act of 1947) and the amendments to that ordinance. Quantitative restrictions are applied to imports of certain commodities. There are certain restrictions on current payments for invisibles. Mauritius is a member of the sterling area, but settlements with other sterling area countries are subject to exchange control. Special regulations apply to settlements with Rhodesia.

EXCHANGE RATE SYSTEM

No par value for the Mauritian rupee has been established with the International Monetary Fund. The official rate is Re 1 = £0.075, corresponding to Re 1 = $0.18. The rates of the Bank of Mauritius for sterling are Rs 13.31⅔ buying and Rs 13.36⅔ selling per £1. Commercial banks are authorized to deal with customers in sterling at spot rates based on the rates of the Bank of Mauritius, and in other foreign currencies at rates based on the London market rates (foreign currencies are defined as all currencies other than the Mauritian rupee). An additional effective rate results from the application of a stamp duty of 35.70 per cent to outward capital transfers other than transfers of banking funds and to payments for gold coins and gold bullion.

REGULATIONS GOVERNING IMPORTS AND EXPORTS

Imports from Rhodesia are prohibited. There is a list of commodities for which a specific license from the Ministry of Commerce and Industry is required regardless of origin. Some 75–80 per cent of the domestic market for most of these commodities is reserved for local producers, leaving the remainder for imports, in order to protect and encourage the development of domestic industry and promote diversification of the economy. Rice and wheat flour are imported by the Government. All other goods may be imported freely from the sterling area by individual traders under open general licenses; but most of these require a specific license when imported from outside the sterling area. General licenses are granted liberally; specific licenses are issued on the basis of domestic requirements. The issue of a license, whether general or specific, carries with it authorization to make the corresponding import payments.

Exports to Rhodesia are prohibited. Special permission from the Financial Secretary is required for exports of articles made wholly or partially of gold, platinum, or silver; diamonds, pearls, other precious and semiprecious stones, and articles mounted with these; and works of art. All exports valued at more than Rs 1,000 and all exports of food valued at more than Rs 50 require a license from the Ministry of Commerce and Industry. The Mauritius Sugar Syndicate is the sole exporter of sugar, and a 6 per cent export tax is levied on sugar exports. The proceeds of exports in any currency other than Mauritian rupees must be offered for sale to an authorized exchange dealer.

REGULATIONS GOVERNING INVISIBLES

Exchange to pay for invisibles related to imports and, up to certain limits, for certain other purposes is provided by the commercial banks without prior reference to the exchange control authorities. The basic allowance for tourist travel is the equivalent of £250 a person a year. The allowance for business travel is the equivalent of £250 a trip or £20 a day up to a maximum of £1,000 a trip for travel in the sterling area, or up to a maximum of £750 a trip for travel to countries outside the sterling area. Requests for more than £250 for a business trip must be referred to the Bank of Mauritius. Payments and transfers to the sterling area and to other countries for many other invisibles— such as salary remittances by foreigners, trade commissions, royalties, and expenses of education—are also subject to established limits. In all cases, however, applications for amounts exceeding the standard allocations may be submitted to the exchange control authorities. Resident and nonresident travelers may take out Rs 350 in domestic currency. Resident travelers may take out foreign currency notes up to the amount of their travel allowance. Nonresident travelers may take out any foreign currency which they declared upon entry.

Receipts from invisibles in any currency other than Mauritian rupees must be offered for sale to an authorized bank. Any amount of foreign notes and coins may be imported by travelers, but not more than Rs 700 in domestic notes and coins.

CAPITAL TRANSFERS

Inward transfers of capital are not restricted; outward transfers are subject to certain restrictions. Residents of Mauritius (other than banks) may transfer a reasonable amount of capital to any country in the sterling area on payment of a 35.70 per cent stamp duty (a duty of 34 per cent plus a surcharge of 5 per cent thereon); subject to permission, which is freely granted, they may also transfer a reasonable amount of capital to countries outside the sterling area on payment of the stamp duty, provided, normally, that the transfer is made through the investment currency market in the United Kingdom. Nonresidents must have permission to transfer capital to any country. Such transfers are also subject to the stamp duty and, if directed to a country outside the sterling area by a resident of the sterling area, must normally be made through the investment currency market in the United Kingdom. Foreign-owned companies may freely transfer abroad dividends, profits, and interest on capital. Permission to repatriate is not granted for capital brought in before April 5, 1966, irrespective of the country of origin, but is, in normal circumstances, given for capital brought in on or after that date. Proceeds from the sale, liquidation, etc., of foreign capital that may not be repatriated must be credited to a blocked account with an authorized bank in Mauritius.

Emigrants may take out, at the official rate of exchange and free of stamp duty, the equivalent of Rs 67,000 from their Mauritian assets when emigrating to any country except Rhodesia; this facility is available when the emigrant is designated a nonresident, which occurs upon departure. The balance of an emigrant's funds must be credited for an indefinite period to a blocked account and may be transferred only with special permission and subject to payment of the stamp duty. Persons emigrating from Mauritius are not entitled to draw their personal travel allowance in addition to the emigration facilities.

GOLD

Residents other than the monetary authorities are permitted to hold gold only in the form of numismatic coins or personal jewelry and ornaments. Monetary gold may not be imported or exported except by the monetary authorities. Imports of gold for industrial purposes are subject to quota and specific import license. Exports of articles made wholly or partially of gold, other than jewelry constituting the personal effects of a traveler, are prohibited. Payments in respect of private imports of gold coins and gold bullion are subject to the stamp duty.

TRADE AND PAYMENTS ARRANGEMENTS

Mauritius maintains no bilateral payments agreements.

CHAPTER 6

Zambia

GENERAL SETTING

The Republic of Zambia is a landlocked country in southern Africa, bounded on the south by Mozambique, Rhodesia, Botswana, and South-West Africa (Namibia), on the west by Angola, on the north by the Democratic Republic of Congo, and on the east by Tanzania and Malawi. The country covers 290,586 square miles and consists of undulating plateaus which range in altitude from 3,000 feet to 4,500 feet. Zambia is drained by the Zambezi River and its two great tributaries, the Luangwa and the Kafue. In the northeast, the Chambeshi River runs into Lake Bangweulu and this in turn flows into Lake Mweru through the Luapula River (see map). The Luangwa and lower Zambezi Rivers, below Victoria Falls, flow in deep, hot valleys through broken, arid country. The climate is tropical, with three distinct seasons: hot from August to November; wet from November to April; and cool from May to July. The annual rainfall varies from 25 to 50 inches, depending on the altitude.

The country is divided into eight administrative provinces: Copperbelt, Central, Eastern,

North-Western, Luapula, Northern, Southern, and Western. The capital city of Lusaka, in Central province, has a population of approximately 354,000 (1971). Other large towns include Kitwe, Ndola, Mufulira, and Luanshya.

The population was estimated at 4.1 million in 1969, of which 50,000 were Europeans and 10,000 were Asians. Owing to a rapidly increasing population—the birth rate remains high and the mortality rate is falling—almost 55 per cent of the people are under 20 years of age. A birth rate of 4.2 per cent per annum and a death rate of 1.7 per cent result in an annual rate of natural growth of about 2.5 per cent. The average density is about 14 inhabitants to the square mile, but the population is not evenly distributed. Economic activity is concentrated in the Copperbelt, near the Congolese border, and along the "line of rail," which is the central area of the country between the Copperbelt and Livingstone in the south. About half of the population lives in Copperbelt province and in Central and Southern provinces near the line of rail. The main languages are Bantu dialects.

In June 1968 there were 2,527 primary schools attended by about 610,000 pupils, of whom 270,000 were girls. There were 22 unaided primary schools, 109 secondary schools, 10 teacher-training colleges, and the University of Zambia. In 1968 government expenditure on education was about K 52.5 million. In 1969, enrollment in primary schools reached 660,000, in secondary schools 48,000, and in university almost 1,300.

Zambia, formerly Northern Rhodesia and a part of the Federation of Rhodesia and Nyasaland, became an independent republic on October 24, 1964. It was admitted to the United Nations on December 1, 1964. On September 23, 1965, it joined the International Monetary Fund (quota on May 31, 1971, $76 million), the International Bank for Reconstruction and Development (capital subscription on May 31, 1971, $53.3 million), the International Development Association, and the International Finance Corporation. It is a member of the Commonwealth, maintains a *de facto* application of the General Agreement on Tariffs and Trade, and is also a member of the African Development Bank, the Food and Agriculture Organization of the United Nations, the United Nations Economic Commission for Africa, and the United Nations Educational, Scientific and Cultural Organization.

TABLE 1. ZAMBIA: GROSS DOMESTIC PRODUCT AT CURRENT PRICES, 1964–69

	1964	1965	1966	1967	1968[1]	1969[1]	1964	1968[1]	1969[1]
	(Million Zambian kwacha)						(Per cent of total)		
Agriculture, forestry, and fishing	53.3	54.8	60.5	66.3	63.1	74.6	11.0	7.0	6.3
Mining and quarrying [2]	239.6	273.7	356.3	352.2	395.7	593.0	49.5	42.3	49.8
Manufacturing	28.2	40.0	60.2	73.2	78.2	84.5	5.8	8.4	7.1
Construction	20.0	39.4	54.0	55.9	67.0	76.0	4.1	7.2	6.4
Electricity and water	5.0	5.3	7.4	8.1	8.9	9.3	1.0	0.9	0.7
Transport and communications	20.6	32.4	32.4	49.4	53.9	54.4	4.3	5.7	4.6
Commerce (distribution)	45.8	71.3	78.3	96.0	105.0	134.0	9.5	11.2	11.3
Financial institutions and insurance	0.6	10.7	11.5	15.8	15.2	15.8	0.1	1.6	1.3
Government administration	21.2	30.4	35.7	42.1	51.1	} 148.4	4.4	5.4	} 12.5
Real estate	10.6	9.2	15.2	18.9	20.9		2.2	2.2	
Community and business services	19.6	34.1	34.6	55.1	59.3		4.1	6.3	
Personal services	19.2	12.1	14.6	15.7	15.9		4.0	1.8	
Gross domestic product	483.7	613.4	760.7	848.7	934.2	1,190.0	100.0	100.0	100.0

Sources: Central Statistical Office, Monthly Digest of Statistics; and data provided by the Zambian authorities.

[1] Preliminary.
[2] Includes royalty payments and copper export tax.

The unit of currency is the kwacha, which is divided into 100 ngwee and the par value of which, agreed with the International Monetary Fund on January 16, 1968, is K 1 = US$1.40. The currency is issued by the Bank of Zambia.

Zambia's economy is based on mineral production, which contributes over two fifths of the gross domestic product and nine tenths of the country's foreign exchange earnings, and employs about 16 per cent of the labor force. Copper accounts for more than 90 per cent of mineral production; other minerals include zinc, lead, cobalt, and manganese, all of which are exported, and (recently) coal. Agriculture is also a vital sector, as it provides employment for more than three fourths of the population. The main obstacles to Zambia's economic development are inadequate transport routes to the sea and lack of trained manpower, though notable progress has been made in these areas.

STRUCTURE OF THE ECONOMY

GROSS DOMESTIC PRODUCT

Zambia's gross domestic product (GDP) is influenced by developments in the mining sector, which during the five years 1965–69 accounted on average for 45 per cent of GDP (Table 1). In 1969 the main sectors contributing to GDP were mining (50 per cent), commerce (11 per cent), construction, transport, and communications (11 per cent), manufacturing (7 per cent), and agriculture (6 per cent). Per capita income was estimated at the equivalent of $218 in 1969.

At current prices, GDP rose by 27 per cent in 1969—compared with an average annual increase of 18 per cent during the four preceding years—reflecting in part a 12 per cent increase in copper output concurrent with an 18 per cent rise in the price on the London Metal Exchange. Output in the agricultural and manufacturing sectors rose by 18 per cent and 8 per cent, respectively, in 1969. In 1970 and 1971, GDP at current prices was expected to decline marginally, as gains in sectors other than mining were expected to be offset by a reduction in the contribution of the mining sector, owing to the flooding of a mine that usually accounts for about 25 per cent of copper output and to a decline in copper prices.

TABLE 2. ZAMBIA: SUPPLY AND USE OF RESOURCES AT CURRENT PRICES, 1964–69

(In millions of Zambian kwacha)

	1964	1965	1966	1967	1968	1969[1]
Resources						
GDP at market prices	502.1	649.8	782.3	891.1	989.7	1,250.0
GDP at factor cost	*483.7*	*613.4*	*760.7*	*848.7*	*934.2*	*1,190.0*
Indirect taxes net of subsidies [2]	*18.4*	*36.4*	*21.5*	*42.4*	*55.5*	*60.0*
Imports of goods and services	213.9	262.7	335.4	416.3	470.4	444.6
Total resources	716.0	912.5	1,117.7	1,307.4	1,460.1	1,694.6
Use of resources						
Domestic consumption	309.2	383.4	435.8	558.0	614.6	662.0
Public	*59.4*	*83.2*	*86.2*	*114.6*	*126.6*	*149.0*
Private	*249.8*	*300.2*	*349.6*	*443.4*	*488.0*	*513.0*
Gross fixed investment	76.2	120.4	175.8	225.3	244.8	232.0
Public	*17.4*	*26.4*	*57.7*	*73.4*	*80.3*	*...*
Private [3]	*58.8*	*94.0*	*118.1*	*151.9*	*164.5*	*...*
Net change in stocks [3]	−18.8	35.5	50.4	48.9	56.2	14.7
Gross domestic expenditure	366.6	539.3	662.0	832.2	915.6	908.7
Exports of goods and services	355.2	373.2	455.7	475.2	544.5	785.9
Total use of resources	721.8 [4]	912.5	1,117.7	1,307.4	1,460.1	1,694.6
National income						
GDP at factor cost	483.7	613.4	760.7	848.7	934.2	1,190.0
Less net factor payments abroad	*69.1*	*45.5*	*58.0*	*50.6*	*52.1*	*59.0*
Gross national product at factor cost	414.6	567.9	702.7	798.1	882.1	1,131.0
Less capital depreciation	*28.4*	*38.6*	*40.6*	*49.6*	*59.8*	*53.4*
Net national income	386.2	529.3	662.1	748.5	822.3	1,077.6
Subsistence income	*34.1*	*35.9*	*40.2*	*44.6*	*49.1*	*50.0*
Wages and salaries	*201.8*	*244.4*	*281.9*	*349.6*	*387.4*	*...*

Sources: Central Statistical Office, *Monthly Digest of Statistics*; Ministry of Development and Finance, *Economic Report, 1969*; data provided by the Zambian authorities; and Fund staff estimates.

[1] Preliminary estimates.
[2] Excludes royalty payments and export tax.
[3] Includes public enterprises.
[4] Statistical discrepancy amounts to K 5.8 million.

Data are not available on the growth of GDP at constant prices. However, allowing for a 9 per cent annual increase in copper prices on
world markets and a 7 per cent rise in domestic prices (as measured by
the cost of living index, the only one available for the whole period), it
can be inferred that GDP in real terms increased in 1965–69 by roughly
10 per cent per annum.

During the four years 1965–68, consumption and investment in the
public sector rose at average annual rates of 22 per cent and 52 per
cent, respectively (Table 2). During the same period consumption and
investment in the private sector rose at average annual rates of 18 per
cent and 31 per cent, respectively. Following the increase in domestic
demand, imports of goods and services rose from K 263 million in
1965 to K 470 million in 1968. Despite the rise in imports, the current
external balance, as defined by national account statistics, showed large,
though fluctuating, surpluses. Exports of goods and services rose from
K 373 million in 1965 to K 544 million in 1968, reflecting both the
expansion in copper production and the increase in the price on the
world market. In 1969, domestic consumption rose by 8 per cent and
accounted for 53 per cent of GDP: public consumption rose by 18 per
cent but the rate of increase in private consumption slowed down considerably. Gross fixed investment actually declined by 5 per cent in 1969
and accounted for 19 per cent of GDP compared with 26 per cent in
1968. There was also a markedly smaller accumulation of stocks in
1969, and total domestic demand remained virtually stable. Imports of
goods and services decreased by almost 6 per cent, and the current
account surplus rose to K 341 million (27 per cent of GDP), owing
mainly to a further large increase in exports.

AGRICULTURE

Only a small fraction of the potentially arable land is cultivated.
The use of agricultural land is governed by a system of private freehold, publicly granted leasehold, and state trust arrangements. The
freehold and the leasehold lands are mostly along the line of rail and
comprise about 12 million acres, of which about one fourth is freehold.
The remaining arable land, nearly 140 million acres, is held in trust by

the State for the benefit of the indigenous population and its use is largely governed by tribal customs.

A Land Acquisition Act was passed in November 1969 giving the authorities the power to acquire unused land. Whenever such action is taken, residents will be compensated for the "unexhausted improvements" of the land, while nonresidents will not be indemnified. The legislation will enable the authorities to take over an area estimated at close to 1 million acres of idle land, most of which had been vacated by foreigners.

The traditional sector of agriculture, which supports one half of the population, accounts for about 78 per cent of agricultural output. The remainder is accounted for by some 600 commercial farms located along the transport arteries and operated by about 1,000 expatriates. Commercial farms produce most of the maize, tobacco, and beef and dairy products. Although the traditional sector accounts for the greater part of cotton and groundnut production, in recent years it has been cultivating maize increasingly. Producers of groundnuts, maize, and tobacco are assured minimum guaranteed prices at which the Government, through cooperatives and marketing boards, will purchase their output. Fruits and vegetables, which are also handled by marketing boards, became subject to minimum guaranteed prices in 1971.

The rate of expansion of agricultural production in recent years has been rather modest, owing in part to the declining output of commercial farms. Although total output at current prices rose from K 53.3 million in 1964 to K 74.6 million in 1969 (40 per cent), its contribution to GDP fell from 11 per cent to 6.3 per cent (Table 1). Exports of agricultural products fell from K 13 million in 1967 to K 7 million in 1968 and K 5 million in 1969; and in the same two years imports of foodstuffs and edible fats rose by 25 per cent, to an average of K 30 million a year.

Cash Crops

Maize.—This is the staple food of the population, and domestic consumption is estimated at 700 million pounds a year. In 1968 and 1969, production suffered a serious setback and marketed output fell sharply, mainly because of adverse weather and the Government's

pricing policies. In mid-September, the Government announced a minimum guaranteed preplanting price for the crop to be marketed in May
of the following year. To give farmers a stable basis for future planning,
preplanting prices usually do not vary by more than 25 ngwee a bag
(200 pounds) from year to year. In the following May, the Government either confirms the preplanting price or adjusts it upward or
downward by no more than 25 ngwee.

With a view to encouraging production to meet export commitments
under an agreement with mainland China, and to allow for the building
up of stocks, a guaranteed preplanting price of K 3.33 a bag was
announced for the 1966/67 crop. The crop of 832 million pounds,
though adequate to meet requirements, involved a considerable financial
loss, as export prices were below the Government's guaranteed prices.
In an attempt to limit the size of the 1967/68 crop in order to reduce
the losses incurred on exports, the preplanting price was reduced by
K 3.10 a bag. Nevertheless, the quantity marketed in 1967/68 was close
to that of the previous year (Table 3). The preplanting price was reduced to K 2.90 a bag for the 1968/69 crop, and production declined to
550 million pounds, resulting in a gap between production and domestic
consumption that was met by stocks accumulated in the previous year.
The preplanting price was raised to K 3.00 a bag for 1969/70, but production increased to only 558 million pounds, necessitating imports of
some 200 million pounds of maize in 1969 and a consumer subsidy of
K 5 a bag. To ensure a more stable production pattern over a period of
time, the Government raised the producer price to K 3.50 a bag in
1970/71 and guaranteed it for three years. The Government also
decided to increase stocks from the then negligible level to 70 million
pounds.

Groundnuts.—Groundnuts are grown primarily in the traditional
sector on small farms in Eastern province. Production in 1968/69
and 1969/70 amounted to 13 million pounds and 17 million pounds,
respectively, compared with 36 million pounds in 1967/68 (Table 3).
The decline was due mainly to drought.

Almost 80 per cent of the marketed production, which is of high
quality and hand shelled, is exported. As the remainder is not sufficient
to meet domestic needs for nuts and oil, it is necessary to import sub-

TABLE 3. ZAMBIA: MARKETED AGRICULTURAL PRODUCTION, 1965/66–1969/70 [1]

	1965/66	1966/67	1967/68	1968/69	1969/70 [2]
Crops	*(Thousand pounds)*				
Tobacco	16,740	11,626	14,727	11,603	11,260
Virginia flue-cured	*14,571*	*10,732*	*13,849*	*11,074*	*10,564*
Burley	*1,697*	*605*	*625*	*529*	*529*
Maize	560,600	832,000	826,400	549,800	558,200
Groundnuts	13,140	24,660	36,180	12,960	16,560
Cotton	5,005	6,105	3,991	9,319	17,382
Sugar	—	—	—	48,000	68,000
Sorghum	—	—	2,800	7,800	2,400
	(Thousand head)				
Cattle	—	56.2	52.0	46.0	39.8
Crops	*(Million Zambian kwacha)*				
Tobacco	4.8	4.8	4.4	4.0	4.1
Virginia flue-cured	*4.4*	*4.7*	*4.2*	*3.9*	*...*
Burley	*0.3*	*0.1*	*0.1*	*0.1*	*...*
Maize	8.6	14.2	12.8	8.0	8.4
Groundnuts	...	1.0	2.0	0.7	0.9
Cotton	0.3	0.4	0.2	0.6	1.0
Sugar	—	—	—	3.8	4.2
Sorghum	—	—	0.1	0.2	0.1
Fruits and vegetables	4.8	4.0	4.4	4.4	4.4
Total	...	24.4	23.9	21.7	23.1
Livestock and dairy products					
Cattle	...	3.1	3.4	4.1	3.8
Poultry	...	2.2	4.1	6.2	8.2
Other livestock	...	0.5	0.4	0.3	0.3
Milk	...	1.2	1.2	1.3	1.2
Total	...	7.0	9.1	11.9	13.5
Total sales value	...	31.4	33.0	33.6	36.6

Sources: Central Statistical Office, *Monthly Digest of Statistics;* Ministry of Development Finance, *Economic Report, 1969;* and data provided by the Zambian authorities.

[1] Years ended April 30. Data are based on deliveries to the marketing boards and statistics of sales of Zambian-produced tobacco.

[2] Preliminary.

stantial amounts of both. The producer price paid by the marketing board generally corresponds to the export price less the cost of marketing and handling. Despite rising export prices, however, producer prices have shown little change because marketing and handling costs have also been rising. They ranged from K 0.47 to K 0.56 a pound in 1969/70 and from K 0.53 to K 0.56 a pound in 1970/71.

Tobacco.—The most important agricultural cash crop is tobacco, which accounted in 1969/70 for about 69 per cent of total marketed agricultural production. Several types of tobacco are grown in Zambia, but by far the most important variety is Virginia flue-cured, which is produced primarily by expatriate farmers. Some Turkish and Burley tobacco is grown, mainly on small African farms.

The Government has established an auction floor at Lusaka, with a capacity to handle trading of 80 million pounds of tobacco per annum, and warehouse and storage facilities. The Tobacco Industry Board is responsible for managing the auction floor, the warehouse and storage facilities, the registration of growers, and the licensing of buyers. The Board has no price-fixing functions. It is, however, entrusted with disbursing a government subsidy to growers which is equivalent to the difference between the minimum price determined by the Government and the average actual price realized on the auction floor. An indication of the Board's operations is given in Table 4, below.

Production of marketed tobacco, which reached a peak of 28.4 million pounds in 1963/64, had declined to 11.6 million pounds in 1968/69. According to preliminary estimates, a further slight decline (about 3 per cent) was anticipated for the 1969/70 season (Table 3). The decline in production was accompanied by an 18 per cent reduction in the average yield, to 769 pounds an acre. Although adverse weather was partly responsible for the smaller crops in 1968/69 and 1969/70, the decline was due mainly to the continued departure of expatriate farmers and to a shift to more profitable agricultural activities, such as cotton.

Although marketed production declined in 1968/69 by 21 per cent, the gross value of sales on the auction floor decreased by only 10 per cent, owing to an increase in the price in 1969 to K 0.35 a pound, from K 0.30 a pound in 1968. A guaranteed price of K 0.36 a pound was established for the three crop seasons beginning 1970/71.

Cotton.—Production of cotton, a relatively new crop in Zambia, rose from 4 million pounds in 1967/68 to 9.3 million pounds in 1968/69 and 17.4 million pounds in 1969/70, owing in part to improvements in insect and disease control and in part to higher producer prices. In order to encourage further production, the Government raised the price paid by the Marketing Board for first-grade unginned cotton by 5 per cent, to K 0.07 a pound in 1969, and announced annual increases of K 0.005 a pound for 1970, 1971, and 1972.

Two gins with a total capacity of 21 million pounds are operational. The first textile mill in Zambia opened in 1969 and can absorb the equivalent of 18 million pounds of unginned cotton a year. Self-sufficiency is estimated at the equivalent of 20 million pounds of unginned cotton a year; this target is expected to be reached by 1972.

Fruits and Vegetables.—Marketed production of fruits and vegetables decreased after 1965, and large quantities have had to be imported. Gross sales remained virtually stagnant in 1969 and 1970, amounting to K 4.4 million in each year. The primary cause for this stagnation appears to be inefficient marketing. Since the ban on imports of fruits and vegetables from South Africa and Rhodesia, emphasis has been placed on increasing local output and improving its marketing. Growers are required to submit data on their estimated output so that storage, marketing, and transport facilities can be planned accordingly. The Marketing Board has established its own warehouse and is constructing a wholesale distribution center. From June 1971, the Board will offer a guaranteed price for fruits and vegetables.

Sugar.—Sugarcane is cultivated on one irrigated commercial farm. The first crop, in 1968/69, amounted to 202,000 tons; the 1969/70 crop reached 283,000 tons. Production of raw sugar in 1968/69 and 1969/70 was 48 million pounds and 68 million pounds, respectively. It is planned to increase the area cultivated from 6,000 to 8,000 acres in order to satisfy a demand for 90 million pounds of sugar.

Other Crops.—Coffee, tea, and sorghum are grown in small quantities for domestic consumption only.

Livestock and Dairy Production

It is estimated that there were 1.5 million head of beef cattle in 1969, of which about 12 per cent was owned by commercial farmers. As the offtake from local herds is not sufficient to meet domestic requirements, beef valued at K 4 million was imported in 1969. The Government has initiated certain schemes to increase the domestic supply of beef, notably the Grazier Scheme and the National Beef Scheme. The former finances the fattening of cattle; the latter is aimed at encouraging farmers in the traditional sector to use improved techniques. The Government subsidizes the construction of paddocks and pens and veterinary services. These schemes are expected to take some years before they have any marked impact on production. In addition, the Agricultural Development Corporation on behalf of the Government operates a number of ranches through its subsidiary, Zambian Cattle Development Limited. The World Bank in June 1969 agreed to finance the development of 12 beef ranches and 5 dairy farms by this subsidiary.

Prior to 1966, Zambia was self-sufficient in milk although some dairy products were imported. However, milk consumption increased sharply during 1968–70 owing to the introduction of subsidized milk schemes for high-density housing areas. Total milk production reached nearly 3.9 million gallons in 1966, but declined in 1969 to 3.4 million, and substantial amounts of powdered milk had to be imported. To meet rising production costs, the producer price for milk was raised in April 1970 by about 10 per cent, to 37 ngwee a gallon.

The poultry industry has been growing at a rapid rate, meeting all local requirements for chickens and eggs; commercial farms have been exporting poultry. The estimated production of poultry has increased from 5,684 short tons in 1964 to 11,000 short tons in 1969. About 40 per cent of egg production and nearly all sales of live poultry are by Zambian farmers.

Agricultural Marketing

Most agricultural marketing is carried out by several statutory marketing boards and cooperatives. There are three principal agricultural marketing boards, the National Agricultural Marketing Board, the Cold Storage Board, and the Dairy Produce Board. These organizations are responsible for the purchase of agricultural products at fixed producer prices announced by the Government and for their marketing.

The National Agricultural Marketing Board was formed in September 1969 by an amalgamation of the Agricultural Rural Marketing Board and the Grain Marketing Board. Before the merger, the latter was the major marketing channel for maize, cotton, and a number of minor crops, such as sorghum, and was also a residual buyer of groundnuts. While the Grain Board, operating principally along the line of rail, was profitable, the Agricultural Rural Marketing Board was not, since its activities were largely in remote provinces. In addition to performing the functions of the two former boards, the National Agricultural Board is the sole importer of seed and distributor of fertilizer, and engages in retail sales of fresh fruits and vegetables. In 1969/70 it purchased 558 million pounds of maize (of which about 400 million pounds from commercial farmers), imported about 200 million pounds of maize, and purchased 17.4 million pounds of cotton.

The Cold Storage Board pays guaranteed prices to farmers for livestock and acts as a wholesaler in the market. Its operations have expanded rapidly; sales rose from K 4.0 million in 1965 to K 7.3 million in 1968. The Board sustained deficits in its operations in 1965 and 1967 but registered a current operating surplus of K 0.5 million in 1968 (Table 4).

TABLE 4. ZAMBIA: SOME INDICATORS OF STATUTORY MARKETING
BOARD OPERATIONS, 1965–68

(*In millions of Zambian kwacha*)

	1965	1966	1967	1968
Grain Marketing Board [1]				
Total assets	5.7	6.1	11.9	11.5
Investments	1.2	0.6	4.8	0.8
Sales proceeds	10.0	12.4	14.6	18.1
Current operating surplus	0.1	0.3	0.8	0.3
Borrowing from Government	5.7	5.6	10.5	10.1
Tobacco Industry Board [2]				
Total assets	0.6	2.7	5.6	5.8
Investments	0.5	1.7	2.5	0.2
Current operating surplus or deficit (−)	—	−0.6	0.4	0.3
Borrowing from Government	0.6	2.5	3.7	4.4
Cold Storage Board [2]				
Total assets	2.8	4.7	5.1	7.0
Investments	0.3	1.1	1.2	1.4
Sales income	4.0	4.7	5.6	7.3
Current operating surplus or deficit (−)	−0.2	0.1	−0.4	0.5
Borrowing from Government	2.9	4.7	5.4	6.9
Dairy Produce Board [3]				
Total assets	1.5	1.6	1.9	2.7
Investments	0.1	0.3	0.3	0.6
Sales income	2.5	3.3	3.7	4.3
Current operating surplus or deficit (−)	0.01	−0.1	−0.05	0.2
Borrowing from Government	0.07	0.3	0.8	1.2

Sources: Central Statistical Office, *Statistical Year-Book, 1969;* and data provided by the Zambian authorities.

[1] Year ended April 30. Merged with the Agricultural Rural Marketing Board in 1969 to form the National Agricultural Marketing Board.

[2] Calendar year.

[3] Year ended June 30.

The Dairy Produce Board, which is responsible for the collection, processing, and distribution of milk and milk products throughout Zambia, has generally operated at a deficit.

There are two types of agricultural cooperatives—marketing and producer. Most marketing cooperatives are organized into unions, the largest being the Eastern Province Cooperative Marketing Association, which deals principally in groundnuts and exports them direct. The marketing cooperatives have sustained large losses, mainly on account of poor management. The operations of producer cooperatives, with a few exceptions in dairy farming and animal husbandry, have suffered from a lack of a sense of cohesion among members and the absence of necessary skills, resulting in the dissolution of many of them.

Agricultural Credit

Agricultural credit is provided by the commercial banks (which lend to commercial farmers and to the statutory marketing boards); by the Grazier Scheme (which finances the cattle industry); and by the Agricultural Finance Corporation. The latter took over the operations of the Credit Organization of Zambia, which was dissolved in 1970.

The Credit Organization, established in 1967, was by far the most important source of short-term, medium-term, and long-term credit to farmers and cooperatives. By the end of June 1969, loans outstanding totaled K 25 million, of which some 60 per cent was not considered recoverable. It is expected that the new organization, which will receive funds direct from the Treasury, will help to establish a sound agricultural credit system.

FISHING

The fish catch is limited because of the landlocked position of the country and the absence of large inland fishing grounds. The domestic output comes mainly from Lakes Kariba, Bangweulu, and Tanganyika and from the Kafue River. The total catch, after declining for several years, rose by an average of about 4 per cent in both 1968 and 1969, when it reached 32,000 tons. A fish processing plant, which was inaugurated in 1969, operates refrigerated storage facilities and a smoke dryer.

INDUSTRIAL PRODUCTION

During the years 1964–68, the index of mining, manufacturing, and generation of electricity rose at an average annual rate of about 3 per cent, reflecting a modest increase in mineral output and a continuing rapid expansion of the manufacturing sector (Table 5). Reflecting the efforts at economic diversification and the desire to promote import-substitution industries, manufacturing industries were encouraged and the index of their production increased by about 90 per cent from 1964 to 1968. Although the manufacturing index fell by 1 per cent in 1969, the index for all industries increased by 11.5 per cent, to 142.5 (1961 = 100) owing largely to an expansion in copper output.

At current prices, the value added in mining, manufacturing, and electric power output more than doubled 1964–69, from K 273 million to K 687 million (see Table 1, above). In 1969, mining accounted for 86 per cent and manufacturing for 12 per cent of the total. While the value added in manufacturing increased almost threefold, from K 28 million in 1964 to K 85 million in 1969, the value added in mining increased less rapidly.

Since April 1968, the Government has acquired majority equity participation in mining and virtually all manufacturing industries. Since June 1970, the equity participation of the Government in manufacturing has been vested in the Industrial Development Corporation of Zambia Ltd. (INDECO), and its participation in mining companies has been vested in the Mining and Development Corporation Ltd. (MINDECO). The share capital of these two holding companies is owned wholly by the Zambia Industrial and Mining Corporation Ltd. (ZIMCO), which is in turn owned by the Government.

TABLE 5. ZAMBIA: INDEX OF MINING, MANUFACTURING, AND POWER, 1964–69

(1961 = 100)

	Weights	1964	1965	1966	1967	1968	1969
Mining	90.1	114.4	122.3	105.2	109.5	119.0	135.5
Manufacturing	7.8	124.4	161.9	172.8	221.2	236.7	233.8
Electric power	2.1	105.0	97.8	90.0	92.2	98.6	103.1
All industries	100.0	115.0	124.9	110.2	117.8	127.8	142.5

Source: Central Statistical Office, *Monthly Digest of Statistics.*

Mining

Mining is the country's largest productive sector, with copper accounting for over 95 per cent of the total value of mineral production. In 1969 the copper industry provided 50 per cent of GDP, 95 per cent of the country's export earnings, and 59 per cent of government revenue (Table 6). Other minerals are zinc, lead, cobalt, and, in recent years, coal. Small quantities of silver, selenium, amethyst, gold, and gypsum are also produced.

Mining rights over the territory of Zambia were acquired by the British South Africa Company between 1890 and 1909. When Zambia became independent in October 1964, an agreement was reached by the British South Africa Company, the U. K. Government, and the Zambian Government whereby the mineral rights were purchased from the British South Africa Company and vested in the President of Zambia on behalf of the Republic.

The Mines and Minerals Act of 1969 sets forth a number of measures aimed at reorganizing the mining industry. The Act provides that all rights of ownership or partial ownership of minerals are to revert to the State, thus ending the situation whereby special grants and rights were held in perpetuity by the mining companies. The State issues prospecting and exploration licenses for a stipulated period of time not

TABLE 6. ZAMBIA: CONTRIBUTION OF COPPER INDUSTRY TO GROSS DOMESTIC PRODUCT,[1] GOVERNMENT REVENUES, AND EXPORT EARNINGS, 1964–69

(*In per cent*)

	Contribution to GDP	Contribution to Government Revenue	Contribution to Export Earnings
1964	44	44	88
1965	40	59	90
1966	45	65	94
1967	39	61	92
1968	40	58	95
1969	50 [2]	59	95

Sources: Central Statistical Office, *Monthly Digest of Statistics;* Ministry of Development and Finance, *Economic Report, 1969;* Copper Industry Service Bureau, Ltd., *Mining Year Book of Zambia, 1969;* and data provided by the Zambian authorities.

[1] At factor cost.
[2] Preliminary estimate.

to exceed 25 years. The Act gives the State the option to acquire a 51 per cent ownership in any mining company established in Zambia.

In December 1969 an agreement was signed by the two copper mining groups then operating in Zambia—Roan Selection Trust and Anglo American Corporation—and the Government. According to this agreement, the State acquired, through ZIMCO Ltd. and MINDECO Ltd., a 51 per cent equity participation in the mining companies. Two new companies were formed to own and operate the mines affected by the take-over. Roan Consolidated Mines Ltd. is to own and operate Mufulira, Luanshya, Chibuluma, Chambishi, and Kalengwa, as well as the Ndola copper refinery, and the new Nchanga Consolidated Copper Mines Ltd. is to own and operate Nchanga, Rhokana, Bancroft, Bwana Mkubwa, and Nampundwe, as well as the Rhokana copper refinery (see Diagram 1). The two mining companies are operated under a ten-year management contract with the Roan Selection Trust and the Anglo American Corporation.

Settlement with the mining companies was based on the consolidated book value of their net mining assets as of December 31, 1969. The agreed total value was set at about K 410 million ($574 million). The Government discharged its obligation of K 209 million by issuing to the companies negotiable, tax-free, government-guaranteed bonds denominated in U. S. dollars and bearing interest at 6 per cent. These bonds and the interest charges will be serviced in half-yearly installments of K 14.1 million during the first eight years and K 7.3 million during the subsequent four years. However, the arrangement calls for a more rapid amortization when two thirds of the dividends received by the Government from the mining companies exceed the scheduled installments.

Copper.—Zambia is the world's third largest producer of copper, after the United States and the U. S. S. R., and accounts for about 12 per cent of world production. Copper deposits are concentrated mainly in the Copperbelt, which lies along the border with the Democratic Republic of Congo. The proven Copperbelt reserves are estimated to be about 745 million metric tons (13 per cent of the world's total), with a metal concentrate of 3.3–3.5 per cent copper.

In 1969 copper production rose by 12.4 per cent, to 747,300 metric tons, surpassing the previous production record of 684,600 metric tons in 1965. During 1969, the industry experienced few of the difficulties suffered in previous years with regard to fuel supplies, transport facilities, and work stoppages. In the first seven months of 1970, output amounted to 406,300 metric tons, compared with 425,400 metric tons in the comparable months of 1969 (Table 7); the decline was expected to be larger on an annual basis because of the flooding of the Mufulira mine, which accounts for about one fourth of total output. Although production in the stricken mine had resumed by November 1970 at a rate of 3,000 tons a month (about one fifth of normal output) and gradual increases were expected, it was difficult to determine when full production would be restored.

The cost of production and marketing has risen sharply since 1964 owing to fuel shortages, transport difficulties, and wage increases. Moreover, exports were diverted to the Far East from the traditional European markets, entailing higher transport costs. According to industry sources, the average cost of producing a metric ton of copper (excluding royalty and export tax but including depreciation) rose by over 60 per cent between 1964 and 1969. Important elements in this increase were rising costs of smelting, inland transport, and labor. Additional increases in costs were anticipated in 1970 and 1971, mainly on account of the cost of rehabilitating the Mufulira mine.

Zambia's mining companies have at different times adopted various ways of selling copper on the world market; the principal means are the fixed producer price system and selling on the basis of quotations on the London Metal Exchange. In 1964, when the average price on the Exchange rose sharply (from K 475 to K 715 a ton) in response to the increase in world demand, the major mining companies announced that they would sell their entire production at fixed prices. The Zambian price was first set at K 480 a ton, and then was raised by steps to K 683 a ton in January 1966. In April 1966, the Chilean authorities raised their contract price by K 325, to K 1,008 a ton. The Zambian producers responded by reverting to basing their prices on the Exchange prices, this time, however, on the three months' forward prices.

Until 1966, Zambia's export prices for copper were substantially lower than the prevailing prices on the London Metal Exchange. The Exchange's average cash price for copper reached a peak of K 1,090 a metric ton in 1966; it fell to K 810 a ton in 1967 but, owing to the

TABLE 7. ZAMBIA: MINERAL PRODUCTION, 1964–JULY 1970

	1964	1965	1966	1967	1968	1969	1969 Jan.–July	1970 Jan.–July
VOLUME (thousand metric tons)								
Copper	642.1	684.6	585.8	616.1	664.8	747.3	425.4	406.3
Copper blister	145.3	163.5	88.3	82.1	93.0	104.9	59.7	60.6
Copper electro-lytic	496.8	521.1	497.5	534.0	571.8	642.4	365.7	345.7
Zinc	46.8	47.5	42.4	45.2	53.2	50.2	30.7	29.9
Lead	13.2	21.3	18.8	19.4	21.8	23.0	15.1	15.7
Cobalt	1.0	1.5	1.5	1.4	1.2	1.8	1.0	1.1
Coal	—	—	114.1	399.3	578.7	397.4	224.0	345.4
VALUE (million Zambian kwacha)								
Copper	279.9	342.9	439.4	443.0	513.5	737.8	387.3	436.3
Zinc	10.3	9.7	8.0	8.4	8.9	8.6	5.1	5.8
Lead	2.3	4.4	3.1	2.7	3.2	4.3	2.8	3.2
Cobalt	3.0	3.4	3.3	3.3	2.6	4.0	2.1	2.4
Coal	—	—	0.2	0.8	1.1	0.8	0.4	0.7
Other	3.6	2.6	3.3	3.9	3.5	4.7	2.1	2.8
Total	299.1	363.0	457.3	462.1	532.8	760.2	399.8	451.2
AVERAGE CASH PRICE (Zambian kwacha per metric ton)								
Copper [1]	693	923	1,090	810	887	1,048	973	1,143
Zinc	233	222	201	195	187	204	196	211
Lead	199	226	187	163	172	207	195	228

Source: Central Statistical Office, *Monthly Digest of Statistics.*

[1] Cash price on London Metal Exchange: spot price until June 1968, and "settlement and cash sellers' price" for electrolytic wire bars since then.

strong world demand for copper, it rose to K 887 a ton in 1968 (Table 7). Since June 1968, Zambian copper has been quoted on the basis of "settlement and cash sellers' price" for electrolytic wire bars.

In 1969, the average cash price on the London Metal Exchange rose to K 1,048 a ton (i.e., by 18 per cent). In that year the total value of Zambian copper exports rose by about 40 per cent, to K 724.5 million. The Exchange price was at a record high of K 1,252 a ton in March 1970 but then declined at an average monthly rate of 5.6 per cent; it averaged K 1,143 a ton in January–July 1970 but was K 740 a metric ton at the end of December.

The Zambian copper industry is planning to expand production through the introduction of a new processing technique and the opening of new mines. The TORCO (treatment of refractory ores) process allows the refining of low-grade oxide ore concentrates, which in the past was not economical. The TORCO process can reduce production costs for ore concentrates currently being processed by conventional methods. With the expansion of production in various existing mines and the opening of new ones, it is expected that production may exceed 950,000 metric tons by 1975.

Toward the end of 1968, the Government established the Metal Marketing Company of Zambia, which was given the right to determine sales policies. Among other things, it was planned that the company would review sales contracts, determine major contractual conditions, review the geographical sales spread, represent Zambia in marketing matters, and participate with producers in negotiations with customers. The Government would own 51 per cent of the capital of the company, the remainder being shared equally by the two copper mining companies. The company has not commenced operations, and with the Government's acquisition of 51 per cent ownership in the mines it is unlikely that it will do so.

Coal.—Before Rhodesia's unilateral declaration of independence in 1965, little attention was given to the development of coal deposits in Zambia because of the existence of large high-grade deposits at Wankie in Rhodesia, whence Zambia imported about 110,000 long tons of coal monthly. A shortage of coal developed in 1966, following the introduction by Rhodesia of a strict one-for-one railroad car swap system at the border between Zambia and Rhodesia. This reduced the

Diagram 1. Zambia: Structure of Mining Industry, 1970

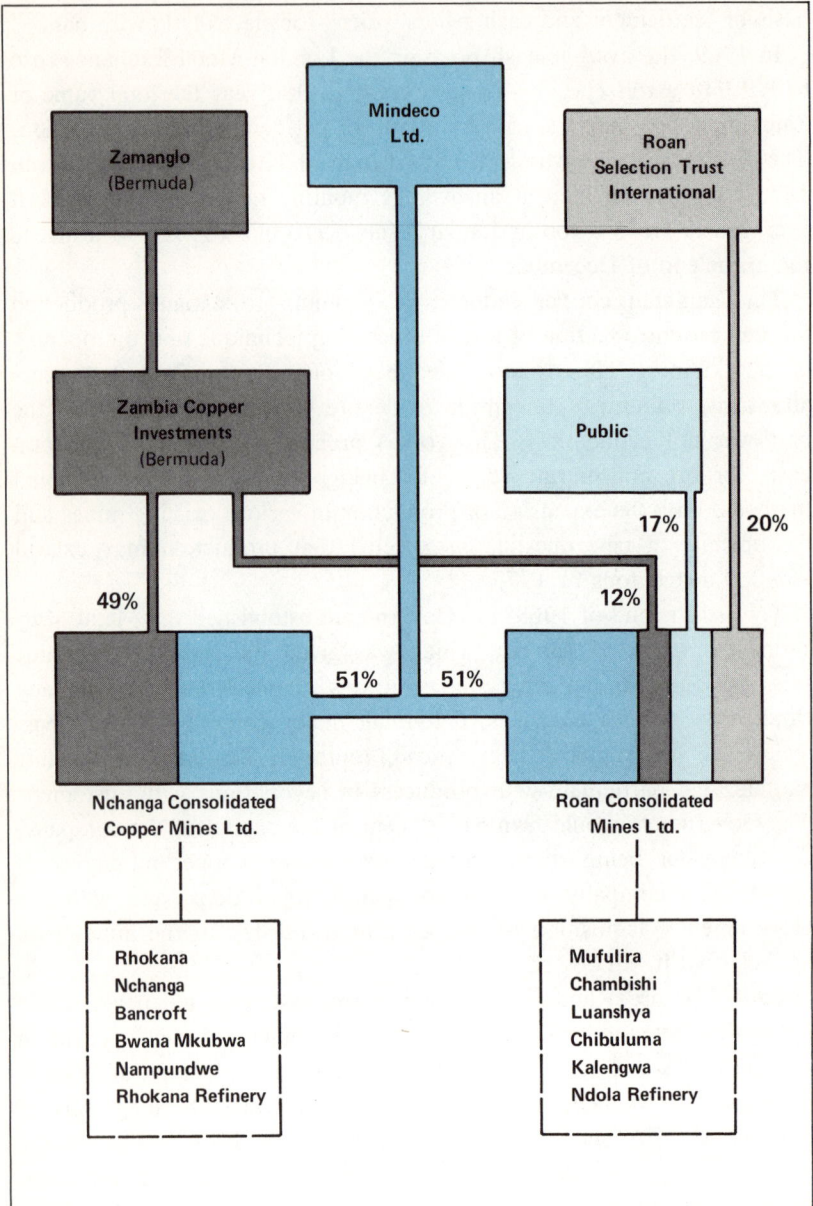

Nchanga Consolidated
Copper Mines Ltd.

Roan Consolidated
Mines Ltd.

Rhokana
Nchanga
Bancroft
Bwana Mkubwa
Nampundwe
Rhokana Refinery

Mufulira
Chambishi
Luanshya
Chibuluma
Kalengwa
Ndola Refinery

Source: Mindeco Ltd., *Prospects for Zambia's Mining Industry,* Lusaka, 1970.

Diagram 2. Zambia: The Indeco Group of Companies, 1970[1]

BREWING AND DISTILLING

Indeco Breweries Ltd. (100%)*
  Duncan, Gilbey & Matheson
    (Zambia) Ltd. (33%)
  National Breweries Ltd. (51%)
  Zambia Breweries Ltd. (51%) and
    subsidiary, Norgroup Plastics Ltd.

BUILDING SUPPLIES
AND ENGINEERING

Steelbuild Holdings Ltd. (100%)*
  Anros Industries Ltd. (72%) and sub-
    sidiary, Metal Industries Ltd.
  Crushed Stone Sales Ltd. (51%)
  Glass Supplies of Zambia Ltd. (51%)
  Hardware Merchants of Zambia Ltd.
    (100%)
  Lusaka Engineering Company (60%)
  Monarch Zambia Ltd. (51%)
  Steel Supplies of Zambia Ltd. (51%)
  Timber Merchants of Zambia Ltd. (55%)
  Zambia Clay Industries Ltd. (71%)

CONSUMER TRADING

Indeco Trading Ltd. (100%)*
  Consumer Buying Corporation of
    Zambia Ltd. (51%)
  Denton & Kennedy of Zambia Ltd. (51%)
  Kafue Textiles of Zambia Ltd. (50%)
  Mwaiseni Stores Ltd. (51%)
  Zambesi Trading Co. Ltd. (51%)
  Z.O.K. Ltd. (51%)

FINANCE

Indeco Industrial Finance Co. Ltd. (100%)
J. H. Minet (Zambia) Ltd. (51%)

PROPERTY

Indeco Real Estate Ltd. (100%)*
  Indeco Properties Ltd. (100%)
  Kafue Estate Ltd. (100%)
  Mwaiseni Properties Ltd. (100%)
  Progressive Development Ltd. (100%)
  Zambia Hotel Properties Ltd. (80%)

MANUFACTURING AND OTHER

A.F.E. Ltd. (29%)
Chilanga Cement Ltd. (45%)
Kabwe Industrial Fabrics Ltd. (100%)
Kafue Steel Corporation Ltd. (100%)
Livingstone Motor Assemblers Ltd. (70%)
Metal Fabricators of Zambia Ltd. (52%)
Miller & Wixley (Zambia) Ltd. (40%)
Nkwazi Manufacturing Company Ltd. (5%)
Scaw-Tow Foundries Ltd. (2%)
The Zambia Sugar Company Ltd. (12%)

PETROL AND CHEMICALS

Indeco Chemicals Ltd. (100%)*
  Agip Zambia Ltd. (50%)
  Indeni Petroleum Refinery Co. Ltd.
    (50%)
  Kafironda Ltd. (33%)
  Nitrogen Chemicals of Zambia Ltd. (90%)
  Shell/BP (Zambia) Ltd. (51%)

RURAL ENTERPRISES

Rucom Holdings Ltd. (100%)*
  Country Hotels Ltd. (100%)
  Indeco Milling Ltd. (100%)
  Lakes Fisheries of Zambia Ltd. (85%)
  Mining Timbers Ltd. (51%)
  Rucom Industries Ltd. (100%)
  Zambesi Sawmills (1968) Ltd. (51%)

TRANSPORT

Indeco Transport Limited (100%)*
  Dunlop Zambia Ltd. (23%)
  Rubber Investments Ltd. (51%)
  Smith and Youngson Ltd. (100%)
  Tazama Pipelines Ltd. (67%)
  Transport Holdings of Zambia Ltd.
    (51%) and subsidiaries, United Bus
    Company of Zambia Ltd. and Freight
    Holdings of Zambia Ltd.
  Zambia-Tanzania Road Services
    Ltd. (35%)

Source: *Enterprise: The Indeco Journal,* Lusaka, No. 2, 1970.

[1] Percentages refer to Indeco's equity participation. An asterisk (*) signifies a holding company.

supply of coal from Wankie and forced Zambian copper producers to cut down their refining operations in 1966 to as much as two thirds of normal.

In the meantime, the Zambian authorities decided to develop domestic coal supplies in order to become independent of Wankie. A coal field at Nkandabwe on the escarpment near Lake Kariba was put into production in June 1966. A new mine at Maamba in Southern province, with coal of better quality, was opened in October 1967, and output from this mine in 1968 was about 220,000 tons. Zambian coal production increased from 114,100 metric tons in 1966 to about 578,700 tons in 1968, but in 1969 declined by over 30 per cent, to about 397,400 tons. The decline was due to the closing of the mine at Nkandabwe; however, with the introduction of a new washing plant and the completion of a cableway that will carry the coal from the mine to the railway, Zambia might become self-sufficient in coal by 1971.

Other Minerals.—Zambia is also a producer of small quantities of zinc, lead, cobalt, and gold. Cobalt is mined in the Copperbelt by the Rhokana Corporation, and silver and selenium are recovered as by-products. Output of cobalt may increase substantially after the opening (planned for 1973) of a new copper mine that has ore with a relatively high cobalt content. As a by-product of copper mining, gold-bearing slime is exported and refined abroad; gold thus recovered amounted to 9,100 ounces in 1969.

Most of the zinc and lead is produced in the Broken Hill area, about 100 miles south of the Copperbelt, by a mining company controlled by the Anglo American Corporation. From 1968 to 1969, zinc production declined by 6 per cent, to 50,200 metric tons, and lead increased by 6 per cent, to 23,000 tons. During 1964 prices on the London Metal Exchange for zinc and lead reached their highest since 1952. Fearing possible substitution, the Zambian producers decided to discontinue selling zinc through the Exchange and independently of the Exchange set lower and more stable prices to customers. In 1966, a growing surplus of lead and zinc in world markets caused a steady decline in the average prices for these metals on the Exchange, and in March of that year the Zambian zinc producers joined the major world producers in reducing selling prices for zinc from K 216 to K 201 a ton. The Exchange's average cash price for zinc continued to decline steadily and in 1969 was at the 1966 level. The average annual price for a metric ton of lead declined from K 199 in 1964 to K 163 in 1967, but rose to K 172 in 1969 and to K 207 in 1970.

Manufacturing

From 1964 to 1968, output of manufacturing industries increased at an average annual rate of 18 per cent, reflecting mainly the production of import substitutes in accordance with the policy of reducing reliance on Rhodesia. A variety of investment incentives are provided through the tax system, including investment allowances, tax holidays, and exemption from customs duties on imports of machinery, spare parts, and raw materials.

Locally manufactured goods consist mainly of processed food, beverages, textiles, furniture, and building materials. Among the projects completed in 1969 were a copper-fabricating plant, a canning factory, a grain bag factory, a textile mill, and a nitrogen plant that is expected to meet two thirds of Zambia's fertilizer requirements. New projects approved in 1970 included an oil refinery, a car assembly plant, and a glass factory.

The Government's industrial development policy is implemented mainly through the Industrial Development Corporation (INDECO). As originally conceived, INDECO was to be primarily a development bank, providing management guidance and loans on commercial terms to private industry. During 1968–70, however, it also became the principal instrument for government equity participation in industry. Compensation to the enterprises was determined on the basis of paid-up equity capital plus reserves, and was to be paid out of future dividends. Certain guarantees, such as the repatriation of profits and dividends, were provided to minority shareholders. In its new and expanded role, INDECO's task is to organize and manage state investments, either as wholly owned subsidiaries or as companies established on a joint venture basis.

The authorized share capital of INDECO was increased in November 1968 from K 20 million to K 50 million, of which K 34.4 million had been paid up at the end of March 1970. At that time, INDECO's total investments (at book value) amounted to K 59.2 million, of which

TABLE 8. ZAMBIA: FINANCIAL INDICATORS OF INDECO, 1964–70 [1]

(In millions of Zambian kwacha)

	December 31				March 31	
	1964	1965	1966	1967	1968/69	1969/70
Paid-up capital [2]	2.03	3.14	7.06	13.36	21.21	34.39
Total assets [2]	2.11	4.90	8.87	16.08	46.68	60.03
Investments [2]	1.23	3.92	6.36	15.08	46.33	59.20
Loans advanced	*1.08*	*1.67*	*1.37*	*3.43*	*2.46*	*1.80*
Equity participation	*0.15*	*2.25*	*4.99*	*11.65*	*43.87*	*57.40*
Investment income, including taxation recoverable	0.14	0.25	0.50	0.75	4.81	6.29
Surplus on current account [3]	0.05	0.08	0.33	0.56	3.77	5.07

Sources: Central Statistical Office, *Statistical Year-Book, 1969;* INDECO Ltd., *Annual Report, 1969–70;* and data provided by the Zambian authorities.

[1] The financial years 1964–67 correspond to the calendar years; the financial years 1968/69 and 1969/70 run from April 1 to March 31.

[2] End of period.

[3] Net profit plus provision for depreciation of fixed assets.

K 57.4 million was equity participation in enterprises and K 1.8 million was loans (Table 8). These investments were distributed among 80 subsidiary and associated companies with major participation in manufacturing, building supplies, hotels, commerce, an oil pipeline, transportation, and petrochemicals (see Diagram 2). Although INDECO enterprises as a whole are profitable, returns as a percentage of turnover have been declining since 1968.

Electricity and Fuel

In 1969, installed electric generating capacity was 712,000 kilowatts, of which almost 50 per cent was on Zambian territory. Within the overall grid, the largest single source of electric power is a hydroelectric installation located in Rhodesia and operated on behalf of the Governments of Zambia and Rhodesia by the Central African Power Corporation. Zambia also obtains electricity from a hydroelectric installation in the Democratic Republic of Congo.

Consumption of electricity in Zambia rose from 2.7 billion kilowatt-hours in 1964 to 3.5 billion kilowatt-hours in 1969, when 18 per cent was generated on Zambian territory (Table 9). Nearly 85 per cent of the total is consumed by the mining industry.

TABLE 9.   ZAMBIA: CONSUMPTION OF ELECTRICITY, 1964–69

(*In millions of kilowatt-hours*)

	1964	1965	1966	1967	1968	1969
Generated domestically	694.6	644.3	578.5	602.3	641.5	614.2
Copperbelt Power						
Company	*373.6*	*349.4*	*306.1*	*314.0*	*354.9*	*371.0*
Kabwe	*263.6*	*234.2*	*206.7*	*219.1*	*242.0*	*211.2*
Lusaka	*15.2*	*14.8*	*15.1*	*12.0*	—	—
Victoria Falls	*32.4*	*35.2*	*40.3*	*43.6*	*35.0*	*22.4*
Other	*9.8*	*10.7*	*10.3*	*13.6*	*9.6*	*9.6*
Plus imports	2,050.4	2,296.5	2,400.5	2,634.5	2,759.3	2,891.8
Kariba (Rhodesia)	*1,848.9*	*2,032.9*	*2,085.7*	*2,625.7*	*2,710.8*	*2,873.3*
Le Marinel (Dem. Rep.						
of Congo)	*201.5*	*263.6*	*314.8*	*8.8*	*48.5*	*18.5*
Less exports	18.2	21.5	9.3	4.6	4.7	5.1
Total consumption	2,726.8	2,919.3	2,969.7	3,232.2	3,396.1	3,500.9

Sources: Ministry of Development and Finance, *Economic Report, 1969;* and data provided by the Zambian authorities.

In order to reduce reliance on power generated in Rhodesia and to meet the increasing demand for electricity, the Zambian authorities are developing hydroelectric facilities at Victoria Falls, Kafue, and Lake Kariba. The Victoria Falls project, which comprises the construction of two hydroelectric plants with a total installed capacity of 100,000 kilowatts, is financed with domestic funds. One plant became operational in 1969 and the other is under construction. The Kafue project is to be financed through a Yugoslav and Swedish consortium at a cost of K 52 million. The Lake Kariba project is estimated to cost K 41 million and will add 600,000 kilowatts of installed capacity by 1975. The foreign exchange costs of the Lake Kariba project will be financed by a loan of K 28 million from the World Bank.

Zambia's difficulties in securing liquid fuel were overcome with the opening in September 1968 of the Tan-Zam oil pipeline from Dar es Salaam in Tanzania to Ndola. The pipeline, 1,058 miles long, was constructed at a cost of K 32 million and was financed in part with an Italian line of credit of K 25 million. It has a capacity of 600,000 tons a year, which could be raised to 1.2 million with additional pumping stations.

TRANSPORT

The domestic transport system consists of 690 miles of railroads, 21,000 miles of roads, and an extensive air transport system. The railway in Zambia is linked with those of Rhodesia and the Democratic Republic of Congo and provides several alternative routes to the sea. The nearest ports are Lourenço Marques and Beira in Mozambique, approximately 1,600 miles by rail from the Copperbelt through Rhodesia. Before Rhodesia's unilateral declaration of independence, almost all exports went by rail to Lourenço Marques and Beira. Copper exports are now shipped to Dar es Salaam in Tanzania and Lobito in Angola, as well as to Beira and Lourenço Marques. In 1969, 35 per cent of copper exports were sent through Dar es Salaam, 17 per cent through Lobito, and the remainder through Rhodesia.

Mainland China has undertaken to finance the construction of a railway that will link Dar es Salaam in Tanzania with the existing Zambian railway system at Kapiri Mposhi. When completed in 1975, the Tanzania-Zambia Railway is expected to reduce transport costs by about 17 per cent.

The road network includes about 3,800 miles of main roads and 13,500 miles of secondary roads. Although the road system is widely spread across the country, and both construction and improvements have increased since independence, it is still inadequate. Resurfacing the Great North Road to Dar es Salaam, at a cost of K 25.6 million, and the Great East Road to Malawi, at a cost of K 22 million, was almost completed in 1970. The capacity of these two roads is about 3,000 vehicles a day. Projects for the future include improvement of the road between Lusaka and the Copperbelt and the opening of new roads in the Copperbelt itself and in the North-Western province to connect isolated copper mines with industrial centers in the Copperbelt.

Apart from the international airport at Lusaka, which can accommodate all types of jet aircraft, there are 141 other airports. Domestic service is provided by the government-owned Zambia Airways Corporation, which operates under management contract with Alitalia.

DOMESTIC COMMERCE

The commercial sector has expanded rapidly since independence. In 1969, commercial activities contributed an estimated K 134 million (11.3 per cent) to GDP, compared with K 45.8 million (9.5 per cent) in 1964. The bulk of trading activity in Zambia has customarily been carried on by expatriates. As part of the Government's efforts to increase Zambian participation in economic activities, the President announced on November 10, 1970 that no foreigners would be allowed to obtain a retail or wholesale trading license after December 31, 1971. All retail trading will be carried out through cooperatives, state companies, and Zambian private businesses. INDECO will play an active role in taking over foreign-owned distribution enterprises. Wholesale trade may eventually be handled by the Wholesale Corporation, which was established in 1967.

ECONOMIC DEVELOPMENT AND PLANNING

FIRST NATIONAL DEVELOPMENT PLAN (1966–71)

The First National Development Plan, which was originally to cover the five years 1966–70, was extended until the end of 1971. Its objectives were (1) to diversify the economy in order to reduce dependence on the mining sector; (2) to increase employment opportunities and raise rural incomes relative to urban incomes; (3) to expand education and training as part of a program of Zambianization (i.e., a program to increase Zambian participation in economic activity); (4) to raise standards of housing, health, and social welfare; and (5) to expand transport and communication facilities.

The Plan called for outlays of K 564 million, to be invested about equally in social infrastructure, economic infrastructure, and power, transport, and public works (Table 10).

Since Rhodesia's unilateral declaration of independence in 1965, Zambia has been redirecting its development effort with a view to achieving self-sufficiency in power and finding routes to the sea other than through Rhodesia. This has entailed substantial investment in hydroelectric facilities, roads, and a petroleum pipeline.

Actual central government investments under the Plan until the end of 1969 and authorized outlays in 1970 exceeded total original estimates by 17 per cent. Agricultural development involved public capital outlays of K 81 million, or 12 per cent of the estimated total. Investments in education, health, and social welfare amounted to K 74 million, 11 per cent of the total. Enrollment in primary schools reached

TABLE 10. ZAMBIA: CENTRAL GOVERNMENT EXPENDITURE UNDER FIRST DEVELOPMENT PLAN, 1966-70

(In thousands of Zambian kwacha)

| | Apr. 1–Mar. 31 1966/67 | | Calendar Years | | | | | | Total, 1966-70 | |
	Planned	Actual	1968 Planned	1968 Actual	1969 Planned	1969 Actual	1970 Planned	1970 Authorized	Planned	Estimated
General administration	4,218	2,727	2,482	4,660	1,982	5,459	1,868	5,277	10,550	18,123
President and State House	26	11	176	89	4	11	—	182	26	293
National Assembly	400	677	1,030	35		11	24	121	604	844
Home Affairs	1,638	1,077	80	456	728	613	804	985	4,200	3,131
Foreign Affairs	312	356	220	268	170	364	80	153	642	2,293
Judicial Department	92	26	64	22	240	2	300	6	852	272
Commerce		3		3	126				190	14
Development and Finance	1,750	577	912	3,787	714	4,387	660	2,525	4,036	11,276
Security administration	8,218	7,473	9,104	2,819	3,470	4,528	4,000	484	24,792	15,304
Police	2,500	2,088	2,036	969	2,490	782	2,920	484	9,946	4,323
Defense	5,550	5,258	6,988	1,821	900	2,895	1,000	...	14,438	9,974
Special Division	168	127	80	29	80	851	80	...	408	1,007
Social infrastructure	49,688	52,764	46,840	48,241	46,372	36,550	45,212	46,544	188,112	184,099
Commission for Technical Education and Training	1,118	412	1,448	840	1,792	777	1,760	3,960	6,118	5,989
Provincial and local government	17,436	21,070	17,314	22,402	18,442	17,759	19,602	23,056	72,794	84,287
Establishment Division	5,624	7,019	3,784	6,959	2,760	2,368	3,058	2,929	15,226	19,275
Labor and social welfare	558	893	582	621	350	172	280	379	1,770	2,065
Health	6,778	4,055	6,946	4,769	4,228	6,524	1,652	8,100	19,604	23,448
Education	18,174	19,315	16,766	12,650	18,800	8,950	18,860	8,120	72,600	49,035
Power, transport, and public works	47,706	50,245	54,706	57,070	46,216	53,594	21,508	46,524	170,136	207,433
Economic infrastructure	49,474	47,142	40,956	80,534	42,462	56,141	37,138	50,034	170,030	233,851
State participation	21,058	25,421	17,834	59,393	18,538	31,544	13,594	19,472	71,024	135,830
Information, broadcasting, and tourism	790	425	412	791	542	696	574	752	2,318	2,664
Lands and natural resources	5,720	3,783	4,814	4,179	4,246	2,447	4,198	3,954	18,978	14,363
Rural development	21,906	17,513	17,896	16,171	19,136	21,454	18,772	25,856	77,710	80,994
Grand total	159,304	160,351	154,088	193,324	140,502	156,272	109,726	148,863	563,620	658,810

Sources: Central Statistical Office, *Monthly Digest of Statistics*; and data provided by the Zambian authorities.

660,000 in 1969, virtually 100 per cent of the Plan target, enrollment in secondary schools reached 48,000, 88 per cent of the target, and university enrollment reached nearly 1,300, some 400 short of the Plan target but still a fourfold increase over 1966 when the university was started. Health facilities have expanded rapidly since independence. The number of hospital beds increased from 6,300 to 12,800 over the period 1964–68, and the number of doctors in government service rose from 81 to 142 and of nurses from 306 to 463. As far as housing is concerned, a total of 18,000 units with supporting facilities have been constructed since the inception of the First National Development Plan. The Plan aimed at creating 100,000 new salaried jobs. By the end of 1969, salaried employment had increased by about 65,000, two thirds of the planned figure.

SECOND DEVELOPMENT PLAN (1972–76)

The second development plan (1972–76), which is currently in preparation, will give priority to rural development, the establishment of industries to process agricultural products, and the establishment of manufacturing industries in areas that at present do not have an industrial base.

PRICES, WAGES, AND EMPLOYMENT

PRICES

Consumer price indices are calculated for lower-income and higher-income groups. The index for lower incomes is weighted on the basis of African consumption patterns and is compiled for six urban areas. The index for higher incomes reflects primarily consumption patterns of foreign families.

During the four years 1965–68, the general price level, as measured by the index of lower-income groups, rose at an average annual rate [1] of 8.6 per cent (Table 11). The sharp price rises were due to several factors: The establishment of new trade routes for imports, as well as

---

[1] Annual figures are averages of monthly figures.

TABLE 11. ZAMBIA: CONSUMER PRICE INDICES, 1965–70

(*Annual averages; January 1964 = 100*) [1]

	Weights	1965	1966	1967	1968	1969	1970 [2]
Lower incomes [3]	100.0	108.1	119.2	125.1	138.6	142.0	144.5
Higher incomes [4]	100.0	104.2	109.5	115.1	125.0	130.4	132.9
Food, beverages, and tobacco	*30.9*	*105.6*	*111.2*	*118.8*	*134.8*	*141.2*	*142.8*
Clothing and footwear	*8.0*	*102.9*	*105.7*	*109.5*	*124.9*	*129.8*	*130.9*
Rent and fuel	*13.6*	*99.8*	*100.2*	*100.2*	*100.4*	*101.1*	*102.3*
Household goods and services	*14.3*	*105.9*	*114.4*	*122.2*	*136.0*	*150.6*	*158.4*
Vehicle expenses	*15.3*	*105.8*	*116.6*	*124.9*	*127.7*	*130.9*	*131.4*
Miscellaneous	*17.9*	*103.5*	*105.4*	*108.0*	*114.8*	*116.8*	*119.8*

Sources: Data provided by the Bank of Zambia and the Central Statistical Office.

[1] Annual figures are averages of monthly figures.
[2] Average for January–August.
[3] New series based on consumption surveys conducted during 1966–68 in Lusaka and five other towns for families with incomes of less than K 60 a month. The components and weights are food, beverages, and tobacco, 64.7; clothing and footwear, 13.6; rent and fuel, 11.1; household goods and services, 6.5; and miscellaneous, 4.1.
[4] Based on a survey of consumption patterns conducted in 1960.

the diversion of imports from Rhodesia to new sources of supply, increased the cost of some imported goods and raw materials. The monetary expansion (which averaged 28 per cent per annum between the end of 1965 and the end of 1968) at a time when the relative supply of imported goods was being generally reduced by delays in delivery also contributed to price increases. Finally, the almost 50 per cent increase in salaries during this period led to a corresponding rise in labor costs per unit of production, as output per worker failed to improve.

The Government has endeavored to limit price increases by imposing price controls. Originally, supervision was exercised over the prices of certain essential commodities, such as flour and maize meal. In 1966 price controls were extended to include beef, rice, tea, bread, and salt, with prices for these commodities frozen at the January 1966 level. Early in 1970 the controlled prices were abrogated and new ceilings were imposed on a few commodities, such as powdered and condensed milk, soap and detergents, margarine, cooking oil, and fats. The new prices are based on permissible profit margins over actual costs. The authorities also directed the state enterprises to reduce the prices of certain commodities that feature prominently in the diet of the lower-income groups.

The above measures, along with the wage freeze, a more restrictive fiscal policy (see Government Finance—Central Government Budget, below), and the leveling off of the cost increases caused by Rhodesia's unilateral declaration of independence, have been successful in abating price increases since 1968. In 1969 and the first eight months of 1970, prices rose at a monthly average of 0.2 per cent, against a monthly average of 0.9 per cent in the comparable 1968 period.

WAGES

Most of the workers in industry and mining belong to unions. The local labor unions belong to a federation, the Zambian Congress of Trade Unions. Government wage policy with respect to the private sector is to encourage collective bargaining through joint industrial councils representing employers and employees. Where adequate bargaining machinery does not exist, wage fixing is undertaken by government-appointed wage boards or councils. The powers of the wage councils are basically the same as those of the wage boards, but the councils can also determine wages in accordance with the length of service. In addition, the wage councils have the responsibility of promoting collective bargaining. New labor legislation is in preparation, the main feature of which will be the institution of work councils for each enterprise. These councils, which will be complementary to the trade unions, are expected to promote participation in management decisionmaking and to contribute to a better relationship between labor and management.

Legal minimum wage rates for unskilled workers in the private sector are set at K 0.55 a day for agricultural employment and K 0.90 a day for other sectors. Minimum wage rates for skilled workers are graduated and are substantially higher. Rates are based on a 45-hour week, and overtime is paid at the rate of one and a half times the applicable minimum rate.

Total wage earnings in Zambia have shown a more rapid growth than employment, reflecting general increases in salaries and wages and the upgrading of positions for Zambians, particularly in the mining sector. During the four years 1965–68, the wage bill rose by an annual average of 17.4 per cent, reaching a peak of K 381 million in 1968 (Table 12). The rate of growth appears to have slowed down in 1969,

TABLE 12. ZAMBIA: NUMBER OF WAGE AND SALARY EARNERS AND
AVERAGE ANNUAL EARNINGS, BY SECTOR, 1965–69

	1965	1966	1967	1968	1969 [1]
EMPLOYMENT (*thousands*)					
Agriculture, forestry, and fishing	35.7	35.4	36.5	34.6	35.0
Mining and quarrying	52.5	54.8	54.7	54.7	55.3
Manufacturing	26.8	30.8	33.4	34.3	37.3
Construction	51.8	71.2	67.5	64.0	59.9
Electricity, water, and sanitary services	4.1	3.8	3.9	4.5	2.8
Commerce	26.7	28.4	30.4	31.6	36.1
Transport and communications	12.3	20.7	20.3	23.5	22.4
Domestic service	35.0	35.0	35.0	35.0	35.0
General services	53.5	56.7	65.3	71.4	79.2
Total	298.4	336.8	347.0	353.6	363.0
Africans	*266.5*	*307.4*	*317.7*	*324.4*	*334.9*
Non-Africans	*31.9*	*29.4*	*29.3*	*29.2*	*28.1*
Public sector	*...*	*107.8*	*114.4*	*122.9*	*131.0*
Private sector	*...*	*229.0*	*232.6*	*230.7*	*232.0*
Public sector as per cent of total	...	32.0%	33.0%	34.8%	36.1%
ANNUAL EARNINGS (*million kwacha*)					
All industries	244.4	281.9	349.6	380.9 [1]	...
AVERAGE ANNUAL EARNINGS PER WORKER (*kwacha*)					
Africans					
Money earnings	428	480	666	789	...
In real terms [2]	396	403	532	569	...
Non-Africans					
Money earnings	3,498	4,090	4,458	4,875	...
In real terms [3]	3,357	3,735	3,873	3,900	...

Sources: Central Statistical Office, *Monthly Digest of Statistics;* data provided by the Zambian authorities; and Fund staff estimates.

[1] Preliminary estimates.

[2] Money earnings deflated by the average consumer price index of lower-income wage earners (January 1964 = 100).

[3] Money earnings deflated by the average consumer price index for higher-income employees (January 1964 = 100).

no major wage increases having been granted because of a wage freeze announced in August and the decision to ban strikes.

Owing largely to the wage adjustments in 1966–67, the average annual money earnings of Africans rose by almost 84 per cent between 1965 and 1968, while those of non-Africans rose by 39.4 per cent. The increase in the annual earnings of Africans was not evenly distributed among industries. The greatest increases were in the construction industry and in commerce, where earnings rose by 96 per cent and 88 per cent, respectively. During the same period, earnings in mining and services rose by 61 per cent and 67 per cent, respectively.

Although the average annual increase in earnings of Africans was in part eroded by the rising cost of living, real earnings rose by about 10 per cent a year between 1965 and 1968. The increase in real earnings for non-Africans during the same period averaged about 4 per cent a year.

Because output per worker in the economy as a whole did not rise noticeably in the years 1965–68, the wage increases resulted in higher labor costs per unit of output. During these four years, labor cost per unit of output for the entire economy increased by an annual average of 9 per cent, while output per worker, which showed large annual variations, rose by 2 per cent a year. In 1966, output per worker for the economy as a whole declined by 11 per cent as a result of both a stagnation of total output in real terms and an increase in employment. Although in 1967 and 1968 output per worker improved, the continuous rise in wages led to further increases in labor costs (Table 13). In the mining industry, after rising by an annual average of 26.6 per cent between 1965 and 1967, unit labor costs fell by 11 per cent in 1968. This reflected a decline in the average wage per worker as a result of Zambianization and smaller wage increases.

The sharp rise in labor costs per unit of output was one of the main reasons for imposing a wage freeze in August 1969. This wage freeze

TABLE 13.   ZAMBIA: INDICES OF PRODUCTIVITY, WAGES,
AND LABOR COST, 1965–68

(*1964 = 100*)

	1965	1966	1967	1968
Economy as a whole				
Output per worker [1]	108	96	106	112
Wages per worker	106	112	130	154
Labor cost per unit of output	99	117	122	138
Mining industry				
Output per worker [2]	104	86	89	96
Wages per worker	103	115	141	135
Labor cost per unit of output	99	133	158	140

Sources: Office of the Vice-President, *Zambian Manpower;* and Fund staff estimates based on statistics for mining production and employment and wages.

[1] Calculated by dividing gross domestic expenditure at constant prices (with adjustment for rural household consumption) by the average number of wage and salaried workers during the year.

[2] Calculated by dividing the metric tons of product a year (mainly tons of copper) by the average number of wage and salaried workers in mining and quarrying.

was relaxed in 1970, when mine workers were granted a 5 per cent wage increase retroactive to November 1969 and a further 5 per cent increase effective November 1970. However, in return for these increases, the Union of Mine Workers undertook to support measures to improve productivity and contain production costs by reducing absenteeism and wildcat strikes.

EMPLOYMENT

According to the 1969 census, the labor force (persons over 15 years of age working or seeking work) numbered more than 1 million, of whom 71 per cent were males. Of the employed population of 757,000, about half were wage and salary earners, of whom 17 per cent were in the public sector (see Tables 12 and 14). The distribution of the employed labor force was 44 per cent in agriculture and related occupations, 25 per cent in the services sector, 8 per cent in mining, and 5 per cent in manufacturing (Table 14).

The number of wage earners rose by about 12 per cent in 1965 and 1966, but at an average annual rate of only 2.5 per cent in 1967–69 (Table 12). Unemployment in 1969 was estimated to have been almost one third of the total labor force; about 80 per cent of the unemployed were in the rural areas. Unemployment among wage earners was close to 50 per cent.

TABLE 14. ZAMBIA: EMPLOYED POPULATION BY SECTOR, 1969 [1]

	Total	African	Non-African
Agriculture, forestry, and fishing	330,300	329,100	1,200
Mining and quarrying	57,600	52,900	4,700
Manufacturing	35,400	33,000	2,400
Electricity, gas, and water supply	8,100	7,600	500
Construction	58,800	53,700	5,100
Commerce	41,400	39,100	2,300
Transport and communications	35,700	33,000	2,700
Services	189,700	181,400	8,300
Total	757,000	729,800	27,200

Source: Central Statistical Office, *Census of Population and Housing, 1969.*

[1] On the basis of the 1969 census. Of the employed population, about half were wage and salary earners in 1969; the remainder were self-employed (see Table 12).

GOVERNMENT FINANCE

BUDGETARY SYSTEM

The Central Government accounts for over 90 per cent of public sector revenue and expenditure. The local authorities supplement their tax revenues, derived mainly from property, by receipts from the supply of certain services, such as water and electricity, and by loans and grants from the Central Government. The annual budgets of the local authorities, as well as the tax rates and service charges, must be approved by the Central Government. The scope of the public sector in Zambia has been greatly enlarged as a result of the economic measures announced in April 1968 and the following years. At present, the Government has a majority ownership, generally 51 per cent of the share capital, in virtually all important mining, industrial, commercial, and financial enterprises in the country.

The Central Government's financial operations are conducted through a current and a capital budget. The current budget provides for normal departmental activities and includes grants and subsidies to state enterprises and to local authorities, as well as transfers to the capital budget. The current and capital budgets are for the calendar year; no grace period is provided for collecting receipts and making payments pertaining to the previous budget. Before 1968, the fiscal year was from July 1 to June 30. To facilitate the transition to a calendar year basis, the fiscal year that began on July 1, 1966 was extended to end on December 31, 1967. The Ministry of Finance is responsible for preparing, executing, and controlling the budget. Although there is no central preaudit of expenditures, each ministry is responsible for ensuring that its expenditures are in accordance with budgetary appropriations. Interdepartmental budgetary transfers are not permitted, but transfers between items within a department may be made with prior approval of the Ministry of Finance. Any excess expenditures must be covered by additional appropriations, which must be approved by Parliament.

All cash operations of the Government are effected through its main account with the Bank of Zambia. Although the Government is a net debtor vis-à-vis the commercial banks, its deposits are considerably in excess of its indebtedness to the banking system as a whole. A large amount of these deposits is in the form of a foreign assets portfolio. Borrowing from the Bank of Zambia is limited to 20 per cent of the Government's budgeted revenues for the current fiscal year, and must be repaid within three months from the end of the fiscal year.

STRUCTURE OF CURRENT REVENUE

Between June 1965 and the end of 1969, revenue rose at an average annual rate of more than 20 per cent. As monetized GDP increased by 15 per cent during this period, revenue as a percentage of GDP rose from 29 per cent in 1966 to 34 per cent in 1969 (Table 15.)

Government revenues in Zambia are greatly influenced by copper production and the price of copper on the world market. Government receipts derived directly from the copper industry [2] rose from K 142 million in 1965/66 to K 235 million in 1969 and to an estimated K 247 million in 1970. Despite these increases, the relative share of receipts from copper in total revenue declined from 67 per cent in 1965/66 to 59 per cent in 1969 and to 60 per cent in 1970. Receipts from all other sources, which rose from K 76 million in 1965/66 to K 166 million in 1969, declined to K 163 million in 1970.

Taxation of Copper Companies

A major reform of the taxation of the copper industry was announced concurrently with the announcement of the Government's intention to take a majority participation in the mining companies. The old system contained three elements: (1) The royalty tax based on the formula used by the British South Africa Company before it sold the mineral rights to Zambia: 13½ per cent of the price of copper less

---

[2] Defined as receipts from the mineral and income taxes imposed on mining companies. Other receipts derived direct from the copper industry, not included in this definition, are as follows: (1) Customs duties on imports of consumer goods by copper companies; these are estimated at about K 3 million, or 10 per cent of customs receipts. (2) Licenses, taxes on motor vehicles, and stamp duties. (3) Fees paid to state and local bodies. Moreover, tax receipts derived indirectly from the mining industry are substantial. For example, income taxes levied on the salaries paid by the mining companies and the 20 largest domestic suppliers to the industry were estimated to equal about 15 per cent of total 1969 income tax receipts from sectors other than mining.

K 16 a ton. It was a levy on production and the price used was the
monthly average of eight prices on the London Metal Exchange at the
time of production, an average which frequently bore little relation to
the prices reported as having actually been received by the companies.
(2) The export tax introduced in 1966: 40 per cent of the price of
copper exported in excess of a price of K 600 a ton, also calculated on
prices on the London Metal Exchange rather than on actual selling
prices. (3) The income tax, which was levied on profits after the deduction of royalty and export tax, at 37½ per cent on the first K 200,000
of profits and 45 per cent on the remainder.

The new reform replaces the export tax and the royalty payment
with a mineral tax of 51 per cent of net profits.[3] Hence, copper companies will pay a total of 73 per cent of profits—a 51 per cent mineral
tax plus the income tax, which is levied at a rate of 45 per cent on the
balance (49 per cent) of profits. The mineral tax is payable within
three months, whereas the income tax is payable with a time lag
ranging between 15 and 18 months, because the fiscal years of the
companies end in March and June.

Since the new arrangement imposes taxes on profits and not on production as was previously the case, it may encourage the development
of marginal mines.

Direct Taxes

The income of residents is subject to personal income tax regardless
of origin, whereas nonresidents are taxed only on that part of their
income earned in Zambia. The incomes of husband and wife are aggre-
gated for tax purposes. However, earnings of salaried working wives are
taxed separately and are, therefore, subject to lower rates. Authorized
deductions from personal income are limited to family allowances and
20 per cent (to a maximum of K 300) of insurance premiums. The
authorized deductions, which had remained unchanged since 1966, were
reduced sharply in April 1969. Family allowances are set at K 450 for
a single person, K 1,300 for a married couple, and K 180 for each
child up to a maximum of six children. The individual income tax is

---

[3] Lower rates are applied to profits derived from minerals other than copper.

TABLE 15. ZAMBIA: SOURCES OF GOVERNMENT REVENUE, 1965–70

(In thousands of Zambian kwacha)

	1965/66	1966/67 18 months	1966/67 Annual basis	1968	1969	1970	As Per Cent of Total 1965/66	1966/67	1968	1969	1970
Tax revenue	190,812	349,634	233,088	272,028	364,307	385,461	87.8	87.4	88.8	90.9	92.6
Mineral taxes	82,472	167,150	111,432	133,979	185,613	177,451	37.9	41.8	43.7	46.3	42.6
Income taxes	80,336	128,148	85,432	86,353	113,816	140,560	37.0	32.0	28.2	28.4	33.8
Mining companies	59,056	78,798	52,532	42,197	49,509	...	27.2	19.7	13.8	12.4	...
Other companies	7,612	19,360	12,907	17,609	30,988	...	3.5	4.8	5.7	7.7	...
P.A.Y.E.[1]	2,330	23,062	15,375	21,003	24,642	...	1.1	5.8	6.9	6.1	...
Other	11,338	6,928	4,618	5,544	8,677	...	5.2	1.7	1.8	2.2	...
Customs duties	16,594	26,174	17,449	21,232	30,965	...	7.6	6.5	6.9	7.7	...
Excise taxes											
Cigarettes	2,562	7,150	4,766	8,341	9,245	...	1.2	1.8	2.8	2.3	...
Dark beer	1,760	3,932	2,622	3,879	5,541	...	0.8	1.0	1.3	1.4	...
Clear beer	3,192	8,096	5,398	11,072	14,543	...	1.5	2.0	3.6	3.6	...
Miscellaneous	1,056	4,558	3,039	3,732	675	...	0.5	1.2	1.2	0.2	...
Licenses and other taxes	2,840	4,426	2,950	3,440	3,909	3,706	1.3	1.1	1.1	1.0	0.9
Other receipts	26,556	50,617	33,478	34,082	36,426	30,876	12.2	12.6	11.2	9.1	7.4
Interest	9,774	21,106	14,070	11,804	15,544	18,778	4.5	5.3	3.9	3.9	4.5
Fees and rents	4,976	13,670	9,114	8,401	9,668	9,412	2.3	3.4	2.7	2.4	2.3
Overseas service aid [2]	} 11,806	5,074	3,382	5,121	5,094	447	} 5.4	1.3	1.7	1.3	0.1
Miscellaneous		10,767	6,912	8,756	6,120	2,239		2.6	2.9	1.5	0.5
Total	217,368	400,251	266,566	306,110	400,733	416,337	100.0	100.0	100.0	100.0	100.0

Sources: Government of Zambia, *Financial Reports*; Central Statistical Office, *Monthly Digest of Statistics*; and data provided by the Zambian authorities.

[1] Pay-as-you-earn.
[2] Funds granted by the United Kingdom to cover mainly travel expenses and pensions of British technical assistants.

applied at progressive rates ranging from 7.5 per cent on annual incomes not exceeding K 500 to 90 per cent on incomes above K 30,000.

Profits of limited liability companies incorporated in Zambia, regardless of origin, are subject to income tax. Companies incorporated abroad are subject to income tax on profits earned in Zambia. Prior to April 1, 1969, the tax rate was 37.5 per cent on the first K 200,000 of profits and 45 per cent on any excess above K 200,000. Since then, profits have been taxed uniformly at 45 per cent. In 1965 the Pioneer Industries Act was promulgated with a view to promoting new investments. The Act provides qualifying industries with a five-year period of income tax relief. Although aimed mainly at attracting new industries, its provisions also apply to existing industries.

Since 1966, taxes on wages and salaries have been collected under the pay-as-you-earn (P.A.Y.E.) system. Taxes are assessed and collected directly on (1) incomes derived from trades or professions of individuals and partnerships; (2) rent and other receipts from land; and (3) profits from business carried out by a company or trust. Income tax assessed directly is normally due and payable within 30 days after the taxpayer is notified of the assessment. The recent increase in revenues from direct taxation was attributed mainly to the improvement in the machinery of tax assessment and collection. However, the Income Tax Department is suffering from a lack of qualified tax officers; nearly 50 per cent of authorized professional positions in the department are vacant. The department is offering in-service training to young professionals recently graduated from university.

Indirect Taxes

The Brussels tariff nomenclature was adopted in January 1970. Imports of certain essential goods, such as maize, vegetables, and fruits, are exempt from import duty. Also exempt are most imports of capital goods and commodities required for the development of the country. Customs duties were raised between 1968 and 1970, especially in 1970. The rates applicable to luxury goods were raised from 30 per cent and 50 per cent to 50 per cent and 75 per cent, respectively. Despite these increases, customs duties in Zambia are considerably lower than in other East African countries; also, the Zambian duties are levied on the f.o.b. price of goods, as opposed to a c.i.f. base in other East African countries.

The rates of import duty can be broadly classified into three groups: (1) a rate ranging between 10 per cent and 20 per cent applicable to most nonessential products widely used by low-income groups, such as textiles, paper products, and wood products; (2) a rate of about 30 per cent applicable to goods used by high-income groups, including certain foodstuffs and appliances; and (3) a rate of about 50 per cent applicable to luxury goods, such as cameras, watches and clocks, cosmetics, and tape recorders, and a rate of about 75 per cent applicable to another category of luxury goods, such as television sets, washing machines, and jewelry. Import duties applicable to automobiles are progressive and vary from 45 per cent on cars valued up to K 1,000 to 925 per cent on cars valued at K 10,000 or over.

STRUCTURE OF CURRENT EXPENDITURE

Government expenditure rose between July 1, 1965 and the end of 1968 at an average annual rate of about 30 per cent, declined in 1969 by 6 per cent, but increased in 1970 by about 11 per cent. As a result, it rose from 27 per cent of GDP in 1966 to 32 per cent in 1969.

Since 1968, there has been a substantial change in the composition of government expenditure: a relative decline in capital expenditure has been more than offset by the increase in current expenditure. The latter rose in 1969 by 6 per cent and in 1970 by 12 per cent. Consequently, the share of current expenditure in total expenditure rose from 52 per cent in 1968 to 59 per cent in 1969 and 61 per cent in 1970 (Table 16).

The increases in current expenditure in 1969 and 1970 were due entirely to larger outlays on economic and social services, which accounted for an estimated 54 per cent of the total in 1970 against 44 per cent and 53 per cent in 1968 and 1969, respectively (Table 17). Salaries, which accounted for about 30 per cent of current expenditure in 1968 and 1969, were expected to account for only 26 per cent in 1970. Subsidy payments have risen substantially beginning in 1968, and in 1970 were about 18 per cent of current expenditure. The subsidies

TABLE 16. ZAMBIA: GOVERNMENT FINANCES, 1968–70

(*In millions of Zambian kwacha*)

	1968	1969	1970
Revenue	306.1	400.7	416
Current expenditure	−209.9	−223.1	−253
Current budget surplus	96.2	177.6	163
Capital expenditure	−193.3	−156.3	−165
Overall surplus or deficit	−97.1	21.3	−2
Domestic financing	**55.2**	**−39.0**	...
Banking system (net)	30.0	−80.3	...
Borrowing (net)	*26.2*	*6.0*	...
Deposits	*3.8*	*−86.3*	...
Other debt operations	1.0	36.0	...
Treasury bills and bonds (net)	*−0.6*	*8.8*	...
Loans and advances (net)	*1.6*	*27.2*	...
Other accounts	24.2	5.3	...
Cash in till and items in transit	*17.9*	*5.3*	...
Special funds	*2.3*	*3.8*	...
Deposits with Treasury	*4.0*	*−3.8*	...
Foreign financing	**40.7**	**18.4**	...
Loans and grants	40.7	18.4	...
Amount received	*47.0*	*23.5*	...
Amortization	*−6.3*	*−5.1*	...
Errors and omissions	**1.2**	**−0.7**	...

Sources: Government of Zambia, *Financial Reports, 1968* and *1969;* and data provided by the Zambian authorities.

were mainly allocated to local authorities and rural councils, to the National Agricultural Marketing Board for imports of food, mainly maize, to the Credit Organization of Zambia, to the Ministry of Education, and to state-owned corporations.

CENTRAL GOVERNMENT BUDGET

1968–69

Because the rise in expenditures in 1968, both current and capital, was in excess of the substantial gains in receipts that followed upon increased copper production and higher copper prices, there was an overall budget deficit of K 97 million in 1968 (Table 16). The deficit was financed mainly by foreign loans and grants and domestic bank borrowing. While current expenditure rose because of expanded services, capital expenditure rose because of Zambia's policy of changing its

TABLE 17. ZAMBIA: DISTRIBUTION OF CURRENT BUDGETARY EXPENDITURE, 1968–70

(*In millions of Zambian kwacha*)

	1968 [1]	1969 [1]	1970 [2]
General			
Administration	52.7	39.3	⎫
Defense and police	25.6	21.5	⎬ 81.5
Pensions and gratuities	13.1	15.5	⎭
Interest on public debt	13.4	15.6	18.4
	104.8	91.9	99.9
Economic services			
Agricultural and rural development	12.3	28.4	24.0
Transportation, power, and public works	21.8	25.3	36.0
	41.2	61.7	69.9
Social services			
Education	31.9	37.4	40.4
Public health	14.8	16.8	23.3
	51.0	55.8	65.8
Local governments	12.9	13.7	17.4
Total	**209.9**	**223.1**	**253.0**
Salaries	61.9	67.7	65.6
Supplies and maintenance	67.9	70.1	83.0
Subsidies	33.7	44.0	46.0
Other	46.4	41.3	58.4

Source: Data provided by the Zambian authorities.

[1] Actual outturn.

[2] Revised estimate.

traditional sources of supply of goods, electricity, and fuel, after Rhodesia's unilateral declaration of independence.

Faced with the emergence of inflationary pressures and the continued rise in current expenditure, the Government took measures to increase receipts and reduce expenditures in order to achieve a balanced budget in 1969. Tax rates on personal income and company profits were raised and permissible deductions were lowered. The machinery of tax assessment and collection was reinforced. These measures raised receipts from personal and company income taxes, other than from mining companies, by 44 per cent (to K 56 million). The continued rise in copper production and higher copper prices raised receipts from the copper industry by 33 per cent (to K 235 million). Total receipts in 1969 rose by 31 per cent, to K 401 million. Although current expenditure in 1969 rose by 6 per cent (to K 223 million), capital outlays were curtailed by 19 per cent (to K 156 million). The reduction in capital expenditure was made possible by the completion of some infrastructure projects connected with the unilateral declaration of independence by Rhodesia. Consequently, overall expenditure declined by 6 per cent, to K 379 million. The resulting overall surplus of K 21 million and receipts from foreign loans and grants made it possible for the Government to increase substantially its domestic deposits and foreign assets portfolio.

1970

In 1970 there was a small overall deficit of about K 2 million. Receipts rose by 3.8 per cent (to K 416 million), while current expenditures and capital outlays rose by 13 per cent and 5.5 per cent (to K 253 million and K 165 million), respectively (Table 16). Receipts from the mining companies are estimated to have risen by 5 per cent. The relatively modest increase was due to a decline in production resulting from the flooding of a major mine and lower copper prices beginning in April 1970. In fact, government receipts from this source would have fallen substantially in 1970 had it not been for the 15 to 18 months' time lag for the payment of income taxes by the mining companies.

Tax receipts other than from mining companies rose by 6 per cent. However, nontax receipts declined, with the result that receipts from sources other than mining increased by about 2 per cent, to K 169 million.

The increase in current expenditure in 1970 was attributed mostly to a number of exceptional and nonrecurrent factors. Substantial expenses were incurred to subsidize imported maize in order to prevent an increase in the domestic price. In addition, a considerable part of the increase was due to outlays connected with the Conference of Non-Aligned Nations held in Lusaka during the year. Wages of government contractual daily workers were also raised following the salary increases in the private sector. The reduction in capital expenditure reflected a further phasing out of investments associated with Rhodesia's unilateral declaration of independence.

SOCIAL SECURITY SYSTEM

The Zambia National Provident Fund, which came into operation in January 1966, is a savings scheme with the principal purpose of providing benefits to persons retiring from employment because of old age, total disability, or permanent ill health. It also offers facilities for voluntary savings that can be claimed at any time a member changes employment or becomes unemployed. Most employees over 18 years of age are required to join, with the notable exception of persons in government service and those employed by local governments or the teaching service, for whom Parliament has already made provision in the existing Pensions Ordinances and Regulations. All employers must contribute, except employers of domestic servants in private households. The employer pays a statutory contribution for every eligible employee, but is authorized to deduct the employee's share of this contribution from his wages. The total statutory contribution is equivalent to 10 per cent of wages, up to a monthly maximum of K 8, except for "low wage earners," for whom the contribution is 7.5 per cent. (A "low wage earner" is an employee whose wage rate does not exceed K 1.50 a working day, or K 39.00 a calendar month, or K 33.00 a calendar month in regular five-days-a-week employment.) The employee's share is normally 5 per cent of his wages, but for "low wage earners" it is 2.5 per cent. In order to give employees better retirement benefits, an employer may make a voluntary, supplementary contribution to the Provident Fund in respect of any employee for whom he is liable to pay a statutory contribution. This extra contribution may be paid solely by the employer as a noncontributory retirement benefit scheme, solely by the employee as a supplementary savings scheme if the employer is willing to deduct an agreed amount each month from wages, or jointly by the employer and employee in such proportion as they might agree. The Provident Fund is administered by an independent board appointed by the Minister of Labor and Social Development, and consists of representatives of employers' associations, trade unions, and government departments.

As of March 1968, a total of 5,351 employers were registered contributors to the Provident Fund in respect of approximately 300,000 employees. The 1968 Ministerial Order that brought employers with under 10 employees into the system increased the number of contributing employers by 2,183. During the nine months ended March 1968, K 7.1 million in statutory contributions was received from contributing employers, bringing the total revenue of the board from contributions to K 12 million.

PUBLIC DEBT

Between June 1966 and December 1969, the domestic public debt rose at an average annual rate of about 12 per cent. At the end of 1969 it amounted to K 219 million, about 55 per cent of 1969 budgetary receipts. Interest on the domestic debt amounted to about K 15.6 million, less than 4 per cent of 1969 budget revenue. Interest on the domestic and foreign debt combined was equal to about 6.5 per cent of 1969 budget revenue. The increase in domestic public debt was mostly in the form of treasury bills and government-registered stocks, which in December 1969 accounted for about 80 per cent of the total public domestic debt. While the Bank of Zambia holds negligible amounts of treasury bills, commercial banks held about one fourth of the amount outstanding at the end of December 1969. The remainder was held by building societies, the Post Office Savings Bank, other financial institutions, and, to a very small extent, individuals.

FISCAL ACTIVITIES OF LOCAL GOVERNMENTS

Following the reorganization of local authorities in July 1970, there are now 54 local authorities comprising 9 principal urban centers, 11 small townships, and 34 rural council areas.

Current expenditures of the local authorities in 1968 amounted to about K 43 million, of which about K 32 million was used by the 9 urban centers and the remainder almost equally by the townships and rural areas. Current revenues of the local authorities consist of proceeds from the property tax, the personal levy (a personal tax, with rates varying from K 1.25 to K 20, depending on income), rents, and the liquor tax. Receipts from these sources finance about 90 per cent of the expenditures of urban centers and townships and 20 per cent of the outlays of rural areas, with the remainder being covered by grants from the Central Government.

In determining the amount of the Central Government's grant to each local authority, a new formula was to be applied beginning in 1971. In the large urban centers, the amount of the grant will depend on the population in the area and the potential yield from property taxes. In the rural areas, the grant will be set so as to cover the difference between expenditures and anticipated income.

In addition to the grants, financial assistance from the Central Government also takes the form of loans for housing and for other infrastructure projects in connection with the water supply, electricity, sewerage, and roads. Government loans for housing rose from about K 6 million in 1969 to about K 10 million in 1970, while loans for other infrastructure projects declined from K 10 million to K 8 million. Local authorities pay interest of 6¼ per cent per annum on these loans, which must be amortized over 40 years for housing and over 30 years for other projects. Borrowing by local authorities from sources other than the Government is limited and requires individual approval from the Ministry of Provincial and Local Governments and the Ministry of Finance. The main source of such borrowing has been the building societies.

MONEY AND BANKING

MONETARY SYSTEM

Until early in 1968, the currency unit of Zambia was the Zambian pound, divided into shillings and pence, with a par value of £Z 1 = US$2.80. The Zambian pound was not devalued at the time the pound sterling was devalued in November 1967. On January 16, 1968, a new currency unit, the kwacha, divided into 100 ngwee, was introduced. The new currency was exchanged for the old at the rate of £Z 1 = K 2, and the corresponding change in the par value to K 1 = US$1.40 was agreed with the International Monetary Fund in January 1968. All old notes and coins ceased to be legal tender by December 15, 1968, although they continue to be redeemable at the Bank of Zambia until further notice.

The currency is issued by the Bank of Zambia, which is required by its statutes to maintain convertible foreign exchange reserves equal to not less than 50 per cent of currency in circulation and other demand liabilities as at June 25, 1965 (the date of commencement of the Bank's operations), plus 25 per cent of any subsequent increase in such liabilities. In practice, external reserves have consistently been in excess of this requirement. In September 1968, Zambia entered into an agreement with the Government of the United Kingdom under which the latter guarantees the value, in terms of U. S. dollars, of the greater part of the official sterling reserves held by Zambia, and in return Zambia undertakes to maintain a certain percentage of its reserves in sterling.

STRUCTURE AND OPERATIONS OF BANKING SYSTEM

The financial institutions in Zambia comprise a central bank (the Bank of Zambia), commercial banks, building societies, specialized credit institutions (such as the Agricultural Finance Corporation), the Post Office Savings Bank, and insurance companies.

On November 10, 1970, the Government announced measures aimed at changing the structure of the banking system and the financial institutions. The measures called for the merger of the five existing commercial banks into two banks with equity participation by the Government of 51 per cent. The assets and liabilities of the three existing building societies, which act as savings and loan associations, were to be wholly taken over by the Government. The operations of foreign insurance companies, which should be phased out by the end of 1971, were to be taken over by the government-owned National Insurance Company. The Government's equity participation in these financial institutions is to be vested in the Financial and Development Corporation (FINDECO), established for this purpose.

Bank of Zambia

The Bank of Rhodesia and Nyasaland functioned as the central bank of the Federation of Rhodesia and Nyasaland until August 1964 when, in anticipation of the dissolution of the Federation, the Bank of Northern Rhodesia was established. The currency in circulation in the three territories of the Federation was the Rhodesia and Nyasaland pound. Following the dissolution of the Federation, and Zambia's independence on October 24, 1964, the Bank of Northern Rhodesia was renamed the Bank of Zambia and a new Zambian currency was issued to replace the federal currency. The assets of the Bank of Rhodesia and Nyasaland were distributed among the three successor central banks [4] in proportion to the amount of old currency redeemed from each territory at the date of the Bank's dissolution. The old currency ceased to be legal tender in June 1965, when the Bank of Rhodesia and Nyasaland was finally dissolved and the Bank of Zambia took over all central banking functions in Zambia. The authorized and paid-up capital of the Bank of Zambia is K 2 million, all of which is subscribed by the Zambian Government. The Bank is required to maintain a general reserve fund to which not less than one fourth of each year's profits must be credited until the reserve fund is equal to the authorized capital of the Bank. Thereafter, and while the reserve fund remains less than three times the authorized capital, at least one eighth of each year's net profits must be allocated to it.

The Bank is administered by a Board of Directors consisting of a Governor, a Deputy Governor, and seven other directors appointed by the Minister of Finance, one of whom is the Permanent Secretary in the Ministry of Finance and has no voting power on the Board.

The Bank is empowered to transact business and deal in assets of various kinds in accordance with the normal principles of central banking. It may buy, sell, discount, or rediscount domestic bills of exchange and promissory notes drawn for commercial purposes, treasury bills, local registered stocks, and other securities of the Government maturing within 25 years from the date of purchase. It may also engage in similar transactions against gold and foreign currencies, bills of exchange, treasury bills, and government securities expressed in sterling or other convertible currencies and maturing in not less than 184 days. The Bank may grant advances against warehouse warrants or similar documents and, with the consent of the Minister of Finance, may subscribe to the shares of any corporation set up with the approval of the Minister of Finance to finance economic development; however, the holdings of such shares may not exceed 25 per cent of the aggregate of the Bank's issued capital and general reserve fund.

The Bank of Zambia is the banker and financial advisor to the Government. It may grant loans and advances to the Government, provided that the total amount outstanding does not exceed 20 per cent of the

---

[4] Bank of Zambia, Reserve Bank of Malawi, and Reserve Bank of Rhodesia.

Government's current budget revenues for the financial year in respect of which the credit is extended. Such loans and advances must be repaid within three months of the end of the financial year, failing which the Bank is prohibited by law from granting further advances to the Government. The Bank also issues and manages government domestic loans and acts as agent for the Treasury in placing treasury bills and medium-term and long-term government bonds.

The Bank of Zambia is empowered to regulate the volume of commercial bank credit by prescribing (1) the minimum liquidity ratio that commercial banks must observe; (2) the minimum percentage of their demand and time deposits that commercial banks must maintain as deposits with the Bank of Zambia; (3) the percentage of any increase in commercial bank advances that should be maintained as deposits with the Bank of Zambia; and (4) sectoral ceilings on commercial bank loans and advances. Thus far the Bank has prescribed a minimum liquidity ratio of 25 per cent, and minimum reserve requirements of 8 per cent for demand deposits and 3 per cent for time and savings deposits. These have remained unchanged since 1965. Liquid assets of the commercial banks and their deposits with the Bank of Zambia have consistently been in excess of the prescribed minimums.

In April 1968 the Bank of Zambia limited to an amount that did not exceed the borrower's paid-up share capital and reserves, new loans or renewals of existing loans by commercial banks to foreign individuals and to enterprises that are not wholly owned by Zambians. Moreover, all such loans were made subject to the prior approval of the Bank of Zambia. To facilitate the granting of small personal loans, banks were permitted to grant, without this prior approval, temporary overdraft facilities up to a limit of K 1,000 for each individual. In August 1969 the restriction on loans to enterprises not wholly owned by Zambians was relaxed and became applicable to those which did not have a majority participation by Zambians. The purpose of this measure was to reduce domestic credit and to induce non-Zambian individuals and enterprises to bring funds into the country and retain a larger proportion of their profits to finance their operations in Zambia.

Although the Bank of Zambia is empowered to act as banker to commercial banks through its rediscount facility, the volume of such activity has been small because of the high liquidity of the commercial

TABLE 18.   ZAMBIA: ASSETS AND LIABILITIES OF BANK OF ZAMBIA, 1965–70

(In millions of Zambian kwacha; end of period)

	1965	1966	1967	1968	1969				1970			
					Mar.	June	Sept.	Dec.	Mar.	June	Sept.	Dec.
Assets												
Foreign assets	142.55	150.41	128.84	142.42	152.12	177.08	213.77	263.45	325.69	403.11	420.26	367.00
Gold	2.54	4.14	4.14	4.15	4.17	4.16	4.16	4.16	4.17	4.17	4.17	4.17
Foreign exchange	52.52	59.70	60.21	87.16	91.69	100.06	112.25	160.02	212.81	290.33	304.89	264.28
SDR holdings	—	—	—	—	—	—	—	—	6.36	6.36	6.35	6.35
IMF gold tranche position	2.31	2.31	4.46	4.60	4.62	4.62	6.38	6.38	7.09	7.08	8.93	13.58
Government holdings of foreign exchange	85.18	84.26	60.03	46.51	51.64	68.24	90.98	92.89	95.26	95.17	95.92	78.62
Claims on government	6.29	5.91	7.95	5.62	8.99	8.89	11.69	-0.79	-4.77	-6.28	3.16	-5.50
Claims on private sector	0.48	0.42	3.75	0.44	0.23	0.41	2.23	2.00	2.00	2.00	2.00	1.00
Unclassified assets	0.09	0.02	0.04	0.04				0.05	0.41	0.27	0.49	
Assets = liabilities	149.41	156.76	140.58	148.52	161.34	186.38	227.69	264.71	323.33	399.10	425.91	364.50
Liabilities												
Reserve money	33.11	41.98	51.53	63.07	60.41	56.78	62.80	72.63	74.62	74.07	67.33	71.03
Currency outside banks	18.55	28.35	35.11	40.30	39.48	37.20	41.30	40.53	39.55	39.76	42.67	42.84
Currency in banks	5.07	4.38	5.63	7.23	6.34	5.81	6.53	8.34	7.57	7.02	7.45	9.03
Bankers' deposits	9.49	9.25	10.79	15.54	14.59	13.77	14.97	23.76	27.50	27.29	17.21	19.16
Quasi-monetary deposits[1]					10.01	20.01	23.51	20.01	30.01	85.50	95.00	66.09
Government deposits	112.20	109.08	81.05	77.30	81.94	101.51	128.44	163.56	196.74	222.43	230.58	197.67
Unclassified liabilities	4.10	5.70	8.00	8.15	8.98	8.08	12.94	8.51	21.96	17.10	33.00	29.71

Source: IMF, *International Financial Statistics.*

[1] Mainly time deposits of mining companies kept with the Bank of Zambia under a special arrangement.

banks. The banks had recourse to central bank facilities only for a short period in 1967 and 1968. In July 1968 the Bank decided to accept for rediscounting only commercial bills whose value was individually K 10,000 or over, and in 1970 it decided to limit the rediscount facility to export credits.

Movements in the assets and liabilities of the Bank of Zambia in recent years reflect almost exclusively developments in the mining sector. The total assets and liabilities of the Bank rose from K 149 million in December 1965 to K 365 million at the end of December 1970 (Table 18). The increase was on account of a sharp rise in foreign assets in 1969 and in 1970. During 1965–70 the Bank's lending operations were small, and they never exceeded 7 per cent of total assets. The low ratio of domestic assets in the Bank's portfolio, in particular in 1970, was due on the one hand to the absence of government borrowing and on the other to the very limited use of central bank facilities by commercial banks.

About 70 per cent of the growth in the Bank of Zambia's liabilities in 1965–70 was accounted for by an increase in government deposits and quasi-monetary deposits. At the end of December 1970 these items represented 54 per cent and 18 per cent, respectively, of central bank liabilities. Before 1969, the Bank did not have any quasi-monetary liabilities. Since then, there has been a sharp increase in this item, owing to the application of the export surrender requirement to mining companies, which held considerable balances abroad prior to 1969. When these balances were repatriated, they were kept mostly as time deposits with the Bank of Zambia and commercial banks. Reserve money (the Bank of Zambia's currency liabilities and commercial bank deposits) more than doubled between December 1965 and December 1970, but its relative importance in total liabilities declined from 22 per cent to 19 per cent. In December 1970 currency outside banks grew at about the same rate as the money supply and accounted for about 21 per cent of it.

Commercial Banks

There are five commercial banks operating in Zambia, four of which are foreign owned. Three of these banks have their head offices abroad,

TABLE 19. ZAMBIA: ASSETS AND LIABILITIES OF COMMERCIAL BANKS, 1965–70 [1]

(In millions of Zambian kwacha; end of period)

	1965	1966	1967	1968	1969 Mar.	1969 June	1969 Sept.	1969 Dec.	1970 Mar.	1970 June	1970 Sept.	1970 Dec.
Assets												
Reserves	14.56	13.63	16.43	22.35	20.50	19.29	20.78	31.43	34.87	34.09	24.65	27.67
Cash	5.07	4.38	5.63	7.23	6.34	5.81	6.53	8.35	7.57	7.02	7.45	9.03
Balances with Bank of Zambia	*9.49*	*9.25*	*10.80*	*15.12*	*14.16*	*13.48*	*14.25*	*23.08*	*27.30*	*27.07*	*17.20*	*18.64*
Foreign assets	10.15	16.80	15.19	4.85	8.11	8.74	8.50	10.22	7.83	11.93	8.10	17.67
Claims on government	21.16	22.99	15.01	43.53	43.23	43.39	35.88	55.90	62.50	71.91	68.86	55.63
Claims on private sector	41.92	66.55	92.38	90.46	94.23	100.25	107.20	110.28	111.18	118.03	122.24	135.03
Unclassified assets	6.01	9.27	14.79	15.62	17.22	18.49	17.32	19.05	19.70	20.92	21.38	22.36
Assets = liabilities	**93.80**	**129.24**	**153.80**	**176.81**	**183.29**	**190.16**	**189.68**	**226.88**	**236.08**	**256.88**	**245.23**	**258.36**
Liabilities												
Demand deposits	64.12	85.08	99.25	132.41	122.93	125.92	125.55	152.16	160.08	168.20	134.65	161.21
Time and savings deposits	31.05	40.06	47.52	58.01	63.24	66.46	70.59	80.22	87.34	96.36	106.68	103.53
Foreign liabilities	1.94	7.02	7.45	4.24	4.37	0.89	3.22	4.35	5.37	3.57	11.74	1.15
Unclassified liabilities	−3.31	−2.92	−0.42	−17.85	−7.25	−3.11	−9.68	−9.85	−16.71	−11.25	−7.84	−7.53
Assets = liabilities	**93.80**	**129.24**	**153.80**	**176.81**	**183.29**	**190.16**	**189.68**	**226.88**	**236.08**	**256.88**	**245.23**	**258.36**

Source: IMF, *International Financial Statistics*.   [1] Including the Merchant Bank.

TABLE 20. ZAMBIA: DEPOSITS AND CREDIT BY TYPE AND BY LENDING INSTITUTION, 1967–70

(In millions of Zambian kwacha; end of period)

Lending Institution	1967 Private sector[1] Deposits	Loans	1967 Public sector Treasury bills and stocks	Loans	1968 Private sector[1] Deposits	Loans	1968 Public sector Treasury bills and stocks	Loans	1969 Private sector[1] Deposits	Loans	1969 Public sector Treasury bills and stocks	Loans	1970 Private sector[1] Deposits	Loans	1970 Public sector Treasury bills and stocks	Loans
Commercial banks[2]	146.8	92.4	15.0	9.5	190.4	90.5	43.5	9.6	232.4	110.3	55.9	11.3	264.7[3]	135.0[3]	55.6[3]	17.0[4]
Building societies	14.9	34.4			18.9	40.0			22.3	42.7			25.8[4]	47.0[4]		
Post Office Savings Bank	7.3	—	6.5		7.8	—	6.9		7.9	—	6.8		8.1[4]	—	7.4[4]	
Credit Organization of Zambia[5]	—	15.9[6]	—		—	18.4[7]	—		—	2.6[8]	—		—	—	—	
INDECO	—	3.4	…		—	—	…		—	—	…		—	3.6[9]	—	

Sources: Central Statistical Office, *Monthly Digest of Statistics*; and data provided by the Zambian authorities.
[1] State-controlled commercial enterprises are included in private sector.   [2] Including the Merchant Bank.
[3] December 1970.   [4] September 1970.
[5] The operations of the Credit Organization (which was established in 1967) were taken over by the newly created Agricultural Finance Corporation in 1970.
[6] June 1967.   [7] June 1968.   [8] March 1969.   [9] March 1970.

while one is incorporated in Zambia and the other is wholly owned by the Bank of Zambia.

Commercial banking facilities, mostly in urban areas, expanded from 80 branches and agencies at the end of 1966 to 144 at the end of 1968 and 150 at the end of November 1970. The expansion of facilities in 1967 and 1968 appeared to have been proportional to the volume of transactions in deposit accounts. Transactions continued to grow in 1969 and 1970 at the same pace as in the previous two years, however, while the number of branches and agencies remained almost unchanged.

At the end of December 1970, about 73 per cent of the demand and time and savings deposits of the private sector were lodged with the commercial banks. Between December 1965 and December 1970, demand deposits and time and savings deposits rose at average annual rates of 21 per cent and 27 per cent, respectively. Between 1965 and 1968 the ratio of savings and time deposits to demand deposits remained fairly constant and averaged about 47 per cent; however, this ratio was 53 per cent at the end of 1969 and 64 per cent at the end of December 1970 (Table 19).

Commercial banks accounted for 72 per cent of credit extended to the private sector at the end of September 1970 (Table 20). Their claims on the private sector, which rose at an average annual rate of 49 per cent between the end of 1965 and the end of 1967, declined by 2 per cent in 1968 but rose by 22 per cent in 1969 and by 12 per cent in 1970. During 1969, credit to manufacturing increased by 12 per cent. A slight decline in construction credit associated with the phasing out of infrastructure activities connected with Rhodesia's unilateral declaration of independence was accompanied by a 48 per cent increase in credit to commerce to finance restocking. At the end of 1969, credit to manufacturing accounted for 29 per cent of total credit, commerce for 28 per cent, construction for 14 per cent, transport and communications for 6 per cent, and agriculture for 4 per cent (Table 21).

The rise in credit to the private sector in 1965–70 absorbed about 55 per cent of the increase in commercial bank resources. In the absence of other investment possibilities, the banks subscribed to treasury bills and government bonds. Their claims on the Government rose by almost 30 per cent in 1968 and by 28 per cent in 1969, but did not

TABLE 21. ZAMBIA: DISTRIBUTION OF COMMERCIAL BANK CREDIT
TO PRIVATE SECTOR, 1965–69

(*In per cent of total; end of year*)

	1965	1966	1967	1968	1969
Agriculture	5	3	2	2	4
Mining and quarrying	16	14	10	5	—
Manufacturing	21	21	17	28	29
Construction	9	9	13	16	14
Commerce	27	23	26	20	28
Transport and communications	—	1	12	4	6
Financial institutions	7	4	8	11	3
Other	15	25	12	14	16
Total	100	100	100	100	100

Source: Central Statistical Office, *Monthly Digest of Statistics.*

show any increase in 1970. The yield of treasury bills declined from 4½ per cent at the end of 1968 to 3½ per cent at the end of 1969.

Commercial bank liquidity remained consistently above the minimum ratio prescribed by the Bank of Zambia, ranging from a high of 53 per cent at the end of 1965 to a low of 39 per cent at the end of 1969. At the end of December 1970 the ratio was about 40 per cent.

Other Financial Institutions

The three building societies operating in Zambia derive their financial resources from share capital and deposits, and provide credit to the private sector in the form of mortgage loans. In the 21 months ended September 1970, the share capital and deposit liabilities of building societies increased by 17 per cent, to K 65 million. Loans outstanding rose by about the same percentage, to K 47 million (Table 20). There was also a 77 per cent rise in the liquid assets of these societies. Under the Building Societies Act of 1968, the Bank of Zambia can prescribe a minimum liquidity ratio for building societies, but as of April 1971 the Bank had not exercised this power.

The Post Office Savings Bank invests its funds largely in domestic government securities and, to a smaller extent, in foreign bonds. In the year ended September 1970, deposits with the Savings Bank rose by about 3 per cent, to K 8.1 million (Table 20).

The Merchant Bank, the only accepting house in Zambia, started operations in April 1965, when it took over the Zambian branch of the

Merchant Bank of Central Africa Ltd. It provides credit by accepting and discounting local trade bills, and its sources of finance are mainly in the form of short-term deposits. The bank has a paid-up capital of K 300,000. Its deposit and acceptance liabilities amounted to about K 19 million in June 1969.

There are two private development finance companies: Barclays Overseas Development Corporation and the African Loan and Development Company, which are subsidiaries of Barclays Bank D. C. O. and the Standard Bank of South Africa, respectively. These companies engage in medium-term financing for agricultural and industrial development, but so far the volume of their operations has been rather small.

A new credit institution, the Agricultural Credit Corporation, was established and took over the operations of the Credit Organization of Zambia in 1970 (see Structure of the Economy—Agricultural Credit, above).

The Industrial Development Corporation (INDECO) undertakes to implement the Government's policy of encouraging industrial growth by state participation, and provides loans to industry and commerce. Its authorized capital was raised from K 4.50 million to K 20 million in October 1966 and to K 50 million in November 1968. Its paid-up capital amounted to K 34.4 million as of March 1970. Loans and investments of INDECO increased from K 4 million in 1965 to K 59 million in March 1970. (See also Structure of the Economy—Industrial Production, above.)

INTEREST RATES

Interest rates have remained fairly stable since 1966, the only change having been in January 1967, when the rediscount rate was raised from 4½ per cent to 5 per cent and other rates were adjusted accordingly. As of December 1970, interest rates charged by commercial banks on their credit operations varied between 6 per cent (on overdrafts guaranteed by the Government) and 7½ per cent (on rediscounts of first-class trade bills maturing between four and six months). The prime rate on overdrafts was 7 per cent. The banks pay interest of 3½ per cent on savings accounts and on time deposits of up to six months, and 4 per

cent on deposits of up to one year. On deposits of over one year but
amounting to less than K 200,000, the banks pay interest of 4½ per
cent; for deposits in excess of that amount the rate is 4¼ per cent.
Building societies pay interest of 3½ per cent on savings accounts and
6 per cent on investment shares. On their mortgage loans, building
societies charge 7½ per cent for residential mortgages and 9 per cent for
commercial and industrial mortgages.

MONETARY AND CREDIT DEVELOPMENTS, 1965–70

The money supply rose at an average annual rate of about 28 per
cent between December 1965 and December 1968, but by only 12 per
cent in 1969. The increase in the money supply outpaced the expansion
in the economy, with the ratio of money to monetized GDP at current
prices rising from 14 per cent in 1965 to 17 per cent in 1969. In 1970,
the rate of expansion of the money supply continued to slow down and
increased by only about 6 per cent (Tables 22 and 23).

The increase in the money supply in the three years 1966–68 was
due mainly to a rapid expansion in bank credit, which was offset in
part by a decline in net foreign assets and an increase in quasi-money.
During this period, bank credit to the Government and the private
sector expanded at average annual rates of 25 per cent and 32 per
cent, respectively. In 1969 the money supply expanded to K 193 million because of an 88 per cent rise in the banking system's net foreign
assets and a 24 per cent increase in credit to the private sector, offset in

TABLE 22.   ZAMBIA: FACTORS AFFECTING MONEY SUPPLY, 1966–70

(In millions of Zambian kwacha)

	1966	1967	1968	1969	1970
Changes in					
Foreign assets (net)	9	−24	6	126	114
Domestic credit	30	51	25	−59	−14
Claims on government (net)	5	22	30	−80	−39
Claims on private sector	25	29	−5	21	25
Quasi-money	−9	−7	−10	−42	−69
Other items (net)	1	1	17	−5	−19
Change in money supply	31	21	38	20	12
Percentage change in money supply	37%	18%	29%	12%	6%

Source: Based on Table 23.

TABLE 23. ZAMBIA: MONETARY SURVEY, 1965–70

(In millions of Zambian kwacha; end of period)

	1965	1966	1967	1968	1969 Mar.	1969 June	1969 Sept.	1969 Dec.	1970 Mar.	1970 June	1970 Sept.	1970 Dec.
Assets												
Foreign assets (net)	150.76	160.19	136.58	143.03	155.86	184.93	219.05	269.32	328.15	411.47	416.62	383.52
Domestic credit	−42.35	−13.21	38.04	62.75	64.51	51.02	26.33	3.83	−25.83	−36.77	−34.32	−10.51
Claims on government (net)	*−84.75*	*−80.18*	*−58.09*	*−28.15*	*−29.72*	*−49.23*	*−80.87*	*−108.45*	*−139.01*	*−156.80*	*−158.56*	*−147.54*
Claims on private sector	*42.40*	*66.97*	*96.13*	*90.90*	*94.23*	*100.25*	*107.20*	*112.28*	*113.18*	*120.03*	*124.24*	*137.03*
Assets = liabilities	**108.41**	**146.98**	**174.62**	**205.78**	**220.37**	**235.95**	**245.38**	**273.15**	**302.32**	**374.70**	**382.30**	**373.01**
Liabilities												
Money	82.67	113.43	134.36	172.71	162.41	163.12	166.85	192.69	199.63	207.96	177.32	204.05
Currency outside banks	*18.55*	*28.35*	*35.11*	*40.30*	*39.48*	*37.20*	*41.30*	*40.53*	*39.55*	*39.76*	*42.67*	*42.84*
Demand deposits	*64.12*	*85.08*	*99.25*	*132.41*	*122.93*	*125.92*	*125.55*	*152.16*	*160.08*	*168.20*	*134.65*	*161.21*
Quasi-money[1]	31.05	40.06	47.52	58.01	73.25	86.47	94.10	100.23	117.35	181.86	201.68	169.62
Other items (net)	−5.31	−6.51	−7.26	−24.94	−15.29	−13.64	−15.57	−19.77	−14.66	−15.12	3.30	−0.66

Sources: IMF, *International Financial Statistics*; Central Statistical Office, *Monthly Digest of Statistics*.

[1] Mainly time deposits of mining companies kept with the Bank of Zambia under a special arrangement.

part by a sharp increase in net government deposits and in part by a substantial rise in quasi-money. The money supply expanded in 1970 to K 204 million because of an increase of 42 per cent in foreign assets and an increase of 12 per cent in credit to the private sector. These expansionary factors were more than offset by another sharp rise in quasi-money, which more than doubled, a further increase in net government deposits, and an increase in unclassified liabilities.

Since 1965, the volume and composition of domestic credit has fluctuated considerably. The Government has maintained a net creditor position with the banking system. The Government's deposits, including the counterpart of its holdings of foreign assets, have consistently exceeded its indebtedness to the banking system and in some years were also larger than the banking system's claims on the private sector. The Government's net creditor position with banks deteriorated by 28 per cent in 1967 and by 52 per cent in 1968, reflecting mainly the partial utilization of government deposits to finance the budgetary deficits that emerged in those years. The Government's net creditor position, which at the end of 1969 was K 108 million, rose by 37 per cent, to K 148 million, at the end of December 1970.

Credit to the private sector grew fairly steadily from 1965 to December 1970, except for a slight decline in 1968. The expansion in credit to the private sector, which averaged some 38 per cent annually between December 1965 and June 1968, was then brought to a halt as a result of the restrictions imposed on loans and advances to individuals other than Zambians and to enterprises that were not wholly owned by Zambians (see Bank of Zambia, above). Between June and December 1968, credit to the private sector declined by 17 per cent, although for the whole year the decline was limited to 5 per cent. Credit to the private sector expanded steadily throughout 1969 and at the end of the year was 23 per cent above that at the end of 1968. Claims on the private sector continued to increase in 1970 and rose by about 22 per cent, to K 137 million.

Net foreign assets, inclusive of government holdings, which showed virtually no change during the three years 1965–68, rose in 1969 by 88 per cent and in 1970 by 42 per cent, reaching K 384 million. The increase in 1970 reflected larger receipts from copper exports and—to the extent of about one third—the repatriation of the foreign exchange balances that mining companies had previously held abroad.

In the 24-month period ended December 1970, quasi-money rose by over 190 per cent, compared with an increase of about 87 per cent in the three years 1965–68. In December 1970 quasi-money represented about 83 per cent of the money supply, compared with 38 per cent at the end of 1965. Again, the repatriation of balances of mining companies was mostly responsible for this increase.[5]

BALANCE OF PAYMENTS

Foreign trade plays a predominant part in Zambia's economy, with exports and imports accounting for 64 per cent and 26 per cent, respectively, of GDP in 1969. Following the UN Security Council's resolution on sanctions against Rhodesia in 1965, Zambia took restrictive measures against both trade and capital movements that resulted in a substantial reduction of transactions with that country. Export receipts depend almost entirely (93 per cent) on copper, and import payments reflect mostly investment outlays on development projects, including those associated with Rhodesia's unilateral declaration of independence. While export receipts during the five years 1965–69 rose at an average annual rate of 21 per cent, reaching $1,067 million in 1969, imports increased at an average annual rate of 10 per cent, to $439 million, and the annual trade surplus, which had averaged $217 million during the four years 1965–68, was about $627 million in 1969 (Table 24).

The relatively large surplus on merchandise account is in part offset by substantial payments for freight and insurance and by outward remittances, mostly by mining companies on account of transfers of investment income and by salary transfers of their employees. During the five years 1965–69, outward payments on account of services and transfers were, on average, equivalent to 28 per cent of export receipts. Capital transactions vary widely because of direct investments carried out by the mining companies and variations in the balances held

---

[5] The reader is referred to the International Monetary Fund's monthly statistical bulletin, *International Financial Statistics,* for later information on monetary and credit developments.

TABLE 24.   ZAMBIA: SUMMARY OF BALANCE OF PAYMENTS, 1965–70

(*In millions of U. S. dollars*)

	1965	1966	1967	1968	1969	1970 [1]
Goods and services	**113.5**	**84.2**	**14.6**	**11.1**	**394.9**	**295**
Exports f.o.b.	513.5	624.7	651.3	746.6	1,066.6	984
Imports f.o.b.	−312.5	−370.4	−465.5	−518.5	−439.3	−439
Trade balance	201.0	254.3	185.8	228.1	627.3	545
Services (net)	−87.5	−170.1	−171.2	−217.0	−232.4	−250
Transfers	**−25.9**	**−13.4**	**0.1**	**−34.9**	**−74.9**	**−139**
Capital movements (net)	**−18.3**	**−38.8**	**37.4**	**40.6**	**−91.5**	**95**
Private	−0.4	16.9	20.4	40.6	−109.8	129
Official	−17.9	−55.7	17.0	—	18.2	−34
Allocation of SDRs	—	—	—	—	—	**8**
Errors and omissions	. . .	**−18.8**	**−85.1** [2]	**−7.7**	**−51.7**	**−99**
Monetary movements (increase −)	. . .	**−13.2**	**33.0**	**−9.1**	**−176.8**	**−160**

Sources: Central Statistical Office, *Monthly Digest of Statistics;* data provided by the Zambian authorities; IMF, *Balance of Payments Yearbook* and *International Financial Statistics.*

[1] Estimates.
[2] Adjusted for the devaluation of sterling.

overseas by them. During 1965–69 net private and official capital out-flows were, on average, equal to 2 per cent of export receipts.

TRADE

Reflecting rising prices for copper, Zambia's export price index, except for a small decline in 1967, increased annually between 1964 and 1969, from 100 to 201. During the same period, again with the exception of 1967, the import price index increased annually from 100 in 1964 to 114 in 1969. Consequently, the terms of trade during the period 1964–69 moved in favor of Zambia to the extent of an average annual rate of 13.5 per cent (Table 25).

Exports

Exports receipts, which in 1968 increased by 15 per cent, rose by 43 per cent in 1969, to K 762 million (Table 26). On the basis of customs data, about 90 per cent of the 1969 rise was due to larger earnings from copper exports, reflecting a 14 per cent rise in volume and a

TABLE 25. ZAMBIA: TRADE INDICES, 1965–69

($1964 = 100$)

Year	Exports			Imports			Terms of Trade [1]
	Volume	Price	Value	Volume	Price	Value	
1965	100	115	115	131	105	137	110
1966	88	178	151	147	108	161	165
1967	90	160	144	191	105	200	152
1968	89	187	166	179	118	212	159
1969	115	201	232	179	114	203	176

Source: Central Statistical Office, *Monthly Digest of Statistics.*
[1] Export price index as a percentage of import price index.

24 per cent rise in the unit value (Table 27). Receipts from other exports, such as zinc, lead, cobalt, and tobacco, also rose and accounted for 4 per cent of total export receipts. Exports of zinc increased by 38 per cent, lead by 16 per cent, and cobalt by 32 per cent. The export prices of zinc, lead, and tobacco in 1969 rose by 14 per cent, 43 per cent, and 11 per cent, respectively, while that of cobalt increased by 7.5 per cent. Exports of tobacco, which had been declining since 1964, mainly because of the departure of foreign farmers, increased by 19 per cent in 1969 although they were still substantially below the level attained in 1964. Although traditionally Zambia has been an exporter of maize, considerable quantities had to be imported in 1969.

Imports

Imports were valued at K 314 million in 1969, a decline of 15 per cent from 1968, owing largely to the completion of infrastructure projects by the Government and the Government's restrictive fiscal policies. On the basis of customs data, imports of machinery and transport equipment (41 per cent of total imports in 1968) declined by 8 per cent in 1969. Imports of manufactured products (30 per cent of total imports in 1968) decreased by 10 per cent, reflecting in part larger domestic production, while food imports (7 per cent of the total in 1968) increased by 26 per cent in 1969. The greater part of this increase was due to larger maize imports caused by lower domestic production. Other imports, including raw materials, chemicals, and fuel, were approximately the same as in 1968 (Table 28).

TABLE 26. ZAMBIA: SUMMARY OF FOREIGN TRADE, 1965–69

(In millions of Zambian kwacha)

	1965	1966	1967	1968	1969 [1]
Exports f.o.b.	366.8	446.2	465.2	533.3	761.9
Imports f.o.b.	−223.2	−264.6	−332.5	−370.4	−313.8
Trade surplus	143.6	181.6	132.7	162.9	448.1
Total exports as per cent of GDP	59.8%	58.7%	54.8%	57.1% [1]	64.0%
Total imports as per cent of GDP	36.4%	34.8%	39.2%	39.6%	26.4%

Sources: IMF, *Balance of Payments Yearbook;* data provided by the Zambian authorities; and Fund staff estimates.

[1] Preliminary.

Direction of Trade

Zambia's exports to the sterling area, including the United Kingdom, were valued at K 227 million in 1969, an increase of 25 per cent over 1968. In terms of relative importance, the market share of the sterling area has been declining annually: from 47 per cent in 1964 it fell to 33 per cent in 1968 and 30 per cent in 1969. The position of the EEC countries has remained fairly stable, accounting for 33 per cent of total exports in 1969, against an annual average of 32 per cent for the years 1964–69 (Table 29). The United States has been a relatively small market for Zambian exports, varying between a high of 5 per cent (in 1967) to less than 1 per cent (in 1965 and 1966). On the other hand, exports to Japan have expanded steadily, accounting for 23 per cent of total exports in 1969, against 11 per cent in 1964.

The direction of Zambia's imports changed considerably between 1964 and 1969 as a consequence of trade sanctions applied against Rhodesia. The ratio of imports from the sterling area and Rhodesia to total imports, after declining sharply during 1964–66, seems to have stabilized at about 62 per cent. While Rhodesia accounted for about half of this share in 1964, it accounted for only 11 per cent in 1969. The U.S. share, after increasing from 5 per cent in 1964 to 11 per cent in 1967, did not change much in 1967–69. The share of EEC countries rose from 6 per cent in 1964 to 13 per cent in 1968, but declined to 10 per cent in 1969. Japan's market share increased steadily from 2 per cent in 1964 to 7 per cent in 1969.

TABLE 27. ZAMBIA: VALUE, VOLUME, AND UNIT PRICE OF EXPORTS OF PRINCIPAL COMMODITIES, 1960–69

	1960	1961	1962	1963	1964	1965	1966	1967	1968	1969
VALUE¹ (million Zambian kwacha)										
Copper	239.2	220.2	217.6	235.6	296.8	343.2	460.6	434.0	516.1	724.5
Zinc	4.8	3.8	4.9	6.5	9.7	9.7	8.2	8.1	9.0	12.4
Lead	1.7	1.5	1.4	1.6	2.3	3.4	4.7	2.7	2.7	6.1
Manganese	1.2	0.9	0.9	0.9	0.6	0.7	0.6	0.5	0.4	—
Cobalt	2.9	1.3	2.1	1.3	3.5	3.6	4.3	5.6	3.4	4.5
Tobacco	3.8	5.0	5.4	3.6	5.7	4.9	4.5	3.7	2.7	3.2
Maize	..	..	..	..	..	1.9	1.8	8.7	2.8	0.4
Timber	..	..	..	0.8	0.8	0.9	0.7	0.6	0.6	0.7
VOLUME (thousand metric tons)										
Copper	556.9	545.1	530.6	574.1	681.2	683.0	598.6	601.3	643.1	730.1
Zinc	29.9	25.4	41.7	47.2	46.3	45.4	41.7	39.9	45.0	53.5
Lead	12.7	10.9	14.5	14.5	13.6	15.4	24.5	17.2	16.3	25.8
Manganese	40.8	42.6	46.3	43.5	27.2	32.7	26.3	24.5	17.5	
Cobalt	1.2	0.5	0.9	0.5	1.4	1.4	1.6	2.1	1.3	1.6
Tobacco	4.5	5.4	6.3	5.9	12.2	9.5	7.3	4.5	3.5	3.8
Maize	..	..	..	..	..	47.2	39.9	197.7	64.0	8.4
UNIT PRICE (Zambian kwacha per metric ton)										
Copper	429.5	404.0	410.1	410.4	435.7	502.5	769.5	721.8	802.5	992.3
Zinc	160.5	149.6	117.5	137.7	209.5	213.6	196.6	203.0	200.0	231.8
Lead	133.8	137.6	96.6	110.3	169.1	220.8	191.8	157.0	165.6	236.4
Manganese	29.4	21.1	19.4	20.7	22.1	21.4	22.8	20.4	22.8	—
Cobalt	2,416.7	2,600.0	2,333.3	2,600.0	2,500.0	2,571.4	2,687.5	2,666.6	2,615.4	2,812.5
Tobacco	844.4	925.9	857.1	610.2	467.2	515.8	616.4	822.2	771.4	842.1
Maize	..	..	..	..	..	40.2	45.1	44.0	43.8	47.6

Source: Central Statistical Office, *Monthly Digest of Statistics.*
¹ Indicates the value of exports of domestic origin.

TABLE 28. ZAMBIA: COMPOSITION OF IMPORTS, 1964–69 [1]

	1964	1965	1966	1967	1968	1969	1964	1965	1966	1967	1968	1969
	(Million Zambian kwacha)						(Per cent of total)					
Food	14.3	16.5	19.8	21.4	24.1	30.4	9.1	7.8	8.0	7.0	7.4	9.7
Beverages and tobacco	2.9	2.8	3.0	2.1	2.2	2.2	1.8	1.3	1.2	0.7	0.7	0.7
Raw materials	3.2	3.7	4.6	4.4	4.4	4.5	2.1	1.8	1.9	1.4	1.3	1.4
Minerals and fuel	17.4	20.6	19.6	31.2	33.2	35.6	11.1	9.8	8.0	10.2	10.2	11.4
Chemicals	16.3	20.1	19.2	20.9	22.7	22.6	10.4	9.6	7.8	6.8	7.0	7.3
Manufactures	55.6	75.7	78.9	93.9	98.1	88.4	35.6	35.9	32.1	30.7	30.2	28.4
Machinery and transport equipment	42.4	69.6	97.9	126.3	134.4	123.0	27.1	33.0	39.8	41.2	41.3	39.5
Other	4.3	1.7	3.0	6.2	6.1	5.1	2.8	0.8	1.2	2.0	1.9	1.6
Total	156.4	210.7	246.0	306.4	325.2	311.8	100.0	100.0	100.0	100.0	100.0	100.0

Source: Central Statistical Office, *Monthly Digest of Statistics.*

[1] Based on customs data, which differ from the balance of payments data.

Table 29. Zambia: Direction of Trade, 1964–69 [1]

	Million Zambian kwacha						Per cent of total					
	1964	1965	1966	1967	1968	1969	1964	1965	1966	1967	1968	1969
Exports												
Sterling area	158.1	182.6	199.9	165.0	181.7	227.3	47	48	40	35	33	30
United Kingdom	109.0	143.2	160.2	128.3	160.0	198.0	33	38	32	27	29	26
South Africa	26.2	24.9	28.1	25.4	11.7	7.8	8	6	6	5	2	1
Rhodesia [2]	13.8	10.9	5.0	2.0	1.0	0.4	3	3	1	1	—	—
Other	9.1	3.6	6.6	9.3	9.0	21.1	3	1	1	3	2	3
United States	8.9	1.6	0.2	23.9	10.8	8.7	3	1	—	5	2	1
EEC	104.4	113.0	167.6	125.1	174.2	252.9	31	30	34	27	32	33
Germany	43.7	50.3	69.4	42.8	70.9	96.1	13	13	14	9	13	13
Japan	37.1	46.2	69.5	95.8	114.9	180.3	11	12	14	20	21	23
CMEA countries [3]	6.0	8.7	10.0	6.6	5.5	6.3	2	2	2	1	1	1
Other countries	21.0	28.2	46.3	53.6	57.3	91.0	6	7	10	12	11	12
Total	335.5	380.3	493.5	470.0	544.4	766.5	100	100	100	100	100	100
Imports												
Sterling area	126.6	162.9	172.9	194.8	202.3	196.7	81	77	70	64	62	63
United Kingdom	26.8	42.1	54.4	62.9	76.2	71.4	17	20	22	21	24	23
South Africa	32.4	41.4	58.5	72.2	76.1	70.0	21	20	24	24	23	22
Rhodesia [2]	61.7	71.1	46.4	32.2	22.6	21.8	40	34	19	11	7	7
East Africa [4]	0.7	1.1	2.2	11.9	7.5	11.2	—	—	1	4	2	4
Other	5.0	7.2	11.4	15.6	19.9	22.3	3	3	4	4	6	7
United States	8.1	13.0	27.2	32.9	33.3	30.1	5	7	11	11	10	10
EEC	8.8	15.5	20.1	37.5	41.2	30.8	6	8	8	12	13	10
Germany	4.2	6.4	8.1	12.2	13.7	12.2	3	3	3	4	4	4
Japan	3.2	7.6	8.9	18.6	18.0	22.6	2	4	4	6	6	7
Other countries	9.7	11.7	17.0	22.6	30.4	31.6	6	4	7	7	9	10
Total	156.4	210.7	246.1	306.4	325.2	311.8	100	100	100	100	100	100

Source: Central Statistical Office, *Monthly Digest of Statistics.*

[1] Based on customs data, which differ from balance of payments data.
[2] Although Rhodesia is legally no longer a member of the sterling area, for statistical comparison it is considered part of the area.
[3] Members of the Council for Mutual Economic Assistance are Albania, Bulgaria, Czechoslovakia, Eastern Germany, Hungary, Mongolia, Poland, Rumania, and the Union of Soviet Socialist Republics.
[4] Kenya, Tanzania, and Uganda.

CURRENT INVISIBLES

The services account comprises mostly investment income and freight and insurance. Investment income in 1969 included receipts of $12.6 million ($9.8 million in 1968), mostly from investments in foreign securities, and outward payments of $96.6 million ($82.6 million in 1968) on account of remittances of dividends and profits, mainly by mining companies. The freight and insurance account in 1969 showed receipts of $33.6 million and payments of $184.8 million, compared with $32.2 million and $159.6 million, respectively, in 1968. While the slight increase in receipts was entirely on account of larger earnings from tourism, the 15 per cent rise in payments was due to increased trade with more distant areas, such as Japan.

Net transfer payments rose from $35 million in 1968 to $74.2 million in 1969, owing mainly to larger transfers by the private sector ($78.4 million in 1969, against $40.6 million in 1968). About $56 million of the transfers by the private sector in 1969 was accounted for by remittances of contract income and emigrants' funds earned by foreigners. Official outward transfers in 1969 were entirely offset by the receipt of $7 million representing the United Kingdom's contributions to the salaries of British subjects working in Zambia.

PRIVATE CAPITAL

Capital movements, which had recorded net inflows of $37.4 million and $40.6 million in 1967 and 1968, respectively, showed a net outflow of $91.5 million in 1969. In 1970 the trend was reversed and a net inflow of $95 million was recorded. The improvement was due to the repatriation in 1970 by mining companies of $130 million of export proceeds previously retained abroad. This inflow was, however, in part offset by an official capital outflow of $34 million, representing payments on account of compensation due to the mining companies.

OFFICIAL LOANS AND GRANTS

After the unilateral declaration of independence by Rhodesia, the United Kingdom provided an increased volume of grants and loans for financing the contingency programs to alleviate the adverse effects of Rhodesia's action on the Zambian economy and to develop alternative supply and transport routes. The United Kingdom agreed to extend aid of $38.8 million in 1967, and in that same year loans amounting to nearly $56 million were obtained from Italy, the United Kingdom, the Export-Import Bank of the United States, the World Bank, Japan, Germany, Denmark, and a French commercial bank. The loan from Italy, for the equivalent of $34.9 million at 6 per cent interest and repayable in 1969–83, was for the Tan-Zam oil pipeline; it was fully utilized by the end of 1968. In 1968, a Yugoslav loan of $72.4 million with a maturity of 10 years (repayment period, 1972–81) at 6 per cent interest was obtained for the Kafue hydroelectric project. In May 1968, an agreement was signed by the Anglo American Corporation and Mitsui and Mitsubishi Shoji Kaisha, under which the Japanese firms will provide $70 million for the expansion of copper production and the introduction of a new process, called TORCO, for treating refractory ores (see Structure of the Economy—Mining, above). Of this total, $42 million is a cash credit repayable over 7 years and $28 million is in the form of suppliers' credits to purchase Japanese plant and machinery. The loans will be repaid by deductions from the proceeds of copper shipments from Zambia to Japan, which are guaranteed at 100,000 tons a year for 10 years starting in 1969.

In July 1970, an agreement was reached between mainland China and Zambia and Tanzania for construction of the Tanzania-Zambia Railway. Mainland China has extended an interest-free loan of $420 million to be shared equally by Zambia and Tanzania. Repayment is to be made over 30 years beginning in 1983, in part by exports to mainland China and in part in third currencies. About 48 per cent of the loan is expected to be used to finance the external costs of the project; the remainder will be available to finance imports from mainland China not associated with the project, in order to generate funds to cover the local currency costs of the project. In June and July 1970, agreements were reached on additional assistance from the World Bank equivalent to $5.5 million for a project to encourage commercial farming by Zambians, and equivalent to $40 million to finance a 600-megawatt hydroelectric power station at the Kariba Dam.

TABLE 30. ZAMBIA: OFFICIAL EXTERNAL DEBT AS OF JUNE 30, 1970 [1]

(In millions of U. S. dollars)

	Outstanding (1)	Received (Cols. 1+3) (2)	Repaid (3)	Undrawn (Cols. 5−2) (4)	Total (Cols. 2+4) (5)	Loans Contracted Before independence (6)	Loans Contracted After independence (7)
World Bank	29.53	44.88	15.36	53.77	98.66	22.40	76.26
Denmark	1.15	1.15	—	1.53	2.67	—	2.67
France	4.68	4.86	0.18	7.52	12.38	—	12.38
Germany	1.18	1.18	—	—	1.18	—	1.18
Italy	32.40	34.87	2.48	—	34.87	—	34.87
Japan	3.72	5.91	2.18	—	5.91	—	5.91
United Kingdom	73.85	84.88	11.03	0.98	85.86	64.82	21.04
United States	4.44	7.81	3.37	25.30	33.11	2.23	30.88
U. S. S. R.	0.76	0.76	—	4.84	5.60	—	5.60
Yugoslavia	24.72 [2]	24.72	—	26.11	50.83 [3]	—	50.83 [3]
Total	176.43 [2]	211.02	34.60	12.01	331.07 [3]	89.45	241.62 [3]

Source: Data provided by the Zambian authorities.

[1] The data do not include loans from mainland China connected with the Tanzania-Zambia Railway.
[2] Of which $22.96 million is repayable in kwacha.
[3] Of which $34.58 million is repayable in kwacha.

EXTERNAL DEBT

Zambia's official external debt at the end of June 1970, at $176.4 million, was equivalent to about 8 per cent of that year's estimated GDP at current prices. Repayments of principal and payments of interest, which in 1969 were equivalent to 1.3 per cent of 1969 export earnings, were expected to increase in 1970 to 2.4 per cent of 1970 export earnings (Tables 30 and 31).

Of the total official lines of credit of $331 million negotiated through June 30, 1970, about 73 per cent was contracted subsequent to Zambia's independence and 10 per cent is repayable in local currency. By the end of June 1970, cumulative disbursements amounted to $211.0 million and repayments to $34.6 million. The main sources of official loans have been, in order of magnitude, the United Kingdom (40 per cent), the World Bank (21 per cent), Italy (16 per cent), and Yugoslavia (12 per cent). The remaining 11 per cent is accounted for by the United States, France, Japan, Germany, Denmark, and the U. S. S. R.

INTERNATIONAL RESERVES

Zambia's international reserves are held by the Bank of Zambia, the Government, and commercial banks. The Government's portfolio of foreign assets is managed by the Bank of Zambia. Commercial banks are permitted to maintain working balances in foreign exchange; since 1965 these have averaged $17 million on a gross basis and $9 million on a net basis. Mining companies maintain foreign exchange working balances under a special arrangement with the Bank of Zambia. In 1969 and 1970 the Bank required the mining companies to repatriate almost all their foreign exchange balances. By the end of September 1970, these balances had declined to about $17 million.

The gross foreign assets, inclusive of SDRs, held by the banking system and the Government increased from $206 million at the end of 1968 to $383 million at the end of 1969 and to $538.5 million at the end of 1970, at which time they were equivalent to 14 months of imports at the 1969 rate. Foreign liabilities were $6 million at the end of both 1968 and 1969 and $2 million at the end of 1970 (Table 32).

Zambia, as a member of the sterling area, participates in the 1968 Basle Agreement and accordingly holds a certain portion of its official

TABLE 31. ZAMBIA: SUMMARY OF OFFICIAL EXTERNAL DEBT,
DISBURSEMENTS AND SERVICING, 1969–71 [1]

(*In millions of U. S. dollars*)

	1969	1970 [2]	1971 [2]
Disbursements	25.9	16.1	. . .
Repayments	−7.1	−14.4	−10.5
Net receipts	18.8	1.7	. . .
Outstanding [3]	158.2	157.1	. . .
Interest payments	7.3	8.8	9.2

Source: Data provided by the Zambian authorities.
[1] Excludes debt repayable in kwacha.
[2] Forecasts by the Zambian authorities.
[3] End of year.

TABLE 32. ZAMBIA: INTERNATIONAL RESERVES, 1965–70

(*In millions of U. S. dollars; end of period*)

	1965	1966	1967	1968	1969	1970
Gold	3.6	5.8	5.8	5.8	5.8	5.8
SDRs	—	—	—	—	—	8.9
IMF gold tranche position	3.2	3.2	6.2	6.4	8.9	19.0
Foreign exchange	207.0	225.1	189.6	193.9	368.3	504.8
Bank of Zambia	*73.5*	*83.6*	*84.3*	*122.0*	*224.0*	*370.0*
Government	*119.3*	*118.0*	*84.0*	*65.1*	*130.0*	*110.1*
Commercial banks	*14.2*	*23.5*	*21.3*	*6.8*	*14.3*	*24.7*
Gross foreign assets	213.8	234.1	201.6	206.1	383.0	538.5
Less Foreign liabilities	2.7	9.8	10.4	5.9	6.1	1.8
Net international reserves	211.1	224.3	191.2	200.2	376.9	536.7

Source: IMF, *International Financial Statistics*, May 1971.

international reserves in sterling. In return, the United Kingdom guarantees in terms of the U.S. dollar that part of the official sterling holdings
held in certain forms (for example, excluding shares and real estate)
which exceeds 10 per cent of the country's total reserves.

EXCHANGE AND TRADE CONTROL SYSTEM [6]

Prior to November 1965 when the UN Security Council's first resolution on sanctions against Rhodesia was adopted, Zambia maintained a
trade and payments system virtually free of restrictions in respect of

[6] As of December 31, 1970. The reader is referred to the International Monetary Fund's *Annual Report on Exchange Restrictions* for later and more detailed
information on exchange and trade controls.

current transactions. Authorized dealers were empowered to sell foreign exchange freely up to certain limits for large numbers of payments for current transactions, while applications for amounts in excess of these limits and foreign exchange for other categories of current payments were approved freely. On the import side, only a few specified commodities required individual licensing. All others were free if originating in the sterling area or were admitted under open general license if originating elsewhere.

To comply with the UN Security Council's resolution, licenses have been required since December 1965 for all imports from all countries with a view to reducing imports from Rhodesia and promoting alternative transport routes circumventing that country. Only a small number of specified commodities now fall within the open general license category, and imports from or via Rhodesia are limited only if considered essential and if there is no alternative source of supply or transport route. For goods originating elsewhere, import licenses are granted liberally and there are no quota restrictions. However, certain goods must be imported via Dar es Salaam.

EXCHANGE RATE SYSTEM

The par value is K 1 = $1.40. The kwacha is pegged to the pound sterling at the par value and is therefore fixed in relation to other sterling area currencies at the par values. The authorized banks base their rates for currencies of countries outside the sterling area on the current London market rates.

REGULATIONS GOVERNING IMPORTS AND EXPORTS

Imports

Most imports from Rhodesia are prohibited. Licenses are granted liberally for goods originating elsewhere, whether the goods are under open general license or subject to individual licensing. There are no quota restrictions on imports and, except for a few items produced locally, there are no import bans. Import licensing aims at reducing imports from Rhodesia and avoiding the Rhodesian transport routes. To promote routes that bypass this country, certain goods are required to be imported via Dar es Salaam.

On August 11, 1969, the Government announced that certain goods, such as iron and steel, timber, glassware, builders' hardware, cloth, and yarn, would be imported by state trading companies. This measure was aimed at preventing overinvoicing by private importers. Thus far, state organizations do not have exclusive rights to import certain commodities, nor do they have specific policies with respect to pricing and profit margins. A National Import Agency is to be established to supply information and supervise the import practices of existing trading companies and state trading organizations. The range of commodities covered by the agency will initially be limited, but will gradually be expanded so that eventually all commodities will be imported through it.

Payment is authorized automatically for all permitted imports, subject to the presentation of the relevant documents showing that the goods have either been received or consigned to Zambia; special arrangements are in force, however, for payments in respect of freight charges on goods carried by Rhodesia Railways. Unless prior permission is obtained, all imports must be paid for within six months of the date of the arrival of the goods in Zambia.

Exports

All exports of a value over K 50 require a license. The main purpose of export licensing is to direct exports to certain transport routes and restrict exports to Rhodesia. Most exports to Rhodesia are prohibited. Certain commodities are subject to licensing mainly to ensure domestic supplies of needed goods and of certain strategic materials. For most goods, however, export licenses are issued freely, and some goods are covered by the open general license.

Export proceeds in foreign currencies appropriate to the country of destination must be surrendered to an authorized bank within six months of the date of shipment.

REGULATIONS GOVERNING INVISIBLES

Exchange to pay for invisibles related to imports, and also, up to certain limits, for other purposes, such as travel, is provided by the commercial banks without prior reference to the exchange control authorities. Special, reduced allocations apply to payments to Rhodesia for some invisibles. The basic exchange allowance for travel to countries other than Rhodesia is K 20 a day for an adult, with a maximum of K 900 for each period of two calendar years, and K 10 a day for each child under 12 years of age, with a maximum of K 450 for two calender years. Each traveler may take out K 10 in local currency on each trip and not more than the equivalent of K 20 in foreign currency notes.

Foreign nationals employed in Zambia under a contract of not more than five years are permitted to remit abroad one half of their earnings if they were recruited outside Zambia and one third if recruited in Zambia, except for foreign nationals employed by the mining companies, who may remit one half of their annual earnings even if they were recruited in Zambia.

The ban on remittance of profits and dividends, which was introduced in April 1968 on a temporary basis, was lifted in March 1970. Under this ban profits and dividends were permitted to be transferred abroad up to a maximum of 30 per cent of equity capital or one half of the net profit, whichever was smaller. This restriction was relaxed in August 1969 by limiting its applicability to companies that did not have a majority Zambian ownership, and was lifted in March 1970.

CAPITAL TRANSFERS

Inward transfers of capital are not restricted. Outward transfers of capital, including those to other parts of the sterling area, are controlled, but nonresidents are normally permitted to repatriate their investments when the authorities are satisfied that the original investment was made with funds brought into the country.

In general, residents are not permitted to transfer capital abroad and, with certain exceptions, are required to offer for sale to an authorized bank any foreign exchange that accrues to them.

GOLD

Residents may hold and acquire gold coins in Zambia for numismatic purposes. With this exception, residents other than the monetary authorities and authorized industrial users are not allowed to hold or acquire gold at home or abroad in any form other than jewelry. Imports and exports of gold in any form other than jewelry require licenses issued by the Minister of Trade, Industry, and Mines; such licenses are not normally granted except for imports and exports by or on behalf of the monetary authorities and industrial users. Monetary authorities do not import gold on behalf of private users.

Gold-bearing slime, a by-product of copper refining, is exported by copper companies for refining abroad and is disposed of abroad at a free market price. The proceeds are not treated differently from other export proceeds. Monetary authorities do not purchase gold-bearing slime.

TRADE AND PAYMENTS ARRANGEMENTS

Zambia maintains no bilateral payments agreements.

MAPS

These maps were designed by the Graphics Section of the International Monetary Fund as an aid to the reader in locating features mentioned in this book. Although every effort has been made to make them accurate, they are not intended to take the place of more formal maps. The boundaries shown are not necessarily authoritative. Moreover, no attempt has been made to distinguish between improved and unimproved roads.

DEMOCRATIC REPUBLIC OF CONGO

Air Service
Railroads
Roads

Cu Copper
Co Cobalt
◆ Diamonds

200 Miles
100   300
400 Kilometers
0   100   200   300

AFRICA

ATLANTIC OCEAN

SUDAN
CENTRAL AFRICAN REPUBLIC
UGANDA
RWANDA
BURUNDI
TANZANIA
ZAMBIA
ANGOLA
GABON
PEOPLE'S REPUBLIC OF THE CONGO
CABINDA

ORIENTALE
EQUATEUR
KIVU
MANIEMA
KATANGA
KASAI ORIENTAL
KASAI OCCIDENTAL
BANDUNDU
KONGO CENTRAL

L. ALBERT
L. EDWARD
L. KIVU
L. VICTORIA
L. TANGANYIKA
L. MWERU
L. LEOPOLD II

Congo
Ubangi
Uele
Mbomou
Aruwimi
Ituri
Lualaba
Lubilash
Sankuru
Kasai
Kwilu
Kwango
Luebo
Lubilash

UGOMA MT. 9,800 ft.

Aba
Kilo-Moto
Mungbere
Isiro
Bunia
Kasese
KAMPALA
KIGALI
Goma
Bukavu
BUJUMBURA
Kigoma
Kalemi
Kabalo
Kasongo
Kindu
Kisangani
Ponthierville
Buta
Bondo
Aketi
Bengassou
Bumba
Lisala
Libenge
BANGUI
Mbandaka
Bikoro
Inongo
Bandundu
Kikwit
Port-Francqui
Luluabourg
Lusambo
Bakwanga
Mbuji Mayi
Luiza
Kapanga
Kisenge
Dilolo
Kakanda
Kolwezi
Ruwe
Jadotville
Kambove
Likasi
Lubumbashi
Kipushi
Shinkolobwe
Tenke
Shituru
Kamina
Bukama
Luena
Luilu
Kabinda
Tshikapa
MALUKU
Kimpoko
KINSHASA
BRAZZAVILLE
Sanga
Zongo
Thysville
Inga Site
Matadi
Boma
Banana
Pointe Noire
MAYOMBE MTS.
Tshela
LUANDA
Lobito

ZAMBIA

ZAMBIA

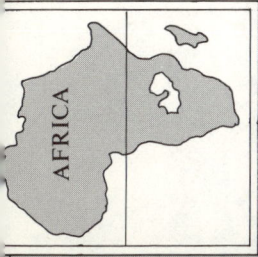

Air Service ✈
Railroads +++
Railroads Under Construction ++ ++
Roads ——
Pipeline ·····
Copper CU

Graphics Section
INTERNATIONAL MONETARY FUND

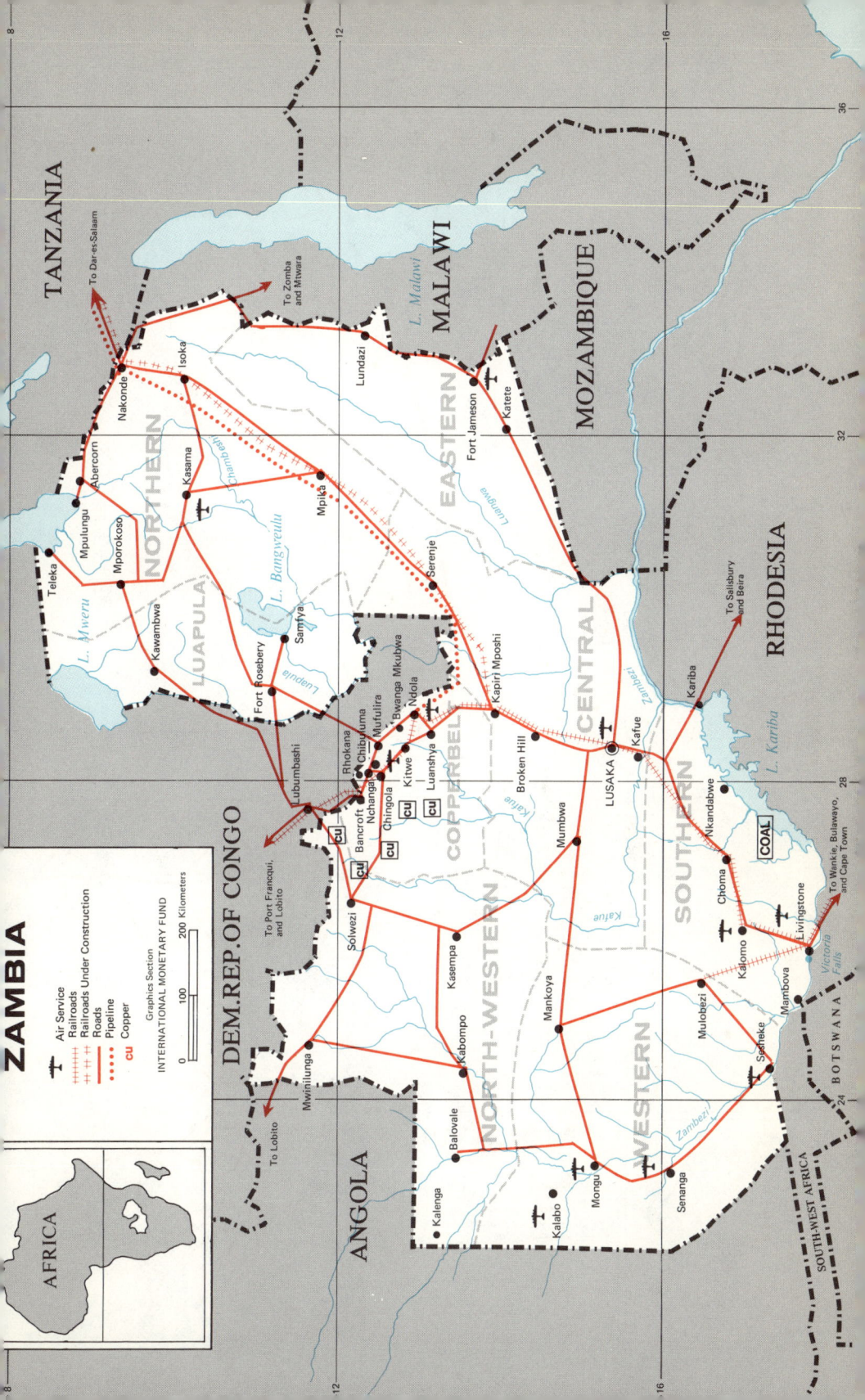

0   100   200 Kilometers

AFRICA

TANZANIA

To Dar-es-Salaam

To Zomba and Mtwara

MALAWI

L. Malawi

MOZAMBIQUE

NORTHERN

Isoka
Nakonde
Abercorn
Mpulungu
Mporokoso
Teleka
L. Mweru
Kasama
L. Bangweulu
Chambeshi
Mpika
Serenje
Lundazi
Fort Jameson
Katete

EASTERN

Luangwa

LUAPULA

Kawambwa
Fort Rosebery
Samfya
L. Bangweulu
Luapula

Lubumbashi

DEM. REP. OF CONGO

To Port Francqui and Lobito

To Lobito

Solwezi

NORTH-WESTERN

Mwinilunga

ANGOLA

Balovale
Kalenga
Kalabo
Mongu
Senanga
Zambezi

Kabompo
Kasempa
Mankoya

WESTERN

Mulobezi
Sesheke
Mambova

BOTSWANA

SOUTH-WEST AFRICA

Rhokana
Chibuluma
Mufulira
Bwanga Mkubwa
Ndola
Kapiri Mposhi
Bancroft
Nchanga
Chingola
Kitwe
Luanshya
CU

COPPERBELT

Broken Hill
Mumbwa
Kafue
LUSAKA
Kabwe

CENTRAL

Zambezi
Kafue

Kariba
L. Kariba

RHODESIA

To Salisbury and Beira

SOUTHERN

Nkandabwe
Chisamba
Choma
Kalomo
Livingstone
Victoria Falls
COAL

To Wankie, Bulawayo, and Cape Town

MALAWI

TANZANIA

ZAMBIA

MOZAMBIQUE

NORTHERN REGION

CENTRAL REGION

SOUTHERN REGION

L. MALAWI

Chitipa

Karonga

Chilumba

Manda

▲ 8,258 ft.
NYIKA PLATEAU

Katumbi

Rumpi

Katoto

Mzuzu

Mbamba Bay

Nkhata Bay

Mzimba

VIPYA MTS.
5,742 ft. ▲

Lundazi

Nkota Kota

Kasungu

Fort Jameson

Mchinji

Dowa

Benga

Lilongwe

Salima

Chipoka

Monkey Bay

To Lusaka

Dedza

Namwera

▲ 6,647 ft.
KIRK RANGE

Fort Johnston

L. MALOMBE

L. CHIUT

Ncheu

Nova F

MOZAMBIQUE

Balaka

SHIRE HIGHLANDS

Liwonde

3,543 ft. ▲

To Nacala

Nkula Falls

Chileka

L. CIMLWA

Tedzani Falls

ZOMBA

Mwanza

Zambezi

Shire

Blantyre-Limbe

Chikwawa

Luchenza

Mlanje

Cholo

9,843 ft. ▲

Milange

Chiromo

Zambezi

Nsanje

To Beira

AFRICA

Air Service
Railroads
Railroads Projected
Roads

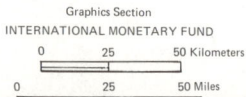

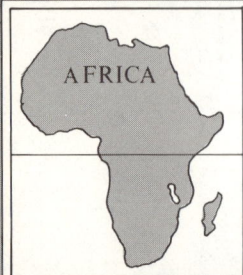

Graphics Section
INTERNATIONAL MONETARY FUND

0   25   50 Kilometers

0   25   50 Miles

MALAGASY REPUBLIC

44   48   52

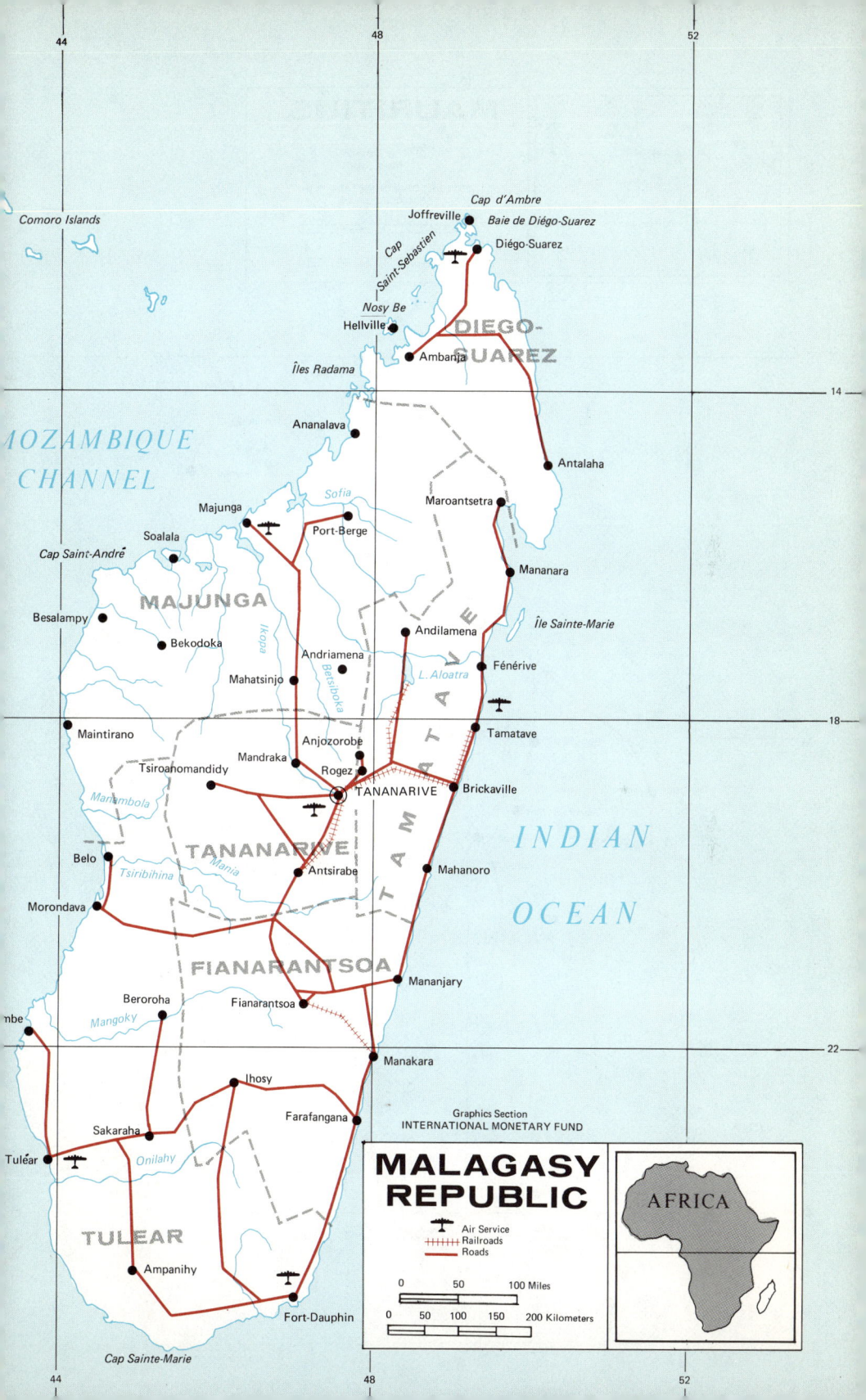

Comoro Islands

Cap d'Ambre

Joffreville

Baie de Diégo-Suarez

Diégo-Suarez

Cap Saint-Sebastien

DIÉGO-SUAREZ

Nosy Be

Hellville

Îles Radama

Ambanja

14

Ananalava

Antalaha

MOZAMBIQUE CHANNEL

Sofia

Majunga

Maroantsetra

Port-Berge

Soalala

Mananara

Cap Saint-André

Île Sainte-Marie

Besalampy

MAJUNGA

Bekodoka

Ikopa

Andilamena

Andriamena

L. Aloatra

Mahatsinjo

Betsiboka

Fénérive

Maintirano

Anjozorobe

Tamatave

Mandraka

Mandrakabe

Rogez

TANANARIVE

Brickaville

Tsiroahomandidy

TAMATAVE

Manambolo

INDIAN OCEAN

TANANARIVE

Belo

Tsiribihina

Antsirabe

Mania

Mahanoro

Morondava

FIANARANTSOA

Mananjary

Beroroha

Fianarantsoa

Mangoky

mbe

22

Ihosy

Manakara

Sakaraha

Farafangana

Tuléar

Onilahy

Graphics Section
INTERNATIONAL MONETARY FUND

TULÉAR

Ampanihy

Air Service
Railroads
Roads

0   50   100 Miles

0   50   100   150   200 Kilometers

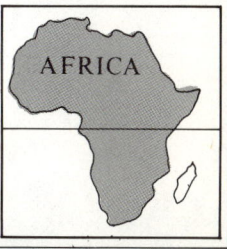

AFRICA

Fort-Dauphin

Cap Sainte-Marie

44   48   52

MAURITIS

✈ Air Service
Main Roads

INTERNATIONAL MONETARY FUND
GRAPHICS SECTION

0   2   4 Miles

0   2   4   6 Kilometers

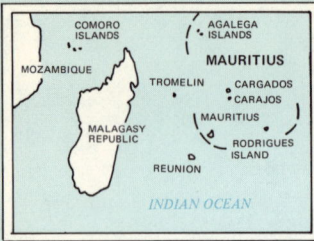

COMORO
ISLANDS

MOZAMBIQUE

AGALEGA
ISLANDS

MAURITIUS

TROMELIN   CARGADOS
CARAJOS

MALAGASY
REPUBLIC

MAURITIUS

RODRIGUES
ISLAND

REUNION

INDIAN OCEAN

57° 30'

20° 00'

RIVIERE

DU

PAMPLEMOUSSES

REMPART

Saint-Antoine

Poudre d'Or

INDIAN OCEAN

Pamplemousses

Port Louis Harbor

PORT LOUIS

MOKA

Saint-Pierre

• 1430 ft.

Beau Bassin

FLACQ

La Russie

Rose Hill

Bambous

Quatre Bornes

1720 ft.

1742 ft.

Phoenix

Mont Blanche

RIVIERE

Vacoas

NOIRE

Curepipe

• 1525 ft.

PLAINES

Ferney

2241 ft.

WILHEMS

Riche-En-Eau

• 2711 ft.

Mahébourg

GRAND PORT

Plaisance
Airport

• 1824 ft.

SAVANNE

Chemin
Grenier

20° 30'

Souillac

57° 30'

INDEX

Index

References (page numbers) are to the text, footnotes to the text (n), tables (t), and diagrams (d); the maps are not included. References to individual countries in Chapters 2 to 6 are indicated by a symbol in bold face type preceding the page number or numbers, as follows: **cng** for Democratic Republic of Congo, **mlg** for Malagasy Republic, **mlw** for Malawi, **mau** for Mauritius, and **zam** for Zambia. References to Chapter 1 are indicated by page numbers only; that is, no symbol precedes the page numbers.

Aketi, **cng** 39, 46
Alaotra Lake, rice cultivation, **mlg** 116–17
Albertville, *see* Kalemi
Aleurites, price stabilization, **mlg** 114
Alitalia, **zam** 396
Alliance Assurance Company, **mlw** 258
Alliance Touristique de l'Océan Indien, **mau** 314
Aloe fiber, **mau** 311
Aluminum smelter, **cng** 43, 44
Andriamena, **mlg** 125, 126–27
Anglo American Corporation, **zam** 386, 392, 437
Angola, **cng** 9
  bordering country, **zam** 370
  coastal fishing, **cng** 28
  rail link, **cng** 39; **zam** 396
Animal husbandry, *see* Livestock and livestock products
Anros Industries, **zam** 391*d*
Antsirabe, **mlg** 126, 134
Arbitration and Control Board, **mau** 304
Area, 1; **cng** 10; **mlg** 109; **mlw** 198, 200, 218; **mau** 297, 303; **zam** 370
Asian population, **mlw** 200, 232; **zam** 371
Atlantic Ocean, access to, **cng** 9, 39; **zam** 396
Auditor General, **mlw** 237
Australia, tourists, **mau** 314
Automobiles and trucks, assembly, **zam** 393

B and C Metal Products, Ltd., **mlw** 227
Bagasse, **mau** 305
Bags, *see* Sacks
Bakwanga, diamond deposits, **cng** 32
Balance of payments, 6–7; **cng** 16–17, 86–100; **mlg** 175–90; **mlw** 280–92; **mau** 358–65; **zam** 375, 429–40
  capital account, **cng** 88*t*, 96–98; **mlg** 176*t*, 185–88; **mlw** 281*t*, 288–89; **mau** 359*t*, 363–64; **zam** 429–30, 436–37
  services account, **cng** 88*t*, 95–96; **mlg** 176*t*, 185; **mlw** 281*t*, 288; **mau** 359*t*, 362–63; **zam** 429–30, 436
  transfers account, **cng** 88*t*, 95–98; **mlg** 176*t*; **mlw** 281*t*, 288; **mau** 359*t*, 363; **zam** 429–30, 436
Banana (port), **cng** 38, 40, 46
Bananas
  preferential markets, **mlg** 114
  production, **mlg** 116*t*, 118; **mau** 309–10

Banca d'America e d'Italia, **cng** 79
Banco Pintu & Sotto Mayor, **mlw** 257
Bancroft, **zam** 386, 390*d*
Bandundu province, **cng** 9
Bangweulu Lake, **zam** 370, 383
Bank of America, **cng** 79
Bank of Baroda, **mau** 348
Bank of Mauritius, **mau** 343–48
  advances to Government, **mau** 344
  assets and liabilities, *see* operations
  capital, **mau** 344
  credit control, **mau** 345–46
  currency issue, **mau** 300, 343–44
  foreign assets and liabilities, *see* International reserves
  functions, **mau** 344–48
  operations, **mau** 346–47
  organization, **mau** 344
Bank of Mauritius Ltd., **mau** 348
Bank of Northern Rhodesia, **zam** 417
Bank of Rhodesia and Nyasaland, **mlw** 256, 260; **zam** 417–18
Bank of Zambia, **mlw** 257; **zam** 373, 405–406, 416–22, 424
  advances to Government, **zam** 406, 418–20
  assets and liabilities, *see* operations
  capital, **zam** 418
  currency issue, **zam** 373, 405, 416
  functions, **zam** 417–19, 421
  foreign assets and liabilities, *see* International reserves
  operations, **zam** 419–20
  organization, **zam** 418
  treasury bill holdings, **zam** 415
Banking Association, **mlg** 156
Banking Control Commission, **mlg** 156
Banknotes, *see* Currency
Banks and banking, **cng** 15–16, 73–86, 87*t*; **mlg** 154–75; **mlw** 256–80; **mau** 343–58; **zam** 373, 416–29
  assets and liabilities, *see* operations
  banking functions of Treasury, **mlg** 150, 165
  branches, **cng** 78; **mlg** 158; **mlw** 258; **mau** 348–49; **zam** 423
  call-money market, **mau** 346
  capital accounts-deposits ratio, **mlg** 164–65, **zam** 419
  capital and reserve funds, obligatory, **mlw** 257; **mau** 349; **zam** 418
  clearinghouse arrangement, **mau** 346
  commercial, 6; **cng** 78–82; **mlg** 158–65; **mlw** 266–70; **mau** 346, 348–51; **zam** 421–24
  commissions, **cng** 83; **mlg** 166
  credit ceilings and controls, 6; **cng** 16–17, 76–77, 80–86; **mlg** 162, 164, 167–73; **mlw** 273; **mau** 345–46; **zam** 419, 421, 424

composition, **cng** 10–11; **mlg** 110;
  mlw 199–200, 234, **mau** 299;
  zam 371
density, 1–2; **cng** 10; **mlg** 110;
  mlw 200; **mau** 298; **zam** 371
dependent on agriculture, 2; **cng** 22;
  mlg 113–14; **mlw** 234; **mau** 303
distribution, **cng** 10–11; **mlg** 110
growth rate, 1; **cng** 10, 13, 17;
  mlg 110, 112; **mlw** 199; **mau** 298,
  300; **zam** 371
urban, **cng** 9; **mlg** 110; **mlw** 199;
  mau 298; **zam** 371
see also Migrant workers
Port Francqui
  proposed rail link with Kinshasa,
  cng 47
  transshipment point, **cng** 38–39
Port Louis
  budget, **mau** 325
  capital, **mau** 298
  hotel, **mau** 315
  industrial free zone, **mau** 312, 314
  port expansion, **mau** 312, 314
  port traffic, **mau** 314, 362
Portland Cement Company (Malawi),
  Ltd., **mlw** 222, 272
Ports, **cng** 38–40; **mlg** 110; **mau** 314,
  319
Portugal, development finance,
  mlw 225
Posts and Telecommunications Department, **mlw** 249
Post and Telecommunications Office,
  budget, **mlg** 140
Post and Telegraph Department,
  mau 354
Post Office Savings Bank, **mlw** 257;
  mau 326; **zam** 417, 424
  deposits, **mlw** 205, 269, 271*t*; **mau**
  354; **zam** 422*t*
  functions, **mlw** 258
  government security holdings,
  mlw 271*t*, 272; **mau** 354; **zam** 415,
  424
  operations, **mlw** 269–72
  transfer of foreign assets, **mau** 347*t*,
  354–55, 358, 364, 365*t*
  treasury bill holdings, **mlw** 263, 272;
  zam 415
  see also Savings Bank
Postal Checking System
  deposits, **cng** 73, 81*t*; **mlg** 150, 161*t*,
  171, 173
  loans to development bank, **mlg** 159,
  164
Potatoes
  marketing, **mau** 310
  production, **mlg** 116*t*; **mau** 309–10

Poultry and poultry products, **zam** 378*t*,
  381
Power, *see* Electricity
Presidency, **cng** 49, 59, 72; **mlw** 244
Prices, 5; **cng** 14, 50–54; **mlg** 112,
  134–36; **mlw** 232; **mau** 300,
  321–22; **zam** 375, 399–401
  controls, **cng** 54; **mlg** 136; **mau** 321;
  zam 400–401
  stabilization funds, *see* Agriculture
  and specific funds
Primary sector
  investment in, **mlg** 129
  share of GDP, **cng** 18–19
  share of GNP, **mau** 300
  see also Agriculture; Forestry; Livestock; Mining
Printing Office, National, **mlg** 140
Produce Marketing Board, **mlw** 214
Programme de Grandes Opérations,
  see Development plans: Major
  Works Program
Progressive Development Ltd., **zam**
  391*d*
Provident Fund, **zam** 413–14
Provinces, **cng** 9; **mlg** 109; **zam** 370–71
  budgets and fiscal administration,
  cng 58; **mlg** 140, 148–49
  see also specific provinces by name
Public agencies, budgets, *see* Budgets:
  consolidated
Public Works Department Workshop,
  budget, **mlg** 140
Pulp industry, **mlw** 218
Pulses
  export price, **mlw** 283*t*
  exports, **mlg** 178*t*; **mlw** 282–83
  production, **mlg** 116*t*; **mlw** 206*t*
Pygmies, **cng** 10
PVC (polyvinyl chloride) plant,
  cng 43–44

Quarrying, *see* Mining and quarrying
Quartz production, **mlg** 125*t*
Quatre Bornes, **mau** 325

Radio and Television Company, Na-
  tional, **mlg** 140
Raffia
  exports, **mlg** 178*t*
  production, **mlg** 116*t*, 121
Railroad, National, budget, **mlg** 140
Railways, *see* Transport
Rainfall, **cng** 10; **mlg** 109; **mlw** 199;
  mau 298; **zam** 370
Ras du sol program, **mlg** 129, 161*t*
Régie de Distribution d'Eau et d'Elec-